Chronology of CULTURE

To The Memory of
S.H. Steinberg
Editor of *The Statesman's Year-Book* 1946-1969

Chronology of CULTURE

A Chronology of Literature, Dramatic Arts, Music, Architecture, Three-dimensional Art, and Visual Arts from 3000 B.C. to the Present

John Paxton · Sheila Fairfield

VNR VAN NOSTRAND REINHOLD COMPANY
NEW YORK CINCINNATI TORONTO LONDON MELBOURNE

First published in paperback in 1984
Copyright © 1979 by John Paxton & Sheila Fairfield
Library of Congress Catalog Card Number 83-6816
ISBN 0-442-27004-6

Printed in the United States of America

Van Nostrand Reinhold Company Inc.
135 West 50th Street
New York, New York 10020

Macmillan of Canada
Division of Gage Publishing Limited
164 Commander Boulevard
Agincourt, Ontario MIS 3C7 Canada

Cloth edition published 1980 by Facts on File, Inc. under the
title *Calendar of Creative Man*

16 15 14 13 12 11 10 9 8 7 6 5 4 3 2 1

Library of Congress Cataloging in Publication Data

Paxton, John.
  Chronology of culture.

  Reprint. Originally published: The calendar of
creative man. New York, N.Y.: Facts on File, 1980,
c1979.
    1. Arts—History—Chronology.   I. Fairfield, Sheila.
II. Title.
NX447.5.P38   1983   700′.9   83-6816
ISBN 0-442-27004-6 (pbk.)

FOREWORD

Chronology of Culture is an illuminating introduction to,
an immense subject. It records man's creative achievement
chronologically over the ages in all its immense variety. The
entries cover all aspects of human creative work from
architecture to needlework, from the symphonies of Beethoven
and the plays of Shakespeare to Indonesian textiles, Mughal
painting, Japanese puppets, the lace glass of Venice and hundreds
more . . .

This is no mere catalogue of bare facts. Each entry gives a
compact commentary on the character and influence of the
achievement recorded — a most courageous innovation in a work
of chronological reference at a time like the present when, as we
all know, experts disagree and new research can overthrow long-
accepted ideas. But these clear and perceptive commentaries
justify themselves: they give life to the facts, place them in their
social setting, make connecting links between them, emphasise
the relationship of different arts to each other, and indicate the
cross-fertilisation of cultures.

We learn that Chinese calligraphy belongs both to art and
literature; that Central American dances, adapted in sixteenth
century Spain, changed the patterns and rhythms of European
dancing; that the etchings of the Lorraine artist Jacques Callot,
depicting the horrors of seventeenth century warfare, influenced
Goya's more famous and more terrible series nearly two hundred
years later. And much more on page after page. Links such as
these stimulate ideas, arouse curiosity, and illustrate the
complexity and the ultimate unity of the best in human
achievement.

The late Dr Steinberg described civilisation as 'a co-operative
achievement and a common heritage.' This book demonstrates
the truth of that statement. It is also a heartening work to appear
in a decade when we are more often confronted by the works of
Destructive Man. Let us not forget that the works of Creative
Man also continue.

C.V. WEDGWOOD

PREFACE

This book is dedicated to Henry Steinberg who compiled *Historical Tables,* now in its tenth edition. In a foreword to the first edition Dr. G.P. Gooch wrote:

'Dr. Steinberg has compiled this extremely useful work in the belief that civilization is a co-operative achievement and a common heritage. To cast one's eye down the column headed Cultural Life is to realise the width of his studies and interests. Peoples are connected with one another by a network of contacts and obligations, visible and invisible. The older the world grows, the greater the debt of each to all and of all to each. Every one of us is a citizen of the world: each nation is a branch of the human tree. Geographical, racial and linguistic barriers blur but cannot destroy the fundamental unity of mankind.'

We decided that the column headed Cultural Life could be expanded and *Chronology of Culture* is the result.

A 'calendar' is necessarily a comparison of *dates;* this publication is therefore a compilation of dated events. It was not possible to include those vast fields of folk and primitive art where changes take place slowly if at all.

Because of this emphasis on dates *Chronology of Culture* is likely to emphasise those cultures in which the identity of the individual artist is considered important, and the dates of his or her life have been recorded. Equally dated events in the earlier periods are few and far between and have therefore been encapsulated in summary essays outlining the major trends in the artistic development up to 500 A.D.

Some selection has been imposed by geography, and the work of the one significant painter of his period in a country not otherwise blessed with visual art has been given precedence over the work of, say, one of many brilliant French impressionists. So sometimes the famous have been omitted in favour of the rare.

Some individual works, however, are so famous that they serve as landmarks for people who have not got an extensive knowledge of art in general. These have been included for that reason, even if they do not represent a significant turning point in the history of art.

The cut-off date chosen was 1970; this seemed sensible in view of the difficulties of evaluating one's own decade; in fact those difficulties apply in only slightly less force to the 1960s, a decade on which opinions are still being formed and still subject to re-assessment.

Obviously a work of this kind depends on the devoted help of many people engaged in searching for and checking facts. Among those giving significant help we should like to mention:

Cedric Beadle	Tess Gonet	Helen Neale
Evelyn Beadle	Beryl Haigh	Anne-Lucie Norton
Caroline Bugler	Michael Hobbs	Maureen Parker
Caroline Dakers	Bob Jones	Joss Pearson
David Dean	Swan Lennard Payne	Stanley Sadie
Ian Dunmuir	Caroline Lucas	Annemarie Swainson
Anne-Marie Ehrlich	Ray Martin	Jenny Uglow
Jessica Orebi Gann	Hugh Meller	Penny White

We thank our many friends within the Macmillan Press but particularly Adrian Soar, the managing director, who encouraged us to go on even when, at times, we felt we had taken on the impossible.

JP

SF

Bruton and Wokingham
November 1978

List of black and white illustrations/acknowledgements

Literature

3000—1000 B.C.

Mesopotamia   The first literate civilization is that of the Sumerians, and is known from examples of cuneiform script to date back at least to *c.* 3000 B.C. Sumerian literature consists mainly of epics, hymns and collections of proverbs and is the source material for much of the later Babylonian epic creation. From 2000 B.C. there are references to the Babylonian hero Gilgamesh, which increase with the creative period of the first Babylonian dynasty, *c.* 1850–1650 B.C. Epic narratives form the bulk of this early heroic poetry.

Palestine   The poems *Aqhat* and *Keret* date from the thirteenth century B.C. and are a mixture of the heroic and the religious. One of the earliest known pieces of Hebrew poetry is the *Song of Deborah*, written in about 1200 B.C. and forming part of the Book of Judges; it is heroic verse in the form for a panegyric. A later form of heroic verse in Hebrew is the lament, typified by David's lament of Jonathan which was written *c.* 1010 B.C.

India   The earliest known texts in any Indo-European language are the four Vedic texts, which comprise the canon of orthodox Hinduism and are written in Sanskrit. The first, a collection of hymns known as the *Rig Veda*, was written towards the end of the second millennium.

1000—500 B.C.

India   The Upanishads, written *c.* 800 B.C., formed the basic text for popular Hinduism, and later for Buddhism.

Greece   Among early epics were Homer's *Iliad* and *Odyssey*, probably composed in the eighth century. Epics were composed by bards to entertain noble houses, and Homer's are probably among the first actually to be written down. The Greeks were the first Europeans to produce a written literature, but most classical Greek literature is in the form of drama until the fifth century B.C., when a move towards prose began. Herodotus claimed that Aesop, the writer of fables, lived during the sixth century B.C.; some of the material Aesop used is found in earlier Hindu works, the *Panchatantru* and the *Hitopedesa*, which may have served him indirectly as sources. The same material was also used by many later writers.

   Greek poetry showed early signs of personal expression, particularly in the lyric form (i.e. to be sung to the lyre); the poetess Sappho lived *c.* 600 B.C., and the poet Pindar wrote his odes *c.* 500 B.C.

China   The Chinese have a strong tradition of historical record; the earliest known history is the *Shu-Ching*, a pre-Confucian collection of ancient historical documents put together in the seventh century B.C. The seventh century also produced the *Shih-Ching* (Classic of Songs), a collection of hymns and other poems.

Mesopotamia   From the seventh century dates the best-preserved text of the story of the hero Gilgamesh; versions of this epic are also found in Hittite. In Nineveh 22,000 clay tablets of historical, literary, scientific and religious texts in Assyrian were found in the excavations of the library of king Ashurbanipal, who reigned from 669–626 B.C.

500 B.C.–1 A.D.

India The teachings of the Buddha (Gautama Sakyamuni) who died in 483 B.C. were at first passed on orally by his followers; later they were collected and written down. Certain of these collections are considered to be of literary merit, particularly the *Jatakas* (stories about the deeds of the Buddha) and the *Dhammapada* (a collection of sayings).

The two great Hindu epics, *Ramayana* and *Mahabharata*, were probably composed between 200 B.C. and 200 A.D. The *Ramayana* tells of the adventures of Rama, an incarnation of the god Vishnu, while the *Mahabharata*, said to be the longest poem in the world, is a mixture of myth, legend and moral and religious teaching. The best known part, the *Bhagavad Gita*, is still used by Hindus as a part of their devotions.

China The first of the books known as the Confucian Classics, which contain the teachings of Confucius together with books of ritual and religious song, was the *I-Ching*, dating from the second century B.C. It was written in Ku-wen, the literary language of the time which remained unchanged for centuries.

One of China's greatest poets was Sau-ma Hsiang-ju (170–117 B.C.), whose work strongly influenced the development of the long prose poem known as 'fu' poetry, which flourished during the Han period. Chinese poetry was always more contemplative than heroic.

In the first century B.C. began the first of a series of official Chinese histories, of which 26 were compiled before the beginning of the twentieth century A.D. The first was written by Ssu-ma Ch'ien and included many poems and legends; it is important to the literary historian because much earlier literature is preserved in it.

Greece The move from verse to prose is reflected in the work of Thucydides, the first truly critical historian, who wrote in the fifth century B.C.; his account of the Pelopponesian war included an analysis of its causes and strategy and of the roles of its leaders. His contemporary Herodotus wrote a more descriptive form of history.

Greek writers also made major contributions to philosophy and aesthetics at this time. The philosopher Plato (c. 427–347 B.C.) discussed the abstract nature of justice in *The Republic* and introduced the prose dialogue as a literary form, while Aristotle's *Poetics* reflects a different approach and argues from the particular to the general.

Rome Until the third century B.C. most of the literature of the Italian peoples was in the oral tradition. Then a Latin poetic idiom began to develop (Ennius, Plautus) culminating in Virgil's *Aeneid*, written during the first century B.C. A different tradition is represented by the highly personal poems of the poet Catullus (c. 84–c. 54 B.C.), the first of their kind to survive in Latin and based on Greek models.

In the first century B.C. prose overtook poetry, inspired by the study of rhetoric (Cicero). From that period come the prose histories of Julius Caesar (100–44 B.C.), who wrote accounts of his own campaigns, and the history of Rome by Livy (59 B.C.–17 A.D.), who used both official annals and the work of previous writers to produce a massive work incorporating both fact and legend. During the succeeding generation Horace wrote his satires, lyrics and odes, concentrating on the pursuit of technical excellence. The only Latin novel to survive complete is *The Golden Ass*, by Apuleius, written in the second century B.C.

Alexandria A famous library was founded c. 300 B.C. and became a gathering ground for writers of subjective poetry, chief among them being Theocritus, the first writer of pastoral idylls.

1–500 A.D.

Germany The Roman historian Tacitus, writing in 98 A.D., referred to songs in which the Germanic peoples celebrated their gods and recorded their history. Some of the songs concerned the mythical past, others were about more recent heroic events.

Greece The scholar 'Longinus' wrote, probably in the first century A.D., a treatise on the nature of the sublime in literature which was influential seventeen centuries later. The *Ecclesiastical History* of Eusebius, dating from the third century, blends the Hellenistic tradition with Christian beliefs.

Rome   The influence of rhetoric led to the decline of the epic form and is seen in the satires of the poet Juvenal (first to second centuries A.D.), which influenced nearly all succeeding European satirists. Imaginative literature gave way to such scholarly works as those of Pliny the Elder and Plutarch. The gradual decline in Latin literature is matched by the rise of a new Christian literature (Augustine of Hippo, Boethius).

India   The period 300–500 A.D. is considered the great age of Indian literature and the classical period of Sanskrit writing. Drama was the characteristic art of the period, and Kalidasa, renowned as lyric poet and dramatist, was perhaps the most important literary figure of the era.

China   During the first and second centuries the typical Chinese 'shih' poetry developed, which was recited rather than sung, while the prose poem and sung poetry continued to flourish. From the third century onwards literary criticism came into being, as did 'occasional poetry', of which T'ao Ch'ien (365–427 A.D.), a recluse who wrote about the virtues of the simple life, was a master, and the short story.

Dance and Drama

38,000—5000 B.C.

Asia, Africa, Europe Cave paintings throughout this area show representations of men and women dancing; dance is probably one of the oldest forms of expression, but the dances devised either do not survive or (where they do survive among primitive peoples) are impossible to date.

5000—3000 B.C.

Egypt 4000 B.C. is a possible date for the earliest of the Egyptian pyramid texts, which are religious dramas about the ascent of the soul or the resurrection of the body; they were probably acted by priests. A Memphite drama, celebrating the coronation of the Pharoah, dates from *c.* 3100 B.C. Paintings and reliefs show dancing as an important part of ceremonial and entertainment, and the dances were performed by professionals.

2000—1000 B.C.

Egypt Ikhernofret's account of the Abydos Passion Play, celebrating the god Osiris, dates from *c.* 1868 B.C., although there is no extant text. The audience took part in crowd scenes.

China It is possible that Chinese drama had its origins in the sacred rituals of ancestor worship; during the Chou dynasty, which began in 1122 B.C., these and other ritual forms of worship began to incorporate a dramatic element.

1000—500 B.C.

Greece Pisistratus, tyrant of Athens, introduced a contest in Tragedy into the celebrations in honour of Dionysus in 534 B.C.; this is the first evidence of a Greek drama. Also at this time Thespis introduced the first actor into a traditional performance of choral narration. He may also have been the first to use a mask.

The Greeks honoured dancing both as a part of their religious worship, and for its theatrical and social enjoyment. They developed miming dance and a kind of dramatic ballet representing battle.

500 B.C.—1 A.D.

Greece During the fifth century tragedy ceased to be purely religious and took on secular themes. In 485 B.C. Aeschylus won his first prize in the tragic contest. He reduced the role of the Chorus and introduced a second actor, which made possible more complicated plots and direct confrontations between characters. Also in this period Epicharmus of Syracuse (550–460 B.C.) wrote mimes; mime had developed originally from the antics of jugglers and acrobats and does not have the religious origins of pure drama.

Sophocles won the tragic prize in 468 B.C. He introduced a third actor and reduced the choral odes to interludes. He also developed the use of painted scenery. The *Oresteia* of Aeschylus was first produced in 458 B.C. and the *Medea* of Euripides in 431 B.C.; he was the first Greek dramatist to deal with psychological rather than social conflict. The *Oedipus Rex* of Sophocles was produced in *c.* 425 B.C., and the great amphitheatre at Epidaurus dates from this period.

The first contest in comedy writing and playing was held in 486 B.C., and in 411 B.C. came *Lysistrata* by Aristophanes (*c.* 448–380), the best known writer of Greek Old Comedy, which developed from the phallic worship of Dionysus. In 392 B.C. he wrote *Ecclesiazusa*, which marked the beginning of Middle Comedy, having less bawdiness and more plot. New Comedy developed *c.* 330 B.C.; this was a comedy of manners, and the most significant dramatist was Menander (*c.* 342–292 B.C.). His plays concerned individuals and the chorus were no longer involved in the plot. Some of his characters – the officious servant, the irritable old man – have become stock comic characters.

The nature of drama was a subject of debate among Greek writers. Plato, in his *Republic*, criticised it as appealing to the emotions rather than to reason and as encouraging blasphemy. Aristotle replied in the *Poetics* that drama had a beneficial function. He analysed the functions and structure of tragedy and his analysis was much referred to (and misinterpreted) by later writers.

Italy   The first known stage was erected in Rome in 346 B.C., but true drama came later. In 240 B.C. Lucius Livius Andronicus introduced the Romans to plays by translating from the Greek. Gnaeus Naevius produced his first play in 235 B.C.; he translated Greek tragedy and comedy and created the Roman historical play ('fabula praetexta'). Plautus wrote very free translations of Greek New Comedy. One of his best known was *Menaechmi*, which inspired Shakespeare's *Comedy of Errors*. His plots were complicated and the plays full of topical allusions. Quintus Ennius began his career as a dramatist in 204 B.C. Many of his plays were translations from Euripides but only fragments survive.

166–160 B.C. was the active period of the comic dramatist Publius Terentius Afer, called Terence, much of whose extant work was based on Menander, although he altered the sources and showed greater originality than any other Roman playwright. The tone of his plays was more sophisticated than that of Plautus, and he was less popular in his own age. His plays were translated at the Renaissance and his influence is traceable in the work of Molière. During the early first century B.C. Pomponius and Novius were writing 'fabulae atellanae', rustic farces involving masked stock characters. They did not invent the form; it probably developed from impromptu performances at markets and fairs.

The two outstanding actors of the period were Roscius (died 62 B.C.), whose name is still a symbol of great acting, and the mime actor Publilius Syrus. Roscius worked out his performance in detail before going on stage, which was unusual at the time. Publilius Syrus established himself in a competition ordered by Julius Caesar in 46–45 B.C.; his rival was Decimus Laberius, the first Latin author to write down his mime plays.

The first permanent stone theatre was built in Rome in 55 B.C.

1–500 A.D.

Rome   Lucius Annaeus Seneca (*c.* 4 B.C.–65 A.D.) wrote melodramatic adaptations of Greek tragedies which were intended for reading aloud and not for performance. His plays reflected the violence and treachery of his age and were popularly revived at the Renaissance, becoming the model for tragic drama.

The Romans developed Greek mimetic dance into the 'pantomime' or dumb-show with explanatory chorus.

India   The Buddhist teacher Asvaghosa wrote plays in about 100 A.D. Only a few fragments survive but they indicate that the plays were written to spread Buddhist teaching. That Indian drama developed to a highly sophisticated level is indicated by the third century treatise by Bharata, the *Natya Sastia*; it covered every aspect of theatre and was influential on all later dramatists. Bhasa wrote *Svapnavasavadatta* in *c.* 350 A.D., basing it on the Hindu epics *Mahabharata* and *Ramayana*. In the early fifth century Kalidasa wrote what was later considered a masterpiece of Sanskrit drama, *Shakuntala*. Dance and drama were closely associated, dancing and acting being considered almost the same thing. Dance was also important in religion and dance rhythms and movements had a strong influence on figure-sculpture.

Music

30,000—10,000 B.C.

Europe, North Africa, Western Asia   Musical instruments such as bone pipes have been excavated from Upper Palaeolithic sites, with further evidence of music-making provided by rock paintings.

4000—1000 B.C.

Western Asia   Evidence of music before the third millennium B.C. is mainly iconographic, provided by cylinder seals, reliefs, etc. Fragments of actual instruments – harps, lyres, pipes, etc. – survive from the Royal Cemetery at Ur in Mesopotamia, dating from the first half of the third millennium B.C., and some instruments have been reconstructed; double reed pipes are attested in Mesopotamia at a very early date. In Anatolia sistrums survive from the late third millennium B.C. and later. This evidence of instruments is supplemented by written evidence, in Mesopotamia from the Sumerian period in the form of copies of literary works inscribed shortly after 2000 B.C. on clay tablets made at Nippur, the religious metropolis of the Sumerians, and in Asia Minor from the Hittite period. These sources name instruments and describe the place of music in ritual, the organization of the cult musicians, etc.

India   Whistles and rattles are almost the only musical survivals from the literate Indus civilization of the third millennium B.C., although relations with Sumeria may be surmised.

Egypt   The earliest clear iconographical evidence, and the earliest surviving instruments, date from *c.* 3000 B.C. From this time onwards there are a large number of pictures showing musical scenes, often including wind instruments and harps, with singers and dancers; sometimes the instruments are named and the texts of the songs given. Many actual instruments survive in good condition owing to the climatic conditions of Egypt; these include clappers, sistrums, and later also wind and string instruments and drums. Changes in general musical practice are attested at various times; increased participation by women, and smaller groups, in the Middle Kingdom; the introduction of instruments of increased range in the New Kingdom. Some representations of Egyptian music have been held to suggest the existence of cheironomy, a system of gestures to indicate various details of the music to be performed, at this date, and it has been suggested that some hieroglyphic inscriptions from as early as the third millennium B.C. may represent analogous written instructions, but the evidence for this, as for early western Asian musical notation, is not unequivocal.

Europe   The variety of surviving instruments increases from *c.* 2000 B.C.; some instruments, such as the aulos or double reed pipe, the lyre and the harp, may have entered Europe from the Near East via Greece.

China   Instruments, for example stone chimes, survive, and are depicted, from as early as the second millenium B.C.

India   The oldest Indian texts relating to music are the *Vedas* and particularly, for musical concepts, the *Sama-veda*, dating from the second millenium B.C.

1000–500 B.C.

Mesopotamia   Reliefs from Nineveh and elsewhere, now in the British Museum, offer plentiful evidence of instrumental ensembles and, seemingly, of secular as well as sacred music-making during the Assyrian period in the first millennium B.C. Even as late as the Hellenistic period, western Asiatic musical iconography shows interesting divergences from Greek practice.

Greece   Early Greek song may have been chiefly epic, sung presumably to simple repetitive melodies, as with epics in other geographical areas in antiquity; but accompanied (lyric) song, both solo and choral, developed from the seventh century B.C. and was later associated with public competitions and, mainly from the fifth century, with drama.

Palestine   Evidence of folk-songs, sacred music and much else occurs throughout the Old Testament, particularly concerning the instruments used in the successive temples in Jerusalem (*c.* 900 B.C.–70 A.D.), although there are still difficulties in identifying some of these. Some suggest possible connections with Mesopotamia, Egypt, Anatolia and Greece. The Psalms and their rubrics also give some evidence of performing practice. This literary evidence may to a limited extent be supplemented by archaeological discoveries, but some instruments of the Israelite period may have been made of wood.

500 B.C.–1 A.D.

Italy   From the sixth century B.C., Etruscan iconographical evidence shows contact with Greek music; Etruscan music was later to influence that of Rome.

Greece   The earliest evidence of Greek interest in music theory can be dated to the late sixth century B.C. (Lasus of Hermione, Pythagoras). In a new musical style of the late fifth and fourth centuries, known to modern scholars as the 'new music', musicians appear to have introduced a novel variety in rhythm and modality, generally giving the music increased importance at the expense of the text (Melanippides, Timotheus, Euripides). In the fourth century Greek musical theory reached a summit of systematic elaboration (Aristoxenus) and the great classics of Greek musical aesthetics were produced (Plato, Aristotle). From the third century B.C. onwards, a few actual notated melodies survive, including a fragment of Euripides's *Orestes, c.* 200 B.C. From this time the music of Greek drama began to spread throughout the Hellenistic and, later, the Roman world, lingering in some places well into the Christian era. Greek drama was first produced in Rome in 240 B.C. by Livius Andronicus. From about 288 B.C. musicians in Athens were organized in professional guilds dedicated to Dionysus; this development reflects an increase in professional music-making in the Hellenistic period. Also in the third century B.C., the hydraulis, ancestor of the modern pipe organ, was invented by Ctesibius of Alexandria.

Rome   With the rise of the Roman Empire there was a great expansion of musical activity, with professionals migrating to Rome from all parts of the Empire. The exotic cults of Cybele and Isis, stressing the role of music in religious rites and representing the Egyptian tradition, were introduced to Rome.

Palestine   Synagogues originated in the second century B.C. and a musical tradition of services of readings and prayers developed which probably influenced that of the early Christian church.

China   An interest in speculative music theory is explicitly attested from the fourth century B.C. but may have existed at an earlier date. A body of doctrine linking music, education and metaphysics, comparable to that of Plato and, in its mathematical aspects, that of the Pythagoreans, was developed in the third century B.C.; some of this may have derived from Confucius (sixth century B.C.). After the third century B.C., with the establishment of Confucianism as a state cult, the so-called *ya-yueh* ('elegant music') was established as sacred Confucian music, to some extent drawing on earlier practice, and remained in use for some centuries. Surviving musical instruments from this period include bells from the period of the Warring States (late fifth to third centuries B.C.); and mouth organs and zithers, as well as possible evidence of a zither notation, from the second century B.C., although no actual melody survives as early as this. Instrumental ensembles were cultivated in the Han dynasty (206 B.C.–220 A.D.); cross-fertilization between Chinese and foreign musical traditions occurred at this period to a greater extent than in later centuries.

1–500 A.D.

Near East and Europe In the early Christian church, hymnody appears to have been important; from the third and fourth centuries A.D. such Syrian collections of hymns as those of Bardesanes and Ephrem Syrus are attested. There is, however, only one hymn (with Greek text) to survive with music from Christian antiquity – Oxyrhynchus Papyrus 1786, from the late third century. The pilgrimage of the Gaulish nun Egeria to Jerusalem in about 384 A.D. yields important evidence of liturgical music, and the first mention of the antiphon. From the fourth century, Latin metrical hymnody began to be cultivated (Hilary of Poitiers, Ambrose) and, from the fifth century, a rich variety of Eastern Christian hymnody survives; Armenia and Georgia had become Christian in the fourth century, Ethiopia in the fifth. After the Christological controversies of the fifth century, the Nestorian and Monophysite churches of the East were separated from Byzantium and Rome, with far-reaching consequences for their musical traditions; it has been suggested that the Nestorian tradition, in its subsequent eastward expansion, influenced the music of Tibetan Buddhism.

Persia Seven modes appear to have existed in Persian music before the sixth century A.D.; in that century the theorist Bārbad seems to have extended the modal system.

India The earliest Indian treatise on music is the *Nāyaśāstra*, whose musical sections may date from the fourth and fifth centuries A.D.; it contains accounts of instruments and details of performing practice. Reliefs and other iconographical evidence of the second century B.C. and later also supply evidence of dances, instrumentalists and instrumental ensembles.

Architecture

4000–2000 B.C.

Mesopotamia   The Sumerian architecture of the Tigris and Euphrates valleys dates back to the fourth millennium B.C. Arches, domes and vaults in sun-dried brick were used for richly ornate palaces, temples and fortifications, all of which were sited on raised platforms or ziggurats. These are the first known city settlements, with the temple as focus. The best known example of a temple is at Warka, the Biblical Erech, in Iraq, dating from the late fourth millennium B.C., where the wall decoration included a series of buttresses, a device used in Mesopotamia until Hellenistic times and signifying sacred buildings. Another spectacular temple was built at Ur, *c.* 2000 B.C., where a number of staircases ascended to diminishing platforms, leading to the shrine placed at the very top of the ziggurat; here the decoration became an integral part of the whole structure. Clay was used for building before brick, and continued to be used for domestic building. The 'tells', mounds made from successive layers of building, are characteristic of Sumerian architecture and are widely distributed throughout the Near and Middle East.

Asia Minor   The Hittite people of Anatolia used both timber and stone for building. Their base unit was the 'megaron', a modest rectangular room with a door at one end set under a deep porch, as discovered in the excavations at Troy dating from *c.* 3250–2600 B.C. The remains of other monuments date mainly from about the fourteenth or thirteenth centuries B.C.

Egypt   The supreme achievement of Egyptian monumental architecture lay in the construction of the funeral complex, consisting of a series of processional halls leading to a pyramid, the tomb of the ruler. The earliest large-scale example was built for king Zoser, founder of the Third Dynasty (*c.* 2780–2680 B.C.), by Imhotep at Saqqara. The form of the pyramid, which developed from a mostaba, a simple funerary structure, reached its full expression in the Great Pyramid of Cheops at Gizeh in *c.* 2600–2480 B.C. Built in stone, it had an internal arrangement of passages, galleries and air-shafts leading to the chamber where the mummified body of the king was placed. This kind of layout was used, with some variation, in all pyramidal structures.

Crete   The earliest known examples of European architecture still in existence are the palaces of Knossos and Phaestos excavated in Crete. They were built about 3000 B.C., possibly by settlers from Egypt, and were probably destroyed by an earthquake *c.* 1700 B.C. They were then rebuilt and the surviving remnants of the so-called palace of king Minos at Knossos reveal its complex assymetrical planning, integrated by its many courtyards, colonnades and gardens with the surrounding countryside. The interiors had brightly painted wall decoration.

North and West Europe   The practice of building megalithic monuments, particularly tombs for collective burial and standing stones, alone or in groups, spread westward across Europe in the third millennium B.C. Some of the work at Stonehenge, England, is thought to date from this period.

2000–1000 B.C.

Mesopotamia   In the second millennium B.C. the Assyrians from northern Mesopotamia inherited the Sumerian architectural tradition. Their contribution lies mainly in the field of decoration and ornament; polychrome brickwork and relief sculpture appeared in the ninth century B.C. The best example of this work is the palace of Sargon, *c.* 722–705 B.C., in the city of Khorsabad (Iraq).

Egypt   The best known of the mortuary temples, at Deir el Bahari (1085 B.C.) dates from the period of the New Kingdom (1570–1085 B.C.). Its pillared halls, colonnades and ramps formed a precedent for all the subsequent temples.

Greece   Further destruction occurred in Crete *c.* 1400 B.C. but by then Cretan building techniques, such as the rectangular megaron, forerunner of the Greek temple, were known in mainland Greece, while the beehive tombs found on the mainland show a northern, megalithic influence. The greatest work of this period is the now ruined citadel of Mycenae, surrounded by its cyclopean walls and entered by the Lion Gate. The lions, carved in relief about the lintel, are the earliest known European examples of architectural sculpture. A significant variation on the Cretan palace prototype was the planning of the citadel on a single axis of courtyards, staircases and rooms. This planning system was to survive the destruction of the Mycenaean culture in about 1200 B.C.

1000–500 B.C.

Persia   Persian architecture became the source of most advances in the Middle East at this period, with its emphasis on large-scale interiors. Excavations indicate that the best example of this is the palace of Persepolis, built *c.* 518–460 B.C. It is a complex of richly decorated buildings which reveal both Assyrian influences, in the use of animal sculpture on the capitals and sculpted wall decoration, and Egyptian influences, in the handling of the architectural masses.

Mesopotamia   In southern Mesopotamia, the neo-Babylonian style combined features of both Sumerian and Assyrian architecture. The city of Babylon (Iraq), rebuilt in burnt brick by Nebuchadnezzar in 605–563 B.C. on a rectangular plan, was dominated by a great palace with hanging gardens, forming one of the Seven Wonders of the ancient world. A second famous building in the city was the Tower of Babel, placed on a platform topped by a massive spiral construction on Assyrian lines.

Asia Minor   Uratrian architecture around Lake Van (Turkey) has unidentified origins. Amongst the stone fortresses, the citadel of Van, built *c.* 800 B.C. and strategically placed on a platform on a cliff edge, is the most striking example of the military architecture of the period, while amongst the temples the best example is that of Altintepe, dating from the seventh century B.C.

Palestine   Nothing survives of the Temple of Solomon, built *c.* 950 B.C. by the Phoenicians, although excavations of the city of Jerusalem, built after David had made it his capital, reveal a complicated system of defences.

Central America   The earliest known buildings are the earth monuments of the Gulf region of Mexico, dating from the Olmec period, *c.* 800 B.C.

500 B.C.–1 A.D.

Greece   By the end of the seventh century B.C. Greek architecture was becoming that of the city as a unit, and the classical architectural orders had emerged. The first of these was the Doric, reminiscent of Assyrian and Egyptian columns and capitals and imitating in stone earlier wooden structures. This was the basis of the typical columnar and trabeated style of Greek temples, of which one of the finest examples is the ruined Parthenon at Athens, dating from *c.* 447–438 B.C. Architectural sculpture also played an important role in these magnificent buildings. From the Doric order developed the more graceful Ionic, in the middle of the sixth century B.C., and the descriptive Corinthian in the fifth century. Although the temples are the culmination of classical Greek architecture, they are not its only achievement. Equally memorable are the huge open-air theatres with semi-circular auditoria, usually cut out of a hillside, and the impressive tombs, of which the demolished mausoleum at Halicarnassus is the most famous example. This monument was built in Asia Minor, demonstrating the spread of the Greek style to other eastern Mediterranean countries.

Egypt   In the fourth century B.C. the Greeks, settling in Egypt, took over the columnar form and built a number of temples still in the traditional Egyptian manner, but at the same time established Alexandria on Hellenistic lines.

India   The development of architecture in the Indian sub-continent ran parallel with the development of religious expression in the form of Buddhism, Jainism and Hinduism. The earliest brick and stone buildings were associated with the rise of Buddhism in the fourth century B.C.; they are mainly carved out of rock surfaces. Later a mount over the relics, such as the Great Stupa at Sanchi, India, dating from the first century B.C., became the building of worship. Buddhist stupas were decorated in order to emphasize the structure while the Jain and Hindu stupas, which evolved from the Buddhist model, were ornamented in a way which concealed the main body of the structure. On the whole the ornament originated in Hellenistic prototypes, although in Hindu temples the introduction of a human figure, often of erotic character, was totally new and original.

Ceylon   As in India, architectural history begins with the rise of Buddhism, when it was introduced from India in the third century B.C. The oldest structure is the third century Thuparama stupa, in the city of Anuradhapura.

China   Our knowledge of ancient Chinese buildings derives only from paintings and relief panels since, due to the use of timber as the main material, few buildings survive. In wooden buildings a column without a capital was the most important architectural element around which screen walls and roofs were placed. During the Han period (206 B.C.–220 A.D.) there was an architectural flowering, and town-planning on a rectangular axial system became a feature. Amongst the early stone structures, the best known example is the Great Wall, begun *c.* 214 B.C., on the north border. It is believed to have been an earth embankment initially and to have received stone facing at a later date, while the imposing watch towers were added in 1368 A.D.

Central America   Most surviving buildings were designed for religious purposes, the most striking being the huge pyramids. Unlike their Egyptian counterparts they were constructed of earth in several stepped stages, surmounted by a flat platform to support a small temple which housed an image of the god. Their base was usually rectangular, such as those at the religious centre of Teotihuacan, Mexico, begun *c.* 100 B.C., but some, for example at Cuilcuilco, Mexico, (now destroyed) were circular. It seems that they were sometimes decorated with sculpture and painted panels. From an early date ceremonial courts and related buildings were constructed in association with the pyramids. The Aztecs and later the Mayans inherited the pyramid from earlier civilizations and there is evidence that they also adapted them for defensive purposes.

South America   The chief distinction of Andean architecture is the high quality of masonry used. The earliest known example is the ruined castle of Chavin de Huantar (Peru), variously dated between 1000 and 100 B.C. Stone was cut to fit without cement round the rubble core of the walls. The same method of construction was still employed by the Incas in the sixteenth century. In the lowlands adobe brick was used, sometimes to build ceremonial pyramids like those in Mexico. Early examples are those at Moche, Peru, dated *c.* 500 A.D.

1–500 A.D.

Rome   With the decline of Greek civilization in the second century B.C., the Greek inheritance passed to the Romans, who enlarged the architectural repertoire by the frequent use of the arch, vault and dome, often employing brick and concrete in their construction. The arch had rarely been used by the Greeks, but the Etruscans in north Italy had built with it from the fourth century B.C. Emboldened by these structural innovations, the Romans often built on an immense scale, notably the now ruined Colisseum in Rome, which dates from 69–79 A.D. There the arcaded wall is the dominating feature and, as often occurred in Roman building, the columns, particularly the Corinthian and Composite orders, serve more for decorative than for practical purposes. The Romans applied the same urban architectural style throughout their vast empire and the Roman tradition continued into the sixth century, but the finest work dates from the first and second centuries A.D.

Persia

Under the Sassanian dynasty (226–642 A.D.) building, mainly of palaces, flourished, forming a link between the old Mesopotamian architecture and that of Byzantium.

Japan

Before the introduction of Buddhism to Japan in the sixth century A.D., Japanese architecture was generally very primitive. Two types of house, the sheltered pit dwelling in the north and the platform house in the south, have been noted by archaeologists. Grander than these were the imperial palaces, but they are only known from early and imprecise written sources. More is known of the imperial tombs which, until the seventh century A.D., were housed in large underground stone chambers. The Shinto shrines at Ise were periodically rebuilt by tradition and replicas of the original third century A.D. shrines survive. Uninfluenced by Chinese precedent, they are simple timber rectangular buildings with floors raised above ground level. The roofs have straight-sided gables.

Visual and Three-Dimensional Arts

35,000—8000 B.C.

Asia, Africa, Europe Palaeolithic or early Stone Age hunters, who have been named 'Cromagnon Man', spread outwards from the Near East. Their name was taken from a French site where their settlement has been excavated; other French sites have given their names to successive palaeolithic cultures (Aurignacian, Gravettian and Magdalenian). These hunters made the first pieces of representational art now surviving in about 25,000 B.C. One aspect was the decoration of everyday objects: they made implements carved in the round as animal figures or incized with decoration, and carved small figurines in animal and human form. Their materials were antler, bone and ivory. The other aspect of this primitive art was cave painting. The Gravettian hunters penetrated to the Ural mountains, where they made monochrome animal paintings such as those found in the Kapova cave. The later Magdalenians were responsible for the painted polychrome animal figures in the caves of Spain and southern France, the best known being those at Lascaux (*c.* 15,000 B.C.) and Altamira (*c.* 12,000 B.C.). The artists used powdered ochre, haematite and manganese pigments which they applied with brushes, pads and blowpipes; caves were also decorated with prints of their hands.

8000—5000 B.C.

Asia, Africa, Europe The Near East was the focus for a new form of rock painting, with animal and human figures in silhouette. These depicted scenes of dancing, battle and hunting for game. An early example is the Anatolian settlement of Catal Huyuk (*c.* 6250 B.C.), which contained shrine rooms decorated with mural paintings based on a cult of fertility and death; some also showed hunting scenes. Religious sculpture for the shrines was made in stone and terracotta, the most important pieces being the fertility goddess and her consort. Plaster relief on the walls sometimes incorporated real animal skulls.

Mesopotamia The technique of pottery making was developed by the first Neolithic or New Stone Age farmers in the villages of the Tigris and Euphrates rivers, and pottery became an art form in its own right from about 6000 B.C. In Mesopotamia it forms a complete cultural sequence to the beginning of the literate Sumerian civilization *c.* 3000 B.C. The use of plain and decorated pottery spread both east and west.

5000—3000 B.C.

Mesopotamia The Tigris and Euphrates valleys continued to form a nucleus for the art of the developing agricultural settlements. Figures and vessels were carved from alabaster, and pottery was decorated with stylized animal figures and geometric patterns; polychrome painted ware has been excavated at Samarra, Tell Halaf and Hassuna.

The earliest rulers in Mesopotamia were the Sumerians, who gradually evolved a new type of civilisation based on urban settlements. Sculptors at Uruk and other Sumerian centres developed a style of human figure sculpture that showed an interest in the dignity of human beings and at the same time reflected an organized hieratic society. Free-standing sculpted figures were always in frontal pose, staring straight ahead, while relief-carving usually showed figures in profile. Sumerian artists were skilled in copper and alabaster and their work established styles that remained influential in Mesopotamia and Egypt for two thousand years.

Egypt Hieratic Sumerian art influenced that of early pharaonic Egypt. The victory palette of king Narmer was a characteristic Egyptian version of the Sumerian style; it was carved in relief on slate to show the exploits of the king. A faience or glazed quartz frit was developed and widely used for beads and ornaments, bowls, vases, tiling and inlay.

Greece In Thessaly a form of painted pottery now called Dimini ware began to be made. It was decorated with bold bands of stripes, spirals and zig-zags, usually in black and red. Painted pottery in various styles was found as far west as Sicily at this period.

Persia Pottery making also spread east to Susa, where pots were decorated with sophisticated animal designs in dark brown or black on a cream ground.

China The Neolithic farming communities of the Yang Shao people in the Yellow and Wei river valleys formed the earliest centre of culture and made painted pottery, including large funerary jars with bold chevron patterning.

Japan The Neolithic Jomon people, who were hunters and fishermen, made pottery but were more interested in modelling than painting, and produced figurines that were sometimes eccentric in form.

3000—1000 B.C.

Mesopotamia Sumerian civilisation continued to develop and funerary objects from the royal tombs of Ur (*c.* 2600–2500 B.C.) included effigies, armour and personal possessions made of precious metals and stones. The 'standard of Ur', also found in a tomb, is now thought to have been the sound-box of a harp; it was decorated with inlaid figures in shell and limestone on a mosaic of lapis lazuli. The cylinder seals used by Sumerian officials stimulated interest in the artistic possibilities of the repeating pattern running in horizontal lines, and were influential on later reliefs, after Sumerian rule had given way to that of the Babylonians and Assyrians.

By about 1500 B.C. the Assyrians had begun to produce their own art, distinct from that of the Babylonians to the south. Their most characteristic work was in stone, which the Babylonians lacked. They made and coloured relief wall panels, the main subject being the king and his exploits. Background events were shown in rows above the foreground subject; human figures were stiff, animals full of vigour.

Egypt In *c.* 3000 B.C. the kingdoms of Upper and Lower Egypt were united, and increased stability led to new artistic developments. The artists of the Old Kingdom (2700–2180 B.C.) excelled at portrait sculpture in stone and wood. For a stone sculpture the figure was drawn, from the front and in profile, on the sides of a shaped block; a grid was used to ensure the correct proportions for an idealized figure. The stone was then sawn, chiselled or pounded away from the outlines to leave a monolithic figure which combined the frontal and the profile view. Pottery began to be thrown on the wheel at this period.

The walls of tombs and palaces were decorated with plaster reliefs, often painted. Reliefs and mural painting showed a strong feeling for nature and often portrayed the landscape and wild life of the Nile valley with an unprecedented realism. The painting medium was not fresco but gouache, with mineral or frit pigments in gum or water. Composition was divided into three horizontal registers, the lowest indicating the foreground.

The sculpture of the New Kingdom (1567–1085 B.C.) showed more interest in the surface texture of the materials, in form and design, than in representation. Earlier sculptors had emphasized likeness, in the belief that to make a likeness was to perpetuate the original. The 'block statue' showed an emphasis on reducing form to its essentials.

The first glassware was made during the eighteenth dynasty (1567–1320 B.C.). Vessels were moulded not blown, and were decorated with coloured glass trails. Simple engraving was practised, treating solid glass like a block of precious stone, and carving it. Mosaic glass was made by fusing coloured rods.

In 1375 B.C. the pharaoh Akhenaten established a city at el-Amarna as a centre for his sun-worshipping religion. The art of this new cult was revolutionary in its lively and informal portrayal of court life. Thebes remained the centre of formal, conservative art.

Crete   The earlier sculpture found in Crete and the Cyclades is in the form of small figures made of white marble in an elegant near-abstract form, and is the work of an independent pre-Minoan farming and sailing community.

Between 2000 and 1500 B.C. Cretan civilization rose to new heights, possibly under Egyptian influence, and fresco painting, of which the best known depicted the sport of bull-leaping, was developed in the Minoan palaces. The artists also painted decorative groups of birds and flowers, as well as framing their painted scenes with borders of abstract pattern. Their main colours were blue, yellow, buff and a reddish brown. The frescoes showed great liveliness and responsiveness to nature, and a strong feeling for beauty. The most characteristic were painted after 1700 B.C.

Greece   From *c*. 1500 B.C. the Mycenaeans from the Greek mainland came to dominate the Minoans and adapted much of their art. Their approach was more formal and austere, with hunting and warfare as the main inspirations; they could not imitate the sensitive, decorative qualities of Minoan art. They introduced the potter's wheel *c*. 1800 B.C.

North and Atlantic Europe   Neolithic farming settlers, arriving later than in southern Europe and the Near East, developed a characteristic stylized and geometric art, much of it in the form of carving on stone, including representations of a funerary or mother goddess.

Asia Minor   The Hittities in Anatolia began to make monumental sculpture *c*. 1450 B.C. The sanctuary of Yazilikaya (thirteenth century B.C.) was cut out of rock and decorated with relief figures of kings, gods and goddesses. Most of their art was religious, but their treatment of human figures was lively and sympathetic. They worked in stone, copper, bronze, silver, gold and iron.

India   A fully developed literate civilization flourished in the Indus valley during much of this period but little is known of its art, apart from terracotta figures and painted pottery.

China   During the period 3000–2000 B.C. the farming settlements of Shantung and Ronan made a fine black pottery in elaborate form. The potter's wheel appeared towards the end of the period.

Between 2000 and 1000 B.C. bronze-casting developed as an art along the course of the Yellow River under the Shang dynasty (1600–1027 B.C.), a loose federation of city state. Styles varied from the simple to the ornate; many vessels were made for ritual purposes and were elaborately decorated with motifs which were engraved in piece-moulds and usually bore a religious significance. Favourite animal subjects were the tiger and the dragon. The decoration used on bronzes was influential on most other art forms until *c*. 100 B.C. Chinese woven silks were first produced at this time.

Central America   In Mexico, Colombia and Ecuador, potters in agricultural settlements began to make female figurines and to model grotesque heads as decoration for their bowls and cups.

South America   Textiles surviving from this period are woven in elaborate designs, many of them with a serpent motif.

1000–500 B.C.

Persia   During this period the Persian peoples grew to dominate the Near and Middle East, both politically and culturally. In Mannae, in the north west, an art of working in ivory and precious metals was developed which had Assyrian elements and, later, reflected Scythian nomad art.

During the sixth century B.C. the Persian empire was founded under a single ruler, and work began on the city of Persepolis in *c*. 518 B.C. The decoration of the city was characterized by stone relief panels depicting ceremonial processions of figures carved in profile in a cold and formal style. Like all empires, Persia adopted art styles from subject and trading nations and in turn disseminated her own styles widely. Persian influence was strong in early Indian art.

Greece   Mycenaean art degenerated during the period 1000–500 B.C. and was represented only by pottery painted in geometric patterns, of which the 'key' pattern was the most typical. In the eighth century the patterning covered most of the vase surface and human figures were introduced, in geometric form. By the late eighth century an oriental style of decoration, through Syrian influence, introduced the lotus flower, palmette and animal motifs. The 'black figure' style of vase painting, making a black silhouette figure and engraving the details on it, flourished at Corinth during 700–600 B.C. and was then taken up by Attic potters who finally surpassed the Corinthians and also later introduced the 'red figure' style of painting a figure in outline, putting in the details with lines of thin paint, and filling up the background between the figures with black. Reds and blacks were achieved through controlled oxydization during firing.

The archaic style of Greek sculpture first appeared *c.* 670 B.C. and is thought to have developed with some influence from Egypt through Syria. Sculptors at first concentrated on the face and the frontal view, learning slowly to understand the profile and the form of the body. The main figures were the nude standing male *(kouros)* and the draped standing female figure *(kore)*, both in rigid frontal pose.

Italy   The sculptured reliefs in stone, bronze and terracotta made by the Etruscans showed Greek and oriental influences and first appeared in 700–600 B.C. The Etruscans were particularly skilled in metalwork, engraving scenes from Greek mythology as decoration on vessels, mirrors and panels. From *c.* 600 their paintings were murals inspired by the decorative traditions of the Near East and, it is thought, by Greek painting, of which little survives from this period. Southern Italy began producing pottery on the wheel *c.* 750 B.C.

China   Bronze cast vessels began to appear in simpler form and the earlier elaboration was transferred to jade. The 'Huai' style of bronze casting first appeared *c.* 600 B.C.; the artists used inlays of gold, silver and copper to produce the religious motifs of earlier bronzes for purely decorative effects. Bronzes were produced in great variety until *c.* 220 A.D.

Central America   The first major Central American civilization was that of the Olmecs on the Mexican Gulf. Their art was mainly in the form of sculpture, particularly their 'big head' sculptures, which were carved from single blocks of basalt up to 3 metres high; they also made small statuettes in a variety of materials including jade. The features of the jaguar, a cult animal, were often incorporated into religious sculpture.

South America   Architecture and sculpture emerged at about the same time (*c.* 1000 B.C.); the religious iconography of the ritual buildings of Chavin de Huantar (Peru) included serpent and cat motifs in stone relief. Artists of this period also made ceramics of massive form and graceful organic shape. The temples of Kotosh and Cerro were decorated with relief panels in stone.

500 B.C.—1 A.D.

Greece   The classical period in Greek sculpture began *c.* 480 B.C. when sculptors had mastered the anatomy of the male body and began to concentrate on varying the pose and using drapery to enhance form. The statues of the Parthenon (447–438 B.C.) typified this period. The great masters of the fifth century were Phidias and Polyclitus; of the fourth century, Scopas, Praxiteles and Lysippus. The female nude did not appear until the fourth century. In relief carving, artists developed an understanding of perspective and mastered the presentation of three quarter profile, giving a greater sense of depth in shallow relief.

The naturalism of the classical period was emphasized in the Hellenistic period (from 323 B.C.). Sculptors explored the most difficult poses and groupings with great virtuosity; their figures were often types in the theatrical sense of the word, sometimes to the point of caricature. Portrait busts were made to show psychological, not representational, likenesses.

Polygnotus of Thasos (active *c.* 450 B.C.) is considered the first notable Greek painter. His figures were painted in flat washes and his background groups were placed higher to indicate distance. Apollodorus of Athens (fifth century) was said to be the first to model figures with light and shade; his technique was further developed by Zeuxis later in the century. Apelles (active in the late fourth century) was considered by contemporaries to be the greatest of Greek painters and a master of chiaroscuro, but none of his work survives.

Italy   Etruscan painting was best typified by murals from the Tarquinian tombs, which were colourful scenes of banquets and general enjoyment.

Egypt   The Syrians or the Egyptians discovered how to blow glass, which provided artists with a far greater scope in creating shapes. Previously vessels were moulded on an earthen core in the furnace on a long rod. Hollowing the rod to make it lighter could have suggested the idea of blowing down it.

Northern Asia, Eastern Europe   The mounted nomads or Scythians of Asia and eastern Europe are thought to have developed their art during the sixth and fifth centuries B.C. They concentrated on making small, portable objects in precious metals, ivory, bone, textiles, leather and wood; the usual motif was a highly stylized bird or animal form taken from an elaborate mythology.

Central, North and West Europe   From the fifth century B.C. onwards the decorative Celtic artistic tradition began to appear. The Celts were especially skilled in metalwork, particularly bronze, which they decorated with curving, abstract patterns and stylized human figures, by means of engraving, inlaying and hammering. They were also skilled in *champlevé* enamelling. Their art was influenced by the Greeks and by the Scythian nomads, with whom they shared a cultural dependence on the horse. Celtic arts spread from central Europe to Spain, Britain and Anatolia. The potter's wheel appeared along the Rhine and Danube *c.* 450 B.C.

Persia   The Macedonian conquest of the Persian empire in 333 B.C. brought Hellenistic traditions which displaced the native style. These were in turn displaced by an oriental art introduced with the Parthian conquest of 250 B.C. By the end of this period Parthian statues and reliefs were reviving the Sumerian tradition of frontal poses, with figures staring straight ahead; this was in time one of the formative influences on Byzantine art.

India   A Hindu culture developed in the Ganges-Jumna basin during the fourth and third centuries B.C., but a greater stimulus to art was the accession of the Mauryan ruler Ashoka in the Punjab in 273 B.C. He ruled much of north India and his conversion to Buddhism stimulated a new school of sculpture, some of it copied from Persian and Hellenistic models, such as the sandstone columns crowned with lions, bulls and elephants. Temples were also decorated with free-standing and deep relief figures of female deities which were entirely Indian in inspiration. The sculptors applied techniques learned in small-scale wood and ivory sculpture.

China   The establishment of the Han dynasty (206 B.C.) is regarded as the true beginning of the arts in China. The first monumental stone sculpture appears during this period, with the figure cut as a block and the details shallow-carved on the four sides. Great strides were made in ceramics, especially in modelled figures such as the tomb figures which replaced the human immolations of earlier times. Lead glazes were first used during the fourth century B.C. Lacquer ware, of which fragments have been found dating to *c.* 650 B.C., developed as an art form during this period; black lacquered surfaces were painted with red, blue, white and yellow lacquers and appeared on many kinds of vessels and furnishings. The Han emperor Wu-ti (140–86 B.C.) developed and made safe the Silk Road, the route along which Chinese woven silks were sent to the west. The trade brought naturalistic ideas of design to China and naturalistic bird, animal and plant motifs began to replace those taken from decorated bronzes. The Han period also produced the first Chinese embroidery still surviving; the technique was based on chain-stitch and knots.

South America   The Paracas Cavernas culture of Peru produced pottery with a thin body and graceful form, decorated with resin pigments which were applied to incized patterns to give a *cloisonné* effect; the main colours were red and yellow but others also appeared. The Paracas necropolis contained woven textiles of a very high standard, ornamented with birds, animals, grotesque monsters and stylized human figures.

I—500 A.D.

Rome   The Etruscan interest in portraying ordinary life was shared by Roman painters, who worked mainly in murals and showed a new concern for landscape and genre scenes. They adapted Hellenistic conventions to scenes of daily life which they painted with lively realism. They also painted illusionistic landscape murals.

The most characteristic Roman sculpture was realistic portrait sculpture and dramatic narrative in relief. Carved stone relief panels portrayed a continuous narrative of real events in a sequence of scenes; Greek influence remained in that the scenes were punctuated by mythological and allegorical figures. This combination remained popular in commemorative sculpture until the twentieth century A.D.

India   The Satavahana dynasty encouraged sculpture and wall-painting, mainly as decoration for Buddhist stupas (shrines), the most famous being at Araravati.

Reliefs from the first century show Buddha as a figure for the first time; he is portrayed as super-human and remote. A different sort of Buddhist art developed at Gandhara in the north-west, based on Hellenistic influences which had travelled across Persia. Ghandara sculptors adapted Hellenistic styles of face and drapery but ignored the Greek and Roman interest in anatomy, forming the bodies of their statues according to rules laid down in Hindu teachings. They gave the figure of Buddha a truly human appearance for the first time. At Mathura in Uttar Pradesh a third style of art developed which became a synthesis of the other two, using Graeco-Roman forms to express purely Indian feelings and ideas.

The succeeding Gupta dynasty encouraged a new national Hindu spirit in art and established a prosperous, aristocratic society. The Ajanta cave temples, cut out of the rock under the Satavahanas, were richly decorated with frescoes and reliefs which are characteristic of Gupta art in their combination of the sensual and the mystical. The conquests of the dynasty took north Indian art all over the subcontinent.

Japan   The Yayoi culture (*c.* 200 B.C.–*c.* 300 A.D.) was based on wet-rice farming, an idea imported from China which brought important cultural changes because of the new way of life that went with it. These changes affected both Japan and south Korea, and the two countries became more closely linked. Through Korea, Japan also came into contact with the nomad people of north-east Asia. The Yayoi people made pottery and bronze articles in graceful shapes which were suitable for a stable domesticated society. After 300 A.D. a new people appeared, characterized by their vast keyhole-shaped burial mounds, in which the distinguished dead were buried with treasures of metal and semi-precious stones. The style of these objects showed strong influences from the nomad cultures which had by this time spread into China.

Central America   In *c.* 300 A.D. began the rise of Teotihuaca (Mexico), a city which became the centre of a civilization which lasted until *c.* 700. This was an organized religious society, building pyramid temples which were richly decorated with carving and frescoes. The earliest artistic objects are terracotta jars with incised and painted decoration; later an almost translucent orange pottery was produced. The stone sculpture depicted the ritual plumed serpent and the figures of gods, especially the fire god.

6-10th Centuries

500
Mayan city of Chichen Itza flourished in Yucatan.

*c.***400–500 India** First written version of Bharata's *Natya Sastra*, a codification of the movements and expressions of Indian dance: it includes drama since the two were always combined. Dance in Hindu teaching was the means by which Siva created the world, and must be central to all drama. Drama must progress through beginning, effort, hope, certainty and success, since it shares the will of the gods, which must be good.

*c.***500–600 Byzantium** Emperor Justinian closed the mime theatres: mime actors had been previously defended in an essay by Choricius of Gaza in 500 A.D.

*c.***480 Italy** Birth of Anicus Manlius Servinus Boethius (d. *c.*524). His treatise, *De Institutione Musica*, the most extensive of the Latin writings on music, is based on Greek sources; it was a standard textbook throughout the Middle Ages.

Egypt: Coptic tapestry with divine figures

ARCHITECTURE	THREE DIMENSIONAL ART	VISUAL ARTS	*INVENTIONS & DISCOVERIES*

THREE DIMENSIONAL ART

220–580 China Pottery of the 'Six Dynasties' period no longer followed bronze vessels in shape; the main type was celadon (grey-green glazed) stoneware from Chekiang.

400–500 Roman Empire The barbarian invasions broke up the Roman glass industry in all parts of the Empire but Byzantium. However the north German provinces continued the tradition, especially in Cologne, making glass with trailed thread decoration.

*c.***400–750 Northern Europe** Merovingian glass, found in pagan tombs of this period, included ribbed ware, drinking horns and 'claw beakers' which had curving, trunk-like appendages curving down from the body of the vessel to its foot.

ARCHITECTURE

500–600 China Earliest surviving buildings of any size, excepting parts of the Great Wall of China: other ancient cultures were always known primarily by their buildings and architects, but China's early architecture is known mostly from written records and later copies. The main buildings were secular, not consecrated, and built in wood. Buddhist rock-cut shrines exist from the fourth century A.D., and also pagodas, the pyramidal structures which are equivalent to Indian *stupas* (sacred mounds or pyramids) and shrine towers.

500–600 Ethiopia Building of Dabra Dammo monastery began: it was completed *c.*900–1000 and, like other early Ethiopian churches, resembles an ancient Syrian basilica in plan. The upper storey is divided into several rooms; wooden panels decorated with geometric designs surround the nave interior.

500–600 India Sarnath Stupa, near Benares, a late Gupta-period stupa (Buddhist sacred mound): it influenced the style of others outside India e.g. in Java, Thailand and Tibet. Built of brick, it consisted of two circular-plan drums, one atop the other, surmounted by a dome. Relief sculpture and statues in niches originally decorated the exterior.

500–600 Egypt Flourishing period of Coptic art: the Coptic church arose from the Egyptian peasantry's rejection of Byzantine authority in church teaching; their wall paintings, relief carvings and embroidered textiles show a combination of peasant character and Syrian-derived motifs.

500–600 India Paintings give evidence of established techniques of making textiles: woven patterns, double-tied dyeing, warp and weft dyed separately and then woven, and tie-and-dye methods are all indicated.

500–600 Italy Mosaic in the church at Parenzo is the earliest known representation of the Virgin enthroned in the central position of honour in the apse.

500–700 China First Chinese evidence of resist-dyeing in silk textiles. It stimulated a freedom in design beyond the Indian Buddhist iconography and Sassanian Persian motifs which characterized Chinese woven textiles of the time.

500–800 Korea Buddhism had a considerable effect on sculpture: the classical simplicity and dignity of Buddhist statuary is characteristic of Korean work.

VISUAL ARTS

500–600 Byzantium Christ crucified was usually portrayed as a majestic, alive, triumphant figure, in a formal long tunic, proclaiming mastery over death.

INVENTIONS & DISCOVERIES

500 Indians understood the use of zero in mathematics.

502
End of Chi
dynasty in
southern China.

503
Baptism of
Clovis, king of
the Franks.

507
Clovis annexed
Visigothic
kingdom of
Toulouse.

511
Partition of
Frankish
kingdom between
Clovis's four
sons.

516
Sigmund became
king of Burgundy
and was later
canonized.

India: Buddhist cave temple at Ajanta

ARCHITECTURE

500–600 India Ajanta monastery, near Bombay: in common with other early Buddhist monasteries, its buildings were carved out of the rock. Architecture features in imitation of earlier wood structures include columns and vault ribs.

500–600 Syria Qalb Louzeh church: now in ruins, it was a late Roman-inspired building. The three-bay nave, with its semi-circular arcade arches supported by piers, and the apse, give it a curiously Romanesque appearance. It is also an early example of a church with two flanking west end towers.

500–600 Turkey St John's church, Ephesus, had domed bays covering the nave and transepts: like its contemporary, the church of the Apostles in Istanbul (since destroyed), it may have influenced the design of the domed Romanesque churches of Aquitaine and St Mark's in Venice. It has since been destroyed.

*c.***500 Mexico** The Cholula (now ruined), a solid earth, stepped, flat-topped pyramid, was the largest of the Mesoamerican pyramids. The base, which covered 45 acres, was far larger than in its Egyptian counterparts.

*c.***510 Honduras** Structure 22 at Copan, the most impressive building of this important classic Mayan site: it is built of block masonry laid in mud. The sculptured frieze culminates in the doorway surrounded by a snake mask.

513 Syria Bosra cathedral was built to an experimental plan combining a circular central tower within a square. It was a prototype for the Byzantine centrally planned churches of Istanbul and Ravenna.

516 China Yung-ning-ssu was according to a near contemporary description, a magnificent Buddhist temple. The centre of the plan was the pagoda on the main axis with the courtyard entrance. The Buddha hall stood behind it. It would have resembled the rock-cut pagodas in the Yün-kang cave shrines of the sixth century. It has been destroyed.

THREE DIMENSIONAL ART

500 Peru Flourishing period of the Nazca artists: they made polychrome pottery, gold funerary masks and jewellery, and gold portrait vases. Peruvian goldsmiths used *cire-perdue* casting; they also decorated by welding applied pieces on to the original, and knew four methods of gilding including *mise en couleur* (adding gold particles to copper or silver and removing the soft metals from the resulting alloy with acid).

*c.***500 Cambodia** The Chen-La kingdom united with the earlier Fou-nan kingdom, began to control parts of Cambodia and Cochin-China: both kingdoms had an Indian-derived culture, and this formed the basis of classical Khmer religious art. Carved reliefs survive on buildings at Sambor Prei Kuk, and Hindu and Buddhist figures in stone and bronze are considered outstanding.

*c.***500 Japan** The Japanese began to translate and adapt the teaching of the Chinese on beautiful gardens. Gardens as a form of art declined in the West with the fall of Rome; early Christian monastic gardens were mainly for herbs and vegetables.

VISUAL ARTS

INVENTIONS & DISCOVERIES

525
Abyssinians conquered Yemen.

526
Amalaswintha, daughter of Theodoric the Ostrogoth, became regent of Italy.

Israel: Christmas service in the Church of the Nativity, Bethlehem

527
Emperor Justinian I began his re-unification of the Roman empire from Constantinople.

529
Benedict of Nursia founded monastery of Montecassino.

530
Gelimer became last king of the Vandals in North Africa.

531
Accession of Chosroes 1 of Persia; climax of Sassanian empire.

523 China The Sung Yüeh pagoda in Honan: this earliest surviving form shows the evolution of the pagoda from the plain watchtower. Under the influence of Indian Buddhist architecture, it became a tiered tower of pavilions, decreasing in size towards the top, and built of brick. Traditional Chinese wood-framed open pavilion pagodas do not survive from this date.

526 Italy The Church of San Vitale, Ravenna: its plan is a double octagon with an additional apse on one side, the model being the circular Roman mausoleum form. Byzantine taste covered the classical form with decoration, mainly mosaic designs and pictures. Completed 548 A.D. exterior belies the fine domes of the centrally planned interior and the superb gold-ground mosaic decoration of the apse. The carved capitals are also characteristically Byzantine, with their cubiform shapes and dosserets (blocks placed on top of capital to support arch).

527 Israel The Church of the Nativity at Bethlehem, Constantine's fourth-century church on the traditional site of Christ's birthplace, was rebuilt in the usual Early Christian manner. An atrium and narthex precede the double aisled basilica. It was completed in 565 and has been restored.

527 Turkey The church of St Sergius and St Bacchus in Istanbul was founded by Justinian: it is one of the finest of the many centrally planned domed Byzantine churches of this period. Its interior decoration of fresco, mosaic and capital sculpture were of very high quality. It has been restored.

*c.***530 Italy** The Tomb of Theodoric in Ravenna, a mausoleum designed for the Ostrogoth King: it is two-storeyed and capped by a single block of marble about 9 metres in diameter and weighing 470 tons.

532 Turkey The Basilica Cistern in Istanbul, designed possibly by Anthemius for Justinian, is the largest of the city's underground cisterns for storing water. It measures about 450 feet and the brick vaulted roof is supported by 336 Corinthian-capped columns.

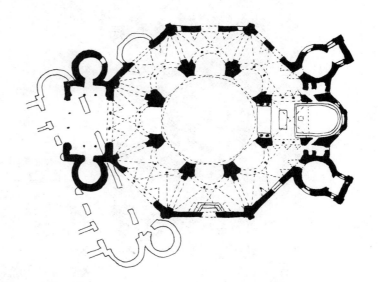

Italy: exterior and ground plan of San Vitale, Ravenna

530–550 Italy The mosaic decorations of St Vitale, Ravenna, make full use of the medium and its ability to reflect light and break up colours by means of cubes set at different angles into a ground that was never completely flat. The designs are complementary to the architecture.

*533
Belisarius
overthrew Vandal
kingdom and
made northern
Africa a
Byzantine
province.*

*534
Franks overthrew
kingdom of
Burgundy.*

*535
Belisarius
occupied Gothic
kingdom of Italy.*

*540
Badwila (Totila)
re-established
Gothic rule in
Italy.*

*550
Migration of
Turks from the
east began.
Anglian
kingdoms of E.
Anglia, Mercia
and Northumbria
established in
England.*

*552
Buddhism
introduced to
Japan.*

*553
Fifth Council of
Constantinople.*

*555
Narses completed
destruction of
Gothic kingdom
in Italy, and
again made Italy
a Byzantine
province.*

*558
Clotaire I
reunited Frankish
kingdom.*

*560
Ethelbert became
king of Kent,
England.*

Italy: mosaic of the Emperor Justinian in the church of San Vitale, Ravenna

532 Turkey The building of the basilica of Santa Sophia in Istanbul by Anthemius of Tralles and Isidore of Miletus. Early Christian churches were based either on the Latin cross, giving the shape of the Roman basilica, or on the Greek cross, which provided for a central main area, usually under a large dome, and side arms bounded by a square or a circle. Santa Sophia combines both traditions: it has the nave and aisles (ending in apses) of the basilica, and an important central area under a huge dominating dome. The dome is made to cover a square area by resting it on the tops of semi-domes, all pierced for extra light. It replaces an earlier building by Constantine. Completed 537 A.D.

*c.*534 **Italy** St Apollinare in Classe was built by Justinian on the site of a temple of Apollo. It is a brick three-aisled basilica, and was originally enriched with marble and mosaics. The remaining mosaics are of high quality.

535 Yugoslavia Porec' cathedral, an early Christian basilica which retains its atrium, octagonal baptistery and campanile: the apse is especially rich in decoration, with marble, porphyry, mother-of-pearl and mosaic. It was completed in 543.

Turkey: Santa Sophia basilica in Istanbul

541 Byzantium Abolition of the office of consul ended presentations of the ivory diptych: derived from the two-panelled Roman writing tablet, the diptych was traditionally carved with scenes, figures and ornaments, and given to the emperor and senators when the consul took office. The form was adapted by the church.

*c.*550 **Byzantium** Emperor Justinian obtained silk worms and silk technology from China, but the art of silk textiles was hampered by royal monopoly.

*c.*550 **Italy** The throne of Bishop Maximian in Ravenna: the most famous ivory carving of its period, it is decorated with panels of scenes from the life of Christ, Joseph and the Virgin; the expert style suggests that it came from a workshop in Constantinople or Alexandria.

560 China The Emperor of the Northern Chou dynasty commissioned a 26-foot high woven hanging as a Buddhist icon. Its size indicates highly-developed textile craftsmanship. In Chinese silks it was traditionally the warp thread and not, as in the West, the weft that showed the pattern.

HISTORICAL EVENTS

563
Columba travelled to Iona and began conversion of Picts.

567
Permanent partition of Frankish kingdom into Austrasia, Neustria, and Burgundy.

568
Lombards invaded northern Italy.

570
Mohammed born in Mecca.

575
Persians overthrew Abyssinian rule over Yemen.

581
Establishment of Sui dynasty in China.

585
Leovigild, king of the Visigoths, overthrew the Suevic kingdom in Spain.

589
Visigoths converted to Roman Catholicism.

596
Pope Gregory I dispatched Augustine as missionary to Britain.

602
Augustine established archiepiscopal see at Canterbury.

603
Lombards in Italy converted to Roman Catholicism.

604
Constitution of 17 articles in Japan.

Japan: Horiuji Temple, Nara

LITERATURE

c.600 Britain The *Gododdin*, by the poet Aneirin, was written as a lament for British heroes killed in battle, at Catterick, against the English. Welsh heroic verse stressed the startling contrasts of vitality and death. Poets accompanied the armies in battle in order to immortalize the courage of the warriors. Aneirin and Taliesin were the most famous of the period; they served rulers of what is now part of Scotland.

c.624 Arabia Probable date of composition of the third part of the Koran. Although intended to be heard, not read silently, the Koran stabilized the written language and marks the true beginning of Arabic literature.

DANCE & DRAMA

c.600–700 India *Malatimadhava* of Bhavabhuti marks the end of the classic period of Hindu drama.

c.600 Japan First appearance of the *bugaku* dances and their musical accompaniment (*gagaku*): the dances came from China through Korea and, unlike other features of Buddhist culture, never became a bourgeois or popular art but were preserved in imperial and aristocratic circles. They retain elements of original Indian dance now lost in India and China.

MUSIC

618 China Orchestras of hundreds of players established.

ARCHITECTURE

*c.*588 **Japan** Shitennoji, at Osaka, the earliest Buddhist monastery in Japan of which visible remains survive (although the original has been altered): its symmetrical plan resembles the Buddhist temples of China known as the 'Kudara'. Buddhism was introduced from China in about 550.

600–700 Japan Horiuji Temple at Nara, one of the earliest surviving Buddhist temples in Japan: it has a complex of monastic buildings planned with the usual Japanese disregard for symmetry. The pillared hall, *Kondo*, is on a stone base and has a curved projecting verandah roof; the five-storey pagoda is supported by a 100-foot central post. (Much altered.)

600–700 Mexico El Tajin is a ritual centre in which the niche pyramid is exceptional in having 364 niches inserted around each of its 7 storeys. Since the dating of ancient American architecture is still subject to conjecture, its date may in fact be placed anywhere between 300 and 900 A.D.

600–700 Mexico Palenque, a group of Mayan-type vaulted temples, with exterior relief sculpture; they were originally topped with carved roof combs. A unique four-storey tower dominates the site.

600 Guatemala Tikal, a Mayan site with a number of towering pyramids and 9 groups of courts and plazas; it was probably completed by this date.

*c.*600 **India** Lād Khān temple at Mysore, an early surviving example of freestanding stone architecture in India: it is a square-planned temple with a double row of square pillars delimiting a nave and verandah.

618 Armenia Surb Hripsime employed ribs in the vault system, at Valarshapat, nearly 500 years before a similar formula was used in Durham Cathedral, England.

THREE DIMENSIONAL ART

*c.*575 **Japan** The introduction of Buddhism was the first important stimulus to sculpture; missionaries brought craftsmen from Korea to make religious statues. The few figures surviving, in bronze and wood, are outstanding for the depth of feeling they convey.

*c.*600 **India** Early examples of the Badami rock temples cut in the Deccan plateau: they are simple architecturally but bear on the walls a mass of deep-relief sculpture, much of it monumental in style and colossal in scale. The characteristic pillar had elaborate stepping and panels of relief decoration; main motifs were the flowering vase, laced strings of jewels, and foliated scrolls. Temples continued to be cut until the ninth century.

*c.*600 **India** Development of the Tantric school of Buddhism, which spread to Tibet, China and Japan: its art is characterized by images of deities as terrible figures with fangs, aureoles of flames, and many heads and hands.

*c.*600–630 **Japan** Most active period of the sculptor Kuratsukuri-no-Tori, who set a style (named 'Tori' after him) of formalized, symmetrical, draped figures in symbolic form. Influenced by the art of the Chinese state of Northern Wei, the style was very austere and massive, but lacked any real feeling for three-dimensional form.

600–1100 China Beginning of the art of painting Chinese pottery with colours from metal ores: copper green, cobalt blue, manganese purple and antimony yellow.

618–906 China During the T'ang dynasty, influence from India resulted in a relaxation of the previous style of sculpture to a plastic, sensual modelling. Sculptors made lions and fantastic animals guarding tombs, and small clay tomb figures.

VISUAL ARTS

600–700 Italy and Byzantium Simultaneous development in Christian art of panel paintings of Christ and the saints.

600–625 India King Mahendra Varman in Tamil Nadu commissioned artists who began to paint frescoes in the Jain caves at Sittannavasal. Painting continued long afterwards.

594
Chinese started printing from a negative relief.

595
Hindus used decimal notation.

606
Accession of Hasha last independent native ruler of northern India before the Moslem conquest.

608
Pulakesin II Chalukya became ruler of the Deccan.

613
Austrasia and Burgundy united.

614
Persians took Damascus and Jerusalem.

618
Foundation of T'ang dynasty in China.

618–619
Persians took Egypt.

622
Mohammed fled from Mecca to Medina (the Hegira); beginning of Moslem calendar.

627
Christianization of Northumbrian kingdom, England.

632
Mohammed died; succeeded by Caliph Abu Bekr.

633
Visigothic Spain became elective kingdom.

634
Fall of Damascus; became capital of Islam.

635
Christianization of English kingdom of Wessex began.

644 China Probable date of the death of Wang Chi (b. ?590), the first notable poet of the Chinese T'ang period. He wrote in a free style, using the vernacular.

632 Arabia Beginning of Arabian music, which was based on older Semitic cultures.

England: purse lid found at Sutton Hoo burial mound

647 India End of the Gupta period (since 320), the great age of dance and drama: the main classical styles of dance from the Gupta period surviving today are Bharata Natyam (solo dances for temple dancers in Tamil areas), Kathakali (dance-drama full of mime from Kerala) and Kathak (court dances from North India). The other important school is Manipuri, a flowing, graceful, style.

626 Italy Death of the Lombard Queen Theodolinda, who gave the earliest surviving precious book-cover to the Basilica of St John at Monza. The cover is divided into four by a gem-studded gold cross; gold leaf, *cloisonné* glass and cameo are used.

*c.***630 Italy** The church of St Agnese Fuori Le Mura in Rome, a late example of an early Christian basilica: it has a characteristic nave and aisles beneath an open timber roof, with an apse to the east and narthex to the west.

625–630 England The royal burial mound at Sutton Hoo contained gold, garnet and glass jewellery apparently from one workshop indicating a high standard of Anglo-Saxon work.

625–638 Italy The silver door of the Vatican basilica was characteristic of the ornamental silver-work of the post-Roman period.

637 Persia Conquest of the Sassanid city of Ctesiphon on the Tigris by the Muslim Caliph Omar: this led to the discovery by Mediterranean Islam of a carpet called 'The Spring of Chosroes', depicting a spring garden, made under the Sassanians. Early Islamic artists, in carpet-making as in other arts, had no indigenous tradition to draw on in their austere, nomadic society. Their main stimulus was the art of the newly-conquered races, especially the Persians.

c. **643 Israel** The Dome of the Rock in Jerusalem, so called because of its wooden dome built over a rocky outcrop whence Mohammed is said to have ascended to heaven: it is the earliest surviving mosque and shows strong Byzantine influence in form, imitating the existing Church of the Holy Sepulchre. Early Moslems were Arabs of nomadic tradition with no native architecture except for the oasis—a rectangular enclosure with a tower, a fountain and a hall for shelter. Mosques have these elements, incorporating features from Semitic, Mesopotamian, Persian, Greek and Byzantine traditions.

*c.***648 Armenia, Russia** The early Armenian church at Mastara: Armenian churches were at first vaulted basilicas, but later followed a square ground plan, covered by a dome, as at Mastara.

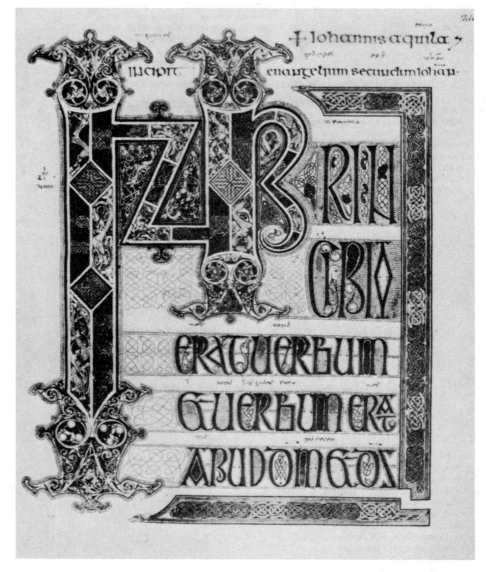

Britain and Ireland: page from the Lindisfarne Gospels

636
Battle of Yarmuk; Arabs took Syria from Byzantine empire.

637
Sassanian empire fell to Arabs; establishment of Omayyad caliphate.

640
Arabs took Egypt.

643
Ambassadors visited China from Persia and Constantinople.

647
Arabs conquered Tripoli.

664
First Arab invasion of India. Synod of Whitby; English church linked to Rome.

670
Arabs began conquest of North Africa.

672
Fujiwara family dominant in Japan.

673
First synod of the English church, at Hertford.

686
Sussex, last heathen kingdom in England, converted.

688
Ine, king of Wessex, subdued Essex and Kent.

c.670 England Caedmon, the Northern peasant poet, wrote his *Hymn* which is the earliest extant English poem. It uses the long, alliterative non-rhyming line with an assurance that suggests the form was already well established. Many later important Germanic poems have it: *Beowulf* in Old English, *Edda* in Old Norse, *Muspilli* in Old High German, and *Heliand* in Old Saxon.

678 China Probable date of the death of Wang P'o (b. ?650), poet and prose writer, who was one of the Four Masters of seventh-century Chinese literature.

691 Byzantium The Trullan Council in Constantinople threatened to depose priests and excommunicate laity who went to watch any theatrical performance.

650 China Tomb of the T'ang emperor T'ai-tsung was furnished with life-size relief panels depicting his favourite horses. T'ang sculptors and potters were particularly successful at expressing the power of the horse in motion; tombs not furnished with such ambitious work normally contained pottery figures of horses, other animals and human beings, sculpted in a lively and realistic style. These images of the beasts and servants of the dead replaced their sacrifice.

*c.***650 India** Cliff-carving at Mamallapuram shows numerous figures on a vast scale, representing a scene from Hindu mythology.

*c.***650 Japan** A wooden statue, the 'Kudara Kannon', of the Buddhist goddess of mercy was brought from Korea to the monastery of Hōryū-ji. A style of sculpture was named after this statue, characterized by tall forms and flowing lines and some feeling for three-dimensional form.

*c.***650 Japan** Development of the Chūgūji style of sculpture, with realistic three-dimensional modelling and concern for surface texture. Materials were wood or bronze. Facial expression was very important in all seventh-century Japanese sculpture.

668 Korea Beginning of the unification of the country under the royal line of the state of Silla: this brought about a unification of art styles and a new art with close affinities to the T'ang art of China.

652 China The Ta-Yen-T'a pagoda, part of the monastery in Tz'u-en-ssu: it consists of 7 diminishing levels, giving the appearance of a pyramid. Its square ground plan is typical of pagoda-building at the time.

661 Spain St Juan de Banos, a rare surviving church of the Visigothic period: it has a cluster of porticuses and the typical horseshoe-shaped arches of Mozarabic (Moslem-influenced Christian architecture) architecture.

662 India A complex of temples at Mamallapuram, Madras carved in rock, displaying a variety of roof levels: it is richly decorated with sculpture. Completed 674 A.D.

669 Hsing-Chiao-Ssua, China A masonry building was erected at Hsuan-Tsang, imitating techniques used when constructions were of timber. Renewed 828 A.D.

670 Tunisia The mosque of Kairouan was begun: most of what remains is ninth-century work.

*c.***670 England** Brixworth church built: it is a large and the only surviving one Anglo-Saxon church to show systematic use of arches in forming the nave arcade.

650–750 Britain and Ireland Ornamented manuscripts were made, showing a native taste for interlacing linear pattern (reinforced by the art of invading peoples during the fifth century), and a Mediterranean influence on figure-drawing. The *Lindisfarne Gospels* (Northumbrian, seventh century) and the *Book of Kells* (Ireland, eighth century) typify the style.

673 China Death of Yen Li Pen, court painter to the T'ang emperor T'ai Tsung: he concentrated on Buddhist and historical subjects.

685
Ravenna
Cosmography,
first gazetteer.

693
Armenia came under Arab rule.

697
Northern Irish church submitted to Rome.

*c.*700 **Arabia** Arabic poetry in the pre-Islamic manner was written by al-Farazdaq and Jarir. The two men were rivals and their poetic warfare is famous.

*c.*700–730 **England** *Beowulf,* the only native English heroic epic, was written by an unknown poet. It is the greatest Old English poem, a study of pagan heroic values written for a Christian, aristocratic society. Like nearly all early poetry, it was written for recitation.

700–800 Italy *Schola Cantorum,* the papal music school, first mentioned; it was founded *c.*600 by Pope Gregory, after whom Gregorian chant was named.

England: after a reconstruction of a helmet of an Anglo-Saxon warrior king, worn around the time 'Beowulf' was written

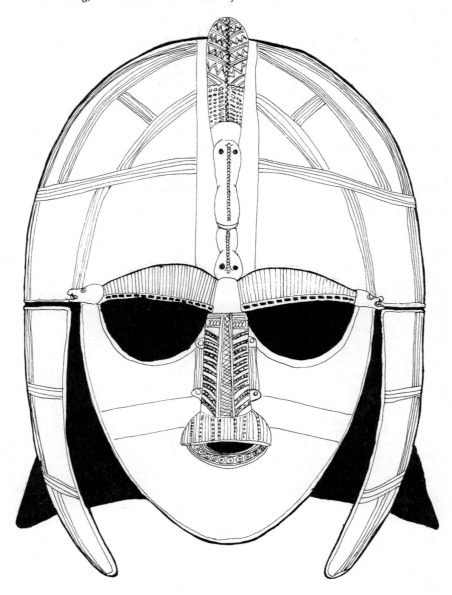

ARCHITECTURE

700–800 Mexico Monte Alban, the sacred capital of the Zapotecs for some 1000 years, was at its zenith: built on a hill site, it has a central plaza surrounded by platform buildings up which rise broad flights of steps. To the east is a ceremonial ball court, and in addition there are many tombs, some richly decorated in ceramics and frescoes.

700–800 Mexico Xochicalco succeeded Teotihuacan as a ritual centre: it is built up on a series of terraces featuring platforms, courtyards and esplanades. The sculptured platform temple to the north-west of the site bears elaborate relief carving, which was originally painted.

*c.*700–900 **China** Ch'ang-an was the first of the planned cities on a large scale. The unit is the courtyard house; a group of them form a square; squares are joined by a grid of streets; main axial street runs north to south. Cities were built for a predetermined number of people and citizens brought in from surrounding villages. Cities were walled with gates.

700–800 China T'ang period pagodas were built on square foundations and often curved gradually inwards, like an Indian shrine-tower, towards the top.

*c.*700–800 **India** Dharmapale Temple and Monastery at Paharpur in Bengal: a complex consisting of a large court, surrounded by cells, in the centre of which is a shrine 30 metres high. Such a plan foreshadows the temples in Java.

700–800 Turkey St Mary Pammakaristos, Istanbul, now Fetiyeh Djamo, is an example of a small structure on the typical Byzantine plan of the Greek cross: it was later converted into a mosque.

700 France St Jean's church at Poitiers, a rare survivor of the seventh-century Merovingian period: it is a basilican church.

THREE DIMENSIONAL ART

700–750 China Pottery ewers reflect Persian and central Asian forms.

700–800 Egypt A cast bronze ewer, called the 'ewer of Marwān II' and found at the site of his death, is characteristic of a type found in Egypt and Syria. It is globular in shape with a long straight neck and decorative engraving.

*c.*700 **India** Caves I and II of the Buddhist rock-cut temple at Ajanta were painted. Narrative paintings cover spans of the walls; individual pictures are of Buddhist icons. The colours were brilliant, mixed with gum and applied on plaster.

700 Central America First indications of metal-working in Mexico and the Mayan areas. Craftsmen used gold, silver, copper, tin and *tumbaga* alloy, gold and copper. The Mixtecs became the leaders in making gold filigree jewellery.

*c.*700 **India** Wall-painting in elaborate floral and figurative designs reached its peak in the Buddhist temple-caves at Ajanta; relief-carving representing Buddhist iconography also continued.

VISUAL ARTS

700–800 Japan Introduction of scroll painting from China. The Chinese used it for landscape; the Japanese developed scrolls up to 30 feet long depicting adventure narratives. The art reached its peak in the twelfth and thirteenth centuries, always in close association with literature

INVENTIONS & DISCOVERIES

695
First Arab coinage in use.

17

HISTORICAL EVENTS	LITERATURE	DANCE & DRAMA	MUSIC

*HISTORICAL
EVENTS*

*701
Codification of
Japanese law.*

701 England A discovery, in Rome, of a fragment of the True Cross inspired the Old English poem *The Dream of the Rood*. Two versions of it were written; the original was carved on a stone cross at Ruthwell in Northumbrian dialect, the second was in manuscript form and written in Wessex *c*.885. It presents an original mystical vision in Anglo-Saxon riddle form.

704 Ireland Death of St Adamnan (b. 625), saint and historian. Attributed to him were a *Life of St Columba*, a mystic poem called *Adamnan's Vision* and one of the earliest European accounts of the Holy Land, *De Locis Sancti*.

*712
Arabs conquered
Seville.*

*715
Pope Gregory II
dispatched
Wynfrith-
Boniface as
missionary to
Germany.*

*716
Arabs besieged
Constantinople.
Accession of
Ethelbald of
Mercia who
controlled all
England except
Northumbria.*

*717
Accession of Leo
III, first of the
Byzantine
Iconoclast
emperors.*

*730
Beginning of
great period of
Mayan empire.*

*732
Charles Martel,
Frankish ruler,
defeated Moors
at Poitiers at the
height of Arab
invasion of
western Europe.*

712 Japan *Kojiki*, the earliest known Japanese book, was a historical chronicle written in Chinese. It records songs and poems, in Japanese, dating from *c*.400, when there was no system of writing. Japanese culture developed rapidly under Chinese influence.

731 England *The Ecclesiastical History of the English People* by the Venerable Bede (625–735), was written in a vivid Latin style with a concern for accuracy. It was widely influential.

732 and 735 Turkey The Orhon Inscriptions were made in Turkish runic characters on two large stones, commemorating two Turkish princes. They are among the earliest examples of the Turkish language, but their style is polished, which indicates that composition in the language was not new.

715 Arabia *A Coded Theory of Arabian Nights* was undertaken by Ibn Misjah, which contained 8 melodic modes and 6 rhythmic modes.

c.730 Japan: Todaiji temple, Nara, the largest wooden structure in the world

705 Syria The Ummayad mosque in Damascus, built on the site of a Roman temple, followed the lines of Christian basilicas: three aisles of equal width with a transept, the crossing being covered by a dome, and a large forecourt. Form and decoration inside a mosque were rhythmic and repetitive, designed as aids to contemplation. The mosque replaced a Christian church, which replaced a temple to Zeus; it was completed in 715 A.D.

725–784 Japan The *Tempyō* style of sculpture, considered to be the best of the Nara (710–784) period: craftsmen were encouraged by imperial patronage and by the influence of T'ang China to improve their technique and widen their range of materials; quality became monumental instead of spiritual as in earlier work while T'ang vigour was tempered by native restraint. Dry lacquer was used extensively. Sculptors also made portrait and other masks for ritual dance.

726 Constantinople Leo III ordered the destruction of all sacred images in human form: this iconoclastic period forced church artists to concentrate on the decorative instead of the figurative. The mosaicists of Sta Irene, Constantinople, began to use richly varied gold backgrounds, with cubes of different shades set at different angles to reflect the light.

716 China Death of the painter Li Ssu-Hsun, founder of the 'blue-and-green' style of landscape painting.

*c.***720–780 China** Hankan flourished, outstanding painter of horses.

c. **730 Japan** Hokkedo, the Todaiji Temple at Nara, was influenced by contemporary Chinese architecture: it has an especially complex wooden bracketing system supporting the roof rafters. The original hall was 275 feet wide. Timber was the usual building material in Japan.

LITERATURE

DANCE & DRAMA

MUSIC

741
*Emperor
Constantine V
renewed
prohibition of
image-worship.*

*c.*740 **China** *Home Longings* by Ts'ui Hao (d. 754) has been considered one of the best T'ang dynasty poems in the seven-word metre.

740 China T'ang emperor Ming Huang (713–756) founded the first drama school: it was called the Pear Garden and produced what appears to have been some kind of opera.

742 Arabia Birth of Ibráhím Ibn Mahán Al-Nadim Al-Mauṣili, Arabian musician (d. 804). He was a celebrated instrumentalist, an unrivalled composer and founded a music school.

749 Arabia Death of Abd al-Hamid al-Katib, considered the originator of the epistolary style in the great period of classical Arabic prose.

*c.*750 **England** Creative period of the religious poet Cynewulf. His surviving poems are *Elene*, *Juliana*, *The Ascension* and the *Fates of the Apostles*. Old English religious verse interpreted Christian themes in terms of Old Germanic heroic society.

750 Arabia Seat of Arabian government moved to Baghdad, which soon became the centre of music. Considerable money was expended on music— 10,000 pieces of silver was paid to one particular singer each month.

India: Kailasa temple at Ellora showing a sculptured panel depicting war scenes

754 Arabia Death of St John of Damascus (b. *c.*700), the first organizer of Christian liturgical song and credited with reform of musical notation.

*755
The Umayyad
Abderrahman
founded Moslem
Caliphate of
Cordoba, Spain.*

740 Turkey The present church of St Irene in Istanbul was built, on sixth-century foundations: it is thought to be the earliest example of a dome mounted on a drum pierced by windows, though the ground plan is still the three-aisled basilican type.

746 China Ching-Ts-Ong, a tomb pagoda of octagonal plan, combining both wooden and masonry structural and decorative features.

c.750 India The Parasuramesvara Temple at Bhuvaneshwar, Orissa, the shrine tower or *Sikhara* of tall, convex-curved sides stands in remarkable contrast to the low horizontal porch-hall, both decorated by sculpture placed in horizontal tiers. This is the best known shrine of many Hindu temples of this type built in Orissa.

750–c.800 England Offa's Dyke, the most formidable of Anglo-Saxon frontiers, consisting of a ditch and rampart 120 miles long.

750–950 India Kailása Temple at Ellora: placed on a platform, it incorporates all the elements of Indian temple architecture including a detached shrine which housed divine images.

750–786 Persia The mosque at Damghan, Tarik-Khana, has a typical plan with an arcaded courtyard in which the fourth side is fronted by the mosque. Remarkable circular piers carrying parabolic arches support a shallow dome. The arches are now a unique survival, though at the time they were widely used.

744–750 Egypt Death of the Umayyad Caliph Marwān II, who is thought to be the caliph described in one of the oldest extant factory inscriptions, on a silk textile from Ifriqiya in Tunisia. Official factories produced the bulk of Islamic textiles; much of its design derived from the Sassanian art of Persia. Each important factory inscribed its textiles with a proof of origin.

750 India Pilgrims to the Buddhist sites in the Pāla kingdom began to take away small copies of the shrine images; these were influential on Buddhist art in many south-east Asian countries.

c.750–900 China Porcelain was developed, probably in Hopei or Kiangsu provinces.

751 Iraq Chinese silk weavers captured in war were settled in Iraq. At first hampered by Moslem austerity, they in time established a thriving industry. Designs were dictated by Islamic doctrine and retained no Chinese influence.

752 Korea Buddhist images in the rock temple at Sokkulam are considered the highest achievement of Korean sculpture. They include a 10-foot figure of a seated Buddha, an 11-headed Kuan-yin (the Bodhisattva or Buddhic deity of mercy) and reliefs of the 10 disciples of the Buddha.

755 Spain Founding of the Moslem Caliphate of Cordoba. The Islamic crescent reaching from Asia to Spain produced a standard Islamic design in textiles, ceramics, metalwork and glass. Spanish textiles were often reproductions of Syrian or Persian designs; the motifs used soon began to penetrate Byzantine work.

756 China An Lu-shan's rebellion: believed to be the date of the buried hoard of the Prince of Pin. Gold and silver vessels found were worked by the *repoussé* technique, by casting, and by the combined techniques of filigree and granulation. Their design shows Sassanian Persian influence.

750
Arabs gained knowledge of Chinese papermaking.

HISTORICAL EVENTS	LITERATURE	DANCE & DRAMA	MUSIC

759 China Probable date of the death of Wang Wei (b. ?699), poet and painter, who was master of the brief, evocative poem.

760 Japan The *Manyōshū*, a collection of *tanka* poems in Japanese. The *tanka*, a poem of 31 syllables in which five- and seven-syllabled lines alternate, has been the standard form for Japanese poetry until recently. The *Manyōshū* is considered fine poetry and of great importance as a source of information on history, myth and language.

*762
Baghdad founded
as capital of
Islamic empire.*

757 Byzantium A wind organ was sent to France by the Byzantine emperor Constantinus Copronymus.

*c.***765 Arabia** Death of Yúnus ibn Sulaimán Al-Kátib, Arabian musical historian and editor, who made the first collection of Arabic songs.

767 Arabia Birth of Abú Muḥammad Isḥáq Al-Mauṣili, Arabian musician (d. 850), one of the greatest musicians of his time, both as a writer and performer, and said to have been first singer to use *falsetto*.

*768
Charlemagne
became king of
the Franks.*

770 China Death of the poet Ts'en Ts'an (b. 715), who wrote of the horrors of war.

*773
Charlemagne
annexed the
Lombard
kingdom of
northern Italy.*

*777
Offa of Mercia
subdued kingdom
of Wessex.*

779 Arabia Birth of Ibráhím Ibn al-Mahdí, Arabian musician (d. 839), leader of the 'romantic' school of music which had a great influence on Arabian music.

783 Persia Death of Bashshar ibn Burd, Arabic satiric poet; he was one of the first Arabic poets to break away from the traditional ode form.

*784
Offa's Dyke
marked frontier
between Mercia
and Wales.*

ARCHITECTURE

*c.*760 **India** Kailasanatha Temple, Ellora, cut out from the rock as a complete building in the round: the pyramidal roof typifies the Hindu temple plan evolved in South India under the Pallavan Kings during the sixth to seventh centuries.

762–776 **Italy** St Maria in Valle, at Cividale: a strange survival of Roman architecture, with vaults and a richly stuccoed interior indicating Byzantine or Saracenic influence.

774–783 **Spain** St Juan de Pravia, the earliest surviving Asturian church: it has a barrel vault over the chancel and contains several royal tombs.

780 **Iraq** The Palace of Ukhaidir at Kerbela is on the plan of the city of Anjar. It is a rectangular enclosure with high external walls within which there was a residential area with a complex of courtyards as well as a mosque.

THREE DIMENSIONAL ART

756 **Japan** The art collection of the Emperor Shōmu, some 3000 objects, was presented to the Tōdai-ji temple at the capital city of Nara. Still extant, it gives a representative picture of the arts admired at the time, most of them of Chinese origin or influence.

762 **Baghdad** The Caliph Al-Mansur laid out a Persian garden at his palace, the Persian style being regarded as the most beautiful. Persian gardens were enclosed against an arid surrounding countryside and stocked with flowers, trees and flowing water. The design reflected the four quarters of the Universe and the four rivers separating them; the effect was strongly architectural with walls and pavilions decorated with tiles and pierced screens. Their outstanding beauty inspired poets, painters and carpet designers for generations.

768–814 **Germany** Charlemagne's court at Aachen patronized embroidery, which showed strong Byzantine influence. The 'eagle' motif commonly used gives the name '*aquilata*' to work done at Charlemagne's court.

772 **Cairo** A glass beaker made at Fostat had lustre painting but pottery of the time had a white, opaque alkaline glaze unsuitable for painting with lustre only later was a tin glaze developed that would take lustre.

784–897 **Japan** The Heian period of sculpture, influenced by stern Buddhist mysticism: figures carved with chisels from a single block of wood tended to be massive and formal, with all emphasis on the facial expression.

VISUAL ARTS

759 **China** Death of Wang Wei (b. 698), outstanding landscape painter.

*c.*760 **China** Death of Wu Tao-Tzu, famous and near-legendary painter. He is credited with inventing monochrome calligraphic bamboo painting.

INVENTIONS & DISCOVERIES

*770
Euclid's* Elements *translated into Arabic.*

*780
Arabs brought decimal numbers from India.*

*785
Floating magnetic compass in use in China.*

*787
Danish attacks
on England
began.*

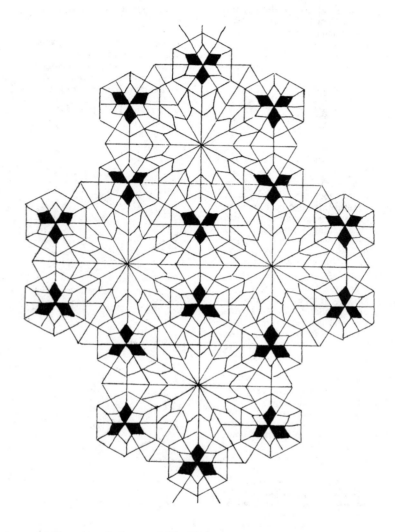

Arabic geometrical pattern of the 8th century

791 Arabia Death of Manṣúr Zalzal Al-Dárib, musician, who reformed the scale on the lute by introducing a neutral third, still known in the sixteenth century as the 'zalzal third'.

*793
Danes destroyed
monastery of
Lindisfarne.*

*794
Japanese capital
moved from Nara
to Kyoto;
beginning of
Heian period.*

799 Italy Death of Paul the Deacon (b. 720), historian and poet, to whom was attributed the *History of the Lombards*.

*800
Charlemagne
crowned Holy
Roman Emperor
by Leo III in
Rome.*

*c.*800–900 **Cambodia** The Khmer city of Angkor emerged as a centre of culture. Dances were influenced by previous invasions from India and parts of Java under Indian influence; they have since been preserved by royal patronage.

786–809 Persia The Tomb of Zobeide in Bagdad: an 8-sided structure surmounted by a pyramidical roof. Alternating arches carry internally the over-hanging pointed niches, a device which could be seen as the origin of later stalactite vaulting.

786–990 Spain The mosque at Cordoba: a great rectangular building of 10 aisles with 33 bays to each, supported by 1200 columns, some carrying tiers of upper arches. The star-ribbed vaults of the tenth century probably inspired later Gothic and Baroque vaulting. It became a Christian church in 1238, and was altered in the sixteenth century.

790–799 France Centula (St Riquier) Abbey was a large Carolingian church with a massive west-work that forms the earliest imposing façade in ecclesiastical architecture. It also had a double transept, west and east, and 9 towers. Its appearance is known from a twelfth century drawing and earlier description. Completed 799 A.D., it was subsequently rebuilt and then destroyed.

792–805 Germany Palatine Chapel, Aachen Aix-la-Chapelle is Charlemagne's mausoleum modelled on San Vitale, Ravenna. Odo of Metz, the architect, used materials and craftsmen from the Byzantine empire. Its ground plan consists basically of an ambulatory around an octagonal centre space, while its decorative character is classical.

794 Japan Kyoto became the new Imperial capital including the Shishinden whose interior space could be enlarged or contracted by using paper covered lattices and bamboo shades between the supporting columns. Private houses were built on the same principle. The Palace was rebuilt in the nineteenth century.

799 Switzerland St Peter's in Niederzell was the first of the great churches of the Reichenau monastic group.

800–900 Peru The huge adobe brick Temple of the Sun, at Moche, five storeys high and crowned with a pyramid; it is the largest ancient construction in South America and rises to 135 feet (over 41 metres).

Spain: the mosque at Córdoba

800–900 Bulgaria The *Madara Horseman*: a figure of a khan on horseback, about 10 feet high, cut in relief on a cliff face after the style of Iranian reliefs.

794
State paper mill set up in Baghdad.

LITERATURE

late 700–800 Arabia Hammad al Rawiya made a collection of 7 pre-Islamic poems by 7 poets: the *Mu'allakat*. Early Arabic poetry was mainly heroic, taking the form of odes that followed a traditional order of subjects, and the poet had his place in a tribal society loyal to an overlord. The subject matter was mostly concerned with desert life.

800–825 Germany First known manuscript of the *Hildebrandslied*, the only preserved Germanic lay.

c.800 Arabia Active period of Abu Nuwas, the Arabic poet of courtly life. Anecdotes about him are found in the *Arabian Nights*.

c.800 India Mannikar Vachagar wrote his poem *Tiravachagam*. He wrote in Tamil, the language of south India.

DANCE & DRAMA

c.800–900 Indonesia Introduction from India of shadow plays based on stories from the two ancient Hindu epics, the *Ramayana* and *Mahabharata*: flat puppet figures were projected on to a sheet by torches behind. From these derive *wayang wong* (imitation of puppet movements by actors) and *wayang golek*, with rounded puppets.

800 Europe Accession of Charlemagne, who forbade actors to dress as priests – though whether in anti-Christian plays or in a kind of ecclesiastical drama is not known.

MUSIC

Indonesia: Chandi Mendut Buddhist Shrine, Java

ARCHITECTURE

800–822 Germany The church of St Boniface at Fulda was modelled on the basilican plan of Old St Peter's, Rome.

800 Indonesia Java, Borobudur is the most impressive monument in the Asiatic world and must have provided a source of inspiration for the temple-mountains of Angkor. There is a series of square stepped-out platforms leading to three circular terraces which culminate in a large circular stupa. It is extremely richly decorated with sculpture depicting Buddhist legends and was excavated in 1907.

*c.***800 India** The sun temple at Martand is a shrine placed in the centre of a rectangular court surrounded by cells. There is a portico for sun-worship ritual which represented a model for later temples.

*c.***800 Indonesia** Chandi Mendut on Java is one of the greatest Buddhist shrines in the Javanese style and is placed on a high plinth with a single large square chamber covered with diminishing roofed storeys. It is highly decorated with sculpture, including a famous Buddha trinity.

THREE DIMENSIONAL ART

800–900 Bulgaria Gold vessels from Nagy Sankt Miklós, which is now in Romania, show influences of Sassanian and Byzantine metalwork.

800–900 Germany The 'Crystal of Lothair', a rock-crystal engraved with the story of Susanna, marked a revival of the art of crystal-carving.

800–900 Japan Main development of *maki-e* lacquering technique, in which designs were built up by alternate applications of lacquer (latex from the tree *Rhus vernicifera*) and sprayed metallic dust.

800–900 Mesopotamia Production of ceramic dishes with moulded relief decoration and all-over coloured glaze in yellow or green. Ornament included a mixture of Hellenistic and Sassanian motifs. Similar, if coarser, ware was made in Egypt and glazed with green or brown. Splashed green decoration on an opaque white glaze also occurs on pottery at this time. It is similar to Chinese T'ang ware but was probably developed independently. Also at this time Mesopotamia developed a thick white tin glaze which could be painted on bright colours; it appeared on Baghdad ware painted brown, blue and green.

800–900 Italy Semitic glass-makers moved to L'Altare, Montforat, away from Frankish rule, leaving no skilled glass-makers in Normandy, Pacardy or other Frankish domains. They became known as Altarists.

800–900 Italy Rome and Ravenna were both centres for the making of glass mosaics.

800–1000 Islam Lustre-ware pottery was developed at Cairo and Baghdad by reducing silver and copper pigments on an already fused glaze. By the year 1000 one-colour lustres predominated.

800–1000 Spain Pottery decorated with underglaze painting was made in a variety of shapes.

800 South America Establishment in Peru and Bolivia of the Tiahuanaco culture. Artists made vessels and pieces of jewellery in hammered gold and silver, realistic figures in stone, sitting or kneeling, with robes of feathers.

VISUAL ARTS

800–900 Bulgaria Revival of Christianity was a strong stimulus to fresco and other mural painting, a tradition in the Thracian period. Painters adapted the system laid down by Constantinople, adding humanistic and naturalistic elements absent in most other Byzantine art.

800–900 Byzantium Figures of Christ crucified begin to show suffering and human vulnerability, stressing Christ's painful death. This dead Christ was rare in Western European art until the thirteenth century.

INVENTIONS & DISCOVERIES

HISTORICAL EVENTS

*814
Death of
Charlemagne;
Louis I, the
Pious, became
emperor of the
Franks.*

*826
Arabs took
Crete.*

*836
Danes sacked
London.*

*840
Confederation of
Slav tribes
formed in eastern
Europe.*

*842
Oaths of
Strasbourg were
the first record of
final separation
of French and
German
languages.*

*843
Treaty of Verdun
divided the
Carolingian
empire.*

*846
Arabs pillaged
Rome.*

*850
Buddhism
replaced by
Jainism and
Hinduism in
India.*

LITERATURE

804 England Death of the scholar Alcuin (b. 735), who carried English traditions of learning to the Germans as counsellor to Charlemagne.

*c.***820 Germany** The *Vita Caroli Magni*, attributed to the cleric Einhard (770–840): it was a rich source of material for later writers on Charlemagne's reign.

821 Germany Death of Theodulf of Orleans (b. 760), Latin poet at the court of Charlemagne. He wrote in a mannered, rhetorical style.

*c.***825 Germany** The epic poem *Heliand* was written; it is the only surviving alliterative heroic epic in Old Saxon.

829–842 Byzantium Greek monumental capital letters, used for carving on stone, were replaced by the miniscule script which was more suitable for connected writing on paper or parchment.

849 Germany Death of Walafrid Strabo (b. 808), cleric and teacher, who wrote fine Latin verse.

851 Ireland Johannes Scotus Erigena (810–860) wrote *De Praedestinatione*.

DANCE & DRAMA

816 Germany The Church Council at Aix-la-Chapelle forbade priests to be present at plays.

MUSIC

*c.***840 Switzerland** Birth of Notker [Balbulus] (d. 912). A monk at the monastery of St Gall, he worked on the development and popularization of the sequences.

France: the oratory at Germigny-des-Pres

ARCHITECTURE

806 France The oratory at Germigny-des-Pres consecrated; built according to the plan of Aix-la-Chappelle at Aachen but with Visigothic horseshoe arches, it was restored in the nineteenth century.

812–876 Yugoslavia St Donato's in Zadar is a centrally planned circular church with triple apsed east end and barrel vaulted nave.

820 Switzerland St Gall Abbey: a still existing plan for the abbey includes apses on the east and west side as well as west towers. Such a plan became common in Germany. The layout of the monastic buildings was intended as an ideal scheme for a monastery.

836 France St Philibert-de-Grandlieu for the first time had an eastern ambulatory at crypt level; it was introduced to allow free passage for pilgrims visiting the saint's shrine. Although finished in 853, it has been altered since.

842 Spain St Maria de Naranco near Oviedo is now a church but was probably originally designed as royal hall over a crypt. It has unusual loggias at the east and west ends. The barrel vault is supported by external buttresses. It was completed in 848.

847 Iraq The great mosque at Samarra has a courtyard with several aisles. The famous minaret placed at one side with a ramp winding all the way to the top must have derived from the ziggurats of Mezopotamia (*c.* 2000 B.C.) of which only one example survives.

848 Spain St Miguel de Lino is an early example of a Spanish church which originally had a complete system of barrel vaulting.

THREE DIMENSIONAL ART

835 Italy The German artist Wolvinius made the altar frontal of St Ambrogio, Milan, in *cloisonné* enamel. *Cloisonné* work with glass and stones had flourished in northern Europe at least since 600 A.D., while *cloisonné* enamelling was a Byzantine art, and was usually done on gold.

843 Constantinople St Methodius finally restored the icon as an object of veneration after a period of iconoclasm lasting from 813.

850 Mexico The lowland Mayas abandoned their ceremonial centres and with this their urban and ritual arts came to an end.

VISUAL ARTS

812–842 Spain Painting of the frescoes in the church of San Julian de los Prados at Santullano, in the small kingdom of Asturias, a region left unconquered by the Moors: they have been described as the latest example of the great classical tradition of decorative painting, with its taste for architectural illusion.

850–900 Spain Spanish Christians moved away from Moslem suppression in the south into Léon and Castile, where they established the Mozarabic style of art, uniting native and Islamic traditions. Its influence spread into Western France.

INVENTIONS & DISCOVERIES

813
Arabs founded school of astronomy in Baghdad.

830
Arab treatise on algebra.

850
Arabs perfected astrolabe.

HISTORICAL EVENTS

855
Louis II became king of Italy and Holy Roman Emperor.

858
Vikings sacked Algeciras; expelled by Moslems in following year.

860
Ethelbert became king of England.

866
Danish kingdom of York established in England.

870
Danes conquered East Anglia.

871
Alfred became king of England.

875
Charles II (the Bald) crowned Holy Roman Emperor.

878
Danes invaded Wessex, defeated by Alfred at Edington. Treaty of Wedmore; Danes kept East Anglia, Essex and part of Mercia.

879
Nepal gained independence from Tibet.

LITERATURE

855–860 Ireland Johannes Scotus Erigena made Irish translations of Latin texts by Pope Gregory.

856 Germany Death of Archbishop Rabanus Maurus of Mainz (b. 784), an influential scholar and teacher.

*c.*860 **Germany** *Muspilli*, an Old High German poem on the fate of the human soul: written in powerful rhetorical style, it had wide influence.

863 Byzantium St Cyril (826–869) and St Methodius (826–865) were appointed to lead a mission to the Moravian Slavs. They devised an alphabet of Old Slavonic in order to translate biblical and liturgical texts. *St Cyril's Gospel* is regarded as the beginning of Slavonic as a literary medium. He may have devised the Cyrillic script which Slavs began to use about this time.

*c.*865 **Germany** Creative period of the poet Otfrid of Weissenburg, author of the earliest rhyming verse in German, which interpreted gospel stories.

869 Germany Death of Godescalc, writer of treatises and poems in Latin.

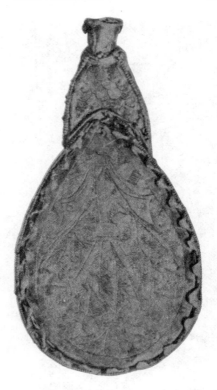

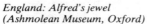

England: Alfred's jewel
(Ashmolean Museum, Oxford)

868 Egypt Beginning of the Tulunid Moslem dynasty, in which religious tolerance led to a blurring of the distinction between Coptic and Islamic arts. Islamic artists had themselves been influenced by earlier Coptic work; Coptic artists had preserved some of the Hellenistic elements from Byzantine art and had turned them into the sort of abstract patterns which Moslem artists appreciated.

871–899 England The reign of Alfred, King of Wessex (871–899), depicted on Alfred's Jewel, made by Kentish artists in gold and *cloisonné* enamel.

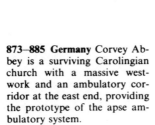

873–885 Germany Corvey Abbey is a surviving Carolingian church with a massive westwork and an ambulatory corridor at the east end, providing the prototype of the apse ambulatory system.

875 Italy St Pietro at Agliote is the earliest known Italian church to incorporate distinctive Romanesque features. It has a barrel vault over the choir.

876–879 Egypt Although the pointed arch of the mosque of Ibn Tooloon in Cairo was used in Syria before this date, it is the earliest example of its use on an extensive scale, replacing the usual horizontal timber beams.

885
*Harold Fairhair
united Norway.*

886
*Alfred captured
and rebuilt
London.*

900
*Moravian state
destroyed by
Magyars
advancing west
from Asia.*

*c.*882 **Germany** Composition of the *Ludwigslied*, a heroic stanzaic poem in Rhenish dialect.

883 **Germany** Notker Balbulus (840–912) wrote his *Gesta Caroli*, a biography of Charlemagne. He was a monk who wrote in Latin.

*c.*890 **France** The *Cantilène de Sainte Eulalie* is the first extant French poem.

891 **England** The first entry was made in the *Anglo-Saxon Chronicle* which provides a main source for English history until *c.*1150.

893 **Byzantium** Tsar Simeon replaced Greek with Slavonic as the official language of Bulgaria. Bulgarian monks translated literature available in the Byzantine empire, including tales and poems brought by travellers and traders from distant countries, including India.

894 **England** Alfred, king of Wessex (849–899), produced, with his scholars, a translation into English of Pope Gregory's *Cura Pastoralis*. Alfred was himself a scholar and historian.

*c.*900 **Japan** *The Story of the Bamboo Gatherer* is the earliest known extant Japanese novel. The author is unknown, but almost all early Japanese literature was written by the aristocracy.

*Ireland: illustration from the
Book of Kells*

900–1100 **France** St Martial school near Limoges flourished.

900 **Europe** *Scholia Enchiriadis* gives the earliest description of polyphony.

879 Cambodia Preak-Ko at Roluos is a temple oriented in east-west direction comprising moats, terraced enclosures and the group of 6 shrines in the centre of the structure.

881 Cambodia The Bakong temples also at Roluos was the first great temple-mountain to survive with the central shrine; one of 8, it was replaced in the twelfth century. The structure gives the impression of a large terraced pyramid.

900–1000 Mexico Tula, the capital and religious centre of the Toltecs (who had assisted in the destruction of the earlier civilizations of central America), was founded. The principal buildings were constructed around a plaza and include the temple of Tlahuizcalpantecuhtil, a traditionally planned five-storey pyramid noted for its sculpture which was originally polychromed.

900–1000 Spain Castle of Baños de la Encina built by the Moors had walls and square towers of pebbles and mortar; it was the most advanced form of castle of the period.

900–930 Indonesia The Lara Jonggrang at Prambanam, Java had over 200 temples incorporated into the overall design of which the temple of Shiva, placed in the centre of the innermost court, was the most important and elaborate.

897–1185 Japan The sculpture of the Fujiwara period was less austere than that of the preceding era, and style was lighter and more natural. Japan was independent of Chinese influence; sculptors ceased to work in cast bronze or dry lacquer, and wood prevailed. The increased demand for sculpture as decoration led to a kind of mass production and an elegant but superficial style.

900–1000 Ireland The 'Tara brooch', an example of Celtic design in metalwork similar to the linear designs in Irish illuminated manuscripts such as the Book of Kells.

900–1000 Mesopotamia Introduction on lustre-ware dishes of bird and animal designs, set against a stippled background. Though stylized, the creatures are more naturalistic than any previous bird or animal motifs. This style was imitated with modifications in the eastern Islamic states.

900–1000 Russia Silver-mounted aurochs' horns, found near Chernigov: they are decorated with *repoussé* work, combining Norse motifs with animal forms of Scythian type in an ancient, pagan iconography. Also in Russia at this period there is evidence of work in carved ivory and in ceramics (glazed tiles and pottery toys).

900–1000 Spain Bronze-casters made hollow animal forms with incised patterning on the surface; they served as fountain heads.

900–1200 Mexico The Toltecs made lead-containing pottery which vitrified in firing; Amerindian potters were skilled at controlling low temperatures.

900–1300 China *Chi-chou* pottery made: this included white porcelain, stonewares and mottled wares.

Ireland: Glendalough Tower

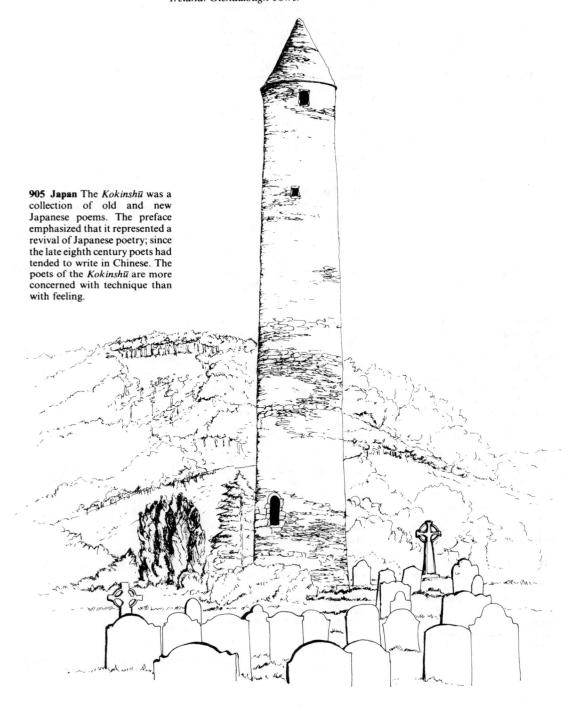

902
Arabs completed conquest of Sicily.

906
First Magyar invasion of Germany.

907
Disorder in China with end of T'ang dynasty; Epoch of the five dynasties followed.

910
Cluny abbey founded by William, duke of Aquitaine.

911
Treaty of St Clair-sur-Epte established the dukedom of Normandy.

905 Japan The *Kokinshū* was a collection of old and new Japanese poems. The preface emphasized that it represented a revival of Japanese poetry; since the late eighth century poets had tended to write in Chinese. The poets of the *Kokinshū* are more concerned with technique than with feeling.

ARCHITECTURE

*c.*900 **Germany** Lorsch Abbey Guest Hall displays an unusual and elaborate system of classical detailed decoration and patterned stonework; it was perhaps the work of Gallic builders.

*c.*900 **Guatemala** The pyramid E Vii Sub is at Uaxactun symmetrically planned with stairs at each side flanked by massive sculptured grotesque faces. All was originally stuccoed and painted.

*c.*900 **Ireland** The Glendalough round tower is a well preserved example of this kind of structure; many towers were built both in Ireland and Scotland from the ninth to the twelfth century. Up to about 30 metres (100 feet) high they probably served as belfries as well as for defensive purposes.

*c.*900 **Italy** St Maria in Cosmedin in Rome has one of the earliest known spacious hall crypts. The twelfth century campanile rises 7 storeys above the church.

*c.*907 **Persia** The mausoleum of Ismail the Samanid at Bokhara is an almost perfect cube, built in brick with superimposed hemispherical masonry dome. Decorative brickwork for the setting of the dome is the earliest example of this technique which later became very popular.

910 **France** Cluny Abbey was founded in Burgundy by William of Aquitaine. Cluniac Benedictines believed that a church should be as beautiful as hands could make it. The church of the Abbey was re-built under abbot St Hugh (1049–1109) although it is now destroyed. Benedictines also urged the duty of pilgrimage and established the route to the shrine of Santiago de Compostela in Spain.

913 **Spain** St Miguel de la Escalada at Léon is a good example of early Mozarabic work, (i.e. mixed Christian and Moslem influence) distinguished by the horseshoe arches of the nave arcade and windows.

915 **Turkey** The church of Achtomar at Lake Van has a square ground plan with niches placed in buttresses and added chapels in the eastern corners. It is richly decorated with sculpture and was completed in 921.

THREE DIMENSIONAL ART

900 **Bulgaria** Earliest surviving icon, made in ceramic tile by a Preslav workshop under Tsar Symeon, depicting St Theodore.

900 **Central America** End of the classical period of theocratic city states, characterised in art by stone sculpture, carved memorial slabs and polychrome pottery. Mexican sculpture was plain and massive; that of the lowland Mayas reflected the luxuriance of the rain-forest surrounding them. Main centres of sculpture were at Palenque and Piedras Negras, Mexico; Copán, Honduras; Quirigua, Tikal, Uaxactun, Piedras Negras and Yaxchilán, Guatemala. The post-classical period lasted until 1520. It was characterized in art by the Mayan *chac-mool*, reclining figures and colossal Olmec sculpted heads. The monumental style of these influenced sculpture throughout Central America; Mexicans, by contrast, were making stone sculptures delicately carved with abstract patterns.

900–1000 **Persia** An elegant ceramic ware was made near Samarkand: the dishes were covered in white slip and then decorated in black, brown or red slip with proverbs and sayings, the letter shapes being distorted to make a pattern. In the later tenth century the scripts became more ornate and the pattern more complex.

Persia: typical dish of the period

VISUAL ARTS

900 **Central America** End of the classical period of theocratic city states, characterized in painting by monumental frescoes in the temples. The best known example of these frescoes is at Bonampak, Mexico: painted on damp plaster, it covers three walls with court and battle scenes in strong colours.

HISTORICAL EVENTS	LITERATURE	DANCE & DRAMA	MUSIC

HISTORICAL EVENTS

917
Edward the Elder subdued Danes of East Anglia and annexed Mercia.

922
Cordoba became autonomous caliphate in Spain.

924
Simeon of Bulgaria devastated Greece, threatened Constantinople.

935
Khitans invaded China from Siberia.

936
Otto I became king of Germany.

954
Fall of Danish kingdom of York.

960
Foundation of Sung dynasty in China.

LITERATURE

916 Bulgaria Death of the scholar and translator Clement of Otrida (b. 840), who was a pupil of Cyril and Methodius.

930 France The cleric Ekkehart (900–973) wrote his epic poem *Walter of Aquitaine.*

*c.*940 **Persia** Death of Abu Add Allah Ja'far Rudaki, the first great Persian poet and the model for later poets of the classical age.

Spain: after a manuscript illumination of the 'Commentary on the Apocalypse' by Beatus of Liébana

955 Syria Death of Al-Mutannabi, regarded as the greatest Arabic poet; his style was noble and rhetorical.

961–971 Italy Creative period of Bishop Lintprand of Cremona, author of *History of Otto I.*

DANCE & DRAMA

960 China Beginning of the Sung Dynasty (960–1127): plays were in classical Chinese, *Wen Li*, a difficult language intended for reading. They were watched by the court; the common people watched marionettes

MUSIC

*c.*935 **France** Odo of Cluny (*c.*879–942) is the reputed author of *Dialogus de Musica.*

916–1125 China The northern Liao dynasty; its culture was influenced by that of T'ang: its earthenwares were made with polychrome glazes, the shapes beaten out over a mould. Celadon ware in the Yüeh tradition was made in Chekiang, mainly at Lung-ch'üan.

918–1392 Korea The Wang dynasty, considered the golden age of Korean pottery; in sculpture, figures were heavier and perhaps more clumsy than contemporary Chinese models.

950–1050 India Out of a large group of Hindu temples at Khajuraho in Central India, the most notable is the Kandarya Mahadev Temple consisting of a series of stone halls (*mandapas*) which build up to the *garbha-griha* (the principal shrine). The group is renowned for the erotic friezes of sculpture consisting of approximately 1000 figures.

950–1120 France St Philibert at Tournus, was designed with an apse ambulatory and radiating chapels. It is remarkable chiefly for the variety of its vaulting system, especially the eleventh century transverse barrel vaults of the nave supported on huge cylindrical columns.

955 France Cluny II was known to have had the earliest example of an apse echelon east end. This and the apse ambulatory east end plan were those normally used in Romanesque churches. It was completed in 981 and has since been destroyed.

955 France St Michel de Cuxa is stylistically Mozarabic. The church was completed in 974 but enlarged in the eleventh century with Lombardic towers and an atrium.

960 Persia Masjid-I-Jami mosque at Nayin is a square court surrounded by pointed arcade arches carried on round columns. In the centre of each side the arch is slightly broader and it is an indication of what was to come, the development of a porch or *iwan* which is a typical feature of Persian mosques.

*c.*950 **Spain** By this date the white-glazed, painted pottery which had been made in Baghdad for some fifty years had spread to Moorish Andalucia. The same colours that were used in Baghdad (brown, green and blue) were established on the Spanish ware.

960–1279 China The Sung dynasty: large wooden sculptures were more delicate and slender than the earlier robust work under Indian influence. There was a new feeling for softness and texture. The main types of pottery were Ting ware, from Hopei, and Chün ware, from Honan; the latter had a lavender-blue glaze suffused with crimson or purple in 'accidental' patterning. i.e. patterns formed by accident from the application of the colour.

960–1279 China The most important development in textiles during the Sung dynasty was that of the silk tapestry or *k'o-ssŭ*, which was woven by the same method as the later Gobelin tapestries of France. The technique was thought to have been invented, but not fully exploited, earlier. Most surviving work had a free, naturalistic, Chinese style unconnected with the Western designs prevalent in T'ang dynasty textiles.

*c.*950–1050 **Spain** Mozarabic manuscript illumination was used to illustrate with miniature paintings a series of *Beatos*, commentaries by Beatus of Liébana on the Book of Daniel and the Apocalypse. The style applied Islamic images to Christian themes.

HISTORICAL EVENTS	LITERATURE	DANCE & DRAMA	MUSIC

962
Otto I of Germany was first Saxon to be crowned Holy Roman Emperor.

965
Eastern empire regained Cyprus from Arabs.

969
Fatimid Arabs conquered Egypt.

972
Bulgaria reconquered by Eastern Empire.

977
Arabs began invasion of southern Italy.

979
Edward the Martyr, king of England, murdered at Corfe castle; succeeded by Ethelred the Unready.

980
First Viking raids on English coast.

987
Hugh Capet became king of France founding the Capetian dynasty.

989
Vladimir of Kiev introduced eastern form of Christianity in Russia.

991
Battle of Maldon; Ethelred defeated by Danes, bought peace (danegeld).

995
King Olaf Tryggveson introduced Christianity to Norway.

965–975 England St Ethelwold in the *Concordia Regularis* refers to the use of a dramatized incident, that of the three Marys encountering the angel at the empty tomb, as part of the Easter Mass. This insertion, in Latin, is found all over Europe, and marks the beginning of liturgical drama.

976–1011 Persia Abu'l Qāsim Firdowsi (941–1019) wrote his poem *Shah-Nameh*, which occupied him for most of his life. The poem is Persia's national epic and is considered a masterpiece of world literature.

*c.*970 **Germany** Hrosvitha of Gandersheim, a nun, wrote 6 plays, modelled on the comedies of Terence, to be acted by her fellow nuns.

967 Arabia Death of Abu'l-Faraj, 'Ali ibn Al-Husain Al-Isfaháni, the Arabic musical historian (b. 897). His *Grand Book of Songs*, the greatest collection of Arabic songs ever made, is said to have taken him 50 years to compile.

980 Arabia Birth of Abú 'Ali Al-Husain ibn 'Abdalláh Ibn Siná, Arabian and Persian theorist (d. 1037). He wrote three works on the theory of music which had a lasting influence.

Cambodia: Pre-Rup Ankor temple-mountain

38

961 Cambodia A Pre Rup at Angkor was the first of the temple-mountains in the shape of a three-storey pyramid with five tower-shrines in brick at its summit which was intended as a permanent shrine for the spirit of the ruler after his death.

961–1000 Germany The Romanesque church of St Cyriakus is a surviving example of a building from the Imperial Ottonian period with apses to east and west, thick walls, exterior blind arcading and alternating piers and columns in the nave.

966–980 Germany The Church of St Pantaleon in Cologne is a forerunner of German Romanesque style. It contains early examples of capitals in the shape of cushions that later became widely used in Germany and England.

967 Cambodia Banteay Srei at Angkor is the most beautiful of the early Khmer temples. The complex of buildings displays structural inventiveness and elaborate decoration.

969 China Lung-Hsing-Ssu monastery at Cheng-Ting-Hsien has three timber-framed buildings placed in line along the court. Mo-Mi-Tien or 'pearhall', the earliest building in the complex, is unique due to narrow vestibules projecting from its four faces.

984 China Tu-Lo-Ssu at I-Hsien, Hopei, is the oldest wooden building of the Liao dynasty comprising a gate and a pavilion of two storeys with a balcony.

989 Russia *Desyatinnaya* or the cathedral of the Dormition of the Virgin at Kiev represented a rare appearance of basilican plan in Russia and thus points to influence from the West. The cathedral collapsed in 1240.

992 France Langeais Castle was built by Fulk Nerra, a great castle builder, and it is one of the earliest known stone built castle halls designed with a rectangular plan.

997 France St Martin's at Tours had the first known complete east end plan of apse ambulatory and radiating chapels which was to become the blueprint for Pilgrimage churches.

969–976 Germany Crucifix made for Archbishop Gero, now in Cologne Cathedral; an early example of what became the characteristic pose of Christ on the cross in church sculpture. It is also the earliest surviving wooden figure over life-size; sculptors had become dissatisfied with small-scale work in ivory or metal.

997–1038 Hungary Reign of Stephen I (St Stephen), whose Queen Gisela established an embroidery workshop; she was said to have developed the 'Hungarian stitch', a satin-stitch worked vertically to make diamond or checked patterns.

963–984 England St Ethelwold, bishop of Winchester, wrote a translation of St Benedict's Rule: the manuscript is characteristic of the Winchester school of manuscript production. English manuscript illustration was noted for vigorous and expressive drawing and had a strong influence on all English and Norman illustration including the Bayeux Tapestry.

*c.*980 Germany Gospel book commissioned by Archbishop Egbert of Trier; it is characteristic of the Reichenau school of illuminated manuscript. The treatment of individual scenes suggests a Roman original of the fourth or fifth century.

*c.*985 India Temples built under the Chola dynasty began to be decorated with painted figures of deities and dancing girls.

988–989 Russia Vladimir, Great Prince of Kiev, adopted the Christian, Orthodox, faith as his country's religion and ordered all pagan works of art to be destroyed. Pagan motifs only survived incorporated into Christian art.

11th Century

LITERATURE

c.1000–1010 **France** The *Chanson de Roland*, poetic cycle of legends celebrating Charlemagne and his court.

c.1000 **England** Earliest surviving translation of the Gospels into English; they were translated from the Latin Vulgate begun by St Jerome in 382.

c.1000 **Japan** *Makura No Soshi* was written by Sei Shonagon (966–?1013), woman author and poet: the book is a miscellany of events and impressions of court life. It was the first of many such works of Japanese writers.

DANCE & DRAMA

c.1000 **India** The beginning of the decline of the theatre came with the Moslem invasion: the Moslems were opposed to drama.

MUSIC

c.1000 **Italy** Guido d'Arezzo (d. *c*.1050) proposed that the stave of four lines be used for writing plainsong. (After 1200 five lines became the norm, although in the sixteenth and seventeenth centuries six lines were used.) He is also noted for his method of teaching the singing of Gregorian chant which spread throughout Europe and is the basis of the modern tonic sol-fa system. *Micrologus* (1025), gives a full account of his methods.

Zimbabwe: large round tower in circular ruin. Part of the stone-walled enclosures which still survive

ARCHITECTURE

1000–1050 England The tower of Earls Barton Church is the best preserved of the Anglo-Saxon period demonstrating the use of surface ornament.

1000–1050 Greece The Katholikon of the Lavra monastery in Mount Athos was the first church built on trifoliate plan in this part of Greece. The arms of the cross are barrel-vaulted and a dome covers the crossing. There is an east apse in addition to the ones at the ends of north and south arms of the cross.

1000–1100 Germany The Gandersheim church preserves the best example of a 'Saxon façade' to the west with a cliff-like west-work incorporating two towers.

1000–1100 Italy St Fedele in Como was built with a trefoil planned east end, inspired by Cologne churches.

1000–1500 Zimbabwe, Rhodesia A complex of stone-walled enclosures survived, the walls of which are topped by monoliths and originally faced with a clay and gravel cement.

c.**1000 Mexico** Mitla was the capital of the Mixtecs; it had no pyramids but large rectangular-planned palaces built around courtyards. The Palace of the Columns was faced with complete stone mosaics. It has been restored.

1000 India Lingaraja temple at Bhubaneshwar, Orissa has a 180 ft (over 54·5 metres) tower above the shrine, which was decorated with very deep-cut carving after building. Its interior is less than half its width; decoration shows influence of earlier traditions in timber or reed.

c.**1000 Denmark** Trelleborg is a Viking settlement containing 16 boat-shaped long houses geometrically grouped in four squares of four.

c.**1000 France** St Martin monastery in Canigou is the first Romanesque group of monastic buildings in the Pyrenees. The church is barrel vaulted, the nave being supported by only 10 columns with no clear storey. It was later restored.

THREE DIMENSIONAL ART

1000–1100 Egypt Cast-bronze figures of animals were made as aquamarites and fountain heads, often with incised detail.

1000–1100 Egypt Lustre-ware bowls were decorated with animal forms which were almost realistic; the surrounding space was filled with panels of abstract design. Dishes with completely abstract or calligraphic ornament continued to be made, many by the unknown potter who signed himself 'Moslem'.

1000–1100 France The style of ivory carving suggests that it was an inspiration for the revival of stone carving.

1000–1100 Greece Mosaic at the monastery of the Hermit Luke (Hosios Loukas) at Phocis: an important example of mosaic decoration in accordance with the official scheme, which placed the images of saints, prophets, apostles and angels in a standard order. The central figure was always Christ 'Pantocrator', Ruler of All.

1000–1100 Russia Evidence exists of glass-making centres at Vladimir, Ryazan and Kiev. Glass mosaic cubes, bangles, rings and vessels were made in pale and dark blue, green and yellow.

1000–1200 Byzantium Beginning of *sgraffito* work in pottery; the engraving of a design on the pot through a coloured slip overlay. Examples are also found in northern Iran.

1000–1200 Italy Tin-glazed pottery was first made in Sicily and Apulia.

1000–1200 Nigeria Flourishing period of Ife terracotta sculpture of human forms: the funerary and ritual pottery was made by men and the functional and house pottery by women.

1000–1200 North America The classic Mimbres pottery of the south-western Pueblo Indians; considered the highest point of their abstract designs, based on plant, animal and human forms. Painted pottery was the most celebrated form of Pueblo art; the pots were built up in coils, not thrown on the wheel.

VISUAL ARTS

1000–1100 India Jain artists began to paint on palm leaf strips, illustrating the sacred text *Kalpa Sutra* with narrative art reflecting a rigorous religious discipline.

1000–1200 France Mural paintings showed great variety of regional style: in the east, painters used bright colours on a dark ground; in the west, the colours were flat and the ground light. Most represented authoritative figures on a flat background, and were influenced by Byzantine tradition.

1000 Central America Earliest existing codices, long folded parchment or paper strips with stories told in miniature paintings: the work indicates that this art of miniature painting was a development from the earlier established arts of fresco and vessel-painting.

c.**1000 Germany** The *Bamberg Apocalypse*, an illustrated manuscript exemplifying the best of the Reichenau school of illumination: its figures are set on a plain gold ground to accentuate their rapt faces and expressive gestures.

1000
Chinese made
gunpowder.

1004
Rule of
Samanides
overthrown in
Persia.
China became
tributary of the
Tungusic
Khitans.

1006
Moslems settled
in north-west
India.

Mexico: Mayan ruins at Uxmal, Yucatán

ARCHITECTURE

*c.*1000 **India** Kandarya Mahdev temple in Khajuraho is a typical example of a large group of temples in central India where a number of *mandapa* (porch-halls) lead to the main shrine. All monuments are placed on a platform but the whole is grouped on firmly defined base. The complex is encrusted with sculpture of nearly 1000 figures.

*c.*1000 **India** The Great Temple at Tanjore is built on a traditional square plan from which rises a monumental, richly decorated pyramidal structure topped by a *stupa* of great height. A *stupa* is a kind of dome, its importance is based on the Buddhist idea of the sacred mound.

*c.*1000 **Mexico** Uxmal at Yucatan is the most beautiful of Mayan cities covering an area of 250 acres. Much remains including a governor's house, 'Pigeon' house, nunnery and pyramid all elaborately decorated in mainly abstract patterned reliefs.

*c.*1000 **Sweden** Lojsta Palace in Gotland is a survivor of the timber hall dwellings built in Scandinavia over a period of several centuries.

1001 France St Benigne in Dijon is remarkable for the remains of its eastern rotunda which was based on the original plan of the Holy Sepulchre, Jerusalem. Several other churches copied the idea. It was completed in 1018.

1001 Germany St Michael church in Hildesheim is planned with east and west transepts and apses in the German tradition. It broke away from the basilican plan by dividing the nave up into three square units and the transept crossings were emphasized by means of chancel arches on all four sides.

1006 Persia Gumbat-i-Qabis is a burial tower in brick with a conical roof and an inscription running around it. Such multi-angular towers quite often containing a small prayer hall, were characteristic of Islamic tomb architecture. Their development is often seen as deriving from the classical martyrium or as a transformation of the conical shaped desert tents into monumental permanent materials.

THREE DIMENSIONAL ART

1000 Peru Andes Introduction of bronze, which was valued highly as a more useful metal than gold.

*c.*1000 **China** *Tzŭ-chou* ware first made in north China.

*c.*1000 **Russia** Kiev became an important centre of *cloisonné* enamelling: the colours were white, pinkish-yellow, turquoise and dark blue. Religious work was Byzantine in style while secular jewellery reflected older native design.

VISUAL ARTS

Mexico: bird god from Uxmal, Yucatán

INVENTIONS & DISCOVERIES

HISTORICAL EVENTS	LITERATURE	DANCE & DRAMA	MUSIC

1008 Germany Berno (d. 1048) became Abbot of Reichenau and began to write books on musical theory.

1012
First persecution of heretics in Germany.

1013
Danes took London, Ethelred fled to Normandy.

1014 England Wulfstan (d. 1023) wrote his *Sermo Lupi ad Anglos,* the most famous of his many homilies.

1015 Italy Sight singing was introduced at Pomposa monastery.

Italy: Saint Miniato's, Florence

1016
Death of Edmund Ironside; Cnut of Denmark recognized as king of England.

1017
Cnut divided England into four earldoms.

1020 England Death of Aelfric (b. 955), the leading scholar of the Benedictine revival of learning in England. He was a distinguished prose stylist in Latin and English.

*c.*1010 **Spain** St Pedro de Casserres is a good example of a small, barrel vaulted, Romanesque church many of which survive in Catalonia and on the French border.

1012 France St Martin's in Angers has a crossing dome supported on pendantives, the oldest of French Romanesque domes; begun 1012, it was the first of many in Aquitaine.

1013 England Greenstead-Juxta-Ongar church in Essex is the only surviving Anglo-Saxon church with wooden walls.

1013 Italy St Miniato's in Florence is essentially an early Christian basilica built over a large eastern crypt, but it introduces wide arcades and diaphragm arches. The novel use of marble and its decorative features suggest a classical flavour. It was completed in 1062.

*c.*1015 **France** Strasbourg Cathedral probably had the earliest of all two-tower façades, although the present façades, date from the 13th and 14th centuries. Two-tower façades, were later widely adopted in Europe.

1017–1050 France Bernay Abbey is the earliest surviving Norman church. It has a triple apse plan inspired by Cluny II.

1020 China Feng-Kuo- Ssu in I-Hsien is part of a monastic settlement in which the wooden hall is the most impressive section, housing 7 Buddhas of colossal proportion.

1020 France Over the west portal of St Genis-des-Fontaines the oldest sculpted Romanesque lintel is preserved. Portals became a favourite area for Romanesque sculptors.

1020–1032 Spain Ripoll Abbey was copied from the plan of Old St Peter's Rome with five aisles and a 'T' cross plan.

1020–1040 Spain St Vincente de Cardona is a typical Catalonian Romanesque church with a barrel vaulted nave and crossing dome. The exterior is surrounded by pilaster buttresses and a frieze of Lombard banding.

1015 Germany Cast-bronze doors of the church of St Michael, Hildesheim, showed figures and scenes in relief. Hildesheim became an important centre of bronze-casting; the church encouraged work that showed both humanity and a strong sense of order and ritual.

England: Anglo-Saxon church in Greenstead-Juxta-Ongar, Essex

1022 Germany Death of the scholar Notker Labeo (b. 950), who translated Boethius, Aristotle and other philosophers into meticulous German.

1022 Japan *The Tale of Genji* by Fujiwara no Nobutaka, called Murasaki Shikibu (978–?1031), woman novelist and poet: a highly polished work, telling the life story of Prince Genji, it is regarded as Japan's greatest novel.

Greece: the church of the monastery, Hosios Lucas

*1025
Mahmud of
Ghazni, Moslem
ruler in India,
conquered
Gujarat.*

*1027
Cnut of Denmark
invaded Norway
and was made
king.*

*1031
Caliphate of
Cordoba
abolished.*

*1034
Malcolm II of
Scotland
murdered;
succeeded by
Duncan his
grandson.*

*c.*1020 **Greece** Whilst the interior ground plan of the Church of the Apostles in Athens consists of a cross-in-square, externally apsidal endings to the arms of the cross penetrate the walls of the church on three sides creating a polygonal layout. The crossing is covered by a dome pierced by windows framed by arches.

*c.*1020 **Greece** The Katholikon and the Theotokos (*c.*1040) the two churches at the Hosios Lucas monastery, are two churches of the best preserved Byzantine monastery in Greece. They form an interesting ground plan by being joined together by Katholikon's north wall. Architecturally Katholikon is more interesting, being built on a Greek cross plan with the cupola carried by a window-pierced drum while the arms of the cross are covered by half domes. It is renowned for its splendid mosaics and marble decoration.

1025–1042 Germany The Limburg Abbey was a massive basilican church with wall shafts capable of supporting a vault and a two-storey façade, probably derived from Strasbourg. It is now ruined.

1030 Germany The Speyer Cathedral was begun in 1030 and later altered. This imperial church incorporates a number of German Romanesque features including a large crypt and towers and Lombard banding exterior decoration. The groin vaulted nave is the highest of all Romanesque vaults and was possibly the earliest large span groin vault in Europe.

1032 India Mount Abu, site of the most important group of Jain temples, typical is the Dilwarra temple, an impressive marble hall displays a mass of intricate sculpture decorating columns and walls. There are characteristic double capitals on the pillars. The lower, which are bracketed, support the raking struts while the upper, corbelled ones, carry the roof beams.

1025 Spain Cluniac monks settled at San Juan de la Peña. The Romanesque styles in art began to eclipse the Mozarabic (half Western, half Islamic) styles.

*1035
Death of Cnut;
succeeded by
Harold Harefoot
in England,
Sweyn in Norway
and Hardacnut in
Denmark.
William became
Duke of
Normandy.*

*1037
Ferdinand I of
Castile asserted
supremacy over
Christian
kingdoms of
Spain.*

*1039
Gruffydd ap
Llywellyn, king
of Gwynedd and
Powys, defeated
the English.*

*1040
Duncan slain by
Macbeth who
became king of
the Scots.*

*1041
Lombards and
Normans
defeated Greeks
at
Montemaggiore.*

*1042
Edward the
Confessor
became king of
England.*

Russia: model of the reconstruction of the cathedral of Santa Sophia, Kiev

1037 France Notre-Dame in Jumiégès is an early Norman church with ambulatory east end and west-work. Its tall but thin walled nave with alternating pier forms suggest they supported diaphragm arches unlike later Norman churches. It was completed in 1067 and later rebuilt.

1037 Russia St Sophia in Kiev is the most influential ecclesiastical structure in Russian architecture and the source of inspiration for 9 centuries to come. It is covered by 13 domes and decorated with mosaics according to Byzantine iconographic tradition. It was completed in 1046 and later altered.

1038 China The Hua-Yen-ssu in Ta-T'ung-Fu consists of two temples with three halls, the ground plan of two being identical, placed symmetrically on either side of the third, differently laid out structure. All of them are covered by bracketed eaves. The most remarkable is the hall comprising the library where a display of architecturally constructed book-shelves is a unique feature.

1040–1069 Germany St Maria im Kapitol in Cologne is an early example of a church with a trefoil-planned choir, a design much copied in Germany thereafter, and especially in Cologne.

*c.*1040–1100   **Switzerland** Payern Priory is the finest Swiss Romanesque church, built to a plan resembling Cluny II.

1042–1095 Italy St Mark's, Venice was built on a Greek cross plan with a central dome and four surrounding domes in the Byzantine style. Most of the interior is painted with figures and/or has mosaics which were completed in the twelfth century.

1042–1056 Greece Nea Moni at Chios is one of the few churches of its type to survive. It is built on a Byzantine plan consisting of a square with no projecting cross arms. The roof is covered by a dome, restored in the nineteenth century, carried on a drum, which in turn is supported by squinches: it is deep and narrow in the four corners and broad and shallow in the axes. The latter rise up from 8 pilasters projecting from the nave walls.

1039–1056 Germany Reign of Henry III, during which the Trier and Echternach manuscript illuminators produced their finest work. Other important *scriptoria* were at Cologne, Regensburg, Aureus and Fulda, the two former showing strong Byzantine influence. The human figure, alive and expressive, was of prime importance in the designs.

1048
William of
Normandy
defeated Geoffrey
of Anjou.

*c.*1050 Byzantium The romantic epic *Digenes Akrites* gave a vivid picture of contemporary life, and exists in at least 7 versions. Byzantine literature also includes many anonymous folk ballads, in a tradition that can be traced back to the sixth century.

*c.*1050 Germany *Ruodlieb*, the first European romance: it was written in Latin by a German noble, and introduced the chivalric code of behaviour into themes taken from folk lore. 'Romance' in this case meant a work of the imagination in verse; the strict French definition of the word was an imaginative work written in vernacular verse to appeal to a popular taste.

1050 Germany The story *Rudlieb* has the first description of a couple-dance: it was a social dance representing courtship, and accompanied by an instrument. The other main type of social dance was the carol or choral, which involved groups of people dancing in formation and singing their own accompaniment.

1050 Germany *Syswillekommon Heirre Kerst* the first German Christmas carol first sung.

Japan: Hoodo Byodin temple, Uji, near Kyoto

1051
William of
Normandy
received promise
of succession to
English throne.

1045–1065 England The second Westminster Abbey, or more correctly, the Collegiate Church of St Peter, Westminster, was built for King Edward the Confessor in London. It was the first church in England to be modelled in the Norman style. It was demolished in the middle of the thirteenth century.

1045 Russia Although in plan St Sophia, Novgorod is similar to St Sophia, Kiev, it already showed structural innovations which prepared the way for the development of north Russian architecture.

1046 Belgium St Gertrude church, Nivelles was consecrated; it is the most imposing eleventh-century church in Belgium, with a massive Romanesque west-work.

*c.***1050 England** St Augustine Rotunda, Canterbury, a unique Anglo-Saxon rotunda inspired by the larger version at St Benigne, Dijon. It was built to link two older churches.

*c.***1050 Italy** The Baptistery probably dates from the fifth century, but its present character is mainly eleventh century and illustrates the thread of classicism that continued in Florence.

*c.***1050 Japan** Hoodo Byodoin temple, Uji near Kyoto, is one of the most lavishly decorated of Jodo temples in which a vision of the Buddhist paradise was evoked. The Hoodo was gilded and decorated with mother of pearl inside and painted vermilion without. Such lavish decoration is the most distinguished aspect of ancient Japanese architecture.

*c.***1050 Turkey** St Saviour in the Chora, Constantinople, also known as the Kariye Djami, was re-built on fourth-century foundations: it is a traditional Byzantine church with a dome on a high drum over the central area. The parekklesion runs full length on the south side of the building. There are later additions, and the church is famous for its fourteenth-century frescoes and mosaics.

1049 France Hugh of Semur became abbot of Cluny; under him it became the centre of a great organization with daughter-churches built and decorated in Cluniac style. Moissac and Souillac are characteristic; their sculpture mixes classical forms with the twisting patterns of northern European art.

*c.***1050 Byzantium** Mosaicists went from Constantinople to work in Russia, Italy and Sicily. The mosaic panels served the same didactic and liturgical purpose as did the later pictorial stained-glass windows of northern churches.

*c.***1050 England** The earliest surviving pieces of medieval European decorative wrought-iron are the elaborate hinges with Nordic motifs on church doors at Stillingfleet, Yorkshire, and Staplehurst, Kent. Their form and decoration were influential on later French work.

1045
Chinese began
printing from
movable type.

1050
Astrolabe
reached Europe.

HISTORICAL EVENTS	LITERATURE	DANCE & DRAMA	MUSIC

1052 Germany Death of Aaron Scotus in Cologne (b. *c.*992, probably in Scotland); he is believed to have introduced Gregorian evensong into Germany.

*1053
Harold Godwinson succeeded his father as earl of Wessex.*

*1054
Final break between Eastern (Orthodox) and Western (Roman) church.*

*1055
Fall of Baghdad and Arab empire to Seljuk Turks.*

*1064
Seljuk Turks took Armenia from Eastern Empire.*

China: wooden pagoda at Ying-chou fu, Shansi

1053 Japan Byodo-in; the Phoenix hall built on a small scale and set in a garden, has characteristically Japanese features, although its design and decoration show Chinese influence.

1058 China Fo-Kung-ssu Ying-Hsien is one of the rare surviving wooden structures from the Liao dynasty, it bridges the gap between buildings constructed in stone and timber.

1058–1075 Italy Sant' Angelo in Formis has eastern inspired pointed arches in the porch and groin vaults, both probably influenced by the lost abbey of Montecassino begun in 1066. The whole interior is painted.

*c.***1060 Norway** Urnes church is an early survivor of the Norwegian stave churches; it has superb Norse carving on the wall planks depicting interlaced animal forms.

1063 Italy Pisa Cathedral's architectural origins are various but with the Baptistery, altered in the fourteenth century, and the Campanile or 'leaning tower', it forms the most magnificent complex of Romanesque architecture. The rows of open arcading that decorate all three buildings are typical Pisan work. The Cathedral was completed in the thirteenth century.

1063 Spain Léon in St Isidoro church the Pantheon of the Kings of the eleventh century is remarkable for the early example of carved narrative scenes in the capitals. It was completed in the twelfth century with the addition of wall paintings.

1063 Spain In Jaca cathedral alternating columns and piers in the nave were used for the first time in Spain, indicating French and Lombard influence in the design.

1064 France The Abbaye-aux Hommes, known as St Etienne, at Caen was founded by William the Conqueror; it has the typical Norman three-storey elevation and a powerful two-tower façade. The 'sexpartite' vault was added in *c.*1120. Contemporary with this church is La Trinité, Caen (abbaye-aux-Dames) founded by William's wife Matilda.

Italy: cathedral and leaning tower at Pisa

1066
*William of
Normandy
defeated Harold
at Hastings,
crowned king of
England.*

1069
*William I
defeated Danish
invasion of
northern
England.*

1070
*Lanfranc became
Archbishop of
Canterbury.*

1066 China Death of the essayist Su Hsun (b. 1009), who wrote in 'old' style prose, modelled on Han authors. Through his influence this style became dominant.

1067 Turkey *Knowledge which brings Happiness* by Yusuf has Hacib, an allegorical poem: it is the first known work in Turkish literature of the Islamic period.

1070 Spain Death of Avicebron (b. 1020), the Spanish-Judaic poet and philosopher.

1071
*William
completed
conquest of
England.
Normans
conquered last
Byzantine
possession in
southern Italy.*

1076
*Seljuk Turks
took Jerusalem
and Damascus.*

1077
*First English
Cluniac
monastery
founded at
Lewes.*

1072 Italy Death of Peter Damian (b. 1007), a cleric and poet who wrote many polemical tracts.

England: Edward the Confessor from the Bayeaux Tapestry

1071 France Birth of Guillaume, Count of Poitiers (d. 1127), the first troubadour whose songs have survived.

1078 Byzantium Death of Michael Psellus (b. 1015), scholar and historian; his *Chronographia* was a vivid personal account of events between 996 and 1077.

ARCHITECTURE	THREE DIMENSIONAL ART	VISUAL ARTS	*INVENTIONS & DISCOVERIES*

ARCHITECTURE

1065–1130 France Ste Foi is a pilgrimage church, at Conquest, one of many on the pilgrimage route to Santiago da Compostella and is famous for its magnificently carved West door tympanum, i.e. space between lintel and arch in medieval doorway.

1066 Belgium In Tournai Cathedral the Romanesque nave has four storeys, and an elevation continued into the trefoil plan of the early Gothic choir. The exterior was planned to have 9 towers, 7 of which were incorporated in the trefoil-planned east end.

1070 England Archbishop Lanfranc began rebuilding the Canterbury cathedral, which had earlier been destroyed.

*c.*1070 **France** The north tower of Bayeux cathedral is the only remaining eleventh century part: it has a unique ribbed vault in the form of two intersecting transverse arches, an early example of the use of ribbed vaults.

*c.*1070 **Germany** Hirsau Abbey was founded as the first of the German Cluniac churches. Its ground plan was similar to the second church at Cluny, a Benedictine · monastery in Burgundy. It was later destroyed.

1077 Austria Hohensalzburg castle was one of many great castles built as a result of the eleventh century investiture contest between successive popes and emperors.

1077 England Lewes Abbey, the first Cluniac church in England was founded. Its later construction in the 12th century copied the plan of the mother church of Cluny III, begun in 1088.

1077 England St Albans Abbey was begun and is the earliest surviving church in the Anglo-Norman style in its most elemental form.

1078 England The Tower of London's massive rectangular White Tower survived from William the Conqueror's original castle. The walls are 4·5 metres (15 feet) thick at the base.

THREE DIMENSIONAL ART

*c.*1070 **England** The Bayeux Tapestry: an embroidery and not a true tapestry, it is sewn in wool on linen. It tells the story of Harold of Wessex in 1065–1066, and of his defeat at Hastings.

England: the White Tower, Tower of London

VISUAL ARTS

1065–1109 Spain Reign of Alfonso VI of Léon and Castile, under whose encouragement the schools of arts in Toledo attracted scholars from all over Europe. Late Mozarabic manuscript illumination reflects the influence of English work.

1066 England The technique of manuscript painting began to alter under continental influence: colours became harsher and line heavier. The tradition of manuscript painting flourished through the fifteenth century.

Greek medicine
brought to
western Europe.*

1080
William I of
England refused
to do homage as
papal vassal.

Sweden: Lund Cathedral

1084
Normans under
Guiscard sacked
Rome.

1078 Spain The old cathedral of Santiago de Compostela is one of the earliest pilgrimage churches and it housed the shrine of St James. It was a vast church with apse ambulatory and radiating chapels and a long 10 bay nave ending in a two-tower façade, and was altered in the eighteenth century.

1079–1093 England Winchester cathedral has Norman transepts which survive from this date demonstrating close kinship with Normandy prototypes. The nave, altered in the late fourteenth century, still retains most of its original great length, typical of Anglo-Norman cathedrals.

1080–1140 England Ely cathedral has a long Anglo-Norman nave with a west transept. It was, and still is, wood ceilinged.

1080–1096 France St Sernin in Toulouse is a large pilgrimage church partly built of brick with typical apse, ambulatory and radiating chapel east end, a long barrel vaulted nave with spacious galleries over the aisles and an equally large transept.

1080 Sweden Lund Cathedral was originally built by Donatus a Lombard architect over a large Lombard-type crypt. The interior is heavy Romanesque with piers and attached cushion capital columns. It has no gallery and it is groin vaulted. It was completed in 1146 but later restored.

*c.***1080–1120 Italy** St Ambrogio, Milan, was rebuilt from the 9th–11th centuries with ribbed vaults; probably the earliest examples in Italy although their date is uncertain. The surviving monk's tower is tenth century and is one of the oldest detached campanili in Italy.

1081 England Old St Paul's in London was planned as a huge Romanesque church. It was completed in the thirteenth century, and then destroyed in the fire of London 1666.

1083–1097 France St Etienne in Nevers was a Cluniac abbey illustrating the mature Romanesque style with an unusual clerestory beneath the nave's barrel vault.

Spain: cathedral of Santiago de Compostela

HISTORICAL EVENTS

1085
Normans evacuated Balkan Peninsula after Guiscard's death.

1086
Compilation of Domesday Book in England.

1087
Death of William I; succeeded by William II (Rufus) in England and Robert in Normandy.

1091
Norman conquest of Sicily completed.

LITERATURE

1085 China Ssŭ-ma Kuang (1019–1086) published his chronological history of China. It was considered a masterpiece of clear and unadorned writing.

1085 China Posthumous publication of the collected works of Tsêng Kung (1019–1083), one of the masters of Sung prose. He had considerable influence on the work of other writers. His own style is clear and unadorned.

1085 Germany The poem *Annolied* mixed history and symbolism in celebrating the canonization of Archbishop Anno of Cologne. It was influential on later work.

DANCE & DRAMA

MUSIC

France: the Romanesque Church at Cluny

ARCHITECTURE

THREE DIMENSIONAL ART

VISUAL ARTS

INVENTIONS & DISCOVERIES

1085–1239 Germany Mainz Cathedral is a vast red sandstone church much altered and rebuilt, but still retaining its Romanesque character.

*c.*1085 **Spain** The cloisters of the abbey at St Domingo de Silos remain and display the finest Romanesque sculpture in Spain.

1088 France Cluny III was the greatest of all Romanesque churches. It had a choir with an ambulatory and five radiating chapels, two transepts, the minor with two apses and crossing tower, the major with four apses and three towers. The nave had pointed transverse arches and double aisles ending in a two-storeyed narthex and two western towers. It was completed in 1121 and largely destroyed during the French Revolution.

1088 Persia Masjid-i-Jami at Isfahan has been much restored and altered, but had the traditional mosque court surrounded by a two-storeyed arcade broken by four iwans (open fronted vaults facing into a court) in the centre of each. The main iwan leads to a rectangular praying chamber, an arrangement used for the first time, covered by a high pointed dome sitting on an octagonal drum. It is a brilliant example of Seljuk architecture.

1089 England Gloucester Cathedral was begun in 1089 and the massive nave columns are typical of the giant order often used in the west of England.

1090–1197 Italy St Nicola at Bari was the first of the important Norman churches to be built in south Italy. The large crypt contains the relics of St Nicholas.

1090
Chinese built water-driven mechanical clock.

1090–1099 Spain Avila town wall was built with 10 gates and 86 towers. They are relatively unaltered and show very little Moslem influence. They later incorporated the east end of the cathedral which formed part of the defensive structure.

1094
Quarrel between
William II and
Anselm,
Archbishop of
Canterbury,
began.

1095
First Crusade
launched by Pope
Urban II.

1099
Crusaders took
Jerusalem.

1100
William II of
England killed in
New Forest,
succeeded by
Henry I.

China: inlaid bronze vase with gold and silver

1092 China Compilation of the first catalogue of ancient bronzes. This stimulated medieval bronze-casters to imitate the earlier forms of the Shang and Chou dynasties.

*c.*1093 **England** Wrought-iron screen for the shrine of St Swithin at Winchester: the oldest surviving piece of its type, it has bars of square section linked by C-shaped scrolls.

1096 Venice Beginning of the Crusades, which gave Venetian merchants contracts with Syrian glass-making centres.

1099 Italy Beginning of sculpture for Modena cathedral by Wiligelmo (d. after 1117), considered the founder of Romanesque sculpture in Italy. His style owed much to the classical.

1093–1133 England Durham cathedral was a building full of innovatory features which mark the transition from the early to late Norman style in England. The most revolutionary of these was the use of ribbed vaults over the nave and choir supported by embryo flying buttresses. Such a vaulting system was to become an essential element of Gothic architecture.

1094 China Ling-Yü pagoda is a tomb pagoda still with a square ground plan; displays unusual wooden rafters similar to those found in T'ieh-t'a in Kai-fēngu. It was later rebuilt.

1095 Spain Loarre castle is the finest Romanesque castle in Spain; it draws on both French and Moslem sources as is typical of Spanish architecture of the period.

1096–1120 England Norwich cathedral is basically Anglo-Norman; it has a rare surviving triple apse planned east end.

1096–1132 France St Madeleine at Vézelay was the first large French church with groin vaulting throughout. It is a rich Cluniac abbey, famous for its superb sculpture on the tympana and capitals.

1097–1099 England Westminster Hall in London is a huge royal hall originally aisled; it is 234·5 feet (71 metres) long.

1099 France Citeaux was founded in 1099 and later destroyed. It was the first of the new Cistercian abbeys. At the zenith of the order there were about 750 abbeys in Europe. Those dating before 1200 were built on the plan 'Bernardian'. They were very austere, planned as a Latin cross with a squared east end. They had no crypt, towers or decorative ornament.

1099–1184 Italy Modena Cathedral was built of brick with and ashlar and marble exterior. It has an internal triforium and originally had diaphragm arches on alternating supports. It was an influential church on Emilian architecture.

Spain: Loarre Castle

late 1000–1100 Europe *Champlevé* enamelling in opaque colours on copper flourished in three independent centres: the Rhine and Meuse valleys. Limoges in France, and Spain. The Meuse work was considered among the major achievements of Romanesque art. Designs were often taken from contemporary manuscripts.

12th Century

HISTORICAL EVENTS	LITERATURE	DANCE & DRAMA	MUSIC

LITERATURE

early 1100–1200 Persia *Kilila va Dimna* by Nizam al-Din Abu'l Ma'li Nasr Allah, a translation into Persian of the Arabic version of the *Fables of Bidpai*. The title is the names of the two jackals who feature in the first fable. The translation served as a model for subsequent prose writers because of its apt vocabulary and clear, balanced style.

1100 Persia The *Rubaiyat* of Abu'l Fath Omar Khayyam (1050–1132), poet and scientist. He was one of the outstanding medieval mathematicians, but is best known to Western readers for this work of poetry, written in quatrains (*ruba'i* = quatrain), which was paraphrased into English in the nineteenth century by E. Fitzgerald.

DANCE & DRAMA

*c.*1100–1200 **Japan** Iso-No-Zenji performed dances wearing man's costume: she is known as the Mother of Japanese drama.

*c.*1100–1200 **France** *The Jeu d'Adam*, in Norman French, is the first known mystery (Bible history) play (though the term 'mystery' was not used of such plays until considerably later). It was given outside the church, not inside as the liturgical dramas were.

MUSIC

1100–1200 England The earliest motet, *Ex Semine Abrahae*, written by an unknown composer; it was later discovered in Worcester cathedral.

Japan: horizontal scroll painting of the 'Tale of Genji'

ARCHITECTURE

1100–1200 Cambodia Angkor Vat is a funerary temple for the deified King Suryavarman II; it is a prodigious monument built by the king himself and is a vast rectangle surrounded by a moat $2\frac{1}{2}$ miles long with stepped pyramids capped by an immense central conical tower; this central tower equals the holy mountain and the axis of the world in Indian symbolism and is within the Indian tradition. The overall design of the complex, however, is quite different from Indian buildings.

1100–1200 Bolivia Tiahuanoco was a ceremonial centre and like others, a station for making observations of the solar year; now in a ruinous state, it was built of stone, some of which were cramped together with copper. Later the stones were dressed to fit.

1100–1200 Burma Ananda temple, Pagan, represents sheer perfection in Burmese architecture. A massive white brick building on a square plan with finally graduated tiered roofs rising to a golden tapering spire, the entrance porticos are elaborately decorated.

1100–1200 Denmark Österlar church in Bornholm was one of a number of small round churches in Denmark which perhaps reflect King Sigurd's pilgrimage to Jerusalem in 1107 in that he was thereafter inspired to build churches in a style similar to the church of the Holy Sepulchre in Jerusalem.

1100–1200 France The fortifications for the town of Carcassone were begun in the twelfth century, and later restored with the wall; its 50 towers, moat and drawbridge are arguably the best preserved examples of a European medieval fortress town.

1100–1200 Germany The Wartburg in Eisenach is a Romanesque house on two floors, each divided into three rooms lit by groups of round headed windows.

1100–1200 Italy The picturesque hill city of San Gimignano, with its 13 surviving tall towers (out of an original 48) begun; the towers were built as private fortifications for rival families and used to abound in other Italian towns such as Florence, Lucca and Bologna.

THREE DIMENSIONAL ART

1100–1150 Syria Incised ceramic 'frit' ware (i.e. of vitreous composition) was made in imitation of Chinese porcelain. Syrian ornament was characterized by free drawing and a design evolved from the Arabic characters of one word. Frit paste was composed of quartz, ground glass and plastic clay and was used to increase strength.

1100–1200 Bulgaria Church of St Nicholas in Okhrida, now in Yugoslavia: the door carved with saints and animals is an early example of 'fantastic' style in woodcarving. Bulgarian carvers of the Samokov, Razlog and Tryavna Schools flourished in the Middle Ages and during the revival of the art in the nineteenth century.

1100–1200 England The Warwick ciborium (Eucharist vessel) and the Balfour ciborium: important pieces of English enamel work with designs based on manuscript work of the Winchester school.

1100–1200 Egypt Ceramic bowls were painted in lustre on an opaque turquoise glaze, a colour popular with Egyptian potters because it did not overwhelm the metallic lustre decoration.

1100–1200 France Relief in Senlis cathedral: the first illustration of the 'Coronation of the Virgin'. The theme was adopted outside France in the thirteenth century.

1100–1200 Russia Embroiderers worked in flat-stitch with silk and gold thread, often using Byzantine textiles as models, or actually embroidering on them; designs were inspired by the linear styles of icon painting.

1100–1200 Sicily Textile workshops flourished under Saracen influence; they specialized in 'cutwork', a form of *appliqué*, and in velvets and brocades.

VISUAL ARTS

1100–1200 France The church of St Savin-sur-Gartempe was painted with four cycles of pictures: apocalyptic scenes, scenes of the Passion, legends of local saints and Old Testament stories. The style is flat, linear and vigorous and has affinities with north European manuscript illumination.

1100–c.1240 Austria A School of wall painting and book illumination was active in Salzburg.

c.1100–1150 Japan First surviving example of horizontal scroll painting: *The Tale of Genji*, attributed to Fujiwara no Takayoshi. Composition of a long narrow scroll to be viewed in sections stimulated original design for linking sequences; painters also developed a gift for rapid, dramatic narrative conveyed in refined brush-line and flat colour wash, combining naturalism with ornamental effect.

Italy: mosaic from façade of Saint Mark's, Venice

ARCHITECTURE

1100–1200 Japan The Todaiji temple Daibutsuden at Nara was part of the largest of the Japanese Buddhist monasteries and is the largest wooden building in the world housing a huge bronze Buddha. The construction system of brackets extending from wooden columns is based on Chinese prototypes in a style known as Tenjikuyo. It was reconstructed in the seventeenth century. Japanese architecture is distinguished by the skilful use of timber construction based on a columnar system of supports and characterized by the subtly curved roof line.

1100–1200 Norway The stone church at Vik represents an older, pagan tradition of building in wood.

1100–1200 Scotland The ruined Kelso abbey was the finest Romanesque church in Scotland with a western transept and tower suggestive of Ely cathedral, England.

1100–1200 Spain The ruined Sahagún Abbey was a Cluniac abbey built of brick probably by Mudéjar (Christian architecture in Moslem style) workmen. It was one of a number of brick churches in the area.

*c.***1100 France** Caen Castle is a rectangular stone keep of a type later built in large numbers especially in England as well as Normandy.

*c.***1100 France** Notre Dame du Port at Clermont-Ferrand is a typical example of the Auvergne school of Romanesque architecture, distinguished by the central octagonal planned tower built over squinches within the raised inner bays of the transepts. The local coloured granite allowed for exterior patterned decoration.

*c.***1100 France** Paray le Monial abbey is a small imitation of Cluny III with similar pointed nave arches and classically fluted pilasters.

*c.***1100 France** St Savin-sur-Gartempe has the most impressive Romanesque nave frescoes in France and is a typical hall church (the vaults of nave and aisles are of approximately the same height) with tall cylindrical nave arcade columns.

THREE DIMENSIONAL ART

*c.***1100–1300 Russia** The most important cathedral furnishings – the vessels, liturgical pieces and gospel covers – for Sta Sophia, Novgorod, were made locally in silver. Novgorod became the centre of a national style in silverwork.

*c.***1100 China** Grey stoneware was made, with an olive-green or brown glaze; it continued until late in the thirteenth century. Moulded decoration was also introduced, the clay being beaten over a mould on a turntable. Carved ware, however, was made on the wheel.

*c.***1100 France** Embroidery was used as a furnishing for new Romanesque buildings, particularly for wall-hangings and curtains in bright colours.

*c.***1100 Germany** Probable date of the five windows in Augsburg cathedral, thought to be the oldest surviving stained-glass windows. Twelfth-century stained glass was held in place by iron bars linked by lead strips. The flexible lead outlines made it possible to cut glass in natural shapes.

*c.***1100 Italy** Byzantine mosaic artists began work on St Mark's, Venice. A Venetian school of mosaic art was established and became influential throughout Italy.

*c.***1100 Italy** Beginning of the Roman fashion for *cosmati* work, in coloured marble and decorative stone inlay; it lasted until 1300.

*c.***1100 Persia** Tartar rule in northern China had opened routes in the north west and brought Chinese metal objects to Khurasan, the centre of metal-working in Persia. Khurasan bronze-casters specialized in high-tin bronze, an alloy of copper with about 20% tin.

VISUAL ARTS

*c.***1100 Bulgaria** Early mural paintings in Boyana church, Sofia: they are considered one of the most important sets of the period.

1101 China Death of Su Shih (b. 1036), poet, essayist, calligrapher and painter. He wrote evocative verse in simple vernacular style.

1103 Magnus III of Norway invaded Ireland.

1106–1107 Russia The abbot Daniil wrote a prose description of his pilgrimage to Jerusalem in a simple, forceful style.

1109 England Death of the Swiss-born cleric Anselm (b. 1033), Archbishop of Canterbury and author of *Monologion, Proslogion* and *Cur Deus Homo.*

*c.***1110 Russia** Composition of the *Nestov Chronicle*, an account of Slav and Russian history between 1040 and 1110 which was attributed to the Kiev monk Nestov. He also wrote a biography of Theodosius.

France: Fontevraud Abbey

1113 Balearic Islands conquered by Pisa.

1117 Henry V of Germany crowned Holy Roman Emperor.

1118 Order of Templars founded.

*c.***1120 France** Creative period of the poet Alberic who wrote the first French romance in a cycle of romances on Alexander the Great.

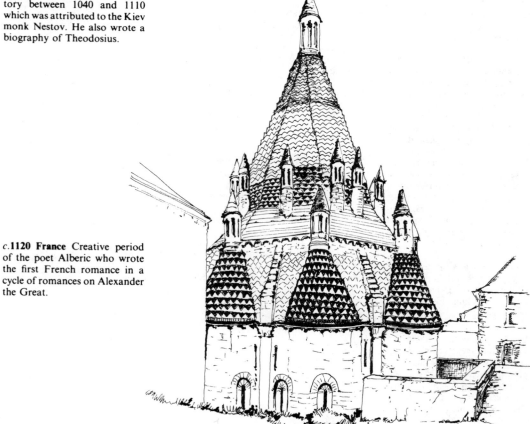

*c.*1100 **Portugal** Guimaraes castle's well-preserved, battlemented square-planned towers and walls make it perhaps the best remaining Romanesque castle on the Peninsula.

1101 France Fontevraud Abbey, a domed monastery church: it is one of about 80 domed Romanesque churches built in western France during the twelfth century. The monastery also has a mid-twelfth century octagonal planned kitchen, which is comparable only with that at Glastonbury Abbey in England, as an example of domestic Romanesque work.

1104–1132 France Church of St Madeleine, Vézelay sculpture carved; it is a Cluniac church and the sculpture was considered as part of the architecture; sculpture reached a climax of energy, luxuriance and grotesqueness in the churches of St Pierre (Moissac) and Souillac, both carved by the same master; their images were increasingly savage and far from Christian, but all stylized into rhythmic ornamentation.

1108–1116 Flanders Renier of Huy (fl. 1100–1125), Flemish sculptor and goldsmith, made a bronze font for Abbot Hellinus. His figures and their attitudes show a naturalism in advance of his time; he is considered the first great goldsmith and bronze-founder of the Meuse school.

1101 China Death of Su Tung Po, noted for calligraphy and bamboo painting.

1107 China Death of Mi Fei (b. 1051), master of the 'ink-splash' style in which ink blots replaced a precise outline to define forms. He was a model for future painters.

1112–1152 Cambodia City of Angkor Vat is of colossal proportions planned as an enclosure surrounded by a moat. The sanctuary, placed on a platform, is richly decorated with sculpture depicting old Indian epics.

*c.***1117–***c.***1168 Italy** St Michele Pavia represents Lombard romanesque at its best. It is rib vaulted with the nave divided into units to facilitate vaulting. The west façade has sculpted friezes in Italian fashion.

1120 England Romsey abbey was begun: it was one of the first churches in England to replace the apse east end with a square-ended chancel, which was to become the normal English plan.

1120–1140 France Autun Cathedral is a Burgundian church with classical features in the Romanesque tradition for the area. It has a magnificent west tympanum carved by Gislebertus. The human interest in the scenes becarved is dominant and the design secondary.

HISTORICAL EVENTS | **LITERATURE** | **DANCE & DRAMA** | **MUSIC**

1125
Lothair of Saxony elected king of Germany.

*c.***1125 England** William of Malmesbury (*c.*1090–1143) wrote his *Gesta Regum Anglorum.*

1125 Russia Death of Monomakh Vladimir, Prince of Kiev (1113–1125), who wrote *Testament*, a vivid personal and political autobiography.

1126
English barons accepted Matilda as future sovereign. Tartars established Ch'in dynasty in north-eastern China.

1127
Imadeddin Zengi became ruler of Mosul.

1126 France Death of Guilhelm IX, Duke of Aquitaine (b. 1071), the earliest known Provençal troubadour. Troubadours fl. from *c.*1100 –*c.*1300 as poets in the Provençal tongue and composers of their own music, expressing the chivalric convention of love for the unattainable woman. Their poetic forms were complex and involved over 900 metric and stanza forms. They were usually of higher social standing than the older minstrels.

1130
Henry I gave a charter to London.

*c.***1130 Germany** Creative period of the poetess Ava, the first woman to work in vernacular German; she was author of a 2500-line poem on the last judgment.

1123–1138 Italy St Zeno Maggiore, Verona is a good example of a wooden roofed Lombard church. It has a stepped basilican façade decorated with blond arcading and pilaster strips. The bronze doors are famous.

1125–1130 France Moissac abbey has a porch vault and was the first in western Europe to be built entirely with pointed arches. The south portal has the finest sculpted decoration in the Languedoc region.

*c.***1125 France** La Charité-sur-Loire abbey was enlarged on the same plan as Cluny III. Its intended monemental west façade with five portals and two towers with spires was never finished.

1127–1134 Ireland Cormac's chapel Cashel of the Kings, contains the best example of a barrel vaulted nave in Ireland and illustrates how Romanesque architecture penetrated Celtic Ireland.

1127 Russia In Bukhara (which used to be in Persia) the Kalan Minaret is exceptionally beautiful, carrying high enclosed galleries decorated with patterned brick work. Completed in 1129.

1130 France Houdan castle is an early example of a circular planned castle keep, a development from the square.

*c.***1130 England** Rochester castle is a typical English rectangular twelfth century tower keep, with walls strengthened by pilaster buttresses rising over 30 metres (100 feet) high and immensely thick at their base.

*c.***1130 France** Notre-Dame-la-Grande at Poitier has the most lavishly decorated west façades of all Poitevan churches and a contemporary painted interior, which was restored in the 19th century.

1131 England Tintern Abbey was one of a number of Cistercian monastery churches built in the more remote areas of Britain in the twelfth century, especially in the north and west. All conform to the regular 'Bernardian' Cistercian plan and at Fountains abbey (1135) Gothic pointed arches appear in the arcade for the first time in England. It was later rebuilt but is now a ruin.

1125–*c.*1135 France The sculptor Gislebertus decorated the whole of Autun cathedral. His art is strongly dramatic; form is reduced to essentials for narrative force. He was allowed to sign his work, which indicates great prestige among his contemporaries.

1127 China The Chin Tartars overcame the Sung court, which fled south from Honan. *Ju* pottery which had elements from both celadon and Chi'in pottery, ceased production in this year. The fast pottery wheel was introduced to meet the greater demands of the non-court market, as were templates for making plates.

France: detail of carving on Notre-Dame-le-Grande, Poitiers

1134
*Moors defeated
and killed
Alfonso of
Aragon at Fraga.*

1135–1150 Germany The *Kaiserchronik*, the first major German history, was written by the monks of Regensburg.

*c.*1136 **France** Creative period of Hugh Primas, a satiric poet of great virtuosity; he wrote in Latin.

France: 12th century French mosaic tiles

1139
*Civil War in
England over
succession to
Henry I.*

1140 China Earliest extant collection of complete works of Wang an-Shih (1021–1086), statesman, poet and essayist. A strictly classical writer, he wrote 'old' style prose and his poems follow T'ang models.

1140 Spain The *Poema de Mío Cid* is the earliest Spanish epic now surviving. Chronicles and histories from this period refer to other epics about Castilian heroes; some of these appear to have dated from the eighth century.

*c.*1140 **France** Creative period of Adam of St Victor, a Breton priest who wrote heavily symbolic rhyming verse.

1141 France Ordericus Vitalis (1075–1142), a Norman monk, wrote his *Historia Ecclesiastica*.

1131–1175 Spain Urgel cathedral is a Catalonian church showing the influence and work of Lombard masons.

1132 Sicily Palermo Palatine chapel illustrates the exotic combination of Norman, Byzantine and Islamic architecture. The mosaics and painted stalactite vaulting ceiling are highly elaborate. It was completed in 1143 by Egyptian Cairo craftsmen.

1135 France Chartres cathedral was rebuilt in early Gothic style of which only the west front with the famous *portail royale* remains. It was completed in 1180.

1137–1144 France The existing choir and west front of St Denis Abbey were built by Abbé Suger. The building itself is revolutionary. It combines the essential parts of Gothic architecture for the first time, particularly the buttressed rib vaults and pointed arches. The unified west façade contained early sculpted jamb figures. Gothic architecture spread through the Ile de France and thereafter throughout Europe.

1139–1149 France Fontenay Abbey is the earliest surviving Cistercian abbey in France designed with characteristic pointed transverse arches.

1140 France Pontigny abbey is a Cistercian church, it illustrates the twelfth century development in Cistercian architecture begun at Clairvaux by St Bernard in 1133, although the building later was destroyed. It is in the Gothic style with a chevet (a polygonal apse with radiating chapels).

*c.***1140 France** Sens cathedral was the first Gothic cathedral to be rib vaulted throughout. The nave, as is usual in early Gothic churches, has a sexpartite vault system.

*c.***1140 Ireland** Christ Church cathedral in Dublin illustrates the influence of the Cistercian west country Gothic style of England.

France: Pontigny Abbey

HISTORICAL EVENTS	LITERATURE	DANCE & DRAMA	MUSIC

HISTORICAL EVENTS

1143
Portugal became independent kingdom.

1144
Geoffrey of Anjou created Duke of Normandy.

1146
St Bernard proclaimed Second Crusade at Vezelay.

1148
Crusaders defeated outside Damascus.

1149
Normans attacked Byzantine empire and lost Corfu.

LITERATURE

1142 France Death of the scholar Peter Abelard. As a theologian and teacher he was associated with a controversial system of dialectics. His book *Historia Calamitatum* tells the story of his life, particularly of his love for and separation from his wife Héloise.

1145 France Death of the scholar William of Conches (b. 1080), author of *Philosophia Mundi* which combined humanist thinking with Platonism.

1147 Wales Geoffrey of Monmouth (1100–1155) wrote *Historia Regum Britanniae*, which provided source material for later treatments of stories about King Arthur.

*c.***1150 Flanders** Creative period of Nivard of Ghent, author of *Ysengrimo et Rainarde*, a 7-book satirical epic with animal characters which was an early example of a continuing tradition.

*c.***1150 France** Rise of the *trouveres*, who were distinguished from the troubadours by their use of the French, as distinct from the Provençal, language. They employed the same chivalric conventions and technical forms in their poetry.

*c.***1150–1200 Wales** Creative period of the poet Cynddelw, called 'Brydydd Mawr' or 'the Great Poet', and considered the best of his time. His poems were mainly in praise of contemporary rulers.

DANCE & DRAMA

*c.***1150 Spain** *Auto de Los Reyes Magos*, a fragment of an Epiphany play: it is the earliest extant play in the Spanish vernacular.

MUSIC

*c.***1150 Western Europe** Bowed instruments such as the vièle and rebec and wind instruments of the flute family became increasingly used in Church music. Many were introduced into Europe by the returning crusaders.

1150–1450 Germany Period when the *Minnesinger* flourished. These corresponded to the troubadours of France.

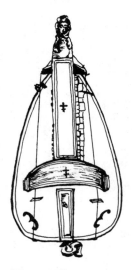

Western Europe: Early bowed instruments

1142 Syria The castle of Krak des Chevaliers was magnificent concentrically walled Crusader castle, one of several the Crusaders built in the Near East (now ruined). It was a massive building with emphasis on defence and storage. The Christian builders applied principles learned from Islamic forts and citadels.

1145 France Noyon cathedral introduced the triforium stage, a low wall-passage between gallery and clerestory, emphasizing the skeletal system of Gothic architecture.

1149 Israel The rebuilt church of the Holy Sepulchre in Jerusalem was dedicated; it has been frequently restored since. Constantine's original church was rebuilt by Crusaders, who added an eastern apse and ambulatory like a normal pilgrimage church. The rotunda had been rebuilt during the first Crusade.

1150 Norway Stavanger cathedral was begun in 1130 and Trondheim in 1152. Both illustrate their dependence on Anglo-Norman architectural style.

*c.***1150 England** Roche abbey is a three-storey church, rib vaulted throughout. It has been described as the first English church with a serious claim to be Gothic.

*c.***1150 France** Angers cathedral was rebuilt with Poitevan dome-like vaults typical of the area.

*c.***1150 France** St Trophime cathedral, Arles and St Gilles-du-Gard (*c.*1135–1195), near Arles display in the west fronts of both churches the finest sculptured façades of Provencal architecture, incorporating a mass of classically inspired details.

*c.***1150 Netherlands** The Churches of Our Lady, Maastricht, a mature Rhenish Romanesque church with an earlier westwork of *c.*1000, it is one of the few Romanesque Dutch churches that was not rebuilt in Holland's prosperous Gothic period.

1144 France Beginning of a period of stained glass production at the abbey of St Denis under Abbot Suger. St Denis became the centre of a French school of window design which was influential in the Netherlands and England. The style used small pieces in strong colours.

1150–1200 Persia Silhouette ware was made by potters; it foreshadowed true underglaze painting. The colour was applied as a slip and the background to the coloured patches was cut away to reveal the white body. The resulting designs were crisply outlined if somewhat stiff.

1150
Magnetic needle known in Italy. Earliest known almanac.

*Russia: cathedral of the
Dormition, Vladimir*

HISTORICAL EVENTS

*1152
Frederick
Barbarossa
elected king of
the Germans.*

*1154
Henry of Anjou
crowned Henry
II of England.*

*1156
Carmelite Order
founded.*

*1159
Henry II
accepted scutage
(shield money)
in place of feudal
military service.*

*1160
Normans
expelled from
North Africa.*

LITERATURE

1153 France Death of Bernard of Clairvaux, leading scholar of the Cistercian order; his rhetorical and mystical Latin style influenced devotional literature of the thirteenth century.

1155 France The *Roman de Brut* by Robert Wace (d. 1174) contains the first mention of the Arthurian Round Table. His stylized descriptions and rhetorical manner were influential on thirteenth century romances.

1158 Germany Death of Otto of Freising (b. 1114), chronicler and author of *Chronica* and *Gesta Friderici I Imperatoris.*

*c.***1160 France** Active period of Beatrice, Countess of Die, a Provençal poetess who wrote vivid personal lyrics.

*c.***1160 France** Benoît de Sainte Maure wrote his long epic *Roman de Troie* which introduced the story of Troilus and Cressida.

*c.***1160 Germany** Active period of 'Archpoet', who wrote in Latin. His best known poem was *Confession.*

MUSIC

1160 France Beginning of compilation of *Magnus Liber Organi* by Léonin, composer and first great representative of Notre-Dame school.

*c.*1150 **Hungary** Pécs cathedral, as in most Hungarian churches, reflects western influence. It combines German and Lombard styles but is unusual in having four towers flanking the east of the nave.

*c.*1150 **Norway** Borgund church is the best surviving Norwegian stave church. It has a nave and aisles, divided by tall mast-like poles with carved heads as capitals, a chancel and exterior ambulatory. The exterior is remarkable for the build-up of gabled roofs to a topmost pinnacle, with carved dragon's heads on lids of gables.

*c.*1150 **Sweden** Husaby church an early stone-built church demonstrates Swedish reliance on German architectural style. The church has an impressive west-work.

1155 **France** Godefroid de Clair made the 'Head Reliquary of Alexander' for Abbot Wibald of Stavelot. He was the leading enameller of the Meuse school.

1154
Map of the world produced at Palermo.

1158–1223 **Portugal** Alcobaça abbey is a remote beautifully proportioned Cistercian church, but unusual in being a hall church indicating Poitevan influence. It is one of the earliest Gothic buildings in Portugal.

1158 **Russia** The cathedral of the Dormition in Vladimir was originally of a simple plan with five aisles and a single dome; later additions of more domes produced a five-domed building which had a considerable influence in Russia thereafter. It was completed in 1161, but has since been rebuilt.

1160 **France** Laon cathedral begun. It is a rare example of a large Gothic church with a near full complement of towers. Seven were planned and five built. Particularly impressive is the west front with twin towers above three cavernous porches with sculpted figures. It makes a total break from the flat surface of Romanesque façades. Completed in early 13th century.

1160 **Japan** Sanjusangendo, Kyoto, is a hall 33 bays long designed to contain 1000 life size images of the Buddhist god Kannon. It was reconstructed in the thirteenth century.

*c.*1160–1170 **Germany** The shrine of St Heribert in Cologne was made in gilt-bronze with *champlevé* enamelling by Godefroid de Clair. It has figure ornament in bronze and enamelled roundels with scenes from the saint's life, and set a style which lasted for a century.

*c.*1160–1170 **England** The Winchester Bible, considered the masterpiece of the Winchester manuscript school which flourished with associated centres at St Albans and Canterbury.

Spain: Salamanca Cathedral

1161
*Canonization of
Edward the
Confessor.*

1162
*Chancellor
Thomas Becket
became
Archbishop of
Canterbury.*

ARCHITECTURE | THREE DIMENSIONAL ART | VISUAL ARTS | *INVENTIONS & DISCOVERIES*

1160 Spain Salamanca old Cathedral was consecrated: it has a ribbed vaulted central dome, a characteristic feature in Salamancan architecture of the period; inspired either by Moorish architecture, or by the Angevin churches of south-west France.

*c.*__1160 England__ Kilpeck church: the best work of the highly individual Herefordshire school of mason-sculptors survives in this tiny church.

*c.*__1160 France__ Private houses at Cluny, rare medieval survivors built of stone in terrace fashion: the ground floor rooms are large with entrance to match and the upper rooms are lit by rows of windows.

*c.*__1160 France__ St Ours at Loches, a typical aisle-less church of Aquitaine, but with two unique octagonal spires over the nave.

*c.*__1160 Germany__ Jerichow abbey, the earliest surviving brick Romanesque church in Germany, where the Romanesque style survived longer than in France and England. A number of churches in north Germany and the Elbe valley were of brick construction.

1161–1189 China The Hua-t'a of Cheng-Ting-Hsien, an octagonal-plan pagoda with unusual decoration, the sculpted lions and elephants being used as caryatids. This combination of decoration and structure shows affinities with Indian architecture rather than Chinese.

1162 Portugal The church of the Convento do Cristo at Tomar, one of the best surviving Templar churches. Typically, it is centrally planned with a 16-sided nave around an octagonal sanctuary.

*c.*__1162–1350 France__ Poitiers Cathedral: it was the first monumental Gothic church to be built on the 'hall church' principle, with nave and aisle vaults of equal height, rather than in the basilican style.

1163
Tartar Ch'in
dynasty
controlled
northern China.

1165
Norwegian
church organized.

1167
Rising of
Lombard League
against Frederick
I of Germany
(Barbarossa).
Frederick I of
Germany
crowned Holy
Roman Emperor.

1168
Storming of Kiev
by the Mongols.
End of Toltec
civilization in
Mexico.

1169
Saladin became
commander of
Syrian army of
occupation in
Egypt.

1170
Thomas Becket
murdered.

1172
Pilgrimage of
Henry the Lion
Duke of Bavaria
to Palestine.

1165–1180 France Active period of the poet Chrétien de Troyes, who wrote romances combining chivalric adventure with romantic and courtly love. The *Conte del Graal* introduces the Grail story into the Arthurian cycle.

1165–1175 France The *Lais* of Marie de France were short narrative poems with strong romantic love themes and a background of folk-lore.

1165 France Gautier d'Arras (1135–1198) wrote the romance *Eracle*.

1170–1190 Germany Active period of the *minnesinger* ('love singer') Friedrich von Hausen, the first German lyric poet to adopt the forms and conventions of the Provençal troubadours. The *minnesingers* expressed love of the ideal woman with more sincerity and less artifice than the French troubadours and *trouvères*.

1170 Wales Death of the poet Hywel ab Owain Gwynedd who, together with his contemporary Gwalchmai, broke away from the convention that one poet must restrict himself to one theme. Their work mixes the themes of love, war and nature.

England: murder of Thomas à Becket

ARCHITECTURE

1163 France Notre-Dame, Paris: this typical early French Gothic cathedral has a compact plan of short nave with virtually no projecting transepts; its chevet choir is an early example of its type. Like its contemporaries, the church was originally planned with a four-storey elevation, reduced to three in the nave. Completed in 1220, it was altered in the mid 13th century with the addition of nave chapels and enlarged transepts.

*c.*1164 **Spain** La Oliva Abbey, a Cistercian church built on the Bernardian plan, it is an early example of Spanish Gothic architecture.

1166—1170 England Orford Castle has a keep built to a polygonal plan designed to increase the defender's view assured the castle walls. It is an early example, of a development from the previous massive rectangular Norman keeps.

1168—1174 England The walls of Dover castle were built around the great keep; they are the first known example in western Europe of concentric lines of defence.

*c.*1170 **Denmark** Kalundborg Church is built of brick on a plan unique for Denmark, the Greek-cross plan: it is part church and part fortress.

*c.*1170 **Spain** Santiago de Compostela Cathedral narthex (portico) incorporates rib vaults, the earliest use of this construction in Spain.

1174—1185 England Canterbury Cathedral choir was rebuilt as the first English Gothic building in the French manner, designed by master mason William of Sens. (died *c.*1180)

THREE DIMENSIONAL ART

1163 Afghanistan Cast-bronze bucket, incised and inlaid with silver and copper and decorated with bands of inscription and illustration, typifies wares made at Herat, which was a centre for bronze-casting of luxury objects.

Egypt: late Fatimid lustre dish

1166 Germany A bronze lion was erected in Brunswick in honour of Henry the Lion: it was the first such free-standing secular statue in Europe. German sculptors excelled in metalwork.

1171 Egypt The fall of the Fatimid dynasty brought an end to the production of lustre-painted pottery. It continued to be made in Persia and in Syria, where Egyptian potters had taught the technique. Syrian lustre ware from Tell Minis had abstract and animal designs, the latter sometimes having an amusing near-cartoon quality.

VISUAL ARTS

INVENTIONS & DISCOVERIES

1163
Silver mines discovered at Freiburg.

1172 France Robert Wace (d. 1174) wrote *Roman de Rou*.

1175–1180 France Active period of Andreas Capellanus, chaplain to Marie, Countess of Champagne, who wrote for her a treatise defining the code of courtly love, as it evolved in Provençal literature.

1176 Manuel I, eastern emperor, defeated by Seljuk Turks.

1175–1190 Germany The poet Heinrich von Veldeke wrote his epic *Eneide*.

1177 Civil war in Norway.

France: Pont St Benezet, Avignon

1180 Persia *Khusrow u Shirin*, a romantic epic by Ilyas Nizam al-Din Abu Yusif Nizami Ganjavi (1140–1203). Nizami was a poet and the most outstanding writer of Persian romantic fiction in his period.

1180 France Perotinus Pérotin, composer, succeeded Léonin at Notre-Dame in Paris; he was the greatest representative of Notre-Dame school and completely revised Léonin's *Magnus Liber Organi*.

late 1100–1200 India Jhanesvar made a Marathi language paraphrase of the great Indian philosophical poem, the *Bhagavad Gita*.

1174–1182 Italy Monreale Cathedral built, representing the climax of Sicilian Romanesque architecture, with almost baroque richness in its exterior decoration; the interior is basilican-planned, but the Romanesque is diluted by pointed Islamic arches and Byzantine mosaics. The cloisters are remarkable for their highly decorated columns.

*c.***1175 Germany** Kirchlinde is a Westphalian Romanesque 'hall church', a design which was to become popular in German Gothic churches.

1177–1185 France Pont St Bénézet, Avignon, the famous Pont d'Avignon, was built by the guild of bridge-builders; it is now partly destroyed. On one pile a small chapel was built. Originally the bridge had 22 arches; there are now only four.

1179–1208 Italy Fossanova Abbey, a Cistercian monastery, was built according to the original Burgundian plan; it is still in use.

*c.***1179 England** Beginning of Ripon cathedral; although it displayed a number of Gothic details, these were applied to massive thick walls, maintaining the Anglo-Norman tradition which continued in north England.

*c.***1180 England** The manor house, Boothby Pagnell, is a rare surviving example of medieval domestic architecture; the ground floor is vaulted and the principal rooms are on the first floor.

*c.***1180 England** Beginning of Wells Cathedral, the first Gothic church in the west of England adapted to English taste, particularly in its emphasis on low horizontal lines. Wells introduced the stylized 'stiff-leaf' capitals which were popular for the next 50 years. It has the finest English West screen façades. Completed in 1240, the east-end was rebuilt in the early 14th century.

*c.***1180–1196** The abbey church of the Cistercian monastery of Poblet, Catalonia, was built with old-fashioned pointed barrel vaults in the nave.

*c.***1175 Syria** Production of lustre ware and underglaze painted ware began at Raqqa, possibly as a continuation of the earlier Tell Minis pottery. Decoration combined calligraphy and floral motifs; form was influenced by Persian pottery. Raqqa decorators were noted for their fluid and original drawing.

1175- 1200 France The tomb of Geoffrey Plantagenet at Le Mans is characteristic of Limoges enamelling, with delicately-drawn figures in coloured enamel on a vermiculated ground (i.e. a background patterned with a network of worm-like lines).

late 1100–1200 Persia Development of the earliest known enamelled pottery, *minai*: colours were painted on the glaze and fixed by a second firing.

late 1100–1200 Russia Beshken the master jeweller of Opiza, flourished. He is known for one Gospel cover, with a traditional plain background.

Syria: late 12th century
Raqquan decoration from lustre
ware

1180
First reference to
European
windmill with
vertical sails.

HISTORICAL EVENTS	LITERATURE	DANCE & DRAMA	MUSIC

HISTORICAL EVENTS

1182
St Francis of Assisi born. Jews banished from France.

1186
Kamakura era in Japan began under domination of Minamato family.

1187
Saladin took Jerusalem. Punjab conquered by Moslem Mohammed of Ghor.

1188
Bulgaria became independent of Eastern Empire.

1189
Frederick I embarked on third crusade.

1191
Richard I of England joined Third Crusade.

1193
Death of Saladin. Richard I of England imprisoned by Henry VI of Germany at Trifels.

1194
Privileges granted to German merchants in England.

LITERATURE

1185 Russia The *Lay of Igor* was written by an anonymous poet in vivid style.

*c.***1186 Denmark** Svend Aggeson (1130–1200) completed his *Historium Regum Daniae*, which is the first history of Denmark and ends at the year 1185.

1190–1195 Germany Hartmann von Aue (1170–1215) wrote his epic poems *Der Arme Heinrich*, *Erec*, and *Gregorius*.

*c.***1190 France** Active period of the poet Alexandre de Bernai, who contributed to the tradition of romances about Alexander the Great.

1191–1204 Germany The first extant version of the *Nibelungenlied* was written; it is based on Germanic legends and probably originated in the sixth century.

1191 Persia Death of Ahwad al-Din Ali Anvari, a poet highly regarded for his panegyrics. Panegyrics and narratives were the two most common verse forms at that period.

1197 China *Ta Yüeh I* by Chiang K'uei (?1158–?1231), poet and musician. His poetry shows the influence of his music.

1198 Spain Death of Averroës (b. 1126), the distinguished Spanish-Arabic philosopher.

Italy: Parma baptistery

ARCHITECTURE

*c.*1180 **Wales** Beginning of St David's Cathedral; it provides the stylistic link between the architecture of the west of England and of Ireland.

1190 **Denmark** Roskilde Cathedral was rebuilt in brick, a material often used in Denmark from the middle of the twelfth century.

*c.*1190 **Germany** Beginning of the church of the Holy Apostles, Cologne; it has a simplified version of the trefoil-planned choir, and a massive west tower.

1192–1275 **France** Bourges Cathedral was built in homogeneous high Gothic style, with an exceptionally fine interior marked by the high arcade piers and restrained decoration.

1192–1280 **England** The choir of Lincoln cathedral was built with an asymmetrical tierceron vault, probably the first of its kind; from it evolved the nave star vaults.

1194–1260 **France** Chartres Cathedral was rebuilt; the interior was reduced to three storeys, producing the classic Gothic elevation with its strong vertical emphasis. The triforium is small and there is no gallery while above, the vault is quadripartite. It is a totally logical elevation making full use of flying buttresses and allowing vast window areas for stained glass. It was the first completed high Gothic church.

1196–1199 **France** Château Gaillard, Les Andelys, was built by Richard I of England; with its three separate lines of defence and 'donjon', or keep, it was, wrongly, considered impregnable.

1196–1296 **Italy** Parma baptistery was built detached from the church, as was often the case during this period in Italy; and it is octagonal outside and 16-sided within, imitating Constantine's baptistery in Rome.

THREE DIMENSIONAL ART

1185–1332 **Japan** The Kamakura period: the restoration of eighth-century Buddhist monasteries of the Nara period, with their sculpture, stimulated a renaissance of the strong and simple style in sculpture: this was also encouraged by contemporary military government and Zen Buddhist teaching. The most prominent sculptor was Unkei (fl. 1175–1218).

1194 **France** Earliest of the stained-glass windows in Chartres Cathedral; about half of the 106 windows were donated by trade guilds and portray their donors at work. Increasing patronage of religious art by guilds established contemporary urban crafts as acceptable subject matter. The church had formerly confined its attention to the timeless occupations of crop-growing and stock raising which appeared in the Bible.

1196 **Italy** Beginning of work on the doors of the baptistry at Parma by Benedetto Antelami (fl. 1178–1219), sculptor. He used elongated figures and formal drapery folds to produce a grave and dramatic expressiveness.

late 1100–1200 **Persia** Khurasan metal workers made objects of sheet brass; a characteristic example is a ewer, made in several parts soldered together, and decorated with *repoussé* figures, incised ornament and silver inlay.

VISUAL ARTS

*c.*1190–1224 **China** Ma Yuan flourished, an artist notable for his principle of 'balanced asymmetry'. He was a member of the Southern Sung Academy and became one of the most imitated of Chinese artists.

1196 **India** The Moslem leader Muhammad of Ghor took Gujarat. The Moslems introduced paper to Jain artists, who continued to paint on it in the long strip format of the palm leaves they had formerly used.

INVENTIONS & DISCOVERIES

1189
Silver florin first coined at Florence.

13th Century

HISTORICAL EVENTS	LITERATURE	DANCE & DRAMA	MUSIC

LITERATURE

1200–1220 Germany Wolfram von Eschenbach wrote *Parzifal*, the best-known medieval romance in German; it is distinguished by its humour and vigour.

*c.***1200–1220 France** *Aucassin et Nicolette*, an anonymous French romance of great popularity.

DANCE & DRAMA

*c.***1200–1300 France** *Jeu de Saint Nicolas* by Jean Bodel: it has a religious subject, a miracle of the saint, but includes secular scenes. This marks a step in the secularization of drama.

*c.***1200–1300 Germany** The poem *The Trojan War* describes contemporary dancers: they combined the stately, gliding form of dancing with spirited free-rhythm dancing in the same choral dance.

*c.***1200–1300 Vietnam** Contact was made, through warfare, with actors of Chinese opera, who were then kept in Vietnam to train local companies: the resultant form of theatre was called *hat boi*, and was completely derived from the earlier Chinese form.

MUSIC

1200–1300 Germany The *minnesinger* fiddle in use (a forerunner of the violin).

1200–1300 Western Europe The term 'motet' first used.

1200–1300 Western Europe The naker, the medieval name for a high-pitched kettledrum, was introduced into Europe.

Germany: a medieval cwrth, like the minnesinger a forerunner of the violin

ARCHITECTURE

early 1200–1300 Cambodia
Angkor Thom is a former capital city planned as a rectangle over 2 km long and surrounded by a moat and walls over 6 m high. At the centre of the city was the King's temple containing an image of Buddha (rebuilt in the 13th century). The city was the greatest architectural achievement of the classical Khmer period but it is significant that building technique was unsophisticated and no mortar was used.

early 1200–1300 Thailand Vat Bhudda Svarya is the oldest building in the south of the country, consisting of a towered shrine and columned hall.

1200–1300 Finland Turku Cathedral built, a simple brick church, it had square piers without capitals, and an uninterrupted vault running the length of the building. It has been restored and rebuilt.

1200–1300 Germany Hanover Town Hall is a large gabled rectangular building panelled and pinnacled in elaborate brick characteristic of the Hanse towns.

1200–1300 Germany The Marksburg, Braubach, is the best preserved, of the Rhine castles, and was built on an impregnable hill. Now restored, it centres on a square tower, around which are grouped residential buildings. The entrance was guarded by a series of gatehouses.

1200–1300 Holland The Muiderslot, Muiden, a rectangular-planned castle with drum towers indicating French influence, is otherwise typically Dutch, being built of brick and surrounded by a moat.

1200–1300 India The Black Pagoda, Konorak, is the remains of an uncompleted temple to the sun; it has been suggested that structural difficulties were the reason for its abandonment.

1200–1300 Italy Lucera Castle was one of the strongest of Frederick II's Italian castles and included his own palace with an upper octagonal tower.

THREE DIMENSIONAL ART

early 1200 1300 France The wrought-iron screen for Ourscamp abbey is characteristic of the more sophisticated and elaborate scroll-work which developed from the original simple, English form.

1200–1300 France Smiths developed techniques of stamping ornament on ironwork that were in advance of the rest of Europe: ornamental hinges were the most important forms.

1200–1300 France Caen was a famous centre for small embroidered articles, pouches and book-covers.

1200–1300 France and England Coloured lead glazes in green, yellow and brown were used on pottery. The colours were made from copper and iron oxides and added to the glaze.

1200–1300 Italy The Altarist glass-makers of Montferrat began to disperse through Europe.

1200–1300 Russia The gold cover for the icon of the Virgin of Vladimir: an early example of fine work in gold, which was so scarce and expensive in eleventh and twelfth century Russia that even important objects were usually made in copper.

VISUAL ARTS

*c.*1200 **Arabia** Collection of poems by Umar Ibnul Farid (1181–1235), regarded as the greatest of Arab mystical poets.

*c.*1200 **Georgia** Shota Rustaveli wrote his epic *Vepkhis Tqaosani*, an allegory which was based on heroic themes.

*c.*1200 **Denmark** Earliest of the ballads which indicate what dancing was like in northern countries: open or closed chain dances by groups of people, never couples, to a sung accompaniment. This form persists in Denmark, Iceland and the Faroes.

Mexico: after a fresco from Temple of the Warriors, Chichen Itza, Yucatán

1200–1300 Japan Kongosan-maiin, Wakyama, illustrates Indian and Chinese influence in the Heian period; the lower storey is topped by a semi-dome supporting a second storey.

1200–1300 Mexico Chichén Itza, Yucatán, the capital of the colonial conquest of the Toltecs was built; it includes a number of temples decorated with magnificent sculpture depicting priests, warriors and gods, and some painted interiors.

1200–1300 Peru Chanchan, the capital of the Chimu Empire, was built over 15 square km and divided into 10 compounds; the material used was adobe brick, some decorated with abstract reliefs carved in the dried clay.

1200–1300 Peru Paramonga was a massive brick fortress built by the Chimu, with its corner bastions and successive lines of defence resembling European sixteenth-century fortification.

1200–1300 Poland Marienburg Castle was built of brick by the Teutonic Knights and became their headquarters in 1309; like their other castles, it was designed along monastic lines.

1200–1300 Sweden The town of Visby, Gorland, is protected by a two-mile wall inspired by the fortifications around Cologne, Germany; it was a centre of Hanseatic power with warehouses notable for their large ornamental gables.

1200–1300 Turkey The Seljuk caliphs built fortified staging posts to protect travellers on trade routes. The caravanserai at Sulan Han, near Konya, is typical; it includes a mosque, halls for merchants and servants, and baths. Dominant in Seljuk architecture is the great gate, derived from Persian tradition, but decorated with carving instead of with tiles as in Persia.

*c.*1200 **Peru** Culmination of the Lambayeque culture, characterized in art by large-scale work in gold and silver which was hammered, wrought in high relief or modelled in the round. Colour was applied with cinnabar, ammonia and copper sulphide. All pre-Hispanic Peruvian gold was hollow, except for small idols from Cuzco, up to 10 ins in height, which were sometimes solid.

*c.*1200 **China** Introduction of cut-glaze decoration on Tz'ŭ-chou pottery of north China.

*c.*1200 **Germany** A group of tapestries, now in Halberstadt Cathedral, has been dated to this period. They include one of 'Charlemagne among the four Philosophers'. Between 15 and 20 dyes were available to medieval weavers, providing vivid colours. Tapestry flourished in the Middle Rhineland, Alsace and Nuremberg.

*c.*1200 **India** End of the 'classical' period, in which Hindu styles were established in many schools of art. Moslem influence becomes stronger after this.

*c.*1200 **Persia** Lustre-ware tiles were produced, moulded and elaborately painted in northwest Persia (Rayy and Kashan). There is evidence of collaboration between potters and manuscript illustrators.

HISTORICAL EVENTS	LITERATURE	DANCE & DRAMA	MUSIC

HISTORICAL EVENTS

1200
*Aztecs
established in
Mexico, Incas in
Peru.*

1202
*Fourth Crusade
launched by
Venice against
Constantinople.*

1203
*Mohammed of
Ghor completed
subjection of
upper India.*

1204
*Crusaders took
Constantinople,
partitioned
Greece,
established Latin
empire;
Byzantine artists
fled to Venice.*

1205
*John of England
lost English
possessions in
France.*

1206
*Genghiz Khan
became emperor
of the Mongols.
Emergence of
Delhi as Moslem
capital of India.*

1208
*England placed
under papal
interdict.*

1210
*Mongols invaded
northern China
under Genghiz
Khan.*

1211
*War between
John of England
and Llywellyn
the Great of
Wales.*

1212
*Children's
Crusade.*

1215
*John of England
signed Magna
Carta.*

LITERATURE

*c.*1200 **India** Chand Bardai wrote the Hindi poem *Prithi Raj Raso* celebrating the life of the Rajput chief Prithi Raj: it was one of the earliest vernacular poems. The Rajput princes had patronized Sanskrit literature. Their departure, like that of Prithi Raj, at the hands of the Moslem invaders, meant a rise of the vernacular languages, like Hindi.

1203 **Germany** Hartmann von Aue (1170–1215) wrote his epic poem *Iwein.*

1205 **France** Death of Peire Vidal (b. 1150), Provençal troubadour, a brilliant stylist with an original and realistic tone.

*c.*1205 **England** The poet Layamon wrote his epic *Brut*, an alliterative romance.

1206 **Japan** *Shinkokinshu*, a collection of Japanese poems, was compiled on the order of the emperor Gotoba. It was the twentieth such anthology since the *Kokinshu* of 905.

1210 **Germany** Gottfried von Strassburg fl., author of an idealized epic *Tristan und Isold.*

1212 **France** Death of Geoffroy de Villehardouin, chronicler and author of *Conquête de Constantinople*, an accurate and realistic account of events 1198–1207; he was a distinguished prose stylist.

1212 **Iceland** Death of Karl Jonsson, the Icelandic saga writer, author of the first part of *Sverris saga.*

1213–1250 **Japan** *Tales of the Taira Clan*, a novel describing the feud between two clans, is a mixture of fact, fiction and tradition. The author is unknown. Military novels of this type were popular at the period, perhaps reflecting the state of the country which was torn by uprisings and civil war.

*c.*1217–1242 **France** Aimeric de Belenoi fl. as a Provençal troubadour; he was considered a delicate, elegant stylist.

1217 **England** Death of Alexander Neckham, the English grammarian and scientist; he wrote *De Naturis Rerum*, a popular handbook of contemporary science.

DANCE & DRAMA

*c.*1200 **France** The story of *Our Lady's Tumbler* records how an illiterate minstrel paid homage to the virgin in dance. Jugglers' and tumblers' dances preserved the classical tradition of acrobatic dance.

*c.*1200 **Germany** The Manesse *minnesinger* manuscript shows jugglers and tumblers dancing with gestures of the hands: lively use of the hands in these dances was peculiar to Germany.

MUSIC

*c.*1200 **Austria** or **Switzerland** Walther von der Vogelweide flourished. His song of the crusader, *Nu Alerst Leb' Ich Mir Werde* (1228), discovered in 1910, is one of the finest *minnesinger* melodies.

1212 **France** Johannes de Garlandia opened a school in Paris and wrote a treatise on music.

1217 **Germany** Neidhart von Reuental, German *minnesinger* (d. *c.*1240), joined the crusade of Leopold, Duke of Babenberg; he was the only *minnesinger* whose songs were printed after the invention of typography.

ARCHITECTURE

1200–1400 Spain The Alhambra, Granada, exemplifies Islamic decorative building; the curve inside what was once a plain arch is now cut out into deep hollows and hanging pendants called 'stalactite' ornament. Columns are slender and screens are fretted to allow maximum interplay of light and space; all surfaces are decorated with repeating abstract patterns.

*c.***1200 Germany** Romanesque Goslar Palace is one of many imperial palaces built by the Hohenstaufens.

*c.***1200 Portugal** Bragança Council Hall is a curious five-sided secular version of a cathedral chapter house.

1203–1278 Spain Lerida Cathedral has a design transitional between Romanesque and Gothic, together with Moorish features.

1209 Germany Magdeburg Cathedral was the first German church to incorporate Gothic elements, its pointed arches in particular.

1211 France Rheims Cathedral was begun, the coronation church of France and the model for Westminster Abbey; it is a superb example of the high Gothic style and important for introducing naturalistic foliage capitals and bar tracery. The 'architect' was Jean d'Orbais.

THREE DIMENSIONAL ART

*c.***1200–1220 Persia** The potter Abū Zayd flourished as one of the leading workers in the Kashan style, which was a development from Rayy lustre pottery.

1201 China First dated piece of overglaze enamelling on pottery.

1204 Persia Earliest dated piece of underglaze-painted pottery, probably made in Kashan. Kashan painted ware was often decorated with blue or black under a turquoise or a transparent glaze.

1205 Meuse Valley Nicolas of Verdun (active c.1180–1205) completed the shrine of St Mary in Tournai Cathedral, made in gold, silver, precious stones and rock crystal. He was a pupil of Godefroid de Clair and is considered the last of the great Romanesque goldsmith-enamellers.

1205–1352 Islam Lustre-painted tiles were used for commemorative niches in mosques.

VISUAL ARTS

*c.***1200 Europe** First appearance of tempera painting, which remained the primary technique for panel painting until the fifteenth century. The term was generally applied to painting with pigments emulsified or mixed with egg. Colours were few and blending difficult; variety was achieved by meticulously building up successive layers of paint.

1210 China Death of Liang-K'ai, a painter and Zen monk who developed a wet-ink technique, in which the figures were formed by the black-and-white effect of ink brushed on to a light ground in broad masses.

1202 Leonardo Fibonacci introduced Arabic numerals to Europe.

Europe: anonymous 13th century Italian tempera painting

Italy: Saint Francesco Assisi

1221
Mongols invaded
sultanate of
Delhi.

1223
Mongols invaded
Russia and
China.

1224
France declared
war on England.

1222 Denmark Saxo Grammaticus' *Gesta Danorum* records legends, heroic poems and events from Danish prehistory to 1222 in easy, flowing Latin.

1225–1250 Italy Sordello of Mantua fl. as a Provençal troubadour of great versatility and originality. Troubadour verse was written in northern Spain and northern Italy as well as in southern France, wherever the Provençal language was used, in fact.

*c.***1225 France** Guillaume de Bretagne fl., author of a Latin epic *Philippeis*, in praise of the French king.

1226 Italy Death of St Francis of Assisi (b. 1182), author of *Canticle of Brother Sun*; he exercised great influence on the literature of personal devotion, particularly on the development of the *lauda*, or vernacular song of praise.

1227
Death of Genghiz
Khan.

1228
James I of
Aragon
conquered
Balearic Islands.

1228 Denmark Death of the poet Anders Sunesen (b. 1167), author of the Latin epic poem *Hexaèmeron*, about the Creation.

1221 Spain Birth of Alfonso el Sabio (d. 1284) who became King Alfonso X of Castile and Leon (1252–1284). A patron of music, he was responsible for a compilation of over **400** *Cantigas de Santa Maria*, hymns to the virgin, in the Galician-Portuguese dialect, which showed the influence of Provençal troubadours.

1229 Germany The Emperor Frederick II brought back professional dancing girls from his crusade: their acrobatic dancing reinforced a native tendency in spectacular dance.

ARCHITECTURE

*c.*1219 **Cambodia** Bayon is the only Buddhist temple-mountain in Cambodia.

*c.*1219 **Italy** St Andrea, Vercelli, was the first Italian church to incorporate Gothic features.

1220–1258 England Salisbury Cathedral, a unique English Gothic cathedral built in one campaign on a virgin site, is a classic example of the severe early English Gothic style.

1220–1288 France Amiens Cathedral is a refinement of the high Gothic style started at Chartres.

*c.*1220 **Germany** Limburg Cathedral, although Gothic, retains the old-fashioned four-storey elevation.

1221–1500 Spain Burgos Cathedral introduced the French high Gothic style to Spain.

1226–1500 Spain Toledo Cathedral is one of the largest and finest of Spanish Gothic churches; the high altar screen is a masterpiece of Gothic sculpture.

1228–1239 Italy St Francesco, Assisi, was the first Franciscan friary and is conservative architecturally, with an upper and lower church. It is chiefly known for its frescoes, a popular Italian form of wall and vault decoration. It was altered in 1253.

1229 France St Nicaise, Rheims, was a superb example of the French high Gothic style, combining features of both Rheims and Amiens cathedrals. Destroyed during the French Revolution, it was one of many churches to suffer at that time.

THREE DIMENSIONAL ART

*c.*1220–1320 **Flanders** French influence predominates in sculpture.

1223 Mesopotamia Date inscribed on a brass ewer, incised and inlaid with silver and made in Mosul by Ahmad al-Dhaki: the design includes medallion-framed scenes of rural and aristocratic life. Ewers and basins were luxury objects, used in rich households for washing the hands before and after meals. Mosul was an important centre of work in inlaid brass.

1224 Venice A glass-blowers' guild is known to have existed.

1225–1250 England Laurence Vitrearius from Normandy was established in the Surrey-Sussex weald as a maker of window glass. Coloured glass was easier to make than clear, and church windows were glazed to provide pictures as well as shelter.

1228–1442 Yemen The Rasulid emirs were patrons of the arts. The period is noted for blown glass which was then enamelled and gilded.

VISUAL ARTS

1218–1241 Bulgaria Reign of Tsar Ivan Assen II, patron of manuscript illumination (earlier manuscripts were plain except for a little decoration of capitals): an important early example of illumination is the *Four Gospels* manuscript decorated by Dobreisho.

1226–1270 France Paris under St Louis became a major centre of painting and book illustration. Manuscripts like the *Psalter* of *c.*1253–1270 showed that illuminators and stained-glass artists influenced each other. The *Legend of St Denis* was illustrated with 60 miniatures of street life and trading in Paris.

HISTORICAL EVENTS	LITERATURE	DANCE & DRAMA	MUSIC
	*c.*1230–1250 Saxony The Englishman Bartholomew de Glanville, also known as Bartholomaeus Anglicus, wrote *De Proprietatibus Rerum*, a Latin encyclopedia of natural science, later translated into English.	*c.*1230 England John Garland, scholar and composer, first mentions the gigue, a British rustic dance adopted by English composers of the sixteenth century.	
	1230–1235 Italy Giacomo da Lentini fl., leader of the Sicilian school of poetry; he introduced the Provençal lyric into Italian poetry, and was credited with the invention of the sonnet.	*c.*1230–1285 France Life of the minstrel Ruteboeuf, who wrote *Le Miracle de Saint Théophile*; he began a vogue for plays about miracles of the Virgin, often called 'Mary Plays'.	
1231 *Beginning of westward spread of Mongols into Persia.*	1230 Austria Death of Walther von der Vogelweide (b. 1170), an Austrian *minnesinger* who used a variety of poetic forms with strong feeling and technical brilliance.		
1232 *Alliance of Mongols and Sung dynasty in southern China.*	1230 France Death of Aimeric de Peguilhan (b. 1195), an accomplished Provençal troubadour.		
	*c.*1235 France Guillaume de Lorris fl., the poet who wrote the first part of *Roman de la Rose*.		
1236 *Ferdinand III of Castile conquered Cordova from the Moors; beginning of Spanish reconquest.*	1236 France Death of Gautier de Coinci, a poet monk whose lyrics attempted reconciliation of courtly love with praise of the Virgin.		
1238 *Mongols took Moscow.*			
1240 *Mongol conquest of Russia complete.*	1240–1250 France *Flamenca*, a Provençal romance, combined realism with courtly conventions.		*c.*1240 England A *rota* or round was found at Reading Abbey, *Sumer is icumen in*. The date is in doubt according to *Grove*, some authorities giving it not earlier than 1280 and others as late as 1310.
	1240 Germany *Kudrun*, a Bavarian narrative poem about the heroic age, by an anonymous poet.		

ARCHITECTURE	THREE DIMENSIONAL ART	VISUAL ARTS	*INVENTIONS &*
			DISCOVERIES

ARCHITECTURE

1230 France The elevation of Beauvais Cathedral is reduced to two-storeys, in which the pier shafts rise to the vault and the triforium is glazed; the vault is the highest ever built at 51·1 m and has to be supported by three tiers of fliers. It was later rebuilt but never completed.

*c.***1230 France** Coucy Castle had a 54·6 m round keep, vaulted at three levels. The walls at its base were more than 8 m thick and it was one of the strongest keeps ever built, though later destroyed.

1231 France St Denis, Nave, was rebuilt by Pierre de Montereau in the high Gothic style; it is one of the first churches to have a glazed triforium storey.

1232 France Angers Castle has 17 drum towers patterned with striped masonry, probably derived from a Byzantine source.

1235–1283 Germany St Elizabeth, Marburg, is a high Gothic church in the French style but peculiarly German by being a hall church, an increasingly popular style in Germany.

1235–1290 Norway Trondheim Cathedral nave, the finest example of Gothic architecture in Norway, is stylistically related to Lincoln Cathedral, England; the west rose window is in the flamboyant style of Rheims Cathedral, France.

*c.***1235 France** Villard de Honnecourt from the Cambrai district was an architect whose notebook is an invaluable source of information on thirteenth-century building methods.

1239 Italy St Michele in Lucca's Tuscan screen façade in marble built.

*c.***1240 England** Lincoln Cathedral chapter house is the largest of the polygonal-planned, English chapter houses; about 30 examples are known of this peculiarly national development.

*c.***1240–1275 France** The west façade of Strasbourg Cathedral nave by Erwin von Steinbach is unusual in having a web of free-standing tracery.

THREE DIMENSIONAL ART

1230–1233 Russia The west and south doors of the Cathedral of the Nativity, Vladimir, were made of damascened copper, each door having 28 square panels: they were considered major achievements in large-scale damascene work (i.e. metal decorated with silver and gold).

*c.***1237/40–1480 Russia** The Mongol occupation disrupted the growth of Russian art as a northern form of the Byzantine tradition. The glass-making centres were destroyed, but wood-carving suffered less than other arts and religious carvings of great complexity survive.

1238–1240 Syria Date of a ceremonial basin made in brass with silver inlay for the Ayyubid sultan al-Malik al-Adil, who commissioned the artist Ahmad al-Dhaki of Mosul in Mesopotamia. Decoration consists of medallion-framed scenes of hunting and war.

*c.***1240 France** Free-standing figures in ivory appear as a new style after a gap in ivory carving of some 50 years.

VISUAL ARTS

Russia: examples of Russian art, 12th and 13th century illustrations

HISTORICAL EVENTS

1241
First commercial treaty between Lübeck and Hamburg; led to development of Hanseatic League.
Mongols expelled from western Europe.

1242
Batu, Genghiz Khan's grandson, established realm of the Golden Horde in Russia.

1243
5 years' truce between England and France.

1247
Pope Innocent IV transformed Carmelites into mendicant friars.

1248
Ferdinand III of Castile took Seville.

LITERATURE

*c.*1240 **Persia** *Masnavi* by Jalal al-Din Muhammad Mowlavi (1207–1273), Persian poet and Sufi mystic, founder of the 'Mowlavies' (whirling dervishes). This long poem contains the Sufi doctrines and is regarded as the supreme example of Persian mystical thought. The poet was more concerned with feeling than with formal expression.

1241 **Iceland** Death of Snorri Sturluson (b. 1178), saga writer and poet, author of *Heimskringla* and the prose *Edda*, which were marked by lively characterization and critical historical analysis.

*c.*1250–1280 **Austria** The poet Wernher der Gartenaere fl.; he wrote *Meier Helmbrecht*, a realistic epic of peasant life.

*c.*1250 **Portugal** Joan Airas de Santiago fl., author of early Portuguese lyrics called *cancioneros*.

DANCE & DRAMA

1243 **India** *The Dutangada* is the earliest surviving shadow play (although the form had existed for centuries): it is based on the *Ramayana* which, together with the other ancient Hindu epic the *Mahabharata*, is one of the most important sources in Indian drama, literature and dance.

MUSIC

1243 **Italy** First Italian *sacra rappresentazione* at Padua.

Italy: exterior of Castel del Monte

*c.*1240 **Italy** Castel del Monte is an extraordinary hunting lodge built for Frederick III with an octagonal plan and towers; it was luxuriously appointed, with decoration including Islamic and classical designs, as well as Gothic vaults.

1243–1248 France St Chapelle, Paris, designed to house relics brought from the Holy Land by Louis IX, represents the logical conclusion of the skeletal Gothic style, being composed almost entirely of glass in the upper chapel walls. The lower chapel has windows of spherical triangular shape, the first known use of this design.

1245 England In Westminster Abbey, London, Henry of Reyns (died *c.*1253), the first architect, incorporated many contemporary French features which suggest Henry may have known Rheims and other near contemporary French churches. Westminster, as a result, appears very un-English. Completed in the seventeenth century.

1247 Denmark Odense Cathedral was built in brick, a spacious church in simple Gothic style; the eastern stepped gable is a characteristic Danish feature.

1248 Germany Cologne Cathedral introduced the French high Gothic style to Germany on a grand scale; intended to be the greatest of all Gothic churches, only the choir was completed by 1322 and the remainder in the nineteenth century.

*c.*1250–1295 **France** The town of Aigues Mortes is planned on the characteristic medieval graph-paper pattern, the tower of Constance providing an additional strong point.

*c.*1250 **France** The new transept to the south of Notre-Dame in Paris, completed by Pierre de Montereau, incorporates vertical jambs that curve into arches without intervening capitals, possibly the earliest example of such a device.

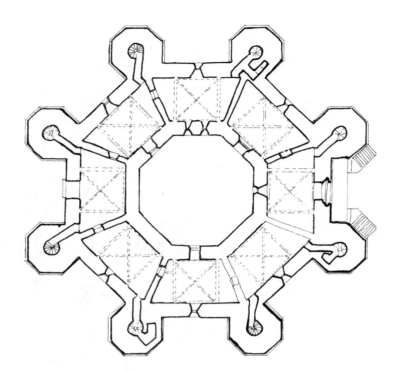

Italy: ground plan of Castel del Monte

*c.*1250–1280 **China** First evidence of decorative carving on lacquer, formerly a utilitarian substance. Decoration involved cutting a slanting line to expose different coloured layers of lacquer, or incising a design which was then gilded.

*c.*1250–1280 **Italy** The gradual resolution of the struggle between Papacy and Empire brought a flowering of 'Italian' art, superseding the various regional arts under different Gothic and Byzantine influences.

*c.*1250–1275 **Italy** The painter called Master of the Magdalen painted in Florence a panel of scenes from the life of Mary Magdalen; it remains within the Byzantine style but introduces a lively narrative force.

*c.*1250 **China** Mu Ch'i flourished, a painter who was a leading artist in the 'ink-splash' style, and in painting with a splayed-out brush-stroke. He was an outstanding painter of flower and bird subjects. He was influential on Japanese painting.

North America: effigy vessel made by New Mexican Indians

1252
Alexander Nevski became last Russian prince of Vladimir.

1256
Persian empire re-established under Mongol rule.

1257
Llywellyn the Great styled himself Prince of Wales, having obtained Anglesey, Snowdon and Powys.

1258
Mongols took Baghdad and overthrew caliphate.

1252 Spain Alfonso X of Castile (1221–1284) succeeded to the throne. He was himself a poet, and the first major vernacular historian, author of *General Estoria* and *Estoria de España*. As a patron, he encouraged translation from Arabic and Latin, and made his court a centre for an important group of Spanish lyric poets.

1255 Germany Ulrich von Lichtenstein (1200–1275) wrote his verse autobiography *Frauendienst*, which revealed the reality behind the courtly love tradition. It was typical of the decline of courtly conventions.

1258 Persia *Gulistan*, a rhymed prose miscellany by Muslih al-Din, Shaikh Sa'di (1194–?1282), poet and writer; he was remarkable for his versatility and his stylistic skill.

ARCHITECTURE

1254–1382 Holland Utrecht Cathedral in a Gothic style which derived from Soisson in France, arrived late in Holland.

1256 England The rebuilding of Old St Paul's, London, choir, which was to have been the largest in Europe, was begun; it was later destroyed.

1258 Persia Ince Minare Madrassa, Konya, was a monumental building of which only the gateway survives; its surface is covered by calligraphic script.

THREE DIMENSIONAL ART

*c.***1250 North America** Indians of the Little Colorado valley used a lead glaze to decorate pottery in black, green, brown or purple; its use spread through the Rio Grande valley.

*c.***1250 China** Traditional incised and carved decoration on pottery became increasingly elaborate and included applied relief. Sometimes a raw clay piece was applied to the glaze and fired again. Large-scale and elaborate Chinese ware was nearly always intended for foreign markets because it was not to Chinese taste.

*c.***1250 England** Establishment of the school of embroidery called *Opus Anglicanum*: the work was ecclesiastical, with pictures of saints and biblical events in medallion frames.

*c.***1250 Germany** First of the sculptures in the west choir of Naumburg Cathedral, considered the finest pieces of Gothic sculpture in Germany. The work continued until *c.*1570, and included 12 statues of benefactors, a crucifixion group and reliefs of the Passion. The style is dignified yet dramatic.

*c.***1250 Syria** Probable origin of Lakabi pottery, in which the colour was prevented from running by an incised outline, although the technique may also have been developed in Persia or Egypt.

1252–1517 Egypt The Mamluk period: in ceramics advances were made in *sgraffito* design and a type of storage jar called an *albarello* was developed.

1252 Turkey The Karatay Medresse building in Konya was decorated with blue and black tiles: this was an early example of Anatolian tile-work by Persian craftsmen. More colours (white, buff, green and yellow) were included later.

*c.***1258 France** The sculpted figure *La Vierge Dorée*, at Amiens, typified a new taste for grace and elegance.

VISUAL ARTS

*c.***1250 England** St Albans monastery included professional trained artists in its community; which was unusual.

1252–1282 Spain Reign of Alfonso X of Castile, who established a school of manuscript illumination. Its most famous books were the codices of the *Cantigas*, poems in honour of the Virgin, which showed the prevailing French Gothic influence.

1259 Bulgaria Second set of murals in Boyana church, Sofia: painted in the Tărnovo style, showing naturalistic detail with antique influence on forms.

INVENTIONS & DISCOVERIES

*1252
Gold florin first
coined at
Florence.*

HISTORICAL EVENTS	LITERATURE	DANCE & DRAMA	MUSIC
1259 *Treaty of Paris defined extent of English possessions in France for which Henry III did homage to Louis IX.*	**1260–1270 Italy** Brunetto Latini (1220/30–1294) fl., an encyclopedist and teacher. **1260 Italy** *Canzone* on the battle of Montaperti by the poet Guittone d'Arrezzo (d. 1294), the chief representative of northern Provençal/Italian poetry, which was influenced by the Sicilian school.	*c.*1260 Germany *Antichristus*, a German Advent play: it was written in a fairly sophisticated and polished style.	**1260 France** *Ars antiqua* (polyphony) at its zenith, especially in Paris.
1260 *Kublai Khan, founder of Mongol Yuan dynasty, became Mongol leader in China.*			
1262 *Iceland came under Norwegian rule.*	**1261 Germany** Death of Albert von Stade (b. 1200), chronicler and poet, author of *Annales* and the epic poem *Troilus*.	*c.*1262 France *Le Jeu de la Feuillée* by Adam de la Halle (1230–1288) is the first purely secular drama in France: it is a satire on the citizens of Arras. Adam's *Le Jeu de Robin et de Marion* is the first French pastoral and, since it contains music, may be said to be the first light opera.	**1262 France** First compositions by Adam de la Hallé (*c.*1240–*c.*1286), *trouvère*, performed.
1264 *Battle of Lewes; Henry III of England defeated by barons under Simon de Montfort.*	*c.*1264 Italy Four poems on the Eucharist by St Thomas Aquinas (1224–1274), the brilliant theologian. A fine Latin stylist in prose and verse, he was author of *Summa Theologica* and *Summa contra Gentiles.*	**1263 Spain** An edict of Alphonso X of Castile forbade clergy to take part in burlesques; they could, however, take part in decent and reverent religious plays.	
1265 *English Parliament, representing shires, cities and boroughs, summoned by Simon de Montfort.*	**1265 Netherlands** Death of the mystic Beatrijs van Nazareth (b. 1206), author of an autobiography and several religious tracts. *c.*1265 Netherlands Hadewijch fl., a mystic and poet who had great influence on the next generation of Western European religious poets; she was author of 45 spiritual love songs as well as prose letters and visions.		
1271 *Marco Polo of Venice began journey through Asia to China where he worked for Kublai Khan.*			
1274 *Coronation of Edward I of England.*			
1275 *Statute of Westminister 1 granted duty on wool to the king.*	**1274 Italy** Death of the Franciscan theologian St Bonaventura (b. 1221), author of *Life of St Francis*, written in Latin prose. *c.*1275–1276 France Philippe de Remy (1248–1296) wrote *La Manekine*, a romance in realistic setting.		

ARCHITECTURE

c.1260–1286 England Little Wenham Hall is a brick manor house on an L-shaped plan with the hall and chapel on the first floor.

c.1260 England In York Cathedral north transept the 'five sisters window' contains the largest of lancet windows, *leit motif* of the early English style.

c.1260–1292 France The Jacobins, Toulouse, is an aisleless hall, typical of friary architecture, but on a grand scale.

1262 France Strasbourg threw off episcopal rule and the growing independence and prosperity of European cities was a stimulus to secular architecture, both public and private.

1262–c.1277 France Only the east end of the church of St Urbain, Troyes, was completed in the Middle Ages but it marks the climax of the late Gothic style in France; it has large traceried windows, glazed triforium, open-work tracery and panels of blind tracery. For the first time, too, the agee arch is used.

1270–1280 Indonesia Chandi Djago, Malong, Java, unique because of the placing of a cell-like shrine at the edge of a pair of superimposed, richly sculpted plinths, presents an also unique approach to a monumental temple, the layout of which consists of a series of courts and buildings culminating in the sacred shrine.

c.1270 Sweden Uppsala Cathedral, built in the French manner by a Frenchman and the first example of the influence on Swedish medieval architecture of foreign styles – especially French, German and English – was begun.

THREE DIMENSIONAL ART

1260–1368 China Yüan period of Mongol occupation: the collapse of the Sung dynasty by 1271 freed potters from court conventions; pottery was now made for merchants, industrial systems were introduced, and a more robust taste developed.

c.1260 Italy The pulpit in Pisa baptistry is the earliest authenticated piece by Niccola Pisano (c.1225–1278) sculptor. He adapted classical conventions to Christian themes.

1261–1263 Persia The tiling, now dispersed, of the Imamzada Yahyā tomb chamber in Veramin: the first major work in lustre pottery after the Mongol invasion. Production of lustre pottery was now mainly in the form of tiles; Kashan lustre tiles in rectangular, star and cross shapes were produced until c.1340.

c.1263 France A series of life-size figures in bronze was cast for Louis IX (St Louis) and placed in St Denis abbey church.

1266 Italy On the death of Manfred (King of Sicily 1258–1266) the Byzantine-inspired Sicilian silk industry moved to Lucca, which became the leading centre of silk weaving in Italy. Lucca workshops specialized in gold-embroidered satin and in silk velvets.

c.1270 Syria Potters at Damascus, possibly refugees from the Mongol invasion of Raqqa, began to make *albarello* drug jars with many decorative features reminiscent of Raqqa ware. *Albarello* jars became famous in Europe throughout the fourteenth century.

c.1275–1300 Persia Pottery after the Mongol invasion continued to be made in Rayy 'monumental' style, with large figures reversed out of coloured glaze. Vessels were made in a wide variety of forms.

VISUAL ARTS

1259 England Death of Matthew Paris (b. c.1200), manuscript painter: his surviving historical manuscripts are *Chronica Majora* and *Liber Additsmentorum*, both illustrated with many marginal scenes and designs by his own hand.

1260 Italy The *Crucifixion* by Cimabue, in Assissi, shows Christ tortured and degraded. The agony and humiliation of the crucifixion were emphasized progressively in Western art from then on.

1261 Italy The painter Coppo di Marcovaldo (b. c.1225) settled in Siena. His religious paintings humanized the Byzantine icon, giving a natural modelling to flesh and to the volumes of the draped body. His figures of the Virgin are still superhuman in scale and splendour, but begin to show human affection towards the Child.

1262 Italy Margarito of Arezzo flourished as a painter of vivid pictures outside the Byzantine convention.

1271 Italy Date attributed, controversially, to the *Madonna and Child* painted in Siena town hall by Guido da Siena. It has the earliest indications of 'modern' naturalism in Sienese painting, while remaining within the Byzantine convention.

1273–1308 Italy Pietro Cavallini flourished, a painter and mosaicist of large-scale work. He introduced a freer and more fluid treatment of Byzantine themes, and a sense of space which foreshadowed Giotto.

1274–1319 Italy Duccio di Buoninsegna flourished in Siena as the major painter of his time. In his panel paintings he used the background, the composition of the group, the juxtaposition of colours and facial expressions to create a unified emotional effect.

INVENTIONS & DISCOVERIES

*1260
Roger Bacon first outlined laws of reflection and refraction of light.*

*1266
Bacon described prototype magnifying glass.*

*1271
Marco Polo left Venice for China.*

1275 France *Girart de Roussillon*, a vivid tale of adventure, is the only Provençal *chanson de geste* now surviving: these French epic poems, chanted to music, were inspired by the heroic age of Charlemagne.

1278 Special liberties granted to Cinque ports.

1279 Kublai Khan became Emperor of China on fall of Sung dynasty.

1280 Germany Death of the German scholar Albertus Magnus (b. 1206), known as 'the father of scholasticism'; his works, *Summa Theologiae* and *Summa de Creaturis*, blend traditional theology and Aristotelianism.

*c.***1280–1285 France** Further important additions to *Roman de la Rose* were written by Jean Chopinel de Meung.

1282 Wales Death of the king Llewellyn the Great inspired Gruffudd ab yr Ynad Coch to write a lament which is his only definitely attributable poem. Its strong emotional force is sustained through more than 70 lines on one rhyme.

*c.***1282 France** Adenet, known as '*le Roi des Ménestrels*', fl. as a court poet and author; he wrote the romance *Cleomadés*.

1285 France Death of Rutebeuf (b. 1250), a satirical poet writing on religious and political themes.

1289 Sweden Death of Petrus de Dacia (b. 1235), a Dominican writer known for his vivid personal letters and biographical accounts.

1280 China Beginning of the Yuan Dynasty, established by the conquering Mongols; it was an exceptionally flourishing period for Chinese dramatists. Yuan dramatists used Sung plots but replaced narrative by dialogue and action. The greatest was Kuan Han-Ching, who wrote *The Sufferings of Tou-E*.

*c.***1280 England** Walter de Odington flourished. He wrote the treatise *De Speculatione Musices* which is particularly important for the study of rhythm in the thirteenth century.

1283 Italy A musical gathering for the Feast of St John in Florence, indicating that the Florentine school of music had early origins.

1282 Defeat and death of Llwellyn of Wales.

1286 Margaret, 'Maid of Norway', became Queen of Scots.

1288 Foundation of Ottoman empire by Osman I.

ARCHITECTURE

1275–c.1370 England Exeter Cathedral was rebuilt in the English decorated style, in which the sculpture tracery and tierceron vaults add up to the total decorative effect.

1277–1282 Wales Rhuddlan Castle, the first of Edward I's great concentrically planned castles by James of St Georges, was built during his conquest of north Wales; others were Conway, Caernarvon, Harlech and Beaumaris.

1278–1350 Italy St Maria Novella, Florence, was built for the Dominicans, the detail and colours suggesting some classical compromises in an otherwise Gothic church; the marble façade was designed by Alberti in 1456–1470.

1280 Italy St Maria Sopra Minerva, Rome, a Dominican church, was the only Gothic church in the city, albeit with classical proportions and a marble veneer.

c.1280 Austria Heiligenkreuz Abbey was a Cistercian church in the Gothic style with a hall chancel.

1282–1390 France Albi Cathedral, built of brick, like several other churches in the Languedoc, is a Gothic cathedral of fortress-like appearance; it has no aisles but internal buttresses forming chapels between each pair and supporting the broadest of medieval French vaults.

1285 England The chapter house at Wells Cathedral, Somerset, is an example of fan-vaulting combining structural need with abstract design.

1289–1377 Italy Siena Cathedral was begun as a Romanesque church but completed in the Gothic style; the façade, designed by Giovanni Pisano (1249–1320), shows greater French influence than other Italian churches of that date.

THREE DIMENSIONAL ART

c.1275–1325 England Second period of the school of embroidery called *Opus Anglicanum*; the work is characterized by the 'Syon cope', which has embroidery in coloured, gold and silver threads on linen, depicting scenes from the life of Christ.

1277 Italy Portrait statue of Charles of Anjou by the sculptor Arnolfo di Cambio (c.1245–1301) who continued the natural realism of Niccola Pisano (1225–1278) for whom he had worked. It is one of the earliest post-classical portrait statues.

c.1277 England Earliest surviving monumental brass, of Sir John Daubernon at Stoke D'Abernon, Surrey. The production of engraved brass on a large scale only began in England in the sixteenth century; before that, brass or latten (an alloy of copper, zinc, lead and tin) was imported from the Continent and engraved.

1278 Italy 'Fontana Maggiore', the Fountain at Perugia, carved by Niccola Pisano with many reliefs in a vigorous and natural style.

1282 Italy The tomb of Cardinal de Brave in Orvieto, by Arnolfo di Cambio, set a style in wall-tombs that was copied for a century.

VISUAL ARTS

England: brass of Sir John Daubernon, Stoke D'Aubernon, Surrey

INVENTIONS & DISCOVERIES

1275
Earliest extant maritime compass.

1280
Glass mirror invented.

1284
Sequins first coined at Venice.

1291
Mamluks
conquered Acre;
end of Christian
rule in Near
East.

1292–1294 Italy Dante Alighieri (1265–1321) wrote *Vita Nuova*, a series of love poems in troubadour style addressed to 'Beatrice'.

1293
First Christian
missionaries
arrived in China.

Italy: one of the cycle of paintings of the life of Saint Francesco of Assisi, Umbria. Attributed to Giotto and his school

1294 Arabia Death of 'Abd al-mu'min ibn Yúsuf ibn Fákhir al Urmawi Safi Al-Din, (b. *c.* 1230), one of greatest Arabian theorists of music.

1295
Matteo Visconti
became tyrant of
Milan.

1297 Netherlands Death of Willem van Afflighem (b. 1210), author of *Sinte Lutgart*, a moving example of early Dutch narrative poetry.

1298
Edward I
defeated William
Wallace and the
Scots.

late 1200–1300 Poland *Bogurodzica*, the oldest known Polish religious song: it is sufficiently accomplished to suggest that the form was not new.

1290–1341 England York Cathedral nave was rebuilt, making this the most spacious of all English churches but size meant that the lierne vault had to be constructed of wood; the tracery of the west windows is a beautiful example of the curvilinear style.

1290–1600 Italy Orvieto Cathedral has an immensely colourful and decorative façade which hides a simple and spacious interior.

1291 England The goldsmith William Torel made life-size gilt-bronze effigies of Henry III and Queen Eleanor, for Edward I. The first large-scale figures cast in England, they were probably imitations of those in St Denis, France, but were still highly original.

1292 Venice Glass factories making soda-glass were established on Murano island.

1292 England St Stephen's Chapel, Westminster, London, of which only the restored undercroft remains, is probably the earliest building designed in the perpendicular style.

1294–1442 Italy St Croce, Florence, by Arnolfo di Cambio is a Franciscan church and one of the largest of the spacious friars' churches.

1294–1421 Italy Work began on Arnolfo di Cambio's Florence Cathedral but stopped at his death in 1301: plans were enlarged on resumption of work in *c*.1350. The design is an Italian classical compromise of the Gothic style.

1297–1305 Italy Cycle of paintings in the Upper Church of San Francisco in Assissi, depicting the life of St Francis, by the Master of the St Francis Legend; the last three scenes are different in style and presumed to be by a different artist.

1298–*c*.1330 England Bristol Cathedral is a unique English hall church with very unusual and varied vaulting, demonstrating the inventiveness of English masons at this time.

1298–1450 Spain Barcelona Cathedral is almost a hall-church; the vault, as often in Spain, is exposed on the exterior.

1299–1344 Italy Palazzo Vecchio, Florence, is the best known of the great municipal palaces of Italy; it was restored in the sixteenth century.

late 1200–1300 Italy Probable origin of *basse-taille* enamelling, using translucent colours on silver or gold: designs were sculpted on the metal base so that colours appeared lighter on the shallowest parts and darker on the deepest. The earliest work was done in Siena; the most important pieces are the silver altars in Pistoia and Florence.

late 1200–1300 Persia Ceramic vessels began to be painted with geometric designs in blue and black underglaze colours. The fashion spread to Egypt and Syria.

14th Century

LITERATURE

1300–1325 Wales The *White Book of Rhydderch*, a manuscript containing some of the stories of the *Mabinogion*, a collection of old Welsh tales considered a masterpiece of medieval poetry. Some of the tales are Arthurian, others are older legends about Celtic gods. The title *Mabinogion* was given to the collection by Lady Charlotte Guest, who translated the stories into English, 1838–1849.

Persia: example of the blue and black ware

DANCE & DRAMA

*c.*1300–1400 **England** First performances of the Chester Cycle of mystery plays: this was the earliest of the great English Cycles. The York Cycle probably dates from 1340–1350, while Wakefield (Towneley) and Coventry are somewhat later. The plays were organized, financed and performed by the craftsmen's guilds.

MUSIC

1300–1400 Germany *Geisslerlieder* were songs sung in procession by flagellants and were the equivalent of the Italian *laudi spirituali.*

1300–1400 Italy Madrigals were first performed.

1300 France Birth of Guillaume de Machaut (d. 1377), a poet and one of the foremost composers of his time, noted for his polyphonic ballads, *ballades notées.*

ARCHITECTURE

1300 Persia The mosque of Ali Shah, Tabriz, is the only building surviving from the former capital; Sultaniya took over this status in 1305.

1300–1400 Finland Perna Church is a three-aisled, barn-like church, in which much of the painting common in Scandinavia survives.

1300–1400 France Vincennes Castle consisted of a perimeter wall with 9 towers and a vast 6-storeyed keep; it has been re-built.

1300–1400 Italy The Doge's Palace, Venice, was begun and later rebuilt with the two lower storeys consisting of open Gothic arcades; the sixteenth-century upper storey was faced in pink and white marble. It had great influence on later Venetian palace architecture.

1300–1400 Mali The mosque of Jenne was built in the native tradition of mud building, shapes being moulded like sculpture.

1300–1400 Mexico Tenochtitlan, Mexico City, was built in the middle of a lake as the Aztec capital; at its centre was a huge pyramid with streets radiating outward. Cortez considered the city unrivalled in Spain but it is now destroyed.

1300–1400 Sweden St Mary's Church, Sigtuna, is a typical Scandinavian brick church, in which German influence is apparent – especially in its hall-church elevation.

THREE DIMENSIONAL ART

early 1300–1400 Byzantium The last great cycle of mosaics, in the church of the Chora in Constantinople. The Byzantine art was seen as liturgical and not aesthetic; the subjects and their attitudes and expressions were determined by church teaching, and innovation brought the charge of heresy or sacrilege.

early 1300–1400 Spain The first identifiable Spain lustre-ware pottery was made, much of it at Malaga.

1300–1400 China Carved lacquer became established and popular, and three master craftsmen are mentioned by name: Chang Ch'èng, Yang Mao and Master Hu.

1300–1400 Italy Tin-glazed pottery, originating in Orvieto, was made throughout Italy.

1300–1400 Japan The introduction of the aristocratic *Nō* theatre stimulated a native Japanese school of decorative textiles. *Nō* costumes had bold patterns and were independent of the Chinese tradition which had previously dominated Japanese textile design.

*c.*1300–1330 **China** *Ch'ing-pai* white porcelain was made, with a transparent glaze which thickened and developed a blue tint. This was the precursor of blue-and-white ware, which appeared towards the end of this period and was first made (until *c.*1350) with imported cobalt for foreign buyers, especially in Moslem countries.

*c.*1300–1350 **Persia** Two wares made by Sultanabad potters: vessels with grey slip painted in black and raised white slip under a transparent glaze; and vessels decorated in underglaze black, blue and turquoise. Some of these had motifs imported from China, such as the lotus flower. The blue and black ware was imitated throughout the Middle East.

*c.*1300 **England and France** The 'blacksmith' style of elaborate, decorative wrought-iron work went out of fashion. It was replaced by a geometric style, in which iron was no longer modelled at welding heat, but worked with carpentry techniques. This change owed much to Islamic influence.

VISUAL ARTS

1300–1400 Bulgaria Zemen monastery: the wall paintings typify Christian art of the Second, Bulgarian, Empire. The art continued after the Turkish conquest of 1396; fifteenth-century frescoes survive at Dragalevtsi, Kremikovtsi and Poganovo monasteries.

1300–1400 England The most typically English manuscripts are a group of East-Anglian *Psalters*: they have highly decorated pages with borders of grotesques.

1300–1400 Japan Introduction by Buddhist priests of the art of *suiboko*, or ink-painting. The medium was black ink on white silk or paper.

1300 Flanders Manuscript illuminators established a connection with England.

INVENTIONS & DISCOVERIES

1300 Earliest known European reference to manufacture of gunpowder.

1301
Death of Andrew III of Hungary, last of the Arpads.

1302
Malik Kafur, general of Alauddin Khiliji, conquered southern India.

1303
Edward I of England granted privileges to foreign merchants.

1304–1312 Spain Possible date of *Amadis de Gaula*, an anonymous novel; its theme is chivalry, and much of the material is Arthurian.

1306 Italy Death of the religious poet Jacopone da Todi (b. 1230/40), possibly the author of the *Stabat Mater*. Most of his powerful poetry is in the vernacular.

*c.***1306 Bohemia** Translation into Czech of *Alexandreis*, an epic by Walter of Châtillon (1135–after 1184), French scholar and poet; it is the story of Alexander the Great. The composition about this time of a group of verse legends marks the effective beginning of Czech literature.

1307–1321 Italy The *Commedia* by Dante Alighieri (1265–1321), who had been exiled in 1302 for his political affiliations: called *The Divine Comedy* by its admirers, this long poem described a journey through hell, purgatory and heaven, and its theme was divine justice. Dante invented the *terza rima* for its composition, and intended its style and vocabulary to be plain and simple. With the *Commedia* Italian literature came to the forefront in Europe. Enormously influential both for its content and its expression, the poem is considered a world masterpiece.

Italy: painting of Dante Alighieri by Andrea del Castagno

1314
Robert Bruce defeated Edward II at the Battle of Bannockburn.

1316
Accession of Grand Duke Gedimin, founder of Lithuanian empire.
Indian kingdom of the Deccan fell to Moslems.

1317
Salic Law, excluding women from succession to throne, adopted in France.

1311 Europe Establishment of the festival of Corpus Christi: this became the traditional day for the performance of mystery plays.

1313 Spain The Jewish dancing master, Rabbi Hacén ben Salomo, taught the Christians of St Bartholomew's, Tauste, a choral dance for performance at the altar.

1311 Germany Heinrich Frauenlob (*c.*1260–1318) founded a literary and musical guild at Mainz and so established the Mastersingers. The movement flourished in German cities in the fifteenth and sixteenth centuries.

1318 Italy Marchettus de Padua, musical theorist, published two treatises on notation *Lucidarium in Arte Musicae Planae* and *Pomerium in Arte Musicae Mensuratae*.

ARCHITECTURE

1304–1518 Austria St Stephen's Cathedral, Vienna, is a hall church design without clerestory or triforium and has a single great roof span; the south tower is a Gothic masterpiece.

1304 Belgium Ypres Cloth Hall is the most impressive of the great Flemish halls with a typically long façade, high-pitched roof and central tower; it has been destroyed and rebuilt.

THREE DIMENSIONAL ART

1300 Persia Abu al-Qasim wrote a textbook on pottery in which he described *Lajvardina* ware; it was decorated with red and white enamel and leaf-gilding on a deep blue or turquoise glaze, in geometric patterns. *Lajvardina* wares were made until *c.*1380.

*c.***1300 Germany** The abbey church of Altenberg, near Cologne, was given *grisaille* windows instead of the customary bright colours. This style was in keeping with Cistercian teaching on austerity and economy; Altenberg is the best surviving example.

1301 Italy Giovanni Pisano (*c.*1250–1330) completed his stone relief panels on the pulpit in S Andrea, Pistoia, depicting the 'Massacre of the Innocents': he was considered a master of tragic expression and drama in sculpture.

VISUAL ARTS

1305–1308 Italy Giotto di Bondone (*c.*1267–1337) painted, in Padua, his scenes of the lives of the Virgin and Christ: the figures are framed in shallow boxes; their squared, massive shapes are reduced to essentials for full emotional and narrative force. Giotto painted directly from his own observation and broke with the copying of medieval formulae. He worked also in Florence, Naples and Milan.

1311 Bulgaria The icon of the Virgin of Bachkovo, presented to Bachkovo monastery by a family from Georgia; mural painting at Bachkovo also shows the monastery's connection with Georgia and dates from the eleventh century.

1315 Italy Simone Martini (*c.*1285–1344) painted *The Virgin in Majesty* in Siena Town Hall. He combined the gorgeous quality and formality of Byzantine style with the graceful decoration of new Gothic fashion.

1317 Italy Simone Martini painted an altarpiece for Robert of Anjou: its composition is an early example of the assured use of perspective.

INVENTIONS & DISCOVERIES

1302
Mariner's compass invented at Naples.

1303
First medical reference to spectacles.

Spain: the Alhambra, Granada

1319
*Magnus VII
united Norway
and Sweden.*

*c.*1320 **Bohemia** *Dalimil*, a verse chronicle: highly patriotic in spirit, it recounted Czech history from legendary times to the time of writing.

1320 **France** Publication of *Ars Nova*, a treatise ascribed to Philippe de Vitry (1291–1361), composer, poet and theorist. His system of notation allowed for a greater variety of rhythmic patterns.

ARCHITECTURE

1306 Italy Palazzo della Ragione, Padua, is an Italian town hall of unparalleled size.

1306–1312 Persia Tomb of Oljeitu, Sultaniya, was a large structure, covered by a dome based on an arcaded octagonal body; the remains of the ribs indicate that the dome must have been of impressive size and rather pointed. The tomb, which was covered in blue tiles, was later destroyed.

1309–1354 Spain The Alhambra, Granada, was a pleasure palace of the West Caliphate, consisting of two oblong courts at right angles to each other of which the 'Court of Lions' is the more elaborate: the whole complex displays elaborate Mozarabic decoration seen especially in arabesques covering most of the surfaces.

1312–1315 Greece Church of the Holy Apostles, Salonika, is a good example of late Byzantine architecture, built in brick on a traditional plan of a Greek cross with barrel-vaulted arms and five domes, of which the central one is carried on pendentives supported by columns. Fragments of mosaic decoration are the last examples of this particular form practised in Byzantine art.

1319 China Kuan-Shêng-Ssui, Chao-Ch'Êng-Hsien, Shansi, was a group of buildings remarkable because they employed a new and unique exploitation of the lever-arm form of construction.

c.***1320 England** Salisbury Cathedral spire is the highest surviving in England, measuring 123·2 m.

c.***1320 Germany** Schwäbisch-Gmund Church is by Heinrich Parler (1350–80), one of the famous family of masons; a classic high Gothic hall church, its plan is simplicity itself, with only minimal transepts and no crossing tower. Tall piers support a net vault, but those in the nave were added in 1491.

THREE DIMENSIONAL ART

1305 Spain Date inscribed on a lamp dedicated to a Nasrid ruler, Muhammad III; the lamp was of bronze with the pierced inscription forming part of the pattern.

1310 Persia A frieze of tiles painted in blue and green and carrying an inscription included one signed by Yūsuf ibn 'Ali ibn Muhammed ibn Abī Ṭāhir. He was the last and most important of a family of lustre potters and is known to have worked with a craftsman of another important family, 'Alī ibn Aḥmad.

1313 Flanders First mention of tapestries made at Arras; the name became a generic term for tapestry hangings. The industry ended with an attack by Louis XI of France in 1477.

VISUAL ARTS

1319–1348 Italy The painter Ambrogio Lorenzetti flourished: his painting *The Allegory of Good and Bad Government*, in Siena town hall, is considered the earliest great landscape by an Italian artist. He painted landscape and human crowds from observation and not to a formula; the single figures indicate a knowledge of classical sculpture.

1320 Italy First dated painting by Pietro Lorenzetti (fl. 1320–1348), brother of Ambrogio: the altarpiece at Arezzo. His figure-groupings show a mature sense of perspective; the forms are statuesque.

| HISTORICAL EVENTS | LITERATURE | DANCE & DRAMA | MUSIC |

Persia: the mosque at Masjid-I-Jami, Varamin

1323
Thomas Aquinas canonized.

1324 France *Ars Nova* attacked by Pope John XXII as unsuitable for sacred music.

1325 Italy Birth of Francesco Landini (d. 1397), Italian poet and composer. Though blind from childhood, he became a virtuoso organist, lutanist and flautist and was the most brilliant of all the 14th century Italian composers.

1327
Edward II of England deposed by Parliament.

1327 Germany Death of Meister Eckhart (b. 1260), the theologian; a mystic, he wrote at a time when German mysticism was at its height.

1326 England *Regulae cum Maximis Magistri Franconis, cum Additionibus Aliorum Musicorum,* an elementary treatise dealing with notation, time-values and modes of rhythm, by Robert de Handlo.

1328
Fall of Capetian dynasty in France.
Robert Bruce recognized as king of Scotland.

1329 Italy Giovanni da Cascia, composer, at court in Verona. He is regarded as the originator of the stylistic reform which spread from Florence soon after 1300.

*c.***1330 Japan** A collection of essays and reflections by Yoshida Kaneyoshi, called Yoshida Kenko (1283–1350), poet and prose writer. Works of high quality were rare in Japan at this period, as the country had been for a long time in a state of unrest, which was not conducive to literary composition.

1332
Division of English Parliament into two Houses first recorded.

1321 Yugoslavia Gračanica Church is a good example of Serbian Byzantine architecture and its layout the ultimate evolution of the cross-in-square type with a central dome and additional domes over the corner chapels, rather than over the arms of the cross; it is a structure of great height, a form much liked by the Slavs.

1322 England Ely Cathedral octagon was a unique timber structure that replaced the collapsed crossing tower.

*c.*1322 **Persia** Masjid-I-Jami, Varamin, has a typical Persian ground plan with four iwans (open vaulted porches) opening into a rectangular court, though only the iwan of a prayer hall with a domed chamber behind it now remains; it has impressive stalactite arches.

1324–1327 Italy The Sienese sculptor Tino di Camaino (*c.*1285–1337) worked for the Angevin court at Naples. His stern and rather massive style introduced northern fashions to southern Italy, where he himself was influenced by the more decorative Gothic style.

*c.*1325–1400 **England** The third period of embroidery called *Opus Anglicanum*. Gothic motifs framed realistic animals and birds, flowers and angels. Colours were subordinated to the design rather than naturalistic.

*c.*1327–1328 **Egypt** Muhammad ibn Sunqur al-Baghdadi made a Koran box of wood; the outside was covered with bronze inlaid with gold and silver, the inlay being done by Haji Yusuf al-Ghawabi. The Mamluk rulers of Egypt were generous patrons of religious art, and their extravagant taste was reflected in ornate mosque furnishings.

1329–1336 Italy The sculptor Andrea Pisano (*c.*1270–1348) worked on one of the bronze doors of the baptistry at Florence. They have 28 relief panels depicting 8 virtues and scenes from the life of St John. Pisano used fewer figures than was fashionable and emphasized the texture of the ground metal.

*c.*1330 **Germany** Freiburg-im-Breigau Minster is renowned for its single openwork spire over the west end: such spires were popular in Germany but this is the only complete fourteenth-century example.

*c.*1330 **Germany** Wiesenkirche, Soest, combines the hall-church idea with high Gothic detail and tracery patterns. Like many contemporary German churches, the vault ribs die into the piers without capitals.

*c.*1330 **Sweden** The tower of Larbro Church, Gotland, retains the only surviving example of medieval timber centering supporting the vault cell.

*c.*1330 **England** Alabaster, quarried in the Midlands, began to take the place of harder stone for funerary sculpture. The earliest surviving example is at Hanbury, Staffordshire; the best is the tomb of Edward II in Gloucester Cathedral, *c.*1331.

*c.*1330 **Italy** Reliquary of the Bolsena *corporale* in Orvieto Cathedral was made in the workshop of the silversmith Ugolino da Vieri of Siena; architectural in form, framing enamel plaques, it was considered the finest work of its type.

HISTORICAL EVENTS

*1333
Zenith of
Moorish
(Arabic)
civilization in
Granada under
Yusuf I and his
son Mohammad
V.
Overthrow of
Hōjō regency in
Japan, start of
Muromachi
period.*

*1336
Edward III of
England
prohibited export
of wool to
Flanders and
moved staple
from Bruges to
Antwerp.*

*1337
Beginning of
Hundred Years'
War.*

*1338
Ottoman Turks
controlled Asia
Minor.*

*1345
Aztecs founded
first major centre
in Mexico.*

*1346
Edward III
defeated French
at Crécy.*

LITERATURE

c.1335 Germany *Kronike von Pruzinlant* by Nikolaus von Jeroschin, who was perhaps the most talented of the knights of the Teutonic order; they wrote chronicles and religious epics.

1340 Spain *Libro de Buen Amor*, poems by Juan Ruiz (d. 1350). The book is a miscellany, in which religious poems and other pious compositions appear side by side with profane material; there are love poems, satires, hymns, fables. This mixture is found in Spanish Arabic literature also. Ruiz is regarded as the greatest Spanish medieval poet.

c.1340–1370 Wales Creative period of the poet Dafydd ap Gwilym, who wrote poems to women and in praise of nature. He used a new metre, the *cywydd*. His work typified the Welsh trait of making unexpected juxtapositions for dramatic effect. There was no important visual art in medieval Wales, but poetry of the time was exceptionally vivid in visual description.

c.1343 Netherlands *Die Chierheit der Gheesteleker Brulocht* by Jan van Ruusbroec (1293–1381), a mystic writing in Middle Dutch prose.

1346 Germany The *Sermons* of the monk Johannes Tauler (c.1300–1371); he used simple language to deal with mystical concepts, thus making them available to ordinary people. The writings of German mystics were widely influential outside Germany.

DANCE & DRAMA

Italy: The Annunciation by Simone Martini

1345 Indonesia Ibn Batuta of Tangier visited Java: there the Arabs probably saw shadow plays, which they adopted themselves. Shadow plays are the only dramatic entertainment of the Sunni Moslems.

ARCHITECTURE

1334 France Avignon Papal Palace was the seat of the popes from 1307 to 1377; it was built in two compaigns to form a large palace centred round two court-yards, with exterior high walls in some cases indented by buttress machicolations and a lavishly decorated interior, which in-cluded the vast Clementine cha-pel.

1334 Italy Florence Cathedral campanile was designed by Giotto and incorporates Rom-anesque, classical and Gothic elements besides Cosmati dec-oration: a proto-Renaissance work.

1337 England Gloucester Cath-edral choir was refashioned to become the first major work in the perpendicular style; the vault has a complex web of lierne (i.e. ribs which do not spring either from one of the main springers or from the centre boss) and the east win-dow is the largest medieval win-dow in Britain.

1339–1426 Holland St Peter's Church, Leyden, is a large lofty brick church, typical of the rather simply designed late medieval Dutch church.

1343 Austria Zwettl Abbey has a classic hall church interior, while a baroque altar and pul-pit, well suited to the simple fourteenth-century work, were later added.

1344 Czechoslovakia Prague Cathedral was begun by Mat-thias of Arras (died 1352), arch-itect of Narbonne Cathedral, France, and continued in 1353 by Peter Parler (1333–1399), who completed the choir and most of the south transept before his death. The vaulting system, including flying ribs, appears to derive from English precedents, and Charles IV em-ployed Italian craftsmen to dec-orate the interior.

THREE DIMENSIONAL ART

1334 Italy Shrine of St Peter the Martyr in S Eustorgio, Milan, by Giovanni da Balduccio of Pisa (active 1315–1349). He was largely responsible for intro-ducing the Pisan Gothic style to Lombard sculptors.

1338–1351 Persia Cast-brass bowls made probably at Fars and inlaid with silver and gold; the form was similar to North Mesopotamian types, which were also copied in Egypt and Syria.

1338–1578 Japan Muromachi (or Ashikaga) period: a con-scious withdrawal from Bud-dhism began among original artists, together with a growing interest in architectural sculp-ture, both in the round and in relief.

1343 England The Schurterre family was established in south-ern England, making window glass.

VISUAL ARTS

1333 Italy The *Annunciation* painted by Simone Martine of Siena (c.1285–1344): it is con-sidered the work most charac-teristic of his graceful Gothic style. He sometimes collabo-rated with his brother-in-law and assistant Lippo Memmi (fl. 1317–1347) who tended to exaggerate Martini's refined qualities in his own work.

c.1337–1377 **Italy** The Floren-tine painter Andrea da Firenze flourished; his frescoes in Santa Maria Novella on the 'Triumph of the Faith' return to the rigid composition of the Byzantine tradition. Severity and meticu-lous detail were in keeping with Dominican teaching.

1340–1341 France Arrival at the Papal court of Avignon of the Italian painter Simone Mar-tini: his work marked a tran-sition between majestic Byzan-tine and graceful Gothic. He was influential on French, Ital-ian and Flemish painters.

1342 Italy *Presentation in the Temple* by Ambrogio Loren-zetti, and *Birth of the Virgin* by his brother Pietro Lorenzetti show a concern with natural description and perspective which anticipated Florentine art of the late fifteenth century.

1343/4–1368 Italy The painter Andrea di Cione, called Or-cagna, flourished as the leading artist of the late fourteenth cen-tury in Florence. He reverted to the Byzantine tradition over-turned by Giotto, and was ver-satile in painting, sculpture and architecture.

1345–1346 Spain Ferrer Bassa (c.1285/90–1348) painted a series of frescoes in the chapel of St Miguel at the convent of Pedralbes, near Barcelona. Ital-ian styles developing in Florence and Siena were reaching Spain through the Papal court at Avig-non; Bassa showed Italian in-fluence in his work, but a native dramatic realism predominated.

*1340
First European paper mill set up at Fabriano, Italy.*

*1346
Gunpowder used at Battle of Crécy.*

HISTORICAL EVENTS	LITERATURE	DANCE & DRAMA	MUSIC

1347
Black Death
devastated
Europe.

1348–1353 Italy The *Decameron* by Giovanni Boccaccio (1313–1375), poet and prose writer: the book is a prose collection of 100 tales, many adapted from traditional stories, and held together by a frame story. Boccaccio may have been influenced in his design by Ovid's *Metamorphoses*; while he in turn had a strong influence on other tale-tellers: Chaucer's *Canterbury Tales*, Marguerite de Navarre's *Heptaméron*. Famous early story cycles include the *Arabian Nights* and the Sanskrit *Hitopadesa*. Boccaccio also wrote love poetry, romances and allegories in Italian, and composed a number of works in Latin including an encyclopedia of mythology. As a forerunner of the Renaissance he was very influential.

1349
Widespread
persecution of
Jews in
Germany.

1349 England Death of Richard Rolle (b. *c.*1300), mystic and hermit, author of a number of devotional books important in early English prose.

c.1350 Iceland *The Lily* a poem by Eysteinn Asgrimsson (?1310–1361), full of religious symbolism, and written in a free, simple style, it is a lay in praise of the Virgin Mary. It is in marked contrast to earlier, 'scaldic' poetry (*scald* = Scandinavian bard), in which material was usually conventional and all the emphasis was placed on technical virtuosity.

1351
Statute of
Labourers
checked English
labour problems
by regulating
wages.

1352 England *Polychronicon* by Ranulf Higden (d. 1363/4), monk and writer: the book, which was very popular, is a universal history. Translated into English, it was later printed by Caxton.

1352 Italy *Le Rime* the collected Italian poems of Francesco Petrarca, called Petrarch (1304–1374), humanist and poet. He collected manuscripts, and wrote important historical and philosophical treatises in Latin. Widely travelled, he met and corresponded with many of the leading literary figures in Europe. He also perfected the sonnet form. He is best known to modern readers for his love poems, written to Laura, which became the model for Italian poetry for over 300 years; they are dignified, delicate, and transparently sincere.

1350 Siam Ayutaya became capital of the kingdom: its society developed a 'fast and slow' dance which is one of the roots of Lakon pure dance. The other main root was the Alphabet Dance, which was originally descriptive and is now almost completely abstract.

c.1350 Europe Death of Johannes de Muris, French, English or (?) Swiss philosopher, astronomer, mathematician and musical theorist; his most important musical work was *Speculum Musices*.

1350 England A small guild of minstrels formed in the City of London, the earliest known professional association for musicians.

ARCHITECTURE

1348 Czechoslovakia Karlstein Castle, a vast structure without flanking towers in the curtain walls—suggesting German influence—was built for Emperor Charles IV. Many wall paintings are preserved, some probably by Italians and the chapel is remarkable for the 3000 semi-precious stones embedded in its lower walls.

England: example of the perpendicular building style showing fan vaulting, Winchester Cathedral

1351 England The cloister of Gloucester Cathedral was built with the earliest known fan vaults.

1352–1411 Belgium Antwerp Cathedral was the largest of Belgian churches, with a nave and triple aisles each side. The 131·1 metres north-west tower was added in the late fifteenth century.

THREE DIMENSIONAL ART

1348 Bohemia Charles, son of King John of Bohemia (*d.*1346) crowned Emperor Charles IV; he established an important and influential centre for the arts in Prague.

1348–1364 Italy Giovanni de Dondi (1318–1389) designed and constructed the Astrarium, a planetary clock with 7 dials and mechanical clockwork, supported on 7 bronze columns. It showed the movement of the 7 known planets, times of sunrise and sunset and an annual calendar.

1350–1500 Turkey *Miletus* ware probably made at Iznik (Nicasa); it was made of clay with white slip painted in geometric patterns of blue, black and green.

1350 England John le Alemayne (a Rhinelander) was working as a glass-maker at Chiddingfold: window-glass was the main art-form in glasswork in northern Europe, and England had several immigrant craftsmen making it.

*c.***1350 England** Introduction of the Perpendicular building style produced a new style of stained-glass window; the artists now tried to produce architectural realism and perspective in their designs and used a restricted colour scheme of blue, red, white and silvery yellow to give an impression of coolness and serenity.

1351 Germany The choir of Kreuzkirche at Gmünd has some of the earliest work by the Parler family of stonemasons, who were important in southern German Gothic stone-carving. Their influence extended into Bohemia where, from 1353, they worked on Prague Cathedral.

VISUAL ARTS

1347 Italy A list of 'best living painters', compiled to choose an artist for Pistoia cathedral, was headed by Taddeo Gaddi (*c.*1300–1366), godson and pupil of Giotto, who combined his master's tradition in narrative painting with his own talent for picturesque effect, incident and detail.

1348 Bohemia Accession of the emperor Charles IV, who made Prague his capital and a centre for the arts. Architects, painters and manuscript illuminators were brought to Prague where they worked in Flemish, German, Italian and French traditions. Influencing each other, they created a new international style.

*c.***1350 Italy** Paintings in Santa Croce, Florence, on the legend of St Sylvester: they are attributed to Maso di Banco, considered one of the most successful developers of Giotto's perspective and massive forms.

INVENTIONS & DISCOVERIES

1351 Groats first coined.

123

*1353
Turks began to
invade Europe.*

*1354
Turks took
Gallipoli.*

Italy: altarpiece at church of Saint Maria Novella, Florence, decorated by Andrea Orcagna

*1355
Iliyas Shah
established
independent
kingdom of
Bengal.*

*1356
Golden Bull of
Emperor Charles
IV regulated
election of
German kings
and constitution
of Holy Roman
Empire until
1806.*

*1358
Hapsburgs made
peace with Swiss
League.*

*1362
English staple
fixed at Calais.*

1362 Germany The first
German prose autobiography
was written by the mystic Heinrich Seuse (c.1295–1366). In
writing of Christ and the soul he
used the vocabulary and conventions of courtly love.

ARCHITECTURE	THREE DIMENSIONAL ART	VISUAL ARTS	*INVENTIONS & DISCOVERIES*

VISUAL ARTS

1354–1357 Italy Altarpiece of the Redeemer, in the Strozzi chapel, Santa Maria Novella, Florence, painted by Orcagna (Andrea di Cione).

1354 China Death of Wu Chên (b. 1280), a landscape painter also famous for bamboo paintings. He was one of the 'Four Great Landscape Masters', who were inspired by the tenth-century landscape school; the other three were Huang Kung-Wang, Wang Mêng and Ni Tsan.

1354 China Death of Huang Kung-Wang, painter of landscapes from a high and distant viewpoint. Together with Ni Tsan (1301–1374), he introduced a clear, slanting brush-stroke and a drier ink. The new brush-line no longer had a calligraphic character and was devoid of the emotional associations of calligraphy for the Chinese.

1355–1356 Bulgaria Gospel book of Tsar Ivan Alexander: an illustrated manuscript by a monk, Symeon, with 366 miniature paintings of gospel scenes showing strong Byzantine influence.

1355 Germany Aachen Cathedral choir was built to resemble St Chapelle, Paris.

1356 Egypt The mosque of Sultan Hassan, Cairo, differs from other mosques in that it is of a cruciform plan placed off a central court; The south arm contains the *mihrab* and beyond it is placed the founder's tomb, a structure covered by a dome displaying stalactite pendentives.

1355 France Death of Jehane Pucelle (b. *c*.1300), miniature painter, whose workshop dominated Parisian painting. His most famous works were the *Belleville Breviary* and the *Bible Hours of Jeanne d'Evreux*, in both of which he did a large share of the work. He was influenced by the early Renaissance in Italy, but his work included motifs from Flemish art.

1359 Russia The carved wooden cross of Ludogoschchinsky is characteristic of the art of unoccupied Novgorod during the Mongol invasion of the rest of Russia. It has a detailed and curvilinear design, and also shows Nordic influence rare in Russian art of this period.

c.**1360 England** At the chapter house of Wells Cathedral tierceron ribs are multiplied, a motif widely used in late Gothic vaulting.

c.**1360–1400 Russia** In Bokhara and Samarkand under Timur (or Tamburlaine) a style of ceramic tile developed, decorated with carved relief in colours. The most celebrated example is the tiled façade to the mausoleum of Shād-e Mulk Aka in Samarkand (1372).

c.**1360 Italy** Sheet-iron screen with pierced ornament made for Sta Maria Novella in Florence; the culmination of a new style in ironwork derived from Islamic models. Decorative ironwork first appeared in Italy *c*.1300.

1360 Francs first coined in France.

HISTORICAL EVENTS	LITERATURE	DANCE & DRAMA	MUSIC

HISTORICAL EVENTS

1363 Timur (Tamburlaine) began conquest of Asia.

1366 Statutes of Kilkenny forbade Anglo-Irish intermarriage, Irish laws and customs.

1368 Mongol Yuan dynasty in Peking overthrown.

1369 Timur became ruler of Samarkand.

1370 Hanseatic League predominant in Baltic.

1371 Accession of Stewarts to Scottish throne.

1372 Mongols driven out of China, establishment of Ming dynasty.

LITERATURE

?1364 France Probable date of the *Livre du Voir Dit* by Guillaume de Machaut (?1300–1377), poet and musician, whose courtly verse and allegory were written in a more personal and realistic way than hitherto. He had an influence on Chaucer. His pupil Eustache Deschamps (?1346–?1406) developed these innovations further.

*c.*1370 England The first of three versions of the poem *The Vision of Piers Plowman* by William Langland (*c.*1332–*c.*1400). The work is a long alliterative allegory about man's search for perfection and truth, and contains criticism of contemporary society.

1371 France Earliest known manuscript of a book of travels by 'Sir John Mandeville' (probably Jehan de Bourgogne); originally written in French, they were later translated into English and printed by Caxton. Part real, part imaginary, the *Travels* include descriptions of fabulous beasts and monsters drawn from Pliny and the Bestiaries.

France: a selection of fabulous beasts and monsters by contemporaries of 'Sir John Mandeville'

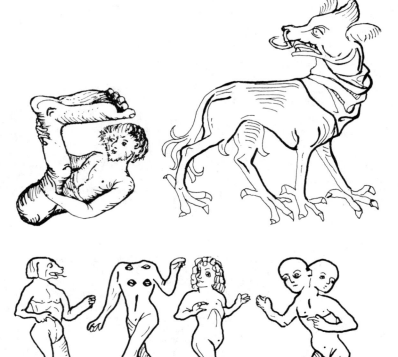

ARCHITECTURE	THREE DIMENSIONAL ART	VISUAL ARTS	INVENTIONS & DISCOVERIES

1364 France Accession of Charles V: he did much to encourage the art of tapestry and commissioned many hangings from Nicholas Bataille (active *c*.1375–1400), who was the most distinguished weaver of his time and was noted for his *Apocalypse* series, designed by Jean de Bondolf.

c.**1367 Italy** Statues of St John and St Paul, in Venice, by Nino Pisano (*c*.1315–1368), one of the earliest sculptors in marble to make life-size free-standing figures.

1368–1644 China Ming dynasty. Porcelain was now the predominant form of ceramic and the best known Ming porcelain is blue-and-white; native cobalt was found and used from *c*.1450. There were four groups of polychrome porcelain: *tou-ts'ai*, *wu-ts'ai*, *san-ts'ai* and *fa-hua*, all made at Ching-tê Chên or nearby. *Wu-ts'ai* was also made in south Fukien and exported from (and named after) the port of Swatow.

1368–1644 China Ming dynasty silks and embroideries included very finely woven *k'o-ssŭ* (silk tapestries) in native Chinese taste, with landscape designs predominating; embroiderers often based their designs on contemporary paintings. Satin-stitch remained the basic technique, with long-and-short-stitch, stem-stitch, and a couched-stitch holding large surface areas of floss silk.

1369 Italy The painter Barna of Siena painted the *Crucifixion* for the Episcopal palace of Arezzo. His figures are noted for dramatic vigour.

1370 Czechoslovakia Karlshof Church, Prague, a rare example of a centrally planned Gothic church, was built for Charles IV by Peter Parler.

c.**1370 Portugal** Tombs of Inez de Castro (d. 1335) and Peter I (d. 1367) are considered the best examples of Portuguese Gothic sculpture.

1370
First use of steel crossbow.

1370–1382 France The Bastille, Paris, is unusual because of the introduction of curtain walls of the same height as the 8 round towers, an innovation copied elsewhere.

1371 Italy Iron screen in Sta Croce, Florence, had two tiers of Gothic tracery, with twisted bars and quatrefoils wrought from bar iron; both motifs appeared in European work throughout the next century. The Italians had an equal flair for sheet-iron ornament in flower and leaf forms.

1373 France Chapelles de la Grange, Amiens Cathedral, introduces the flamboyant style of French architecture, in which the tracery forms long curvelinear shapes.

1373
Dutch developed early form of canal lock.

HISTORICAL EVENTS	LITERATURE	DANCE & DRAMA	MUSIC

LITERATURE

1373 Sweden Death of St Bridget (b. 1302), the visionary: her autobiography, *Revelationes*, was dictated in Swedish and translated into Latin. Vivid and outspoken, it was widely read.

1375 Scotland *Brus* by John Barbour (*c*.1320–1395): a long poem in octosyllabic lines, telling the adventures of Robert the Bruce. It was lively and historically accurate.

1376 Death of Black Prince, heir to English throne.

1377 England Record of a visiting entertainment to Richard II: 130 London citizens, disguised with masks and accompanied by musicians, danced and drank with their hosts. A dance performance in which hosts and visiting troupe joined in ('commoning') was popular in Europe, particularly Italy. It went out of fashion in England during the fifteenth century.

1377 Italy The Papal Chapel musicians returned to Rome from Avignon.

Italy: the Pazzi Chapel by Brunelleschi

1378 Beginning of Great Schism, with two elected popes.

1378 Bohemia *The New Council* by Smil Flaška z Pardubic a Rychmburka (before 1350–1403): a satirical allegorical poem.

1378 Bohemia Death of the Holy Roman Emperor Charles IV, who wrote, in Latin, one of the earliest ever autobiographies. He also encouraged Czech literature, in particular lives of the saints; one of these, *The Legend of St Catherine* is acknowledged as a masterpiece of medieval poetry.

1380 Union of Norway and Denmark.

1380–1400 England *The Canterbury Tales* by the poet Geoffrey Chaucer (1340–1400). He used as his sources Boccaccio, the French *Roman de la Rose*, Ovid and Boethius, though he adapted freely. Ironic, detached, though with great compassion and humour, he is considered a master story-teller. Written in heroic couplets, *The Canterbury Tales*, which is unfinished, was a collection of tales after the manner of the *Decameron*, but it included a prologue and a series of portraits of the tellers, which were unique in medieval literature. Chaucer ranks as one of the outstanding poets of all time.

1374 China Death of Ni Tsan, the most original of the Four Great Masters of Landscape. His style was restrained and calm.

1375 France Cartoons for the great series of tapestry known as the *Angers Apocalypse* made for the Duke of Anjou by Jean de Bondolf (active *c.*1368–1381) painter: he mastered the elegant and mannered sophistication of French court style but brought to it a direct Flemish realism in the depiction of landscape and figures.

*c.***1375 Caucasus** Beginning of pottery making at Kubachi: a soft white ware with a thin glaze which was inclined to crackle.

*c.***1375–1400 France** The Royal Gold Cup, presented to Charles VI, was decorated with scenes from the legend of St Agnes and with symbols of the Evangelists, executed in *basse-taille* enamel. Little survives of medieval French silver or gold, but pieces like this indicate a high standard of work.

1377 Germany Ulm Minster is dominated by its colossal west tower and spire: the highest ever built, it was completed in the nineteenth century and measures 185·1 m.

1377 Italy Filippo Brunelleschi (died 1446), the first and one of the greatest Renaissance architects was born in Florence; his work included the Pazzi Chapel in St Croce, a small domed building, with a porch with Corinthian columns projecting into the cloister, which shows a complete intuitive grasp of the emergent Renaissance spirit.

*c.***1379 England** Canterbury Cathedral nave was rebuilt in perpendicular style by Henry Yevele (died 1400), greatest of English Gothic architects.

*c.***1380 England** Bodiam Castle was one of the last castles built in England for purely military purposes; symmetrically planned, it is also an early example of a castle fitted with gun loops.

1378 Russia Theophanes the Greek (*c.*1307–*c.*1405) painted a serie of frescoes in the Church of the Transfiguration at Novgorod. He was a Byzantine who followed a late Byzantine style, more Hellenistic than oriental, but developed it with his own technique of modelling figures with light and shadow. He was also important as a book illustrator.

1379 Germany The painter Master Bertram of Minden painted the Grabow altar in Hamburg: he was apparently influenced by the Bohemian school.

*1377
First European
use of quarantine
against plague;
beginning of the
theory of
infection.*

HISTORICAL EVENTS

1381
Peasants' Revolt in England.

1385
Portugal became independent of Castile.

1390
Last Byzantine possessions in Asia Minor lost to Turks. Timur defeated Tartars.

1392
Timur sacked Baghdad.

1395
Timur defeated and divided Golden Horde.

1396
Bulgaria under Turkish rule.

1397
Union of Kalmar between Sweden, Denmark and Norway.

1398
Timur established rule at Delhi.

LITERATURE

1380–1446 Russia *Lithuanian Annals* is the earliest extant Byelorussian literature.

1385 England *Troilus and Criseyde* by Geoffrey Chaucer.

1390–1393 England *Confessio Amantis* by the poet John Gower (*c.*1330–1408): this long poem was a collection of stories, in octosyllabic couplets, examining the concept of courtly love from a theological stand point. Gower's sources were both classical and medieval.

1398 Spain *Lo Somni* by Bernat Metge (1350–1413), Catalan writer and translator. He introduced the work of Petrarch to the Iberian Peninsula and with it a strong Italian influence. This book consisted of four dialogues in which medieval allegory was expressed in classical style.

DANCE & DRAMA

1384 England *The Play of the Lord's Prayer* at York portrayed the Seven Deadly Sins: allegorical plays such as this one are now called moralities, but the term was not then in use.

1384 Japan Death of Kwanami Kiyotsugu (b. 1333), the first known writer of Japanese *Nō* drama, the aristocratic drama of Japan. *Nō* drama may have developed from the Kagura-dances performed at Shinto temples. The plays ascribed to Kwanami are a mature art form, which implies the existence of earlier, cruder work. Seami Motokiyu, actor son of Kwanami, further improved and polished the *Nō* form. Comic interludes, *kyogen*, were performed in the same programme.

MUSIC

1397 Italy Death of Francesco Landini.

1387 Italy The design of Milan Cathedral caused dissent between architects summoned from north Europe and their Italian counterparts. The doors and windows of the façade are baroque, while the roof is decorated with hundreds of pinnacles which visually heighten the stepped rectangular body of the church; the tracery is late Gothic curvelinear. Building continued until the nineteenth century.

1387 Portugal Batalha Abbey is a very eclectic building, incorporating Spanish, French, Italian and English Gothic elements while the cloisters are in the richly carved Manoeline style in which even the structural members are lavishly decorated over their entire surface.

*c.***1387 Rumania** Cozia Abbey is in the Byzantine tradition as are most Rumanian medieval churches; it is trefoil-planned with a central dome and west narthex.

1392 Germany St Martin's, Landshut, is a typical German hall church of great elegance: the slender 21 m high piers are only a metre wide and its tower rises to 133 m. It was completed in the sixteenth century.

1395 Turkey Ulu-Cami Mosque, Bursa, is the earliest example of a structure displaying vaulted piers, a design which became very popular in mosque structures in Bursa; the prayer space is covered by 20 equal domes, placed in four ranks of five.

1398 Turkey Beyazid Külliye, Bursa, was the earliest example of a complete *külliye*, a series of buildings for public use: medrese or theological college, hospital, library, lunatic asylum, bath, fountains, and alms kitchens – a self-contained community within the greater city of Bursa.

1399 England Westminster Hall, London, was reconstructed with the finest of all hammerbeam roofs.

1389 Burgundy The sculptor Claus Sluter (d. 1406) became master sculptor at the charterhouse of Champmol, near Dijon, and was responsible for most of the work there. He designed the portal, the Calvary (of which the base, called the Puits de Moïse, survives) and the tomb of Duke Philip the Bold. His work expressed a spiritual intensity and realism far beyond Gothic realism; his use of draped mourning figures to support the Duke's bier was a conventional choice, but the emphasis of the design is on the drapery, its folds expressing the grief of the mourners.

1389 Russia Embroidered hangings commissioned by the Great Princess Marià show the figures of the Virgin and St John on an ivory ground; plain, empty backgrounds were characteristic of Russian embroideries until the sixteenth century.

1390–1403 or 1413 France Andre Beauneven flourished sculptor of the royal monuments at St Denis abbey. He introduced realism into the formal, monumental style; the Guesclin and Sancerre tombs in St Denis were made under his influence.

late 1300–1400 Germany Emergence of Rhineland stone-ware at Siegburg or possibly Dreihausen: it was characterized, especially that made at Cologne, by applied decoration in relief.

1385 China Death of Wang-Mêng, one of the Four Great Masters of Landscape. His style involved covering the whole of the paper with brush-strokes and he was a formative influence on painting in China until the nineteenth century.

1388–1422 Italy Lorenzo Monaco flourished, a monk trained as an illuminator of manuscript in the monastery of Maria degli Angeli. His paintings on a larger scale, murals and altarpieces, retained the techniques of miniature painting. He worked in the graceful, decorative style of Simone Martini.

*c.***1390–1420 Burgundy** The 'school of Burgundy' consisted of Flemish artists employed by Duke Philip the Bold, who had married Margaret of Flanders. They brought a strong Flemish realism into French painting, in addition to the Italian influence already active. They were important in forming a new International Gothic style.

1391 Burgundy Melchior Broederlam (fl. 1381–1409) painted panels for Baerze's retable (altarpiece) at the Chartreuse de Champmol. This is the earliest extant example in panel painting of the Franco-Flemish style.

1393–1411 Japan Josetsu flourished, considered the first great practitioner of *suiboko* ink-painting, a form introduced by Buddhist priests during the fourteenth century. Early work, inspired by Chinese ink-painting of the Sung and Yen periods, was a vehicle for the austerity and simplicity of Zen Buddhism.

1397 England The *Wilton Diptych*: a painting showing Richard II being presented to the Virgin by his patron saints. The artist was not English and the painting follows International Gothic style.

15th Century

HISTORICAL EVENTS	LITERATURE	DANCE & DRAMA	MUSIC

HISTORICAL EVENTS

1400
Inca empire established in Peru and Chile.

LITERATURE

early 1400–1500 Russia *Zadonshchina* by the priest Sophronia of Ryazen, a long poem describing the Russian defeat of the Tatars at Kulikovo; it is one of the best-known works of early Russian literature.

1400–1500 England Although there are few great names in English poetry at this period, there is a large body of anonymous carols, lyrics and ballads which have survived. Among the best known are *I sing of a Maiden* and *Sir Patrick Spens*.

1400–1500 Romania The first known Romanian manuscript, a translation of the Gospels.

1400 Spain *Poema de Yucuf*, an anonymous poem about St Joseph; it is interesting because it is written in Spanish Arabic script, evidently for Spanish Moors. Medieval Spanish society included Christians, Jews and Moors together.

1400 Turkey The *Mevlid* by Imam Suleyman Celebi (d. 1422): this work, his only one, is a panegyric on the Prophet, and is acknowledged as a masterpiece.

*c.***1400 England** First known manuscript of *Sir Gawain and the Green Knight*, a Middle English poem on the Arthurian theme. The manuscript also contained three other poems, *Pearl*, *Patience*, and *Purity*, possibly, though not certainly, by the same poet. They show a high standard of literary composition

*c.***1400 Switzerland** *Der Ring* by the writer Heinrich Wittenweiler: it is a didactic work, presented as a grotesque, vulgar and comic rustic epic to make the message more appealing.

DANCE & DRAMA

*c.***1400–1500 England** Development of the characteristic Morris dance, with 6 men, a fool, a man dressed as a woman and a hobby horse: they danced in two rows. This form indicates that English morris is later than Romanian *călușari*, which has the same elements but an older, circular, formation.

*c.***1400–1500 Germany** German dance was impervious to fashionable influences: aristocratic and middle class society continued to favour national folk dances. Their favourite slow introductory or opening dance was called (elsewhere) the allemande.

*c.***1400–1500 Italy** First emergence of the dancing master, as a socially important figure. Many were Jewish. The establishment of teaching as a profession brought the establishment of theory, and so separated courtly dance from folk dances. Domenico Piacenza was an important theorist.

*c.***1400–1500 Italy** Probable origin of the galliard, a lively dance of complex, springing steps: it was sometimes also called the *cinq-pas* or the *Romanesca*. It often became a virtuoso solo performance of elaborate steps, many of them derived from morris steps but lacking the accompanying arm and body movements.

*c.***1400–1500 Siam** Lakon drama-dances were imported from Cambodia: their stories come from a variety of sources and they are danced by women. As with the aristocratic Khon dances, the hand-gestures and many of the movements originated in India, whence they spread in the seventh and eighth centuries.

*c.***1400 Europe** Old customs of carnival and semi-religious dance performances began to be sorted out as *mascarades* and *intermedi*: the former were either processions of tableaux or recitals of dance, songs and speech; the latter were invasions of dances or banquets by groups of singers, dancers and musicians. They used tableaux dances, ordinary social dances and theatrical, costumed dances choreographed for the occasion and also *moresques* (improvised Morris and other grotesque dances).

MUSIC

1400 Netherlands Birth of Guillaume Dufay (d. 1474), Burgundian composer, leader of the first Netherlands school of polyphonic music and one of the most important composers of the period.

1400–1500 China The T'ai-Miao Shrine, Peking, is conceived on the layout of a palace and perpetuates the traditional monumentality of scale as well as decoration.

1400–1500 Mexico Calixtlahuaca is the best example of circular Aztec temple of four storeys.

1400–1500 Mexico Santa Cecilia Sanctuary is the only Aztec pyramid which retains its sanctuary; the simple rectangular elements give it a very modern appearance. It has been restored.

1400–1500 Mexico Tenayuca, Mexico City, illustrated the technique of superimposed building practised in pre-Columbian architecture; the Aztecs added the last and 8th layer to the old pyramid, which appears to have been rebuilt every 52 years. (Tenayuca may have been built earlier than the dates given.)

1400–1500 Peru Sacsahuamán is an Inca fortress built of huge stones, with terraced curtain walls following a zigzag plan.

1400–1500 Spain Coca Castle, the finest example of Mudéjar military work in Spain, was built mainly of brick; the exterior is elaborately decorated and fitted with gun loops and common embrasures.

1400–1500 Spain The magnificent Peñafiel Castle has two lines of curtain walls and is typically Spanish in that it retains a very tall keep and has almost no windows facing outside the walls.

1400–1520 Turkey Beyazid Mosque, Bursa, was symmetrically set out in plan, with very restrained decoration and great care was taken in building materials used.

*c.***1400–1500 Russia** Shah-i-Zinda Necropolis, Samarkand, consists of two groups of buildings built on either side of a ceremonial path; the domes display variation in contour, from tall ones on high drums to shorter bulbous ones. All have ceramic mosaic facings, in part from the fourteenth century.

1400–1500 China The plain white porcelain known as 'Blanc de Chine' was made at Ching-tê Chên and Têhua: the decoration was often so fine as to be visible only in a beam of light.

1400–1500 Germany Silver ceremonial drinking vessels began to be made. They had extravagant ornament and were designed for appearance rather than for use; both religious and secular silver of the period was heavily decorated with enamel and precious stones.

1400–1500 Germany Luneberg and Wienhausen were centres of woollen embroidery for domestic furnishing.

1400–1500 Italy Embroidery flourished under noble and papal patronage, and Italy became the main European source of pattern books, especially for linen drawn-thread work.

1400–1500 Italy Revival in western Europe of the garden as an art form: designs were a conscious imitation of classical styles and do not indicate any knowledge of the flourishing Islamic art of garden design.

1400–1500 Italy Discovered in Venice that oxide of manganese would clarify glass and remove the green and brown tints of iron in the silica; the resulting clear glass resembled rock crystal and was called crystal.

1400–1500 Japan Emergence of specialist workers in decorative metal who made sword-guards as ornamental pieces: the Gotó school was noted for high-relief designs in precious metals.

1400–1500 Spain Church screens were made of decorative ironwork, in the form of closely-spaced vertical bars and horizontal cross bars decorated with pierced sheet-iron ornament. In appearance the style was that of 'Locksmith' work, but traditional 'Blacksmith' work still played a part in construction, although it was associated with smaller objects, while these screens culminated in examples 40 feet high.

1400 Turkey Pottery at Iznik at this date had a reddish clay body with thin white slip in geometric patterns.

*Italy: 'The Gate of the Garden'
from Romance of the Rose,
1481*

HISTORICAL EVENTS	LITERATURE	DANCE & DRAMA	MUSIC
		*c.*1400 **Spain** The poem *La Danza de la Muerte* contains the first reference to the *basse-danse*: a slow, dignified dance of walking steps, not Spanish in origin. It had at first no regular plan of steps, but was danced in three forms, each capable of variation.	
1401 Owen Glendower assumed title of Prince of Wales.			
		1402 France The Confrérie de la Passion, an association of Paris Burghers, was licensed by Charles VI to present mystery plays: this is the first known use of the word 'mystery'.	
	1405 Bohemia Death of Tomáš Štítný (b. *c.*1333), a moralist and one of the first writers of prose to use the Czech language. **1405 Bohemia** *Ackermann aus Böhmen* by Johann von Tepl (*c.*1350–*c.*1415), a Bohemian writer using rhythmical German prose. It was a dispute between Death and a widower, and contained both medieval and Renaissance elements. It was enormously popular; there are 18 manuscripts.		**1405 Arabia** Publication of *Compiler of Melodies*, the greatest work of the Arabian and Persian musical theorist 'Abd Al-Qadir Ibn Ghaibi Al Hafiz Al-Maraghi (*c.*1350–1435).
1406 English defeated Welsh. *1407 First charter granted to Merchant Adventurers by Henry IV of England.*			**1407 Poland** First manuscript of the *Bogurodzica*, Mother of God, which was the earliest Polish religious song and used on all state occasions from the earliest times to the present day.
	1405 France Death of the chronicler Jean Froissart (b. 1337). While the accuracy of his historical viewpoint has been questioned, his skill as a writer was considerable. He wrote a natural style with vivid descriptions and skilful portraiture. **1410 Bohemia** *De Orthographia Bohemica* by Jan Hus (?1369–1415), theologian and religious reformer. He wrote theological works in both Latin and Czech and is also known for his letters, his hymns, and his reform of Czech orthography.		

ARCHITECTURE

1402 Belgium Brussels Town Hall is a richly decorated Gothic building fronting the Grande Place and is a fine example of the many medieval municipal buildings of the Low Countries; it has been restored.

1402–1520 Spain Seville cathedral is one of the largest ever built; it owes its irregular rectangular plan to Islamic mosques but, unlike them, its nave is impressively high.

1403 Turkey The remains of the Yeshil Mosque, Bursa, reveal affinities to the vaulted hall of the Beyazid Mosque: the central area is covered by a dome, and around it is a complicated arrangement of minor rooms.

1404 Italy Leone Battista Alberti (died 1472) was born; he was author of the first architectural treatise of the Renaissance and an architect who combined practical advice from his own experience with an incomplete interpretation of Greek theories. From Vitruvius, via Alberti, came the concept that buildings should be in proportion to the human body, and all their dimensions interrelated. Alberti especially stressed the importance of setting to a building: earlier architects had designed magnificent palazzos and placed them on side streets.

1404–1434 Russia The Tamerlane family mausoleum Guri-i-Mir, Samarkand, Turkistan, was constructed with a new type of dome which is lobed and with slightly bulbous ribs; layout is rectangular with a courtyard bearing a minaret at each corner. There is extensive tile work in the interior.

THREE DIMENSIONAL ART

*c.***1400 Italy** Humanist scholars began to use a script based on Roman inscriptional capitals and Carolingian small letters: this was the basis for 'Roman' lettering.

1401–1452 Italy Work on new bronze doors for the Florence Baptistry, supervised by Lorenzo Ghiberti (1378–1455), provided a workshop in which a whole generation of Florentine artists was trained. Ghiberti was also a goldsmith and stained-glass artist; his work on the doors was remarkable for his use of perspective in low relief.

1402 Syria Damascus was invaded by Timur, who destroyed the glass industry and removed the artists to Samarkand: as a result Syrian competition was eliminated, leaving Venice in a stronger position.

1409–1425 Russia Princess Agrafevna's palace embroiderers worked the altar-cloth for the Cathedral of the Virgin's Birth, Suzdal; Until now all church embroidery had been done by nuns. The palace workshops continued the Novgorod tradition of working in flat-stitch, and in colours of pale blue, pale brown, violet, raspberry and pale green.

1411 France A statute concerning iron-workers mentions the making of decorated locks: French smiths specialized in small-scale pieces such as locks, of great complexity and beauty.

VISUAL ARTS

Italy: 'The Winged Eye', emblem of Lorenzo Ghiberti

*c.***1404–1409 Spain** Death of Pedro Serra who, with his brother Jaime (d. 1399), was a leading figure in Spanish painting from *c.*1350. Their work showed Sienese influence.

1405 Russia Andrei Rublev (*c.*1360–*c.*1430) worked as assistant to the painter Theophanes the Greek.

1411 France Polde Limburg (fl. 1399–*c.*1416) and his brothers entered the service of the Duc de Berry and painted *Les Belles Heures* and *Les Tres Riches Heures*. These two illuminated manuscripts were more influential in Flanders, in their treatment of landscape and composition, than in France. They are nevertheless considered a high point of French International Gothic style.

HISTORICAL EVENTS	LITERATURE	DANCE & DRAMA	MUSIC

1415
Henry V of England defeated French at Agincourt.

1417
End of Great Schism.

1418
German Hansa constituted.

1415 Netherlands *De Imitatione Christi* by the mystic Thomas a Kempis (1380–1471): written in poetic prose and showing deep devotion and considerable psychological insight, the work became the most widely circulated religious book after the Bible. Within a few years of its composition, it was known throughout Europe.

*c.***1420 Bohemia** Theological and ethical writings of the moralist Petr Chelčický (1390–1460). Much early Czech literature was didactic or devotional in character.

1415 Austria Oswald von Wolkenstein (*c*.1377–1445), *minnesinger*, entered the service of King Sigismund.

1421
Peking made capital of China.

1422
First siege of Constantinople by Turks.

1422 France *Quadrilogue Invectif* by Alain Chartier (?1385–?1429), a political writer and poet. His prose style was modelled on classical Latin rhetoric.

1423 Scotland *The Kingis Quair* by James I, King of Scotland (1394–1437) was a love poem in the courtly convention, but the lovers were convincingly portrayed and the story ended in their marriage, whereas true courtly love was adulterous.

Russia: 'The Trinity' by Andrei Rublev, painted between 1422-27

1428
Foundation of Aztec empire in Mexico.

ARCHITECTURE

1413–1421 Turkey The tomb at Yeshil Mosque, Bursa, is adjacent to the mosque; a multi-faced lower structure rises by pendentives to a ring carrying a single dome on a low drum, while ceramics decorate both interior and exterior.

1417 Spain Gerona Cathedral nave was begun; the aisleless nave has a span of 22·3 m, the widest of all medieval naves.

1419–1433 France Strasbourg Cathedral spire designed by Ulrick Ensinger (1350–1419) and continued by Johannes Hultz (?–1449) is a magnificent late Gothic design.

1419–1444 Italy The Foundling Hospital, Florence, by Brunelleschi, the earliest truly Renaissance building, has a ground-floor arcade supported on Corinthian columns, with antique-inspired detail.

1420–1435 Italy Construction of the dome of Florence Cathedral by Filippo Brunelleschi was carried out.

1421–1444 Italy The building of the Foundling Hospital courtyard, Florence, by Brunelleschi was begun; it is an early Renaissance building carrying on, but refining and developing, the Romanesque, rethinking it in the light of Greek theories and forms. Renaissance builders were more concerned with a graceful and harmonious definition of space than with structural ingenuity, as were the Gothic.

1425–c.1460 Italy St Lorenzo, Florence, is by Brunelleschi; it was basilican planned, the first Renaissance building to have entablature blocks and was painted white inside to contrast with the grey stone, (pietra serena).

THREE DIMENSIONAL ART

1415–1420 Italy *Saint George* (now in the Bargello, Florence) by the sculptor Donatello (Donato di Niccolo di Betti Bardi, 1386–1466), who combined an appreciation of classical forms with keen observation of human form and character.

1418 France The sculptor Jacques Morel (d. 1459) was appointed master of works at the Cathedral of Lyon. He was noted for his skill in carving draperies for ornamental effect.

1420 Italy Relief panel in the church at Or San Michele, Florence, of *St George and the Dragon* by Donatello; his reliefs made an original use of perspective for emotional and dramatic effect. He put into practice the Brunelleschi perspective system.

*c.***1420 Egypt** First works by the potters' workshop of Ghaybī ibn al-Tāwrīzī, which continued making painted ceramic tiles and other wares for several generations.

1422–1425 Russia Icon of the Blessed Trinity by Andrey Rublev (d. *c.*1430): it was set in enamel work characteristic of the Moscow style; delicate colours were dropped on to the surface of *repousse* metal work.

1425 Italy Reliefs on the portal of S Petronio, Bologna, by Jacopo della Quercia (*c.*1374–1438). This was his last important work; he used only three figures to a panel, and this dramatic economy was admired by Michelangelo.

VISUAL ARTS

1412–1415 Spain Luis Borrassa (d. *c.*1425) painted the great composite altar of Santa Clara. His work shows French and Sienese influences and is representative of the International Gothic style. He had a strong interest in lively narrative and bright colour.

1419 Italy Discovery of Horapollo's work on Egyptian hieroglyphs. This aroused an interest in symbolic pictures which led to the production of a modern equivalent to the hieroglyph: the emblem, or device.

1422 Russia Andrei Rublev (*c.*1360–*c.*1430), considered the greatest Russian religious painter, decorated the Cathedral of the Trinity at Troitsky-Sergieva. His paintings for it included his best known work, the Icon of the Old Testament Trinity. His style was flowing and linear, and he did not develop the interest in modelling of his early master Theophanes.

1423–1426 Italy First recorded painting by the Sienese artist Sassetta (d.1450): the altarpiece for the Arte della Lana chapel. He painted in an original, lyrical style that kept alive fourteenth-century ideals of religious painting.

1427 Italy Death of the painter Gentile da Fabriano (b. *c.*1370), considered a leading artist in the decorative Gothic style, although little of his work has survived.

1428 Italy Death of the painter Masaccio (Tommaso Guido, b. *c.*1401), considered the most influential artist of his time. He studied the architectural perspective of Brunelleschi and the modelling of Donatello, and used light to define the construction of his painted forms. His treatment of sacred subjects was grave and monumental.

INVENTIONS & DISCOVERIES

HISTORICAL EVENTS	LITERATURE	DANCE & DRAMA	MUSIC

HISTORICAL EVENTS

*1429
Jeanne d'Arc
raised siege of
Orleans.*

1430 Netherlands Gilles Binchois (*c*.1400–1460), composer, established at the court of Philip the Good of Burgundy, where he remained until his death.

c.1430–*c*.1495 **Belgium** Johannes Okeghem (also Ockeghem and Ockenheim), Flemish composer, regarded as founder of second Netherland school.

*1431
Jeanne d'Arc
burnt at Rouen.*

1431 Belgium The *Chapelle de Bourgogne* was founded in Brussels by Philip the Good, Duke of Burgundy; this marked the beginning of Brussels' fame as one of the most important musical centres in Europe.

1432 Iceland Death of Lofthur Guttormsson, the poet; his *Hattalkill* was a cycle of 90 love songs in varied metres.

*1434
Cosimo de'
Medici became
first Medici ruler
in Florence.*

1434 Portugal Fernão Lopes (*c*.1380–*c*.1460) began his history of the Portuguese kings; three chronicles are extant. His view of history was remarkably objective and his understanding of human nature profound. He wrote a natural balanced style, without pedantry.

*1435
First Swedish
Riksdag
established at
Arboga.*

1436–1511 Belgium Joannes de Tinctoris, Flemish theorist and composer. He wrote many important theoretical works and founded a public music school at Naples.

1437 France First known carillon in Europe was at Dunkirk, though carillons had been known by the Chinese very much earlier.

ARCHITECTURE

France: Portail de Saint Maclou, Rouen

1434–1446 England Tattershall Castle is a brick tower house combining the advantages of the keep with the country residence; it is an elaborate version of the many tower houses built in north England and Scotland at the time.

1434–c.1514 France St Maclou, Rouen, is the richest example of French flamboyant architecture, a style that flourished in Normandy especially.

1434 Italy St Maria Degle Angeli, Florence, is by Brunelleschi and is an unfinished centrally planned building, the first of the Renaissance.

1436–1483 Italy St Spirito, Florence, is Brunelleschi's second great basilican church.

THREE DIMENSIONAL ART

1430 Russia First of the embroideries produced by Archbishop Evfimy's workshop, in which profound religious feeling was expressed with economy and restraint. The design of embroidery in this period shows the influence of the painter Andrey Rublev.

1430 Russia Death of the painter Andrey Rublev, whose work now began to influence styles in woodcarving. The best known carver in Rubler-inspired style was Dionysios Amarosy of Zagorsk; his work was in turn influential on carvers of the early sixteenth century.

c.1430 Italy Luca della Robbia (1399–1482), sculptor and maiolica (glazed and decorated Italian ware) potter, began producing modelled pottery figures. His successors Andrea (1435–1525), Giovanni (1469–1529) and Girolamo (1488–1566) della Robbia made true ceramic sculpture.

1431–1438 Italy Singing Gallery in Florence Cathedral by Luca della Robbia (1399) is typical of his skill in depicting cheerful, energetic humanity; his figures of the Madonna set a style which exploited the sentimental appeal of mother and child.

1435 Russia The silver panagiria (a lidded cup supported by the figures of angels) made for Sta Sophia by Peter the silversmith: it showed the influence of the Romanesque style of western Europe.

VISUAL ARTS

1428–1431 Italy The painter Masolino da Panicale (c.1383–c.1447) was at work in Rome. He had worked with Masaccio, and showed his influence during this period. He combined the main trends in Italian painting: an interest in organizing space and volume, and an interest in decorative colour.

1431–1432 Italy The painter Antonio Pisano, called Pisanello (c.1395–1455), finished Gentile's frescoes for the Lateran basilica, Rome. From then on he was recognized as master of the International Gothic style, noted for his draughtsmanship. He was an original in the art of portrait medals, in which he was considered preeminent.

1431 Germany The altarpiece at Tiefenbronn, Constance, is the only known work by Lukas Moser, a painter innovative in his interest in landscape, his light effects, and the grouping of his solidly modelled figures.

1433 Italy Earliest documented painting by Fra Angelico (1387–1455), a monk of the Dominican order. His paintings often used medieval compositions and motifs in an anti-modern, anti-humanist spirit in keeping with Dominican teaching.

1434 Netherlands *Arnolfini and his Wife* by Jan van Eyck (d. 1441): it is considered a masterpiece of realistic painting. Van Eyck invented a new method of using oil paints, which made possible the colours, textures and representation of light, depth and space in this picture. The details of his innovation are still unknown. Oils gradually became more popular than tempera, as being capable of more natural effects.

1437 Italy Fra Filippo Lippi (c.1406–1469) painted the *Tarquinia Madonna*: it shows the influence of Masaccio in its use of three-dimensional composition and massive forms.

1437 Spain Bernardo Martorell (fl. 1433–1452) painted the altarpiece of Pubol. Influenced by Borrasá, Martorell enlivened the Gothic conventions with a keen naturalistic observation. He was also a miniaturist and stained-glass artist, and was credited with introducing the gilded stucco relief technique.

INVENTIONS & DISCOVERIES

1430 Introduction of matchlock as trigger mechanism.

1431 Portuguese discovered the Azores.

*c.*1440 **France** *Les Quinze Joyes de Mariage*, an anonymous piece of early French realistic fiction.

*c.*1440 **Spain** *El Siervo Libre de Amor* by Juan Rodríguez del Padrón (*c.*1405– after 1440), poet and novelist: the book, in part autobiographical, is a novel of chivalry and shows French influence.

?1440 France Probable date of *Retenue d'Amours* by the poet Charles d'Orléans (1394–1465). By this time the courtly conventions were becoming outworn; however, Charles still wrote in that style, with skill, sincerity and psychological insight.

1443 Sweden Death of Thomas Simonsson, bishop and poet, known as the author of the two earliest patriotic Swedish poems: *Frihetsvisan* and *Trohetsvisan*.

1444 Spain *El Laberinto de Fortuna* by the poet Juan de Mena (1411–1456), an allegorical work; the vocabulary and syntax showed strong Latin influence.

1445 Spain The *Cancionero de Baena*, a collection of Spanish courtly lyrics by several poets. The lyrics tended to follow French models; before 1500 the strongest influence on Spanish literature was French. Other notable anthologies are the *Cancioner de Stúñiga*, late fifteenth century, and the *Cancionero General* (1511).

*c.*1440 **Spain** The first gipsies began to arrive in Spain: there they adopted the Andalusian Moorish traditions of song and dance and preserved them after the Moors themselves were expelled between 1501 and 1609. In time these traditions were modified by gipsy life; courtly elements disappeared and violence was introduced.

*c.*1440–1521 **Netherlands** Josquin des Prés, was the most celebrated composer of his day and his music has remained in high esteem through the ages. He wrote over 30 masses including *Ave Maris Stella*, *De Beata Virgine*, *Da Pacem* and *Mater Patris Pange Lingua* and more than 50 motets. Stylistically, his music forms a bridge between the music of the later Middle Ages and that of the Renaissance.

1445–1527 Germany Heinrich Finck, composer and *Kapellmeister* at Stuttgart and Salzburg. His compositions included masses, motets and part-songs.

ARCHITECTURE

1438 Turkey The name (Üç Şerefeli Mosque) of the three-balconied mosque, Edirne, derives from the structure of four tall minarets which carry three balconies each; the minarets are of different size and decorated with checkered patterns. The mosque itself, the first centrally planned structure in Turkey, is covered by a main central dome, supported by flying buttresses, and is accompanied by several smaller domes.

1439 Germany St Laurence Nuremberg choir is late Gothic with very slender piers supporting high vaults of star-shaped pattern.

1440 Germany Dinkelsbuhl House is a fine large gabled half-timbered house of a type common in Germany before World War II.

1443 France The house of Jacques Coeur, Bourges, is the finest surviving French medieval town house; irregularly planned around a courtyard, it has 7 newel staircases (a staircase in which the steps circle a central pillar).

1443 Italy Castel Nuovo, Naples, was designed with sharp-angled bastions, an early instance of this form of defence against cannon fire.

1444 China Chih-Hua-Ssu, Peking, is a temple representing the official Ming style, which endured for four centuries in China.

1444 Italy Donato Bramante born (died 1514). He was the first of the great high Renaissance architects based in Milan.

1444 Italy Palazzo Medici-Ricardi, Florence, was begun by Michelozzo di Bartolommeo (1396–1472). It is the first Renaissance palace with an austere façade surrounded by an arcaded courtyard.

1446–1451 Italy Palazzo Rucellai, Florence, Alberti's first independent work, is three storeys high and introduced double windows with pilasters between. The whole is capped by a heavy cornice and is an adaptation of the Roman colosseum.

THREE DIMENSIONAL ART

Turkey: the Uc Serefeli Mosque

*c.*1445 **Italy** The first tapestry workshop was set up at Ferrara by Lionello d'Este.

VISUAL ARTS

*c.*1440 **Italy** Death of Cennino Cennini (b. 1370), artist and writer, who published *Il Libro dell'Arte*, a technical manual influenced by methods in Giotto's workshop.

1442–1451 Germany Active period of Stefan Lochner, leading artist of the Cologne school. His major work is the *Dombild* altarpiece in Cologne cathedral.

*c.*1442 **Italy** Fra Filippo Lippi reverted to Gothic features in his interest in decoration. He began to use Gothic landscapes and started his practice of including a sequence of incidents in one unit of space. This, his later, style was an important source for the pre-Raphaelites.

1443–1445 Spain *The Virgin of the Councillors* by Luis Dalman (fl. 1428–1460) echoed Van Eyck's altarpiece in Ghent. Dalman had visited Flanders in 1431–1437, the first recorded contact of a Spanish artist with the Flemish school.

1444–1447 Germany Death of Conrad Witz, a German artist who worked in Switzerland. His painting *Christ Walking on the Water* is considered outstanding in German landscape.

1444–1450 Italy Andrea del Castagno (*c.*1423–1457) painted frescoes of the Passion in Florence: monumental in the manner of Masaccio, they caused a stir for their harsh realism and dramatic presentation.

1444 Netherlands Death of the Master of Flémalle, probably Robert Campin. His figures had a sculptural solidity and realism, heightened by lighting, which broke from the decorative International Gothic style.

*c.*1445 **Italy** Domenicho Veneziano (d. 1461) painted his *St Lucy* altarpiece, in Florence, one of two surviving signed works. He was influential in his use of colour and light.

*c.*1446 **China** Active period of Tai Chin, a professional painter at a time when most of the major artists were amateurs who considered painting an automatic process stimulated by a state of inspiration.

INVENTIONS & DISCOVERIES

1445 Portuguese Diniz Diaz discovered Cape Verde Islands.

HISTORICAL EVENTS	LITERATURE	DANCE & DRAMA	MUSIC

1447
Break-up of
Timur's empire;
India, Persia and
Afghanistan
gained
independence.

1448
Accession of
Constantine XI,
last eastern
emperor.

LITERATURE

DANCE & DRAMA

*c.*1450 **Europe** First evidence of the pavane, a stately dance of gliding steps to a 32-bar tune. It was danced in couples and sometimes in procession, a little more quickly than the *basse-danse* but still rather solemn.

*c.*1450 **Europe** Social dances for couples began to dispense with the original interludes of danced pantomime: the separate acting out of wooing or display continued in the galliard, courante and canaries until *c.*1550.

*c.*1450 **France** *Maître Pierre Pathelin*, one of the earliest French farces, played by the Enfants Sans Souci, a Parisian student society of amateur actors.

*c.*1450 **Germany** Performance of the *Neidhartspiel*, one of the best-known carnival plays, or *Festnachtspielen*, in Austria and Germany: these are short farces. The greatest writer of carnival plays was Hans Sachs (1494–1576).

*c.*1450 **Italy** Guglielmo Ebreo of Pesaro published a treatise on dancing, *De praticha seu arte tripudii vulghare opusculum*: it is said to continue the teaching of an earlier theorist, Domenico of Piacenza.

*c.*1450 **Japan** Development of the Japanese puppet play.

1450 **France** First record of the *Mystère du Nouveau Testament* by Arnoul Greban: it exists in 6 other versions also.

MUSIC

1450 **Italy** A chair of music was established at Bologna University.

1452 **Germany** Conrad Paumann (1410–1473), a blind organist, published *Fundamentum Organisandi*, one of the earliest of keyboard tablature.

1453 **England** Death of John Dunstable, composer, one of the first to bind the five items of Ordinary of the Mass into one whole.

1451 **Wales** Dafydd ab Edmwnd, a poet of love and nature, introduced stricter forms of measure at the Carmarthen eisteddfod. The technical complexity of medieval Welsh verse reached its peak with him.

1453
Fall of
Constantinople
and end of
Eastern Empire.
Hundred Years'
War between
England and
France ended.
Metropolitan of
Moscow assumed
headship of
Orthodox church.

?1454 **Portugal** Probable date of *Crónica da Tomada de Ceuta* by Gomes Eanes de Zurara (1410–1474), a chronicler who continued the work of Lopes. His style was often pedantic; it showed the influence of Latin writers, particularly Livy.

1447–1449 Italy Paintings by Fra Angelico of the lives of St Stephen and St Lawrence, for the Pope's private chapel: they had an emphasis on narrative, which was for him a new development.

1449 Italy Andrea del Castagno painted the *Assumption* in Florence: this marked a change in his style from forceful to decorative.

*c.*1450 **England** Sherborne Abbey was rebuilt with the first large-scale fan vaults over choir and nave.

*c.*1450 **Italy** Castello Sforzesco, Milan, one of the grandest castles built by the powerful families in north Italy in the fourteenth and fifteenth centuries, was begun; such architects as Bramante, Filarete and Leonardo da Vinci worked on it.

*c.*1450 **Peru** Building began on Cuzco, the capital of the Incas; massive irregularly shaped stone blocks, closely fitted together with mortar, were used. It was planned around a central plaza which included a citadel.

*c.*1450 **Peru** The city of Machu Picchu was typical of Inca use of megalithic stonework to build up a terraced site; it was destroyed during the Spanish conquest.

*c.*1450 **Scotland** The details of Melrose Abbey show the influence of continental, and especially French, architecture; the window tracery is perpendicular. It was later rebuilt but is now in ruins.

1452 Italy *De re aedificatoria*, written by Leone Battista Alberti, was published, the first architectural treatise of the Renaissance emulating Vitruvius (flourished 46–30 BC). He gave a copy to the Pope, who was inspired by it to rebuild, rather than merely improve, St Peter's basilica.

1452 Italy Leonardo da Vinci was born (died 1519). He built nothing but produced a number of influential architectural schemes and designs and was particularly interested in centrally planned churches.

*c.*1450 **China** Clear yellow monochrome pottery was introduced during the Ming period.

*c.*1450 **Germany** Creative period of 'Master E.S.', engraver and goldsmith, who was among the first to achieve tonal effects in line engraving with hatchings.

*c.*1450 **Germany** Publication of the thirteenth-century *Biblia Pauperum*, textbook on the Old Testament prefiguration of the life of Christ, as a block-book. Block-books were printed entirely from woodcuts and were only suitable for short texts in continuous demand. They disappeared *c.*1500.

*c.*1450 **Italy** Venetian glass artists began to make pedestal-foot goblets, coloured and decorated with gilt and enamel. Venetian glass was suitable for moulding but too fragile to engrave, other than by a fine diamond-point. It was made coloured, clear or opaque white; enamelled pictures were painted on dark glass and fired. *Latticinio* had a thread of pattern in the glass; 'crackle' glass was made by cooling and re-heating, or by adding particles to the surface.

1453 Italy Pulpit panels in S Lorenzo, Florence, show the culmination of the sculptor Donatello's inclination towards the rugged and emotional: he was the most influential individual artist of his time.

1453 Russia Turkish invasion of Constantinople; Russia became the chief representative of the Orthodox church. This was a stimulus to the creation of icons, gospel covers, censers and liturgical vessels in silver and gold.

1454 France Enguerrand Charonton (fl. *c.*1447–1461) painted *The Coronation of the Virgin* at Avignon. His style combined Mediterranean influence, on his landscape, and Flemish influence, on his scenes of Hell.

HISTORICAL EVENTS	LITERATURE	DANCE & DRAMA	MUSIC

1455
Civil War (Wars of the Roses) in England.

1458
Acropolis of Athens fell to Turks.

1456 France *Le Petit Jehan de Saintré* by Antoine de La Sale (1385/6–?1460) was the first full-length work of prose fiction in French. Although it contained material on quests and tournaments, which was becoming *passé*, there was also much realism and contemporary detail.

1457 England Burning of the controversial religious books written by the theologian Reginald Pecock (c.1390–c.1460). He wrote in English, whereas most previous prose had been in Latin; English was still developing as a medium for argument and logic.

1458 Spain Death of Auziàs March (b. 1397), regarded as the greatest Catalan poet. He wrote troubadour lyrics, and his work showed the influence of Petrarch and Dante.

1458 Spain Death of the poet Iñigo López de Mendoza, Marques of Santillana (b. 1388). He introduced the Italian sonnet form in Spain and attempted to use the hendecasyllable, though with limited success. He is considered the first Spanish Renaissance poet.

1461 France *Le Testament* by François Villon (?1431– ?), a poet remarkable for his highly personal and powerful treatment of the themes that preoccupied most medieval writers, particularly the vanity of human aspirations and the ever-present shadow of death. His work included passages of obscenity as well as moral reflections.

1455 Italy Antonio Cornazano published *Libro dell'arte del danzare*, a treatise on the dance following the teaching of Domenico of Piacenza, theorist of dance.

*c.*1460 **Netherlands** Publication of a manuscript, now in Brussels, detailing the music and steps of *basses-danses*: by this time the *basse-danse* was always followed by an after-dance, the *saltarello*, which was far more sprightly. The manuscript indicates that the after-dance was united with it in being danced to the same tune, adapted to another rhythm.

1455 Netherlands Adriaen Pietersz, born in Bruges, was the earliest known organ builder in Flanders, and constructed an organ at Delft. The organ still exists, though much restored.

1460 Germany The beginning of the compilation of *Buxheimer Orgelbuch*, the largest and most important organ book of the fifteenth century, completed in 1470; it was removed to the Bavarian State Library in Munich in 1883.

1463 England The first degree of B. Mus. at Cambridge was conferred on Henry Abyngdon (c.1418–1497), English singer, organist and composer.

1464
Peace in England under Edward IV.

1464–1498 France The *Memoirs* of Philippe de Commynes (?1447–1511), a chronicler working first at the court of Charles the Bold and later with Louis XI. His skill lay in his ability to select and link together events of real importance.

1465 France *Le Jouvencel* by Jean de Beuil, a war novel: it was one of a number of early novels which pointed the way to later realistic fiction.

ARCHITECTURE

1457 Czechoslovakia Pernstein Castle was reconstructed in the late Gothic style.

1458 Italy The Pitti Palace, Florence, was possibly designed by Brunelleschi and was to become the largest of Italian palaces outside the Vatican; its austere astylar façade is built of large blocks of stone. It was completed in the seventeenth century.

1460 France Toul Cathedral's façade is the most impressive of large-scale, flamboyant-style façades.

1460–1563 Italy Pienza cathedral, the Bishop's and Piccolomini palaces are by Bernardo Rossellino (1409–1464) and built for Pius II as part of a new town scheme.

*c.***1460 Italy** The ducal palace, Urbino, was perhaps by Luciano Laurana (*c.*1420–1479); the arcaded courtyard and main entrance façade are the most important existing parts, while the interior craftsmanship is superb.

1462 China The main hall of K'ai-Fu-Ssu, Hopei, is rather conservative, for externally it is still dominated by curving eaves which, together with the low porch, are reminiscent of picturesque massing found in the time of the Sung dynasty.

1463–1471 Turkey The Külliye of Mohomed II, Istanbul, a large complex on the site of Justinian's church, contains no innovations, but is a simplification of the earlier medreses in Bursa; the mosque is an eighteenth-century replacement of the original.

1463 Yugoslavia The Gothic Rector's Palace, Dubrovnik, by Onofrio Giordano della Cava had a Renaissance porch added.

1465 Italy *Trattato d'archittura* by Antonio Filarete (1400–1470) was written; it criticized Gothic and favoured the antique and circulated in manuscript form only, being published in the nineteenth century.

*c.***1465 France** Langeais is an example of the fortress-type Loire château.

THREE DIMENSIONAL ART

1454 Italy First written reference to white tin-glazed pottery painted in bright colours, especially blue, green, brown and purple, known as maiolica. It was Spanish-Islamic in style and was imported into Italy via Majorca. Later it began to be copied at Faenza (hence faience) and Deruta.

*c.***1454 Germany** *Indulgence* printed at Mainz; the earliest existing piece of printing. Printers connected with it were Johann Gutenberg (*c.*1394–1468) Johann Fust (d. 1466) and Peter Schöffer (d. 1503).

1457 Germany Johann Gutenberg retired from printing, and his associates Fust and Schöffer produced a Psalter which is the first printed book to have a dated imprint.

1462–1473 Germany Active period of sculptor Nicolas Gerhaert van Leyden who worked in Trier, Strasbourg and Vienna in Burgundian style. He was an unconventional artist whose religious subjects and portraits showed unusual warmth and humour.

*c.***1463 Italy** Discovery of Venetian *cristallo* glass-making technique, attributed to the Berovieri family of Murano.

1464 Italy Death of Maso Finiguerra (b. 1426), noted as a goldsmith and maker of niello plates, i.e. plates with an engraved design filled in by decorative metal alloy. He was also one of the first to use copper engraving.

1465 Italy German printers set up a printing press at Subiaco. Printing and typography spread from Germany to Venice, Rome, Paris, Lyon, Rouen and Utrecht.

VISUAL ARTS

1455 Spain Jaime Huguet (fl. *c.*1448–1492) painted the altarpiece of San Antonio Abad. He continued and matured the Catalan tradition of Bernardo Martorell, and was a formative influence on future artists in Catalonia and Aragón.

1455 Spain Jorge Ingles painted the *Entierro de San Jerónimo*, an altarpiece which is one of the first examples in Castile of the Hispano-Flemish style, combining Flemish realism with the interlacing patterns of Moorish art.

1460–1470 Portugal Nuño Gonçalves (fl. 1450–1471) painted 6 large panels of court and society figures praying in the presence of a saint, probably St Vincent. His style had a powerful realism resembling Flemish and Burgundian schools.

1460 Italy Andrea Mantegna (1431–1506) was appointed court painter to the Gonzaga family at Mantua, whom he painted in a series of frescoes in their palace. The figures appeared in informal groups making up narrative pictures; the scenes were divided by classical motifs. Mantegna was noted for his understanding of the antique, his humanist scholarship and his skill in perspective. The Mantuan frescoes are the first to be truly illusionist.

1461 Spain Death of Jaime Baco, called Master Jacomart, court painter to Alfonso of Aragon. He worked for some years in Naples and in 1451 returned to Valencia where he was the most influential painter of his time. His only surviving documented work is an altarpiece for the town of Cati.

1464 Netherlands Death of Rogier van der Weyden, who with Jan van Eyck was the main influence on Flemish painting, especially realistic portraiture, in his time. In his sacred paintings he used a strong line to express tragedy or deep feeling.

1465 Italy The Venetian painter Giovanni Bellini (*c.*1430–1516) painted his *Agony in the Garden*, notable for its expressive treatment of dying light: the effect was based on actual observation of landscape, put to imaginative use. A concern with light became characteristic of Venetian landscape painting.

INVENTIONS & DISCOVERIES

1456 Quadrant first used for navigation.

147

1467
Turks conquered Herzegovina.

1468
End of first period of Aztec conquest in Mexico.

1469
Lorenzo de' Medici became leader of Florentine republic.

1466–1472 Russia *Journey Beyond the Three Seas* by Afanasy Nikicin, a merchant: it was an account in clear and simple language of his travels through Persia and India, and contained one of the earliest descriptions of India and its people in any European literature.

Italy: the pulpit from Sta Croce Church, Florence, decorated by Benedetto da Maiano

1475 Scotland *The Testament of Cresseid* by the poet Robert Henryson. His work included fables, and the first pastoral in English, *Robene and Makyne*.

1475 Italy Carving on the altar of the Montoliveto church, Naples, shows angels in a chain round dance: this was a popular form not accepted for public performance in society.

1475–1552 Italy The *frottola* was a sort of strophic song with a popular theme and preceded the madrigal.

ARCHITECTURE

1466 Spain Burgos Cathedral lantern begun by Hans of Cologne (?–1481), although the Moors covered vaults with elaborate pattern, at Burgos this idea is carried out in ribbing derived from German high Gothic: the effect remains Moorish but the structure is not.

1469 Germany The north aisle of Brunswick Cathedral was rebuilt with piers decorated with spiral shafts and angular abaci (slabs forming the uppermost part of a capital), an example of the exotic flowering of late Gothic architecture.

1470 Italy St Andrea, Mantua, was begun by Alberti and is his greatest work: it has a Roman triumphal-arch entrance and coffered barrel vaulted nave supported on classical styled piers.

1471 Germany Meissen Albrechtsburg is a totally irregular castle, incorporating every form of late Gothic architecture.

1471–1633 Turkey Top Kapi Saray, Istanbul, are residential and governmental buildings whose development evolved over centuries and comprises several courtyard and terraced gardens with pavilions and summer houses.

1474 Russia The Cathedral of the Dormition in the Kremlin, Moscow, is by Aristotele Fioravanti (c.1418–c.1480) an Italian architect; built to resemble the twelfth-century Cathedral of the Dormition at Vladmir the internal galleries were abolished and thus the interior is very spacious.

1475 Finland Olavinlinna Castle is one of several castles built in Finland, in this case designed as a defence against the Russians; it is concentrically planned.

THREE DIMENSIONAL ART

1470 France The first French printing press was established in Paris at the Sorbonne.

1470 Germany Iron screen for church of St Ulric in Augsburg combines the techniques of the 'blacksmith' style and the later geometric chiselled style, which flourished simultaneously in Germany.

1470 Italy The printer Nicolas Jenson, working in Venice, adapted Roman script to typography. His Roman type was one of the most successful.

1472–1475 Italy Pulpit in Sta Croce, Florence, by Benedetto da Maiano (1442–1497) follows the narrative tradition of Donatello: he was noted for the very fine architectural frames he designed for his reliefs and figures.

1474 Spain The first Spanish printing press was set up in Valencia.

c.1475 Germany Jörg Syrlin (d. c.1490) carved the choir-stalls in Ulm cathedral. He abandoned the attributes conventionally distinguishing figures of prophets and sibyls, and instead gave each of them an individual personality.

VISUAL ARTS

c.1467 Spain Fernando Gallego (1440/5–after 1507) painted the retable (altarpiece) of San Idelfonso in the cathedral of Zamora. He was considered the most important representative of the Hispano-Flemish style in Castile, and influenced a generation of artists.

1468 Netherlands *Portrait of Tommaso Portinari and his Wife* by Hans Memling (d. 1494), celebrated portrait painter. His portraits appeared in Italy, where they influenced Bellini.

1470–1480 Italy Sandro Botticelli (1445–1510) painted the *Prima Vera* for Lorenzino de Medici. He reacted against the dramatic realism of Masaccio and returned to the decorative line and pattern of Gothic painting, into which he assimilated images from classical art. He established an ideal of ethereal feminine beauty which was equally convincing in pagan or Christian figures.

c.1470–1480 Germany Active period of the 'Master of the Life of the Virgin', a painter of the Cologne school whose work was influenced by Flemish masters. The panels on the *Life of the Virgin* show a realistic narrative style.

1471–1481 Austria Michael Pacher (? 1465–1498), painter and wood-carver, painted the scenes from the *Life of the Virgin* for the high altar in St Wolfgang on the Abersee. He was influenced by van der Weyden but also by the Italian painter Andrea Mantegna (1431–1506), from whom he derived the technique of taking a low viewpoint in order to give his figures a monumental quality.

1472 Italy Leonardo da Vinci (1452–1519) enrolled as a painter in the fraternity of St Luke's Florence. He was at the time thought to be a pupil of Verrochio, and an angel in Verrochio's *Baptism* is attributed to him.

1475–1476 France Altarpiece of *The Burning Bush* at Aix-en-Provence was painted by Nicolas Froment (fl. c. 1450–c.1490) in sculptural style.

INVENTIONS & DISCOVERIES

*1472
Danish Dietrich Pining discovered Newfoundland.*

*1474
Method of lunar distances for longitude introduced.*

Spain: church of Saint Juan de los Reyes, Toledo

1476 Italy In Rome, the first plainsong books with music were printed.

*1479
Union of Aragon and Castile under Ferdinand and Isabella.*

1477 England *The Dictes or Sayengis of the Philosophres* was printed by William Caxton (1422–1491); it was the first book printed in England for which we have an exact date. The choice of printed books available to those who could read was governed by Caxton's selection; his early books were all of an 'improving' nature.

1477 Netherlands Pierre de la Rue (d. 1518), composer, was in residence at the Burgundy court. As a contrapuntal composer he is said to have been second to Josquin des Prés.

*1480
Ivan III threw off Mongol rule in Russia and took title of Tsar.*

1480–1496 Italy *L'Arcadia* by Jacopo Sannazzaro (?1456–1530), a humanist and poet writing in both Latin and Italian: a pastoral romance, consisting of 12 eclogues alternating with 12 passages of prose, it illustrated clearly how Renaissance literature was firmly founded on classical tradition.

1480 Germany Carved figures in the Munich Ratssaal illustrate energetic, acrobatic male dancers in a 'Moorish' dance. Folk dance continued vigorous, while courtly dance was restrained by manners and costume.

1480 Italy *Orlando Innamorato* by the poet Matteo Maria Boiardo (1441–1494): a romantic epic, combining stories of King Arthur with those of Charlemagne.

ARCHITECTURE

1475 Italy Michelangelo Buonarroti born (died 1564). He represents the Italian Renaissance at its height: architect, sculptor, painter and poet.

1475 Italy Sebastiano Serlio, architect, was born (died 1554); he wrote an illustrated treatise which influenced French architecture and caused him to be summoned to work for Francis I at Fontainebleau. That château was decorated by Italian artists Francesco Primaticcio (1504–1570) and Giovanni Rosso (1494–1540), in imitation of Romano's Palazzo del Té.

1476–1520 Mexico Malinalco was one of the last Aztec temples and unique in being cut out of the mountain side, inside are animal and bird sculptures.

c.1479 Spain San Juan de los Reyes, Toledo, is a royal sepulchre built for Ferdinand and Isabella, whose profuse decoration derives from Islamic and Gothic sources.

1480–1492 Spain The ducal palace, Guadalajara, had a typically Spanish central courtyard and two storeys with highly decorated arcading and partly twisted columns; it was later destroyed.

c.1480 Spain Manzanares el Real is one of the most sumptuously decorated castles in Spain: the west towers are studded with round bosses, while the inner gallery is a rich example of Spanish flamboyant architecture.

THREE DIMENSIONAL ART

1476–1479 Germany The 30-foot tabernacle in bronze for the Marienkirche in Lübeck showed the continuing fashion for and skill in bronze-casting which persisted in Germany long after it had declined elsewhere in Europe, where bronze was seen as more suitable for monumental Romanesque work than for the more refined and elegant Gothic.

1476 England William Caxton (c.1422–1491) set up the first English printing press in Westminster. He had learned printing from visits to Cologne and Bruges, where he printed the first book printed in English, *Recuyell of the Histories of Troy*.

c.1476 Italy The bronze *David* by Andrea del Verrochio (c.1435–1488): it was characteristic of his graceful treatment of a youthful figure. Verrochio trained as a goldsmith and also worked under Donatello.

1477–1489 Poland Veit Stoss (c.1450–1533), German sculptor and carver, carved the altarpiece for the church of St Mary, Cracow. His art was dramatic, with figures carved in the round, often over life-size; he was less concerned with anatomy than with the impact of shapes, whether drapery or human features.

c.1480–c.1520 Netherlands The series of tapestries in *milles-fleurs* style called *The Lady with the Unicorn* was probably woven in Brussels. Other centres of *milles-fleurs* tapestry are thought to have flourished in Tournai (Flanders) and the Loire valley and the Marche (France).

1480 Bavaria Sculptor and wood-carver Erasmus Grasser (c.1450–1526) made his most characteristic work, *Moreska Tänzer*: he was noted for a lively and expressive style.

VISUAL ARTS

1475–1565 Portugal Active period of the 'Portuguese primitives', prolific painters following Flemish example. They were skilled portraitists and preferred brilliant colours.

1475 France Jean Fouquet (c.1420–c.1481) became *Peintre du Roy*. His paintings depicted monumental figures built up from broad planes. His art was based on draughtsmanship.

1475 Netherlands Death of Dieric Bouts, an artist strongly influenced by van der Weyden. His painting of *The Last Supper* from the Louvain altarpiece shows a grasp of true perspective, but he was mainly noted for his poetic approach to landscape background and his colour sense.

c.1475 Netherlands Hugo van der Goes (fl. c.1467–1482) painted the Portinari altarpiece, commissioned by Tommaso Portinari of Florence.

INVENTIONS & DISCOVERIES

1480 Leonardo da Vinci invented parachute.

HISTORICAL EVENTS	LITERATURE	DANCE & DRAMA	MUSIC

MUSIC

1481–1553 Spain Mateo Flecha the Elder, director of music at the cathedral of Lerida, served as *maestro de capilla* to the Infantas Maria and Joanna. His *ensaladas* were published in 1581 by his nephew, also Mateo Flecha (1520–1604).

Italy: Palazzo della Cancellaria, Rome

HISTORICAL EVENTS

1483 Spanish Inquisition came under joint direction of church and state.

1484 Papal bull Summis desiderantes against witchcraft and sorcery.

1485 Battle of Bosworth; beginning of Tudor dynasty in England.

LITERATURE

1485 England *Le Morte d'Arthur* by Sir Thomas Malory (d. 1471) was printed by Caxton. Malory's version of the Arthurian legend was mainly derived from the thirteenth-century French romances. It was written in simple but vigorous prose, and established prose as a medium for literature in England, capable of being used for entertainment and not merely for business or instruction as hitherto.

MUSIC

*c.*1485–*c.*1549 **England** Hugh Aston [or Ashton], a composer whose compositions, particularly his *Hornpipe for Virginals*, anticipates much Elizabethan music.

1488 Swabian League formed in south Germany.

1487 Germany Conrad Celtes (1459–1508) became the first German *poeta laureatus*. A lyric poet and humanist, he discovered the tenth-century plays of Hrothswitha of Gandersheim.

1489 Italy *Miscellanea* by Angelo Poliziano (1454–1494), humanist and poet. He was a famous scholar, lecturing on classical literature and philosophy, and wrote Greek and Latin as well as Italian. His poetry combined the best elements of classical and contemporary popular literature. He is best remembered today for his Italian love lyrics.

1489 Italy A ballet of scenes from classical mythology was presented at the wedding of the Duke of Milan. As episodes of pantomime faded out of social dance they became popular as entertainments on their own.

1487 Italy One of the earliest printed books on the theory of music was published at Bologna, written by Nicolaus Burtius (b. 1450?).

1487 Scotland Birth of Robert Carver (d. *c.*1546), the greatest sixteenth century Scottish composer.

ARCHITECTURE

1481 Italy Baldassare Peruzzi was born (died 1536). A high Renaissance architect who designed many buildings in Rome.

*c.***1482 Italy** St Maria Presso S. Satiro, Milan, was rebuilt by Donato Bramante; his first important architectural work, it has an extraordinary *trompe d'oeil* (illusionistic) chancel.

1483 Italy Sanzio Raphael was born (died 1520), an exponent of high Renaissance Classicism, although his buildings are few.

*c.***1483 Japan** Kinkaku and Ginkaku, Kyoto, are two garden pavilions intended to be covered with silver foil, a type of ornament later used to excess in Japan; they were built in a carefully landscaped garden.

1484 Russia The cathedral of the Annunciation in the Kremlin, Moscow, is on the site of an earlier building and owes more to the past than to contemporary architectural innovations.

1485 Italy Antonio da Sangallo the younger was born (died 1546). He was the leading high Renaissance architect in Rome after Raphael's death.

1486 Germany Matthäus Roriczer (died *c.*1494), a mason, published his textbook *On the Ordination of Pinnacles*, which illustrates how medieval masons worked according to a system of proportions.

1486–1498 Italy Palazzo della Cancellaria, Rome, was the first important Renaissance building in the City; the architect is unknown.

1486 Italy Vitruvius' first-century treatise *De Architectura*, which became a basic Renaissance source book, was printed in Italy.

1489–1506 Italy Palazzo Strozzi, Florence, is a typically massive palace built around a central courtyard, as are found in most Italian towns.

THREE DIMENSIONAL ART

1481–1512 Turkey Inlaid armour was decorated by the *kuftgari* technique, which was more suited to steel than the cutting or punching methods used on brass or bronze: the surface of the steel was roughened and gold wire hammered on to it.

1483 England The Edward IV screen in St George's Chapel, Windsor, was considered the finest European piece of architectural chiselled iron-work.

1483–1500 Spain Gil de Siloe active, sculptor of reredoses at Valladolid and Burgos, and of the tombs of John II and Isabella, and Prince Alfonso. His style showed Flemish and *mudejar* (or Moorish) influence; he was the last important Spanish Gothic sculptor.

1488 Italy Equestrian statue of the condottieri Bartolomeo Colleoni by Verrocchio shows the sculptor's interest in depicting toughness and old age, in contrast to his graceful figures of youth. Leonardo da Vinci was his pupil.

1489 Spain Tombs of Alvaro de Luna and his wife, in Toledo Cathedral, accredited to Sebastián de Almonacid (active *c.*1475–1500) and his school: considered to be among the most important pieces of Hispano-Flemish work.

VISUAL ARTS

1481–1482 Italy The *Adoration of the Kings* (unfinished) by Leonardo da Vinci (1452–1519) introduced elements of excitement and agitation in place of the conventional reverence.

1482 Italy Leonardo da Vinci (1452–1519) painted *The Virgin of the Rocks* (the first version, now in the Louvre) in Milan. The disturbing element is limited to the strange setting; the spirit of the central group is gentle.

1485 Japan Death of Geiami, ink-painter, considered one of the foremost artists of the mature *suiboko* style.

1486–1495 Persia Series of 32 miniature paintings by Kamul Ud-Din Bihzad (*c.*1460–1535). He was the strongest influence on a school of painting developed in Herat *c.*1480–1500. He revitalized the miniature-painting conventions and influenced succeeding generations. He was noted for his sense of colour harmony and his animated figure drawing.

1486 Italy Francesco Francia (*c.*1450–1515) of Bologna began painting. His elegant style set a fashion in Bolognese painting of the Mannerist school.

1488 Italy Giovanni Bellini (*c.*1430–1516) painted the *Madonna with Saints* in the church of St Maria dei Frari, Venice. It was considered the most characteristic work of his serene and contemplative style, and the first truly Venetian painting, mainly concerned with colour and light and free of outside influences.

INVENTIONS & DISCOVERIES

1482 Portuguese established settlements on Gold Coast.

1483 Russians began to explore Siberia.

1487 Portuguese Bartholomew Diaz sailed round Cape of Good Hope.

HISTORICAL EVENTS	LITERATURE	DANCE & DRAMA	MUSIC
		1490 Italy *The Passion of Revello*: it was written in cultured Italian, not dialect or Latin, and shows the influence of the French mysteries.	**1490–1502 England** The Eton Manuscript is the oldest, and in some respects the largest, collection of early Tudor music. It originally contained about a hundred motets and magnificats for from 4 to 8 and, in one case, 9 voices.
			*c.***1490–1545 Italy** Pietro Aaron, a teacher of music in Rome, abandoned many of the traditional views and advocated that accidentals should not be at the discretion of performers but should be written in the manuscript.
	1491 Spain *Arnalte y Lucenda* by Diego de San Pedro, novelist and poet (possibly Jewish): a novel of courtly love, the book draws on Boccaccio and Rodríguez del Padrón.		
1492 End of Moslem era in Spain with conquest of Moorish kingdom of Granada.	**1492 Spain** Publication of a Spanish grammar by the humanist Elio Antonio de Nebrija (?1444–1532); it was the first grammar of a European vernacular language.		**1492 Italy** The earliest European reference to the armonica was in *Theoria Musicae* published in Milan by Franchino Gafori (1451–1522). This instrument developed from 'musical glasses' which originated in Asia; although originally percussive it was later played with moistened tips of fingers.
			1492 Italy Publication in Venice of *Opera*, a study of the theory of music by Boëthius (480–524) a Roman philosopher.
	1494 Germany *Narrenschiff* by Sebastian Brant (1457/8–1521), a poem in rhymed couplets, satirized over 100 contemporary follies. Brant used the German vernacular at a time when most writers used Latin.		
		1495 Netherlands First record of *Everyman*, probably the best-known of all moralities.	
		1497 Spain *Representacion del Amor* by Juan del Encina (1468–1537): a secular play with religious inspiration, in that, although it is a nativity play, the main interest is in the shepherds.	

ARCHITECTURE

1490 Czechoslovakia Prague Cathedral's royal gallery was built for Vladislav II with vault ribs resembling lopped branches, a device used in such other late Gothic buildings as the south façade of Sens Cathedral, France.

1490 Russia The Granovitaya Palta in the Kremlin, Moscow, was built by Italians Marco Ruffo (flourished 1480–91) and Pietro Antonio Solari (1450–c.1493); the façade is covered by diamond-shaped studding as on buildings in Italy and Spain.

1491 Turkey Sinan was born (died c.1588), the most famous of Turkish architects, who produced a prodigious number of buildings throughout the Ottoman Empire during his long life.

1492 Germany The Simpertus Arch of St Ulrich and Afra, Augsburg, was built with vault ribs with three-dimensional curves, an example of several contemporary experiments employing double-curved ribs.

1493–1508 France The Palais de Justice, Rouen, is a very rich example of French municipal architecture in the flamboyant style.

THREE DIMENSIONAL ART

c.1490 Germany Beginning of the active period of Tilman Riemenschneider (1468–1531) as a woodcarver of large-scale altarpieces and figure groups. He was considered one of the best woodcarvers in the Gothic style in Germany.

1493–1519 Germany Reign of the Emperor Maximilian I who commissioned Hans Reutlingen of Aachen, goldsmith, to make a silver book-cover for the *Reichsevangeliar*. This is considered the most splendid of late medieval silversmiths' work.

1493 Germany Hartman Schedel's book *Weltchronik* produced by the workshop of Michael Wolgemut in a combination of woodcut and letterpress: Dürer learned woodcutting technique and design under Wolgemut (1434–1519).

1494 Establishment in Venice of the Aldine Press by Aldus Manutius (c.1450–1515), the first printer to design a small book useful for the student.

c.1495 Italy Tomb of Pope Innocent VIII by the goldsmith and bronze-founder Antonio Pollaiuolo (c.1432–1498): he was reputed to have anticipated Leonardo in his scientific study of anatomy.

1497 Italy Michelangelo Buonarroti (1475–1564) was commissioned to carve his first *Pieta*, considered the culmination of the Florentine tradition in sculpture.

VISUAL ARTS

1490–1500 Italy The Venetian painter Vittore Carpaccio (active 1490–1523) painted his cycle on the *Life of St Ursula*. He specialized in narrative paintings crowded with detail.

1490 Japan Death of Masanobu (b. 1453), credited with founding the *Kano* school of painting: this reflected not the scholar-artist but the highly-trained professional with the ideals of an aristocratic military tradition.

1490 Spain *Pietà* in Barcelona cathedral by Bartolomé Bermejo (fl. 1474–1495), one of the earliest Spanish oil paintings. Bermejo worked in Hispano-Flemish style with powerful realism.

c.1490 Italy Leonardo da Vinci made his drawing of a *cannon foundry*. Throughout his working life he made numerous drawings of armaments, and once described himself as 'an artificer of instruments of war'. The drawing conveys the awesome size and power of the cannon, and the violent physical effort of the massed workers surrounding it.

1491 Germany Death of Martin Schongauer (b. c.1430), painter and engraver. His engravings were widely admired and imitated, and are considered the first versions of popular religious images to be valuable as art. His paintings show the influence of van der Weyden, whose work he copied, but lack the Fleming's interest in realism.

1495–1497 Italy *The Last Supper* by Leonardo da Vinci.

1496 Spain Queen Isabella brought the Fleming Juan de Flandes (d. c.1519) to be court painter in Castile. Commercial contact between Spain and the Netherlands fostered a taste for Flemish art during the period c.1440–1500.

INVENTIONS & DISCOVERIES

*1490
Da Vinci observed capillary action of liquids in narrow tubes.*

*1491
Portuguese expedition to Angola.*

*1492
Christopher Columbus discovered West Indies.
Da Vinci designed a flying machine.*

*1493
Columbus discovered Jamaica.*

*1495
Giorgio Martini invented military mines.*

1498 Germany Low German version of the fable of *Renard the Fox*; the work is satirical, characteristic of Low German literature at this period.

Germany: detail from 'The Apocalypse' by Dürer

1499 Switzerland became an independent republic.

1499, 1502 Spain *La Celestina*, the first great Spanish novel: written from classical and medieval sources, it told the story of the ill-fated lovers Calisto and Melibea and their go-between, the bawd Celestina. The earlier version (published 1499) was in 16 acts, most of which are attributed to Fernando de Rojas, a novelist of Jewish origins. He may also have been responsible for a further five acts added in 1502. The novel was a source of inspiration to many Spanish playwrights and novelists.

late 1400–1500 France Extreme formalism in poetry was practised by the 'Grands Rhétoriqueurs', a group led by Georges Chastellain (?1405–1475), historiographer to Charles the Bold, Duke of Burgundy.

1499 Spain *Calisto Y Melibea* by Fernando de Rojas: although this is a novel in dramatic form and was probably never intended for the stage, it is the first Spanish work to portray lifelike characters through dialogue.

1499 England The University of Oxford instituted degrees in music.

ARCHITECTURE

1498–1515 France The east wing of Blois Château was built with the famous staircase in which Renaissance style is applied to the Gothic concept of a spiral stair.

1498 Germany The walls of Nuremburg Custom House are only three storeys high but the enormous roof rises a further 6 storeys, a typical German feature.

1499 Italy Giulio Romano born (died 1546), one of the first mannerist architects and Raphael's assistant.

THREE DIMENSIONAL ART

1498–c.1541 Spain Felipe Vigarny (Biguerney) active; a sculptor from Langres, he brought Flemish and Burgundian features into Spanish Renaissance art. He carved Christ bearing the cross for the high altar of Burgos Cathedral in 1498; his last work was in Toledo Cathedral choir-stalls. He was praised for his versatility, which was characteristic of the Renaissance.

1498–1504 Spain Reredos of Toledo Cathedral in polychrome wood represents, with that of Seville Cathedral (1482–1525) the culmination of Castilian coloured wood sculpture.

1498 Portugal Vasco da Gama brought ornate cotton cloth called 'chintz' to Europe from the east. Its attraction was its fast colour and durability.

1498 Russia Helen of Moldavia, wife of the Tzarevich, directed her own embroiderers in making a panel of the Palm Sunday procession: she used Wallachian stitches and colours. Her mother-in-law Sophia Paleologina, a Byzantine princess, had her own workshop which used Roman as well as Wallachian techniques.

1499 Persia Beginning of the Safavid dynasty (ended 1736), the most celebrated period in the design of carpets. These are divided into categories according to their design: animal, hunting, garden vase and medallion. Many were made in silk.

late 1400–1500 Italy Discovery of the classical Greek statue called the *Apollo Belvedere*, considered for 400 years the finest achievement of Greek art, and widely copied.

late 1400–1600 Italy Production of *sgraffito* pottery, especially at Bologna, was inspired by Islamic and Byzantine ware.

VISUAL ARTS

1498 Germany *The Apocalypse*, woodcuts by Albrecht Dürer (1471–1528). Dürer was also a painter, but has always been more celebrated for his woodcuts, engravings and drawings. In his youth he was taught drawing by his father, a goldsmith, and apprenticed to a book illustrator and woodcut artist. He came into early contact with humanism and pre-Reformation religious thought, and both are reflected in his subject matter.

1499–1504 Italy Frescoes in Orvieto cathedral on the *End of the World* and the *Last Judgment* by Luca Signorelli (1441?–1523): they showed a sculptural approach to figures and movement, and vigorous treatment of the nude. In this respect he was considered second only to Michelangelo.

INVENTIONS & DISCOVERIES

1498 Columbus discovered Trinidad and mainland of South America, John Cabot explored Labrador, Hudson Bay and east coast of North America., Portuguese Vasco da Gama reached India by sea.

1499 Amerigo Vespucci and Alonso Hojeda discovered Guiana and Venezuela.

16th Century

LITERATURE

early 1500–1600 Spain *El Abencerraje* was an anonymous Spanish novel about a Spanish commander who frees his prisoner, a Moor, so that the latter can marry his fiancée. The material was used by later writers, including Lope de Vega.

1500 Germany First collection of stories of 'Till Eulenspiegel': the son of a Brunswick peasant, Till is the hero of these farcical tales in Low German, which recount the pranks he plays on authority by pretending to misunderstand their directions. Anecdotes of this type, popular in German literature during the fifteenth and sixteenth centuries, were called *schwank*.

DANCE & DRAMA

*c.*1500–1600 **France** First record of *Moresque* and *Les Bouffons* dances in Europe: the *Moresque* was a Morris jig, *Les Bouffons* was a sword dance. Both were danced by men only.

*c.*1500–1600 **France** The sarabande became a court dance: having begun as a lascivious dance which was temporarily suppressed, it had been much refined.

MUSIC

1500–1600 England Harmonizations of the Gregorian tones in the Anglican chant were adopted by English composers and used in the English psalter after the Reformation.

*c.*1500 **Italy** Birth of Andrea Amati in Cremona (d. *c.*1575), the earliest recorded member of the family of violin makers who flourished in the sixteenth and seventeenth centuries. Nicolo Amati (1596–1684), probably the greatest member, became master of Antonio Stradivari (1644–1737).

*c.*1500 **Italy** Birth of Giovanni Animuccia (d.1571). A friend of St Philip Neri, he composed *Laudi spirituali* for his oratory. He published a book of masses in 1567.

*c.*1500 **Spain** Birth of Cristobal de Morales, composer (d. 1553).

Italy: an example of an Amati-made violin, 1620

ARCHITECTURE

1500–1600 China The Lingering Gardens of Suchow are in the tradition of Chinese buildings blending with surrounding gardens and natural landscape; here they also make characteristic use of water.

c.1500 England The roof of the church of St Wendreda, March, Cambridgeshire, is a double hammerbeam, decorated with wooden angels. English builders of provincial churches produced a spectacular perpendicular style for rival patrons.

c.1500 France Albi Cathedral. Coro, is a good example of the most developed form of late Gothic architecture, in which infinitely complex forms and detail were especially adaptable to small-scale works; a further example occurs in the cathedral south porch of 1519.

c.1500 France Josselin Castle, Brittany, was orginally an immensely strong fourteenth-century castle, transformed into a country house with flamboyant-style decoration.

c.1500 France The church of St Maclou, Rouen, typifies flamboyant and spectacular Gothic with much decoration for its own sake; the recurring motif is the 'flame' shape that gave the name. The structure is hidden by layers of lace-pattern stonework.

c.1500 Peru Machu Picchu is a ruined Inca town built entirely of stone cut to regular size; it is sited on terraced platforms on a steep mountainside.

c.1500 Portugal The Belem Monastery tentatively introduces Renaissance ornament to late Gothic doorways and piers.

c.1500 Portugal The Convento do Cristo, Tomar, is a western extension to the old Templar church; its rich decoration suggests Eastern influence. The lower west window of the chapter house is a monument to Vasco da Gama.

THREE DIMENSIONAL ART

early 1500–1600 Italy Niculoso Italiano of Pisa began to design tiled panels which made a single picture, in place of the traditional repetitive Moorish abstract design.

1500–1600 America Introduction of the potter's wheel.

1500–1600 Caucasus Blue-and-white pottery introduced at Kubachi, copied from Ming blue-and-white ware.

1500–1600 France Establishment of a school of ivory-carving at Dieppe.

1500–1600 Germany Ironsmiths were stimulated by designs drawn by Dürer and another German engraver, Virgil Soils (1514–62); motifs based on the arabesque, and calligraphic interlace, remained the foundation of their style for a century.

1500–1600 Italy Production of maiolica pottery at Castel Durante, Caffaggiolo, Gubbio, Urbino and Venice. Potters from Faenza went to France, Spain and the Netherlands, and maiolica from northern Europe is called faience.

1500–1600 Italy Merchants imported Chinese porcelain, which was well known and much copied in Europe by 1600.

1500–1600 Japan The introduction of cotton was a stimulus to the technique of resist-dyeing, to which the material was well suited. The Japanese had imported the technique from China in the seventh century and developed it in their own way.

1500–1600 Russia Embroidery styles changed with the introduction of couched metal threads and filled backgrounds.

1500–1600 Ukraine Revival of the medieval glass industry, making mosaic cubes, bangles, rings and vessels.

1500 Turkey Introduction at Iznik of a white pottery, slip-washed in white then coloured and finished with a transparent glaze.

VISUAL ARTS

1500 Germany The Italian engraver Jacopo de' Barbari (active c.1497–1516) was brought to work for the Emperor Maximilian. His engravings were important in spreading the 'new Italian style' through Germany and the Netherlands, where he influenced Jan Gossaert ('Mabuse') and the Flemish painter Bernaert van Orley (c. 1490–1541).

1500 Italy Sandro Botticelli (1445–1510) painted the *Mystic Nativity*: it is characteristic of his later work, in which decoration was subordinated to an ecstatic intensity. Its inscription, 'on the Apocalypse', implied an expectation of the end of the world.

1500 Italy Pietro Vannucci Perugino of Umbria (c.1450–1523) painted the Audience Chamber of the Collegio del Cambio at Perugia, working with Raphael. His contemporary Agostino Chigi called him 'the best painter in Italy' and he was admired by the pre-Raphaelites. He has also been considered over sentimental.

c.1500 India Mandu in central India was ruled by a tolerant Moslem ruler Nazir-ud-din (1469–1512) under whom art flourished. The best-known work was the *Niamat-nama*, a work on food and its preparation illustrated with scenes of court life. Persian and Jain influences mingle in its style.

INVENTIONS & DISCOVERIES

1500
Pedro Cabral discovered Brazilian coast and secured it for Portugal.

HISTORICAL EVENTS	LITERATURE	DANCE & DRAMA	MUSIC

1501
Persecution of
Moors in Spain.

1502
End of second
period of Aztec
conquest in
Mexico.

1503
Julius II became
Pope.

1501 Dalmatia Death of Djordje Držić (b. 1461), whose poems were mainly imitations of Petrarch. He is the earliest poet of this region whose work still survives.

1503 Scotland *The Thrissil and the Ros* by William Dunbar (*c.*1460–*c.*1515), court poet to James IV. Highly versatile, technically vigorous and accomplished, he wrote satire, burlesque, and all the conventional medieval forms: allegory, love debate, vision, complaint etc. He used the alliterative line, octosyllabic couplets and a variety of stanza forms.

1501 Italy Ottaviano de Petrucci (1466–1539), music printer, established in Venice in 1498, where he published *Harmonie Musices Odhecaton* which was printed with moveable type, the notes being printed in black and the staves separately in red.

1502 Flanders First book of masses by Josquin des Prés (*c.*1450–1521), composer. His motets also began to be published at this time.

Italy: Tempieto of Saint Pietro in Montorio, Rome, by Bramante

1505 Flanders A book of masses by Mabriano de Orto (d. 1529), composer, printed by Petrucci.

ARCHITECTURE

1502–1510 Italy Tempieto of St Pietro in Montorio, Rome, by Bramante is a tiny circular building with a Doric peristyle and a source work for Bramante designs for St Peter's Rome.

1503–1512 England Henry VII's Chapel, Westminster Abbey, London, by Robert (died 1506) and William (died 1527) Vertue, is a late perpendicular building with a complex system of pendant vaults and lavish decoration.

1503 France Salses Castle, Roussillon, was revolutionary in no longer having high walls easily destroyed by artillery; instead it is concealed and protected by the natural lie of land. It was later destroyed.

1505–1509 Russia The cathedral of St Michael the Archangel, Moscow, was rebuilt by the Italian Alevisio Novi (flourished 1490–1510) to serve as the burial place of the Tsars. The interior depended still on the style used in Vladimir, while the exterior for the first time displays Renaissance decorative details and was an important source of inspiration for buildings that followed.

THREE DIMENSIONAL ART

*c.*1500 **Europe** Introduction of geometrical facet-cutting for gemstones, a process which had been discovered by Indian lapidaries: this greatly stimulated the use of diamonds, previously considered too hard to cut and uninteresting uncut. European jewellery was made thereafter as a setting for the brilliance of an individual stone.

*c.*1500 **Germany** Beginning of the fashion for carved and painted altarpieces, in which south Germany was particularly prolific.

*c.*1500 **Italy** Discovery of classical Greek sculpture, which had lost its colour, and Roman sculpture, which had never been coloured, influenced a move away from polychrome medieval figures, and towards work that revealed and exploited the natural surface of the material.

*c.*1500 **Japan** Potters began to make simple rustic ware for the tea ceremony, *raku* pottery. It was mainly hand, not wheel, made, of low-fired earthenware soft-glazed with one colour.

*c.*1500 **Venice** Beginning of the movement towards clear glass resembling rock crystal; this had at first a greyish tone.

1501–1504 Italy Michelangelo Buonarroti carved *David*; larger than life-size and in marble, it was considered the embodiment of the Renaissance heroic spirit.

1501 Italy Invention of a new typeface by Aldus Manutius, based on the fashionable cursive script. His convenient octavo-size books required a smaller type than that used for library folios. The italic letter derives from this type of 1501; he also designed a Greek type which set a fashion for three hundred years.

1501 Spain Enrique de Arfe of Léon was commissioned to make a monstrance for Léon Cathedral, which took 21 years to finish: he was the best-known Spanish silversmith of the period and his son and grandson followed him in the craft.

VISUAL ARTS

1503 Italy *Mona Lisa* by Leonardo da Vinci: the painting is characteristic of his use of shadow and subdued colour to convey the mysterious.

1504–1508 Italy The Florentine painter Fra Baccio Bartolommeo (*c.*1475–1517) was a formative influence, with Raphael, on the new Christian imagery of the Virgin and Saints: the Virgin became the pivot of the whole composition, and the Holy Family was seen in a landscape. Bartolommeo was particularly noted for his drawings, which best expressed his religious mysticism.

1504–1504 Italy Leonardo da Vinci painted a fresco *The Battle of Anghiari* for the Palazzo Vecchio, Florence. It was destroyed in 1565; the drawings remain and indicate the artist's concern with human and animal bodies in violent action.

1504 Germany Lucas Cranach (1472–1553) painted the *Rest on the Flight into Egypt*, which shows the Holy Family resting in a German landscape. Cranach's early pictures were innovatory in using landscape to establish a mood.

1504 Italy Michelangelo Buonarotti (1475–1564) was commissioned to paint a battle scene for the Palazzo Vecchio. The surviving cartoon of one section, *The Bathers*, was a model for younger artists, including Raphael; it was one of the main stimuli to the Mannerist concern with the nude figure in violent action.

*c.*1504–1508 **Italy** Raphael (Raffaello Sanzio, 1483–1520) spent some years in Florence where he was impressed by the work of Michelangelo and Leonardo. During his Florentine period he painted versions of the Virgin and Child which emphasize the human family group, and express holiness as an inner quality, not stated by conventional symbols.

*1504
Cape Breton
discovered by
French fishermen.*

HISTORICAL EVENTS	LITERATURE	DANCE & DRAMA	MUSIC

1506 England *The Pastime of Pleasure*, a poem by Stephen Hawes (*c.*1475– before 1530) combining romantic with didactic allegory.

1506 Germany *Rudimenta Linguae Hebraicae* by Johann Reuchlin (1455–1522), a humanist who introduced the study of Hebrew into Germany; the book is a Hebrew grammar and lexicon. His tolerance of sacred Jewish literature made him enemies who are satirized in the anonymous *Epistolae Obscurorum Virorum*, a famous vindication of humanism.

1507 Dalmatia Love poems by Sisko Menčetić (1457–1527), whose work showed Italian influences.

1507 Germany *Melopoeiae sive Harmoniae Tetracenticae* (by Tritonius) printed by Erhart Oeglin, the first work to be printed in Germany using Petrucci's invention of moveable metal types.

1507 Italy The first printed instrumental music, Francesco. Spinaccino's *Lute Intabulatura*, marked the rapid growth of instrumental music at this time.

*1508
Baghdad became
Persian province.*

1508 Italy *Cassaria* by Lodovico Ariost (1474–1533), one of the first Italian comic writers: his plays are about city life of the period, but modelled on ancient Roman comedies.

Germany: 'The Emperor Maximilian on Horseback' by Hans Burgkmair

ARCHITECTURE

1506–1626 Italy St Peter's, Rome, rebuilt; the design of Bramante, commissioned by Pope Julius III, was later altered by numerous other architects including Raphael, Peruzzi, Antonio de Sangallo the younger, Michelangelo (who began the dome), Giocomo della Porta and Dominico Fontana, who lengthened the nave and added the façade. The rebuilding of the basilica occupied every pope until its completion.

1506 Poland Royal castle on Wawel Hill, Cracow, was built by Italians and has one of the earliest surviving Renaissance courtyards outside Italy.

1507 Hungary The chapel of Archbishop Tomas Bakocz, Esztergom, now part of the cathedral, is one of the earliest surviving Renaissance works north of the Alps based on Florentine buildings.

1507 Italy Giacomo Barozzi da Vignola born (died 1573), the leading architect in Rome following Michelangelo's death, and author of the influential *Regola delli cinque ordini* of 1562. He built the church of the newly founded Jesuit order in Rome (the Gesù), which combines medieval and Renaissance ideals of form. The nave was widened with a dome above the crossing, and the façade has large-scale scrolls uniting the wide lower with the narrow upper storey.

1508–1515 England King's College Chapel vaults, Cambridge by John Wastell (?–1515) were built; the chapel itself, begun in 1446, was completed with the finest of all fan-vaulted roofs.

1508 Italy Andrea Palladio born (died 1580), one of the most influential of Italian architects, particularly in Britain; he used classical forms with strict regard for proportion, particularly in domestic building, and the classical temple frontage, combined with dramatic flights of steps, on country villas.

1508–1604 Italy St Maria della Consolazione, Todi, by Cola da Caprarola (flourished 1494–1518) has a design based on the ideal of the Renaissance architects: centrally planned with a dome.

THREE DIMENSIONAL ART

1506 Italy Discovery of the sculpture group Laocoon, thought to be Hellenistic. Its influence, especially on Michelangelo, was due to its emotional impact.

1506 Portugal The Belem monstrance, made from gold brought from India by Vasco da Gama: it was Gothic in form, with a design of pinnacled towers above a group of apostles. Portuguese smiths of this period were especially noted for skill in embossing and chasing.

1507–1516 Italy Andrea Briosco, 'Il Riccio (1470–1532), sculptor, made the bronze Easter candlestick for the Santo in Padua, considered one of the greatest examples of expert bronze-casting. He treated Christian subjects in the idiom of classical mythology, and was famous for the beautiful finish of his bronzes.

1508–1519 Germany Bronze shrine of St Sebaldus in his church at Nuremberg was made by the Vischer family, important sculptors and bronze-founders who were influenced by Italian styles.

VISUAL ARTS

1506 Japan Death of Sesshu (*b.* 1420), considered the greatest fifteenth-century ink-painter. He began painting in a meticulous style and later adopted *Haboku* or the 'thrown ink' style which he took to a near-abstract degree. His school spread through most of Japan.

1507–1509 Spain Fernando Yanez collaborated with Fernando de Llanos (both fl. 1506–1525) to paint 12 panels of the life of the Virgin for the main altarpiece of Valencia cathedral. The style indicates that one of them was the 'Fernando Spagnuolo' working in 1505 with Leonardo da Vinci on *The Battle of Anghiari*.

1508–1512 Italy Michelangelo Buonarotti painted the ceiling frescoes of the Sistine chapel. The work gained him recognition as the greatest artist of his age.

1508–1509 Netherlands Jan Gossaert, called Mabuse (1478–1533 6) went to Italy in the service of Philip the Bastard, Duke of Burgundy. He was the first artist to bring Italian treatment of the nude and of mythology to the artists in the Netherlands.

1508 Germany *The Emperor Maximilian on Horseback* by Hans Burgkmair is the earliest dated chiaroscuro woodcut: this technique produced a three-dimensional effect by printing from several blocks in dark and light tones.

1508 Italy Raphael (1483–1520) began work on the frescoes for the Stanza della Segnatura in the Vatican, taking for his theme the relationship between classical learning and the Christian faith. Raphael is considered to have been the influence towards synthesis of these two primary inspirations of Renaissance art.

HISTORICAL EVENTS	LITERATURE	DANCE & DRAMA	MUSIC

1509 England *Moriae Encomium* by Desiderius Erasmus (d. 1536), the Dutch humanist and scholar; he was famous throughout Europe even during his life-time. His writings were in Latin.

1509 Germany *Fortunatus* was an anonymous prose narrative concerned with the search for riches, one of the great preoccupations of the sixteenth century.

*c.***1510 England** Dance performances by visiting troupes whose hosts joined in with them ('commoning') were reintroduced from Italy and became an element of the masque.

1510 Italy The first Roman musical publication *Canzoni Nove con Alcune Scelte de Varii Libri de Canto*, was published by Andrea Antico (b. 1470–8).

France: a bridge by Philibert de l'Orme. Gallery above by Jean Bullant

1511 France *Le Jeu du Prince des Sots* by Pierre Gringore (1475–1544), a political satire on Pope Julius II written to please Louis XII: it was a *sotie*, which is more topical than a farce but has a weaker plot. Gringore also wrote the first French play on a national theme: a mystery on the life of Louis IX.

1511 Germany The first extant music tutor for instruments, Sebastian Virdung's *Musica Getutscht*, has instructions for organ, lute and flute.

1512 England *God Be in My Head*, was translated into English from *Jesu soit en ma teste et mon entendement*, the earliest hymn with an exact date (1490).

1512 Germany Publication of *Spiegel der Orgelmacher und Orginisten* by Arnolt Schlick (b. *c.*1460), organist, lutenist and composer; it was the earliest appearance in print of organ pieces in German tablature.

1513
Scots allied with France defeated by the English at Flodden; death of James IV.

1513 Italy *Il Principe* by Niccolo Machiavelli (1459–1527), historian and political theorist: widely read in Europe, it is one of the most famous books on the art of government ever written, advocating political expediency with sharp intelligence and literary skill.

1513 England *Hickscorner*, an anonymous English moral interlude: it was similar to a morality but more humorous

1513 Germany Organ book in tablature written by Hans Kotter (*c.*1485–1541), Alsatian organist and composer; it is one of the earliest examples of the German school of organ playing.

1513 Italy Election of Pope Leo X. A member of the Medici family, the pope brought many leading French musicians to Rome and established a large professional body.

ARCHITECTURE

1508 Turkey In the Beyazid II Mosque, Istanbul, by Hayreddn, the use of space is very similiar to that of Hagia Sophia: undivided interior, covered by one main dome surrounded by two half domes; outside are the earliest surviving fully developed Ottoman minarets: multi-faced stalactite, balconied and very slim.

1509–1511 Italy Villa Farnesina, Rome, by Baldassare Peruzzi is an early example of a villa planned with a centre block and projecting wings; inside are brilliant frescoes by Raphael, Peruzzi and others.

*c.***1510 France** Philibert de l'Orme born (died 1570); he built the Tuileries with Jean Bullant (*c.*1520–1578) and the château at Anet (*c.*1552), where he used Gothic detail to decorate classical forms, while in the screen for St-Étienne-du-Mont, Paris (*c.*1545) he used Renaissance detail to decorate forms derived from Gothic.

*c.***1510 Portugal** Convent of Christ at Tomar, in the Manueline Gothic style, was very ornate and fantastic, using decorative motifs such as ropes, seaweed, shells and other sea images.

1512 Germany The nave of St Barbara, Kuttenburg, was built with double curved ribs producing an extreme effect of weightlessness, characteristic of late Gothic German vaulting.

1512 Spain Casa de las Conchas, Salamanca, is so called because the façade is decorated with carved scallop-shell decoration; the lower windows are barred with elaborate Moorish iron work.

1513–1546 Italy Palazzo Farnese, Rome, by Antonio da Sangallo the younger and Michelangelo is the largest in Rome and one of the most magnificent of Renaissance palaces.

THREE DIMENSIONAL ART

1509 Italy Roman goldsmiths were reorganized as a guild and built a church to their patron St Eligius. Rome remained a centre of fine gold and silver work; other centres were Turin, Genoa, Naples and Venice.

1509 Spain Italian sculptor Domenico di Sandro Fancelli (1469–1519) made the tomb of Cardinal Hurtado de Mendoza in Seville Cathedral: he was one of the first sculptors to introduce the Italian Renaissance style into Spain.

1511 Flanders The stained-glass artist Dirk Vellert (active 1511–1544) was made a master of the guild of St Luke in Antwerp: his painted glass is found in Germany, England and Spain.

1512 Spain Damián Forment (d. 1540), sculptor, carved the reredos of the church at Saragossa. His work forms a transition from Gothic to Renaissance; he had abandoned Gothic by 1527 in his reredos for the monastery church at Poblet, Tarragona.

VISUAL ARTS

1509 China Death of Shén Chou, outstanding calligrapher and painter in ink. He introduced genre scenes into his landscapes and was possibly the first to do so.

1510 Italy Marcantonio Raimondi (*c.*1480–*c.*1534), an engraver inspired by Dürer, began engraving the paintings of Raphael: he contributed greatly to the spread of Raphael's work, and that of other Renaissance artists, through Europe.

1510 Italy Death of the Venetian painter Giorgio Giorgione (b. 1475). His painting *The Tempest* is his first in which figures and landscape are subordinate to atmosphere, and this is done by manipulating colours. He was probably a pupil of Giovanni Bellini, whose influence he shows. His own innovations in conveying atmosphere were influential in their turn.

1510 Italy On the death of Giorgione, his pupil Titian (Tiziano Vecellio, *c.*1487–1576) completed many of the unfinished paintings. Titian's own work showed the influence of Giorgione until *c.*1515, when he painted *The Three Ages of Man.*

*c.***1510 Germany** The *Isenheim Altar* by Mathias Grunewald (Mathis Neithart called Gothart, *c.*1460–1528): his characteristic style was linear late Gothic, with strong colours, distorted limbs and faces, and great depth of expression. He stopped painting *c.*1525 when his patronage by the archbishop of Magdeburg was apparently ended by religious differences; his last religious paintings show more than usual strain.

1512 Germany *St Jerome in the Wilderness* by Albrecht Dürer (1471–1528) was one of his earliest works in drypoint engraving on copper. The engraving point throws up a ridge, or burr, beside its deeper lines, which retains ink and therefore provides part of the printed line.

1512 Italy Raphael (1483–1520) painted his *Sistine Madonna* showing the Virgin and Child as triumphant but nonetheless recognizably solid and human figures. He was concerned in much of his work with the mystery of the Incarnation, of divinity within human form.

INVENTIONS & DISCOVERIES

*1509
Peter Henle of
Nuremberg
invented watch.*

*1510
Da Vinci outlined
principles of
water turbine.*

*1512
Spaniard Juan
Ponce de Leon
discovered
Florida.*

*1513
Portuguese
crossed Panama
isthmus and
discovered Pacific
Ocean.*

HISTORICAL EVENTS	LITERATURE	DANCE & DRAMA	MUSIC
1515 *Thomas Wolsey created Cardinal, Archbishop of York and Chancellor in England.*	**1515–1521 Scotland** *Eclogues* by Alexander Barclay (?1475–1552) were the earliest pastoral poems in English. He also adapted Brant's *Narrenschiff* to satirize English society, in *The Shyp of Folys*.	**1515 England** *Magnyficence* by John Skelton (*c*.1460–1529): one of the best-known English moralities. **1515 Italy** *Sophonisba* by Giovanni Giorgio Trissino (1478–1550), not acted until 1524, was regarded as the first Italian tragedy: Trissino had read, but misunderstood, Aristotle's *Poetics*.	
1516 *Accession of Charles I in Spain united Spain, Sicily, Burgundy, Netherlands and Spanish America.* *1517* *Martin Luther protested against sale of indulgences; beginning of Reformation. Ottoman Turks entered Cairo; end of Mamluk empire.* *1519* *Charles I of Spain became Emperor Charles V.*	**1516 England** *Utopia* by the humanist Sir Thomas More (1478–1535): the book is an allegorical account of an ideal society. **1516 Italy** *Orlando Furioso*, a romantic epic by the poet Ludovico Ariosto (1474–1533): the poem is a sequel to Boiardo's *Orlando Innamorato*. A skilful narrator and psychologist, Ariosto ridiculed knights and the code of chivalry which they followed. He was a detached writer, though capable of conveying deep emotion when necessary. **1516 Portugal** *Cancionero Geral* was an anthology of fifteenth- and sixteenth-century Portuguese poetry, composed at court as a form of diversion. Many of the contributing poets wrote in both Portuguese and Spanish. One of the best-known poets in the collection was Francisco de Sá de Miranda (1481–1558), who introduced Italian influences into Portuguese poetry. **1518 India** Death of the mystic Kabir (b. 1440), whose hymns have been translated by Rabindranath Tagore. He had considerable influence on the founder of the Sikh religion, Nanak.	**1516 Italy** *Rosmunda* by Giovanni Rucallai (1475–1525): as a dramatist, Rucallai followed the precepts of Trissino. **1517–1519 Portugal** *Trilogis de Las Barcas* by Gil Vicente (*c*.1465–*c*.1537), dramatist to the Portuguese court: he wrote moralities which strongly influenced the development of the *auto sacramental*, (Spanish mystery), but also produced lavish allegorical spectacles to entertain the court. **1517 Spain** Bartolome de Torres Naharro (*c*.1480–*c*.1530), Spain's first dramatic critic, published *Propalladia*, in which he described and demonstrated two types of comedy: comedy of manners and romantic comedy.	**1516 England** John Gaschet, probably the first English provincial music publisher, settled in York and published his first book, a Missal. **1516 Italy** A school of music was founded in Rome by Pietro Aaron (*c*.1490–1545), the Italian theorist. The first of his many works of writings on music, *Libri Tres de Institutione Harmonica*, was published. **1519 Flanders** First known works by Jean Richafort (*c*.1480–*c*.1547), composer, pupil and distinguished successor of Josquin des Prés.

ARCHITECTURE

1514–1536 England Hampton Court Palace was built for Cardinal Wolsey but used as a royal palace; it retains some Tudor late Gothic work, especially the Great Hall, built of brick with large perpendicular windows and a fine hammerbeam roof. It was altered later.

1514–1529 Spain The university façade, Salamanca, has Plateresque design incorporating both Gothic and Renaissance motifs applied to the surface of the building. An ornate style peculiar to Spain at this period.

1515–1524 France Blois Château, Francis I wing, includes the famous spiral staircase and introduces Renaissance architecture to France.

1516 Italy Villa Madama, Rome, by Raphael and others is unfinished but intended to recreate a classical villa with a great hillside garden; the interior decoration was also by Raphael and his pupils.

1519–1550 France Château Chambord built; Frenchmen saw Italian Renaissance buildings during the Franco-Italian wars (c.1500–1520) and so classical elements were incorporated in French buildings, sometimes, as at Chambord, modifying the form, but usually for decoration on a Gothic structure.

1519–1533 Poland Sigismund Chapel, Wawel Hill, Cracow, set the pattern in Poland for a Renaissance chapel as a centrally planned building carrying a dome with a lantern.

THREE DIMENSIONAL ART

1515 Flanders Pieter Coecke van Aelst, one of the leading Flemish weavers, made a set of tapestries illustrating *The Acts of the Apostles* for Pope Leo X, working from cartoons by Raphael: the tapestries were in Renaissance style and made a break with Flemish Gothic tradition.

c.1515 France Statue of St Martha in the Church of the Magdalene, Troyes, marks a return to a controlled, intense style of sculpture which is quite different from the emotional, dramatic treatment of the previous century.

1517 Germany Death of Konrad Seusenhofer (born 1450/60), leading member of a family of armourers who were all in the service of the Emperor. Others were Hans (1470–1555) and Jörg (1500/1505–1580).

1517 Spain Bartolomé Ordoñez (d. 1520) sculptor, carved a series of reliefs in Renaissance style for the choir of Barcelona Cathedral: his work showed the first impact of the Italian Renaissance.

1518 Spain Return from Italy of the painter and sculptor Alonso Berruguete (c.1488–1561) to become court painter to Charles I (later Emperor Charles V): he made composite reredoses of paintings, carved relief and figures sculpted in the round; that of St Benito, Valladolid (1526) is typical.

1519 Netherlands Accession of the Emperor Charles V (Charles I of Spain): he commissioned many Flemish tapestries and hangings woven in Brussels, Oudenarde, Bruges, Ghent, Lille, Louvain and Valenciennes achieved a high reputation throughout Europe.

1519 Spain The iron choir screen in Seville Cathedral was made by Sancho Muñez: an early example of Renaissance style in Spanish iron-work, it had pillars decorated with repoussé work, Corinthian capitals and spindled balusters with elaborate cresting.

VISUAL ARTS

1515 Italy Death of the painter Vincenzio Foppa (b. c.1427), who was important in developing the Renaissance style in Lombardy and Milan.

1516–1518 Italy Titian (c.1487–1576) painted his *Assumption of the Virgin* for Santa Maria dei Frari, Venice. This was the first of a series of important altarpieces culminating in the Pesaro altarpiece of 1519–1526. His style at this period anticipated the baroque in its drama and contrasts of primary colour. At the same time it showed a celebration of the human body which was equally strong in pagan and Christian subjects.

1516 Netherlands Death of Hieronymus Bosch, a painter from northern Brabant who became successful and was imitated in his lifetime. He painted grotesque fantasies peopled by horrific creatures, but his most influential gift was for landscape.

1517 Netherlands Quentin Massys (1465–1530) painted portraits of Erasmus and Petrus Egidius as presents for Sir Thomas More. He was a noted portraitist, and painted many satirical studies of bankers and men of business.

1518 Germany The altar of St Florian, near Linz, by Albrecht Altdorfer (c.1485–1538) typified his interest in placing figures in landscape. His feeling for landscape was similar to that of Cranach. Both were influential on the 'Danube school'.

1519 Germany Hans Holbein (1497/8–1543) painted his portrait of Bonifacius Amerbach in Basel. Its style suggests contact with Italian work; the colours and modelling are warmer and more subtle than in earlier paintings.

*1514
Portuguese established bases for Chinese trade at Malacca.*

*1515
Introduction of German wheellock pistol.*

*1517
Spaniard Fernando de Cordova discovered Mexico.*

*1519
Portuguese Ferdinand Magellan began first circumnavigation of the world.*

LITERATURE

1520 Germany *Eccius Deolatus* was a satire of the Reformation, possibly by Willibald Pirckheimer (1470–1530), a leader of Nuremberg cultural life and a true 'Renaissance Man': courtier, soldier, scientist and humanist.

1521 Dalmatia *Judita* by Marko Marulić (1450–1524), poet and scholar: an epic poem on the biblical Judith, it was the first known work printed in Croatian.

1521 Germany *Gesprächsbüchlein* by Ulrich von Hutten (1488–1523), knight, humanist, and journalist. His earliest writings were in Latin; after 1520 he used German. He was the first German writer to use dialogue in popular literature. His work was satirical, and he appears in later German literature as a militant supporter of freedom and herald of the Reformation.

1522 Germany Translation of the New Testament into German by the reformer Martin Luther (1483–1546). He translated the Old Testament in the following year. He based his work on the Hebrew of Reuchlin and the Greek of Erasmus, following the sense, rather than the literal meaning, of the original and using vivid, colloquial German.

1522 Germany *Von dem grossen Lutherischen Narren* by Thomas Murner (1475–1537), monk and satirist. His work was vigorous and witty, written in homely German.

1522 Spain Commentary on St Augustine's *City of God* by Juan Luis Vives (1492–1540), a humanist writing in Latin.

DANCE & DRAMA

1520 Italy Angelo Beolco, known as Ruzzante, (*c.*1501–1542) performed in Venice. Although his plays are fully written out and not a basis for improvisation, he has often been associated with the origins of the *commedia dell'arte* tradition of popular improvised drama. Each member of a *commedia dell'arte* troupe was the exclusive player of a particular character. The theatrical descendants of many of these characters still survive: Harlequin, Columbine, Pierrot, Punch. But the *commedia dell'arte* tradition itself is now lost.

*c.***1520 Rome, Italy** Records of Italian aristocrats learning to dance *alla francesca*: France had by this time displaced Italy as the leader of fashionable dance, though not as leader in professional dancing. Italian professionals were still in demand for entertainments in France.

1521 England Coplande published *The Maner of dauncynge of Bace daunces after the use of Fraunce.*

Germany: portrait of Martin Luther by Lucas Cranach

MUSIC

1520 France Robert Fayrfax (1464–1521), English composer, led royal singers in France at the Field of the Cloth of Gold, an event which gave an opportunity for French and English musicians to hear each other. William Cornyshe (d. *c.*1523) composer, supervised the Chapel Royal ceremonies.

1520 Italy Birth of Vincenzo Galilei (d. 1591), amateur lutenist and composer and father of the astronomer Galileo Galilei. His writings on music were of considerable interest including *Il Fronimo* (Venice 1568).

1520 Italy Birth of Andrea Gabrieli (d. 1586), organist and the most original composer between Willaert and Palestrina.

1521 England The first known printed collection of carols was produced by Wynkyn de Worde (d. 1534), the Alsatian printer, who had settled in London.

1521 Netherlands Birth of Philippe de Monte, composer (d. 1603), a most prolific writer who composed nearly 1200 madrigals and songs, as well as church music.

ARCHITECTURE

1520 Italy The architecture and sculpture of the St Lorenzo, Medici Chapel, Florence, are by Michelangelo, and together create an imposing mannerist mausoleum.

1521–1541 Dominican Republic Santo Domingo Cathedral is a late Gothic colonial architecture and has a Plateresque west façade.

THREE DIMENSIONAL ART

1520–1530 Spain Iron screen to the Royal Chapel, Granada Cathedral, was made by Master Bartolomeo, sculptor and smith: its three tiers of twisted bars were divided by two large-scale friezes and surmounted by a cresting of arabesques and candelabra decorated with scenes from the life of Christ. Spanish screens of the Renaissance surpassed anything previously achieved in iron; the art declined after *c.*1600.

c.1520 England The Italian sculptor Giovanni da Maiano made terracotta roundels of the Roman emperors for Hampton Court. Although not distinguished in themselves they are among the earliest decorations in Renaissance style on English buildings.

1522–1566 China Overglaze green enamel, made from copper, was introduced for ceramics.

VISUAL ARTS

1520 Italy Antonio Allegri Correggio (*c.*1489–1534) painted the dome of St Giovanni Evangelista in Parma, using the illusionist technique of Mantegna which he developed to a degree resembling baroque style. His ceiling paintings and altarpieces had unorthodox composition with bold effects of form and light. His work was studied by Annibale Carracci and other painter-decorators.

1520 Italy On the death of Raphael in Rome, several of his works were completed by his pupil and assistant Giulio Romano (*c.*1499–1546). In this and in his own later work Romano showed a melodramatic development of Raphael's style. He is considered one of the first Mannerist painters.

c.1520 Netherlands Joachim Patenier (*c.*1480–1524) painted *Paysage avec haut Fourneau*: one of the earliest industrial paintings, showing a blast-furnace. The Reformation inspired artists to glorify the common man at the expense of the Spanish Catholic establishment.

1521 Italy *The Marriage of St Catherine* by Francesco Mazzola Parmigianino (1503–1540) shows his distinctive style of linear figure painting with elongated forms. His slightly exaggerated Mannerist elegance was very popular and widely imitated, particularly the elongation of the figures, taken to extreme in the *Madonna with the Long Neck*. He was one of the earliest Italian artists to take a serious interest in etching, for which he made his own designs and plates.

1521 Netherlands Dürer described Joachim Patenier (*c.* 1480–1524) as a very good landscape artist. He was the first Netherlandish artist to allow landscape to dominate the scene: in this respect he presages Bruegel. In his colour scheme—brown or green foreground, green middle distance and blue background—and in his structures of landscapes he followed convention and created an artificial scene.

1522–1560 China Active period of Ch'u Ying, noted for his detailed paintings of court and banquet scenes and of beautiful women.

HISTORICAL EVENTS	LITERATURE	DANCE & DRAMA	MUSIC

*1523
Europeans
expelled from
China.*

LITERATURE

1523 Germany *Die Wittenbergische Nachtigall*, an allegorical poem in support of Luther by Hans Sachs (1494–1576), poet and dramatist and a master cobbler. His work was genial, humorous and sensible, and included *schwank* and *meisterliede* (moralistic poems following strict formal patterns, derived from the work of thirteenth-century poets like Walther von der Vogelweide). He wrote in homely rhyming verse. He appears in Wagner's opera *Die Meistersinger Von Nurnberg*.

1524 Germany First of the *Geistliche Lieder* by Martin Luther: Luther's hymns and those of his followers, many of them adapted from secular songs of the period, are Germany's major contribution to sixteenth-century European literature. A revival of religious poetry followed their appearance.

1524 Italy *La Mandragola* by Nicolo Machiavelli (1469–1527): a comedy of contemporary Italian morals which completely accepts the corruption of Renaissance society.

1524 Germany Publication of the first German Protestant hymn-book, *Geystliche Gesangk Buchleyn*, containing some hymns by Martin Luther (1483–1546).

1525 Italy *Prose Della Volgar Lingua* by Pietro Bembo (1470–1547), writer and scholar. He supported the use of Italian as a fit medium for literature instead of Latin, suggesting Petrarch as a model. He wrote the first Italian grammar book.

1525 France *Breviarium Noviomense* was printed by Pierre Attaignant (d. 1552) who is said to have been the first in Paris to print music from moveable types.

1525 Italy Birth of Giovanni Pierluigi da Palestrina (d. 1594), composer, noted for the restraint and simplicity of his liturgical music.

*1526
Babur became
first Mogul ruler
in India.*

1526 India The Mughal emperor Muhammad Zahiruddin Babur (d. 1530) established the Mughal dynasty in Delhi, following the conquest of India. His colourful and entertaining autobiography is considered a masterpiece.

1526 England John Taverner (c.1495–1545), organist and composer, appointed Master of Choristers at Oxford and remained there for about three years, composing most of his famous church music in this time.

1526 Spain Antonio de Cabezon (1500–1566), one of the outstanding sixteenth century composers of keyboard music, a blind organist and clavichordist, was appointed to the Spanish court; he was one of the chief developers of musical forms and keyboard techniques.

ARCHITECTURE

1523 Italy Biblioteca Lauren-
ziana, Florence, is by Michelangelo and the vestibule is the
architect's most perverse and
original mannerist building.

1524–1616 Spain St Estéban,
Salamanca, illustrates the
unique qualities of Spanish
architecture in combining
Plateresque, Gothic and Moorish styles.

1526 Italy Palazzo del Tè, Mantua, by Giulio Romano is a villa
planned around a central courtyard with a number of mannerist features; the Room of
Giants is a masterpiece of illusionary painting by Giulio
himself, who was a pupil of
Raphael, and his pupils.

1526–1550 Spain Unfinished
additions to the Alhambra,
Granada, by Pedro Machuca
(died 1550). The circular colonnaded courtyard introduced
Italian Renaissance architecture
to Spain.

THREE DIMENSIONAL ART

1525–1526 England The
Howard Grace Cup in silver and
ivory shows both Gothic and
Renaissance characteristics, although English metalwork was
slow to show Renaissance
influence.

1526–1531 Netherlands Effigy
of Margaret of Austria by Conrad Meit of Worms (c.1475–
1545) shows the first major
influence of the Italian Renaissance.

1526 India The Mogul ruler
Babur created a garden at Agra
on the Persian model, the first of
a number of great gardens designed for Moslem rulers in India and culminating in those at
the Taj Mahal. They embodied
the classical Persian symbolism
in their geometric design, emphasis on water and shade and
architectural setting.

VISUAL ARTS

1523–1526 Germany Hans
Holbein (1497/8–1543) designed 51 plates on *The Dance of
Death*, which reflected Reformation ideas. He had worked as
a printer's designer intermit-
tently since c.1515.

1523 China Death of T'ang
Yin, as academic painter known
for his paintings of women. He
used rich colours and a delicate
outlining technique; his popularity gave rise to many
limitations.

1523 Netherlands Death of
Gerard David, a painter noted
for his domestic scenes from the
life of Christ—in one painting
he shows the Virgin feeding the
Child with porridge. His work
was popular in his lifeime and
much copied.

1524 Netherlands The painter
Jan van Scorel (1495–1562) settled in Utrecht. His painting of
The Jerusalem Pilgrims was probably the earliest example of
Dutch group portraiture. He
was important in bringing together Northern and Re-
naissance elements in his work,
and his skill in landscape and
portraiture influenced Maerten
van Heemskerck (1498–1574)
and Moro.

1525 Japan Death of Tosa
Mitsunobu (b. 1434), con-
sidered the founder of the Tosa
school of painting: this claimed
to follow the fifteenth-century
masters and took its subjects
from old Japanese native tradition.

1525 Japan Death of Soami,
major ink-painter, considered
with Geiami one of the foremost
artists of the mature *suiboko*
style.

1526–1528 Italy Jacopo Ca-
rucci Pontormo (1494–1551)
painted the *Deposition* in Santa
Felicita, Florence: it is considered one of the major works of
the early Mannerist style in
Florence. Pontormo's style was
an unstable combination of Renaissance classicism and the
more nervous Mannerism.

1526 Germany Albrecht Dürer
(1471–1528)painted two panels
of the *Four Apostles* for the town
of Nuremberg. They reflect his
concern with proportion and his
contact (1505–1506) with Venetian painting.

INVENTIONS &
DISCOVERIES

*1525
Introduction of
square root sign
to Europe.*

HISTORICAL EVENTS	LITERATURE	DANCE & DRAMA	MUSIC

1527 Reformation effected in Sweden and Denmark.

1527 Switzerland *Chianzun dalla guerra dagl Chiastè da Müs* by Gian Travérs (1483–1563), Romansch poet and playwright: a vigorous political poem, it is the first extant work in Romansch.

1527 Flanders Adriano Willaert (*c.*1485–1562), composer, appointed *maestro di cappella* of San Marco, Venice, where he remained until his death. A distinguished composer of chansons and madrigals, he had a strong influence on later Italian composers.

1527 Spain Birth of Francisco Guerrero (d. 1599), a prolific composer of both sacred and secular works.

1528 Netherlands A collection of poems by Anna Bijns (1493–1575), a Dutch poet in the *rederijker* tradition. These were middle-class writers organized in 'Chambers of Rhetoric', societies like guilds, and practising certain established poetic and dramatic genres. They also held competitions. The name comes from the French *rhétoriqueurs*.

1528 Europe First appearance of violin bow having a nut to control tension of hair. Simpler types of bows had previously been used.

1528 Italy *Il Libro del Cortegiano* by Baldassare Castiglione (1478–1529), courtier, diplomat, and writer. The book is about the 'Renaissance Gentleman', and current social, political and philosophical ideas. It is considered a literary masterpiece, and was read throughout Europe.

1529–1530 France Attaignant published two volumes of tunes for dancing.

1529 Flanders First publication of works by Nicolas Gombert (*c.*1505–*c.*1556), one of the most important and prolific musicians of the school of Josquin des Prés.

1529 France First collection of songs by composer Clément Jannequin, (*c.*1475–*c.*1560) published by Attaignant.

1529 Germany Publication of *Musica Instrumentalis Deutsch* by Martin Agricola (1486–1556), writer on musical theory.

1530 League of Schmalkalden formed by Protestant states in Holy Roman Empire.

1530 Spain *Diálogo de la Lengua* by Juan de Valdés (?1490–1541), philologist and theologian. He spent the latter part of his life in Italy and was somewhat influenced by Bembo. The book discussed the need for a natural style and careful choice of words; it was not published until 1737.

1530 France Earliest known contract of *commedia dell' arte* players in France.

1530 France Étienne Briard, a music engraver, settled at Avignon; he replaced the square characters hitherto in use by round ones and devised a simple means of expressing the duration of a note.

?1530 Netherlands Probable date of *Basia* by Janus Secundus (1511–1536), a poet writing in Latin. This work, his most famous, is a love lyric.

1530 Italy Valerio Dorico published *Madrigali de Diversi Autori*; authors were Costanzo Festa (d. 1547) and Philippe Verdelot (d. *c.*1540).

1531 Italy *De Architecture* by Vitruvius (70–15 B.C.) was translated into Italian: Book V deals with theatre construction and was extensively used by Renaissance theatre designers.

1526 Germany Hans Holbein (1497/8–1543) painted the *Madonna of Burgomaster Meyer*. The figures of the Madonna and Child are outside the German tradition and represent a Renaissance ideal. The figures of the donors are realistic portraits.

1527 or 1528 Switzerland Death of Urs Graf, (b. *c.* 1485) goldsmith engraver and designer of stained glass.

1528–1540 France Palais de Fontainebleau was rebuilt by Gilles Le Breton (flourished 1527–1552) and it is especially famous for the richness of its interior decoration by Italian craftsmen. Their use of stucco and painted panels had great influence in Europe.

1528–63 Spain Granada Cathedral was designed by Diego de Siloé (*c.*1495–1563) and is a combination of classical architecture applied to a Gothic plan by an Italian-trained architect.

1530 France Francis I brought the Italian mannerist painter Giovanni Batista Rossa Fiorentino (1494–1540) to work at Fontainebleau, where his main work was the decoration of the Galerie François I. He helped to found a French mannerist style, partly by the wide dissemination of his designs in engraving.

1530 France Death of Jean Perreal (fl. from *c.*1483), painter, sculptor, decorator and architect: his main interest in painting was portraiture and his contemporary reputation was high.

1529 France Geofroi Tory (1480–1533), printer, wrote and published *Champ Fleury*, a discussion on the design of Roman letters: he was influential in developing French Renaissance book design.

*c.***1530–1590 Italy** Central period of the style of painting called mannerism, in which the serene harmony of the classical ideal of the Renaissance became valued mainly for its elegance. Artists sought to improve on this elegance with increasingly fertile invention in line, movement and contrast; their ingenuity sometimes overbalanced into a self-conscious virtuosity, the results becoming eccentric or bizarre. The style was influential throughout Europe.

*c.***1530 Spain** Juan de Herrera was born (died 1597); trained in Italy, his high Renaissance style was influential in Spain and its colonies.

*c.***1530 Italy** Palazzo Pompeii, Verona, by Michele Sanmichel (1484–1559) was one of several buildings in Verona and Venice by this architect in a classical mannerist style.

1530 France First appearance, in printing by Robert Estienne (1503–1559), of types designed by Claude Garamond (1480–1561). He cut Roman, Greek, Italic and Black letter types; his Roman types prevailed in French printing until the eighteenth century.

*c.***1530 Italy** The Venetian painter Titian (*c.*1487–1576) turned to a restrained and contemplative style on the death of his wife. His colours became quieter and his compositions still. This style lasted until *c.*1543, when his former vigour was re-stimulated by mannerist influence.

1531–1612 Germany The medieval castle of Heidelberg was enlarged with Renaissance-style buildings.

1531 Italy Andrea Alciati published *Emblemata*, the first and most influential emblem book. Emblem books were collections of visual images and devices, jewels, animals, flowers and so on, with explanations of their symbolism; their sources were Biblical, classical and medieval.

1530 Portugal established colonies in Brazil.

HISTORICAL EVENTS	LITERATURE	DANCE & DRAMA	MUSIC

HISTORICAL EVENTS

1531
Pizarro captured Inca capital of Cuzco.

1533
Accession of Ivan IV (the Terrible) in Moscow.

1534
Henry VIII recognized as supreme head of English church. Foundation of Society of Jesus (Jesuits), Paris.

1536
Suppression of monasteries began in England.

LITERATURE

1531 England *The Boke of the Governor* by Sir Thomas Elyot (?1490–1546), diplomat, scholar and translator; he grasped the importance of the relationship between subject matter and style.

1531 Germany *Bergreihen*, one of the numerous collections of secular songs, many of which were adapted as hymns by Luther and his followers. Songs from these collections were still popular three centuries later.

1532 France *L'Adolescence Clémentine* by the poet Clément Marot (1496–1544). He used the medieval forms: *ballade, rondeau* etc., but was also the first Frenchman to use the sonnet, imported from Italy.

1532 France *Pantagruel* by François Rabelais (1490–1553/4), scholar, physician and writer: the book contained satire, burlesque, adventure, fantasy and exposition of his theories, and was written over a period of 20 years. *Gargantua* (1534) became book I, *Pantagruel* then became book II, followed by three further books, the last of which is possibly not authentic. His work is gross and humorous, his language inventive. Rabelais expresses the spirit of early humanism with its new-found freedom.

1533 Denmark *The Right way to the Kingdom of Heaven* by Christiern Pedersen (1480–1554), a historical and ecclesiastical writer. He edited a Danish/Latin dictionary, and helped to translate the Bible.

DANCE & DRAMA

1534 Spain Death of Enzina the playwright (b. 1469): his work included dance, which remained a traditional ingredient of Spanish plays.

1536 France Antonius de Arena published *Ad compagnones qui sunt de persona friantes, bassas dansas et branlos practicantes.* Its contents on the dance included a regular form for the previously unregulated *basse-danse.*

1538 Mexico Spanish religious plays were acted in Mexico on the feast of Corpus Christi.

MUSIC

1532 Germany Publication of *Musica Teusch auf die Instrument der Grossen. und Kleynen Geygen auch Lautten* (a book of instructions for the viol and lute) by lutenist Hans Gerle (d. 1570).

1533 Italy Publication of *Scintille di Musica* by Giovanni Maria Lanfranco, ecclesiastical writer on music; it gave valuable information about contemporary musical instruments.

1535 Spain Cristobal de Morales (c.1500–1553) joined the papal choir in Rome, where he remained for 10 years before returning to Spain.

1536 Italy Adriano Willaert (c.1485–1562) published his first collection of madrigals, followed by a second collection in 1559.

1536 Spain Publication of *Libro de Musica de Vihuela de Mano, Intitulado El Maestro* by Luis Milan (b. c.1500), lutenist and composer.

1537 Italy First book of madrigals published by Costanzo Festa (1490–1545). One of the earliest composers of the Roman church school, he holds a prominent position in historical development of Italian school of madrigalists.

1539 Germany First of five volumes of secular songs edited by Georg Forster (c.1514–1568), musical editor.

1539 Italy Jacques Arcadelt (1505–1567), Dutch composer, moved from Florence to Rome, where he became the first *magister cappellae* at the Julian Chapel. His first book of four-part madrigals, probably his most important volume, was published at this time and was reprinted for over 100 years.

1539 Italy Musical *intermedi* written for wedding of Cosimo I de Medici of Florence and Eleanora of Toledo; it was one of the first *intermedi* for which music has survived and it specifies the various ensembles of instruments which were used.

ARCHITECTURE

1532–1589 France St-Eustache, Paris, was designed with a Gothic plan and proportions but classical detail.

1532–1536 Italy Palazzo Massimialle Colonne, Rome, by Baldassare Peruzzi cleverly incorporated the palace on an irregular site with a curved façade; it has a number of curious mannerist decorative features.

1532 Russia The church of Ascension at Kolimenskoe, near Moscow is a unique structure in brick with a tall and angular mass of a central tower which encloses a rather simple interior.

1535 Czechoslovakia The Belvedere, summer palace of Prague Castle, was built by Italian architects on designs deriving from Brunelleschi's Foundling Hospital in Florence.

*c.***1536 Italy** The Villa Criciole, near Vicenza, by Giangiorgio Trissino (1478–1550) is based on Vitruvian descriptions and was an important influence on the Palladian villa.

1537 Italy Biblioteca Marianna, Venice, is by Jacopo Sansovino (1486–1570), an outstanding architect of sixteenth-century Venice, who introduced the high Renaissance style to the city; he also designed the Mint, the Loggia and also many palaces and churches.

1537 Italy First volume of *L'Architettura* by Sebastiano Serlio (1475–1554) was published; this was the first of 6 volumes which were to become the most popular source books on architecture in Europe in the sixteenth and seventeenth centuries.

1537–1553 Spain The Alcazar, Toledo, is a medieval castle rebuilt in the high Renaissance style with an especially fine two-storey arcade of Corinthian columns surrounding the central patio; it is now largely destroyed.

THREE DIMENSIONAL ART

1532 Germany The Apollo fountain, Nuremberg: probably made by the sculptor and bronze-founder Hans Vischer (1489–1550), who copied the figure from an Italian source.

1533 Netherlands Jean Mone (*c.*1500–*c.*1550), sculptor, made the High Altar of Notre Dame at Hal: he was court sculptor to Charles V of Burgundy and one of the main workers in the Italian style during the early sixteenth century.

1533 Russia Archbishop Makariy commissioned an elaborate wooden iconostasis, or screen, for Sta Sophia, Novgorod; it is the earliest surviving example of its kind, carved in flat, linear style for decorative rather than sculptural effect.

1534 Italy The Medici chapel in Florence was left unfinished when Michelangelo returned to Rome. Figures of Giulano and Lorenzo de Medici are set above figures of Day and Night, Dawn and Evening.

*c.***1535 Netherlands** Jacques Dubroeucq (1500 or 1510–1584), sculptor, returned from Italy where he studied work by Ghiberti, Michelangelo and Sansovino. He became the leading Renaissance sculptor in the Netherlands and the only Flemish sculptor to attempt large-scale work.

1539 Mexico Establishment of the first printing press by Juan Pablos of Seville.

VISUAL ARTS

1531 Italy Death of Andrea del Sarto (b. 1486), a painter concerned with classical composition who was influenced by Raphael and Fra Bartolommeo. His best known works were the frescoes for St Annunziata in Florence and the *Last Supper* in St Salvi. He created a dreamy, gentle ideal of feminine beauty.

1532 France François I brought the Italian painter Francesco Primaticcio (1504–1570) to work at Fontainebleau. He began the fashion for subjects of classical mythology and tempered the more exuberant Italian mannerism to French taste.

*c.***1533 Italy** Arrival in Venice of Jacopo da Ponte Bassano (*c.*1517–1592), who painted biblical subjects as rustic genre scenes. He and his son Francesco were among the first to popularize the pastoral.

1535–1555 Netherlands Pieter Aertsen (1508–1575) worked in Antwerp, painting mainly in monumental style. He was the founder of a long family dynasty of artists; the Aertsens were successful painters for many generations.

1539 Japan Death of Motonobu (b. 1476), son of the founder of *Kanō* painting; he established its distinctive firm brushline. *Kanō* artists worked in bright colours and in bold black and white, with a mainly decorative aim.

INVENTIONS & DISCOVERIES

1535 Frenchman Jacques Cartier discovered St Lawrence river. Spaniard Grijalva discovered California.

HISTORICAL EVENTS	LITERATURE	DANCE & DRAMA	MUSIC

LITERATURE

1540 Italy Death of Francesco Guicciardini (b. 1483), statesman, historian and political writer. *Storia d'Italia*, his most important book, is an account of Italian political history from the arrival of Charles VIII to the death of Clement VII. A book of such scope had never been attempted before but, like all his writings, it was not published during his lifetime.

1543 Spain Publication of poems by Juan Almogáver Boscán (*c*.1490–1542), and Garcilaso de la Vega (1503–1536). Close friends, they wrote in Italian metres. Boscán translated Castiglione's *Il Cortegiano* into Spanish. Garcilaso was the superior poet, and in his best work completely assimilated Italian material to recreate it in Spanish. He was considered the major Spanish poet of his time.

1544 France *Délie*, a love poem by Maurice Scève (?1501–?1560). He was the first to introduce the Petrarchan style of poetry into France, and was the leader of a group of poets similarly influenced by Italian literature, the Lyon group.

1545 Spain *Linguae Vasconum Primitiae*, a book of verse by Bernard Dechepare, was the first work to be written entirely in Basque. Dechepare, a priest, urged fellow Basques to use the vernacular for literature, but his appeal met with limited success.

c.**1545 England** Earliest printed version of *Phyllyp Sparowe* by John Skelton (*c*.1460–1529), poet laureate and scholar, published posthumously. Much of his verse is humorous (though this is not, it is an elegy) and some is satiric. He wrote mainly in 'Skeltonics', a metrical system of his own.

DANCE & DRAMA

1540 Germany Hans Newsidler published *Lautenbüchlein*, a book of dances including an after-dance: a gay dance always following a slower dance, in the rhythm of the *ländler*. The most popular German after-dance was the *quaternaria*, very similar to the *ländler* in rhythm and possibly its forerunner.

1543 Italy *L'Altile* by Giambattista Giraldi, called il Cinthio (1504–1573): he was greatly influenced by Seneca, as were most writers of the period, though he was less rigid than many. In *L'Altile* he uses a medieval, not a classical, story.

1545 Italy First record of a *commedia dell'arte* performance at which the members of the troupe were named. They were led by Maffeo dei Re of Padua. Women appeared in *commedia dell'arte* performances.

1545 Italy *The Second Book of Architecture* by Sebastiano Serlio (1475–1554) describes and illustrates three basic sets: tragic, comic and satiric These were the basis of European set design for the next 300 years. He also discussed the use of coloured lights in stage settings.

MUSIC

1540 England Thomas Tallis (*c*.1505–1585), composer and organist, left Waltham Abbey to work in Canterbury.

1540 France The first types were made for the French printing family, Ballard, who enjoyed a monopoly of printing music for more than 200 years.

1540 Poland The *Capella Rorantistarum* (Chapel of Roratists), a Polish religious and musical establishment, as formed by King Sigismond in Cracow.

1542 England Christopher Tye (b. *c*.1500), composer, established as master of choristers at Ely; he had considerable influence on history of English church music.

1542 Italy Forty-five madrigals in four parts, by Domenico Maria Ferrabosco (1513–1574), dedicated to Guidobaldo, Duke of Urbino, published at Venice.

1542 Switzerland The first edition of the *Genevan Psalter* was published; the musician who had, possibly, the greatest connection with it, was Louis Bourgeois (1510–1561). The musical settings were monophonic at Calvin's insistence. Later, in 1565, Claude Goudimel (*c*.1505–1572), published four-part harmonizations of the Genevan Psalter which became very popular throughout Europe.

1543 Netherlands Tielman Susato (d. *c*.1561) musician and publisher, established at Antwerp, where he published more than 50 volumes of music before his death.

1543 Italy Birth of Alfonso Ferrabosco (d. 1588), composer, in Bologna; he was the most important Italian musician to live in England during the sixteenth century.

1544 Italy St Philip Neri established the Oratory in Rome, where the practice of congregational singing of *Laude* was begun.

1545 Netherlands Phalèse, Flemish music-publishing house, established by Pierre Phalèse; it held a leading position in Netherlands for more than a century.

1541 John Calvin established theocratic government in Geneva.

1545 Council of Trent established to reform Catholic church.

ARCHITECTURE

1539 Italy The Campidoglio, Capitoline Hill, Rome, are buildings begun by Michelangelo, whose interest lay in large-scale design and massive construction: he used the colossal order, pilasters carried up through two storeys instead of defining one, on three palaces around a square, approached by a long stepped ramp, and all related in façade treatment.

1539 Scotland The façade of Falkland Palace, Fife, was built by French masons, importing a style directly related to the Renaissance buildings of the Loire valley.

1540 Turkey Mihrimah Mosque, Istanbul, by Sinan demonstrates refined method of transition from cube-like hall to a dome; stalactite decoration is confined to the pillar capitals.

1544 Turkey The Sahzade Mosque, Istanbul, was the first large mosque by Sinan and reveals the influence of Hagia Sophia.

*c.***1545 Denmark** Martin Bussaert (?–1551) began Egeskov Castle, which was built mainly for defence but incorporated in a solid medieval structure the Renaissance proportions of storeys; a Dutchman he became the earliest exponent of Renaissance styles in Denmark.

THREE DIMENSIONAL ART

1540–1545 France Benvenuto Cellini (1500–1571), Italian goldsmith and sculptor, made a gold and enamel salt-cellar for Francis I, considered the most important surviving piece of Renaissance goldsmith's work.

1540 North America The arrival of the Spaniards in Navajo territory introduced the Navajo to stock raising; this stimulated an art form in woven wool, of which the designs were geometric patterns or pictures of horses, cattle and men.

1540 France Columns of the organ-loft in St Maclou, Rouen, attributed to Jean Goujon (c.1510–1568): their pure classicism indicates knowledge of Italian work.

1542 France Active period of Bernard Palissy (c.1510–c.1590), potter trained as a stained-glass artist, began: his wares had rich polychrome glazes and were decorated with natural forms cast from life.

*c.***1542 Italy** Establishment of the Medici tapestry factory in Florence. It was predominant in Italy until c.1630. One of its major commissions, a series to furnish the Palazzo Vecchio, was designed by Vasari and woven by Jan van den Straecht.

1545–1554 Italy Benvenuto Cellini made his bronze *Perseus*, which is considered his masterpiece.

1545 Italy The final version of the tomb for Pope Julius by Michelangelo Buonarroti (1475–1564) was set up; this was a greatly reduced version of the original idea, which had involved 40 figures.

VISUAL ARTS

1540–1555 India The Mogul prince Humayun was in exile in Persia, where he met and took lessons from the court painters Aga Mirak, Sultan Muhammad and Muzattar Ali, themselves pupils of Bihzad.

1540 India Court painters of Mewar, in Rajasthan, illustrated the story of Rana Ratan Singh and his Rani Padmini. Rajput painting used colours for their decorative brilliance and a style of drawing that was formalized, with no attempt at portraiture. Prosperity in trade made Rajasthan a source of livelihood to many Mogul-trained artists, who adapted themselves to Hindu and Rajput themes for local patrons.

1541 Italy Michelangelo Buonarroti (1475–1564) completed *The Last Judgment* in the Sistine chapel. This was commissioned in 1534 by Pope Clement, reflecting a spirit of penitence after the sack of Rome by a Spanish-German force in 1527. By the time it was finished it had become a work of stern warning, reflecting the revived authority of the Church.

*c.***1543 Italy** Titian (c.1487–1576) painted three ceilings for Santa Maria della Salute, Venice: *Cain and Abel, Sacrifice of Isaac*, and *David and Goliath*. The violent subject matter was made more so by the startling angle of view.

1543
First statement of heliocentre system by Nicolas Copernicus. Georg Hartmann of Nuremberg discovered declination of magnetic needle. De Fabrica Corporis Humani by Andreas Vesalius opened era of modern biology.

1544
Silver mines at Potosi, Peru, discovered.

HISTORICAL EVENTS	LITERATURE	DANCE & DRAMA	MUSIC

HISTORICAL EVENTS

1547
Ivan IV crowned Tsar of Russia at Moscow.

1549
First Act of Uniformity in England; first Anglican prayer book in use.

LITERATURE

1549 England Publication of the first Prayer Book of Edward VI. The second appeared in 1552. Composed largely by Archbishop Cranmer, they had considerable influence on English prose style.

1549 France *Défense et Illustration de la Langue Française* by the poet Joachim du Bellay (1522–1560). He argued that the French language was capable of carrying the finest literature if the medieval traditions were discarded and the classical writers accepted as models. This was the doctrine of the Pléiade, a group of poets led by Pierre de Ronsard (1524/5–1585) and including du Bellay, Jean-Antoine de Baïf (1532–1589), Étienne Jodelle (1532–1573), Pontus de Tyard (1521–1605), Rémy Belleau (1528–1577) and Jean Dinemandi, called Dorat. Through them the sonnet, the ode, and the alexandrine line were established in France.

1549 Switzerland *Raeteis* by Simon Lemnius Margadant (1505–1556), a Romansch writer: the work is a national epic.

1550 France A French translation of the Spanish chivalric novel *Amadis de Gaula* reintroduced the long prose romance into French literature.

1550 Italy *Vite de più eccelenti architetti pittori e scultori Italiano* by Giorgio Vasari (1511–1574), architect, painter and art historian. The work is a series of biographies showing the artistic development of the subjects. It is still considered of value.

DANCE & DRAMA

1546 Italy *Orazio* by Pietro Aretino (1492–1556), was a Renaissance treatment of an ancient Roman subject: this type of drama was popular among Italian writers.

1548 France Construction of the Hôtel de Bourgogne, the first building in Paris actually designed as a theatre.

1548 France Religious drama was suppressed by law, because it was said to bring religion into disrepute. The Confrérie de la Passion, an actors' company whose origins lay in religious plays, were given the monopoly of acting in Paris.

*c.***1550 Europe** Replacement of staid court dances by livelier new ones: Arbeau's treatise *Orchésographie* (publ. 1588) describes 23 varieties of branles, as well as the allemande, canaries courante, gavotte, *Pavane d'Espagne* and *La Volta* as being in fashion at this time. Branles were almost folk dances, some of them being mime or action dances.

*c.***1550 Spain** Lope de Rueda (*c.*1505–1565) Spanish playwright and first actor-manager, worked with his own travelling company, both in inn-yards and noble houses. He invented the *paso*, a comic one-act play. One of his plays, *Los Engañados*, shares the same anonymous Italian source as Shakespeare's *Twelfth Night*.

1550 England *Ralph Roister Doister* by Nicholas Udall (*c.*1505–1556), England's first comedy: written for performance by schoolboys, it shows the influence of Plautus and Terence.

1550 Sweden *Tobiae Comedia* by Olavus Petri (1493–1552), the first extant play in the Swedish vernacular.

MUSIC

1547 England John Day (1522–1584), one of earliest English musical typographers, started his business in London.

1547 Flanders A volume of *ricercari*, one of the earliest books of organ music to be printed, was published by Jacques Buus (d. 1565), composer.

1547 Poland Waclaw of Szamotuly (*c.*1533–*c.*1567), composer, appointed to the royal chapel at Cracow.

1547 Switzerland *Dodecachordon*, a work on church modes to prove the existence of 12 modes and not 8, published by Henricus Glareanus (1488–1563), musical theorist and teacher.

1548 Spain Birth of Tomás Luis de Victoria (d. 1611), composer.

1549 France First songs (*Chansons*), published by Du Chemin of Paris, by Claude Goudimel (*c.*1510–1572), prolific composer of songs and psalms.

*c.***1550 France** Robert Ballard and Adrian Le Roy established as publishers.

1550 England Publication of *The Booke of Common Praier*, noted by John Marbeck (*c.*1510–*c.*1585), English church musician, composer and writer; it contained the first setting to music of English liturgy as authorized by Act of Uniformity (1549).

ARCHITECTURE

1546 France The Louvre, Paris, was rebuilt to the design of Pierre Lescot (1510–1578); intended as a vast royal palace, it was not completed until the end of the nineteenth century. The whole history of the French Renaissance style of architecture is illustrated in the building.

1546 Italy Michelangelo Buonarroti was appointed architect of St Peter's; as a sculptor he designed buildings which had drama in form and in contrasting effects of light. This broke away from the purity of Renaissance building, which enclosed space in perfect proportion.

1547 Italy Villa Farnese, Caprarola, by Vignola and others is a huge palace, planned with a pentagonal exterior and circular inner courtyard; in one angle of the villa is a large circular open staircase built in 1550.

1550 Italy *Vite de più eccellenti architetti pittori e scultori italiano* by Giorgio Vasari (1511–1574) first published. Michelangelo in particular was eulogized by Vasari.

1550 Italy St Andrea, Rome, by Giacomo Barozzi Vignola is the earliest example of a church with an elliptically planned dome.

1550–1555 Italy Villa Giulia, Rome, by Vignola and others was built for Pope Jullius III to a complex design in which architecture and landscape are complementary; its curved and straight façades combine with the intriguing vistas.

1550–1561 Poland The town hall in Poznan was originally a medieval building with a Renaissance loggia in front of a Gothic façade built by Giovanni Battista Quadro di Lugano (?–*c.*1590).

THREE DIMENSIONAL ART

1546 England John Day, printer, began work for Archbishop Parker. He produced several new type founts and even printed a book in Anglo-Saxon letters.

1546 Italy Bartolommeo Campi (fl.*c.*1543–*c.*1554), goldsmith engraver and armourer, made a suit of parade-armour in Roman style for Guidobaldo II, Duke of Urbino.

1547 France *Fontaine des Innocents* by Jean Goujon (*c.*1510–1568), sculptor, who introduced a mannerist style similar to the work of Primaticcio in painting and decoration: Goujon's work was always decorative and elegant but also classical in form.

1548 France Death of the Italian gem-carver Matteo del Nassaro (b. 1515) who founded a school of carving in France: shell-cameo carving was already established there, but Italy and especially Milan was the centre of *intaglio* gem carving, and Milanese artists worked all over Europe.

1550 France The decorator and furniture designer Jacques du Cerceau (*c.*1510–1584) published a book of furniture designs which were a strong influence on French style throughout the century.

*c.*1550–*c.*1700 **Turkey** Pottery centre fl. at Iznik, Anatolia, making white earthenware painted in turquoise, blue and brick-red. It influenced maiolica made at Padua, seventeenth century English delft ware, and eighteenth century faience made at Berlin.

*c.*1550 **Netherlands** Borders of tapestries began to be developed as part of the overall design. Earlier examples with elaborate borders, such as *Susanna and the Elders*, *c.*1500, were rare.

*c.*1550 **Netherlands** By this date emigré Altarist and Venetian glass-makers had established houses in Antwerp and Liège.

*c.*1550 **Russia** Iron made available by the Muscovite conquest of Siberia led to the development of decorative wrought-iron work in lacy patterns.

VISUAL ARTS

1547 Spain Pedro de Campania (1503–1580; the Spanish name of a Flemish painter, Pietr de Kempeneer), painted his *Descent from the Cross*. He exercised a strong influence in Andalusia as a pioneer of Mannerism.

1548 Portugal Francisco de Holanda (1517–1584) wrote his *Da Pintura Antigua*, containing one book of art theory and one of dialogues between himself and Michelangelo, Colonna, Clovio and other Italian artists. This was influential in spreading Italian styles in Portugal.

INVENTIONS & DISCOVERIES

*1548
Silver mines at Zacatecar, Mexico, discovered.*

Italy: Saint Andrea, Rome, by Vignola

1552 Spain A history of the conquest of Mexico, by Bernal Diaz del Castillo (?1498–after 1568): it was a vivid account of Cortés' expedition, written at first hand experience, because the official account, by Lópes de Gomara, struck him as inaccurate. His style relied heavily on the spoken language and was lively and compelling.

1553 Portugal *Consolação às Tribulações de Israel* by Samuel Usque, a writer of Spanish-Jewish extraction: it consisted of three pastoral dialogues on the persecution of the Jews throughout history.

1554 Portugal *Menina e Moça* by Bernardim Ribeiro (?1482–1552), novelist and poet: the book was a sentimental novel, and included passages of chivalry and pastoral.

1554 Spain *La Vida de Lazarillo de Tormes*, attributed to Diego Hurtada de Mendoza (1503–1575), poet, historian and humanist: vigorous and amusing, it was the first picaresque novel.

1555 Dalmatia *Fishing and Fisherman's Talk* by Petar Hektorović (1487–1573): this work, the most original of the period and region, included realistic passages, natural description, and popular poems.

1555 Portugal *Comédia Eufrosina* by Jorge Ferreira de Vasconcelos (1515–?1563), playwright and novelist: a novel in dialogue, it showed the influence of the Spanish *La Celestina*.

1556 Spain *Guia de Pecadores* by Fray Luis de Granada (?1504–1588), a religious writer. Forbidden to Roman Catholics by its inclusion in the Index of 1559, the book was later reissued and translated into many languages, including Polish and Japanese. Fray Luis modelled his style on Cicero.

1555 Accession of Akbar the Great, climax of Mogul rule in India.

1556 Division of Spain and Holy Roman Empire.

1552 France *Cléopatre Captive* by Etienne Jodelle (1522–1573) was the first French neoclassical tragedy. He was one of the Pleide, a group of poets who reformed French verse on models taken from a study of Greek and Roman literature.

1556 France First appearance at the French court of the leaping and turning dance *La Volta*. Its origin was said to be in Provence, but its elements appear in German dances of an earlier date.

1552 Hungary First collection of lute pieces written by Bálint Bakfark (1507–1576), Hungarian, later Polish, lutenist and composer, one of most brilliant performers of his time.

1553 Spain Book of divisions for bass viol and *cymbalo* by Diego Ortiz (b. *c.*1525) who was one of first to use the principle of divisions (variations).

1554 Italy First works by Giovanni da Palestrina (*c.*1524–1594), including masses and motets. He was appointed musical director of St John Lateran Church, Rome in 1556, of Santa Maria Maggiore, Rome in 1561 and at the Vatican Basilica in 1578.

1555 Italy First publications by Costanzo Porta (*c.*1530–1601).

1555 Netherlands First publications of works by Roland de Lassus (1532–1594).

1556 Germany Roland de Lassus appointed to the Bavarian court chapel at Munich. From this stemmed the great growth in the reputation of the music there, until it became an established musical centre.

1556 Switzerland A first edition of the Sternhold and Hopkins Psalter, with tunes, was published in Geneva. it was 1560 before an edition was published in English.

1557 Flanders Antoon Moors (*c.*1490–*c.*1562) built an organ at Schwerin which had a lasting influence on organ-building in Germany because of the disposition of its stops.

1557 Italy Birth of Giovanni Joanne a Cruce Clodiensis Croce (d. 1609), Italian composer; an important writer of both secular and liturgical music, he had great influence on English madrigalists.

ARCHITECTURE

1551–1580 Turkey Suleymaniÿe Mosque, Istanbul, by Sinan, like previous mosques by him, includes a number of public buildings from schools to shops; structurally the mosque echoes Bayazit Mosque and Hagia Sophia.

1552 Italy St Maria in Carignano, Genoa, by Galeazzo Alessi (1512–1572) was based on Bramante's designs for St Peter's Rome by the leading Genoese architect of the High Renaissance.

1555–1560 Russia Vasili Blazhenny, Moscow, is a unique church rising from an octagonal ground plan and encircled by radiating chapels; the climax is achieved in a cluster of bulbous domes.

1556–1559 Germany Hexenburgermeister House, Lemgo, is a building typical of sixteenth-century German architecture with tall façade and rich scroll and strap-work decoration ascending in stages to reach the gable.

1556 Italy Carlo Maderna was born (died 1629), a leading architect in Rome in the early seventeenth century.

1557–1565 Austria Landhaus, Graz, was one of few Austrian classical courts with a three-storeyed arcaded gallery supporting a pitched roof with dormers; damaged in World War II.

THREE DIMENSIONAL ART

1551 Germany Portrait bust of the Emperor Charles V, with removable armour, by Leone Leow (1509–90), Italian born sculptor, goldsmith, coin-engraver and medallist. His sculptures were mainly portraits; some of his work was finished by his son Pompeo (d. 1610)

1554 England Bowes Cup in silver and rock crystal exemplified the classical style, introduced after the designs of Hans Holbein the Younger (1497–1543) had stimulated English smiths in the Renaissance idiom. German techniques were influential, and produced a somewhat rigid style.

c.1554 Bavaria Death of Loy Hering (b. c.1485), sculptor, who specialized in small pieces and reliefs. He was one of many who used Dürer's engravings as a pattern book, but he also showed some familiarity with Italian styles.

1556–1606 India The technique of enamelling was developed during the reign of Akbar, Mogul emperor. Previous jewellers used gold and gems, choosing the stones for their colour and their contribution to the overall design of the piece; they had relatively little interest in cutting the stone for brilliance, although a silver foil setting was often used to add brightness. After the introduction of enamelling the usual technique was *champlevé*.

1557 France Robert Granjon (1513–1589 influential painter and type-designer, designed *civilité* type: it was a version of the script called 'cursive françoyse' and was used to teach handwriting.

VISUAL ARTS

1551 Portugal Death of Gregorio Lopes, a court painter who expressed the luxury of contemporary Portuguese life.

1553 Germany Death of Wolf Huber (b. c.1490), an engraver and draughtsman primarily concerned with landscape.

1554 Netherlands Anthonis Mor van Dashorst, called Moro (1517/20–1576/7) painted his portrait of *Mary Tudor*, considered one of the best of his austere royal portraits. He was leading portraitist to the Spanish-Burgundian nobility, and court painter to Philip II.

c.1554 Italy Titian began painting in a fluid technique: he had used light to build forms in his early work; now he used it to dissolve them. The style lasted for the rest of his working life.

1555 Netherlands Pieter Bruegel the Elder (c.1525–1569) returned from a journey through the Alps on which he had made pure landscape sketches. Only Dürer produced anything comparable in fidelity and sensitivity. Bruegel engraved and published his landscapes, concentrating on graphic work until c.1562.

1556 Italy Taddeo Zuccaro (1529–1566) painted his first important commission, decorating the Capella Mattei in Santa Maria della Consolazione, Rome. He and his brother Federico developed a smooth style of historical painting which incorporated influences from Correggio, Michelangelo and Raphael, and was widely imitated.

INVENTIONS & DISCOVERIES

1552 Bartolommeo Eustachio discovered Eustachian tubes and Eustachian valve.

1554 G. Cardano produced absolute alcohol. Richard Chancellor received in Moscow by Ivan IV.

1557 Portuguese founded settlement in Macao.

HISTORICAL EVENTS	LITERATURE	DANCE & DRAMA	MUSIC

HISTORICAL EVENTS

1557
First national bankruptcies in France and Spain.
First Covenant signed in Scotland.

1558
Elizabeth I became Queen of England.
Geneva became independent of Berne.

1559
Treaty of Câteau-Cambrésis; France abandoned her claims in Italy.

1560
Scots Parliament abolished papal jurisdiction and adopted Calvinism.

LITERATURE

1557 England *Songs and Sonnets*, a collection of lyrics compiled by Richard Tottel (*c*.1530–1593) and Nicholas Grimald (?1519–?1562), was printed by Tottel; the book became known as *Tottel's Miscellany*. It contains work by Sir Thomas Wyatt (1503–1542), who introduced the sonnet to England, and by Henry Howard, Earl of Surrey (?1517–1546/1547), who devised what is now called the Shakespearean sonnet. Many English lyrics of the period were intended to be sung, not read, hence the title.

1558 Poland *Wizerunek*, a long poem by Mikolaj Rej (1505–1569), poet and prose writer, the first to write only in Polish.

1558 Portugal *Castro* by António Ferreira (1528–1569), playwright and poet. A follower of Sá de Miranda (1481–1588), he helped to establish the new Italian style. He was opposed to the use of Spanish by Portuguese writers.

1558 Portugal *Peregrinação* by Fernão Mendes Pinto (1510–1583); an adventurer, and later a missionary, he claimed to be one of the first Europeans in Japan. The book is an account of his travels in the East, vivid, exciting and enormously popular. For a long time it was regarded as fantasy, but is now accepted as basically factual, though doubtless embroidered.

1559 France French translation of Plutarch's *Lives*, by the scholar Jacques Amyot (1513–1593). In the first half of the sixteenth century, many learned French writers used Latin or Greek—a result of the rediscovery of the ancient classical literatures.

1559 France Posthumous publication of the *Heptaméron* by Marguerite de Navarre (1492–1549), a patroness of letters, and herself a writer of poetry and prose: this book, which contains 72 short stories and is unfinished, is an imitation of the *Decameron*.

DANCE & DRAMA

1560 England *Gammer Gurton's Needle* (anonymous), the first English farce.

c.**1560 Europe** After this date, dances combining procession and episodes of 'actions' began to decline. The opening dances like the allemande, which were dignified, had lost their pantomime episodes earlier and were now followed by the livelier after-dances.

MUSIC

1558 Czechoslovakia The earliest book on musical theory written and printed in Czech was published by Jan Blahoslav (1523–1571), the Moravian hymnologist.

1558 Italy First publication of *Istitutioni Armoniche* by Gioseffe Zarlino (1517–1590), Italian theorist, one of the most learned of his day.

1559 France *Le Premier Trophée de Musique* published by Robert Granjon, typefounder and music printer; it was the first work to be printed in Granjon's new system of round notes, an idea of which he was one of the first exponents.

1560 Germany Elias Nikolaus Ammerbach (*c*.1530–1597), an authority on fingering and decorations, was appointed organist at St Thomas's Church, Leipzig.

England: Little Moreton Hall, Cheshire

1559–1580 England Little Moreton Hall is one of the best preserved of the many gabled half-timbered houses in England.

1559 Germany Munich Residenz is a complex of several buildings built over a period of time, placed around 6 courts of which two are in Renaissance style and were built by Friedrich Sustris (1524–*c.*1591); the grotto court has Florentine characteristics.

1559–1584 Spain The Escorial, Madrid, by Juan Bautista de Toledo (died 1567) and, later, Juan de Herrera was Philip II's palace built as a vast rectangle; on a rigid grid plan; remote and austere, it is built of granite and incorporates a church, monastery and college. It was the first of the royal·buildings of Europe built on a vast scale and was later much imitated.

1560–1574 Italy Uffizi Palace, Florence, is Vasari's only significant work and is mannerist in style.

1560 Turkey In the interior of the Rüstem Pasha Mosque, Istanbul, by Sinan large spherical spandrels as in the Mihrimah and Süleyman mosques are replaced by smaller half domes, the bases of which are related to the walls by stalactites.

1558 Italy Giovanni Battista della Porta published *Natural Magic*, the first published account of the use of the *camera obscura* as an aid to the artist: light entering a dark room through a little hole will form on the opposite wall an inverted image of whatever stands between the light-source and the hole.

*c.***1560 Peru** Establishment of a school of painting at Cuzco which influenced the whole of central Andean art. European ideas were interpreted and decorated in terms of folk art. The flat treatment and bright, gilded patterns of flowers and birds were derived from the pre-Conquest tradition. The European motifs were usually taken from religious prints.

HISTORICAL EVENTS

1562 John Hawkins started slave trade between Africa and America. First revolt against Spanish rule in Netherlands.

1566 Death of Suleiman the Magnificent; Ottoman empire at its peak.

1567 End of Muromachi period in Japan.

1568 English college for education of Catholic priests established at Douai.

LITERATURE

1560–1570 Russia A history of Muscovy was written by Prince Andrey Mikhaylovich Kurbsky (1528–1583), a boyar, while living in exile in Lithuania. It is in marked contrast to official histories of the period, which glorified Russia and her rulers at the expense of truth. He is also famous for his angry letters to the Tsar.

1563 Dalmatia Some poems of Dinko Ranjina (1536–1607), who rejected the influence of Petrarch and strove for greater originality.

1563 England *Actes and Monuments* by John Foxe (1516–1587), the Protestant martyrologist: the work, known as *Foxe's Book of Martyrs*, is inaccurate but vigorous.

1567 Portugal *Palmeirim de Inglaterra* by Francisco de Morais (1500–1572), courtier and novelist: the book is a romance of chivalry, a type of literature which enjoyed great popularity following the publication of the fourteenth-century anonymous Spanish chivalric novel *Amadis de Gaula* in 1508. Cervantes, who disapproved of the genre, was complimentary about this book.

1567 Spain First part of the *Araucana* by Alonso de Ercilla y Zuñiga (1533–1594): an epic poem in three parts, the work tells of Ercilla's experience fighting in Chile. He shows sympathy for the Indians and excels in descriptive writing. He published the two further parts in 1578 and 1589.

1568 Netherlands *Het Bosken* by the Dutch poet Jonker Jan van der Noot (1539/40–c.1595), whose poetry shows the influence of the French Pléiade. He is considered the first Renaissance poet of the Netherlands.

1569 Dalmatia *Planine* by Peter Zoranić (1508– ?) was the first Dalmatian pastoral novel.

1569 Denmark *Den Danske Psalmebog* by Hans Thomisson (1532–1573), hymn-writer: the collection, which remained in use for 130 years, contained both original hymns and translations.

DANCE & DRAMA

1562 England *Gorboduc* by Thomas Sackville (1536–1608) and Thomas Norton (1532–1584), the first English tragedy, was performed before Elizabeth I: it shows the influence of Seneca. Classical imitations were intended for a private, educated audience, not for the general public.

1564 Philippines Beginning of the Spanish occupation: Spanish dance and drama predominated in the large cities.

MUSIC

1561 England Richard Edwards (c.1522–1566), poet, playwright and composer, appointed Master of the Children. He produced various plays at court.

1562 Italy Council of Trent began discussions on church music, which led to reforms. It recommended that vocal and instrumental displays be prohibited and musical settings should promote clarity and intelligibility of the words.

1562 Netherlands Birth of Jan P(i)eterszoon Sweelinck (d. 1621), organist and composer, the last important composer of the brilliant 'Netherlands' period.

1564 Italy The first violins made by Andrea Amati (c.1520–1578) date from this year. Amati, who may have begun his career as a maker of flutes and viols, more than any other maker deserves credit for the design of the modern violin, having bridged the gap between viol and violin; his design of the violin remains virtually unchanged today.

1564 Italy Giulio Caccini (1545–1618), the singer and composer, entered the service of the Medici court at Florence; he was one of the first composers to use the *basso continuo*, and although not the inventor of monody certainly promoted it.

1566 Scotland *Scottish Psalter* published by Thomas Wood, musician.

1567 Italy Birth of Claudio Monteverdi (d. 1643), the first great operatic composer.

1568 Italy *Il Fronimo* by Vincenzo Galilei (1520–1591), lutenist and composer, was published; it indicates the form of tablature employed by Italian lutenists of the period and their method of tuning.

1568 Italy Gasparo da Salò (1540–1609), violin maker, established at Brescia; he was one of earliest makers of stringed instruments who used pattern of violin as distinguished from that of viol.

1561–1566 Belgium The town hall, Antwerp, by Cornelis Floris (*c.*1514–1575) is a large rectangular building with an ornate centrepiece and the outstanding example of Flemish mannerism.

1561 France *Nouvelles inventions* by Philibert de l'Orme was published in France, and, with his other work *L'Architecture* (1567), had a great influence on French architecture, especially on practical matters described in the latter book.

1563–1667 Mexico Mexico City Cathedral combines Baroque and more austere classical features; it has nineteenth-century additions.

1566–1610 Italy St Giorgio Maggiore and Il Redentore, Venice, are both by Palladio and notable for the method of using interpenetrating pediments on the façade to adapt to the basilican elevation.

1567–1575 England Longleat House, a great Elizabethan 'prodigy house', was revolutionary by incorporating classical pilaster orders over the whole façade.

1567 Italy Villa Capra, Vicenza, was completed by Palladio the most symmetrical of his elegant villas with hexastyle porticoes on each side; several copies were built in England.

1568–1584 Italy Il Gesù, Rome, by Vignola and Giacomo della Porta is the mother church of the Jesuit order; an addition of three bays to the nave breaks the otherwise centralized plan which, together with the proto-baroque façade was very influential.

1569–*c.*1580 India The city of Fatehpur a Sikri was built by Akbar the Great; Indian Mogul rulers originated in Persia and their architecture combines Islamic, European and native Hindu elements. Akbar's palace is pink sandstone and its form traditional Islamic, while detail is original and reflects Hindu taste.

1561 England Elizabeth I granted a charter to the Broders' Company. Embroiderers' guilds encouraged the spread of the art, which had stressed the secular since the dissolution of the monasteries in 1536.

1563–1570 France Tomb of Henry II and Catherine de Medici, by Germaine Pilon (1537–1590) sculptor: his work shows a development towards naturalism, greater freedom of movement and a feeling for materials; in later work his naturalism became more emotional.

1564 Italy Death of Michelangelo Buonarroti (b. 1475). His last work, a *Pieta*, departed completely from his former expressive use of the male nude; the figures of the Virgin and the dead Christ combine in an abstract expression of emotional intensity, all rules of anatomy abandoned. It was this intensive quality above all else which brought him the admiration of his contemporaries.

The gardens at the Villa Lante, laid out by Giacomo da Vignola (1507–73) were the earliest of the great Renaissance gardens in Europe. They revived an art which had been little practised since Roman times, and were widely copied in Italy and France.

1568 Switzerland Jost Amman (1539–1591), wood-engraver, illustrated his best known book, *Panoplia Omnium Artium*, which provides valuable pictures of contemporary artistic techniques: Amman was a prolific illustrator.

1562 Italy *The Finding of the Body of St Mark* by Jacopo Robusti Tintoretto (1518–1594) of Venice. Tintoretto planned his compositions by making wax models which he arranged on a stage and lit with directional lamps. This enabled him to achieve a three-dimensional effect, with bold foreshortening and startling angles. The method broke from the Venetian tradition of composing in lines parallel to the plane of the picture, and brought the spectator into the scene.

1563–1569 Netherlands Pieter Bruegel the Elder painted his best known works: the *Months* series, the peasant village scenes, grotesque allegories such as *The Triumph of Death*, an anti-Spanish protest, and religious subjects in everyday village settings which gave them added force. His influence on landscape and genre painting was immense. In his grotesque graphics and paintings he acknowledged the influence of Hieronymus Bosch.

*c.*1567 **China** Death of Wèn Chêng-Ming, painter of the revolutionary *Wu* school of Suchouin. He combined the wet-ink and dry-brush techniques, and had great influence on later painters. He painted mainly landscapes.

1568 Italy Danielo Barbaro of Padua substituted a lens for the original 'small hole' of the *camera obscura*. A more extensive picture could be obtained and focused on a sheet of paper. The 'camera' was literally a room and the artist worked inside it.

1565 Manufacture of pencils began in England.

HISTORICAL EVENTS	LITERATURE	DANCE & DRAMA	MUSIC

LITERATURE

1569 Spain Publication of a Spanish translation of the Bible, by Casiodoro de Reina (?–after 1581), a Spanish friar who turned Protestant.

1570 Hungary A collection of poems by Bálint Balassi (1554–1594), a lyric poet and innovator in verse forms.

1570 Portugal *Os Lusíadas* by the poet Luís Vaz de Camões (?1524–1580): an epic on Vasco da Gama's discovery of a sea-route to India, it covered the whole of Portuguese history. Its spirit was humanistic, it glorified man and his achievements, and it was regarded as the major epic of the Renaissance. Camões also wrote lyrics in the traditional short metres.

1570 Romania *Psaltirea* by the deacon Coresi, about whom almost nothing is known beyond the fact that he printed 22 religious books, the first extant printed books in Romanian.

1571 Bohemia Death of Jan Blahoslav (b. 1523), humanist and religious writer: an eminent scholar, he translated the New Testament and also compiled a Czech grammar.

1571 Spain Basque translation of the Gospels, by Lizarraga: it had considerable influence on the development of the language.

1571 Spain Probable date of the history of the rebellion of the Moriscos by Diego Hurtado de Mendoza. His models were Tacitus and Sallust. The work was published posthumously in 1627.

1575 Italy *Gerusalemme Liberata* by Torquato Tasso (1544–1595). The poem is an epic in the classical manner about the first crusade. Tasso, however, is more concerned with individuals than with history or religion. At this period, poetry was still regarded as the highest form of literature. The outstanding and most popular work of Italian literature of the time, Tasso's epic had considerable influence on other European writers.

HISTORICAL EVENTS

*1571
Thirty-nine
Articles of Faith
sanctioned in
England.
Battle of Lepanto
broke Turkish
sea power.*

*1572
St Bartholomew's
Day massacre of
Huguenots in
France.
Francis Drake
began attacks on
Spanish harbours
in America.*

DANCE & DRAMA

*c.*1570–1600 **Spain** *Siete Infantes de Lara* by Juan de la Cueva (*c.*1550–*c.*1610): he was the first Spanish dramatist to use episodes from native history. His plays show the influence of Seneca.

1570 England *Cambyses, King of Persia* by Thomas Preston: nothing is known about the author, but the play is a peculiarly English mixture of comedy and tragedy and links the morality play with historical drama. *Cambyses* was a 'popular' play.

1571 France The Gelosi, one of the best-known *commedia dell' arte* troupes, performed in Lyons. Their leading members were Francesco and Isabella Andreini.

1573 Italy *Aminta* by Torquato Tasso (1554–1595), was a pastoral: this type of drama, giving an artificial picture of the lives of shepherds and shepherdesses, had developed from pastoral poetry. It was very popular in Italy and, to a lesser extent, in France.

MUSIC

1570 France Earliest known celebration of St Cecilia's festival at Évreux, Normandy.

1570 France Académie de Poésie et de Musique founded in Paris by J. A. de Baif, but dissolved 1584.

1571 England Publication of a book of secular songs by Thomas Whythorne (b. 1528), composer.

1571 Germany Birth of Michael Praetorius (d. 1621), musical scholar and composer.

1571 Italy Tomás Luis de Victoria (*c.*1548–1611) succeeded Palestrina as *maestro di cappella* at the Roman Seminary.

1572 England Birth of Thomas Tomkins (d. 1656), organist and composer.

1573 Germany A comprehensive collection of liturgical music for Lutheran Church published by Johannes Keuchenthal, clergyman and musical editor.

1574 Germany Elector John George of Brandenburg founded a *Hofkapelle* in Berlin.

1574 Spain Death of Pedro Fernández de Castilleja (b. *c.*1490), known as 'master of the Spanish masters'; his pupils included Morales and Guerrero.

1575 England William Byrd (1543–1623), composer, and Thomas Tallis (*c.*1505–1585), composer and organist jointly published *Cantiones Sacrae*. They were also granted a monopoly for printed music and music paper.

1575 England Birth of John Coperario (Cooper) (d. 1625), viola da gambist, lutenist and composer. He visited Italy (*c.*1604) where he italianised his name and style, and had a great influence on English chamber music for viols.

1575 Mexico Hernando Franco (*c.*1525–1585), composer of Spanish birth, appointed chapel master at Mexico City cathedral; he is the earliest polyphonic composer of Mexico whose works are still extant.

ARCHITECTURE

1569–1575 Turkey Selim Mosque, Edirne, by Sinan has an octagonal ground plan as employed in Rüstem Pasha Mosque; a circle of alternating supporting walls and half domes carries the weight of the main dome on to 8 pillars.

1570 Italy *Quattro libri dell'architettura* by Palladio was published; the ideas and designs contained in this treatise proved highly influential, especially in Britain.

1571 Turkey Sokulla Mehmet Pasha Mosque, Istanbul, is by Sinan, who designed the centrally domed hall in a style which, for once, did not depend on the example of Hagia Sophia.

1573 England Inigo Jones born (died 1652), the royal architect who introduced the authentic Renaissance style to England.

1573 Turkey Piyale Pasha Mosque, Istanbul, by Sinan is a simple pillared hall similar to the Ulu-Cami in Bursa.

THREE DIMENSIONAL ART

1571 Spain Juan de Juni (*c.*1507–1577), sculptor, carved the *Entombment* in Segovia Cathedral. His early work was in elaborate mannerist style; this later work is dramatic and emotional and foreshadows Spanish baroque.

*c.***1571 England** Introduction of delft ware to London, via Norwich, by potters from Antwerp.

1572 France Hugues Sambin (*c.*1515–*c.*1601) published *Oeuvre de la diversité des termes*: a collection of designs for woodcarving and other ornament, it was a source for furniture-makers, particularly in France, who produced elaborately carved cabinets.

1573–1615 Japan The Momoyama period, in which Japan was united and prosperous under the military leader Hideyoshi: it was noted for luxurious articles and is thought to be the period when the *inrō*, seal box hanging from a girdle and one of the most important forms for lacquer artists, was first made as a work of art.

1573 Austria Iron screen surrounding the tomb of the Emperor Maximilian at Innsbruck, designed by Paul Trabel, was made by Jorg Schmidhammer of Prague: it was considered the finest example of the sixteenth century German style which was based on delicate calligraphic interlace.

1575–1587 Italy A type of porcelain made with *frit* (fired ground glass) was commissioned by Francesco de Medici in Florence; it was painted in blue on white, and lead-glazed.

VISUAL ARTS

1572 Italy Death of the painter Agnolo Bronzino (b. 1503), noted for his portraits. His mastery of draughtsmanship and his assured, detached style set a fashion in European portraiture.

*c.***1575 Netherlands** Paul and Mattheus Bril (d. 1626 and 1583) went to Italy to work as landscape artists. Paul Bril represented a transition from Flemish fantastic treatment of landscape to Italian idealized style. He influenced Agostino Tassi and, through him, Claude.

INVENTIONS & DISCOVERIES

1569 Mercator chart invented for navigation.

1572 Tycho Brahe first to observe a new fixed star.

HISTORICAL EVENTS	LITERATURE	DANCE & DRAMA	MUSIC
			1575 Spain Fernando de las Infantas (b. 1534), Spanish composer and theologian, established in Rome. Through his intervention the reform of '*Graduale Romanum*' was suspended, which had some influence on the history of church music.
	1576 Dalmatia Death of Mavar Nikola Vetranić (b. ?1482), a Benedictine monk who wrote mystical poems and nature lyrics, and also an allegorical poem showing the influence of Dante.	**1576 England** James Burbage built The Theatre, the first permanent theatre in London.	
	1577 England *The Firste Volume of the Chronicles of England, Scotland and Ireland* by Raphael Holinshed (d. ?1580), English chronicler. The work was widely read and used as a historical source by many writers, including Shakespeare.	**1577 France** The Gelosi troupe were summoned to play before the French king, Henri III, at Blois.	**1576 Spain** Esteban Daza, lutenist, published a book in tablature containing many transcriptions for lute of Spanish madrigals.

1577 Spain Publication of *De Musica Libri Septem* by Francisco de Salinas (1513–1590), theorist, organist and writer on music. He was the first Spanish musician to write down folksongs as they were sung in his own time. |
| *1578 Russians crossed the Urals.* | **1578 France** The first of the two *Semaines* by Guillaume de Salluste du Bartas (1544–1590), poet and militant protestant: this first poem, in 7 cantos, tells the story of the Creation. The *Semaines* were very popular and may have influenced Tasso and Milton.

1578 France *Sonnets pour Hélène* by Pierre de Ronsard (1524/5–1585), a poet influenced by Pindar, Horace, Anacreon, and in particular, Petrarch. A dominant literary figure, he was the leader of the Pléiade. | **1578 France** Valleran Lecomte's company leased the Hôtel de Bourgogne from the Confrérie de la Passion players: they were thus the first professional theatrical company to establish themselves in Paris. Among them was Marie Venier, the first French actress whose name is known.

1578 Poland *The Dismissal of the Grecian Envoys* by Jan Kochanowski (1530–1584) is the first important secular play in Polish. | |
| *1579 Portuguese established trading station in Bengal.* | **1579–1593 Bohemia** Translation of the Bible into Czech.

1579 England Plutarch's *Lives of the Noble Greeks and Romans* was translated from the French of Jacques Amyot by Sir Thomas North (1523–?1601). North's book was Shakespeare's chief classical source.

1579 England *The Shepheardes Calender* by Edmund Spenser (c.1552–1599) was a landmark in English poetry; with its deliberate archaisms and dialect words, it ushered in a new conception of vernacular poetry. Spenser's most ambitious work is the unfinished allegory in the mode of a romance of chivalry, *The Faerie Queene*, begun in 1590. | | **1579 Flanders** Flemish family of harpsichord makers, Ruckers, established in Antwerp. |
| *1580 First commercial treaty between England and Turkey. Philip II of Spain annexed Portugal.* | **1580–1600 India** Reign of the Shah of Golconda, Mohammed Kuli Kutb, a patron of poets writing in Urdu, the Indian Moslem vernacular. He also wrote poetry himself. | **1580 Germany** Description by Montaigne of a 'turning dance' he saw at Augsburg: dances in which couples held each other closely face-to-face while making the 'turn' were peculiarly German, if slow to reach the far north. They were considered improper by many and were responsible for the growth of an anti-dance movement in Germany. Their direct expression survived adaptation to court. | **1580 Italy** First madrigals written by Luca Marenzio (1553–1599), composer. He is considered to be greatest Italian master of the madrigal, of which he wrote more than 200.

1580 Poland *Melodies for the Polish Psalter* written by Mikolaj Gomólka (b. c.1535), instrumentalist and composer. |

England: frontispiece of 'The Shepheardes Calendar' by Edmund Spenser

1577 Spain El Greco (1541–1614) settled in Toledo. He was born in Crete, with its Byzantine tradition of painting, and trained in Italy where he was influenced by Tintoretto and Michelangelo. His painting of *Christ Stripped of his Garments* (1579) shows the fusion of these influences with elements from his Spanish surroundings.

1578 Russia The church of the Benedictines L'vov, combines Byzantine features with a Renaissance treatment of architectural elements; it has a beautifully carved doorway.

1578 France Henry III founded the Order of the Holy Spirit: this proved a great stimulus to heraldic embroidery.

1579–1580 India Jesuit missionaries from Europe visited the Mogul ruler Akbar and gave him a picture of the Madonna. He also had a Bible with Flemish illustrations. Western trends in portraiture began to appear in later Mogul painting.

1579 Spain Death of the painter Juan de Juanes Macip. His painting of the *Assumption of the Virgin* indicates direct contact with the paintings of Raphael and his school. His work was influential in Valencia.

1580–1588 England Wollaton Hall by Robert Smythson (c.1536–1614), the architect of many large sixteenth-century houses; Wollaton has a unique keep-like central block and Flemish strapwork, as well as classical pilasters and niches, decorate its façade.

1580–1584 Italy Teatro Olimpico, Vicenza, by Palladio was based on the antique Roman theatre described by Vitruvius.

1580–1590 France Germaine Pilon sculpted the *Virgin of Pity* and *St Francis*. His use of naturalism for emotional effect marks a transition between the mannerist and baroque style.

*c.*1580 **Germany** Iron screen to the Fugger Chapel in St Ulric's church, Augsburg, made by Hans Mezger, outstanding ironsmith of his day, in the light interlaced style.

1580–1600 England Nicholas Hilliard (c.1547–1619) fl. as a miniature painter. He followed a graceful linear style and modelled his portrait faces with flesh tones and not with shadows. This technique was influential on Elizabethan portraiture. Hilliard was the leading English miniaturist and his reputation extended to France. The linear portrait typified by his work is the only sign of mannerism to appear in English art.

HISTORICAL EVENTS	LITERATURE	DANCE & DRAMA	MUSIC

HISTORICAL EVENTS

1581 Northern Netherlands (United Provinces) proclaimed independence from Spain. Russians began conquest of Siberia.

1582 Adoption of the Gregorian calendar in Catholic countries.

1584 Sir Walter Raleigh annexed Virginia.

1585 Antwerp sacked by Spaniards, lost its importance in international trade to Amsterdam.

LITERATURE

1580 England *Euphues and his England* by John Lyly (1554–1606), poet, novelist and dramatist. His style was artificial and elaborate. The book was the first English novel of manners.

1580 Poland *Laments*, poems by Jan Kochanowski (1530–1584), poet and playwright. His early poems were in Latin, but later he wrote entirely in Polish; his work showed strong classical influence. He was considered the best Polish poet before the nineteenth century.

1580 England *Astrophel and Stella* by Sir Philip Sidney (1554–1586), courtier, soldier, critic, poet and prose writer. The book was a collection of sonnets on one theme, a sonnet sequence. Other famous sonnet sequences were written by Spenser and Shakespeare.

1580 France Books I and II of *Essais* by Michel de Montaigne (1533–1592). The word *essai* ('attempt') was first used in a literary sense by Montaigne, to describe an experimental form. Montaigne's essays were a series of brief, irregular observations, full of digressions, about the world from the writer's personal point of view. They appear spontaneous but were in fact highly polished.

1580 Netherlands Translation of the Psalms by Philips van Marnix van St Aldegonde (1540–1598), poet and theologian. He also wrote in Latin and French.

1580 Spain A commentary on the poems of Garcilaso de la Vega, by Fernando de Herrera (1534–1597), humanist and man of letters. Elegance and fitness were his criteria; his own poetry was considered excellent.

1586 Netherlands *Zedekunst* by Dirck Volkertsz Coornhert (1522–1590), poet, playwright, moralist and engraver. His poetry showed the influence of the *rederijkers*; his prose showed his concern for the purity of the Dutch language. This work was the first ethical treatise in any vernacular.

DANCE & DRAMA

1581 France *Ballet Comique de la Reine* performed at the marriage of Marguerite of Lorraine and the Duc de Joyeuse: produced by the Italian, Baltazarini, it brought together old material from *mascarades* and *intermedi* into one united whole, telling the story of Circe.

1581 Italy Fabritio Caroso published *Il Ballarino*, an important treatise on the male dancer.

1582 First extant manuscript of a Jewish religious play, modelled on the German *Festnachtspiel*.

1585 France Civil unrest meant the end of large-scale ballet performances and a return to the earlier *mascarades*: these later combined with ballet to evolve towards an operatic form, with dancing secondary.

MUSIC

1581 Italy *Il Ballarino*, an important treatise on dancing, published in Venice by Fabrizio Caroso, an Italian dancing-master.

1582 Italy Birth of Gregorio Allegri (d. 1652), a priest who became a papal singer in 1629. He composed much church music, including a 9-part *Miserere* which is sung in the Sistine Chapel in Holy Week.

1582 Italy First compositions by Claudio Giovanni Antonio Monteverdi (1567–1643).

1582 Italy *Directorium Chori . . . Opera Joannis Guidetti Bononiensis . . . .*, revised services of the Roman Church, was published. Although Palestrina was commissioned to undertake the revision, the actual writing was done by Giovanni Guidetti (1530–1592), an authority on Italian church music.

1584 Italy Birth of Antonio Cifra (d. 1629), one of most prolific composers of his time.

1585 England Death of Thomas Tallis, composer and organist (b. *c*.1505).

1585 Germany Birth of Johann Lippius (d. 1612), Alsatian theorist and a pioneer in the change of viewpoint from polyphony to harmony.

1585 Germany Birth of Heinrich Schütz (d. 1672), the greatest German composer before Bach, who developed a dramatic, free-style composition in his setting of scriptural texts.

1585 Italy *Officium Hebdomadae Sanctae*, one of Victoria's most important works, published in Rome.

1586 Germany First chorale book by Lucas Osiander (1534–1604), theologian and musician.

1586 Italy First work designed for a symphonic combination of instruments only by Andrea Gabrieli (1520–1586). On his death, his nephew, Giovanni Gabrieli (?1557–1612) succeeded him as organist of San Marco where he remained until his death. Apart from his own contribution to the development of balance between voices and instruments, he published the bulk of his uncle's works.

ARCHITECTURE

*c.*1580 **Switzerland** Spieshof Basel is the most important Swiss building in the classical style in the sixteenth century; it has four storeys with superimposed orders.

1582–1597 **Germany** St Michael, Munich, is an outstanding Renaissance building based on Il Gesù, Rome, combined with the German use of detail; it has a magnificent three-tiered painted altar with classical decoration.

1585 **Spain** The unfinished Valladolid Cathedral by Juan de Herrera was planned as a huge church, but only the plain Palladian-style nave of Herrera's design was completed.

England: from a late 16th century tapestry, the life of an Elizabethan gentleman

1586 **Laos** That Luang, Vientiane, is a stupa (an edifice designed to contain relics) consisting of a low dome topped with a tall spire, surrounded at the base by a series of smaller spires; the tiled cloistered enclosure around it is reminiscent of Chinese architecture. It was restored in the eighteenth and nineteenth centuries.

THREE DIMENSIONAL ART

1583–1613 **China** Active period of the bronze-caster Hu Wênming, who made vessels of original design at a time when it was fashionable to copy classical models: he was noted for using cast ornament in relief and part gilding.

1583 **Italy** Figure group *The Rape of the Sabines* by the Flemish-born sculptor Jean Boulogne (Giovanni da Bologna), (1529–1608) considered his masterpiece. His output, especially in bronze, was enormous and very popular; reproductions of his work appeared until the twentieth century. He personified the mannerist style.

1585 **Germany** Death of Wenzel Jamnitzer, (b. 1508), leading goldsmith of his time in Nuremberg: he is credited with originating the German fashion for casting animal, insect and reptile forms from nature. He was succeeded by his equally successful grandson Christoph (1563–1618).

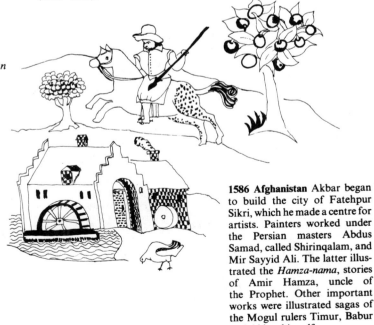

VISUAL ARTS

*c.*1580 **Mexico** The Spanish painter Baltasar de Echave Orio (*c.*1548–1620) settled in Mexico Together with his son Baltasar de Echave Ibia and grandson Baltasar de Echave Rioja (d. 1682), he was a formative influence on Mexican painting.

1581 **Bohemia** The Flemish painter Bartholomeus Spranger (1546–1611) settled in Prague as leader of the later mannerist movement. He painted very formal 'spiral' compositions in the style of Correggio, whose work he had encountered when travelling in Italy. While in Italy he also met the Dutch painter van Mander, who introduced his style to the Haarlem academy.

*c.*1585 **Italy** Paolo Caliari Veronese (*c.*1528–1588) painted *The Triumph of Venice*. His work is considered the culmination of Venetian magnificence and pageantry. His decorative murals and ceilings were extensions of the architecture of the buildings.

1586 **Afghanistan** Akbar began to build the city of Fatehpur Sikri, which he made a centre for artists. Painters worked under the Persian masters Abdus Samad, called Shirinqalam, and Mir Sayyid Ali. The latter illustrated the *Hamza-nama*, stories of Amir Hamza, uncle of the Prophet. Other important works were illustrated sagas of the Mogul rulers Timur, Babur and Akbar himself.

INVENTIONS & DISCOVERIES

*1584
Sir Walter
Raleigh
discovered
Virginia.*

*1585
Englishman John
Davis tried to
find North-West
Passage and
discovered Davis
Straits.*

HISTORICAL EVENTS	LITERATURE	DANCE & DRAMA	MUSIC

MUSIC

1586 Italy Giovanni Battista Giacometti appointed *maestro di cappella* at Mantua; he was one of earliest virtuosi on the violin.

HISTORICAL EVENTS

1587 Mary Queen of Scots beheaded at Fotheringhay.

1588 Defeat of Spanish Armada against England.

1589 Beginning of Bourbon dynasty in France with accession of Huguenot Henry of Navarre.

LITERATURE

1587 Germany *Historia von D. Johann Fausten* was compiled by Johann Spies. The Faust legend dates from before 1540, but this book is the first published account. Attempts have been made to trace the origins of the Faust figure back to various historical prototypes, including Solomon; the magical practices and the blood-pact with the Devil were certainly present in early Persian and Jewish occultism. The search for knowledge at any price was one of the major sixteenth-century preoccupations.

1588 England *Pandosto* by Robert Greene (1558–1592), poet, playwright, pamphleteer, and writer of prose fiction. His fiction is closer to the modern novel than Lyly's, but still not very readable today.

1590 Netherlands *Hertspiegel*, a poem by Henric Laurens Spiegel (1549–1612), a Dutch poet, playwright and prose writer. In his mature work he used alexandrines, a new metre in Dutch poetry.

DANCE & DRAMA

1587 England *Tamburlaine the Great* by Christopher Marlowe (1564–1593): the first English blank-verse tragedy for the public theatre.

1587 Portugal *Castro* by Antonio Ferreira (1528–1569), the first Portuguese writer to use a combination of native subject matter and classical models.

1587 Spain Actresses were permitted to appear professionally in Madrid.

1588 China *The Peony Pavilion* by T'ang Hsien Tsu (1550–1616), a romantic drama which is still popular.

1588 England Death of Richard Tarlton, celebrated for his performances of the comic jig which often ended a theatre performance: it was a type of song-and-dance act, the fore-runner of the German *Singspiel*.

1588 France Thoinot Arbeau (Jehan Tabourot, Abbé of Lengres), published his *Orchésographie*, describing the dances of the fifteenth and sixteenth centuries. He shows that steps used in court dances like the galliard were also used in morris jigs.

1589 England *The Spanish Tragedy* by Thomas Kyd (1558–1594) popularized the Senecan play in England.

1589 Italy Bernardo Buontalenti (1536–1608) designed scenery and stage machinery for a series of interludes of spectacle with music, as part of the wedding celebrations of the Duke of Tuscany: these *Intermezzi* were the origins of opera. His scenery aroused great interest, and his drawings and engravings, which still exist, are important records in the history of stage scenery. He may have invented a system of flat side wings, sliding in grooves; earlier designers used three-sided prisms which were turned to indicate a change of scene – the *periaktoi* of the ancient Greeks.

MUSIC

1588 England Second publication of *Psalmes, Sonets and Songs of Sadnes and Pietie* by William Byrd (1543–1623), composer, one of the first to write songs for solo voice with an instrumental accompaniment forming an integral and indispensable part.

1588 England Birth of Nicholas Lanier(e) (d. 1666), English musician of French descent. Composer of many songs, he is believed to have introduced the *stylo recitativo* into England.

1588 England First printed collection of Italian madrigals with English words, *Musica Transalpina*, compiled by Nicholas Yonge (d. 1619). Although Italian madrigals had been known in England for some 40 years, this anthology, together with the work of Morley, provided the impetus for English composers to take up the form.

1589 France Publication of *Orchesographie . . .*, earliest extant treatise on dancing containing notation of different dance tunes, written by Thoinot Arbeau (1519–1595).

1589 Italy The *intermedi* called 'de la Pellegrina' performed for the wedding of Ferdinando Medici and Christine of Lorraine in Florence, which were perhaps the most lavish entertainments of the century. They also included some of the earliest extant music by members of the group around Count Bardi.

1586 Spain Death of Luis de Morales, who expressed the religious intensity of his time in popular devotional paintings.

*c.***1587 Germany** Blue and purple pottery glazes were developed at the Raeren stoneware factory. Stoneware manufacture spread from the Rhine to the Netherlands and England during the late sixteenth century. It is the only non-earthenware made in Europe before the introduction of Eastern techniques.

1588 Italy The Grand Duke Ferdinand of Florence established a factory making *pietre dure* mosaics; coloured stones such as agate, porphyry and lapis lazuli were used to make naturalistic panel designs of birds, flowers and landscapes.

England: after a contemporary illustration of 'The Spanish Tragedy' by Thomas Kyd

1589 Afghanistan Completion of the illustrated version of the classic Hindu epic *Mahabharata*, now called *Razmnama*, by the Persian-influenced artist Daswanth. This was done for the Mogul ruler Akbar: the 'Akbar' style which developed at his court used brilliant colour, linear drawing, faithful portraiture and composition in rising tiers.

1589 Japan Death of Sesson, an ink-painter who carried on the school of the fourteenth-century master Sesshū.

1590–1597 England Hardwick Hall by Robert Smythson is a typical 'prodigy house'; symmetrical in plan, it is flat-roofed and has large mullioned and transomed windows on every front.

1590 Netherlands The line-engraver Hendrick Goltzius (1558–1617) studied classical sculpture and Renaissance art in Rome, which influenced him in adopting a classical style. His landscape drawings were forerunners of seventeenth-century work.

1590 Janssen invented compound microscope.

HISTORICAL EVENTS	LITERATURE	DANCE & DRAMA	MUSIC
		*c.*1590 **England** *Love's Labour's Lost* by William Shakespeare (1564–1616), a highly versatile writer, who wrote mainly for the public stage. As there was little or no scenery in the Elizabethan theatre, atmosphere and setting were conveyed by the poetry, and character was much more important than it would be in a highly elaborate, spectacular production.	
	1591 Denmark First printed edition of Danish ballads; they are all anonymous, but of great artistic merit.	**1591 Ceylon** Establishment of the Kandya monarchy, who were, until the nineteenth century, patrons of the dance: Kandya dance, imported from India in a Hindu form *c.*second century A.D., was preserved in a secular form compatible with Buddhism. The dance even came to be used as part of a Buddhist festival.	
	1591 Spain Death of Juan de Yepes (b. 1542), the mystic and poet cannonized in 1726 as St John of the Cross. His most important works, three mystical poems, are in Italian metres. He also wrote prose commentaries on them.		**1592 England** The *Whole Booke of Psalmes* published by Thomas East (d. 1609), musical typographer, publisher and composer, famous as publisher of Elizabethan madrigalists.
		1592 Germany Robert Browne, English actor, gave his first performance in Germany under the patronage of the Duke of Brunswick. Troupes of English actors did much to raise standards of acting and appreciation of theatre in Germany about this time. They also created the character 'Hanswurst', descended from the medieval jester, whose crude fooling remained popular for over 100 years.	**1592 England** First songs by George Kirbye, (*c.*1565–1634) published in *Whole Book of Psalms*.
			1592 Italy Publication of the first part of *Prattica di Musica Utile et Necessaria si al Compositore . . . si anco al Cantore* by Ludovico Zacconi (1555–1627).
	1594 Portugal *Várias Rimas Ao Bom Jesus* by Diogo Bernardes (?1532–1596). These are devotional poems. He was also a distinguished writer of pastoral poetry.	**1594 Spain** Lope de Vega published *Maestro de Danzar*, in which he describes among other dances a *Moresque* or Moorish dance as a solo display performance. The term also described choral dances pantomiming the struggle between Christians and Islam, and other choral dances influenced in form by Moorish Spain.	**1594 Italy** A work on vocal figuration and ornamentation was published by Giovanni Battista Bovicelli.
			1594 Italy *Amfiparnaso, Commedia Harmonica* by Orazio Vecchi (1550–1605), composer and poet, published at Modena.

1590–1636 Japan Katsura Imperial Palace, Kyoto, is superbly sited in a specially composed landscape on a riverbank. Building materials are simple but the result is a highly sophisticated complex of palace halls and tea pavilions.

1591–1608 Italy St Andrea della Valle, Rome, by Carlo Maderna (1556–1629), and Giacomo della Porta (c.1533–1602), is a Maderna's masterpiece, especially the great crossing dome.

England: the Swan Theatre, where Shakespeare played, 1596-97

1594 Japan Nishi-Hongau-Ji-Shoin, Kyoto, is a high priest's residence with the main hall divided into rooms by sliding doors; vertical columns were further pared down in size than formerly and book shelves, reading desk, a stage for *No* dramas, a separate temple and garden were important features.

1591 Italy *The Madonna and Child with Sts Joseph and Francis* by Ludovico Carracci of Bologna (1555–1619). He was cousin to the painter Annibale Carracci and, with him, an influence on the next generation. His classicism was subordinated to emotional tension and expressive force.

c.1592 Italy Beginning of the first active period for the Venetian painter Michelangelo Merisi da Caravaggio (1573–1610) who established himself in Rome: he was criticized for painting directly on to canvas, in oils, from the model, a method traditional to Venice but not to central Italy. He built his compositions with deep colour, strongly marked shadow and strong beams of light. His naturalism and solidity were a strong counter-influence to Mannerism.

1593 Bohemia Death of the Italian painter Giuseppe Archimboldo (b. 1537) who became court painter in Prague and was noted for his paintings of grotesque symbolic figures. The twentieth-century Surrealists revived interest in him.

1594 Italy On the death of Tintoretto, Jacopo Negretti Palma Giovane (1544–1628) became the leading painter in Venice. He was trained by Titian; when Titian died, Giovane completed his last painting.

1595 Italy Annibale Carracci of Bologna (1560–1609) was invited to Rome by Cardinal Farnese to work on the fresco decoration of the Farnese palace: This occupied him for 10 years. His style was influenced by Raphael and, although developing during the 10 years, remained within the High Renaissance; his decoration of the Farnese gallery was considered the third great classical decoration in Rome, after Michelangelo's Sistine ceiling and Raphael's *Stanze*. He was also a caricaturist, bringing the caricaturist's economy and force to his figure composition.

1592 Remains of Pompeii discovered. Della Szienza Meccanica by Galileo Galilei outlined new principles of mechanics in support of Copernican theory.

HISTORICAL EVENTS	LITERATURE	DANCE & DRAMA	MUSIC

DANCE & DRAMA

1596 England Sir John Davies' poem *Orchestra* is the earliest poem on dancing in English: it describes May dances as 'spirited' and court dances, which evolved from them, as 'grave and solemn'.

1596 England The Dutch scholar Johann de Witt made a drawing and description of the Swan theatre, London, from which we derive much of our knowledge of the Elizabethan theatre buildings.

MUSIC

1596 Italy *Hippolyti Baccusi, Eccl. Cath. Veronae Musicae Magistri, Missae Tres, tum Vivâ Voce tum Omni Instrumentorum Genere Cantatu Accommodatissimae, cum Octo Vocibus*, one of first works to have instruments playing in unison with voices, was published by Ippolito Baccusi (d. 1609).

1597 England *First Booke of Songes* by John Dowland (1563–1626) published. It marked the introduction into England of the *obbligato* type of accompaniment. He was a virtuoso performer and a notable song writer, publishing four volumes.

HISTORICAL EVENTS

1597 Japan banished Christian missionaries.

LITERATURE

1597 England *Essays* by Francis Bacon (1561–1626), statesman, lawyer, philosopher and essayist. All his writing, in whatever field, was thoughtful and highly competent. His style in the *Essays* was pithy and witty.

1597 England *A Plaine and Easie Introduction to Practicall Musicke* published by Thomas Morley (1557–1603).

1597 England Publication of *Madrigals to 3, 4, 5, and 6 Voyces* by Thomas Weelkes (d. 1623).

1597 Italy First part of treatise on organ-playing published by Girolamo Diruta (b. *c.*1550). This was far in advance of any contemporary publication as it attempted to treat organ as a separate instrument from clavier.

1598 Bohemia *Silva Quadrilinguis* by Daniel Adam Veleslavin (1545–1599), a humanist, whose work is representative of the golden age of the Czech language. His style, elegant and mannered, was regarded as the model for Czech writers. In addition to his historical writings, he is known for his dictionaries, of which this work is one.

1598–1599 England Building of the Globe theatre, London.

1598 England *Every Man in His Humour* by Ben Jonson (1573–1637): he created the comedy of humours in England and was the first English satiric dramatist.

1598 Italy *Della Poesia Rappresentativa E Del Modo Di Rappresenture le Favole Sceniche* written by Angelo Ingegneri (*c.*1550–*c.*1613) stressed the importance of stage lighting, and advocated darkening the auditorium completely and concealing the stage lights. A darkened auditorium did not, however, become usual until the nineteenth century because earlier audiences wished to be seen – the play was often less important than the social gathering.

1599 England *Hamlet* by William Shakespeare.

*c.*1597 Italy Birth of Antonio Maria Abbatini (d. 1680), composer. With Marco Marazzoli he wrote *Dal Male du Violon*, the earliest known comic opera, which was performed in Rome in 1653.

1598 England *Canzonets to Fowre Voyces* published by Giles Farnaby (*c.*1565–1640). His writing for virginals was second only to Byrd.

1598 England Publication of *The First Set of English Madrigals to 3, 4, 5 and 6 voices* by John Wilbye (1574–1638).

1599 England *The Psalmes of David in Meter*, one of the earliest collections to give the melody in the soprano part, was published by Richard Alison.

1599 Mogul leader Akbar began conquest of the Deccan.

1599 England Publication of a collection of madrigals by John Farmer, important composer of the Elizabethan period.

ARCHITECTURE

1596–1619 Poland Jesuit church of Sts Peter and Paul, Cracow, by Giovanni Trevano (flourished 1596–1632) is one of the first baroque structures in Poland modelled on Il Gesù, Rome.

1597 Italy St Susannah façade, Rome, by Carlo Maderna (1556–1679) is a baroque elevation crowded with orders and set with niches rather than windows, a pattern repeated many times in churches thereafter.

1598 France François Mansart born (died 1666), the first of the great architects in the classic French style. He designed several châteaux and churches.

1599 Italy Francesco Borromini born (died 1667); a highly original baroque architect who rivalled Bernini, he designed churches almost exclusively.

THREE DIMENSIONAL ART

1597 England Gerard's *Herbal* used as a pattern-book for embroideries of flowers and fruit: Embroidery was by this time popular with the merchant class.

late 1500–1600 Persia Revival of lustre ware, using rich ruby and flame colours on alkaline glazes.

late 1500–1700 Venice Glassmakers made lace glass or *latticine*, containing lacy patterns in opaque white.

VISUAL ARTS

1595 Netherlands Gilles Coninxloo (1544–1607) settled in Amsterdam. His later landscape paintings, studies of atmosphere and the moods of nature, influenced other Flemish and Dutch painters.

1596 Netherlands Jan Brueghel (1568–1625) returned to Brussels after working in Italy. He became established as a still-life painter, considered the greatest of his age. His landscapes were mainly small woodland scenes with figure groups, meticulous in style and brightly coloured.

1598 Italy Arrival of the German painter and etcher Adam Elsheimer (1578–1610), who had trained in the realistic Flemish style and now learned Italian use of colour. He painted many small works, sometimes on copper, with simplicity and narrative skill. His work was widely disseminated, through engravings, and influential well into the seventeenth century.

1596
Galileo invented thermometer.

Italy: Saint Susannah, Rome, by Carlo Maderna

17th Century

LITERATURE

1600 France *Ode au Roi Henri le Grand* by the poet François de Malherbe (1555–1628), known as the creator of classical poetry in France. His work is dignified, rhetorical, and tending to abstraction. The 'classic' alexandrine is his creation.

DANCE & DRAMA

*c.*1600–1700 **Japan** Development, alongside *kabuki*, of the *bunraku* puppet theatre, which has near life-size puppets with eyes, eyebrows and fingers separately controlled: puppeteers specialize in male or female rôles. The art was for centuries based on Osaka.

*c.*1600–1700 **Philippines** Christian missionaries began the *moro-moro* plays, presenting stylized battle scenes between Christians and Moslems: They were grafted on to a native dramatic form. The set is always the same, with the rival forces coming out of two towers on either side of the stage, and there is an epic-style poetic text.

1600 England Will Kemp, dancer and comedian, danced in morris steps from London to Norwich and recorded the achievement in *Kemp's Nine Daies Wonder*.

*c.*1600 **England** The masque had come to include three formal dances: the Entry, the Main and the Going-Out dance, performed by amateurs. The anti-masque, which preceded it instead of a spoken prologue, was usually a grotesque dance; it was performed by professionals. Dancers of the true masque went down to dance with the audience as in traditional 'commoning'.

*c.*1600 **Spain** Dances originating in Central American colonies and refined in Spain, the *zarabanda, chacona, pasacalle* and *folía* began to be popular in the rest of Europe. Their energy reinvigorated the courtly dance, but they were modified by a new feeling for gliding movements; the leaping and kicking steps became fewer in social dances.

MUSIC

1600–1700 England The arch-lute was used extensively for playing the base part in compositions.

1600 England First of five books of lute-songs published by Robert Jones, lutenist and composer.

1600 Italy *La Rappresentazione di Anima, e di Corpo* first performed in Rome; it was written by Emilio de' Cavalieri, (*c.*1550–1602), one of earliest composers of opera and an important contributor to monodic music for the stage.

1600 Italy The opera *Euridice*, with music by Giulio Caccini (*c.*1550–1618) and Jacopo Peri (1561–1633), performed in Florence, as the first full manifestation of the monodic principles being discussed there.

ARCHITECTURE

1600–1700 Bolivia San Francisco, La Paz, is remarkable in combining a traditional basilican-planned church with primitive decoration of Indian origin; pre-Columbian art survived most strongly in Bolivia and Peru and when fused with European elements is termed *mestizo*.

1600–1700 Ecuador Church of the Compania, Quito, is a Jesuit church in imitation of the Gesù, Rome, with an elaborate eighteenth-century baroque façade.

1600–1700 Japan Hikone Castle is an example of the large castles built in Japan in the sixteenth and seventeenth centuries; it has stone ramparts and upper walls of timber and plaster construction and its design may have owed something to Western influence.

1600–1700 Japan Yokokan Pavilion, Fukui, is a tea house in which architecture was reduced to the most elemental and simple forms; the wall partitions are moveable.

1600–1700 Japan The mausoleum of Shogun Ieuasu and Iemitsu, Nikko, is one of the most impressive tombs of the Shoguns; a complex of buildings contained within a triple enclosure, it is highly decorated in coloured and gilded carving, metal work and sculpture.

1600 Persia The two-storeyed Allahverdi Bridge, Isfahan, has niches built as an extension of the promenade of the Chagar Bagh.

1600 Russia Nicholas Church, Panilovo, is the earliest surviving example of a wooden octagonal church in Russia, preceding a whole group of churches, all of which share a common ground plan of a square apse and anteroom, placed next to the main octagonal body.

1600 Scotland Fyvie Castle is a good example of the Scottish baronial style, in which the traditional square defensive pele tower was elaborated by the addition of corbelled-out turrets (tourelles), of French origin.

*c.***1600 France** Henry IV began the replanning of Paris, introducing the idea of small-scale terrace houses forming great squares; an example is Place des Vosges, begun in 1605.

THREE DIMENSIONAL ART

early 1600–1700 Germany Stoneware potters at Kreussen began to decorate wares with enamel paints.

1600–1700 Bulgaria Furnishing of Rozhen monastery, noted for the wood carvings on its iconostasis.

1600–1700 India Carpets of this period were as highly prized by Europeans as those of Persia. Design was more naturalistic, including pictures of men and animals as well as flower motifs; Hindu influence tempered Moslem tendencies to abstraction.

1600–1700 Western Europe Portuguese and Dutch imported Ming pottery which was copied in Portugal, Germany, Spain and the Netherlands, culminating in the blue-and-white, underglazed copies, made in Delft, of ware of K'ang-hsi's reign (1662–1722).

1600–1700 Russia Peter the Great established workshops in wood-carving and metalwork at St Petersburg. Wood-carvers by this time had developed a rounded, sculptural art which influenced some of the later Russian architects.

1600–1700 Russia Boxes made at Archangel from walrus ivory were decorated with an olive-branch design; this became a favourite motif for scrimshaw carvers, especially Americans carving on whale's teeth.

*c.***1600 India** Sculpture in temple buildings began to take the form of elaborate groups of figures incorporated in piers.

VISUAL ARTS

1600–1617 France Active period of the painter Jacques Bellange, who developed an original style of mannerism. He succeeded in expressing genuine religious faith through an apparently conventional form.

*c.***1600 Japan** The influence of Zen Buddhism on *suiboko* (ink-painting) artists declined: they became more interested in technical virtuosity, beginning to use a jagged, angular brush-stroke for dramatic effect.

INVENTIONS & DISCOVERIES
1600
De Magnete *by William Gilbert described terrestrial magnetism. Johann Kepler calculated elliptical paths of planets.*

India: detail from Indian carpet, 17th century

203

HISTORICAL EVENTS	LITERATURE	DANCE & DRAMA	MUSIC

HISTORICAL EVENTS

1601
Ricci, Jesuit missionary, admitted to Peking.

1602
East India Company formally established.

1603
Death of Elizabeth I, start of Stuart rule in England.

1605
Gunpowder Plot discovered in London.

LITERATURE

1601–1610 Netherlands Love lyrics by Pieter Cornelisz Hooft (1581–1647), poet, playwright and prose writer. Profoundly influenced by his travels in Italy, he was concerned with beauty more deeply than any other Dutch poet. He was a member of the Egelantier, an important *rederijker* guild, in Amsterdam; the city was the centre of the literary life of the period. His friends included a number of distinguished musicians. He was the most important Dutch writer of the seventeenth century.

1601 England *The Progresse of the Soule* by John Donne (1572–1631), divine and poet in the metaphysical tradition. The metaphysical poets frequently treated religious subjects, and used striking, even fantastic, imagery, compressing complex ideas into a few words. Donne's work included sermons, and both religious and secular poetry.

1605–1615 Spain *Don Quixote* by Miguel de Cervantes Saavedra (1547–1616), novelist, playwright and poet. First conceived as a satire on the novel of chivalry, the book developed into a story of an egotistical idealist disillusioned. It has been variously interpreted according to the standards obtaining at the time: in the seventeenth century it was regarded as a fantastic burlesque; in the eighteenth it was seen as a satire on people who acted against good sense; in the nineteenth it was the tale of a misunderstood idealist. Translated into many languages, it had a profound influence on many European literatures and is considered a world masterpiece.

1607 France First part of *Astrée* by the novelist Honoré d'Urfé (1567–1625): the book, a pastoral romance in the style of *Amadis de Gaula*, was written in five parts and completed in 1627. Enormously popular, it set a style of courtship and gallant conversation.

DANCE & DRAMA

1602 England *Twelfth Night* by William Shakespeare was presented at the Middle Temple.

1603 France *L'Ecossaise* by Antoine de Montchrétien (1575–1621) was one of the first plays to deal with contemporary or very near contemporary events: it is about Mary, Queen of Scots.

1603–1604 Japan O-kuni, inventor of the Japanese popular (*kabuki*) theatre, was invited to play before the Imperial court.

1604 Italy Cesare Negri (b.1530) published *Le Grazie d'Amore* or *Nuove Inventioni di Balli*, a treatise on the techniques of dancing in the form of 55 rules.

1606 England *Volpone* by Ben Jonson (1573–1637).

1607 England *The Knight of the Burning Pestle* by Francis Beaumont (1584–1616) and John Fletcher (1579–1625) ridiculed the middle classes. Audiences were increasingly made up of the sophisticated upper classes, while theatres were smaller and roofed in, demanding a different style of acting from that of the older, unroofed theatres.

1607 England *The Revenger's Tragedy* by Cyril Tourneur (1575–1626): the revenge play, usually set in Italy, where the English believed all manner of dark deeds were perpetrated, was very popular during the seventeenth century.

MUSIC

1601 England *A Booke of Ayres* was published by Thomas Campian (1567–1620).

1601 Germany Publication of *Lustgarten Neuer Teutscher Gesang* by Hans Leo Hassler (1564–1612), organist and composer.

1602 Italy Birth of Francesco Cavalli (d. 1676). A brilliant and prolific composer of opera, of which more than 40 were performed, he may be regarded as most significant figure in the field of opera in Venice.

1602 Italy Lodovico Grossi Viadana (c.1564–1645), composer, published a set of *concerti* making full use of (unfigured) *basso continuo*. He has often been regarded as inventor of this form.

1603 France Publication of a collection of lute pieces *Thesaurus Harmonicus Divini Laurenci Romani* by Jean Baptiste Besard (b. c.1567).

1604 England First madrigals published by Thomas Bateson (c.1570–1630).

1604 Mexico *Liber in Quo Quatuor Passiones Christi Domini Continentur* the only neo-Hispanic imprint exclusively devoted to music, published by Juan Navarro (c.1550–c.1610), Mexican composer of Spanish birth.

1605 England Orlando Gibbons (1583–1625), organist and composer, appointed organist of Chapel Royal, where he remained until his death. His great reputation was founded on his church music, none of which was printed during his lifetime.

1605 Italy *L'Organo Suonarino* by Adriano Banchieri (c.1567–1634), composer, theorist and poet, was published in Venice; it contained the first precise rules for accompanying from a figured bass.

1606 Italy Production, in Rome, of the first open-air opera.

1607 England *Musicke of Sundrie Kindes* published by Thomas Ford (c.1580–1648), lutenist and composer.

ARCHITECTURE

*c.*1600 **Japan** Kojoin Kyakuden, Ostu, is a house in the Shoin style and it is a small version of the more palatial buildings of the period on a rectangular plan and one storey high; room sizes depended on the size of mats used, which normally measured about 2 m by 1 m. Sliding wall partitions were usual and room functions interchangeable.

1601–1606 Persia The Sheik Luttullah Mosque, Isfahan, has a simple ground plan on traditional lines; magnificent tile cladding covers every conceivable surface.

1602 Holland The Butchers' Guildhall, Haarlem, by Lieven de Key is a mannerist building distinguished by elaborate gable ends and dormers decorated with strapwork and obelisks.

1607 England Charlton House, Greenwich, London, is a Jacobean house displaying typical features: on an H plan, built of brick with stone quoining, it has an elaborately decorated centre entrance bay and ogee-capped end turrets.

THREE DIMENSIONAL ART

1605–1627 India Earliest surviving embroideries, made for the Mogul court, are tenthangings of brocaded velvet or cotton worked in silk and metal thread.

1607 France Flemish weavers were permitted to set up a tapestry workshop in Paris. They successfully established a French school of tapestry, the first to have lasting influence since the English occupation of 1418–1436 destroyed the earlier tradition.

VISUAL ARTS

1602 France Death of Toussaint Dubreuil (b. 1561), a Flemish painter trained in France, whose work at Fontainebleau and the Louvre formed a bridge from mannerism to seventeenth-century classicism.

1602 Italy The Bolognese painter Domenichino (Domenico Zampieri, 1581–1641) went to work on the Farnese palace in Rome under Annibale Carracci. He retained the Renaissance interest in the firm line even when moving towards a baroque style, and became a leading artist of the Bologna school. He was influenced by Raphael and in his turn influenced the French painter Poussin.

1603 Italy *Crucifixion of St Peter* by Guido Reni (1575–1642), a Bolognese artist who painted incidental balanced pictures independent of the prevailing influences of Caravaggio and Annibale Carracci.

1604–1608 Netherlands Sir Peter Paul Rubens (1577–1640) worked in Italy, studying and copying the work of Michelangelo, Titian, Tintoretto and Correggio. He also made a study of antique forms. His work carried on the Renaissance combination of religious depth and sensuality.

*c.*1604 **Netherlands** Roelandt Savery (*c.*1576–1639) travelled to Prague to paint for Rudolf II. His drawings of the emperor's menagerie inspired him, on his return, to paint studies of individual animals which were the first of their kind in Holland. His flower paintings, though few, were very influential.

1605–1627 India Reign of the Mogul emperor, Jahangir, patron of the arts, whose own interest in nature stimulated a school of bird and flower paintings; the best known of his artists was Mansur. Portraits of Jahangir are the earliest to show a nimbus behind the head: this was a symbol originating in Persian sun-worship, copied by Buddhists and Byzantine Christians, and brought to Moslem India in Christian portraiture.

INVENTIONS & DISCOVERIES

1602 Galileo discovered laws of gravitation and oscillation. Bartholomew Gosnold explored Cape Cod.

1606 Galileo invented proportional compass.

HISTORICAL EVENTS	LITERATURE	DANCE & DRAMA	MUSIC
1608 Jesuit state of Paraguay established.	**1608–1609 France** *Satires I–XII* by the poet Mathurin Régnier (1573–1613). *Satire IX* is against Malherbe. Régnier was highly regarded by Boileau.		**1607 Italy** Production of Monteverdi's first opera *La Favola d'Orfeo* in Mantua where he was court composer to the Gorzaga family from 1590–1612.
1609 Moors expelled from Spain.	**1609 England** Sonnet sequence by William Shakespeare (1564–1616), poet and playwright.	**1609 England** Ben Jonson's *Masque of Queens* included a *Danse Figurée*, based on medieval tableaux dances derived from Italy. English masques still retained the main types of dance used in the older *mascarades* and *intermedi*.	**1609 England** *Ayres* (28 songs with accompaniment for lute and bass viol) and *Lessons for 1, 2 and 3 Viols*, published by Alfonso Ferrabosco (1575–1628), violist and composer, who lived in England.
	1610 Italy *Sidereus Nuncius* by Galileo Galilei (1564–1642), a scientist important in literary history for his vigorous, lucid and elegant prose.		**1609 England** Publication of *Pammelia* by Thomas Ravenscroft (*c*.1590–*c*.1633), theorist, musical editor and composer, it was the earliest English printed collection of rounds and catches.
	1611 Spain *El Polifemo* and *Las Soledades* by the poet Luis de Góngora y Argote (1561–1627), whose latinate vocabulary and syntax and use of hyperbole and mythological references formed a style which has become known as 'gongorism'. He used the devices with great skill and sensitivity, but his imitators were frequently less successful. In the nineteenth century, 'gongorism' implied an over-inflated style. Both Lope de Vega and Quevedo were critical of Góngora's work, but he did have a strong influence on seventeenth-century poetry and is regarded as one of the greatest of Spanish poets.	**1610 France** Accession of Louis XIII, who banned the dance *La Volta* as indecorous. Both the pavane and the galliard soon died out; the latter was thought too lively for current taste. **1611 England** The masque *Oberon Faery Prince* was devised by Ben Jonson and the architect, Inigo Jones (1573–1652), the first Englishman to become known for scenic design. Masques were elaborate productions which had little story but were rich in music, gorgeous costumes and spectacular effects. Opera, ballet and pantomime all owe something to the masque.	**1609 Germany** *New Ausserlesene Paduanen . . .*, the first published collection by William Brade (*c*.1560–1630), the English violist and composer, appeared in Hamburg.
	1611 Spain Death of Pedro de Ribadeneyra (b. 1527), biographer, historian and religious writer. A Jesuit, he wrote the life of St Ignatius Loyola, which is the first Spanish biography.	**1611 England** *The Tempest* by William Shakespeare was presented at court. **1611 Italy** Flaminio Scala made a collection of scenarii used by *commedia dell' arte* troupes as a basis for their improvisation.	**1611 Spain** Death of Tomás Luis de Victoria (b. 1548).
	1612 England *Poly-Olbion* by Michael Drayton (1563–1631), poet and playwright. He wrote well in a variety of forms and metres. This work is a patriotic epic.		**1612 England** *Parthenia*, a collection of virginal music, printed by William Hole, one of the earliest music engravers.
1613 Michael Romanov elected Tsar of Russia, founded Romanov dynasty.	**1612 Germany** *Aurora* by Jakob Böhme (1575–1624), the mystical philosopher. He worked out his own original philosophy which was widely influential especially, much later, on the Romantics.	**1613 Russia** The first Romanov Tsar, Michael III, ordered the construction of the first known theatre in Russia. The actors were probably German. **1613–1614 England** *The Duchess of Malfi* by John Webster (*c*.1580–1625) writer of 'revenge' tragedies.	**1614 England** Publication of a collection of metrical psalms and hymns *The Teares or Lamentacions of a Sorrowfvll Soule* by Sir William Leighton (d. *c*.1616), musical editor and amateur composer.
	1612 Italy *Vocabolario*, the first important Italian dictionary, was published by the Accademia della Crusca in Florence.		**1615 Germany** *Synopsis Musicae Practicae*, with numerous examples of hymns for four voices, published by Bartholomäus Gese (*c*.1555–1621).
1615 Dutch seized Moluccas from Portuguese.	**1615 Germany** A translation into German of Mateo Alemán's *Guzmán De Alfarache* (first published ?1599–1604) introduced the Spanish picaresque novel to Germany. The translator was Agidius Albertinus (1560–1620).	**1615 Spain** Publication of the collected plays of the writer Miguel Cervantes (1547–1616).	**1615 Italy** Giovanni Paolo Maggini (1581–*c*.1632), Italian violin maker, established his business at Brescia.

*1608
Dutch
constructed first
telescope.*

1609–1617 Russia Boim Chapel, L'vov, combines the local L'vov style with elements of contemporary Italian architecture; it has rich sculpted decoration on the façade.

1609 Spain The expulsion of the Moors ended Moorish influence on Spanish decorative arts, particularly embroidery, which they now continued in Algeria. Moorish embroidery had black outline stitches on white; this, in a more complex form, became known as 'Spanish work'.

1609 France The Flemish painter Frans Pourbus the Younger, third generation of a family of artists, became court painter to Marie de Médicis. His portraits were formal and emphasized the details of his patrons' costume and jewellery.

1609–1617 Turkey The Blue Mosque, Istanbul, is the crowning glory of the largest of all the royal Ottoman mosque complexes surrounded by 6 minarets; it was sumptuously decorated with Venetian glass, ostrich eggs, crystal, marble and, above all, tiles, with patterns of blue stencilling.

1609 Spain Juan Martinez Montanes (1568–1649), leading sculptor of the Sevillian school, began his first major work, the reredos at S Isadore, Santiponce; he continued the tradition of sixteenth century coloured sculpture but with more realism and emotional appeal. His workshop was influential on younger artists.

*c.*1610 **Peru** Death of the Jesuit artist Bernardo Bitti (b. 1548), whose work influenced painters in Peru, Ecuador and Bolivia well into the eighteenth century.

1612 France Louis le Vau born (died 1670), a great French baroque architect, especially famous for his houses.

1610 Italy Beginning of the active period of Agostino Tassi (*c.*1580–1644), creator of theatrical decoration schemes in illusionary architectural settings. He also painted a frieze of marine and coastal scenes in the Palazzo Doria-Pamphili which influenced his pupil, the French painter Claude, in his early work. Tassi's landscapes were mannerist in their use of bizarre forms.

1612 Japan Bosen Tea Room, Kyoto, is a 12-mat room designed especially for the tea-drinking ceremony and associated cultural activities; small tea houses had been built exclusively for this purpose, in landscaped gardens, from about the fourteenth century.

*1611
Kepler invented
astronomical
telescope.*

1612–1638 Persia Masjid-I-Shah, Isfahan, is a complex consisting of a mosque, a palace and a royal caravanserai, and it is the culmination of Persian mosque building, tiled both inside and out, the predominant colour being blue.

1614–1628 Austria Salzburg Cathedral by Santino Solari (1576–1646) is a Roman baroque-styled building in Latin-cross plan with apsidal transepts and dome placed on an octagonal drum; the interior is similar to Il Gesù, Rome.

1613 England Nicolas Stone (1583–1647), sculptor of tomb monuments, began work in London: he was the most accomplished English sculptor of his day.

1613 Spain El Greco (1541–1614) painted his *Assumption*: it was criticized for its Mannerist distortion and for the elongated forms characteristic of his work; he was also noted for his use of cold colours and harsh light to convey intense religious feeling.

*1614
John Napier
invented
logarithms.*

1614 Holland Zwiderkerk, Amsterdam, by Hendrik de Keyser (1565–1621) was the first post-Reformation church in Holland and one of several he designed adapted for Protestant use; the towers are particularly fine.

1615–1624 France Luxembourg Palace, Paris, by Salomon de Brosse (1565–1626) is a typical example of a large French hotel with one-storey street façade flanked by tall pavilions, an inner courtyard, and the main house at the rear.

1615 Japan End of the Momoyama period, which produced architectural sculpture of high quality; after this date it degenerated into elaborate formalism on a grand scale.

*c.*1615 **Netherlands** Hendrick Terbrugghen (1588–1629) became a leader of the Caravaggian school in Utrecht, after a journey to Italy.

HISTORICAL EVENTS	LITERATURE	DANCE & DRAMA	MUSIC

1616
Manchu Tartars invaded China. Richelieu became French Secretary of State.

1616 France Completion of *Les Tragiques*, begun 1577, by Théodore Agrippa d'Aubigné (1551–1630), poet and militant protestant. He was one of France's greatest religious poets. A long poem in 7 books, it exposed the misery and fanaticism of religious wars.

1617 Germany The Fruchtbringende Gesellschaft, a society to refine literature and improve the language, was founded by the Prince of Anhalt. Tastes in poetry at the time were learned and aristocratic.

1617
Treaty of succession between Austrian and Spanish Hapsburgs.

1617 Netherlands Foundation of the Duytsche Academie by Samuel Coster (1579–1665), surgeon and playwright. The object was to bring learning to the ordinary people in their native language, but the various courses, in languages, philosophy and mathematics, did not survive long. The Academie then confined itself to drama, and later merged with the Egelantier Chamber of Rhetoric.

1617 Portugal Death of Bernardo de Brito (b. 1568) who wrote the beginning of a history of Portugal which was later continued by other writers. The historical value of his work is doubtful, but he was a superb stylist and his work marks the beginning of the classical period in Portuguese writing.

?1618–1619 Germany Probable dates of the two volumes of *Oden und Gesänge* by Georg Rudolf Weckherlin (1584–1653), courtier and poet. He was influenced by the French Pléiade and the English Elizabethans, and wrote the most important German court poetry of the period. Later in life, he revised his poetry, following the rules of Martin Opitz.

1619 Portugal *Corte na Aldeia a Noites de Inverno* by Francisco Rodrigues Lobo (1580–1622), novelist and poet. His work included ballads, eclogues, an epic, and pastoral novels, besides this book, his best, which is not unlike Castiglione's *Cortegiano*. It is considered an excellent example of the best Portuguese prose.

1617 Japan Creation of all-male *kabuki* troupes, called *wakasha kabuki*, by Dansuke.

1618 Italy The Teatro Farnese was built in **Parma** by Giambattista Aleotti (1546–1636): the stage had a proscenium arch and the seating arrangements were much closer to those of a modern theatre than in earlier buildings. It was intended for spectacular productions and equipped with elaborate stage machinery for this purpose.

1618 Italy Earliest extant manuscript of *The Comedy of a Marriage*, probably by Leone de Somi (1527–1592), and the first known Hebrew play: it shows the influence of the *commedia dell' arte*.

1618 Spain Lope de Vega (1562–1635) began work on the preparation of his plays for publication: tradition credits him with 2000. His keen sense of the theatre, masterly handling of verse and skilful use of intrigue make him an outstanding figure not only in his native Spain but throughout Europe.

1616 Czechoslovakia Collegium Musicum established in Prague.

1617 Italy Claudio Monteverdi (b. 1567) appointed choirmaster at San Marco, Venice where he remained until his death, during which time he composed most of his dramatic music.

1619 England Francis Tregian (1574–1619), English musician, compiled *Fitzwilliam Virginal Book*.

1619 Germany *Psalmen Davids Sammt Etlichen Motetten und Concerten mit 8 und mehr Stimmen* published by Heinrich Schütz (1585–1672); this marked the beginning of his long mature creative period, having been established as musical director of electoral chapel in Dresden in 1617.

1618
Thirty Years' War began in Holy Roman Empire.

1619
First American Parliament met in Jamestown, Virginia.

ARCHITECTURE

1615 Germany Augsburg Town Hall by Elias Holl, the first truly Renaissance building in Germany has a beautifully proportioned façade; it was rebuilt to the original design after World War II.

1615 Sweden Nicodemus Tessin the elder born (died 1681), a leading Swedish baroque architect whose son, Nicodemus Tessin the younger (1654–1728), succeeded him in that role.

1616–1635 England London, The Queen's House, Greenwich, by Inigo Jones (1573–1651) is a revolutionary house in that it resembles a Palladian villa, examples of which Jones had seen on a visit to Italy 1613–1614, and is thus the first wholly classical building in England.

1617–1693 Brazil The São Bento Abby, Rio de Janerio, has a lavishly decorated baroque interior with a wooden barrel vault, and is one of the earliest baroque churches in Brazil.

1617 Spain Bernardas Church, Alcala de Henares, by Sebastian de la Plaza is an early baroque work after Gionanni Lorenzo Bernini (1598–1680).

1617–1620 Spain Plaza Mayor, Madrid, by Juan Gomez de Mora was planned by Herrera (c.1530–1597) and completed in his restrained classical style; the buildings around the square are four-storeyed with arcaded shops on the ground floor.

1619 England The Banqueting House, London, by Inigo Jones (1573–1651) is a Palladian-styled town house built in the middle of Tudor Whitehall.

1619 Japan Like most surviving pagodas, this one at Yasaka dates from the seventeenth century but resembles those built earlier; the ground storey contained the Buddhist shrine, those above serving as belvederes with curved projecting roofs supporting bells.

THREE DIMENSIONAL ART

c.1617–1621 Germany Dated work by the amber-carvers Georg Scriba and Charles Marutus of Königsberg. Work in amber is considered to have reached its highest artistic level in this period, especially in Germany.

1617 Holland Isaac Elsevier (1596–1651) set up a printing works in Leiden which was later carried on by Bonaventure and Abraham Elsevier. They specialized in books for the University and other learned works.

1619 England Foundation of the Mortlake tapestry factory, under the patronage of Charles I. It was directed by Sir Francis Crane (d. 1636), whose Flemish weavers produced outstanding work between 1620 and 1635; they made their own versions of Raphael's *Acts of the Apostles* and worked also from cartoons by Francis Cleyn, who was appointed their designer in 1624.

VISUAL ARTS

1616 Netherlands *The Banquet of the Officers of St George Militia Company* by Frans Hals (1581/5–1666) was innovatory, being a life-size group portrait celebrating the new republic with strong characterization of individual men. Before Hals, only Cornelisz van Haarlem (1562–1638) had painted group portraits of similar vigour.

1616 Netherlands Death of Cornelis Ketel, a successful portrait artist.

1617 England Death of Isaac Oliver, a miniaturist who had worked under Hilliard and continued his tradition in a more matter-of-fact style. His portraits had more naturalism and less elegance than his master's.

c.1618 Netherlands Sir Anthony van Dyck (1599–1641) went to work in Rubens' workshop and stayed for two years. His early paintings show the influence of Rubens.

1619 Spain Diego Rodriguez de Silva y Velazquez (1599–1660) painted *The Immaculate Conception* and *The Adoration of the Magi*. His figures were naturalistic, portrait-like and painted on a warm ground. His paintings of everyday subjects such as *The Old Woman Cooking Eggs* (1618), treat humble figures and objects with seriousness and dignity. He did much to destroy the formal distinction between 'serious' and genre painting.

INVENTIONS & DISCOVERIES

1616 W. Snell formulated Law of refraction of light.

1617 Triangulation method of land measurement invented by Snell.

1619 First systematic use of decimal point.

1619 Portugal *Vida de Dom Frei Bartolomeu dos Martires* by the historian Frei Luis de Sousa (c.1555–1632). Of little value historically, his work was superbly written; he is considered one of the masters of Portuguese prose.

1620
Pilgrim Fathers left Plymouth in the Mayflower.

1620 Germany *Epigrammatus Libri Tres* by Jakob Bidermann (1578–1639), a playwright and poet who wrote in Latin.

1620 Russia A history of the troubled period before the accession of the first Romanov Tsar, written by the monk Avraamy Palitsyn (d. 1626): his account was powerful and dramatic.

1620 Italy The term *cantata*, denoting a solo song with continuo, was first used for a collection of songs by the prolific composer Alessandro Grandi (d. 1630).

1621
Papal Chancery first adopted 1 Jan as beginning of year.

1621 England *The Anatomy of Melancholy* by Robert Burton (1576/1577–1639/1640), prose writer and divine: the book is a typical Renaissance account of authorities on melancholy.

1621 Netherlands *Costelyck Mal* by Constantijn Huygens (1596–1687), statesman and poet. He wrote in French, Italian and Latin, besides Dutch. An intellectual, he enjoyed word-play; he regarded poetry as one of the ornaments of life, but secondary to his work.

1621 Austria Birth of Jacob Stainer (d. 1683), Austrian violin maker; he was first to introduce into Germany Italian principles of construction.

1619 Portugal The Carmelite Churches, Oporto, are twin churches illustrating the stylistic development of early to late baroque in Portugal; in the later church (1756–1768), ceramic murals were used as decoration, a characteristic of seventeenth- and eighteenth-century Portuguese architecture.

*c.*1620–1625 **Italy** Series of sculpture groups by Gianlorenzo Bernini (1598–1680); *Aeneas and Anchises, David, Rape of Proserpine* and *Apollo and Daphne*: their dramatic force and the sense of movement captured in marble made them a departure from current 'mannerist' fashions.

1620–1628 India Reign of Karan Singh II of Rajasthan, who made Udaipur a centre of painting after the end of the Mogul wars. Colours were now used to express emotion and not for purely decorative effect.

1620–1621 Italy Death of Bartolommeo Manfredi (b. 1580) whose imitation of Caravaggio's early style introduced Carravaggio's ideas to French and Dutch painters.

1620–1630 Netherlands Frans Hals (1581/5–1666) had his most successful and popular period. He painted five large group portraits using bright colours and a modified 'Caravaggist' treatment of light.

*c.*1620 **Netherlands** Gerrit van Honthurst (1590–1656) returned from Italy to become a leader of the Caravaggian school, with Terbrugghen. His liking for candlelight effects earned him the nickname 'Gerrit of the Night-Scenes'. This style was later abandoned, but it was probably an influence on the French painter de la Tour. Gerrit van Honthurst became a successful court painter.

1621–1628 Netherlands Sir Anthony van Dyck (1599–1641) worked in Italy; here his previous vigorous, Flemish, style developed into the refined style of his most famous work. His influence on portraiture in Flanders and in England was great.

Italy: 'David' by Gianlorenzo Bernini

1621 Czechoslovakia Valdstejn Palace, Prague, by Andrea Spezza (?–1628) is a combination of Renaissance style, employed on the loggia, and Roman baroque, used on the façade and the courtyard.

1621 Holland Death of Hendrick de Keyser (b. 1565), influential sculptor and architect: his chief work was the tomb of William of Orange, considered the first important piece of Dutch sculpture after new independence and prosperity stimulated the art. His realism and style of characterization influenced English work through his son-in-law Nicholas Stone.

1621 Italy Giovanni Lanfranco (1582–1647) painted his 'Assumption' in the dome of St Andrea della Valle, Rome. He carried Correggio's illusionist technique to a height that inspired a generation of baroque illusionist decorators.

1621 Netherlands Death of Ambrosius Bosschaert (b. 1573) who with Jan Brueghel was the most important of early Flemish flower painters. He worked mainly in Holland where he and his sons established flower painting as a genre. He often painted on copper.

HISTORICAL EVENTS	LITERATURE	DANCE & DRAMA	MUSIC

LITERATURE

1622 Netherlands Posthumous publication of poems by Gerbrand Adriaensz Brederode (1585–1618), poet, playwright and painter. He was a member of both the Egelantier Chamber of Rhetoric and Coster's Academie.

1622 Italy *La Secchia Rapita* by Alessandro Tassoni (1565–1635), literary critic, political writer and poet: mock heroic poem, which deals with imaginary adventures against a background of historical fact. Tassoni aimed to amuse, while satirizing contemporary life.

1623 Denmark Translation of the *Psalms* by Anders Christiensen Arrebo (1587–1637), poet and clergyman. He also wrote a long religious poem in alexandrines, *Hexaëmeron*, which owed much to du Bartas.

1623 Denmark *De Zeeuwsche Nachtegaal*, a collection of poems by Zealand writers, chief among them Jacob Cats (1577–1660). He wrote homely moral stories in undistinguished verse, and showed no trace of any influence of the Renaissance. His work was very popular and he had many followers.

1623 India Death of Tulsi Das (b. 1532), who wrote the *Ramcharita Manasa* (the *Ramayana* epic told in Hindi).

1623 Italy *Adone* by Giovan Battista Marino (1569–1625) was a long mythological poem on the story of Venus and Adonis; Marino deliberately set out to astonish the reader by his verbal skill, and his work abounded in metaphors and sensuous imagery. He was widely admired.

1623 Scotland *Flowers of Sion* by William Drummond of Hawthornden (1585–1649), poet and pamphleteer. His poems were in the Elizabethan tradition.

1624 Germany *Buch von der Deutschen Poeterey* by Martin Opitz von Boberfeld (1597–1639), poet and literary theorist. By either adapting or translating, he provided examples of all the major baroque genres for other writers to follow, and initiated the seventeenth-century German literary reform.

DANCE & DRAMA

1623 England The first folio edition of Shakespeare's plays was published by John Heminge (1556–1630) and Henry Condell (d.1627), seven years after the writer's death. Shakespeare himself appears to have made no attempt to publish his work.

1624 Japan The first theatre in Tokyo was established.

MUSIC

1623 France Publication of *Hymnes de l'Église pour Toucher sur l'Orgue avec les Fugues et Recherches sur leur Plainchant* by Jean Titelouze (1563–1633), one of the noblest creations of early baroque organ school.

1624 Germany Publication of *Tabulatura Nova* by Samuel Scheidt (1587–1654), a work for organ which marked an important step forward in technique.

HISTORICAL EVENTS

1624 Richelieu became first Minister in France.

| ARCHITECTURE | THREE DIMENSIONAL ART | VISUAL ARTS | INVENTIONS & DISCOVERIES |

THREE DIMENSIONAL ART

1622 Germany George Schwanhardt (1601–1667) began work as a glass engraver in Nuremberg. He developed the technique of the earlier artist Caspar Lehmann (1570–1622) of engraving with the wheel and diamond; he also polished the engraved surface, which was an innovation.

VISUAL ARTS

1622–1625 France The Flemish artist Peter Paul Rubens (1577–1640) painted a series on the life of Marie de Médicis, considered outstanding in baroque decorative painting. His method was to make a sketch which was carried out by assistants and finished by himself. His most famous attributes were his speed and accuracy in drawing with the brush, and his luminous colour. He was recognized as the foremost artist of his day.

1622–1623 Netherlands *The Ferry* and *Winter Scene* by Esias van de Velde (*c*.1591–1630), a founder of Dutch realistic landscape painting.

1623 England, The Queen's Chapel, St James's Palace, London, by Inigo Jones was the first ecclesiastical building in the classical style to be built in England.

c.**1623 India** Great Temple, Madura, was one of the late monumental complexes built on traditional lines; the gopura (tall gateway) is famous for its exterior sculpture of life-size figures.

England: The Queen's Chapel, St James' Palace, London, by Inigo Jones

1624 Italy Guarino Guarini born (died 1683); he trained as a mathematician and used this knowledge to create some highly intricate compositions. All his most important buildings were built in Turin.

1624 Italy The canopy over the high altar of St Peter's, Rome, was commissioned from Gian Lorenzo Bernini (1598–1680) sculptor and architect; this made a focal point for the long interior, drawing attention back to the centre under the dome.

1624 Spain Diego Rodriguez de Silva y Velazquez (1599–1660) painted the full-length portrait *Oliváres*, characteristic of his attempt to break with the austerity of Mor van Dashorst (1517/20–1576/7). He was influenced by Titian, but exceeded him in naturalism.

c.**1624 Netherlands** Death of Willem Buytewetch (b. *c*.1591), original and lively genre painter and etcher.

*1624
Van Helmont
introduced the
term 'gas'.*

HISTORICAL EVENTS	LITERATURE	DANCE & DRAMA	MUSIC

1625
Charles I of
England married
Henrietta Maria
of France.

LITERATURE

DANCE & DRAMA

1625 England *A New Way to Pay Old Debts* by Philip Massinger (1583–1646), English writer of comedies and romantic dramas.

MUSIC

1625 Italy *La Liberazione di Ruggiero dall' Isola d'Alcina*, the first opera to be written by a woman, Francesca Cannini (b. 1588), was produced.

1626 Dalmatia *Osman* by Ivan Gundulić (1589–1638), a poet and playwright strongly influenced by Tasso; his work included pastoral and religious poetry. *Osman*, his masterpiece, was an epic celebrating the Polish defeat of the Turks in 1621 and symbolizing Christianity triumphant over the powers of darkness. It showed great artistry.

1626 Spain *La Historia de la Vida del Buscón* by Francisco Gómez de Quevedo y Villegas (1580–1645), satirist, moralist, novelist and poet, who wrote in all genres with great skill and insight. A feature of his style was *conceptismo*, an extended metaphor or pun elaborated into a paradox. This book is a parody picaresque novel.

1626 Russia At the celebrations of the Tsar's wedding nomadic entertainers were introduced instead of the traditional church choir for the diversion of the guests.

1626 England William Heather (1563–1627) appointed first Professor of Music at Oxford University

1626 England Henry Lawes (1596–1662), composer, singer and player, joined the Chapel Royal. He wrote many songs and music for masques.

1626 Italy Posthumous publication of six-part madrigals by Don Carlo Gesualdo, Prince of Venosa (1560–1613).

1627
Korea became
tributary of
China and Japan,
excluded all
foreigners.

1627 Germany Johann Hermann Schein (1586–1630) published his *Cantional*, a collection of chorale tunes.

1625 England Francis Bacon's essay *On Gardens* described the typical garden of the sixteenth and early seventeenth century in England: a walled enclosure, with small beds in patterns marked out with low hedges. Topiary was also an Elizabethan fashion, but the English style was less elaborate than the Dutch; gardens of the period in Holland were exceptionally formal and artificial.

1626 France Establishment at Chaillot of a national carpet factory making hand-knotted *savonnerie* carpets, screen panels and chair seats.

17th century design for garden mazes

1625–*c*.1632 Netherlands Rembrandt Harmensz van Rijn (1606–1669) concentrated on religious and allegorical painting, while the main concern of contemporary Dutch artists was with their surroundings and with portraiture. At this time Rembrandt also began his series of over 100 self portraits: physiognomy was an important early study in his portrayal of emotion.

1625 Netherlands Daniel Seghers (1590–1661) became leading flower painter of the Flemish school after the death of Jan Brueghel. Seghers was a monk; his work often took the form of a flower garland framing figures in religious paintings by other artists.

1626 England The Italian painter Orazio Gentileschi (1563–*c*.1647) came to work at the court of Charles I. He was a follower of Caravaggio, one who had actually met him, and helped to spread Caravaggio's ideas in northern Europe.

1626 Naples, Italy *Drunken Silenus*, the earliest dated surviving painting by the Spanish artist José de Ribera (1591–1652): his early work was influenced by Titian and Caravaggio. He was also an etcher with a taste for the grotesque that was widely copied.

1627 France Claude le Lorrain (Claude Lorraine, 1600–1682) settled finally in Rome, where he spent the rest of his working life painting the Roman countryside. With Poussin, he was the main influence on French classical art. The incidents of his paintings, taken from classical or biblical stories, were subordinated to the light and atmosphere of the landscape; his use of light and form was influential on English landscape painting of the eighteenth and nineteenth centuries.

1627 France The painter Simon Vouet (1590–1649) returned after fourteen years in Italy. He developed a moderated baroque style which suited French taste, and introduced techniques of illusionism which influenced decorative painting for the rest of the century. He also stressed professional competence, and many of the next generation of artists received a thorough training in his studio.

HISTORICAL EVENTS	LITERATURE	DANCE & DRAMA	MUSIC

*1628
English
Parliament
passed Petition
of Rights.*

1628 Italy Giacomo Carissimi (1605–1674) appointed *maestro di cappella* at Sant' Apollinare in Rome, a post he held until his death. He had a great influence on Italian music, mainly through his pupils, among whom was Alessandro Scarlatti (1660–1725).

1629 Japan *Onna kabuki* drama troupes, consisting of women and men dressed as women, were suppressed as immoral.

1629 Italy Gregorio Allegri (1582–1652), the Italian singer and composer, was appointed to the Papal Chapel, where he became an important contributor to church music.

*1630
Sweden under
Gustavus
Adolphus invaded
Holy Roman
Empire.*

1630 Netherlands *Overysselsche Sangen en Dichten*, poems of Jacobus Revius (1586–1658), clergyman, historian and poet. He was a Calvinist and strongly patriotic. His sonnets were particularly remarkable.

1630 Russia A chronicle of the troubled period of Russian history from the late sixteenth to the early seventeenth century, by Ivan Timofeyev, a Russian scribe: his account was reliable, his style rhetorical.

1630 France *Sylvanaire* by Jean Mairet (1604–1686): in the preface he set out the rules of classical tragedy, notably the three Unities of time, place and action, derived from Aristotle. The Unities were for generations a battleground in the French theatre.

1630 Spain *El Burlador de Savilla* by Tirso de Molina (1571–1639), the first playwright to make use of the legend of Don Juan: it was later used by Molière, Mozart and Byron, among others.

1631 Spain Posthumous publication of poems by Luis de Léon (?1527–1591), religious writer and poet. He wrote theological works in Latin, Bible commentaries and translations, and his own poetry in Spanish. He modelled his odes on those of Horace. Although his poetry circulated widely in manuscript during his life-time, it was not until the eighteenth century that other poets began to use him as their model.

Netherlands: Rembrandt's etching 'Dr Faustus'

ARCHITECTURE

1628 France Château de Balleroy by François Mansart is a typical well-preserved Mansart house; it has a tall centre pavilion with a cupola, and lower side blocks with steeply rising roofs and dormer windows.

1629 Spain St Isidro el Real, Madrid, is by Francisco Bautista, a Jesuit priest who designed this church to resemble the Gesù in Rome; the design had considerable influence in Spain.

1630–1653 India The Taj Mahal, Agra, by Ali Mardan Khan is the best known Islamic tomb monument; it is sited in a picturesque landscape displaying a complex but symmetric structure covered with most beautiful lattice work in marble.

1631 Italy, Guglia di St Gennaro, Naples, by Cosimo Fanzago is a vigorous baroque church by the leading exponent of the style in seventeenth-century Naples.

1631–1687 Italy St Maria della Salute, Venice, by Baldassare Longhena (1595–1682) is magnificently sited at the head of the Grand Canal and is the architect's masterpiece; the church is unusual in having an octagonally planned nave, surmounted by a dome joined to the outer walls by scrolled buttresses.

THREE DIMENSIONAL ART

1630–1660 France Florimond Badier, bookbinder, flourished working in the mosaic and *pointille* styles.

c.1630 Italy Establishment in Rome of the Barberini tapestry workshop.

1631 England Edward East (1602–1697) founded the Clockmakers' Company. He was clockmaker to Charles I and a pioneer in making long-case clocks and watches.

VISUAL ARTS

1628 Netherlands Rembrandt made his earliest etchings: he was the first artist to regard etching as something more than a labour-saving substitute for line engraving—labour-saving because the acid, not the artist, cut into the metal. He used the medium to make free, spontaneous drawings directly on the plate.

1630–1640 Spain Francisco Zurbaran (1598–1664) painted single figures of monks and saints. His compositions were simple, his forms sculptural and monumental. He influenced Spanish colonial painters but was not widely known in Europe.

1630 Spain *Philip IV in Brown and Silver* by Velazquez (1599–1660) showed a change in the painter's use of colour and light: the earliest chiaroscuro copied from Caravaggio was replaced by an even light uniting subject and background; the colours became silvery, the painting impressionistic.

c.1630 France Nicolas Poussin (1593/4–1665) began to paint subjects from classical mythology. He was regarded as the founder of French classical painting, insisting on design as the most important factor in a picture, rather than colour. He himself was influenced by Titian until about this time; his later style was calmer and more austere.

1631–1632 Naples, Italy The Spanish artist José de Ribera (1591–1652) painted *St Peter*; a work characteristic of his new style of religious painting. He broke from the ideal 'types' of the mannerists and made his sacred, and secular, subjects individuals, with characters of their own. A feeling for the value of the individual was established in Spanish painting through his work and that of Velazquez.

1631 Netherlands Adriaen Brouwer (1605/6–1638) moved from Haarlem in Holland to Antwerp in Flanders. His work displayed elements from the Flemish style, with its rich colours, and from the Dutch style with its exploitation of monochrome. His best known works are genre pictures, but his landscapes are considered finer.

INVENTIONS & DISCOVERIES

1628 William Harvey published essay outlining his theory of the circulation of the blood.

217

HISTORICAL EVENTS	LITERATURE	DANCE & DRAMA	MUSIC
	1632 Germany *Soldatenlob* by the poet Julius Wilhelm Zincgref (1591–1635), an admirer of Opitz.		**1632 Italy** Birth of Jean-Baptiste Lully (d. 1687), skilled musician and choreographer and composer of many ballets, operas and incidental music for the stage. He moved to Paris in his youth and made his career at the French court.
	1632 Poland Collection of poems of Maciej Kazimierz Sarbiewski (1595–1640), a poet writing in Latin. He specialized in occasional verse, using Pindar and Horace as his models.		
	1632 Spain *La Dorotea* by Lope Félix de Vega Carpio (1562–1635), playwright, poet and novelist. Highly versatile, he wrote epics, pastorals, short stories, odes, sonnets, mythological poems, burlesque and ballads, and was a master of lyric-writing. This book was a dialogue novel inspired by *La Celestina*, and is regarded as a masterpiece.		
1633 Laud became Archbishop of Canterbury.	**1633 England** *The Temple* by George Herbert (1593–1632/3), clergyman and metaphysical poet. An excellent classical scholar, he wrote clear, economical, and dignified English.		**1633 Italy** *Musiche Varie a Voce Sola* published at Venice by Benedetto Ferrari (1597–1681), one of the earliest composers of solo cantatas.
	1634 France Foundation of the Académie Française: its function was to formulate rules to ensure that the language remained pure, eloquent, and a fit vehicle for both arts and sciences. There was to be a dictionary, first issued 1644, a grammar, finally published 1932, a *Poétique* and a *Rhétorique*, both, as yet, unwritten.	**1634 England** *Comus*, a masque by the English writer John Milton, was presented at Ludlow castle.	**1634 France** Birth of Marc-Antoine Charpentier (d. 1704), French composer.
		1634 Germany First performance of the Oberammergau Passion Play.	
	1634 Wales Death of Thomas Prys (b. *c.*1564), poet, soldier, landowner and pirate. His experiences of the adventurous life in London and at sea brought new topics into Welsh verse. He gave up piracy for the stability of life on his estate; his most moving poem is an appeal, unsuccessful, to his cousin and heir to do the same.	**1634 Italy** A commemorative book of the opera *Sant' Alassio* was published with engravings of the principle scenes: the settings were by Bernini. Operas had very elaborate settings; the ordinary theatrical performances followed similar trends but were in general simpler.	

ARCHITECTURE

1632 England Sir Christopher Wren born (died 1723); Wren was a scientist and architect and immensely prolific both in the work of rebuilding London following the fire of 1666, and as Surveyor General in the King's Works.

1633 Holland The Maritshuis, The Hague, by Jacob van Campen and Pieter Post (1608–1669) is a fine example of Dutch Palladian architecture that later influenced the architecture of Restoration England.

1635 France Blois Château, Orleans Wing, by François Mansart is a distinguished building of Renaissance Classicism in which Mansart introduced the roof design which now bears his name.

1635–1659 France Sorbonne Church, Paris, is by Jacques Lemercier (c.1585–1654). The architect had studied in Rome and designed this domed church as the first wholly classical church in France.

THREE DIMENSIONAL ART

1632 England Tomb of Lord Teynham at Lynsted by Epiphanius of Evesham (1570–after 1633) sculptor, shows the freshness and humanity which he brought to funeral monuments.

1633 Germany Lorraine, the main centre for making coloured glass, was devastated by war and the glass makers dispersed. Coloured glass being no longer available, artists began to make windows by painting pictures on clear glass with vitreous enamel; the art of designing for the mosaic method was lost until its revival in the 1860s, in England.

1634 North America John Mansfield was the first recorded silversmith in Massachusetts Bay colony: Boston was an important centre of silversmithing in the colonial period.

1635 Russia Elias Koyet, a Swede, founded the first glass factory, at Dukhanino near Moscow.

VISUAL ARTS

1632 Netherlands Death of Abraham Janssens, a Flemish painter who moved from a mannerist to a classical style and was particularly successful in his earlier work, up to 1620.

1632 Netherlands Death of Jan Porcellis, a Flemish-born painter working in Holland. His paintings mark the transition in Dutch marine art from brightly coloured ship studies to monochromatic atmospheric paintings of sea, sky and weather.

1632 Netherlands Rembrandt (1606–1669) painted the *Anatomy Lesson of Dr Tulp*, which brought him instant recognition. He was the leading portraitist in Amsterdam until c.1642, at the same time painting large-scale religious pictures in baroque style.

1633 France Jacques Callot (1592/3–1635), engraver, published *Les Grandes Misères de la Guerre*, a series of engravings expressing his horror at Richelieu's invasion of Lorraine. His work was a source for Goya's *Disasters of War*.

c.1633–1639 Italy Pietro Cortona (1596–1669) painted a ceiling fresco in the Barberini palace, Rome, as an allegory of Divine providence and the power of the Barberinis. This was considered one of the most important and characteristic spectacular illusionist paintings of the baroque period.

1634 Netherlands Death of Hendrick Avercamp (b. 1585), a landscape artist who exploited the flatness of the Dutch landscape as a setting for many pictures of sport and enjoyment.

1635 Netherlands Death of Joost de Momper (b. 1564), whose landscape paintings were transitional between the imaginary, constructed scenes of sixteenth-century landscape art and the naturalistic style of the seventeenth century. He added to the conventional colour scheme and was influential on younger artists.

c.1635 Netherlands Gerrit Dou (1613–1675) began to move from imitating his master Rembrandt towards a personal style of precision, smoothness and great detail, sometimes achieved with a magnifying glass. He was imitated for two hundred years.

1636 Hungary *Prédikáciok* by Péter, cardinal Pázmány (1570–1637), a polemic writer. He did much to raise the standard of prose writing in Hungarian.

1637 England *Religio Medici* by Sir Thomas Browne (1605–1682), physician and writer: the book contained essays on a variety of subjects, but especially his religious beliefs. His style was involved and often obscure.

1637 England Death of Ben Jonson (b. *c.*1572) poet, playwright and critic. He brought European neo-classicism to English fashionable society.

1637 England *Account of Religion by Reason* by Sir John Suckling (1608/9–1642), a poet, dramatist and prose-writer, and a supporter of Charles I. He is remarkable for the grace and felicity of his poetry, which was popular at court.

1637 Germany *Sonn- und Feiertagessonette* by Andreas Gryphius (1616–1664), poet and playwright. He was considered the most moving and sincere German poet of the period, a deeply religious and pessimistic writer.

1638 Italy Death of the poet Gabriello Chiabrera (b. 1552), a skilful writer of lyrics and light verses (*canzonette*).

1638 Spain *Notitia Utriusque Vasconiae* by Arnauld Oinhart of Soule: a regional Basque history with poems and proverbs. It was the most important secular work in pre-nineteenth-century Basque literature.

1636 France *Le Cid* by Pierre Corneille (1606–1686) performed, with the celebrated actor Montdory playing the lead: the play is a tragi-comedy and aroused controversy because the playwright disregarded the Unities.

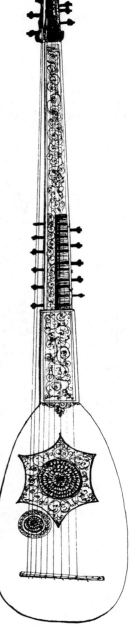

17th century musical instrument, a chitarrone

1636 France *Harmonie Universelle*, giving descriptions of contemporary instruments, written by Marin Mersenne (1588–1648).

1637 England Ancient Society of College Youths (bell-ringers) founded in London.

1638 France Death of Nicolas Formé (b. 1567), singer and composer; he created the classical French motet.

1639 Italy Production in Rome of first comic opera *Chi Soffre, Speri* by Marco Marazzoli (d. 1662), and Virgilio Mazzocchi (1597–1646).

1639 Spain *Guitarra Espanola, y vandola en Dos Maneras de Guitarra . . .*, the earliest known treatise on the Spanish guitar, was published in Gerona by Juan Carles Amat (1572–1642); there is some evidence that the book was originally published in Barcelona in 1586.

*c.*1635 **Netherlands** Death of Hercules Seghers (b. 1589/90), an original painter and etcher of landscape who was best known for mountain scenes of a romantic and atmospheric grandeur. He was a pupil of Coninxloo and himself influenced Rembrandt.

1636 **France** Jacques Sarrazin (1588–1660), considered the leading sculptor of his time, abandoned the Italian classicist manner and adopted a more personal style influential on French classicism. He trained most of the next generation of sculptors in his studios.

1636 **Spain** Death of Gregorio Hernandez (b. 1576), sculptor of religious subjects: he continued the dramatic emotional style of Juan de Juni but with greater realism. He was the first to require naturalistic colouring from the polychromists who painted his work, in place of the traditional gold and brilliant colour.

1636 **China** Death of Tung Ch'i-Ch'ang, leading art theorist of the *Wên-jên* (scholar-amateur) school that dominated painting in the Ming dynasty. He taught the representation of nature through symbols based on the work of the old Masters; observation of real landscape and natural objects was unnecessary. His theories were followed by *Wên-jên* artists for 200 years.

1636 **Netherlands** Jan Davidsz de Heem (1606–1683/4) moved to Antwerp from Holland. His work became the climax of the Flemish baroque; he painted flower pieces and still life of great opulence.

1637 **Denmark** Although in the nave of Trinity Church, Copenhagen, the arcade columns are basically classical, set on plinths, the vault is still ribbed in the medieval tradition.

1637 René Descartes developed analytical geometry.

1637–44 **Brazil** Frans Post (1612–1680), Dutch painter and engraver, recorded landscapes and scenes of Indian and colonial life in north-east Brazil during the governorship of Prince John of Nassau.

1637 **Italy** *Death of Adonis* and *Apollo and Marsyas* by José de Ribera (1591–1652), in Naples: they are the earliest mythological paintings by a Spanish artist. The Spaniards on the whole disliked mythological subjects. At about this time de Ribera abandoned his early dramatic chiaroscuro for an overall luminosity which became spiritual in his sacred paintings.

1638 **Italy** Rome, St Carlo Alle Quattro Fontane by Francesco Borromini (1599–1677) is an ingeniously designed church in which convex and concave wall surfaces are juxtaposed both on the façade and in the interior; Borromini used the classical vocabulary with greater freedom than Bernini.

1639–1649 **Holland** St Mary's, Leyden, by A. van's Gravensande (died 1662) is an unusual baroque design, for the country, planned as an octagon and domed.

1639 **North America** The first printing press in the English colonies in America was set up in Massachusetts.

1637 **Japan** Death of Honnami Koetsu (b. 1558), considered one of the greatest calligraphers of his age, and also a potter and landscape gardener. He was taught by the painters of the *Momoyama* school and shared their flair for brilliant colour. He invented a poem-scroll decorated to convey its mood rather than its story, and did much to bring together decorative art, calligraphy and literature.

HISTORICAL EVENTS	LITERATURE	DANCE & DRAMA	MUSIC

1640
*Portugal revolted
and became
independent of
Spain.*

1640 America First edition of *Bay Psalm Book* published at Cambridge, Massachusetts.

1640 Germany First organ built in Germany by Sebastian Kilgen; established in America in 1851, where the Kilgen Organ Company has built several thousand organs.

1641 England The first collection of cathedral music was published by John Barnard, canon of St Paul's Cathedral, London.

*1642
Beginning of
English Civil
War.*

1642 England *Cooper's Hill* by Sir John Denham (1615–1668/1669), courtier, poet and playwright: this poem was written in heroic couplets, which he handled with great skill, and contained passages of description and of contemplation. Heroic metre has five stresses, or 10 syllables, to the line.

1642 England Public theatres were closed.

1643 Germany *Lyrica* by Jakob Balde (1604–1668), a poet writing in Latin; he was known as the German Horace.

1643 Italy Death of Claudio Monteverdi (b. 1567).

*1644
End of Ming and
beginning of
Manchu dynasty
in China.*

1643 Germany *Hundert Grabschriften* by Christian Hofmann von Hofmannswaldau (1617–1679), a poet deeply influenced by Opitz and leader of a group of Silesian writers.

1644 Germany *Das Geistliche Waldgedicht oder Freudenspiel Genannt Seelewig. Gesangweis auf Italiänische Art Gesetzet,* the first German operatic work, by Sigmund Gottlieb Staden (1607–1655).

1643 Germany *Himlische Lieder* by Johann Rist (1607–1667), a Lutheran pastor and poet, best known for his hymns, of which there are over 600. He wrote in the style of Opitz.

*1645
Oliver Cromwell
defeated
Royalists at
Naseby.
Turks began
conquest of
Crete.*

1645 France *La Festa Teatralle Della Finta Pazzia* was produced in Paris. It was the French people's introduction to Italian opera and they were unimpressed; but the production is of interest because the libretto and scenery were by Giacomo Torelli (1608–1678) who invented a number of stage machines, including the 'carriage and frame system' of changing side wings.

1645 Italy Publication of *Harmonia Organica in Tabulaturam Germanicam Composita . . .* by Johann Erasmus Kindermann (1616–1655); it was one of earliest specimens of German copper-plate engraving and also important historically regarding organ composition and playing.

1645 Germany *Seven Words from the Cross* by Heinrich Schütz (1585–1672) anticipated Bach's *St Matthew Passion* in using four viole da gamba to accompany Christ's words.

1645 France First mention of the dance which the French called *polonaise*, said to have originated in triumphal marches of Polish warriors, and noted for its dignity.

ARCHITECTURE

1640 France Hotel Lambert, Paris, by Louis Le Vau (1612–1670) demonstrates the trend to more adventurous planning of rooms and has a hint of baroque; the gallery with its superb decoration and river views is an exceptional room.

1641–1674 Sweden The Riddarhusat, Stockholm, by Simon (?–1642) and Jean de la Vallée (1620–96) and Joost Vingboons (flourished 1650–70) Dutch Palladian in style by foreign architects, who were frequently in Sweden in the seventeenth century; the assembly hall, however, has a sateri (hipped) roof, the first such example on a major Swedish building.

1642 France Château de Maisons, Paris, by François Mansart was built on an E-shaped plan with emphasis on the centre and two wings; the exterior is notable for the effective use of classical orders, high roofs and chimney stacks. Mansart's fine interior survives intact.

1642 Italy St Ivo alla Sapienza, Rome, by Francesco Borromini is built on a triangular plan, with a spiral lantern. Borromini used simple geometric shapes and then decorated their austerity with line, texture, spatial effect, use of light, false perspective and other devices.

1645–1667 France Church of the Val de Grâce, Paris, by François Mansart and Jacques Lemercier (c.1585–1654) is a domed classical church probably influenced by Palladio's Il Redentore, Venice and, in its turn, influencing Wren's St Paul's, London.

THREE DIMENSIONAL ART

1640 France Establishment of the Imprimerie Royale, which was intended to enhance national prestige by the production of splendid books.

1640 Spain Death of the Italian sculptor Pietro Tacca (b. 1577): his equestrian statue of Philip IV of Spain, his last work, shows the king on a rearing horse. This pose was introduced in paintings by Rubens and Velazquez and subsequently adopted by sculptors; it became standard for royal statues in the baroque style.

1643 Netherlands Death of Francesco Duquesnoy (b. 1594), sculptor of small bronzes. He worked mainly in Italy but established an influential studio in Flanders.

1644 Italy Death of Pope Urban VIII: this meant that the sculptor and architect Bernini fell from favour. He abandoned work on St Peter's and for private patrons for 11 years.

VISUAL ARTS

c.1640–1665 Netherlands Active period of Aelbert Cuyp (1620–1691), an outstanding landscape artist whose work influenced English painters, especially the nineteenth-century Norwich school.

c.1640–1670 Netherlands Bartholomeus van der Helst (1613–1670) was the leading portraitist in Amsterdam; his style influenced his contemporaries, even converting those taught by Rembrandt.

1642 Netherlands *The Corporalship of Captain Banning Cocq's Civic Guards*, known as 'The Night Watch', by Rembrandt (1606–1669): it was innovatory as a group portrait in that the figures were subordinated to the action.

1642 Netherlands Ludwig von Siegen (1609–after 1676) who is credited with inventing the mezzotint process, published his first print.

1643 France The portraits painted by Phillippe de Champaigne (1602–1674) began to show the influence of the Jansenist sect, which made his already restrained style even more severe. He was the leading portraitist of his day.

1643 Japan Death of Nonomura Sotatsu, the narrative painter, who symbolized the return to ancient Japanese tradition and worked for a reunification of painting with literature. He used the Tarashikomi technique, applying rich colour over a wet wash, for delicate bird and flower paintings.

c.1643 England Arrival of Sir Peter Lely (1618–1680), born in Westphalia, to work as a portrait painter. He painted in an impressive and decorative style and became the dominant portraitist of his day. He was principal painter to King Charles II.

1645 France Abraham Bosse (1602–1676) published the first textbook on etching: *Traité des Manières de Graver en Taille Douce*. The earliest etchings date from the first part of the sixteenth century. Bosse's own technique was still heavily influenced by line engraving; he used a hard ground and his line scored the metal.

1642 Dutchman Abel Tasman discovered Tasmania and New Zealand.

1643 Evangelista Torricelli invented barometer.

HISTORICAL EVENTS	LITERATURE	DANCE & DRAMA	MUSIC

DANCE & DRAMA

1645 Spain *El Gran Teatro del Mundo* by Pedro Calderon de la Barca (1600–1681), writer of many *autos sacramentales* which were not only biblical narratives but highly dramatic and poetic pieces of theatre. He also wrote historical plays and comedies which were translated into English, German and French.

England: engraving of Robert Herrick

HISTORICAL EVENTS

1646
Charles I surrendered to Scottish army at Newark.

1647
Scots sold Charles I to English Parliament.

1649
Charles I beheaded, England proclaimed Commonwealth.

LITERATURE

1646 Portugal *Rythmas Varias* by Violante do Céu (1601–1693). Her poetry is full of word-play and conceits, a style very popular in Portugal during the seventeenth and eighteenth centuries.

1647 France *Remarques sur la Langue Française* by Claude Favre, Sieur de Vaugelas (1595–1650), a grammarian. He took for his standard the language of the court, and condemned provincial and popular terms; this encouraged artificiality.

1647 Netherlands *Poëzy* by Joost van den Vondel (1587–1679), poet, prose-writer and playwright. His early work was influenced by the Bible (he was deeply devout) and by French writers, particularly du Bartas. Later he met Hooft and his circle, and was introduced to mythology and the classics. In plays, satires, lyrics and prose he was equally distinguished.

1647 Sweden *Hercules*, a didactic epic by Georg Stiernhielm (1598–1672), philosopher, philologist, lawyer, scientist and poet. He was instrumental in raising the status of poet in the eyes of the public.

1648–1654 Denmark A translation into Danish of Honoré d'Urfé's *Astrée*, by the poet Soren Terkelsen, began the fashion for pastoral poetry in Denmark.

1648 Bohemia *Testament of the Dying Mother, the Unity of Brethren* by Comenius (Jan Amos Komenský, 1592–1670), philosopher, educationist and protestant minister. His Czech religious writings were of great literary merit; he also wrote highly influential educational works. He is the more outstanding because, after the Thirty Years War, Czech was seldom used for literature until the revival in the eighteenth century.

1648 England *Hesperides* by Robert Herrick (1591–1674), clergyman and poet. He wrote epigrams and lyrics on love and country life.

1649 England *Steps to the Temple* by Richard Crashaw (1612/13–1649), a religious poet noted for his intense symbolism.

DANCE & DRAMA

1648 Russia The Tsar Alexis ordered all theatrical properties to be burned and prohibited all worldly amusements.

MUSIC

1648 England John Playford (1623–1686), music publisher, established in London. He had a virtual monopoly of music publishing until his death.

1648 Germany Birth of Arp Schnitger (d. 1718), German organ builder. His instruments represented the peak of German baroque style.

1649 Italy Production of *Orontea*, first opera by Pietro Antonio Cesti (1623–1669), a most prolific composer and the most widely known of the Venetians.

ARCHITECTURE	THREE DIMENSIONAL ART	VISUAL ARTS	INVENTIONS & DISCOVERIES

VISUAL ARTS

1645 Netherlands *The Holy Family* by Rembrandt (1606–1669): it marks his change of interest away from appearance and physiognomy and towards the portrayal of inner qualities. His landscape drawings of the same period are concerned with mood and atmosphere.

ARCHITECTURE

1646 France Jules Hardouin Mansart born (died 1708), was a great nephew of François Mansart but an architect more in the grand manner of Le Vau.

1646–1668 Sweden Skokloster Castle by Jean de la Vallée and Nicodemus Tessin the elder (1615–1681) is a severely classical house, rusticated overall, including the octagonal corner turrets; both architects were of French origin.

1646 Netherlands Return of the painter Willem Kalf (1619–1693) who had worked in Paris. He became established as a leading painter of still life.

1647 Blaise Pascal postulated existence of the vacuum.

1647 Netherlands *The Young Bull* by Paulus Potter (1625–1654), a famous life-size painting in absolute realism. His smaller paintings and etchings of animals in landscape were more successful.

1648–1655 India The Moslem painter Sahabdin of Mewar, Rajasthan, illustrated the texts *Bhagavata Purana* and *Sukar Kshetra Mahatmya*. Rajput painting at this time was described as a robust style in primary colours.

1648 France Death of Louis Le Nain (b. *c*.1593), foremost among three brothers who painted naturalistic genre scenes new to French art and who were all founder members of the Academy in the year of Louis' death. He painted peasant scenes on a large scale in a colour scheme of grey and green.

1648–1652 France Tomb of Henry de Montmorency at Moulins, by François (1604–1669) and Michel (1613–1686) Anguier, sculptors, who broke from the influence of Jacques Sarrazin into a more supple French classicism.

1648 Holland Amsterdam Town Hall by Jacob van Campen (1595–1657) is a huge Palladian block, unusually for Holland, entirely constructed of stone, and now used as the royal palace.

1648 Italy Piazza Navona, Rome, by Bernini was planned on the lines of the Emperor Diocletian's stadium; Bernini also designed two of the three axial fountains.

1649 England *Lucasta* by Richard Lovelace (1618–1658), courtier, scholar, musician, connoisseur of painting, and lyric poet. He first translated Catullus into English.

?1649 India Death of Tukaram (b. 1608), who wrote simple hymns which are still popular today.

1650 America *The Tenth Muse Lately Sprung up in America* by the English-born poet Anne Bradstree (1612–1672), the first established American poet.

1650 England *Silex Scintillans: Sacred Poems and Private Ejaculations* by Henry Vaughan (1621–1695), the Anglo-Welsh metaphysical poet. Many of his poems are on the mystical significance of nature. His later work was influenced by Herbert.

1650 Poland Publication of the satires of Krzysctof Opalinski (*c*.1610–1662), an outspoken poet whose work was modelled on Juvenal.

1651 Charles II defeated by Cromwell, escaped to France.

1651 England *Leviathan* . by Thomas Hobbes (1588–1679), the philosopher, translator and prose writer. His political philosophy was advanced; his critical standards were neo-classical in that he regarded the epic as the highest form of literature and distrusted extremes of emotion.

1651 France *Roman Comique* by Paul Scarron (1610–1660), comic poet, novelist and playwright: it was a realistic novel, one of the few of the period.

1651 Hungary *Obsidio Szigetiana* by Miklós, Count Zrinyi (1620–1664), essayist and poet. His writing showed baroque influence. This work was an epic, more vivid and colourful than previous Hungarian historical poems.

1651 Spain Publication of the first part of *El Criticón* by Baltazar Gracian y Morales (1601–1658), novelist and moralist (the other two parts were published in 1653 and 1657): the book was an allegory of human life. He wrote a number of treatises, including an important one on style. To fix his meaning in the minds of his readers he wrote a deliberately difficult style, so that his books had to be read slowly and carefully.

c.**1650 Spain** The plays of Calderon and contemporary playwrights included Spanish dances of Moorish origin: these were dramatic ballets in which the dancers sang and spoke.

c.**1650 England** End of the court masque; it survived only as a base for theatre opera.

1650 England First publication of John Playford's *The English Dancing Master*, which describes country dances popular since the early sixteenth century and possibly earlier. Country dances had simple steps but elaborately evolved 'figures'; they were popular with all classes and reached court by 1600, making English dancing bright and lively when continental taste was more sombre.

1650 France *Andromede* by Pierre Corneille, a spectacle opera with machines by Torelli: it was the first production of its kind.

1651–1669 France Louis XIV, patron of the dance, danced in a succession of ballets including the *ballets-comiques* of Molière.

1650–1670 Belgium St Michel, Louvain, by Pieter Huyssens (1557–1637) is a typical baroque church by this Jesuit architect, with a west façade inspired by Roman baroque churches.

1650 England Coleshill House, Warwickshire, by Sir Roger Pratt (1620–1684) was an example of the 'double pile' houses designed by an amateur admirer of Inigo Jones and was widely imitated in England.

*c.*1650–1664 **Holland** The Flemish sculptor Artus Quellinus (1609–1668) carved his best known work, the elaborate decoration for Amsterdam Town Hall; he was trained by Frans Duquesnoy's studio and became the chief Flemish baroque sculptor.

*c.*1650 **China** Ceramic sculpture, usually figures of gods, began to be made at Tehua pottery, and continued until *c.*1850.

*c.*1650 **Holland** The Dutch faience pottery industry was concentrated in Delft by this date. Maiolica ware, of which faience is an example, made use of colours that benefited from very high firing temperatures; deep shades of brown, purple, blue, turquoise, green, orange and yellow as well as black.

*c.*1650 **Italy** Giovanni Lorenzo Bernini (1598–1680) designed his most theatrical group, the *Ecstasy of St Teresa* in the Cornaro chapel S Maria della Vittoria: his dramatic presentation of religious figures made him the foremost artist of the Counter-Reformation.

*c.*1650 **Japan** Kakiemon, potter of Arita introduced overglaze enamelling on porcelain: his name was applied to asymmetrical wares popular during the eighteenth century.

1650 France *The New-born Child* by Georges de la Tour (1593–1652) showed his achievement of a monumental simplicity. His frequently recurring device of light from a hidden source was most probably derived from Dutch painters.

1650 Netherlands Abraham van Beyeren (1620/1–1690), considered one of the greatest Dutch still-life artists, turned from making studies of fish to painting rich banquet tables.

1651 Japan Death of Sansetsu (b. 1590), a leader of seventeenth-century *Kanō* painting, together with Naonobu (1607–1650), Tanyu (1602–1647), Sanraku (1559–1632) and Tsuneobu (1636–1713). From the seventeenth to the nineteenth century the highly prolific *Kanō* artists vied with the rival Tosa school for official patronage, and were the leaders of the contemporary movement in painting.

1650
Thomas Hobbes applied mechanistic principles to psychology.

HISTORICAL EVENTS	LITERATURE	DANCE & DRAMA	MUSIC

LITERATURE

1652 Portugal *Arte de Furtar*, an anonymous Portuguese satire on corruption, resembling the picaresque novel. It has been attributed to Manuel de Melo.

1653 England *The Compleat Angler* by Isaac Walton (1593–1683). His style was grave and gentle, with close attention to detail.

1654–1660 France *Clélie, Histoire Romaine* in 10 volumes by the novelist Madelaine de Scudéry (1607–1701), who was a leading hostess in Parisian literary society. Her salon was satirized by Molière. She wrote pseudo-historical novels of a sentimental nature, developing the genre established by d'Urfé.

1655 China Collected writings of Sung Lien (1310–1381), the most important man of letters of his period.

HISTORICAL EVENTS

1653 Cromwell appointed Lord Protector in England.

DANCE & DRAMA

1653 France The first instance of royalty payments: Philippe Quinault (1635–1688) received a percentage of receipts from the production of *Les Rivales*, instead of the customary lump sum.

MUSIC

1652 Austria An opera house established in Vienna.

1653 England Matthew Locke (*c.*1630–1677) wrote (with Christopher Gibbons) music for Shirley's masque *Cupid and Death*. This was his first work for stage, in which field he was the most eminent of Purcell's predecessors.

1653 England William Young (d. 1671), violist and violinist, published at Innsbruck a collection of 11 sonatas dedicated to the Archduke Ferdinand. They were the earliest known set of sonatas for strings and continuo by an English composer.

1653 France First of over 30 ballets composed by Jean-Baptiste Lully (1632–1687).

1655 Germany Birth of Johann Christoph Denner (d. 1707), musical-instrument maker and inventor of the clarinet.

1655 Italy Birth of Bartolommeo di Francesco Cristofori (d. 1731), harpsichord maker and inventor of pianoforte.

1656 England An opera house established in London.

Italy: dome of Saint Agnese, Piazza Navona, Rome, by Francesco Borromini

ARCHITECTURE

1652 France Hôtel de Beauvais, Paris, by Antoine Le Pautre (1660–1744) is a town house built on a very irregular site with great ingenuity by an architect best known for the ambitious designs in his book *Desseins de plusieurs palais*, published in 1652.

1652 Italy The scheme of a central dome and two-tower façade of St Agnese, Piazza Navona, Rome, by Francesco Borromini was very influential.

1652 Norway Kvikne Church, Hedmark, is typical of its period in Norway: built with board walls and topped by a slender spire, the interior is richly painted.

1653 Russia Church of the Georgiou Virgin, Moscow, is a magnificently achieved transition from the square body of the church to the slender cupolas by the way of *kikoshniki*, a decorative kind of wooden roofing.

1656 Austria Johann Fischer von Erlach born (died 1723); the leading Austrian baroque architect, he trained in Italy and wrote an architectural treatise which included illustrations of Chinese and Egyptian buildings.

1656–1667 Italy St Peter's Piazza, The Vatican, and Colonnade by Gianlorenzo Bernini is a huge elliptical space surrounded by columns four deep, supporting a hefty entablature; smaller versions of the piazza were copied elsewhere in Europe.

1657–1661 France Château of Vaux le Vicomte by Louis Le Vau is the grandest of French châteaux built at great speed and expense for Nicolas Fouquet; a team of artists produced interiors of baroque splendour, whilst Le Notre (1613–1700) designed the gardens.

THREE DIMENSIONAL ART

1652 Spain Alonso Cano (1601–1667) and his assistant Pedro de Mena (1628–1688) worked at Granada as sculptors in the cathedral: both worked in the baroque style, de Mena being the more theatrical. His *St Francis* (*c.*1663) was much admired.

*c.***1652 Holland** Christiaen van Vianen (d. *c.*1669), one of a family of Utrecht silversmiths, published *Modelles Artificiels*, a collection of designs by himself and his father Adam (d. 1627). The family exploited the lobed or 'auricular' shapes thought to have been invented by Paulus van Vianen (d. 1613) and characteristic of silverwork in Utrecht.

1656 Italy Death of the goldsmith Corinzio Colleoni (b. 1579) who worked in Rome and was there succeeded by his nephew Bartolomeo.

VISUAL ARTS

*c.***1653 France** Nicolas Poussin (1593/1594–1655) entered his last phase of painting, in which his austere classicism was replaced by poetic imagination.

*c.***1654 Netherlands** Emanuel de Witte (1617–1692) settled in Amsterdam, having been trained as a painter in Delft. He is best known for his church interiors which are characterized by dramatic play of light.

1654 Netherlands Gerard Terborch the Younger (1617–1681) settled in Deventer in Holland, after working in England, Italy and Germany. He specialized in interior scenes and small portraits often on copper.

1656 Netherlands Death of Jan van Goyen (b. 1596), pioneer of realistic landscape painting. His work shows a special concern for air, light and clouds; in colour range it is almost monochrome.

1656 Spain Death of Francisco Herrara the Elder, a painter who represented the transition from mannerism to baroque in Spanish art.

1656 Spain Francisco Rizi (1608–1685) was appointed painter to the king. He was renowned for his mastery of perspective.

1656 Netherlands Earliest dated painting by Jan Vermeer (1632–1675), whose reputation as an artist was only established in the late nineteenth century. He is known to have possessed work by Fabritius, but his painting is not representative of any main school. His predominant yellows, blues and greys were composed simply in patterns suggestive of abstract art.

1657 India Painting of the *Shahjahan-nama*, an illustrated story of the reign and exploits of Shahjahan, who established a centre for the arts at the Red Fort, Delhi. His painters specialized in portraits with highly decorative settings; the chief artists included Muhammad Faquirullah Khan, Mir Hashim and Muhammad Nadir.

INVENTIONS & DISCOVERIES

*1652
Otto von Guericke invented air-pump.*

*1655
First pendulum-clock designed by Christian Huygens.*

*1656
Stockings first manufactured in Paris.*

*1657
Fountain pens first manufactured in Paris.*

HISTORICAL EVENTS	LITERATURE	DANCE & DRAMA	MUSIC

1658
*Death of
Cromwell;
succeeded by son
Richard.*

1658 China Chin Jen-jui edited and published a text of the thirteenth century play *Hsi-Hsiang Chi*, by Wang Shi-fu, describing it as one of the greatest works of Chinese drama.

1658 France *Le Docteur Amoureux* by Jean-Baptiste Poquelin, called Molière (1622–1673) was played before Louis XIV: he was so pleased with it that he gave Molière's troupe permission to remain in Paris, sharing the Petit-Bourbon theatre with the resident *commedia dell' arte* troupe under Tiberio Fiorelli.

1659 France *Divers Portraits* by Jean Regnault de Segrais (1624–1701), poet and prose writer. His collection of character sketches composed in the salon of the Duchess of Montpensier began a vogue for 'portraits'.

1659 Germany Death of Simon Dach (b. 1605), professor of poetry at Konigsberg and leader of the Konigsberg circle of poets. His poetry was sincere and straightforward; he also wrote hymns.

1659 Austria *Pietas Victrix* by Nicolaus Avancinus (1612–1686), a Jesuit professor of rhetoric at the University of Vienna. Jesuit plays began as exercises in Latin to be performed by pupils; by the seventeenth century they had become highly elaborate productions and a serious rival to the professional theatre. Calderon, Corneille, Goldoni, Molière, Voltaire were all ex-pupils of Jesuit colleges who had come under the influence of school drama.

1659 England Birth of Henry Purcell (d. 1695), the greatest English baroque composer, noted for his expressive word-setting.

1659 France The 'première comedie française en musique', the *Pastorale d'Issy*, by Robert Cambert (1628–1677) and the Abbé Pierre Perrin (1625–1675), was performed near Paris.

1659 Netherlands *Tablatuurboeck van Psalmen en Fantasijen Waarvan de Psalmen soo in de superius, tenor als bassus met 2, 3 en 4 part* published by Anthoni van Noordt (d. 1675), Dutch musician. It is probably the first example of music engraving in the Netherlands.

1660
*Restoration of
Charles II of
England.*

1660 Germany *Geharnschte Venus* by Kaspar Stieler (1632–1707): graceful and spontaneous, these poems were considered among the best of the seventeenth century. he also wrote pious books and a manual of letter-writing which was very influential.

1660 Portugal *Epanáforas de Vária História* by Francisco Manuel de Melo (1608–1666), moralist, historian and poet. He wrote a large quantity of verse, but is remarkable for his prose writings, which were shrewd, witty and polished. He wrote in both Spanish and Portuguese.

?1660 Poland *Poeta* by Lucasz Opalinski (1612–1662), brother of the poet Krzysct of Opalinski; it was the first critique of poetry in Polish.

1659 Germany *Papinianus* by Andreas Gryphius (1616–1664): he wrote the first literary tragedies in German. His work shows the influence of Corneille.

1660 England At the Restoration the public theatres had been closed for 18 years. Ordinary people had lost the habit of going to the theatre, and the new audiences tended to be fashionable sophisticates who enjoyed above all the comedy of manners. Charles II gave permission for two theatre companies only to operate in London and forbade all others. The two official theatres were the Theatre Royal, Drury Lane, under Thomas Killigrew, and Covent Garden under Sir William Davenant.

The part of Desdemona in Shakespeare's *Othello* was played by a woman, the first actress in the English professional theatre.

1660 Italy Birth of Pietro Alessandro Gaspare Scarlatti (d. 1725), composer of many operas in the Neapolitan style, and one of the most important influences in the history of opera.

1660 Spain Performance of earliest Spanish opera by Juan Hidalgo, composer.

1661
*Louis XIV
assumed absolute
power in France.*

1661 Poland Collection of poems by Jan Andrzej, count Morsztyn (1613–1693), a lyricist considered the greatest poet in the baroque style. He was influenced by Marino; he also translated Corneille and Tasso into Polish.

1660 France The 'Salle des Machines' built at The Tuileries by Gaspare Vigarani (1586–1663), a rival of Torelli: it was especially designed and equipped for the presentation of spectacular shows to entertain the French court.

1661 Poland *Merkuriusz Polski*, the first Polish periodical, was published by Jan Aleksander Gorczyn who also published a handbook on music in 1647.

ARCHITECTURE

1658–1670 Italy St Andrea del Quirinale, Rome by Gianlorenzo Bernini is a church incorporating several typical baroque features: an elliptical plan, a monumental entrance with semicircular porch and an interior drawing on all the arts for theatrical effect.

1659–1670 Italy Lecce Cathedral façade by Guiseppe Zimbalo (1617–c.1710) is exuberant baroque by the leading exponent of the style in Lecce.

c.1660 Sweden Drottningholm Palace by Nicodemus Tessin the elder (1615–1681) is a royal summer palace designed in the French manner after Versailles, with a fine landscaped park.

1661 England Nicholas Hawksmoor born (died 1736), a brilliant draftsman, who worked for Wren and Vanbrugh as well as producing his own work, especially his 6 London churches.

1661 France Collège des Quatre Nations, Paris, by Louis Le Vau was conceived as part of the great Louvre rebuilding scheme and introduced Roman baroque architecture to France; the church was one of several domed churches built in seventeenth-century Paris.

1661–1756 France Versailles Palace was enlarged by Louis Le Vau, J. H. Mansart and others, as a massive building but retaining the scale of the original château of 1624; the interior decorations and gardens are the most successful part of the whole design.

THREE DIMENSIONAL ART

1658 France Establishment of the tapestry workshop at Maincy: this marked the revival of tapestry making after the disruptions of civil war.

The gardens of Vaux le Vicomte were designed by André le Nôtre (1613–1700) according to the principles evolved by the Mollets, a family of outstanding French gardeners. These principles were a further development of Italian schemes: the French designs were based on long avenues radiating from the front of the house and patterns of parterre at the back. French gardens influenced those of royal and great houses all over Europe.

c.1658 France Iron gates made for the Château de Maison, Poissy: these exemplified the French baroque style, which was influenced by architectural form and stimulated by the fashion for landscaped gardens needing secure but decorative railings and gates. Strong vertical and horizontal frames were decorated with massed leaves, masks, scallops and rosettes and with flowing scroll-work. The style flourished until c.1690.

1660–1664 Holland Rombout Verhulst (1624–1698) sculptor, worked with Artus Quellin on Amsterdam Town Hall. He settled in the Hague and became famous for portrait busts and monuments, especially that of Admiral de Ruyter which he made for the New Church, Amsterdam.

c.1660 France Building of the palace at Versailles stimulated the making of solid silver furniture: outstanding among the silversmiths was Pierre Germain (1645–1684).

1661 North America Samuel Belding (1633–1713) and John Allis began to make cabinets in Hadley, Connecticut River Valley: they are thought to have been the makers of many of the early American coffers called 'Hadley chests'.

VISUAL ARTS

1657 Spain Juan de Valdés Leal (1622–1690), the last great baroque religious painter in Andalusia, began his series on the *Life of St Jerome*. In his work, baroque drama and movement were taken to excess and sometimes became grotesque.

1658 India Shahjahan was deposed by his son Aurangzeb, a ruler intolerant of art. Much existing temple ornament was destroyed during his reign, and no art commissioned.

c.1660–1670 India The painter Ustad Hamid Ruknuddin flourished in Bikaner, a centre of arts under Mogul influence.

c.1660–1670 Netherlands Jan Steen (c.1626–1679) worked in Haarlem and painted two of his best known pictures, *St Nicholas' Feast* and *As the Old Sing, the Young Pipe*. He was considered the most versatile Dutch artist except for Rembrandt and was particularly successful in painting children. He is most famous for his feast and tavern scenes.

1660–1670 Netherlands The pictures of Pieter de Hooch (1629–1683) of Delft, painter of interior domestic scenes, recorded a change in Dutch living style, from simplicity to ostentation.

c.1660 Netherlands Jan van der Heyden (1637–1712) began to paint a new precise style of townscape, in harmonious colours and bright, sunny light.

1660 Spain Bartolomé Esteban Murillo (1617–1682) became first president of the academy of painting in Seville, of which he was a founder. His idealized, atmospheric sacred paintings were popular and influential; his paintings of children in poverty established a new genre in Spain.

1661 Italy Death of Andrea Sacchi (b. 1599), Roman classicist painter and follower of Raphael.

*1661
Manometer
invented by
Huygens.*

HISTORICAL EVENTS	LITERATURE	DANCE & DRAMA	MUSIC

DANCE & DRAMA

1661 France Louis XIV established the Royal School of Dancing with Charles Beauchamps (1636–1705) as director. He was the first to teach the 'five positions' of the feet basic to ballet technique, and introduced the minuet. In his time social dancing became pedantic, with much attention to correct technique.

MUSIC

1662 Scotland First edition of *Songs and Fancies* published by John Forbes (d. 1675), music printer and publisher; it was the only book of secular music published in Scotland in the seventeenth century.

LITERATURE

1662 America *The Day of Doom* by Michael Wigglesworth (1631–1705), an English-born clergyman; the poem was a best-seller, the first in America.

1663 Poland *Sielanki Nowe Ruskie* by Bartlomiej Jozef Zimorowicz (1597–1677), poet and prosewriter; his verse was elegant and cosmopolitan.

1663 Turks overran Transylvania, attacked Austria and Hungary.

1664 China Death of Ch'ien Ch'ien-i (b. 1582), one of the most popular poets of the seventeenth century.

1663 England Construction of the first Drury Lane Theatre, London.

1663 England *The Divine Services and Anthems usually sung in the Cathedrals and Collegiate Choirs of the Church of England* by James Clifford (1622–1698). It was first publication of its kind to appear in London.

1664 Hungary *Murányi Venusz* by the poet Istrán Gyöngyösi (1629–1704). His highly polished baroque style set a new standard in poetry. This work is an epic in the manner of Ovid.

1664 France *Tartuffe* by Molière was produced privately; it created so much resentment that it was not shown publicly until three years later. Until Molière wrote comedies which were accepted by intelligent and influential people, particularly the court, comedy was not taken seriously as an art form in France.

1664 Russia A political pamphlet bitterly critical of Russian rulers was written by Grigory Karpovich Kotoschikhin, a Russian in exile in Sweden.

1664 Russia The English ambassador to the Russian court attended a performance of an unnamed comedy in the German quarter of Moscow.

1665 Great Plague in London.

1665 France First version of *Réflexions ou Sentences et Maximes Morales* by François VI, Duc de La Rochefoucauld (1613–1680), moralist. He spent the last 15 years of his life revising and polishing his maxims, which showed great insight and were written with elegance and wit.

1665 Spain Juan Cabanilles (1644–1712) was appointed organist to the metropolitan cathedral in Valencia. He was one of the greatest organists in Europe before J. S. Bach, and paved the way for the sonata.

1666 Great Fire of London.

1666 Denmark *Den Danske Mercurius*, the first Danish newspaper, was founded by the poet Anders Christensen Bording (1619–1677). The news was in rhymed alexandrines. Bording's other work included pastorals.

1666 France *Le Misanthrope* by Molière.

1666 Italy Antonio Stradivari (1644–1737), violin maker, established at Cremona.

1667 England *Paradise Lost* by John Milton (1608–1674): an epic poem on the fall of man, written in blank verse. Poet, pamphleteer, historian, scholar and civil servant, and a supporter of Cromwell, Milton wrote strongly on behalf of the Commonwealth. He was thoroughly grounded in classical literature, and also technically highly accomplished. His vocabulary showed strong Latin influence.

1667 France *Andromaque* by Jean Racine (1639–1699), who adhered strictly to the rules of French classical tragedy without appearing to find them at all restricting.

1667 Peace of Breda between England and Holland.

1667 Sweden Poems by Samuel Jonae Columbus (1642–1679), scholar and poet. His early work was in Latin but he later used Swedish, under the influence of Stiernhielm.

ARCHITECTURE

1663 England The Sheldonian Theatre, Oxford, by Sir Christopher Wren (1632–1723) is his first building based on a Serlian adaptation (i.e. from Serio's 'L' architecttura') of a Roman theatre, with Wren's scientific ingenuity demonstrated in the trussed roof.

1663–1671 Germany Theatinerkirche, Munich, by Agostino Barelli and Enrico Zuccalli has a classic cruciform plan with chapels placed in the thickness of the walls similar to St Andrea della Valle, Rome. Interior is painted white, with gilding used for the high altar only. There were additions in 1715.

1663 Italy The Scala Regia, The Vatican, by Gianlorenzo Bernini is a baroque masterpiece of a staircase, making bold use of the limited space available, together with ingenious lighting and cunning perspective effects.

1664 England Sir John Vanbrugh born (died 1726), an architect in the baroque style, who was earlier a soldier and playwright.

1667 France The Louvre, Paris, was by Claude Perrault (1613–1688) and others, after Bernini's designs had been rejected in favour of this long façade: above a plain ground floor, paired columns were set in front of a loggia.

1667 Spain The unfinished Granada Cathedral façade by Alonso Cano (1601–1667) has triple recesses, which are unusual in baroque design, the usual system of applying classical orders being ignored.

1667 Spain Cartuja Church, Jerez de la Frontera, has a classic Spanish baroque façade.

THREE DIMENSIONAL ART

1663 France The Gobelin tapestry factory was founded in Paris by Colbert, Minister of Finance to Louis XIV. Charles Lebrun was director and chief designer; he employed many weavers from the previous Maincy factory.

1664 France André-Charles Boulle (1642–1732) the most celebrated cabinet-maker of the period began work: he perfected marquetry in coloured woods, tortoiseshell, pewter and brass. His name was given to furniture which continued to be made by his family until c.1750.

1666 England The need to rebuild and re-furnish after the Great Fire of London stimulated commissions for craftsmen like the woodcarver Grinling Gibbons (1648–1721). He was foremost of his age in the naturalistic carving of fruit, flowers, leaves and shells grouped in baroque style.

1666 France François Girardon (1628–1715), sculptor, made *Apollo tended by nymphs* for the grotto of Thetis at Versailles, considered the most purely classical work of seventeenth century French sculpture: his style derived from Sarrazin and embodied the classical doctrines of the Royal Academy.

1666 Spain José de Mora (1642–1724), a pupil of Cano, became court sculptor to Charles II, although his most moving work was religious.

VISUAL ARTS

*c.***1661 France** Charles Lebrun (1619–1690), painter and decorative artist, was established as the chief influence on decoration at Versailles. He was the driving force behind the grandiose schemes of Louis XIV and Colbert, and he also implemented Colbert's policy of central control and unified style in all artistic work. He later became a strong influence on Academy policy.

1663 France The Academy was re-organized by Colbert and Lebrun: it became a body under the control of the court, and imposed court taste.

1664 Netherlands The *Regents* and the *Regentesses of the Old Men's Alms House* by Frans Hals (1581/5–1666) are considered the finest paintings of his career. They represent the darker colours, restraint and economy of brush-work of his later work.

1665 Netherlands The painter Gerard de Lairesse (1641–1711) settled in Amsterdam to work as a painter and etcher. He was the leading classicist painter of his time in Holland and published *Het Groot Schilderboek* a treatise on academic theories of painting, by which standards he found Rembrandt wanting.

1665 Netherlands Death of Pieter Jansz Saenredam, whose paintings of church interiors recorded the Gothic churches of Haarlem and Utrecht.

INVENTIONS & DISCOVERIES

*1662
Robert Boyle postulated Boyle's law on gases.*

*1663
Guinea first minted in England.*

*1665
Micrographia by Robert Hooke described new uses of the microscope.*

*1666
Isaac Newton developed theory of gravitation. Newton and Leibnitz independently invented calculus.*

**HISTORICAL
EVENTS**
*1668
Bombay made
over to East
India Company.*

LITERATURE

1668 France *Fables* books I–VI by Jean de La Fontaine (1621–1695). He revived the verse fable, using material from Aesop and the *Fables* of Bidpai, writing with economy, elegance, and sharp realism.

1669 Germany *Simplicissimus* by the novelist Johann Jakob Christoph von Grimmelshausen (1622–1676). Most of his works were popular, as opposed to courtly, tales. One of the most important works of German literature, this book is a picaresque novel in which the hero seeks spiritual salvation. It combines deep religious feeling and lively description.

1669 Portugal *Lettres Portugaises*, passionate love-letters supposedly written by a Portuguese nun, Mariana Alcoforado (1640–1723) to a French nobleman. There is no known Portuguese original and their authenticity is doubtful. They were widely popular.

1671 England *Samson Agonistes*, a poetic drama by John Milton (1608–1674).

1671 Germany *Himmlische Liebesküsse* by Quirinus Kuhlmann (1651–1689), religious poet. He used a wide variety of metrical forms, including free verse, and was remarkable for his freedom in the use of language. Almost expressionist in style, and powerfully symbolic, his work was unique in German letters of the period.

1672 Japan *Kaivi* by Matsuo Manefusa, called Bashō, (1644–1694), a poet and writer of travel books. He was a master of the *haiku* form: a poem of only 17 syllables, combining sharp observation with ambiguous thought, which developed at this period. After 1603 Japan was unified under a strong central government. The new peace and stability led to a great renewal of literary activity and many of the new authors were from the military and merchant classes.

1672–1673 Russia Autobiography of Petrovich Avvakum (1620–1682), the archpriest, who was opposed to the ritual reforms of Patriarch Nikon. It was written in lively spoken Russian, not church Slavonic, the literary language. He also wrote epistles and sermons.

DANCE & DRAMA

1671 France First production of an opera-ballet, *Pomone*, in the public theatre. The dances were by Beauchamps, director of the Royal School of Dancing.

1672 France The opera-ballet *Fêtes de Bacchus et de l'Amour* was produced by Jean-Baptiste Lully. Louis XIV authorized him to direct a school of dancing for the stage at the Royal Academy.

1672 Russia Actors from the German quarter of Moscow performed at the celebrations for the birth of the Tsar's son Peter (the Great). A wooden theatre was built for the performance.

1673 England *The Country Wife* by William Wycherley (1640–1715), English comic dramatist: his plays were indecent but they did attack the lax morals of the time.

1673 France Racine accepted a chair of drama at the Académie Française, after it had been refused by Molière. The Académie had stipulated that Molière must give up acting, which he would not do.

1673 Netherlands *Asiré Hatiqva* by Joseph Penco de la Vega (1650–1703), a morality play: it was the first Hebrew play printed.

MUSIC

1668 Denmark Dietrich Buxtehude (1637–1707), organist and composer, became organist at St Mary's Church, Lübeck, where he continued until 1703. During this time he exerted a great musical influence on northern Europe.

1668 France Birth of François Couperin (d. 1733), organist, harpsichordist, teacher and composer.

1669 England An M.A. degree (Oxford) was conferred on Henry Aldrich (1647–1710), the musician and architect. He wrote an important treatise on harmony.

1669 England The Sheldonian Theatre was built at Oxford, by the munificence of Archbishop Sheldon, for the performance of 'Act Music'. This was incidental music played on the occasion of the 'Act', public exercises required by candidates for degrees before the introduction of written examinations.

1671 France Birth of Antoine Forqueray (d. 1745), viola da gamba player whose *Pièces de Viole* are some of the finest of their kind.

1671 France *Pomone*, a pastoral by Robert Cambert (c.1628–1677) with a libretto by Pierre Perrin, was performed at the opening of the Academie de Musique as an operatic institution. The first London performance was in 1674.

1671 Italy Birth in Venice of Tommaso Albinoni (d. 1750), a violinist who became one of the first composers to write concertos for solo violin.

1672 England Pelham Humfrey (1647–1674) appointed Master of the Children of the Chapel Royal; he was a talented lutenist and prolific composer.

1672 Germany Death of Heinrich Schütz (b. 1585).

1673 Poland *The Perfect Polish Hymn-Book* was published at Brzeg by Jan Accoltuhus, a Protestant priest and composer.

ARCHITECTURE

1668 Germany Passau Cathedral by Carlo Lurago has a saucer-dome roof, a type which in the eighteenth century became typical of German baroque churches; interior, which has been rebuilt, is richly painted and has stucco decoration.

1668 Italy St Lorenzo, Turin, by Guarino Guarini (1624–1683) is a baroque church remarkable for its use of 8 interrelated arches to support a circular lantern resting on an octagon: the baroque concern with light and space led to increasing interest in, and experiment with, the structural techniques by which light and space could be best exploited. The Sidone Chapel in Turin Cathedral (1667–1690), also by Guarini, has a similar dome.

1670 England Rebuilding of London began under the control of Wren, following the fire of 1666: the 51 new city churches were built in a great variety of designs especially notable for their highly individual steeples.

1670–1762 Mexico Tepototlán Church and colleges founded by Jesuits and built in the most lavish Spanish baroque style; decoration in the church is everywhere but especially round openings and upper sections of the building.

1670 USA Bacon's Castle, Surrey County, Virginia, is the finest surviving brick-built seventeenth-century house in the USA in the English Jacobean style.

1671–1687 Russia St John the Baptist Tolchkovo, near Yaroslavl, features an attractive interplay of the domes covering the main body of the church as well as the chapels: an impressive silhouette is created.

1672 Denmark Charlottenburg Palace, Copenhagen, was, like many Danish buildings of the period, designed by a foreigner, Evert Janssen, a Dutchman using a Dutch Palladian style.

1673–1709 England St Paul's Cathedral, London, was rebuilt by Sir Christopher Wren; despite original plans for a centrally planned church, St Paul's, baroque-inspired, was built with a conventional Latin-cross plan and is Wren's masterpiece.

THREE DIMENSIONAL ART

1668 Russia The Izmaylovo glass factory, the first recorded in Russia, was founded, employing Venetian glass-blowers.

1670 England Return from Italy of the sculptor John Bushnell (d. *c*.1701) whose work, although uneven, was important in revealing to the English the possibilities of Italian baroque.

1671 England Thomas Tompion (1639–1713) was admitted a Brother of the Clockmakers' Company: he is considered one of the greatest of all clockmakers.

c.**1673 England** Baroque portrait bust of Sir Christopher Wren by Edward Pierce (*c*.1635–1695), considered his best work. He had worked for Wren on many of the City of London churches as a sculptor and stonemason.

VISUAL ARTS

England: Saint Mary le Bow Church by Christopher Wren

1672 Spain Juan de Valdés Leal (1622–1690) painted two *Allegories of Death* for the Hospital de la Caridad, Seville. These are considered his most remarkable paintings in that they revert to a medieval quality of expression.

INVENTIONS & DISCOVERIES

1669 Hennig Brandt discovered phosphorus.

1671 Newton constructed reflecting telescope.

1673 Centrifugal force determined by Huygens.

HISTORICAL EVENTS	LITERATURE	DANCE & DRAMA	MUSIC

LITERATURE

1674–1675 England Part I of *The Pilgrim's Progress* by John Bunyan (1628–1688), preacher and prose writer. He had no literary training, but was both intelligent and imaginative, and the book is regarded as England's greatest allegory.

1674 Denmark *Aandeligt Sjungekor*, poems by Thomas Hansen Kingo (1634–1703), poet and hymn-writer. He is considered the greatest Danish writer in the baroque style.

1674 England Death of Edward Hyde, Earl of Clarendon, statesman and historian. An outstanding prose stylist, he wrote a history of the rebellion and civil war in England.

1674 France *L'Art Poétique* by Nicolas Boileau (1636–1711), poet and critic. He formulated the classical doctrine in which 'nature' and 'reason' are paramount. He was the champion of the Ancients in the 'Quarrel of the Ancients and the Moderns', a literary argument between classicists and humanists.

1676 Germany *Der Politische Näscher* by Christian Weise (1642–1708), poet, playwright and novelist; he was representative of the contemporary German middle classes.

1678 France *La Princesse de Clèves* by the novelist Marie Madelaine, Comtesse de La Fayette (1634–1693). A close friend of La Rochefoucauld, who collaborated with her to some extent, she developed the method of sentimental analysis used by d'Urfé and Madeleine de Scudéry, but her psychology was truer and more subtle, and the book was a landmark in the history of French fiction.

1679–1702 Sweden *Atland Eller Manheim* by Olaus Rudbeckius (1630–1702), scholar, historian and doctor. The book argued that all human culture had originated in Sweden. It reflected the upsurge of confidence after the Thirty Years War and the realization of the potentialities of the Swedish language.

1679 Portugal *Sermões* by António Vieira (1608–1697), a Jesuit writer whose sermons and letters are of interest. The anonymous *Arte de Furtar* was published, spuriously, under his name.

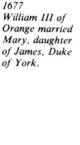

1677 William III of Orange married Mary, daughter of James, Duke of York.

DANCE & DRAMA

1675 Russia Death of Johann Gottfried Gregori who had organized plays to entertain the Russian court. His actors were children, at first German, later Russian.

1676 Russia On the death of the Tsar Alexis the court theatre was closed and its contents destroyed.

1677 England *The Rover, or the Banished Cavalier* by Mrs Aphra Behn; she was the first Englishwoman to earn a living by writing.

1677 France *Phèdre* by Racine: he excelled in the portrayal of women and his plays have provided many great actresses, including Rachel and Sarah Bernhardt, with their best rôles.

1677 Japan *The Evil Spirit of Lady Wisteria* by Chickamatsu Monsayemon (1652–1724): this is a *kabuki* play. Most dramatists preferred to write for the aristocratic *No* theatre.

1678 English *All For Love* by John Dryden (1631–1700) English poet and dramatist: it was a new version of Shakespeare's *Antony and Cleopatra*.

1679 Germany Production of Alessandro Scarlatti's first opera *Gli Equivoci nel Sembiante* in Rome.

Japan: from an ancient sketch of a 'kabuki' actor

MUSIC

1674 England Nicholas Staggins (d. 1700) appointed Master of the King's Music.

1674 Germany Birth of Reinhard Keiser (d. 1739); he exercised an important though not lasting influence on German opera.

c.1675 Italy Birth of Antonio Vivaldi (d. 1741), virtuoso violinist, composer and priest. He is an important figure in the development of the *concerto grosso*, of which he wrote over 400.

1676 England *Musick's Monument: or a remembrancer of the best practical musick, both divine and civil, that has ever been known to have been in the world* by Thomas Mace (c.1613–c.1709), one of the most important and informative sourcebooks for English seventeenth century instrumental music.

1677 England Henry Purcell (1659–1695) succeeded Matthew Locke (c.1630–1677) as Court Composer in Ordinary of the Violin. He was appointed organist at Westminster Abbey in 1679 and of the Chapel Royal in 1682.

1678 England Thomas Britton (1644–1714), English patron of music, inaugurated weekly concerts at Clerkenwell, London.

1678 Germany First regular opera began in Hamburg.

1679 Germany *Die Drey Tochter Cecrops* written by Johann Wolfgang Franck (b. c.1641), the earliest example of a German opera still extant.

ARCHITECTURE

THREE DIMENSIONAL ART

VISUAL ARTS

1674–1675 England Arrival of Sir Godfrey Kneller (1649–1723), who established a workshop and an extensive team of assistants to produce fashionable portraits. He recorded most of the prominent men of his day.

1675–1689 Scotland Drumlanrig Castle was the last residence to be built in the Scottish castle tradition, but makes some concessions to classical detailing.

*1675
Antony van
Leeuwenhoek
discovered red
blood corpuscles.*

1676–1684 England Trinity College library, Cambridge, by Sir Christopher Wren is generally regarded as the best of his university buildings and features an eclectic use of classical sources.

1676 England William Sherwin developed a fast-dyeing process for calico: the success of cotton was seen as a threat by wool, linen and silk manufacturers.

*1676
Repeating clock
and watch
invented by
Barlow.*

1677–1696 Poland The palace of Wilanow, Warsaw, grew gradually from a modest house into a baroque palace with the addition of wings and towers; it is now part of the National Museum of Warsaw.

1677 Netherlands Death of Aert van der Neer, a painter famous for his night scenes and winter landscapes. He is considered one of the greatest Dutch colourists.

1678–1695 Czechoslovakia Castle of Vranov on the Dyje is beautifully sited on a hill overlooking the river gorge; the main room is the oval salon displaying fine wall painting and sculpture.

1678 Italy Filippo Juvarra born (died 1736), who designed a vast number of both secular and ecclesiastical buildings in Turin before being summoned to Spain in 1735 to work for Philip V.

1678 Holland Believed to be the date at which Dutch potters like Lambert Clettius began to imitate Chinese teapots in unglazed red stoneware. These imitations had become popular and widespread by *c*.1700 and later their manufacture spread to Staffordshire, England. China provided the main influence on eighteenth century European ceramics.

1679 France Château de Marly by J. H. Mansart was built for Louis XIV and planned with a rectangular central block for the king and rows of pavilions extending either side of the parterre for his courtiers; it has since been destroyed.

1679 Netherlands Death of Jan van de Capelle, painter of marine pictures celebrated for their silver-grey tones.

1679–1691 France Church of the Invalides, Paris, by J. H. Mansart is the most baroque of Parisian churches with a dome derived from St Peter's, Rome.

1679 Italy The Palazzo Carignano, Turin, by Guarino Guarini is his best known secular building, in which his debt to Borromini is reflected in the curving façade and oval salon.

HISTORICAL EVENTS	LITERATURE	DANCE & DRAMA	MUSIC

HISTORICAL EVENTS

1683
William Penn signed peace treaty with North American Indians.

1684
Holy League formed against Turkey.

1685
Death of Charles II of England. Rebellion and defeat of Duke of Monmouth.

LITERATURE

1680 Russia A rhymed *Psalter* by Simoen Polotsky (1629–1680), monk, preacher, playwright and poet. He used a form of rhymed couplets with an equal number, 11 or 13, of stressed syllables to the line; this metre was taken from the Poles. Polotsky is important for his metrical innovations, rather than for the quality of his verse.

1681 England *Miscellaneous Poems* (folio posthumous) by Andrew Marvell (1621–1678), poet, civil servant and politician, and a supporter of Cromwell. His poems were in the metaphysical tradition.

1681 England *Absolom and Achitophel* by John Dryden (1631–1700), poet playwright, prosewriter and translator. His range and his technical skill were considerable. He valued clear thinking and ·graceful, lucid expression. He was a brilliant satirist; this poem was important both as an accomplished satire and as political propaganda. The link between politics and literature was strengthening at this period.

1682 Turkey Death of Evliya Celebi (b. 1611), a travel writer of the classical period. Turkish classical writers used a vocabulary and grammar strongly influenced by Arabic and Persian, and only an educated minority could appreciate literature. However, at about this time the folk poet Karacaoglan wrote his poetry, which owed nothing to foreign influence.

1683 Norway Collection of poems by Petter Dass (1647–1707), a poet writing in Norwegian. His major work was a description of life in the North, *Nordlands Trompet*: vigorous and free from ornamentation, it is considered a major work of seventeenth-century literature, but, like most of his work, was published posthumously. At this time, Norway was under Danish influence; there were few writers, and they generally wrote in Danish, not Norwegian.

1685 Denmark Peder Pedersen Syv (1631–1702), the grammarian and linguist, published a Danish grammar. He also collected 100 medieval ballads, previously unprinted, and a large number of proverbs.

DANCE & DRAMA

1680 France Creation of the world's first national theatre: the Théâtre Française (later the Comédie Française). It was an amalgamation of Molière's old troupe with the companies from the Hotel de Bourgogne and the Theatre de la Marais.

1681 France Jean-Baptiste Lully produced the ballet *Le Triomphe de l'Amour*, in which professional female dancers appeared on the stage for the first time. Their costume was inherited from the court ladies who had appeared in private performances: high heels, heavy panniered skirts, tall wigs and masks. They were thus limited to formal court dances.

1682 France First mention of the 'pirouette' dance-step, by Ménétrier. Many acrobatic dance-steps were used by tumblers and jig dancers long before they appeared in ballet.

1685 Italy Ferdinando Galli da Bibiena (1657–1743) was working at the Teatro Farnese. Ferdinando and his brother, sons and grandson were scenic artists in the baroque style; they worked all over Europe and their influence on settings was considerable. Ferdinando is believed to have discovered the diagonal perspective in scene design.

MUSIC

1681 Germany Birth of Johann Mattheson (d. 1764), organist, harpsichordist, singer and composer. His many books are a valuable contribution to the history of the music of the period.

1681 Germany Birth of Georg Philipp Telemann (d. 1767) a prominent representative of the Hamburg school.

1683 England *Sonnatas of III Parts* by Henry Purcell (1659–1695), published by Thomas Cross, music engraver, printer, publisher and music seller. He was practically the inventor of sheet music and held a virtual monopoly of London's music-engraving trade.

1683 France Birth of Jean-Philippe Rameau (d. 1764), theorist and composer.

1683 Germany The Klotz family of violin makers established at Mittenwald.

1684 Italy Alessandro Scarlatti (1660–1725), was appointed *maestro di cappella* of the royal chapel, Naples, where he remained until 1702, returning again in 1709.

1685 England From about this date, William Bull, (appointed Trumpeter Extraordinary to Charles II in 1666), made and repaired brass instruments.

1685 England *Division-Violin*, the first printed book for the violin in England, was published by Henry Playford (1657–1709).

1685 France *Livre d'Orgue* published by Nicolas Gigault (c.1624–1707), organist and composer.

1685 Germany Birth of Johann Sebastian Bach, organist and composer, at Eisenach.

1685 Germany Birth of Johann Georg Gebel (d. 1750), organist and composer; he invented a clavichord with quarter-tones and a large clavicembalo with 6 complete octaves.

1685 Germany Birth of George Frideric Handel (d. 1759), English (naturalized) composer of German birth.

1685 Italy Birth of Giuseppe Domenico Scarlatti (d. 1757), harpsichordist and composer.

THREE DIMENSIONAL ART

1680 North America An oak chest signed by Nicholas Disbrowe (1612–1683), English-born cabinet-maker of Hartford, Connecticut, is the earliest piece of American furniture with a maker's name.

*c.***1680 North America** French Huguenot silversmiths began to arrive in New York, adding a French influence to the existing Dutch and English styles.

1682 France Jean Bérain (1640–1711), designer and engraver, was appointed Dessinateur de la Chambre et du Cabinet du Roi: his work in the grotesque and arabesque styles led to the later rococo. He was influential in popularizing Oriental motifs.

1683 France The death of Louis XIV's adviser Jean-Baptiste Colbert (b. 1619) weakened the strong classicist influence on state-commissioned arts and allowed the emergence in his own country of the sculptor Pierre Puget (1620–1694), who worked in baroque style. His previous work was done in Italy and included work for Pietro da Certona on the Pitti Palace. He assimilated Roman baroque and established it in France.

1684 England The Flemish sculptor Arnold Quellin (1653–1686), nephew of the distinguished baroque sculptor Artus Quellin (1609–1668), worked in England with Grinling Gibbons (1648–1721) and introduced him to Flemish baroque, which influenced his carving.

1685 Germany The need to rebuild after the fire of Dresden stimulated commissions by Augustus the strong of Saxony. His chief architect Matthaeus Pöppelman (1662–1736) designed the Zwinger palace for sports and festivities; it was decorated by the sculptor Balthasar Permoser (1651–1732) who was strongly influenced by Bernini.

1685–1693 France Claude and Jacques Simonin published two books of patterns for artist-gunsmiths which were influential in spreading the French style of gun design through Europe.

VISUAL ARTS

1680–1682 Netherlands Death of Willem Claesz Heda (b. 1593/4), leading painter of still life in monochrome, together with Pieter Claesz.

1680 France The Academy issued a comprehensive set of rules covering all aspects of painting. This led to rebellion and argument between the followers of Poussin, who held that 'drawing and design come first, and must be used to create the ideal', and those of Rubens, who held that 'colour forms composition, and the aim is realism'. The Academy decided for Poussin, and retained this policy for many years.

1681 Spain Death of Juan Andres Rizi, outstanding portrait painter; he also wrote *Tratado dela Pintura Sabia*.

1682 France Nicolas de Largillière (1656–1746) established himself as a portrait painter with great success. He was friend and rival to Hyacinthe Rigaud.

1682 France *The Presentation of the Virgin* by Charles de La Fosse (1636–1716) showed the influence of Rubens to a degree unusual in French painting. De La Fosse took the side of Rubens in the Academy controversy on design versus colour.

1682 Netherlands Death of Jacob van Ruisdael, the outstanding landscape artist, who provided all Europe with an imagery of the Dutch landscape. He was concerned with the insignificance of human beings before the powers of nature.

1685–1688 Spain *Charles II adoring the Host* by Claudio Coello (1642–1693): this painting typifies baroque illusionism, repeating inversely the architecture of the room where it hangs.

ARCHITECTURE

1683 USA Capen House, Topsfield, Massachusetts, is colonial New England in style; the house has a timber frame jettied out at first-floor level and is weatherboarded and shingle-roofed.

France: details of decorations for gun mountings by Claude and Jacques Simonin

INVENTIONS & DISCOVERIES

*1682
Pierre Baille established weaving mill with 100 looms at Amsterdam.*

*1684
Robert Hooke invented optical telegraph (heliograph).*

HISTORICAL EVENTS	LITERATURE	DANCE & DRAMA	MUSIC

LITERATURE

1685 Italy *Bacchus in Tuscany* by Francesco Redi (1626–1698), physician, biologist, philologist, and poet: the poem used a variety of metrical effects.

1687 England Death of the poet Edmund Waller (b. 1606), who virtually created the neo-classical style of poetry which came to be so highly regarded in eighteenth-century England.

1687 France *Le Siècle de Louis le Grand* by Charles Perrault (1628–1703). This poem was the first blow in the 'Quarrel of the Ancients and the Moderns', in which he was on the side of modernity. His chief opponent, defending classicism, was Boileau. Either Charles or his son, Pierre, was responsible for a collection of fairy tales called *Contes de ma Mère L'Oye* (1697).

1688 France *Les Caractères de Théophraste Traduits du Grèc, avec Les Caractères ou Les Moeurs de ce Siècle* by the moralist Jean de La Bruyère (1645–1696). He satirized contemporary 'types', developing the art of the portrait begun by Segrais. His standpoint was that of the intelligent middle-class. He is regarded as one of the great French prose stylists.

1689 Germany *Grossmüthiger Feldherr Arminius* by Daniel Caspar von Hohenstein (1635–1683), poet, playwright and novelist. The book, which is unfinished, was a political novel; the hero moved at the highest social levels. The predominantly courtly and learned tastes of the period were well exemplified in contemporary novels.

1690 England *An Essay Concerning Humane Understanding* by John Locke (1632–1704), educationist and philosopher.

1690 Italy Foundation in Rome of the Accademia dell' Arcadia to reform Italian poetry. The members rejected recent baroque developments in literature and sought to return to the simplicity and purity of the ancient Greeks. They organized contests for pastoral poetry.

DANCE & DRAMA

1686 Germany *Der Bestrafte Brüdersmord*, German version of *Hamlet* by Johannes Velten (1640–1695): he was manager of a company of actors which survived until 1771 under a variety of famous managers including die Neuberin and Schroder.

1687 France Jean Balon (1676–1739) succeeded Beauchamp as choreographer to Louis XIV. His use of mime foreshadowed the work of Noverre (1727–1809).

MUSIC

1686 Italy Birth of Nicola Antonio Porpora (d. 1766), composer.

1687 England *Vinculum Societatis*, the first musical work with the 'new tied note', published by John Heptinstall, Thomas Moore and Francis Clark.

1687 France Death of Jean-Baptiste Lully (b. 1632), composer.

1687 Italy Birth of Francesco Geminiani (d. 1762), violinist and composer. His book *The Art of Playing on the Violin*, written in English, was the first of its kind ever published in any country, and the rules he gives are still recognized today.

1688 England Barak Norman, English viol and violoncello maker, established in London; he was probably the first to make 'cellos in England.

1688 France Birth of Louis Bertrand Castel (d. 1757), theorist, one of the first to investigate the scientific relationship between colour and sound.

1689 England Purcell's first opera *Dido and Aeneas* produced in London.

Italy: violin decoration of late 17th century

1693 France François Couperin (1668–1773) was chosen by Louis XIV to be one of four organists of the royal chapel.

1693 Germany Handel began studying with Zachau, organist at Liebfrauenkirche in Halle.

1688 Glorious Revolution; William III landed in England.

1689 Peter I became Tsar of Russia.

1692 Massacre of Glencoe, Scotland.

ARCHITECTURE

1686 Germany Cosmas Damian Asam born (died 1739); with his brother Egid (1692–1750) he built and decorated some of the finest south German and Austrian baroque churches.

1687–1696 England Chatsworth House east façade by William Talman was the grandest of the massive rectangular façades he designed for his several grand country houses.

1687 Germany Johann Neumann born (died 1753), the greatest of German rococo architects.

1689 England Hampton Court Palace was enlarged by Sir Christopher Wren: the Tudor royal palace was in part rebuilt in a restrained brick-built classical style around the Fountain Court and the result is very much a compromise on the grand-palace design Wren had envisaged.

1689–1710 France The Royal Chapel, Versailles, by J. H. Mansart is of Gothic proportions but with baroque exuberance, although this is restrained compared with the baroques of southern Europe.

1690–1753 Sweden Stockholm Royal Palace is by Nicodemus Tessin the younger (1654–1758) and others; he had travelled widely and the palace architecture illustrates his interest in Roman baroque.

1691 Italy St Ignazio Church, Rome, has a ceiling painted in false perspective by Andrea del Pozzo to open the interior space: baroque structural illusion techniques were difficult to use in a long, plain rectangular space, so painting was often used instead.

1691 South Africa Groot Constantia is an example of Dutch colonial architecture common in South Africa; it was rebuilt c.1780.

1693 Italy Rebuilding of Catania, Sicily, began under the direction of Giovanni Vaccarini and others, following a serious earthquake; the cathedral was one of several fine buildings erected.

THREE DIMENSIONAL ART

*c.*1685 **England** Revocation of the French Edict of Nantes brought many Huguenot refugees, silversmiths and other craftsmen, to England. Native craftsmanship improved to meet the higher standard of casting and ornamenting; influential immigrant goldsmiths included Pierre Harache the Elder, Pierre Platel and Simon Pantin.

1686 France The import and imitation of oriental cottons was banned. This did not affect the free port of Marseilles, where the manufacture of 'Indian' cottons flourished.

1689 France Edict ordering the melting down of all table vessels of silver and gold; these had to be replaced with ceramic vessels, production of which was greatly stimulated. The edict was repeated in 1709.

1689–1699 England The French ironsmith Jean Tijou worked at Hampton Court and, among other things, made twelve ornamental panels and two gates for the Fountain Garden (1690); these are considered his best work, outstanding in baroque ironwork. Tijou also worked on St Paul's Cathedral, London, Burghley House, Stamford, and Ampthill House Bedfordshire. He was specially skilled in *repoussé* work, a technique derived from silversmithing and not traditional in English ironwork.

1690 Flanders Death of David Teniers the Younger (b. 1610), painter, who had a strong influence on tapestry design. Weavers in Flanders followed closely the styles of contemporary painters, especially Teniers and Rubens.

1693 England Jean Tijou (fl. 1688–1712), French ironsmith, published *A New Booke of Drawings Invented and Designed by Jean Tijou*; this was the first pattern book for decorative ironwork published in England, although many had been published in France.

1693 France A design committee set up by Louis XIV devised the *romains du roi* typefaces for the Imprimerie Royale. They were the first to be designed with the engraver's tools rather than the pen in mind and they broke completely with calligraphic models.

VISUAL ARTS

1689 Netherlands *The Avenue at Middleharnis* by Meindert Hobbema (1638–1709), considered the last of the Dutch landscape masters.

1690 France Pierre Mignard (1612–1695) was made First Painter to the king. He revived the allegorical portrait.

1691 Japan Death of Mitsuoki (b. 1617), last great artist of the *Tosa* school of painting; under him it revived from a general decline into superficiality.

INVENTIONS & DISCOVERIES

1687 Newton's Philosophiae Naturalis Principia Mathematica *postulated a mechanistic universe.*

1688 Abraham Thevart first cast plate glass. William Dampier explored Australia.

1693 First scientific astronomical tables composed by Edmund Halley.

HISTORICAL EVENTS	LITERATURE	DANCE & DRAMA	MUSIC

MUSIC

1694 Sweden Birth of Johan Helmich Roman (d. 1758), composer and conductor of Finnish origin known as the 'father of Swedish music'.

1695 England Death of Henry Purcell (b. 1659).

1696 France Publication in Paris of *Éléments ou Principes de Musique dans un Nouvel Ordre. . . . avec l'Estampe et l'Usage du Chronomètre* by Étienne Loulié, French music master and writer on music. He was the first to invent an instrument for beating time (more than a century before Maelzel) and his book contains an engraving and description of his metronome.

LITERATURE

1695 Sweden Jesper Swedborg (1653–1735), bishop, philologist and hymnwriter, and Hakvin Spegel (1645–1714), archbishop, poet and scholar, wrote a hymn book which contained some of the finest poetry of the period. Swedborg also wrote a grammar, and was concerned with the reform of spelling.

1696 France Death of Marie de Rabutin-Chantal, Marquise de Sévigné (b. 1626): her letters, most of them written to her daughter, were a lively comment on contemporary life, both public and private; about 1,500 survive.

1696 Netherlands Estienne Roger, Dutch or (?) Flemish music publisher, established in Amsterdam; he is believed to be one of the first to introduce the practice of punching notes on copper as a substitute for engraving.

1696 Portugal *Luz e Calor* by the moralist Manuel Bernardes (1644–1710); he was a superb stylist and is regarded as a master of prose.

1697 England Concerts began at Hickford's Room, London, one of first regular public concert rooms.

1698 England *A Short View of the Immorality and Profaneness of the English Stage* by the Revd Jeremy Collier (1656–1726): he attacked not only contemporary dramatists but also Shakespeare–he criticized *Hamlet* as highly immoral. Much of his criticism of the Restoration stage was just, but he blamed the corruption of morals on the theatre, whereas the theatre merely reflected the society of the time.

1698 Denmark Death of Leonora Christina, Countess of Slesvig and Holstein (b. 1621), whose autobiography *Jammersminde*, written during a long imprisonment, is a major work of Danish prose. It combined deep feeling with brilliant expression, and established her as Denmark's greatest woman writer. It was not published until 1869.

1697 France *L'Europe Galante* by Andre Campra (1660–1744) was first produced and was performed until 1755; it became the model for all future ballets.

1698 Italy Birth of Giuseppe Guarneri (d. 1744), the greatest of the family of violin makers, and second only to Stradivari.

1698 Italy Birth of Giovanni Battista Sammartini (d. 1775), organist and composer.

1699
Peter the Great of Russia began administrative reforms.

1699 France *Télémaque* by François de Salignac de la Mothe Fénelon (1651–1715), theologian and author. This imaginative account of the deeds of Telemachus, son of Odysseus, was written for his pupil, the Duc de Bourgogne. Fénelon did not wish its publication, and the work brought him into disfavour because of its liberal ideas, especially those which implied criticism of the King.

1698 England *The Provok'd Wife* by Sir John Vanbrugh (1666–1726), an architect: his output in the theatre was small, but important because it extended the scope of the comedy of manners.

1699 England Three sonatas for violin, among the very first English sonatas for this instrument, were published by William Croft (1678–1727), organist and composer.

1699 England William Pearson, music printer, established in London; he made many improvements in musical typography following on from Heptinstall.

1699 Germany Death of the poet Friedrich Rudolf, Freiherr von Canitz (b. 1654). Influenced by Boileau, he wrote satires in a restrained, sober style. He was also known for his hymns.

1699 Germany *Hexachordum Apollinis* written by Johann Pachelbel (1653–1706), organist and composer. He wrote elaborate variations on chorales and is considered to be one of the spiritual ancestors of J. S. Bach.

1694–1707 Austria Dreifaltigs-keitskirche, Salzburg, by Johann Fischer von Erlach (1656–1723) is externally on the lines of St Agnese in Piazza Navonna, Rome, while the interior is based on St Andreal Quirinale, Rome.

1694 England Greenwich Hospital, London, by Sir Christopher Wren and others is the most successful of Wren's great secular building programmes and is baroque in character to suit its scale.

1696–1707 Austria The Kollegienkirche, Salzburg, by Johann Fischer von Erlach (1656–1723) is one of several baroque works carried out by the architect in Salzburg.

1696 Austria Palace of Schönbrunn, Vienna, was begun by Johann Fischer von Erlach and is the imperial summer palace, the 'Versailles' of Austria.

1698 France Jacques Ange Gabriel born (died 1782), the greatest eighteenth-century architect in France and architect to the king.

1698 Germany Royal palace, Berlin, by Andreas Schütter was one of many fine baroque buildings in Berlin, most of which were destroyed in World War II.

1699–1712 England Castle Howard by Sir John Vanbrugh was designed in an expansive baroque scale new to England, with kitchen and stable blocks linked by covered colonnades to the centre block which is crowned by a dome.

1699–1731 Spain St Luis Church, Seville, by Leonardo de Figueroa (c.1650–1730) is a brick church in the Mudéjar tradition by the leading Sevillian baroque architect; it is richly decorated and includes a coloured-tile façade.

1699 USA Established as capital of the state, Williamsburg, Virginia, is built in English seventeenth-century style; the public buildings especially are notable and there is evidence that Wren supplied some of the designs. Williamsburg was restored in 1931–1933.

*c.***1695 Japan** Death of Hishikawa Moronobu (b. *c.*1625), the most famous print-maker of the *Ukiyo-E* or 'pictures of the floating world' school of genre pictures. The movement seems to have begun spontaneously during the sixteenth century in response to the popular taste of workmen and tradesmen. At first their interests and entertainments were the subject of paintings: with Moronobu the paintings were succeeded by prints.

Japan: 'The Saffron Flower' by Moronobu

1699 North America Death of the New York silversmith Cornelius van der Burgh (b. 1653): his style combined English and Dutch characteristics.

late 1600–1700 England Powdered fling became the English silica for glass-making; previously Venetian quartz had been imported. Flint produced a glass that cracked on the inside; to counter this, George Ravenscroft experimented (c.1675) by adding lead. He produced a solid metal which diffused light brilliantly but was heavy to work, so the elaborate Venetian styles were abandoned for plainer shapes.

late 1600–1700 India Artists of the Punjab state of Basohli developed an original style of painting based on the Rajput school of Udaipur. The colour scheme was extended by pinks and acid greens and yellows; faces were dominated by huge eyes, and the figures were set off against their background by dark outlines. The most popular theme was the *Rasamanjari* by a sixteenth-century Bihari poet. An important series on this was painted (1694–1695) by Devi Das.

*1698
Thomas Savery
constructed
primitive steam
engine.*

18th Century

HISTORICAL EVENTS	LITERATURE	DANCE & DRAMA	MUSIC

LITERATURE

DANCE & DRAMA

MUSIC

*c.***1700–1800 England** The 'after-piece', usually a short comedy written for the purpose or adapted from an existing full-length play, became part of the evening's entertainment at the English theatres. It was introduced to attract the middle classes, whose business commitments prevented their being able to reach the theatre by 6 p.m., the usual time for the performance to start. They could now, however, arrive later and, at a reduced price, still see a complete play.

1700 England *The Way of the World* by William Congreve (1670–1729), the highwater mark in the English Restoration theatre.

1700–1800 Trinidad The Calypso originated from the plantations of Trinidad.

1700 England John Blow (1649–1708) published a volume of songs, *Amphion Anglicus.*

1700 England John Eccles (1668–1735) appointed Master of the King's Music.

1701 Denmark *Ars Poetica* by the poet Tøger Clausen Reenberg (1656–1742). His work was satirical, and often didactic, typical of the period.

1701 France First definite description of the *entrechat* dance step, in Feuillet's *Chorégraphie.* The book also described in choreographic symbols the five fundamental positions of the feet in ballet, taught earlier by Beauchamps.

1701 Russia Peter the Great built the first public theatre. He encouraged people to attend by making it cheap and convenient to do so. Johann Kunst was ordered to write a play celebrating one of Peter's recent victories, but the play was never written and the theatre closed in 1707.

1701 England *A Collection of Songs in Several Languages,* dedicated to William III, and *A Collection of Songs in English,* were published by John Abell (1650–1724) singer and lutenist.

*1702
War of Spanish
Succession
began.*

1702 England John Weaver (1673–1760), dancing master, created the pantomime-ballet *The Cheats of Scapin,* a comic ballet pantomiming the action in the tradition of the Elizabethan stage jig. Originally jig dancers had used a comic dance and a song; the sung lines were gradually replaced by more expressive miming during the seventeenth century.

1702 Russia The Moscow Religious Academy produced *Allegorical,* a play in honour of Peter the Great.

ARCHITECTURE

early 1700–1800 Peru Cajamarca Cathedral was one of three churches in the city demonstrating the exceptional vivacity of the baroque style in Peru.

early 1700–1800 Portugal Reign of King João V (1706–1750), patron of architecture, during which decoration, especially of façades, was important, but structural ingenuity was not.

1700–1800 Burma Shwe Dragon Buddhist temple, Rangoon, is in a style going back to India before Christ, but richly decorated in native Burmese tradition and surrounded by shrines in Burmese wood-architecture style.

1700–1800 Finland Harmina was replanned on the pattern of Scamozzi's sixteenth-century unified plan for Palmanova, which was based on concentric octagons.

1700–1800 Portugal The medieval church of St Francisco, Oporto, was extravagantly decorated in carved and gilded woodwork in the overpowering manner of Portuguese baroque.

1700 Italy Bartolommeo Rastrelli born (died 1771); trained in Paris, he moved to Russia in 1716, where he worked chiefly for Tsaritsa Elizabeth Petrovna, his buildings reflecting his French rococo training.

*c.*1700 **Belgium** The guild houses in Grande Place, Brussels, were rebuilt on narrow medieval sites in many variations of baroque, often culminating in fanciful gables.

*c.*1700 **China** The Throne Hall, Peking, is the centre of the axial plan of Peking, the city of the imperial family, and is approached through successive gates and halls on the main axis; the Throne Hall is built on a three-tier marble terrace.

1702–1736 Austria Malk Abbey was rebuilt by Jakob Prandtauer (1660–1726) and, like many Austrian abbeys, is dramatically sited above the Danube; its façade is undulating baroque, above a curious Palladian arch, and it was one of several abbeys the architect rebuilt.

THREE DIMENSIONAL ART

early 1700–1800 China Tinglaze enamel for ceramics was introduced from Europe: it produced colours known as *famille rose* and facilitated a very delicate style of painting. Blue-and-white ware began to decline.

early 1700–1800 Germany Ignaz Bottengruber, outstanding painter of ceramics, active at Vienna and at Breslau.

early 1700–1800 Holland A sober native style of glass-engraving replaced the early Italian influence. English glass made at Newcastle-on-Tyne was the most popular form among Dutch engravers.

1700–1800 Germany Johann Kunckel (1630–1703) developed *goldrubinglas* (gold ruby glass) characterized by deep colours, including blue and green, and produced at Potsdam.

early 1700–1800 Russia Sparrow Hills glass factory was established by English masters and glass-blowers, who trained Russian craftsmen. By 1750 it had been moved to near St Petersburg and called the St Petersburg Crystal factory.

1700–1800 Indonesia Techniques of dyeing introduced to Celebes, Java and Mandura by Indian Moslems made multicoloured batik fabrics possible; batik was previously a monochrome process.

1700 England First of the Acts of Parliament banning the import of calico for printing.

*c.*1700 **Portugal** Emergence of a typical Portuguese style of tile decoration, using blue on white for large panel pictures framed by baroque ornament. These were popular for buildings in Portugal and Brazil.

1702 Flanders Death of Jean Delcour (b. 1627) who, with his pupils, formed a group apart from the main-stream of Flemish sculpture and strongly influenced by Bernini: his tomb for Bishop Allamount in Ghent cathedral is characteristic. Native Flemish sculpture declined after the early eighteenth century.

VISUAL ARTS

early 1700–1800 Germany Discovery of the synthetic pigment 'Prussian blue'. Chemical advances between 1700 and 1900 doubled the number of pigments available to artists.

1700–1800 Europe The 'camera', once a room, was developed as a movable box. The image was projected through a lens and reflected up on to a glass lid from which the artist traced it off.

*c.*1700 **India** By this date a distinctive style of painting had developed in Kishangarh: green dominated the palette, and figures were drawn in elongated form against panoramic landscapes.

1701 France *Louis XIV* by Hyacinthe Rigaud (1649–1743) typified his successful portraits of royalty. He originated the technique of indicating rank, not character, by attitude and facial expression, and created an image of royalty that remained popular.

Portugal: 18th century Portuguese tiles

1702 India Death of Zeb-unnisa, daughter of the iconoclastic ruler Aurangzeb. In a time of little artistic activity she continued to encourage calligraphy and the copying of manuscripts.

| HISTORICAL EVENTS | LITERATURE | DANCE & DRAMA | MUSIC |

1703
St Petersburg
founded by Tsar
Peter I (the
Great).

1703 America Tony Aston, an Irish actor, appeared at Charleston, South Carolina. Little is known of either him or his visit but it is the first recorded instance of a professional actor performing in America.

1703 France A dictionary of music, the first of its kind, was written by the French composer, Sébastien de Brossard (1655–1730).

1703 Germany Johann Sebastian Bach (1685–1750) was appointed violinist to Duke of Weimar, but went almost immediately to Arnstadt as organist, and in the following year wrote his first cantata *Denn Du Wirst meine Seele*.

1703 Germany George Frideric Handel (1685–1759) left university where he was studying law and went to Hamburg where he obtained employment at the Opera House; his first opera *Almira* was produced there in 1705.

Germany: composer
Buxtehude's birthplace in
Holstein

1704
English defeated
French at
Blenheim.

1704 Italy Antonio Vivaldi (c.1675–1741) was established as a teacher at Conservatorio dell' Ospedale della Pietà, Venice, where he remained until 1740. He was appointed concert master there in 1716.

1705 Japan The Japanese Puppet Theatre in Osaka was named 'Takemoto-za' in honour of the puppet master Takemoto Gidayu.

1705 Russia Feofan Prokopovich (1681–1736) produced a tragi-comedy in which the hero is a thinly disguised portrait of Peter the Great. He tried to found a secular drama but was not successful.

1705 Germany Performance in Hamburg of the first opera, *Almira*, by George Frideric Handel (1685–1759), containing 41 German and 15 Italian airs.

1705 Germany J. S. Bach made his famous journey on foot, some 200 miles, to Lübeck, to hear *Abendmusiken* directed by Dietrich Buxtehude (1637–1707), the Danish composer and organist. Both Handel and Johann Mattheson had applied for the post to be successor to Buxtehude but on hearing that one of the conditions of the appointment was to marry Buxtehude's daughter, they both withdrew.

1706 France Publication of the *Recueil de Contredanses* by Raoul Feuillet: it was the first collection of English country dances (mostly 'longways' dances with two parallel lines of dancers) to be published in France. The English dances or their derivatives had spread through Europe by 1750, replacing the more dignified court dances. The term *contredanse* came into general use in France at this time, meaning English 'longways' country dance.

1706 France First published work by Jean Philippe Rameau (1683–1764), *Premier Livre de Pièces à Clavecin*.

1706 Italy Birth of Giovanni Battista Martini (d. 1784), composer, theorist and teacher; he completed three volumes on ancient music *Storia della Musica*, and taught many celebrated composers.

1707
Act of Union
united English
and Scottish
Parliaments.

1707 England John Shore (c.1662–1752), trumpeter and lutenist, appointed Sergeant-Trumpeter to the Royal Household. He was a most celebrated player and is said to have invented the tuning-fork in 1711.

ARCHITECTURE

1702 Germany Abbey Church of Ettal, Oberammergau, was reconstructed by Enrico Zuccalli (1642–1724); the medieval building is on the lines of Roman rather than German baroque. The dome and the interior are by Joseph Schmuzer (1683–1752) after 1745.

1704 USA Abraham Ackerman House, Hackensack, New Jersey, is stone-built and illustrates the influence of contemporary Dutch architecture.

1705–1724 England Blenheim Palace by Sir John Vanbrugh and Nicholas Hawksmoor was built for the Duke of Marlborough at the nation's expense on a vast and sprawling baroque scale.

1706 France Chapel of les Invalides, Paris, by J. H. Mansart has a dome which rises to half the height of the building and is the dominant feature of it; the masonry dome is topped by a false dome of wood to increase the height.

1706 Persia Madrassah Madir-I-Shah, Isfahan, is the largest eighteenth-century Persian mosque built on a traditional plan which has the principal iwan leading to the domed prayer chamber.

THREE DIMENSIONAL ART

*c.***1702 Germany** The amber carver Gottfried Turan of Danzig completed a set of carved panels that were to form an amber room for Frederick IV of Denmark; they were eventually bought by Peter the Great of Russia for his palace at Tsarskoye Selo. This work was the culmination of a century of outstanding amber-carving in Brandenburg, which had been patronised by the Electors and protected by the formation of a guild. The art declined in the eighteenth century.

1703 Russia Foundation of St Petersburg, where Peter the Great brought together craftsmen from Russia and western Europe. Ivory carvers from northern Russia, who had worked in a tradition established by 1000 A.D., had begun to cater for Muscovite and European taste in the seventeenth century, usually working in walrus ivory.

1707 France Portrait bust of Robert de Cotte by Antoine Coysevox (1640–1720), sculptor: he introduced a new psychological penetration into French portraiture and his work was noted for keen observation of the details of the features and of characteristic expression.

VISUAL ARTS

Italy: after a contemporary sketch of Vivaldi

1705 China Death of Chu Ta, forerunner of the Individualist school of painters who rebelled against copying the Masters. He used empty space to great effect, with an economy of brushstrokes and ink washes. His angles of vision were new and unusual. The influence of the Individualists was considerable, but delayed by conservative academics.

1707–1712 India A version of the *Shahjahan-nama* was painted for Bahadur Shah.

1707 Netherlands Death of Willem Velde II, considered a major marine painter. He worked in Holland and in England, and was concerned with recording weather and light. His younger brother Adriaen (1636–1672) concentrated on landscapes in painting and etching.

INVENTIONS & DISCOVERIES

*1706
Henry Mill
invented carriage
springs.*

*1707
Denis Papin
invented
steamboat.*

HISTORICAL EVENTS	LITERATURE	DANCE & DRAMA	MUSIC

MUSIC

1707 Germany First organ built in Frauenstein by eminent Gottfried Silbermann (1683–1753).

1707 Germany Death of Dietrich Buxtehude (b. 1637), composer.

DANCE & DRAMA

1708 France *Le Legataire Universel*, by Jean-Franҫois Regnard (1655–1709): the valet is the central character, which was unusual at that time and foreshadowed Beaumarchais' *Figaro*.

1708 Germany J. S. Bach went to Weimar as court organist to Duke Wilhelm Ernst, having been organist at Mühlhausen in 1707.

1708 Italy Handel's first oratorio *La Resurrezione* performed in Rome. He had left Germany for Italy in 1706.

1709 First mass German emigration to America.

1709 America *The Secret Diary of W. B. of Westover* by William Byrd (1674–1744), a writer and statesman who was educated in England. His style was polished and witty.

1709 France *Turcaret* by Alain Rene le Sage (1668–1747) was a satire on the *nouveau-riche* who exploit the poor, and reflected the growing resentment in France against taxation.

1709 Italy First performance of the opera *Agrippina* by George Frederick Handel, the outcome of the composer's long stay in Italy.

1709 Italy Bartolomeo Cristofori (1655–1731) constructed the first mechanism for a true pianoforte at Padua.

1710 England *Almanide* (anonymous), the first opera to be wholly sung in Italian in London, followed by *Idaspe Fedele* by Francesco Mancini (1679–1739), Italian composer.

1710 France Couperin (1668–1773) was established as a national figure and known as 'le Grand'.

1711–1714 England *The Spectator*, a literary periodical edited by Joseph Addison (1672–1719) and Sir Richard Steele (1672–1729). Addison's fame chiefly rests on the *De Coverley Papers*, essays setting forth the views of the imaginary Sir Roger de Coverley. His style, both familiar and elegant, the language of the educated middle classes and the characteristic note of the eighteenth century, was commended by Dr Johnson. Steele was chiefly concerned to improve the standards and taste of his readership, writing lively and humorous essays and character sketches to that end.

1710 Germany Birth at Weimar of Wilhelm Friedemann Bach (d. 1784), the eldest and one of the most distinguished sons of Johann Sebastian.

1710 Germany Handel became *Kapellmeister* to Elector Georg of Hanover and visited London for the first time.

1710 Italy Birth of Giovanni Battista Pergolesi (d. 1736), composer.

1711 China Death of Wang Shih-chen (b. 1634), a poet whose work illustrated his theory that poetry depends on spiritual harmony between words and rhythm.

1711 France *Rhadamiste et Zénobie* by Prosper Jolyot de Crébillon (1674–1762): his plays were more melodramatic than anything that had been seen hitherto on the French stage. They remained popular until the Romantics produced work which was yet more melodramatic.

1711 Mexico Production in Mexico City of *La Partenope* by Manuel Zumaya (c.1680–c.1740), composer. This was the first opera to be publicly presented in the New World.

1712 Slave revolt in New York. Last execution for witchcraft in Britain.

1712 England Handel's second visit to London, where he took out citizenship and remained until his death. *Il Pastor Fido* performed in London.

1709 Germany Johann Friedrich Böttger (d. 1719) and Ehrenfried Walther von Tschirnhausen (d. 1708) discovered the technique of making true Chinese porcelain.

1711 Germany The Zwinger, Dresden, is by Daniel Poppelmann (1662–1736) and Marcus Dietze (flourished 1680–1704), who established the Saxon baroque style; it was originally a wooden amphitheatre incorporated in the royal palace. The eighteenth-century Zwinger, outer courtyard, was to comprise a vast courtyard surrounded by a single-storeyed gallery connecting two-storeyed pavilions. The wall pavilion, built 1716, is an especially fine baroque structure with rich sculptural decoration. The Zwinger was damaged in 1945 but in part rebuilt since then.

1711 Germany Schloss Weissenstein, Pommersfelden, by Johann Dietzenhofer (1663–1726) is a monumental palace with projecting wings encircling a court on one side with a stable block one end, placed opposite the façade; there are extremely rich interiors, with fine staircase hall and decoration in sculpture, paint and shells in the Hall of Shells. Dietzenhofer came from a family of baroque architects.

1711–1770 Portugal Marra Palace by Joào Ludovice is one of the largest baroque palaces in Europe, dominated by its abbey church in the Roman baroque style.

1712 England St Alphege, Greenwich, London, by Nicholas Hawksmoor was the first of 6 churches he designed in London: all demonstrate his interest in classical Roman architecture.

1710 Germany Meissen porcelain factory was founded under the directorship of Böttger. In the same year Leipzig Fair gave the first public display for sale of a hard, fine, red stoneware by Böttger, copied from imported Chinese teapots made at Yi-hsing. Glazed with lead glaze and lacquered, it was made until *c*.1740.

1711 England Thomas Robinson, ironsmith, made a gate and screen for New College, Oxford, which are early examples of the English reaction against the heavy magnificence of continental baroque. English baroque ironwork became plainer, lighter and elegantly proportioned; the style continued until the introduction of neo-classicism.

1710–1734 India Sangram Singh II ruled Rajasthan. Under his patronage the cult of Krishna became the main subject for artists. He commissioned two series of paintings of the *Gita Govinda* in 1723 and an illustrated version of Sundar Das's *Sundar Sringára*, by the painter Jagannath, in 1725.

1712–1716 England Visit of the Venetian painters Sebastiano (1659–1734) and Marco (1676–1729) Ricci, who worked as decorative artists. On returning to Venice they worked for an English patron, Joseph Smith, who commissioned a series of religious paintings. Their work begins the eighteenth-century revival of Venetian painting: Sebastiano was a formative influence on Tiepolo, while Marco was the founder of a school of landscape painting.

HISTORICAL EVENTS	LITERATURE	DANCE & DRAMA	MUSIC

MUSIC

1712 England Organ built for St Magnus's Church, London Bridge by Abraham Jordan (I and II) father and son, which incorporated their invention of the swell, in the form of a sliding shutter.

1712 France Birth of Pierre Simon Fournier, engraver and type-founder (d. 1768); he replaced lozenge-shaped notes by round ones and greatly improved the engraving of music in France.

1713 England *Cato* by Joseph Addison (1672–1719), English journalist and playwright: it was a tragedy on French neoclassical lines.

1713 Italy *Merope*, by Scipione Maffei (1675–1755): Maffei set out to reform Italian tragedy, using the French and the ancient Greeks as his models. He also tried to found a National Theatre in Verona.

1714 Accession of Elector of Hanover as George I of Britain.

1714 England *The Tragedy of Jane Shore* by Nicholas Rowe (1674–1718): he differed from earlier English tragic dramatists in placing the emphasis on pathos.

1714 Germany Birth of Christoph Willibald Gluck (d. 1787), composer.

1714 Germany Birth at Weimar of Carl Philipp Emmanuel Bach (d. 1784), second son of Johann Sebastian.

1715 France Court ballets ended, with the death of Louis XIV, and ballet moved to the theatre.

1714 Italy Birth of Niccolò Jommelli (d. 1774), composer who wrote many operas and was one of first to use accompanied recitative.

1715–1724 France *Gil Blas de Santillane* by Alain René Lesage (1668–1747), novelist and playwright: written as a Spanish picaresque novel, it satirized French manners.

1715 England First performance of *Amadigi di Gaula* by Handel (1685–1759) with a libretto by John James Heidegger.

1715 France Pierre Buffardin (1690–1768), the French flautist, was appointed to the court chapel at Dresden, where he remained until 1749; he was one of the first to raise the technique of the flute to the level of modern virtuosity.

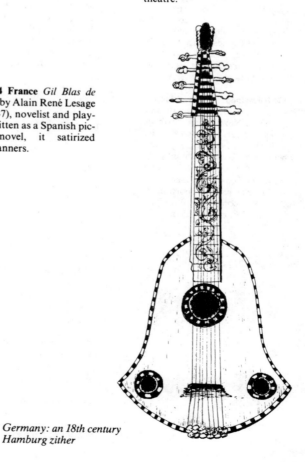

Germany: an 18th century Hamburg zither

1713 France Jacques Soufflot born (died 1780), a great neo-classical architect, and also an admirer of the Gothic style.

1714 Austria Palace, Vienna, for Prinz Eugen by Johann Lucas von Hildebrandt (1663–1745) consisted of two separate structures: the Lower Belvedere of 1714–1715 and the Upper Belvedere of 1721, the latter is a magnificent palace with decorative pavilions reminiscent of Borromini's architecture.

1714 Russia Church of the Transfiguration, Kishi, is the most elaborate of all Russian timber-built churches; no fewer than 22 domes are clustered above the octagonal and Greek-cross plan.

1714 Russia Cathedral of Sts Peter and Paul, St Petersburg, by Domenico Trezzini (1670–1734) was built as part of Peter and Paul Fortress; it is neo-classical rather than a baroque structure and presents a break with the domed churches of Russia.

1715 England First volume of *Vitruvius Britannicus* was published by Colin Campbell (?–1729); the author was influential in establishing Palladianism in Britain, a style which lasted for about a century.

1715–1740 England All Souls College North Quad, Oxford, by Nicholas Hawksmoor is the most unusual of his university buildings, which usually were of classical Roman inspiration, while this is mainly Gothic.

1715 Germany The abbey church of Weingarten is the best example of the German Vorarlberg school; numerous artists were employed on this immense structure imposingly positioned, overlooking the town, which has a two-towered façade with undulating front. The interior is based on Il Gesù, Rome, but with characteristic German baroque free-standing piers. Saucer domes and cupola on drum are placed over the crossing.

1714–1725 *c.*1750 **Germany** During the reign of George I of England and Hanover, the Lauenstein Glass House was established in Hanover; its glasses showed strong English influence and George I is believed to have supplied the House with English craftsmen.

1715–1725 France Gilles-Marie Oppenord (1672–1742), designer and decorator, was an important influence on the French *Régence* style. His work is known mainly from published designs.

1714 China Death of Tao Chi (b. 1667), an Individualist painter noted for unusual composition and observation of the moods of landscape.

1715 Japan Death of Nishikawa Sukenobu (b. 1671), considered one of the few artists who excelled in colour prints and in painting. He specialized in elaborate polychrome prints.

*1714
Gabriel David
Fahrenheit
constructed his
mercury
thermometer.*

HISTORICAL EVENTS	LITERATURE	DANCE & DRAMA	MUSIC

LITERATURE

1716–1733 Netherlands Poems of Hubert Korneliszoon Poot (1689–1733), writer of nature lyrics. Minor by European standards, he was nevertheless the only considerable Dutch poet of the period. The increased use of French was in part responsible for the small output of Dutch literature in this period.

1716–1728 Portugal *Fénix Renascida*, an anthology of poetry, was published by Matias Pereira da Silva. Most of the poems dated from the previous century, and many were in Spanish.

DANCE & DRAMA

1716 America Charles and Mary Stagg presented plays in the newly built playhouse in Williamsburg, Virginia.

1716 England Presentation of the ballet *The Loves of Mars and Venus* by John Weaver (1673–1760), dancer, teacher and choreographer. He introduced for the first time the *ballet d'action*, which dispensed with words and songs and depended entirely on dance. The form did not survive him in England, but was reintroduced.

HISTORICAL EVENTS

1717 Treaty of Amsterdam marked Russian entry into European diplomacy.

LITERATURE

1717–1758 Hungary Belles-lettres by Kelemen Mikes (1690–1761), a translator and essayist: his translations were from French religious works and the French influence shows in the style of these letters. At this period, Hungarian literature did not flourish, largely because of wars and the divided state of the country.

1717 Germany *Unvorgreiffliche Gedanken Betreffend de Ausübung und Verbesserung der Deutschen Sprache* by Gottfried Wilhelm von Liebnitz (1646–1717), a philosopher, diplomat and mathematician who believed that the universe was an organic whole made up of a hierarchy of units which mirrored each other. He wanted a historical study of German to be made, and the language to be more widely used.

1717 Italy *Le Rime* by Paolo Rolli (1687–1765), librettist and poet. His verse was in the Arcadian tradition, modelled on Catullus and Anacreon.

MUSIC

1717 France Publication of *L'Art de Toucher le Clavecin* by François Couperin, one of the most important treatises dealing with interpretation of early eighteenth century French music.

1717 Germany Johann Sebastian Bach went, as conductor of court orchestra, to Cöthen, where most of his chamber music, including the Brandenburg concerti, was written.

1718 Germany Birth of Friedrich Wilhelm Marpurg (d. 1795), writer of many important theoretical and critical works on music.

1718 Italy Performance of *Sofonisba* by Leonardo Leo (1694–1744), the opera which established his reputation. He was first of the Neapolitan school to have complete mastery over modern harmonic counterpoint.

ARCHITECTURE

1716 Austria Karlskirche, Vienna, by Johann Fischer von Erlach (1656–1723) is a masterpiece of complete originality in full-blown baroque style: the façade incorporates a portico similar to the Pantheon, surrounded by a column reminiscent of Trajan's, placed either side and the interior is monumental, characteristic of Austrian baroque.

1716 Russia Petrovdvorets, St Petersburg, by Trezzini, Alexander le Blond (1679–1719) and Rastrelli (1700–1771), who altered it to a baroque structure with lavish rococo decoration.

1716 USA Peter Harrison born (died 1775), architect who built Longfellow House, Cambridge, Massachusetts, 1759; English Palladian style was adapted to American conditions with weatherboarding; styles derived from stone buildings were built in rubble covered with stucco, decorated with wood and brick.

1717 Austria St Jakob's Church, Innsbruck, by Johann Herkommer (1648–1717) is chiefly remarkable for the magnificent baroque interior, painted and stuccoed by the Asam brothers.

1717 England Vanbrugh Castle, Greenwich, London, by Sir John Vanbrugh was the architect's own house, disguised as a castellated and turreted castle; it is an early example of Gothic revivalism.

1717 France Robert de Cotte (1683–1767) was an architect of many Parisian mansions decorated in the rococo style, including Hôtel de la Vriellière.

1717–1731 Italy The Superga, Turin, by Filippo Juvarra (1678–1736) is the most spectacular of his churches and is surmounted by a dome and preceded by a columned portico; behind the church is a large monastery in a contrasting and simpler style.

1718 Denmark Fredensborg Castle was enlarged by J. C. Krieger and others: the old royal hunting lodge was restyled as a Palladian villa of modest size. At the end of the eighteenth century it was further enlarged.

THREE DIMENSIONAL ART

1716 England Appointment of Paul de Lamerie (1688–1751) as goldsmith to the king: considered the most outstanding goldsmith and silversmith of his time in England, he was among the first to introduce rococo elements into English silver design.

1716 Russia Arrival of Nicolas Pineau (1684–1754) French sculptor and decorator, who became the chief decorative artist at the Tsar's court. His most important work was the carved cabinet of Peter the Great.

1717–1724 Europe Publication by Père d'Entrecolles, Jesuit missionary to China, of his observations on Chinese porcelain-making methods encouraged and influenced the European porcelain industry.

c.1717 Germany Death of Franz Gondelach, artist in glass and crystal, who worked at Cassel and was considered the foremost glass-artist of his time. Engraved crystal vessels were popular in Germany from c.1600 until c.1750.

VISUAL ARTS

1716 Japan Death of Ogata (b. 1658), reviver of the *Korin* school of decorative painting. His work combined direct naturalism with a love of pattern; it was popular in Japan and in the West, and ensured international interest in *Korin* painting.

1717 France Jean-Antoine Watteau (1684–1721) painted *L'Embarquement pour l'Île de Cythère*, considered his most characteristic work. He was an early practitioner of 'divisionism', a technique of juxtaposing pure colours so that they are mixed by the eye. Watteau set an original French style: it was developed from both Venetian and Flemish painting (especially the work of Rubens), and broke completely from the academic classical style. He painted genre pictures and scenes of escapist, elegant pleasures.

1717 Italy The painter Giovanni Paolo Panini (c.1692–1765) settled in Rome and became famous for his pictures of Roman ruins, which started a fashion.

INVENTIONS & DISCOVERIES

1718
Halley discovered independent movement of fixed stars. Leopold of Dessau invented iron ramrod.

1719 Italy *Artino Corasio* the first of five *canzonette* by Pietro Trapassi, called Metastasio (1698–1782), librettist and poet. He was a major lyric poet in the Arcadian tradition.

1719–1720 Denmark *Peder Paars*, a mock-heroic poem by Ludvig, Baron Holberg (1684–1754), satirist, essayist, playwright and historian. He came into contact with European thought during his travels in England, France and Italy, and was especially impressed by the French. He used his experiences in the foundation of a modern Danish literature.

1719 England Handel appointed director of the Royal Academy of Music, London.

1719 Germany A printing-press was set up at Leipzig by Bernhardt Christoph Breitkopf (1695–1777); this was the foundation of Breitkopf and Härtel, the music publishers.

Germany: an 18th century German porcelain tea-pot

1720
Tibet became tributary of China.

*c.***1720 Central America** African slaves coming to the plantations brought with them a dance, the *tángano*, which became popular and was the ancestor of the tango.

1720 England First opera season of Royal Academy in London, which was an artistic and financial success for Handel, and began a series of operas which he wrote during the following 21 years.

1718–1729 Germany The plan of Aldersbach Abbey by Cosmas Damian Asam and Egid Quirin Asam is simple but the stucco work, painting and sculpture create a rococo masterpiece.

1718 Italy Palazzo Madama, Turin, by Filippo Juvarra was one of several great baroque palaces built for Victor Amadeus II by Juvarra.

1719 Austria Göttweig Abbey was enlarged by Johann von Hildebrandt (1663–1745); it is typical of the architect's work, the interior decoration being rich baroque in paint and stucco, with the stylistic influence mainly Italian.

1719–1753 Germany The Würzburg Residenz, Würzburg, is one of the most remarkable interiors of the whole complex, the Staircase Hall, by the architect Balthasar Neumann (1687–1753), stuccoist Giuseppi Bossi (flourished 1735–43) and painter Tiepolo (1692–1769), being conceived as a ceremonial staircase: one sweep of stairs leads to a half landing from where it doubles, leading to a galleried upper landing.

1719 Italy Stupinigi Hunting Lodge, Turin, by Sicilian Filippo Juvarra is a huge baroque country house consisting of a centrepiece and extended wings.

1719–1750 Switzerland Einsielden Abbey near Lake Zürich was rebuilt by Caspar Moosbrugger (1656–1723) and has a large baroque interior in the German tradition with painted, sculpted and gilded decoration, but the exterior is much simpler.

1720 Hungary Eszterhazy Palace, Fertod, is by Erhard Martinelli (1684–1747) and was later extended; the ground plan is in baroque tradition, all the details of decoration being rococo. The entrance to the main block leads through a magnificent horseshoe-shaped courtyard along a curving staircase of stone and iron.

England: portrait of Josiah Wedgwood by George Stubbs painted in enamel on Queen's ware plaque, 1780

1719–1864 Austria Vienna produced the first porcelain to rival Meissen.

1719 France Charles Cressent (1685–1768) became cabinetmaker to the Regent, Philip of Orléans. He specialized in furniture with gilt-bronze mounts, and introduced the *bombé*-shaped (convex) commode typical of Louis XV's reign.

1720–1730 England Development of creamware pottery, an off-white, lead-glazed earthenware which reached its peak under the partnership (1754–1759) of Thomas Whieldon and Josiah Wedgwood.

1720–1730 Germany Johann Gregor Höroldt (d. *c.*1731) developed an extensive range of enamel colours for ceramic decoration at Meissen.

1720 Holland Earliest known piece of engraved glass by the gifted engraver Frans Greenwood (1680–1761). He and his two most noted successors, Jacob Sang (fl. *c.*1750) and David Wolff (d. 1808), all specialized in diamond-point stipple-engraving.

1720 China Death of Wang Hui (b. 1632), last surviving artist of the 'Four Wangs' whose paintings were considered the last important work in traditional style. The other three were Wang Shih-Min (1592–1680), Wang Chien (1598–1680) and Wang Yuan Ch'i (1642–1715).

1721
French occupied Mauritius.
Peter I proclaimed Russian empire.

1721 Greenland Colonization by Denmark/Norway; at the time, there was a rich and well-developed native Greenlandic folk-lore, which was entirely oral, including songs, poems and myths, though no long works. Much of this was later suppressed by the Danes.

1721 Denmark Ludvig Holberg (1684–1754) a Norwegian by birth, became director of the Danish Theatre in Copenhagen. Widely travelled in England, France and Italy, he returned to Denmark to create a native drama, using the Danish language and Danish and Norwegian subjects, and modelled on the comic traditions of the countries he had visited.

1721 Scotland Publication of *A Treatise of Musik, Speculative, Practical and Historical* by Alexander Malcolm (b. 1687), scientist and author; it was first important treatise on the theory of music issued in Scotland.

Austria: the Belvedere summer palace, Vienna

1722 England *Moll Flanders* by Daniel Defoe (1660–1731), journalist, pamphleteer and novelist. Vividly written, full of detail and virtually plotless, his books read like good factual reporting. Though they contain both fact and fiction, it is impossible to separate the two.

1722 England *The Conscious Lovers* by Sir Richard Steele (1672–1729) was one of his four English comedies expressly written to make virtue appealing and so improve morals.

1722 France Publication, in Paris, of *Traite de l'Harmonie* by Jean Philippe Rameau (1683–1764), a treatise which propounded the modern theory of harmony.

1722 Germany Earliest of all musical periodicals, *Musica Critica* by Johann Mattheson (1681–1764).

ARCHITECTURE

1721 Austria The Belvedere Summer Palace, Vienna, built for Prince Eugen by Lukas von Hildebrandt (1668–1745), military engineer and architect; elegance and decoration predominate and there are some oriental features: Fischer von Erlach had published *Outline for an Historical Architecture* in 1721, including Egyptian and Chinese architecture for the first time, as well as Roman and Greek.

1721 Bavaria The high altar at Weltenburg is by Cosmas Damian (1686–1739) and Egid Quirin Asam (1692–1750), in whose work the theatrical completely dominates the architectural; decoration is paramount in this period in Germany: architects worked in teams with stucco artists, painters and decorative designers.

1721 England St John's, Westminster, London, is by Thomas Archer (1668–1743), who had studied in Italy and in this church produced the most Italian baroque church in England.

1721 England St Martin in the Fields, London, is by James Gibbs (1682–1754), an Italian-trained architect; his design of the western portico and spire for this church was widely copied in England and America.

1721 Italy The Spanish Steps, Rome, by Francesco de Sanctis (1693–1740) and Alessandro Specchi (1668–1729) are part of an elegant baroque ensemble of piazza, with Bernini's fountain of 1628, the steps in triple ascent, and St Trinità dei Monti by Specchi.

1721–1770 Italy Rosario Gagliardi active (flourished 1721–70), Sicily, who incorporated traditional Sicilian features into baroque style such as the cathedral of St Giorgio, Ragusa, begun 1746; Sicilians liked surface decoration and Gagliardi made this truly architectural.

1722 England Mereworth House by Colin Campbell (died 1729) is an exact imitation of Palladio's Villa Rotonda; English architects mainly ignored the rococo and went back through Inigo Jones, the Renaissance and the Romans.

Italy: the Spanish Steps, Rome, by Francesco de Sanctis and Alessandro Specchi

1722 North America Death of the silversmith John Coney (b. 1655) whose prolific output spans the styles of three periods, baroque Louis XIV and Queen Anne, in their colonial adaptations.

*c.***1722 England** William Caslon, (1692–1766) type designer, cut his first (Hebrew) type: he began as an engraver of gunlocks and became the first British type-founder to offer his own uniformly designed range of type.

HISTORICAL EVENTS

1725
Death of Peter I
of Russia;
succeeded by
Catherine I.

LITERATURE

1723 France *Odes* by Jean-Baptiste Rousseau (1671–1741), one of the most noted poets of the day. He was especially remarkable for topical odes. His style was dignified and rhetorical.

1726 Ireland *Gulliver's Travels* by Jonathan Swift (1667–1745), satirist, novelist, pamphleteer and poet. He wrote on political, religious and literary matters. This book was a savage satire on mankind. Swift deplored the fact that men are irrational and swayed by emotion.

1726 Spain A Spanish dictionary was issued by the Academy (founded 1714). The seventeenth century had been Spain's golden age; the eighteenth was remarkable not for creative activity but for study and discussion of Spanish history and culture.

DANCE & DRAMA

1723 France Bonnet published *Histoire de la Danse Sacrée et Profane.*

1726 France Stage debut of the dancer Maria Camargo (1710–1770), who introduced ballet slippers and shorter skirts, and was therefore able to execute livelier steps such as an *entrechat* of four crosses and various leaping steps.

1727 France The dancer and choreographer Marie Sallé (1707–1756) joined the Paris Opéra ballet. The strict conventions of the Opéra hampered her ambitions to produce *ballet d'action* (ballet where the dancing is self-sufficient in expression, with no need of speech or song), and other more creative companies were closed down by the jealousy of the powerful Opéra. She left for London in 1730.

1727 Germany Johann Christoph Gottsched (1700–1766), German man of letters, and Caroline Neuber (1697–1760), called 'die Neuberin', actress-manager of the best theatrical company of the time, collaborated to introduce drama on French neo-classical lines: their attempts were ill-received by a public loyal to 'Hanswurst'. Their association was short-lived, but it marks the turning-point in the history of the German theatre.

1727 Netherlands *Migdal Oz* by Moses Hazim Luzzatto (1707–1747), one of the foremost Hebrew poets: the play is a pastoral. There was no established Jewish theatre anywhere at this time, plays being performed at religious festivals or on other special occasions.

MUSIC

1723 France First opera by Jean Philippe Rameau, *L'Endriague*, produced in Paris.

1723 Germany J. S. Bach went to Leipzig as Cantor at St Thomas's, where he remained until his death in 1750. His oratorio *St John Passion* was first performed.

1724 England Beginning of Three Choirs Festival—Gloucester, Worcester and Hereford.

1724 Italy Publication of the first part of *50 Psalms* by Benedetto Marcello (1686–1739), composer, the second part being published by 1726. These psalms constitute one of finest productions of musical literature.

1725 Austria *Gradus ad Parnassum* was published in Latin by Johann Joseph Fux (1660–1741), organist and composer, in Vienna. This important work, which formulated rules of contrapuntal composition, has passed through innumerable editions, been translated into four languages and is still found useful today.

1725 Italy Death of Pietro Alessandro Gaspare Scarlatti, composer (b. 1660).

1725 Scotland First publication by Richard Cooper, music engraver (d. 1764), the first to engrave music in Scotland.

1726 France Johann Joachim Quantz (1697–1773), German flautist, theorist and composer, visited Paris, where he made several improvements in the flute, including a second key; he later invented the sliding top for tuning the instrument.

1722–1853 Spain Cadiz Cathedral was begun by Vincente Acero; a monumental church, it is the only completely baroque cathedral in Spain.

1722–1729 Spain The frontispiece of the Hospicio San Fernando, Madrid, by Pedro de Ribera (*c.*1683–1742) is exuberantly decorated Churrigueresque work (florid baroque style named after the churriguera family of architects and sculptors); he was the leading Madrid architect in this style.

1723–1784 Portugal Bom Jesus do Monte, near Braga by Carlos Amarante (1748–1815) is a pilgrimage church sited on a hill-top reached by a sculpture-decorated staircase; the approach and façade are rich baroque in style.

1724 Bolivia *The Four Evangelists* were the last paintings by Melchor Pérez Holguin (*c.*1660–*c.*1725), founder of the Potosi school of painting. He was a mannerist painter whose use of detail and decoration echoed Bolivian folk tradition.

1725 England Chiswick House, London, by Lord Burlington (1695–1753) and William Kent (1685–1748) was based on Palladio's Villa Rotonda and, together with its aristocratic designer, was influential in the spread of Palladianism in Britain and Ireland.

1725–1750 France Chantilly porcelain factory made wares in Japanese kakiemon style.

1724 France Maurice de la Tour (1704–1788) set up in Paris as a portraitist in pastels or 'dry colours', a favourite medium with eighteenth-century portrait painters. He became one of the most successful portraitists, outstanding for treating colour and finish as secondary to draughtsmanship; many artists were attracted to pastels, because the colour values were novel.

1726 France The planning of Hôtel Matignon, Paris, by Jean Courtonne (1671–1739) illustrates the eighteenth-century French tendency for the ingenious arrangement of rooms on a small scale behind symmetric and elegantly classical façades.

1726 France Appointment of Juste-Aurèle Meissonnier (1695–1750) as Dessinateur de la Chambre et du Cabinet du Roi. He had begun as a silversmith and his designs for silver established the most asymmetrical phase of the rococo style.

*1726
John Harrison
invented a
compensating
balance for
clocks.*

1726–1734 USA Westover, Charles City County, Virginia, is a very fine house equal in design and quality of construction to contemporary English buildings; like many similar houses in the eastern states, the architect is unknown but the debt to plates in Gibbs's *Book of Architecture*, published 1727, is sometimes noticeable.

1726 France Jean-Baptiste Oudry (1686–1755), painter, was appointed director of the Beauvais carpet factory. François Boucher (1703–1770) worked for the factory as a designer.

*1727
Stephen Hales
isolated oxygen.*

1727–1764 Spain La Cartuja, Granada, by Francisco Izquierdo (1669–1725) shows Moorish influence in the decoration with rich and varied materials used, including marble, tortoiseshell, ivory and mother of pearl.

1727–1751 USA Christ Church, Philadelphia, by John Kearsley (1684–1722) is a colonial church, in which some detailing and the west steeple owe their design to Gibbs.

HISTORICAL EVENTS	LITERATURE	DANCE & DRAMA	MUSIC

LITERATURE

1728–1731 France *Manon Lescaut* by L'Abbé Antoine François Prévost (1697–1763), a novelist and writer of travel books and philosophy. He translated the English novelist Samuel Richardson into French. This book was a sentimental novel, written as moral instruction.

DANCE & DRAMA

1728 England *The Beggars' Opera* by John Gay (1685–1732): an English ballad-opera containing political satire and also making fun of the fashionable Italian opera.

1728 England Last edition of John Playford's *The Dancing Masters*: the first (1650) had recorded 104 dances; the last listed nearly 900, divided into ring or round dances, 'square-eights', dances for two couples and dances for two files of dancers (longways dances).

MUSIC

1728 England The oldest firm of keyboard instrument makers still extant, John Broadwood and Sons, was founded in London by the Swiss harpsichord maker, Burkat Shudi (Burkhard Tschudi).

1728 England The first ballad opera, *The Beggar's Opera*, by John Gay (1685–1732) was produced.

1728 Germany Birth of Johann Andreas Stein, pianoforte maker (d. 1792) who invented several important modifications to the instrument.

1728 Italy Foundation of a school of violin playing at Padua by Giuseppe Tartini (1692–1770), violinist, teacher and composer.

1729 North and South Carolina became British crown colonies.

1729 Russia Satiric poems by Antioch Dmitrievich, Prince Kantemir (1709–1744), who wrote exclusively in conversational Russian. He used the Polish syllabic verse form, though he was aware of its limitations and realized the possibilities of tonic verse, an iambic metre with regular feet. During the reign of Peter the Great, Church-Slavonic was restricted to the Church. Peter was more interested in technical and scientific development than in literature, but a practical language was required for text books and manuals, so 'spoken' Russian as a literary language began to develop. Peter also introduced the civic alphabet to replace the complicated Church-Slavonic characters.

1729 Germany *St Matthew Passion* by Johann Sebastian Bach first performed.

1729 Netherlands Birth of Pierre van Maldere, violinist and composer (d. 1768) believed to have introduced the bi-thematic technique into the first movement of a symphony.

1730 Germany *Kritische Dichtkunst* by the critic Johann Christoph Gottsched (1700–1766). An admirer of French literature, he tried to establish similar tastes in Germany.

1730 Russia Accession of the Empress Anna: although there was still no native drama, she encouraged visits from Italian *commedia dell' arte* troupes.

1730 France Jean Philippe Rameau met Voltaire, whose ideas were to have a great influence on his life and works.

1730 Germany Production in Venice of *Artaserse*, opera by Johann Adolph Hasse (1699–1783), one of most popular composers of his time.

1730 Scotland *The Seasons*, four long poems in blank verse, by James Thomson (1700–1748): the work showed the influence of Milton in its vocabulary, and contained scientific and philosophical material popular at the period. It is interesting because Thomson's passages of natural description were unusually sensitive and detailed at a time when nature was not generally admired.

1730 Turkey Death of the poet Ahmed Nedim (b. 1681), whose poetry gave a vivid picture of the wealthy and cultured city of Istanbul at that time. He also wrote songs, which are still sung. The best poets of this period had ceased to imitate Persian classics and developed their own style.

England: 'A Harlot's Progress' by William Hogarth

ARCHITECTURE

1728 France Étienne-Louis Boullée, architect born (died 1799), whose designs were an extreme reaction against baroque, and stressed plain shapes of enormous size with no illusion or softening; few of his designs could be build because of their size.

1728 Germany Steinhausen Church, by Dominikus Zimmerman (1685–1766) and Johann Baptiste Zimmerman (1680–1758), is one of several beautifully decorated baroque churches in southern Germany with a predominantly white colour scheme.

1728 Ireland The Old Parliament House, Dublin, by Edward Pearce (1699–1733) is one of the best Palladian buildings in Ireland where the style flourished; the domed House of Commons, now destroyed, may have derived from Burlington's Chiswick House, London.

1728 Poland University at Wroclaw by Domenico Martinelli is an outstanding baroque complex, culminating in a long river façade.

1728 Scotland Robert Adam born (died 1792), whose work returned to classical forms of antiquity, not their Renaissance-derived imitations; the feeling of the late eighteenth century was for stern moral purpose: architecture must be 'natural', true, that is, to its function. Adam excelled in using the natural early classical forms in domestic settings: scale, decoration and colours were no longer dramatic but harmonious as background for domestic life.

1729–1740 Spain Plaza Mayor, Salamanca, by Alberto de Churriguera (1676–1750) and Andrea Garcia de Quiñones (flourished 1750–55) is a magnificent baroque square surrounded by arcades beneath houses; Alberto was the most able of the famous Churriguera family of architects.

1730–1742 Hungary University church, Pest, by Andreas Mayerhoffer (flourished 1720–54) is an outstanding example of full-blown Austrian Baroque.

THREE DIMENSIONAL ART

1728 Spain Founding of the royal glass factory at La Granja (the only major one in Spain). From c.1775 it produced crystal glass with gilded and engraved patterns.

c.1728 England William Kent (1685–1748) designed his first garden: Chiswick House. He put into practice ideas which had been developing in England since c.1700, in reaction against the neat English and grand French traditions of artificial gardens. Kent still worked on a limited area but designed it in imitation of natural woodland, grassland or lake-side. Copses replaced stiff plantations, meandering streams replaced straight canals. Gardens after this were extended into parks covering hundreds of acres, providing landowners with a comfortably tamed countryside all round their principal seats.

c.1730 Bohemia Invention of *Zeischengoldglass*, a style of glass in which the sides of a beaker were decorated on gold or silver leaf and it was then encased in an outer glass, which was converted on to the original. The best known exponent of the art was the Austrian glass-maker Johann Josef Mildner (1763–1808).

c.1730 England First known pieces of English cut-glass; shallow cutting was used until c.1800 when the typical deep-cut diamond pattern developed.

VISUAL ARTS

1728 France Jean-Baptiste-Simeon Chardin (1699–1779) was received into the Academy. His small pictures of still life or everyday life were a further development of Dutch realism. He achieved new depths of colour tone by overpainting and was unrivalled in presenting solid form. He is considered one of the greatest of French painters; his feeling for essential form went far beyond surface realism.

c.1730 England William Hogarth (1697–1764) began his sequences of narrative pictures which were 'similar to representations on the stage' and full of visual symbols; the earliest was *A Harlot's Progress*. His skill at conveying character made his pictures a successful medium for satire on affectation, foolishness and human failings as well as social abuses.

c.1730 Italy 'The Stone-Mason's Yard' by the Venetian painter Giovanni Canaletto (1697–1768) marks the culmination of his early style, painted with freedom and strong light effects. From this time on he began to paint topographical studies of meticulous accuracy. In this he was partly influenced by the topographical artist Luca Carlevaris, but he went far beyond mere topography in his ability to show sunlight and the open air.

1728 Bering Strait discovered.

1729 James Bradley discovered aberration of light of fixed stars.

<table>
<tr>
<td valign="top">

</td>
<td valign="top">

1731–1741 France *La Vie de Marianne* by Pierre Carlet de Chamblain de Marivaux (1688–1763), novelist and playwright. He was a sensitive observer of character, but he used the picaresque form, which was best suited to action.

1731–1735 Netherlands *De Hollandische Spectator* by Justus van Effen (1684–1735), an essayist whose early work was in French; later he wrote in Dutch, in spirited and unforced style.

</td>
<td valign="top">

1731 England *The London Merchant* by George Lillo (1693–1739) was an English middle-class, domestic tragedy.

</td>
<td valign="top">

1731 America The earliest known public concert in North America took place in Boston, Massachusetts.

1731 Italy First operas by Giovanni Battista Pergolesi (1710–1736) performed in Naples.

</td>
</tr>
<tr>
<td valign="top">

1732 James Oglethorpe founded colony of Georgia.

</td>
<td valign="top">

1732–1734 Sweden *Then Svänska Argus*, a periodical on the lines of the *Spectator*, was founded by Olof von Dalin (1708–1763), historian, journalist, poet and playwright. He introduced the French classical style to Sweden and his work, with its emphasis on good taste and reason, marked the beginning in that country of what is known as the Enlightenment.

</td>
<td valign="top">

1732 France *Les Fausses Confidences* by Pierre Carlet de Chamblain de Marivaux (1688–1763), French comic dramatist: his most important rôles are for women, and his subtle, rather precious style is sufficiently remarkable to have been given the name *marivaudage*.

1732 Italy *La Clemenza di Tito* by Pietro Armando Dominico Trapassi, called Metestasio (1693–1782): this is a melodrama, a new form which developed from the pastoral and in which words and music are equally important.

</td>
<td valign="top">

1732 Austria Birth of Franz Joseph Haydn (d. 1809), composer.

1732 England Covent Garden Theatre opened in London.

1732 Germany Publication of *Musicalisches Lexicon oder Musicalische Bibliothec* by Johann Gottfried Walther (1684–1748), composer and musical lexicographer.

1732 Italy Giovanni Battista Pergolesi (1710–1736) appointed *maestro di cappella* to Prince of Stigliano at Naples.

1732 Italy *Sonate da Cimbalo di Piano* written by Lodovico Giustini. These sonatas are probably earliest printed music for pianoforte.

</td>
</tr>
<tr>
<td valign="top">

</td>
<td valign="top">

1733 England *Essay on Man* by Alexander Pope (1688–1744), the satiric poet, who was regarded during his lifetime as the greatest poet in Europe. He believed that his task as a poet was to set high standards, both moral and aesthetic. He translated Homer's *Iliad* and *Odyssey* and his own poetry is strictly classical, written in highly polished heroic couplets.

</td>
<td valign="top">

</td>
<td valign="top">

1733 England Performance of the opera *Rosamund* in London by Thomas Augustine Arne (1710–1778).

1733 France Death of François Couperin (b. 1668).

</td>
</tr>
</table>

ARCHITECTURE

*c.*1730–1770 **England** Bath was replanned and built in the form of a Palladian-style Roman city by John Wood the elder (1704–1754) and his son (1728–1781) into such terraces as Royal Crescent; this was novel in England and copied in other towns including Bristol, Brighton and Cheltenham in the eighteenth century.

*c.*1730 **France** The decorative rococo interiors of the Hôtel de Soubise, Paris, by Germain Boffrand (1667–1754) contrast with the more classical exteriors. This is typical of Boffrand, a prolific rococo architect.

1731–1791 **USA** Independence Hall, Philadelphia, is essentially Georgian, built of brick with white quoining. The tower—rebuilt in 1832—with its timber lantern is outstanding work for America at that period.

1732–1762 **Italy** Trevi Fountain, Rome, by Niccolo Salvi (1697–1751) consists of an artificial rocky outcrop, inhabited by sculpted figures, from which fountains gush; the backdrop is a façade in the form of a Roman triumphal arch.

1732–1750 **Portugal** Nossa Senhora de Assumpçao by Niccolo Nasoni (died 1773) is situated on a narrow site, the church having a curious elleptically planned nave, entered from the side since the elaborate baroque entrance is blind.

1732 **Spain** The Transparante, Toledo Cathedral, by Narciso Tomé (active 1715–*c.*1740) is a dazzling piece of baroque ingenuity, whereby the view of the sacrament was enhanced by light flooding from a special window out through the Gothic vaults—the ultimate in theatrical baroque.

1733–1746 **Germany** St John Nepomuk, Munich, by Cosmas Damian Asam and Egid Quirin Asam is a masterpiece of Bavarian baroque; the architectural layout and decoration in pale tones form a harmonious unit. There is a magnificent centrepiece over the altar and richly painted ceiling.

THREE DIMENSIONAL ART

1731 **Germany** Death of Johann Melchior Dinglinger (b. 1664), goldsmith and jeweller to Augustus of Saxony. His work embodies the grotesque taste in its extravagant combinations of gold, cameos, enamel and precious stones.

1731 **Germany** Beginning of active period of Johann Joachim Kaendler (d. 1775), modeller and sculptor in Meissen porcelain who made the first European porcelain figures.

1733 **Austria** Johann Georg Oegg (fl. 1720–1767), ironsmith, entered the service of Bishop Karl von Schönborn and began the gates and screens for the Residenz-schloss. His work is in an exuberant rococo style and is considered among the best German ironwork.

1733 **France** Jean-Baptiste Oudry (1686–1755), painter, was made director and chief designer of the Gobelin tapestry works. He insisted on the exact reproduction of the artist's cartoon with no freedom of interpretation for the weavers. His own designs for the *Hunts of Louis XV* were considered outstanding in their treatment of natural landscape.

VISUAL ARTS

1731–1733 **Japan** Visit of the southern Chinese painter of birds and flowers, Shên Nan-p'in. His work inspired the Nagasaki school of painting which lasted through the nineteenth century. The school was also influenced by European work, as Nagasaki was the only city open to foreigners.

1732 **England** Arrival of the French designer and book illustrator Hubert-François Bourguignon Gravelot (1699–1773) who was important in introducing French rococo style into English illustration.

INVENTIONS & DISCOVERIES

1731 John Hadley invented navigational sextant.

LITERATURE

DANCE & DRAMA

MUSIC

1734 England The French dancer Marie Sallé choreographed the *ballet d'action Pygmalion* and danced Galatea, wearing a plain muslin without the wig, mask, powdered hair or heavy court costume which were previously the rule. She was described in this and *Bacchus et Ariane*, in the same year, as expressing 'all the great passions perfectly declaimed by means of dances, attitudes and gestures'. She also danced her *ballets d'action* in Paris, and influenced Noverre.

1734 Russia Arrival of the French dancer Jean-Baptiste Landet (d.1748); he became ballet-master of a poor children's school in the following year and was influential in founding the Imperial Theatre School.

1734 Ireland Death of John Neale, who together with his brother William Neale (d. 1769) was the earliest Irish music publisher of any note.

1734 Sweden Birth of Abraham Abrahamsson Hülphers (d. 1798), topographer and music historian, known as the 'father of Swedish musical history'.

1734 Russia A permanent opera was formed at the Imperial Court in St Petersburg by the Empress Anne. It employed an Italian company, led by Francesco Araia (1709–1770).

1735 England Maurice Greene (1695–1755) appointed Master of the King's Music.

1735 Germany Birth at Leipzig of Johann (later John) Christian Bach (d. 1782), the youngest son of Johann Sebastian by his second wife.

1736 England John Beard (1717–1791) first sang as a tenor at Covent Garden Theatre. He was the first to do so at a time when *castrati* normally sang the leading parts in opera.

1736 Italy Death of Giovanni Battista Pergolesi (b. 1710).

1737 Spain *Poetica* by Ignacio Luzán Claramunt de Suelvas y Guerra (1702–1754). In this book he set down the rules of neo-classical literature. He was, however, aware of the virtues of other modes of writing, and believed that enjoyment was the real criterion.

1737 Spain *Poetica*, by Ignacio de Luzan (1702–1754), attempted to impose neo-classical rules on Spanish drama. The Spanish court, disliking the imitation French classics offered to them, found their pleasure in Italian opera.

1737 England Henry Roberts, music and ornamental engraver, issued the first publication of *Calliope, or English Harmony*.

1738 England Royal Society of Musicians of Great Britain founded in London.

1738 Italy Domenico Scarlatti (1586–1757, son of Alessandro, 1660–1725) prepared for publication his first keyboard works; he was in some ways the founder of modern keyboard execution and had a great influence on later composers.

ARCHITECTURE

1734 England Holkham Hall by William Kent (1685–1748) is one of the greatest Palladian houses in Britain by an architect equally well known as a garden designer and interior decorator; his patron.

1734 Germany The Amalienburg, Munich, by François Cuvilliés (1695–1768) is a single-storey building with interiors decorated with great delicacy and subtly coloured; it is the architect's most impressive work.

1734 Holland The Royal Library, The Hague, by Daniel Marot (1661–1752) reflects the architect's Huguenot origins in its rococo ornament; he worked for William of Orange in Holland and England but is known for his illustrated volumes of *L'Architecture française*.

1735–1739 Spain The royal palace of La Granja near Segovia by Filippo Juvarra and Giovanni Sacchetti (1700–1764) was enlarged into an Italianate baroque version of Versailles with gardens to match.

1736 France Claude-Nicholas Ledoux born (died 1806), architect of the neo-classical style; his buildings combine simple shapes and austere treatment. The pure neo-classicism was too simple to appeal to the Napoleonic era, which stressed the grandiose and ostentatious.

1737–1767 Germany Ottobeuem Abbey by Johann Fischer von Erlach (1656–1723) is the most lavish of the rococo churches by the most prolific of the south German architects of the period, who built a total of 54 churches.

1738–1764 Spain Royal palace, Madrid, by Filippo Juvarra and Giovanni Sacchetti was built around a great court in heavy baroque style. Some interiors are very fine, in particular the throne room, with a Tiepolo ceiling, and the porcelain room.

1738–1758 Russia The cathedral of St George, L'vov, is a conglomeration of Italian and east European traditions and has a cruciform, centrally planned space with a dome over the crossing supported by a rectangular drum; it has a magnificently modulated baroque façade.

THREE DIMENSIONAL ART

1734 Canada The retable of the Ursuline chapel in Quebec was carved by the Levasseur family, leading woodcarvers of eighteenth-century Canada. Their style was derived from French *Régence*, the style of the regency of Philip of Orléans (1715–1723), which introduced lightness and elegance and a smaller scale in reaction to the grand manner of Louis XIV's reign.

1734 France Mennecy porcelain factory was founded in Paris. It moved to Mennecy in 1748 and made soft-paste porcelain.

1735 England Equestrian statue of William III made for Bristol by John Rysbrack (1694–1770): it was the finest of its kind in England in the eighteenth century. Rysbrack's work showed baroque influence and an interest in the antique.

1735 France Death of Jacques Caffieri (b. 1678) who with his son Philippe (1714–1774) was considered the outstanding bronze-founder of his day.

1737 Holland First dated glass engraved by Jacob Sang (fl. *c.*1750), considered a virtuoso in wheel-engraving and an important pioneer of diamond-point stipple-engraving.

VISUAL ARTS

*c.***1735 India** Active period of the painter Fateh Chand, whose work shows a softening Hindu naturalistic influence on the Mogul style.

1738–1739 India The sack of Delhi by the Persian Nadir Shah led to a dispersal of artists to other regions. The brothers Manak and Nain Sukh went to the Kangra Valley in the Punjab Himalayas; they contributed an elegance and delicacy to the romantic Kangra art.

INVENTIONS & DISCOVERIES

1738 John Kay invented fly-shuttle enabling weavers to produce double the quantity of calico.

HISTORICAL EVENTS	LITERATURE	DANCE & DRAMA	MUSIC

MUSIC

1738 Germany The full version of Johann Sebastian Bach's *Mass in B Minor* performed.

1739 Austria Birth of Karl Ditters von Dittersdorf (d. 1799), violinist and composer.

1739 Denmark Collection of poems by Hans Adolph Brorson (1694–1764), a writer of hymns and sacred verse; his poetry was deeply felt and inspired by mysticism.

Italy: Giovanni Canaletto's etching, 'A le Porto del Dolo'

1739 England The oratorios *Saul* and *Israel in Egypt* by Handel were first performed in London.

1739 England Jacob Kirkman (1710–1792), harpsichord and pianoforte maker, of Alsatian origin, established his own business on the death of his employer Hermann Tabel.

1739 Germany Carl August Grenser (1720–c.1807), woodwind-instrument maker, established himself in Dresden with his nephew Johann Heinrich Grenser. They are said to have been first to make bass clarinets in 1793.

1739 Portugal *La Spinalba* the comic opera by Francisco Antonio d'Almeida was first performed; it is the first Italian opera by a Portuguese to be preserved intact.

1740
Death of last Hapsburg emperor, War of Austrian Succession.

1740 England *Pamela, or Virtue Rewarded* ((two volumes) by Samuel Richardson (1689–1761), printer and novelist: written in the form of letters, full of vivid and realistic detail, the work described a servant girl's resistance to attempts at seduction by her employer. Richardson wrote to teach; he began his career as a writer by producing exemplary letters, and was entirely without humour. But he analysed human feelings with accuracy, sensitivity and conviction, and established them as the essential subject of the psychological novel.

1740 Switzerland Johann Jakob Bodmer (1698–1783) and Johann Jakob Breitinger (1701–1776), often referred to as the Swiss Critics, wrote suggesting English poets as models for German writers, instead of the French preferred by Gottsched. A bitter controversy resulted as to which was supreme, imagination or reason.

1740 Russia Die Neuberin's German company visited Russia. This was the Russians' introduction to European neo-classical theatre.

*c.***1740 France** Development of a square dance, founded on the *cotillon* or a similar folk dance, for four couples: it was at first described as a *contredanse* and later as the quadrille. This is the first example of a French folk dance being turned into a formal social dance.

1740 England The masque *Alfred* by Thomas Augustine Arne (1710–1778) which included the song *Rule, Britannia* was first performed at Cliveden, Bucks.

1740 England *A Musical Dictionary . . .* by James Grassineau (c.1715–1767), English musical lexicographer, was published. Although largely derivative (mainly from Brossard's *Dictionnaire de Musique* which he had translated) it was the first work of its kind in English.

1740 England Birth of Samuel Green, English organ builder (d. 1796). There exist more cathedral organs by him than by any other builder.

1740 England John Snetzler (c.1710–c.1800), German (anglicized) organ builder settled in England; he built the organ for first performance of Handel's *Messiah* in Dublin.

1740 Italy Death of Domenico Alberti (b. 1710), singer, harpsichordist and composer. Although it is not very probable that he invented the 'Alberti' bass (a type of accompaniment) he brought it into great prominence in his sonatas.

ARCHITECTURE

1738 Spain Santiago de Compostela Cathedral façade by Fernando de Casasy Nóvoa (active 1711 – died 1794) has a baroque twin-tower façade, added as the first stage in a total refacing of the entire Romanesque building; it is one of many baroque façades added to older churches in Spain.

1738–1742 USA Drayton Hall, South Carolina, is one of the best Palladian-style houses in the Deep South with a typical two-storey colonnade beneath the front pediment.

*c.***1739 Ireland** Carton House, Kildare, by Richard Cassels is one of the finest houses in Ireland, designed by this German architect in the English Palladian style.

1740 Germany Schloss Charlottenburg wing, Berlin, by Georg von Knobelsdorf (1699–1759) has a very rich rococo interior designed by the court architect to Frederick the Great.

1740 Spain The palace of the Marques de Dos Aquas, Valencia, illustrates the tendency for riotous decoration to be concentrated around doorways – in this case in white alabaster – and windows.

*c.***1740 Russia** Scottish architect Charles Cameron born (died 1812), who took British Palladian styles to Russia.

THREE DIMENSIONAL ART

1739 Austria Fountain in the Neuer Markt in Vienna by Georg Raphael Donner (1693–1741): it was influential in bringing the classical style, derived from sixteenth century Italian sculpture, to Austria. Donner was exceptionally skilled in the use of lead.

*c.***1739 North America** Caspar Wistar (1696–1752), a German, established the first successful American glass factory, in New Jersey. He made free-blown ware decorated with applied form especially the 'lily-pad' motif known as the South Jersey style; the style, lasted until *c.*1850. American glass-making began as an industry, not a craft, and designers did not make their own glasses.

1740–1777 Western Europe Spread of hard-paste porcelain to factories throughout Europe, a process hastened in 1750–60 by Hohann Jakob Ringler (d. 1804) and Johann Benckgraff, who spread their knowledge of porcelain manufacture at Vienna. New factories included Italy (Doccia, 1740), Holland (1759), Switzerland (1763), Denmark (Copenhagen, 1775), France (Sèvres, 1770), and Sweden (1777).

VISUAL ARTS

1740–1750 Italy The Venetian artist Giovanni Canaletto (1697–1768) concentrated on etchings and pen-and-wash drawings.

1740 England William Hogarth painted his portrait of *Captain Coram* which he regarded as his greatest, because of its confident baroque style. The public have preferred his portraits of *A Shrimp Girl* and *Hogarth's Servants*, which are considered among the most spontaneous and successful of eighteenth-century English paintings.

*c.***1740 Japan** Okumara Masonobu (1691–1768) invented the 'pillar print' or long vertical print. He excelled in prints with a perspective background in Western style, and was also credited with inventing the *Urushi-E* technique of covering the print's colours with transparent lacquer.

*c.***1740 Japan** Introduction of limited colour printing for *Ukiyo-E* popular prints. Earlier prints were done from black outline blocks and hand-coloured; they were called *Tan-E* when mainly vermilion and *Beni-E* when mainly rose-red. The true colour print was called *Benizuri-E*.

INVENTIONS & DISCOVERIES

1740 Benjamin Huntsman of Sheffield produced crucible steel.

HISTORICAL EVENTS	LITERATURE	DANCE & DRAMA	MUSIC

HISTORICAL EVENTS

*1741
Elizabeth became
Empress of
Russia.*

LITERATURE

1742 France *Les Confessions du Comte de* *** by Charles Pinot Duclos (1704–1772), novelist and historian. He wrote about vice, on the pretext of teaching a moral lesson.

1743–1758 Spain *Vida*, the confessions of Diego de Torres Villarroel (1693–1770), poet and prose writer: cynical and entertaining, it was written in an easy style, and read like the ultimate in picaresque novels. He also wrote some interesting burlesque and satirical verse.

1743 Sweden Poems on the death of her husband by Hedvig Charlotta Nordenflycht (1718–1793), a poet and literary hostess. The members of her salon were particularly stimulated by the ideas and work of French writers.

1744–1747 Wales *Aleluja* by William Williams Pantycelyn (1717–1791), a hymn writer, who was prominent in the religious movement to revive Welsh literature. He used English, not classical Welsh, metres.

DANCE & DRAMA

1741 France *Mélanide* by Pierre Claude Nivelle de la Chaussée (1692–1754), chief writer of the French *comedie larmoyante* (comedy combined with sentimental pathos). he appealed to the sentimental tastes of a middle-class audience, and his work marks the beginning of bourgeois drama in France.

1743 France *Mérope* by François Marie Arouet, called Voltaire (1694–1778), French philosopher and man of letters: this was the first occasion on which a French audience called for the author.

1743 France The manager Jean Monnet obtained the concession for the Opéra Comique at the Foire St Laurent. His productions included *ballets-d'action* by Marie Sallé and by the French dancer Louis Dupré, who had danced in Weaver's and Sallé's ballets in London. Jean-Georges Noverre (1727–1809), Dupré's pupil, danced in the company. Monnet's success angered the Opéra, who ended his concession.

1743 Russia A French company began a 15-year stay in Russia, performing the works of Molière and Voltaire among others. French replaced German as the court language.

1744 France Death of André Campra (b.1666), writer of ballets, who added a repertoire of livelier dances to the court dances used on the stage. His most successful opera-ballets were *L'Europe galante* and *Fêtes Venitiennes*.

MUSIC

1740 Italy Birth of Giovanni Paisiello (d. 1816) who wrote about 100 operas as well as cantatas, oratorios, etc.

1741 England The Madrigal Society was founded in London by the elder John Immyns (d. 1764). The society has had regular meetings ever since.

1741 France Birth of André Ernest Grétry (d. 1813), French composer of Walloon descent. A prolific composer, he had some 50 operas produced in Paris.

1741 Germany Johann Stamitz (1717–1757), Bohemian composer, conductor and violinist, appointed to court at Mannheim, where he remained until his death. He developed the sonata form and created a new style of orchestral playing.

1741 Italy First opera by Christoph Willibald von Gluck (1714–1787) *Artaserse* produced in Milan.

1741 Italy Death of Antonio Vivaldi (b. *c.*1675).

1742 Ireland First performance of *Messiah* by Handel in Dublin.

1744 England A version of *God Save the Queen* was published in *Thesaurus Musicus*, possibly earliest printed version.

1744 England *Six Concertos for the Organ or Harpsichord with Instrumental Parts* written by William Felton (1715–1769), clergyman, organist, harpsichordist and composer.

*1746
Final defeat of
the Jacobites at
Culloden.*

1746 America *A Treatise Concerning Religious Affections* by Jonathon Edwards (1703–1758), a clergyman. Early American writing was intended to instruct, rather than to entertain.

1746 Japan *The House of Sugawara* by Takeda Izume, *kabuki* writer: originally written for puppets, the play was later performed by actors.

1747 England David Garrick (1717–1779) joined the management at Drury Lane. A dramatist and a talented actor, he brought about a number of reforms in the theatre, including concealed stage lighting and the removal of the audience from the stage, where they sat between the side wings. Above all, he changed the style of English acting from declamatory to naturalistic.

1744 Germany J. S. Bach wrote Book II of the *Well Tempered Clavier*, the first book having been written in 1722.

1747 France Jean Le Rond d'Alembert (1717–1783), mathematician, made researches into vibrating strings.

1747 France Birth of François Tourte, violin-bow maker (d. 1835).

ARCHITECTURE

1743–1772 Germany Church of Vierzenheiligen by Balthasar Neumann (1687–1753) on an older foundation is an outstanding example of German baroque; series of three ovals in the vaulting as in the ground plan. Discreet painted decoration, rich sculpture and altars are integral parts of the structure, while the exterior is formed by two towers and a modulated frontispiece between them.

1743 Guatemala Town hall, Antigua, is a typical colonial government building, classical in style, with arcaded loggias on both floors of its 9-bay façade.

1744–1754 Bavaria Church of Die Wies by Dominikus Zimmerman (1685–1766) is an oval building, lit and decorated to ensure brightness and grace; white stucco, gilt and clear, but not strong, colours were used.

1744 Russia Dominican church, L'vov, is an example of monumentality expressed in baroque, partly of Italian and partly Bavarian origins; the ground plan is elliptical, surmounted by a large oval dome on a drum supported by 8 piers.

1745 Germany Palace of Sanssouci, Potsdam, by Georg von Knobelsdorff is one of several Potsdam buildings by the architect in collaboration with the king; the rococo style is derived from French sources.

1747 Russia St Andrew's Cathedral, Kiev, by Bartolommeo Rastrelli exemplifies the mature baroque style in Russia.

THREE DIMENSIONAL ART

1742 France Jacques Dubois (1693–1763) became a master cabinet-maker. His style is considered the culmination of rococo.

1742 Sweden Foundation of the Kosta glassworks, which became famous for cut and engraved crystal and, later, for sculptured glass.

1743 Italy Capo-di-Monte factory established in Naples: it made soft-paste porcelain figures of a high quality.

1743 Japan Death of Ogata Kenzan, potter, whose work was influenced by Zen painting.

1744 Austria Johann Josef Niedermeyer became chief modeller of figures for the Vienna porcelain company.

1744 Russia Law passed requiring all factories to impress and mark their glass; the Empress Elizabeth Petrovna created a state monopoly of glass in St Petersburg and the industry did not flourish.

*c.*1744–1757 **England** Porcelain factories at Chelsea, Bow, Derby and Lowestoft strengthened soft-paste porcelain made of *frit* (ground glass) with calcined ox-bones.

1745–1750 France Paul Hannong of Strasbourg developed vitreous enamels for colouring pottery; low-temperature firing fused pigments into the glaze at 700–900C. These were used on faience.

1745 Britain The Excise Act taxed glass by weight; glasses therefore became smaller with less lead content and more decoration was used as a compensation, especially on the stem.

1746 England Henry Copland (active from 1738), designer employed by Thomas Chippendale the Elder, published *A New Book of Ornaments* which introduced rococo ornament for English furniture, replacing the Palladian style.

1747-1767 Germany Porcelain figures influenced by contemporary wood carvings were made at Nymphenburg, Munich, by Franz Antan Bustelli (fl. 1723–1763), modeller. They declined after 1767.

VISUAL ARTS

1743–1750 Italy Excavations at Herculaneum provided a stimulus to the neo-classical style. The historical painter Joseph-Marie, Comte Vien (1716–1809) visited them and became interested in neoclassicism. He taught the painter David.

1744–1773 India Reign of Govardhan Chand of Guler in the Kangra Valley, patron of the arts. Under him the romantic Kangra style developed through a fusion of influences from Basholi and Delhi. Painters used enamel-like colours and delicate, leafy landscapes. Artists from Guler passed on, after 1775, to the later centre of Tira Sujanpur and the patronage of Sansar Chand.

*c.*1745–1761 **Italy** *Carceri d'Invezione*, a series of etchings by Giovanni Battista Piranesi (1720–1778): the work is outstanding among etchings for its use of perspective for romantic effect. At about the same time Piranesi made the *Vedute* series of etchings on ancient and modern Rome, which helped to form the romantic idea of the city.

1747 Italy Death of the Neapolitan baroque painter Francesco Solimena (b. 1657), fresco artist and teacher with European influence.

INVENTIONS & DISCOVERIES

1742 Celsius proposed 100-division thermometer scale.

LITERATURE

1748 France *De L'Esprit des Lois* by Charles-Louis de Secondat, Baron de La Brède et de Montesquieu (1689–1755), social and political philosopher and writer. After the death of Louis XIV, philosophy rather than religion provided the ideologies underlying both life and art. The French believed that progress would come through Enlightenment. 'Man in society' became the dominant study, and forms of literature in which this could be discussed — essays, letters, treatises etc. — came to the fore.

1748 Germany *Der Messias* by the poet Friedrich Gottlieb Klopstock (1724–1803), a disciple of Bodmer and Breitinger: a biblical epic in unrhymed hexameters, the poem was deeply felt, and showed the supremacy of emotion in the development of German literature.

1748 Scotland *The Adventures of Roderick Random* by Tobias George Smollett (1721–1771), a novelist who wrote picaresque novels using his own experiences as a ship's surgeon. His work was vivid, lively and entertaining, and sometimes coarse.

1749–1759 Netherlands The first history of the Netherlands and Amsterdam was written, by Jan Wagenaar (1709–1773), a journalist, topographer and historian.

1749–1756 Sweden *Arcana Coelestia* by Emanuel Swedenborg (1688–1772), philosopher, scientist, mathematician and mystic. After a spiritual crisis in 1743–1745 in which he saw visions of angels and of Christ, he abandoned scientific works and wrote mystical and prophetic books in Latin. Their style, however, showed evidence of his scientific training.

1749 England *The History of Tom Jones, A Foundling* by Henry Fielding (1707–1754), magistrate, pamphleteer, playwright and novelist. He began his career as a novelist by satirizing Richardson's *Pamela*. His own genius was for comedy, and he developed the rambling narratives of Cervantes and Marivaux to produce a kind of comic prose epic. Through him, the novel of action was established in England.

DANCE & DRAMA

1748 France *Sémiramis* by Voltaire: the crowd scenes and spectacle in performances left no room on stage for members of the audience, who were removed at Voltaire's insistence. Voltaire moved away from the rigid traditions of classical tragedy and paved the way for melodrama.

1749 America The Virginia Company of Comedians was formed by Thomas Kean and Walter Murray. They used a converted warehouse in Philadelphia as their theatre, and among their repertoire was Shakespeare's *Richard III*.

1749 Russia *Khorev* by Alexei Petrovich Sumarokov (1718–1777) was performed by the cadets of a newly founded college for the sons of the nobility. The cadets formed a Society of Lovers of Russian Literature, of which Sumarokov was a member. He ranks as the first Russian dramatist of note.

MUSIC

1748 England Publication of *Harmonics, or The Philosophy of Musical Sounds* by Robert Smith (1689–1768), mathematician. This important work anticipated that by Helmholtz by a century.

1749 Italy Production of *L'Arcadia in Brenta*, first comic opera by Baldassare Galuppi (1706–1785).

1749 Italy Birth of Domenico Cimarosa (d. 1801), composer.

1750 America *The Beggar's Opera* by John Gay (1685–1732) performed for first time in New York, having been first performed in London in 1728.

1750 England *La Serva Padrona*, an *opera batta* by Giovanni Battista Pergolesi (1710–1736) was first performed in London.

1750 Germany Death of Johann Sebastian Bach at Leipzig.

1750 Italy Death of Tommaso Albinoni (b. 1671); he is chiefly known now for his *Adagio for Organ and Strings*.

*c.***1750 England** Popularity of ballad operas, in which dialogue was interspersed with songs set to popular tunes.

ARCHITECTURE

1748 Russia Smolny Convent, St Petersburg, by Bartolommeo Rastrelli, who was a prolific architect of baroque buildings in Russia; here full-blown three-dimensional baroque masses, with rococo decoration, are employed in an immense layout comprising the convent building and a cathedral. The layout indicates a re-employment of the traditional Russian ground plan.

1784 Switzerland Abbey church of St Gallen by Peter Thumb (1681–1766) and Johann Beer (1696–1780) of the two families of architects who intermarried and produced a number of Vorarlberg baroque churches, mainly Benedictine abbeys in south-west Germany and Switzerland; St Gallen Abbey has a remarkable rococo library.

1749 England Strawberry Hill, Twickenham, began to be rebuilt by Horace Walpole (1717–1797) and his 'Committee of Taste'. They chose to build an asymmetrically planned Gothic-style building which was to be very influential.

1749 USA King's Chapel, Boston, by Peter Harrison (1716–75) was an original design adapted from Gibbs; Harrison was the most able of New England architects in the eighteenth century.

1750 USA Parlange, Pointe Coupée Parish, Louisiana, is a typical French plantation house, surrounded by a colonnaded verandah on both storeys—a desirable feature in the hot and wet climate.

c.1750 France Nancy was replanned by Emmanuel Héré de Corny (1705–63) and is the finest of several eighteenth-century French town-planning schemes, in which a series of squares were treated with rococo charm.

c.1750 Mexico Spanish styles began to be adapted by native builders with a taste for overall surface decoration even more extravagant than the original (Moorish) tradition; whole ceramic pillars and panels were added to Spanish tiling.

THREE DIMENSIONAL ART

1748–1755 England Production of Chelsea porcelain figures with the distinguishing 'red anchor' mark. 'Gold anchor' vases were made from 1755.

c.1748 Russia Discovery of hard-paste porcelain by Dmitri Vinogradov (d. 1758); his factory became the Imperial Porcelain Manufactory in 1803.

c.1748 England Landscape designer and gardener Lancelot ('Capability') Brown (1716–1783) executed his first independent design at Warwick castle. He improved on the work of his master William Kent, with his knowledge of horticulture, geology and hydraulics. He did much to popularize the carefully-contrived 'natural' parkland combining simple shapes with a grand scale which embraced most of the scene visible from the house and involved massive movements of earth.

c.1750 China Tapestry weavers began to paint fine details on *k'o-ssŭ* (silk tapestry) panels, instead of weaving them in. This marked the beginning of a decline in *k'o-ssŭ* which had reached its highest peak after 1700.

c.1750 England Founding of Derby porcelain factory: it specialized in landscape painting for decoration.

c.1750 Europe Plaster of Paris began to be used to make cheap, porous pottery moulds. This encouraged a new technique of slip-casting; a thin clay slip was poured into a porous mould, the water is absorbed in the mould, and the clay solidifies in shape.

c.1750 France Appearance of the neo-classical style in metalwork; this was less stimulating for metalworkers than the preceding rococo style. Cast iron began to replace wrought iron in decorative work, being more suitable for the severity and angularity of neo-classicism. This change took place a little later in England.

c.1750 Russia The glass-maker Bakhnetev and the chemist Lomonosov (d. 1765) developed white opaline glass and smalt (heavy coloured glass); they also revived the glass-cube mosaic.

VISUAL ARTS

1748 India Accession of Sawant Singh of Kishangarh, patron of the arts. The most famous painting he commissioned was the close-up profile group of *Radha and Krishna* (c.1750), painted with fine brush-work as two profile heads on a plain ground.

1749–1771 India Reign of Ummed Singh at Bundi. Under his patronage Bundi painters excelled in *ragamala*—paintings illustrating the moods of the traditional forms of music. They achieved a more expressive drawing style and a more varied texture, without losing the Rajput intensity of colour.

1750 Italy The fresco artist Giovanni Battista Tiepolo (1696–1770) was commissioned to decorate the palace of Wurzburg. He was the most celebrated and sought-after Italian artist of his day; his frescoes since 1726 had shown grandeur and imagination, and complete control of light, space and colour. He was also a successful etcher, conveying in that medium the same sense of light and space.

1750 Netherlands Death of Rachel Ruysch (b. 1664), outstanding Dutch flower painter in delicate colour and great detail.

c.1750 France Invention of 'crayon manner' engraving, used to reproduce crayon drawings and combined for the purpose with stipple engraving. It was eclipsed by lithography in the early nineteenth century.

INVENTIONS & DISCOVERIES

*1748
Abbé Nollet
recognized
osmosis.*

*1750
Muschenbrock
constructed the
pyrometer.*

HISTORICAL EVENTS	LITERATURE	DANCE & DRAMA	MUSIC

LITERATURE

1751–1765 France Denis Diderot (1713–1784) edited the *Encyclopédie*, a compendium of contemporary liberal and progressive thought. From 1751–1758 his co-editor was Jean le Rond d'Alembert (1717–1783). A Radical, though not an original thinker, Diderot also wrote plays and novels.

1751 England *An Elegy Wrote (sic) in a Country Churchyard* by Thomas Gray (1716–1771). His poetry was highly polished, expressing his feeling for rural life in grave harmonious lines.

1752 China Posthumous publication of the collected works of the poet Chao Chih-hsin (1662–1744). He attacked the poetic theories of Wang Shih-chen and was the author of a study of T'ang poetry.

1752 Germany First collection of poems by Christoph Martin Wieland (1733–1813), poet and novelist. These early poems are imitations of Klopstock. His later verse was more worldly. He also wrote light satiric prose.

1755 England *A Dictionary of the English Language* by Samuel Johnson (1709–1784), scholar, writer, moralist and critic. He was learned in the classics, and his writing showed a strong Latin influence. His honesty, common sense, learning and firmly-held principles had a formidable influence on English letters. No other man of letters had been held in such high esteem by contemporary society.

HISTORICAL EVENTS

1752 Arcot, India, captured from French by Clive.

1754 Anglo-French war in North America ended French dominion.

DANCE & DRAMA

1752 America Lewis Hallam Snr (1714–1756) led the first theatrical company to be purposely sent from London to America. They settled in Williamsburg.

1753 England Jean-Georges Noverre (1727–1809), choreographer and dancer, was brought to work for David Garrick in London; Garrick's miming talent inspired him and influenced his later work – Noverre's *ballets d'action* laid great emphasis on mime.

1753 Italy *La Locandiera* by Carlo Goldoni (1707–1793), who worked to replace the improvised comedies of the dying *commedia dell' arte* tradition with fully written-out plays.

1755 Germany *Miss Sara Sampson* by Gotthold Ephraim Lessing (1729–1781), a middle-class tragedy; it was the first play in Germany with natural dialogue and a realistic subject.

MUSIC

1751 Italy *The Art of Playing on the Violin* was written by Francesco Geminiani (1687–1762), violinist and composer; it was first book of its kind ever published in any country.

1752 England *An Essay on Musical Expression* by Charles Avison (1709–1770), organist, composer and writer on music.

1752 England Birth of John Dodd, greatest of English bow makers and member of the Dodd family of bow makers (d. 1839).

1752 England Felice Giardini (1716–1796), Italian violinist and composer, became leader of the Italian Opera in London, with which he was connected for some 40 years. During this time he had considerable influence on musical and operatic life in England.

1752 England Birth of John Marsh, composer and amateur musician (d. 1828), believed to have been the only English composer of the latter part of the eighteenth century to write symphonies.

1752 Germany *The Art of Fugue* by Johann Sebastian Bach was published by Friedrich Wilhelm Marpurg.

1752 Italy Birth of Muzio Clementi (d. 1832), pianist and composer.

1753 Germany Domenico Ferrari (d. 1780), violinist and composer, joined the orchestra of the Duke of Württemberg at Stuttgart; he was considered to be greatest living violinist.

1753 Switzerland Jean-Jacques Rousseau (1712–1778), philosopher, author and musician, wrote his *Lettre sur la Musique Française*, which contains a complete exposition of his musical philosophy. He had a great influence on French music.

1755 England William Boyce (1711–1799) appointed Master of the King's Music and took up office in 1757. His music included the song *Hearts of Oak* for the play *Harlequin's Invasion* (1759).

ARCHITECTURE

*c.*1750 **Mexico** Ocotlan Sanctuary. Tlaxçala, was built to honour the appearance of the Virgin in the sixteenth century; the façade has remarkable brick towers and an elaborate shell-like niche and belfries between.

1751–1788 France École Militaire, Paris, by Jacques Ange Gabriel (1698–1782) was his largest commission; it is a restrained classical building surmounted by a four-sided dome. More practical than decorative, the quality of construction is superb.

1751 Italy Caserta Royal Palace by Luigi Vanvitelli (1700–1773) was the last great Italian baroque palace and built by Carlo III; it has 1200 rooms and magnificent gardens.

1751 Mexico Government palace, Guadalajara, by Nicholas del Castillo and José Conque; it was provincial Spanish architecture with a mixture of Churrigueresque, baroque and Mudéjar, a blend of Moslem and Christian styles.

1753 France *Essai sur L'architecture* by Marc-Antoine Laugier (1713–1769) was published; he propounded a rationalist theory of neo-Classicism which was to prove influential.

1753 Spain Alternations to the El Pilar Cathedral, Saragossa, by Ventura Rodriquez (1717–85) in which, Herrera's earlier work was resumed in a more severe classical style; the exterior, of brick, with its many coloured tiles and domes is impressive.

1754–1768 Denmark Amalienburg Palace, Copenhagen, by Niels Eigtved (1701–1754) is one of four palaces grouped around an octagonal piazza, joined later by colonnades; the fine French-style exteriors hide rich baroque decoration within.

1754–1762 Russia Winter Palace, St Petersburg, by Bartolommeo Rastrelli is the most important building in the city placed alongside the river Neva; the façade has three main storeys and two superimposed Corinthian orders on one side and a vast square on the other, and is now the Hermitage Museum. There have been several restorations.

THREE DIMENSIONAL ART

1751–1759 France Jean-Baptiste Lamour (1698–1771), ironsmith, made a series of gates and screens on a huge scale for the Place Stanislas in Nancy. He was considered the master of French rococo ironwork; his exuberant decoration was always disciplined by its architectural framework.

1752–1753 France François Boucher (1703–1770), designer, succeeded Oudry as director of the Gobelin tapestry works.

1752 France Claude-Charles Saunier (1735–1807) was made master of the guild of cabinet-makers. His work shows the change in French taste with the first introduction of classical features to the Empire style, which was basically neo-classical but included revivals of ancient Egyptian motifs.

1753–1768 Germany Fürstenberg porcelain factory produced its most important figures.

*c.*1753–1756 **England** Battersea enamel factory developed printed decoration for porcelain; copperplate engravings were printed on paper and transferred, still wet, to the glaze. Only one colour was used as cobalt was the only pigment which would withstand the firing of the glaze. The factory employed the engraver Robert Hancock (1731–1817) to work on enamels.

1754 England Thomas Chippendale the Elder (1718–1779) published *The Gentleman and Cabinet-maker's Director*, a book of furniture designs considered to be mainly his own. This was the first large-scale work of its kind in England and established him as the main force in English rococo furniture-design.

1755 England Statue of Sir Isaac Newton at Trinity College, Cambridge: considered the masterpiece of Louis Roubiliac (*c.*1705–1762), French-born sculptor working in England. He introduced a lively rococo style to portrait sculpture.

VISUAL ARTS

1751 Japan Death of Gion Nanki (b. 1677), founder of the *Nanga* school of painting which was an adaptation of the Chinese *Wên-jën Hua* style of landscape, if more clear-cut and explicit.

1752 England Thomas Gainsborough (1727–1788) began as a portrait painter in Ipswich. He painted mainly head and half-length portraits, with some small groups in landscape settings. His landscapes were influenced by Dutch painting at first.

1752 France The Swedish painter Alexander Roslin (1718–1793) settled in Paris. His portraits were famous for his insight into character.

1753–1793 India Reign of Bijai Singh of Jodhpur. Under his patronage the Mogul influence on painting declined and was replaced by the Rajput style with its emphasis on colour.

1754 Netherlands Death of Jacob de Wit (b. 1695), the ceiling painter. He is credited with inventing a technique of decorative painting in grisaille, imitating marble relief.

1755 Germany The art historian Johann Winckelmann published *Gedanken über die Nachahmurg der griechischen Werke in der Malerei und Bildhauerkunst*, later published in English as *Reflections on the Painting and Sculpture of the Greeks*. He was the first to identify the Greeks as the originators of the classical ideal, and the Romans as their imitators. Renaissance artists had admired 'the ancients' generally. He was a formative influence on the neo-classical style.

INVENTIONS & DISCOVERIES

1751 Chaumette invented breech-loading gun.

1752 Benjamin Franklin demonstrated lightning to be electricity.

LITERATURE

1756 Dalmatia A cycle of Croatian poetry and prose was collected by the poet Andrija Kačič—Miošič (1704—1760) and arranged by him to record the history of the South Slavs, with a view to arousing their national consciousness.

1756 England *Inquiry into the Origin of our Ideas on the Sublime and the Beautiful* by Edmund Burke (1729—1797), the Irish politician, writer and orator, an associate of Samuel Johnson. The work was the first English treatise on aesthetics.

1756 Portugal Foundation of the Arcadia Lusitana, a literary academy which endeavoured to free Portuguese literature from the influence of Spain. The standards were neo-classical, and by returning to the earlier pastoral modes the members hoped to check the tendency towards elaborate imagery and extravagant expression.

1757 America *The Way to Wealth* by Benjamin Franklin (1706—1790), statesman, essayist and scientist. He set up his own printing press. His style is simple and original, whereas many early American writers tended to copy established writers in English.

1757 Italy *Lettere Virgiliane* by Saverio Bettinelli (1718—1808), critic, historian and poet. He attacked what he regarded as the worst aspects of Italian literature: imitation and confusion. Even the *Divina Commedia* came under fire. A supplement to the work contained poems by 'three excellent authors', Bettinelli and two of his friends. They offered themselves as models of a new didactic poetry on philosophy and science, written in blank verse.

1757 Russia A Russian grammar was compiled by Mikhail Vasilyevich Lomonosov (1711—1765), a poet, playwright, and grammarian who was an important figure in the reform and development of the Russian language. He systematized the spoken language for the first time; Church Slavonic was to be used only for heroic epics and odes which required a grand, rhetorical style. He finally established the tonic metre (an iambic metre with regular feet), and also wrote distinguished prose.

DANCE & DRAMA

1755 Russia *Sinav and Truvor* by Sumarokov was performed at court. Among the company was Feodor Volkov (1729—1763) a former amateur actor whose company had been invited to perform at court in 1752. He had been given a place at the cadet college and later became their leading actor.

1757 Germany Konrad Ekhov (1740—1778) founded the first German acting academy. His own acting style was natural, not declamatory. His academic course included analyses and discussions of plays.

1757 Russia Sumarokov's company, which now included women, was given a court subsidy, becoming the first professional Russian theatre company.

MUSIC

1755 England Cahusac founded an instrument-making business in London. They made flutes, violins and other small instruments, and may have been the earliest manufacturers in London.

1755 Italy An essay *Saggio sopra l'Opera in Musica* by Francesco Algarotti (1712—1764) advocated abandoning the outworn conventions of early eighteenth century opera.

1755 Russia The first opera to be written in the Russian language, *Cephalus and Prokris*, by Francesco Araia (1709—1770), had its first performance at St Petersburg.

1755 Russia First concert by a horn band in Moscow. These bands were extremely popular for nearly a century.

1756 Austria Birth of Wolfgang Amadeus Mozart (d. 1791), virtuoso and composer, at Salzburg.

1756 Scotland The first publication of *The Rudiments of Music* by Robert Bremner (1713—1789), Scottish music publisher.

1757 America First public concert in Philadelphia.

1757 Italy Publication of *Thoroughbass made Easy* by Niccolo Pasquali (d. 1757), violinist and composer.

1757 Italy Death of Giuseppe Domenico Scarlatti (b. 1865), harpsichordist and composer.

*1757
Clive took
Calcutta and won
battle of Plassey.*

ARCHITECTURE

1755 France Place de la Concorde, Paris, by Jacques-Ange Gabriel (1698–1782) is a fine example of large-scale urban planning, incorporating picturesque wooded and river views as well as architecture, in contrast to earlier more rigidly confined squares.

1757–1792 France The Panthéon, Paris, was begun by Jacques Soufflot (1709–1780) and is masterpiece of neo-Classicism in which the influence of ancient Roman monumentalism and Wren's St Paul's dome are both recalled; it is one of the earliest buildings reinforced with iron.

THREE DIMENSIONAL ART

c.1755 France French influence began to predominate over Meissen rococo style in porcelain. Neo-classicism became the fashion; the Sèvres factory was important in this development.

1756 England Art of transfer printing on porcelain taken from Battersea enamel factory to Bow china factory by the French-born engraver Simon François Ravenet (1706–1774) and Robert Hancock (1731–1817).

1756 France Vincennes porcelain factory moved to Sèvres, became the royal factory and began to make soft-paste porcelain.

1757 England John Baskerville (1706–1775) published his edition of *Virgil*, which established him as a master of fine printing. He began work as a writing master and a letterer of tombstones, and he developed a rounded Roman letter on which modern Baskerville type is based.

1757 England Portrait bust of Lord Chesterfield by the sculptor Joseph Wilton (1722–1803), successful portrait sculptor in the classical manner.

VISUAL ARTS

1756 England Death of the painter John Wootton, who specialized in horses as subjects and introduced the classical landscape into English painting.

Richard Wilson (1714–1782) began to paint English landscape, after four years in Italy; he was influenced by Claude's paintings and by Roman landscape. It was Wilson who established English landscape painting in the neo-classical style.

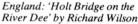

England: 'Holt Bridge on the River Dee' by Richard Wilson

HISTORICAL EVENTS	LITERATURE	DANCE & DRAMA	MUSIC

HISTORICAL EVENTS

LITERATURE

1758–1770 Spain *Fray Gerundio* by the satirist José de Isla (1703–1781): the work was a picaresque novel, satirizing pulpit oratory.

1758 Denmark Death of the poet Ambrosius Christoffersen Stub (b. 1705/1709). In form his lyrics were conventional and inclined to artificiality, but they also showed a love of nature and strong personal feeling.

1758 Sweden Odes in the style of Thomson by Gustav Fredrik, Count Gyllenborg (1731–1808), courtier and poet. His work included satires, lyrical poetry, didactic poetry and fables.

1759 Wolfe took Quebec from French.

1759 France *Candide* by François-Marie Arouet, called Voltaire (1694–1778), philosopher, historian, playwright, novelist and poet. He also contributed to the *Encyclopédie*. He attacked the 'enemies of reason', the philosophical optimism of Rousseau, oppression, injustice and privilege. Nearly all his writings carried a serious message, but he was a master of light, readable prose, which conveyed his meaning exactly, but palatably, and made his thought available to even the most frivolous reader.

1760–1767 England *The Life and Opinions of Tristram Shandy* by Laurence Sterne (1713–1768), novelist. The book had virtually no plot, and relied on character drawing. The arrangement of pages and chapters was deliberately eccentric, but the oddities of the book were carefully designed, the wit of a learned man.

1760–1770 Sweden *Epistles* by the poet Carl Michael Bellman (1740–1795). He was a great entertainer, accompanying his own lyrics on the lute, often adapting folk-songs or contemporary tunes. His themes were taken from the picturesque, if sordid, life of old Stockholm.

1761 France *Contes Moraux* by Jean-François Marmontel (1723–1799), playwright and novelist. There was a trend among later eighteenth-century French writers to use the novel for moral instruction.

DANCE & DRAMA

1760–1765 Austria The balletmaster Gasparo Angiolini (1731–1803) created *ballets d'action* for Count Durazzo, director of the Austrian Imperial Theatres in Vienna; he worked with the composer Gluck and the librettist Calzabigi, a ballet reformer. Durazzo was important as a director who understood, and provided, ideal working conditions; many contemporary companies could not provide any stability for a ballet-master or guarantee any continuation of his work.

1760 Germany The choreographer Jean-Georges Noverre was appointed *maitre de ballet* to the Duke of Württemberg's theatre at Stuttgart. He established a French ballet company trained in dramatic interpretation rather than in virtuoso exhibitions, and published *Lettres sur la Danse*, which was a formative document of dramatic ballet. Noverre took over the post from Franz Hilferding (1710–1768) whose work as a ballet-master strongly influenced him; Hilferding went on to St Petersburg.

1761 Austria The ballet *Don Juan* was presented in Vienna by Gasparo Angiolini (1731–1803), ballet-master to the Austrian Imperial Theatres, to music by Gluck. Angiolini succeeded Hilferding as ballet-master at St Petersburg in 1766.

MUSIC

1758 France Christoph Willibald von Gluck (1714–1787) began a new phase, writing for French comic operas.

1758 Sweden Per Brandt (1713–1767) became conductor of the Royal Orchestra at Stockholm and was the first to organize public concerts there.

1759 England Death of George Frederick Handel (b. 1685).

1760 Bohemia Birth of Jan Ladislav Dussek (d. 1812), Bohemian pianist and composer.

1760 England First volume of a collection of cathedral music published by William Boyce (c.1710–1779), English organist, composer and musical editor. This collection had a great influence on the repertory of cathedral choirs for at least 150 years.

1760 Netherlands *Messe des Morts* by Francois Joseph Gossec (1734–1829), first performed; it was written for two orchestras, one concealed, an innovation in orchestral writing. Gossec was a forerunner of Berlioz in orchestral experimentation and exerted great influence on the development of instrumental music in France.

1761 England The Noblemen and Gentlemen's Catch Club was formed in London for the encouragement of composition and performance of canons, catches and glees.

ARCHITECTURE

1758 England Hagley Temple, Worcestershire, by James 'Athenian' Stuart (1713–1788) is the earliest Doric revival building by the author, with Nicholas Revett, of the *Antiquities of Athens*.

1758–1794 Portugal Queluz Palace by João Baptista Robillion (?–1785) and Vincente de Oliviera (1706–1786) is a charming rococo summer palace with a pink and white decorated garden façade, and is characteristic of Portuguese rococo architecture.

1759 USA Christchurch, Cambridge, Massachusetts, by Peter Harrison (1716–75) is an English colonial church built, typically, of timber and comparable with contemporary English provincial churches. The Wren/Gibbs tradition continued in the USA until the nineteenth century.

1761 England Syon House Middlesex was rebuilt by Robert Adam (1728–1792), who was also responsible for his own brand of neo-classical interiors in this and in several other country and town houses.

1761 France Petit Trianon, Versailles, was by Jacques-Ange Gabriel, who continued in the classical tradition of Mansart with a minimum of artifice or enrichment; the small intricate scale, as in several of his other houses, is very different from its massively pompous predecessors.

1761 Italy *Della magnificenza ed architettura dei Romani* by Giovanni Piranesi (1720–1778) was published, one of several influential works by him which championed ancient Roman architecture.

THREE DIMENSIONAL ART

1759 England Josiah Wedgwood (1730–1795) set up his own business. He established the neo-classical style in English ceramics and was a strong force in the industrialization of pottery.

1759 France The calico-printing factory at Jouy was established by C. B. Oberkampf (d. 1816). He led the field in block, copperplate and roller printing, and the fabrics, called *Toiles de Jouy*, were often designed by important contemporary artists.

1759 Spain Capo-di-Monte porcelain factory moved from Naples to Buen Retiro, near Madrid: the ware acquired a distinctively Spanish neo-classical flavour.

1761–1762 Germany Decoration of the church at Rott-am-Inn by Ignaz Günther (1725–1775), wood-carver in the rococo style: it combined elegance with emotional religious feeling and he succeeded in giving figures a dance-like animation.

1761 England Matthew Boulton (1728–1809) established a factory which made metalwares and was the only British producer of ormulu. Boulton did much to promote well-designed ormolu and Sheffield plate (silver plated on copper), some of which was designed for him by the Adam brothers.

1761 France Étienne-Maurice Falconnet (1716–1791), sculptor, published his *Reflexions sur la sculpture*, a defence of the modern movement against the ancients. His most famous work was the equestrian statue of Peter the Great (1766–1769), notable for the arrested motion of the rearing horse.

1761 Germany Opening of Johann Ernst Gotzkowsky's porcelain factory at Berlin; it made a white-paste porcelain which was decorated by painters from Meissen.

VISUAL ARTS

*c.***1758–1773 America** Creative period in Boston of John Singleton Copley (1738–1815), considered the most distinguished eighteenth-century portraitist of America. He moved to Europe in 1774, and, with some exceptions, his work lost its originality and realism.

1758 England First known views of Coalbrookdale, the iron-working centre in Shropshire, by Thomas Smith and George Perry. This industrial centre in a beautiful natural setting inspired a series of landscape artists from Smith to Turner and Cotman, and was painted in the 'sublime', picturesque and romantic-impressionist styles for 50 years. Industrial scenes inspired English painters with a mixture of awe and exhilaration.

1760 England The Scottish artist Allan Ramsay (1713–1784) was made painter-in-ordinary to George III. His portraits reflect a continental elegance acquired in the course of his travels.

*c.***1760 Italy** The Venetian painter Francesco Guardi (1712–1793) began to paint scenes of Venice. He abandoned the firm outline and meticulous detail of Canaletto and concentrated on the dissolving effects of light, reflection and water.

1761 Germany A. Kircher published *Ars Magna Lucis et Umbrae*, a text book on the magic lantern. Lanterns had been used since the seventeenth century, and developed technically during the eighteenth century. From the 1790s various systems evolved to 'move' the image: the 'phantasmagoria' moved the lantern while maintaining the focus, so that the clear image became larger or smaller.

1761 Spain Anton Raffael Mengs (1728–1779) painted *Parnassus*, the first ceiling painting to break away from baroque illusionism. Mengs had met the German art historian Winckelmann in 1755 and was stimulated by his neo-classicism; he became famous as a pioneer of the style.

1758 Threshing machine invented.

1759 First canal in England.

LITERATURE

1761 Sweden *Atis Och Camilla* by Count Gustav Philip Creutz (1731–1785), a politician and poet who was a member of the poet Hedwig Nordenflycht's circle. Creutz was a friend of Voltaire, and acted as a link between French and Swedish cultures. This work was a pastoral love poem.

1762 France *Du Contrat Social ou principes du Droit Politique*, by Jean-Jacques Rousseau (1712–1778), philosopher and writer. He believed in the fundamental goodness of man, which modern society, so-called 'progress', tended to corrupt. This view brought him into conflict with the champions of Enlightenment, not least Voltaire. His concept of the noble savage and his belief that power by rights belongs to the people later appealed strongly to the Romantics.

1762 Scotland *Fingal* by James Macpherson (1736–1796), an epic poem purported to be a translation from the Gaelic works of Ossian, a third-century bard. Probably largely invented by Macpherson, it is symptomatic of the reaction against strict classicism. A second epic, *Temora*, appeared in the following year. Dr Johnson recognized and denounced them as forgeries, but Goethe admired them and apparently took them seriously.

1763–1765 Italy *La Frusta Letteraria*, a periodical produced by Giuseppe Buretti (1719–1789), critic and prose writer. He was a friend of Samuel Johnson, and lived for a time in England, whose literature he admired. He endeavoured to encourage serious writing on serious subjects and attacked the Arcadians, whom he regarded as trivial.

1763–1772 Italy A translation into Italian of Macpherson's *The Works of Ossian* was made by Melchiorre Cesarotti (1730–1808), critic and poet. He also translated ancient Greek writers, including Homer, and wrote in favour of the virtues of reason, good taste, and freedom from artificial rules.

DANCE & DRAMA

1761 France Gaetan Vestris (1729-1808) became ballet-master of the Paris Opéra: he was considered the greatest male dancer of his age, and an expressive mime.

1761 Italy *Gli Amore Delle Tre Melarance* by Carlo Gozzi (1720–1806) who was seen as the herald of the Romantic movement in France and Germany. He was a bitter opponent of Goldoni, who tried to revive the *commedia dell' arte*.

MUSIC

1762 Austria First production in Vienna of *Orfeo and Euridice* by Christoph Willibald von Gluck.

1762 England Royal Artillery Band formed.

1762 England Joseph Hill (1715–1748) founded the firm of W. E. Hill & Sons, dealers and repairers.

1762 Germany Birth of Jacob Augustus Otto (d. 1830), violin maker and author of a valuable treatise on the construction of the violin.

1763 France Birth of Étienne Nicolas Méhul (d. 1817), French composer.

1763 France Wolfgang Amadeus Mozart (1756–1791) at the age of seven played before the court at Versailles. His first compositions included works for solo piano and violin and piano.

1763 Germany Birth of Franz Danzi (d. 1826), German composer of Italian origin. As an opera composer he was forerunner of Weber and romanticism.

1762–1773 Switzerland Jesuit cathedral, Solothurn, by Gaetano Pisoni (1713–82) has an impressive baroque exterior in Italian style, the interior being a combination of Italian and German baroque.

*c.***1762–1778 England** William Beilby (1740–1819), glass enameller, worked at Newcastle-on-Tyne: his designs were mainly armorial at first but later became naturalistic.

USA: Unitarian church, Lancaster, Massachusetts, 1816, designed by Charles Bulfinch

1763 USA Charles Bulfinch born (died 1844), architect of Boston churches and of the Massachusetts State House (1795–1800), a combination of Palladian and pure Classicism.

1763–1774 America Henry Stiegel (1729–1785) a German, flourished as a glass-maker, with factories in Pennsylvania: he was the first American glass-maker to insist on controlling the quality of his glass.

1763 America Arrival from England of Thomas Affleck (d. 1795), leading cabinet-maker in the Chippendale style, in which he succeeded the New York cabinet-maker William Ash (1717–1785).

1763 England The American painter Benjamin West (1738–1820) settled in London and became the first American artist with an international reputation. He became President of the Royal Academy and created a centre for American artists in London.

LITERATURE

1763 Italy The first part of *Il Giorno* by Giuseppe Parini (1729–1799), prose writer and poet: a long satiric poem in four books, it describes a day in the life of a nobleman and reveals his uselessness and that of his class. Parini also wrote important odes on topical social themes. Although his subject matter was in tune with the reforming measures suggested by Bettinelli and others, his style was classical and restrained.

1763 Wales Collection of poems by Goronwy Owen (1723–1769). During this century Welsh literature declined, and two movements were created to save it from extinction; Owen was an important writer of the literary movement, using bardic metres.

1764 England *The Castle of Otranto* by Horace Walpole, first Earl of Orford (1717–1797), letter-writer and amateur author. The book was a 'Gothic' novel, a tale of terror and mystery, a new development totally unlike the work of previous eighteenth-century novelists. It illustrated the growing unrest at the clear, reasonable, enlightened attitude of the period.

1765 England *Reliques of Ancient English Poetry*, three volumes of medieval ballads and romances collected and published by Thomas Percy, bishop of Dromore (1729–1811) with critical essays. These are the genuine article, unlike *The Works of Ossian*, and fulfilled a growing need, though the discovery of the original manuscripts was pure chance. The rediscovery of medieval literature did much to stimulate the growth of the Romantic movement in literature.

1766 England *The Vicar of Wakefield* by Oliver Goldsmith (1728–1774), Irish poet, novelist, essayist and playwright. His tone was gentle, his style simple and polished. Although he thought of himself as a classicist, his approach to nature and the countryside anticipated the Romantics.

DANCE & DRAMA

1765 Poland The Teatr Narodowy, the first Polish public theatre, opened in Warsaw.

MUSIC

1764 Austria First performance of *Symphony No. 22 in E-flat*, 'The Philosopher' by Franz Joseph Haydn (1732–1809), followed by the *Great Mass in E-flat* in 1766.

1764 England *The Shepherd's Artifice* performed, first work of Charles Dibdin (1745–1814), English composer, author and entertainer.

1764 England Wolfgang Amadeus Mozart visited London where he met J. C. Bach (1735–1782) whose music he admired. He remained in London for a year, giving many concerts with his sister, and alone.

1764 France Death of Jean Philippe Rameau (b. 1683).

1765 Austria Wolfgang Amadeus Mozart finished his first symphony and the following year wrote his first church music.

1766 England Birth of Samuel Wesley, organist and composer (d. 1837), the greatest English organist of his time.

1766 France Birth of Rodolphe Kreutzer, violinist and composer (d. 1831). His *40 Etudes ou Caprices pour le Violin* holds a unique position in the literature of violin studies and has been published in numerous editions.

1766 Hungary Franz Joseph Haydn became sole *Kapellmeister* to Prince Esterhazy, having been appointed second *Kapellmeister* in 1761. He held the position until 1790.

ARCHITECTURE

1764 England Benjamin Latrobe born (died 1820); after training in Europe, he emigrated to the USA in 1795, where he built a number of public buildings and churches in classical and Gothic styles, including the Hall of Representatives in Washington and the Roman Catholic cathedral in Baltimore.

England: Ralph Allen's Sham Castle, built in 'Gothic' style

1765 USA Jumel House, New York, is a rare eighteenth-century building in that city with a giant-portico, the first of its kind in the USA.

*c.*1765 **Spain** The Porcelain Room of the Madrid Royal Palace was modelled on the Neapolitan original; the style is Chinese, which was then popular.

*c.*1765 **USA** Brandon, Prince George County, Virginia, is a large house with Palladian features, typical in the eastern states during the eighteenth century.

1766–1794 Brazil Ouro Preto was probably by Antonio Lisbôa (1738–1814); it is a Franciscan chapel, built in elegant Portuguese rococo style by the greatest Brazilian sculptor and architect of the period, and has a curving two-tower façade and an aisleless interior.

1766 France Hôtel Alexandre, Paris, by Étienne-Louis Boullée (1728–1799) is one of the few buildings actually built by him: his imaginative, often impracticable, series of neo-classical drawings were better known.

THREE DIMENSIONAL ART

1765–1767 England Josiah Wedgwood produced an improved creamware pottery called Queen's ware (1765) and a black basalt ware (1767).

1765 France Georges Jacob (1739–1814) became master cabinet-maker: he specialized in chair-making and was considered the best in his field. He favoured the classical and was a formative influence on the Empire style. His factory was taken over by his sons in 1796, of whom François-Honoré, taking the name Jacob-Desmalter, became cabinet-maker to Napoleon I.

1766 England Portrait bust of Lawrence Sterne by Joseph Nollekens (1737–1823), who excelled as a portrait sculptor.

VISUAL ARTS

1765 Denmark The painter Jens Juel (1745–1802) returned after working for five years in Hamburg, where he had come under the influence of Dutch painting. His work was mainly in family groups and informal portraits of naturalistic style.

1765 England Arrival from Berlin of the artist Henry Fuseli (1741–1825) who brought a German imagination to the depiction of the horrifying and fantastic. He was admired in the twentieth century by the expressionist and surrealist painters.

1765 France François Boucher (1703–1770) was made King's Painter. He painted complex decorative schemes for royal residences which influenced fashion in interior decoration until the Revolution. His paintings expressed perfectly the contemporary taste for the artificial and the sensual combined.

*c.*1765- 1784 **Japan** Isoda Koryúsai flourished: he was famous for his 'pillar prints' (long prints) of women in gorgeous dresses.

*c.*1765 **Japan** Katsukawa Shunsho (1726–1792), designer and print-maker, with Mamoru Buncho (fl. 1764–1790), introduced a new type of realistic portrait head; these were at first mainly of actors but later became generally popular. As a painter he was famous for painting beautiful women.

*c.*1765 **Japan** Introduction of full polychrome printing for *Ukiyo-E* colour prints, using twenty or thirty printing blocks. The results were called *Nishiki-E*, 'brocade-like' pictures. The prints owed much to the designer, engraver and printer having a sympathetic understanding of each other's work; artists were unrestricted by any 'school', so their subjects were fresh and boldly treated.

1766 England George Stubbs (1724–1806), anatomist and painter, published *The Anatomy of the Horse*: anatomical studies of scientific precision which were considered a unique combination of science and art. This led to the patronage of Stubbs' paintings by owners and breeders of horses and by natural scientists.

1764 James Hargreaves produced final version of spinning jenny.

1765 James Watt invented a separate condenser for the steam engine.

1766 Henry Cavendish discovered hydrogen to be an element and analysed air.

HISTORICAL EVENTS	LITERATURE	DANCE & DRAMA	MUSIC

1767
Aly Bey took
Cairo in attempt
to restore
Mamluk empire.

1767 Germany *Phädon Oder Uber Die Unsterblichkeit Der Seele* by Moses Mendelssohn (1729–1786), a Jewish philosopher. His crisp, lucid books expressed the philosophy of the *Aufklärung*, or rational enlightenment.

1767 America Lewis Hallam built the John Street Theatre, New York.

1767 Austria Count Durazzo of the Austrian Imperial Theatres brought the choreographer Jean-Georges Noverre to work in Vienna, with a nucleus of dancers he had already trained in Stuttgart.

1767 Germany The first National Theatre was opened in Hamburg by Konrad Ackermann (1710–1771). The venture failed.

1767 Germany First issue of the periodical, *Hamburgische Dramaturgie*, a vehicle for Lessing's dramatic criticism. He is considered one of the world's finest dramatic critics.

1767 Germany *Minna von Barnhelm* by Lessing: a play remarkable for its convincingly German, three-dimensional characters.

*c.***1767 Russia** Return from Vienna of the dancer, teacher and choreographer Timofei Boublikov (1744-1815), who established Russian folk dance as part of ballet. He had trained at the Russian court school of dancing for cadets set up in 1738.

1767 Austria First production in Vienna of *Alceste* by Christoph Willibald von Gluck.

1767 Austria First performance of Mozart's first dramatic work, a sacred play with music, *Die Schuldigkeit des Ersten Gebotes*.

1767 England Henry Fougt, printer and publisher, took out a patent for an improved metal type. He was a pioneer of cheap sheet music, the typography of which was excellent.

1768 England The Birmingham Music Festivals established.

1768 France Jean Louis Duport (1749–1819), violoncellist, made his debut. He is considered to be originator of modern technique of his instrument.

1769 France *Les Saisons* by the poet Jean-François de Saint-Lambert (1716–1803): the work was a pastoral, modelled on *The Seasons* of James Thomson. It reflected a townsman's view of the countryside, not an intimate knowledge.

ARCHITECTURE

1767–1775 England The Royal Crescent, Bath was built by John Wood the younger; the Wood family originated the idea of using the Roman circus and half-circus shape as street plans while the houses were in Renaissance style.

1767 Sweden The Exchange, Stockholm, by Erik Palmstadt (1741–1803) is severely classical; the architect designed several neo-classical buildings in Sweden.

1768 England The Adelphi, London, by Robert and James (1730–1794) Adam was an ambitious project that failed financially; the great terrace of houses was decorated on the exterior with delicate classical detail normally reserved for interiors. Little remains.

1768 Russia The Marble Palace, St Petersburg, by Antonio Rinaldi (c.1709–1794), who introduced marble facing on the façade of classical proportions; very few baroque elements remain in this essentially neo-classical building.

1769 USA Monticello, Albermarle County, Virginia, by Thomas Jefferson was his own house based on designs chosen from Robert Morris's *Select Architecture* and Gibbs and Leoni's *Palladio*; his designs for Virginia's university and state capitol buildings (Richmond) are nearer the neo-classical.

THREE DIMENSIONAL ART

1767 England Death of William Vile, one of the most celebrated cabinet-makers of his day, and cabinet-maker to George III; he worked in the rococo style.

1768 England Discovery of kaolin in Cornwall by William Cookworthy: he used it in hard-paste porcelain, which he had previously made with American clay.

England: coin cabinet by William Vile

VISUAL ARTS

1766 France The Swedish painter Peter Adolf Hall (1739–1793) settled in Paris and established himself as a portrait miniaturist. His near-impressionist brush-work was unusual in this field.

*c.*1766 **France** *The Swing*, one of the best known paintings by Jean Honoré Fragonard (1732–1806), whose work is identified with frivolous taste and luxury under Louis XV; in spite of his great skill and versatility his career did not survive the Revolution.

1768–1776 England The Reverend William Gilpin (1724–1804) made his tours of Britain and recorded his impressions with drawings, which he began to publish as plates in 1782. Gilpin was the most important influence in forming the 'picturesque' taste, which he attempted to analyse in essays.

1768 England Sir Joshua Reynolds (1723–1792) was elected president of the new Royal Academy. He was the most important artist of his day and one who did much to raise the status of painters. His lectures expressed a belief in the dignity of painting and in a rational ideal which was opposed to the new spirit of romanticism.

1768 England Joseph Wright's painting *A Philosopher giving that Lecture on the Orrery etc.* was published as a mezzotint by William Pether, (1731–1795), the successful engraver and print-seller. He published many of Wright's pictures and ensured that they were widely known.

1768 France First aquatints by Jean Baptiste Le Prince (1733–1781), who was the first to develop a successful technique.

1769 America Charles Willson Peale (1741–1827) returned, after training in England, to work as a portrait and still-life artist in Philadelphia. He became an outstanding portraitist in neo-classical style.

1769 France Jean-Baptiste Greuze (1725–1805) was accepted into the Academy. His genre paintings of rural virtue were highly valued in his own time; posterity has preferred his portraits, in which his talent was not debased to popular taste.

INVENTIONS & DISCOVERIES

1767
Louis Antoine de Bougainville circum-navigated the world.

1768
James Cook sailed on first voyage of discovery to Antipodes.

1769
Richard Arkwright invented water-powered spinning frame.

HISTORICAL EVENTS	LITERATURE	DANCE & DRAMA	MUSIC

HISTORICAL EVENTS

1771
Russia completed conquest of Crimea.

LITERATURE

1770–1780 Poland *The Monitor*, a literary periodical, similar to the English *Spectator*.

1771 Denmark Collection of poems by Johannes Ewald (1743–1781), considered the greatest Danish lyric poet. He was inspired partly by the old myths, sagas and medieval ballads. His autobiography, *Life and Opinions*, modelled on Laurence Sterne, was also noteworthy.

1772–1775 Russia A series of Russian historical articles, including a dictionary of writers, was printed by Nikolay Ivanovich Novikov (1744–1818), publisher and satirical journalist. He was also responsible for the first magazine for children in Russia.

1772 America *A Poem on the Rising Glory of America* by Philip Morin Freneau (1752–1832), patriotic poet and newspaper editor.

1772 Germany A group of young writers formed an association called the Hainbund. They wrote mainly nature poetry, lyrical and simple in style. They admired Klopstock, but regarded Wieland as decadent because he was influenced by foreign writers.

1772 Hungary The philosopher György Bessenyei (1747–1811) returned to his country after military service abroad, during which he had come under the influence of Voltaire. He saw that contemporary Hungarian culture was amost non-existent, and set about creating a new literature. Among other works, he wrote treatises on the language.

DANCE & DRAMA

1770 Italy The Duke of Parma offered an annual prize for the best Italian tragedy, in an attempt to improve standards.

*c.*1770 **England** Introduction of the French folk dance the *Cotillon* in a ball-room form as the cotillion. The French square dance and the English longways dance were the two forms of *contredanse* widely spread in Europe; they inspired other countries to make ballroom dances out of their folk dances.

1771 Denmark Foundation of the Royal Theatre ballet company in Copenhagen.

1771 England *The West Indian* by Richard Cumberland (1732–1811): a typical example of the sentimental comedy then in vogue in England.

1771 England Philipe Jacques de Loutherbourg (1740–1812) became Drury Lane's scenic director. He was particularly known for fluctuating lighting effects like clouds and fire, and for sound effects such as guns, rain and wind.

1771 Italy The French choreographer Jean-Georges Noverre introduced the *ballet d'action* to Milan, which remained a centre of Italian ballet. (Milan was ruled by the Austrian Empress for whom Noverre had been ballet-master in the Austrian Imperial Theatres).

1772 Denmark *Love Without Stockings* by Johann Wessel (1742–1785), a member of the Norwegian Club, a group of Norwegian writers living in Copenhagen. It is a parody of *Zarine*, a neo-classical tragedy by Nordahl Brun (1745–1816) and demolished not only that particular play but the whole neo-classical tradition as far as Scandinavia was concerned.

1772 Germany *Emilia Galotti* by Lessing was produced by Friedrich Ludwig Schroder (1744–1816). Schroder reformed acting style, introduced Shakespeare to German audiences and encouraged the *Sturm und Drang* (storm and stress) movement. This was part of the German Romantic movement, and the plays were about individuals in conflict with their environment or in the grip of mighty passions.

MUSIC

1770 America First performance of Handel's *Messiah* in New York.

1770 Germany Birth of Ludwig van Beethoven (d. 1827), German composer of Flemish descent, at Bonn.

1770 Italy Wolfgang Amadeus Mozart visited Italy for first time, staying for about a year. His first opera was written and performed there.

1771 Austria Florian Gassmann (1729–1774), Bohemian conductor and composer, founded the oldest Vienna music society, Tonkünstler-Societät (Pensionverein für Witwen und Waisen österreichischer Tonkünstler), after 1862 called Haydn-Societät.

1771 Germany Death of Anton Joseph Hampel, Bohemian horn player, credited with the introduction of hand stopping and designing an improved orchestral horn.

1772 England First Chester Music Festival.

1772 Germany First German performance of Handel's *Messiah*.

ARCHITECTURE

1771 France Pavillon de Louveciennes by Claude Ledoux (1736–1780) was the first building in France to be designed throughout in the neo-classical style.

1771 West Indies Pocito chapel, Guadeloupe, is an oval-planned church with a dome. It may have derived from a temple plan published by Serlio and is one of very few centrally planned Spanish-American churches.

THREE DIMENSIONAL ART

1770 Bavaria Death of Joseph Anton Feichtmayer (b. 1696): an important member of a family of sculptors and stuccoists, he was noted for his religious sculpture, much of it in coloured wood and carved in flamboyant style.

*c.***1770 France** First introduction of hard-paste porcelain of the German type, as opposed to soft-paste porcelain: it was first made at the royal factory of Sèvres, due to the discovery of local kaolin.

1771 Italy Giambattista Bodoni (1740–1813), began to cut typefaces. His most influential type was that used for an edition of *Horace's Poems* in 1791. His style dominated printing for 50 years.

1772 Bavaria Death of Johann Michael Feichtmayer, sculptor and stuccoist, (b. *c.*1710): he worked on the Bruchsal palace and the abbey churches of Zwiefalten and Ottobeuren.

1772 Germany David Roentgen (d. 1807) took over his father's furniture workshop, where he had worked since 1761: he was the outstanding European cabinet-maker in neo-classical style, and excelled in pictorial marquetry.

VISUAL ARTS

1770–1778 Italy The artist Henry Fuseli (1741–1825) left his work in England to study Michelangelo's art. His own lifelong attempt to imitate Michelangelo's portrayal of the sublime was frustrated by his extravagant technique and imagination.

1770 Japan Death of Suzuki Harunobu (b. *c.*1720), master of *Ukiyo-E* colour prints. He excelled in line and subtlety of colours, and tried to raise *Ukiyo-E* from popular subject matter to themes from poetry, history and tradition.

*c.***1770 Poland** Daniel Nikolaus Chodowiechi (1726–1801) began producing book illustrations, especially pictures of Polish life and scenes around Danzig.

1771 England The Alsatian painter Philip de Loutherbourg (1740–1812) settled in England; he became a strong influence on painters of landscape and the industrial scene, in the contrived, baroque tradition.

1772 Mexico Completion of the painted wooden ceiling at the church of St James, Tupátaro, near Pátzcuaro. It had 47 sections painted with a central figure or scene in a decorative border; the colours used were red, green, brown and black on white. It was possibly painted in celebration of a local miracle, and has been considered one of the greatest works of Indian Christian art in Latin America.

INVENTIONS & DISCOVERIES

1770
Cook discovered Botany Bay.

1772
Daniel Rutherford discovered nitrogen.

Italy: 'Oedipus Cursing his Son Polynices' by Henry Fuseli

HISTORICAL EVENTS	LITERATURE	DANCE & DRAMA	MUSIC

HISTORICAL EVENTS

1773
Boston Tea Party.

1774
Warren Hastings appointed Governor General of India.

1775
Beginning of American War of Independence.

1776
American Declaration of Independence, drafted by Thomas Jefferson, was carried by Congress.

LITERATURE

1774 Germany *Werther* by the poet Johann Wolfgang von Goethe (1749–1832); the work made his reputation in Europe. In the following year he moved to Weimar, a tiny state which became the centre of German literary life. Goethe, Schiller, Herder and Wieland all lived and worked there. Goethe and Schiller were the core of the German classical movement.

1774 Spain *Caras Marruecas* by José de Cadalso y Vazquez (1741–1782), soldier, essayist and neo-classical poet. The work was a series of essays analysing and satirizing various aspects of Spanish life—culture, character and customs.

1775 Germany *Lenore* by the poet Gottfried August Burger (1747–1794). He wrote powerful popular ballads and lyrics which were modelled on folksong. One of his sources of inspiration was the English ballad.

1776–1778 Finland *De Poesi Fennica* by Henrik Gabriel Porthan (1739–1804), a Finnish-Swedish scholar, historian and folklorist. He was responsible for a revival of interest in folk-songs and in medieval Finnish history.

1777 Italy *Della Tirannide* by Vittorio Alfieri (1749–1803), a playwright and poet who also wrote political treatises such as this work. He thundered against tyrants, but was noted more for the power of his utterances than for his thought. His poetry was important stylistically because it was deliberately harsh and lacking in melody. His influence on subsequent writers was considerable.

1777 Sweden Collection of love poems by Johann Henric Kellgren (1751–1795), critic and poet. A staunch supporter of neo-classicism, he was literary adviser to King Gustav III. His satires on the establishment were published in the *Stockholm Posten*, a paper which he helped to found.

DANCE & DRAMA

1772 Russia *O Tempora*, a comedy by Catherine the Great.

1773 England *She Stoops to Conquer* by Oliver Goldsmith (1730–1774) was a complete breakaway from the current English sentimental plays and an immediate success.

1773 Germany *Götz von Berlichingen* by Johann Wolfgang Goethe (1749–1832) was the first German play inspired by a study of Shakespeare and the first play of the *Sturm und Drang* movement.

1773 Sweden Foundation of an opera and ballet company in Stockholm, with a French ballet-master.

1775 Denmark Vincenzo Galeotti (1733–1816), an Italian ballet-master trained by Noverre and Angiolini, became ballet-master at the Royal Danish Ballet. He stayed 41 years and founded a tradition of *ballet d'action* in Copenhagen.

1775 France *Le Barbier de Seville* by Pierre-Augustin Caron, called Beaumarchais (1732–1799): it was considered revolutionary because of the character of Figaro, the valet who criticizes his master, and was only performed after a struggle with the French censorship.

1776 India The British opened a theatre of their own in Calcutta: its first productions were *The Disguise* and *Love is the Doctor*.

1777 England *The School for Scandal* by Richard Brinsley Sheridan (1751–1816): a comedy of manners as witty as any of the Restoration plays but without their bawdiness.

MUSIC

1773 England Publication of *The Present State of Music in Germany, the Netherlands and the United Provinces* by Charles Burney (1726–1814).

1774 England James Hook (1746–1827) organist and composer, appointed to Vauxhall Gardens, where he remained for nearly 50 years. He was a prolific composer in many fields, especially in light entertainment music.

1774 Germany Publication of *De Cantu et Musica Sacra a Prima Ecclesiae Aetate usque ad Praesens Tempus* by Martin Gerbert von Hornau (1720–1793), German musical historian. This history of church music has formed the foundation of all scholarship in church music.

1774 Italy First performance of the opera *La Finta Giardiniera* by Pasquale Anfossi (1727–1797) in Rome. This opera had a great influence on Mozart.

1774 Italy Birth of Gasparo Luigi Pacifico Spontini (d. 1851), composer.

1775 Europe The piano began to supersede the harpsichord as an accompanying instrument; eventually it superseded it completely because it has a greater output of sound, can be played softly or loudly, is able to sustain notes, and remains in tune owing to its reinforced frame.

1776 England Publication of *General History of the Science and Practice of Music* by Sir John Hawkins (1719–1789), musical historian, antiquarian and attorney. Though extremely unmethodical it contains much valuable information.

1776 England The first of four volumes of a history of music was produced by Charles Burney (1726–1814). The last volume appeared in 1789.

1776 England A concert organization 'The Concert of Antient Music' was established in London.

1777 France First pianoforte constructed in France by Sebastien Erard (1752–1831), Alsatian instrument maker, famous for his improvements to harps and pianofortes.

ARCHITECTURE

1774 Denmark Frederick V Chapel, Roskilde Cathedral, is neo-classical in style by one of the best neo-classical architects of the eighteenth century, C. H. Harsdorff (1735–99).

1774 France St Philippe du Roule, Paris, by Jean Chalgrin (1739–1811), a pupil of Boullée. who based the plan of this church on an early Christian basilica with a Doric portico.

1774–1778 Norway Stiftsgarden Palace, Trondheim, is 19 bays long and, is the largest wooden building in Scandinavia in the classical style. Many other similar houses on a smaller scale were built but were destroyed by fire.

1775 Belgium Place Royale, Brussels, was designed by Nicholas Barré (flourished 1730–88) and Gilles Barnabé Guimard (?–1792), French architects who produced this almost neo-classical scheme.

1775 France Saltworks, Arc-et-Senans, by Claude Ledoux combines an elemental Doric portico before a rusticated wall, conjuring up visions of the primeval.

1776 England Somerset House, London, began to be rebuilt by Sir William Chambers (1723–1796); the masterpiece amongst several public buildings designed by Chambers, who here used a wide range of classical sources.

1776–1796 Ireland The Four Courts, Dublin, by James Gandon (1743–1823) was his masterpiece in the Palladian classical style; he borrowed ideas from Chambers and Wren.

1777–1790 Scotland Culzean Castle by Robert Adam is one of many picturesque Gothic castles built in Britain during the eighteenth and early nineteenth centuries.

THREE DIMENSIONAL ART

1773 America Death of Christopher Townsend (b. 1701), second generation of a family of Quaker cabinet-makers in Rhode Island: John Goddard (1723–1785) was apprenticed to them and the two families together form the 'Newport Group', outstanding in American furniture design during the eighteenth and early nineteenth centuries.

1774–1775 England Josiah Wedgwood produced Jasper ware: a vitreous pottery containing barium sulphate, barium carbonate and felspar, and coloured with metallic oxides, it had a dense body which could be turned on a lathe, and is Wedgwood's most original production.

1774 Portugal Joaquim Machado de Castro (1731–1822), sculptor, completed the bronze equestrian statue of Joseph I in Lisbon.

1775–1787 England John Flaxman (1755–1826), sculptor, worked for the potter Josiah Wedgwood, designing portrait medallions and relief ornament for plaques: the discipline of this small-scale work influenced his later large sculptures.

1776–1880 Russia Porcelain factory at Verbilki, Moscow, was founded by Francis Gardner, an Englishman.

VISUAL ARTS

1773 England Engraving of *Joseph of Arimathea* by William Blake (1757–1827): it shows him already possessed of a mystical vision. He was apprenticed to an engraver for whom he drew church monuments; this led him to a study of Gothic art and confirmed his love of linear pattern.

1774 England Thomas Gainsborough (1727–1788) moved to London and began to paint portraits in delicate colours and rapid brush-work. He acknowledged the influence of van Dyck, of whose portraits he made a study. He also continued to paint landscapes, often imaginary, for pleasure, since he had left the country for the town.

1774 Netherlands The artist Léonard Defrance (1735–1805) returned to his home town of Liège after working in Italy, France and Holland; he began to paint scenes of working life including social comment as well as visual effect.

1775 Japan *The Hundred Poets and their Poems in Brocade*, polychrome colour prints by Katsukawa Shunsho (1726–1792): a very influential work, considered his best.

1776–1791 Spain Francisco José Goya y Lucientes (1746–1828) painted the designs for a series of tapestries for the royal factory. The style is romantic and decorative in rococo spirit.

1776 England Portrait of Richard Cumberland by George Romney (1734–1802): it is considered one of the best works by a painter of fashionable portraits of women and children; Romney was famous for his portraits of Emma Hamilton.

INVENTIONS & DISCOVERIES

1774
Joseph Priestley isolated oxygen.

1775
James Watt perfected the steam engine.

1777
David Bushnell invented the torpedo.

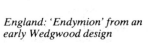

England: 'Endymion' from an early Wedgwood design

MUSIC

1777 Netherlands Felix Meritis Society founded in Amsterdam.

1778 Germany Machine (screw) heads for cellos and double basses were invented by Anton Bachmann (1716–1800), court musician and instrument maker.

1778 Hungary Birth of Johan Nepomuka Hummel (d. 1837), pianist, conductor and composer.

1778 Italy La Teatro alla Scala opened in Milan with *Europa Riconosciuta* by Antonio Salieri (1750–1825).

1779 England John Stanley (1713–1786) appointed Master of the King's Music. A composer and organist, he had been blind from the age of two.

1779 France Louis Francois Pique (1758–1822), French violin maker, established in Paris; he was regarded as one of the best makers.

1780 Germany A new music-printing machine was invented by Heinrich Philipp Bossler, the German musical theorist, printer and editor.

LITERATURE

1778 England *Evelina* by Fanny Burney (1752–1840), diarist and novelist. She used the letter form originated by Richardson and her plots were conventional, but she had a gift for natural dialogue and for character drawing.

1778 Germany *Stimmen der Volker in Liedern*, a collection of folk-songs from many lands by the critic Johann Gottfried Herder (1744–1803). He believed that literature should be original, and particularly approved of folk-song because it is just that. He was also impressed by Shakespeare. By introducing these elements to German writers, chief among them Goethe, he determined the trend of subsequent literature.

1778 Sweden Death of the Swedish naturalist Carl von Linné, called Linnaeus (b. 1707). His work was not literary, strictly speaking, but he deserves mention as a pioneer of clear, direct prose, and for his strong love of his country which he expressed in his writing.

1779 Poland *Satires* by Ignacy, Count Krasicki (1735–1801), poet, playwright and novelist, regarded as the greatest Polish writer of the century. In addition to satires he wrote fables, mock epics, comedies, a heroic epic, and two novels on Polish life. He also translated from Macpherson's *Works of Ossian*, from Lucian and from Plutarch.

DANCE & DRAMA

1778 America George Washington, who was interested in the theatre, attended a performance of Addison's *Cato* at Valley Forge.

1778 Denmark *The Fishers* by Johannes Ewald (1743–1781), Denmark's first tragic writer: his earlier plays show strong German influence, but this is a purely Danish work.

1778 Italy Building of La Scala theatre, Milan: it was subsidized by the holders of season-tickets for boxes, who in practical terms controlled its policies. They wanted variety and had little interest in building a repertoire or developing an art. In ballet, this meant many productions under many ballet-masters, none of them preserved for more than a few performances.

1780 France Malpied published his second treatise on the art of the dance; the positions of the feet are still as laid down by Beauchamps.

1780 Spain Invention of the bolero, by the dancer Sebastian Cerezo, or Zerezo; he may have developed it from an older and similar dance.

*c.*1780 Germany/Austria First appearance of the waltz, thought to be derived from the South German folk dance the *ländler*. Waltz tunes were published in England from *c.*1790 and used as country dance tunes. The waltz as a dance appeared in England in 1812 and was considered improper because no previous dance had required the partners to do more than touch hands.

1781 Sweden *Passionerna* was the prize-winning entry in a poetry competition organized by a Stockholm literary society. It was written by Thomas Thorild (1759–1808), poet, critic and philosopher. It led him into controversy with Kellgren—the usual eighteenth-century debate on the relative values of reason and the imagination. Thorild admired English and German writers, and in this he was the precursor of the Romantic movement in Sweden.

1781 England The choreographer Jean-Georges Noverre came to work in London, after being frustrated by internal politics in an attempt to reform ballet at the Paris Opéra. He firmly established the *ballet d'action* in Europe before his retirement in 1794.

1781 Germany *Die Raüber* by Johann Christoph Friedrich von Schiller (1759–1805), a romantic play in the *Sturm und Drang* tradition, was staged at Mannheim, home of Germany's third National Theatre.

1781 Austria Mozart arrived in Vienna, where he lodged with the Webers, married their daughter Constanze, and remained based for the rest of his life.

1781 England William Forster (1739–1808), music seller and publisher, entered into an agreement with Franz Joseph Haydn (1732–1809) for the purchase and publication in England of Haydn's compositions.

ARCHITECTURE	THREE DIMENSIONAL ART	VISUAL ARTS	*INVENTIONS & DISCOVERIES*

ARCHITECTURE

1778 France The Theatre, Besançon, by Claude Ledoux was revolutionary neo-classicism: it consisted of a massive cubic theatre, semicircular amphitheatre and pedimented Ionic portico. Now destroyed.

1780 Spain Vich Cathedral was rebuilt by José Morato in a severe neo-classical style, which began to displace the Baroque in Spain at the end of the eighteenth century.

1781 Germany Karl Friedrich von Schinkel born (died 1841), the greatest early nineteenth-century German architect and a very original designer of neo-classical buildings, including the Berlin Old Museum (1823–1828), typifying his early Grecian style; other buildings in a more austere monumental style inspired early twentieth-century architects.

THREE DIMENSIONAL ART

1780–1790 England Development of underglaze printing on ceramics, in which the design was printed directly on to the body of the ware before glazing: it was done mainly in blue and white.

*c.*1780 **America** The silversmith Benjamin Pierpont worked in Boston. making cups in a plain style derived from English domestic wares. English fashions continued to influence Boston silver after the revolution; it was always more restrained in design than the work of New York and Philadelphia, the latter being especially exuberant.

*c.*1780 **England** Caughley pottery, Shropshire, made the first known willow pattern plate. The design became standardized *c.*1830.

*c.*1780 **France** Jean-Antoine Houdon (1741–1828) acknowledged the leading portrait sculptor in Europe. His commissions included a statue of George Washington as the modern Cincinnatus.

1781–1785 France François-Ambrose Didot (1730–1804) flourished as a type-designer. He reformed the French scale of type sizes and introduced the making of woven paper to France. His family were influential in the field until 1876.

1781 Japan The book *Soken Kisho* mentioned 54 famous *netsuke* carvers by name: earlier *netsuke* were often unsigned, or made by carvers whose main line was in larger-scale work; among the carvers mentioned as outstanding were Yoshimura Shuzan and Tomotada.

VISUAL ARTS

1778 England Joseph Wright (1734–1797) had his first exhibition at the Royal Academy. His paintings celebrated aspects of industry and science; his technique in dramatic lighting was influenced by Dutch 'candle-light paintings, which began with van Honthurst (1590–1656), and were later developed by Godfried Schalken (1643–1706). His aim was realism, scientifically observed, especially in depicting the mechanics of manual labour.

1779–1803 India Reign of Pratap Singh at Jaipur, an important centre of Rajput art; under his patronage Mogul influence was replaced by a local Rajput style. He employed some 50 painters; a characteristic example of their work was *Krishna's ring dance* (*c.*1800) with massed figures and rhythmic line combined in a tense design, to show swirling movement.

1780–1790 Japan Torii Kiyonaga (1752–1815) dominated contemporary work in *Ukiyo-E* prints; he led the fourth generation of the Torii family of artists. He first made landscape an integral part of the composition in colour prints, and first made full use of triptych form. He was famous for portraits of women in a rhythmic style and elongated form.

1780 Sweden The painter Elias Martin (1739–1818) returned to Stockholm after 12 years in England, where he had studied the work of Gainsborough, Wilson and Hogarth. He became celebrated for pictures of Stockholm and landscape scenes in the romantic style; water-colour was considered his best medium.

1781 England Sir Joshua Reynolds (1723–1792) visited Flanders and came in contact with the work of Rubens, whose influence brought greater warmth to Reynold's portraits. He was outstanding for his ability to combine the 'Grand Manner' of flamboyant baroque with an acute perception of character.

INVENTIONS & DISCOVERIES

1778 Friedrich Mesmer first practised 'mesmerism' in Paris.

1779 Samuel Crompton perfected the spinning mule.

1780 William Withering discovered the use of digitalis in medicine.

1781 Frederick William Herschel discovered the planet Uranus.

HISTORICAL EVENTS

*1782
Rama I founded
new dynasty in
Siam, with
capital at
Bangkok.*

*1783
Peace of
Versailles;
Britain
recognized the
independence of
U.S.A.*

*1784
Pitt's India Act
placed East India
Company under
government
control.*

LITERATURE

1782 France *Les Liaisons Dangereuses* by Pierre Ambroise Choderlos de Laclos (1741–1803), politician, soldier and novelist. The book, which was about the licentious private lives of the aristocracy, caused great indignation. He excelled in the analysis of sexual motives.

1782 Netherlands Collection of poems by Jacobus Bellamy (1757–1786), whose songs, often unrhymed, showed pre-Romantic features.

1782 Spain *Elogio de las Bellas Artes*, a criticism of the arts in Spain by Gaspar Melchior de Jovellanos (1744–1811), statesman and man of letters.

1783 Russia *Felitsa* by the poet Gavriil Romanovich Derzhavin (1743–1816), who followed the trend set by Lomonosov, but was highly individual in his use of colour and baroque imagery. His fame was widespread; he was known in China and Japan as well as Europe. Russian literature at this period was strongly influenced by French, as indeed was all European literature.

1783 Serbia Autobiography of Dositej Obradović (?1742–1811), an educationist, translator and writer of travel accounts. His translations, the most popular being *Aesops Fables*, were intended to introduce European culture in order to enrich that of the Serbs and to point the need for education. He avoided Church Slavonic, and used the spoken language with commendable skill, considering that as a literary language it was in its infancy.

1784–1785 Netherlands *William Leevend* by the novelists Elisabeth Wolff-Bekker (1738–1804) and Agatha Deken (1741–1804), who were also poets. They collaborated on novels in letter form, which showed great psychological insight and sensitive portrayal of typical Dutch life. Although this was only their second novel, it is considered a masterpiece.

1784 Germany *Was Ist Aufklärung* by the philosopher Immanuel Kant (1724–1804) was a summary of the ideas of the 'Age of Reason', which was already passing by the time the book was written.

DANCE & DRAMA

1781 Sweden Antoine Bournonville (1760–1843) became choreographer of the Royal Swedish Ballet. He had trained under Noverre, and had been leading male dancer with Galeotti's Royal Danish Ballet.

1782–1784 Italy *Saul* by Vittorio Amedeo Alfieri (1749–1803), a writer who chose heroic subjects and observed the Unities. He wrote to kindle a hatred of tyranny and a passion for liberty in his audience.

1782 Russia *The Minor* by Dennis Ivanovich Fonvisin (1744–1792), who combined the traditions of his native Russian folk comedy with eighteenth-century French comedy.

England: 'Vauxhall Gardens' by Thomas Rowlandson

1784 France *Le Marriage de Figaro* by Beaumarchais: this criticized society rather than an individual and reflects the movement towards revolution in France. Beaumarchais also led other dramatists in the fight to stop actors tampering with plays and to obtain a better financial deal for writers.

MUSIC

1782 Italy Birth of Niccolo Paganini, composer and violinist (d. 1840) who made his debut as violin virtuoso in Genoa in 1793.

1783 Austria First performance in Salzburg, of Mozart's *Mass in C minor* from which he drew the material for his cantata, *Davidde Penitente (1785)*.

1783 England The Glee Club formed in London.

1784 Belgium Birth of François Joseph Fétis (d. 1871), Belgian musicologist and historian whose many publications made an important contribution to musical instruction and literature.

1784 Germany Birth of Louis Spohr (d. 1859), German violinist and composer.

| ARCHITECTURE | THREE DIMENSIONAL ART | VISUAL ARTS | INVENTIONS & DISCOVERIES |

1781 England Philipp de Loutherbourg (1740–1812), stage designer and painter of picturesque landscapes and dramatic set-pieces, opened in London his show *Eidophusikon*, a spectacle of three-dimensional stage effects produced with light projection.

1782 France Le Hameau, Versailles, by Richard Mique (1728–1794) is a mock farm built for Marie-Antoinette; it represents the French interest in the picturesque *jardin anglais* and accompanying follies.

1782 Italy First of many works on mythological subjects by the sculptor Antonio Canova (1757–1822): he later worked in Rome under Bonaparte family patronage and his neo-classical style dominated most European sculpture of the early nineteenth century.

1781 Sweden The court painter Pehr Hilleström (1732–1816) first visited the Falun coppermine; thereafter he made the mining and metal-founding industries his main subject, especially the spectacular appearance of furnaces, white-hot metal and the forge.

1782 Sweden Carl Gustaf Pilo (1711–1793) painted *The Coronation of Gustavus III* (unfinished). He was remarkable among Swedish painters in being totally free of French influence.

1783 Russia The Great Palace of Tsarkoe Selo, Pushkin, built by Bartolomeo Rastrelli (1700–1771); it was altered by Charles Cameron (1740–1812) in the style of classical antiquity.

1783 Japan Death of Yosa No Buson (b. 1716), artist in the *Nanga* style whose work, together with that of the fan-painter and calligrapher Ikeno Taiga (1723–1776), gave the *Nanga* school a fresh impetus.

1783 First demonstration of hot air and hydrogen balloons.

1783 Russia The Academy of Sciences, St Petersburg, by Giacomo Quarenghi (1744–1817) is a massive rectangular block and has a central portico with a pediment revealing a Palladian manner often employed by Quarenghi.

1784 England *Vauxhall Gardens* by Thomas Rowlandson (1756–1827) was characteristic of his elaborate satirical pictures. His work showed French influence on its line and subject matter but was English in its humour and its colour tones.

1784–1794 USA John Frederick Amelung, a German, flourished as a glass-maker in Maryland. He closely imitated European forms and produced a better glass than his predecessors.

1784 France The *Oath of the Horatii* by Jacques-Louis David (1748–1825) typified his severe neo-classicism and the new feeling for stern republican virtue after the Revolution. He became the symbol of a new French art, founding an Institute to replace the old Academy.

LITERATURE

1785 China Death of Chiang Shih-ch'uan (b. 1725), a poet and playwright writing in a realistic style unusual at the time.

1785 England *The Task* by William Cowper (1731–1800), poet and letter writer. Conventional in form, his work showed his ability to derive pleasure and create poetry from slight and trifling incidents.

1785 Italy *Poesie Campestrie* by Ippolito Pindemonte (1753–1828), prose writer and poet, whose work includes a novel, a tragedy, letters and moral commentaries. These poems were lyrics on solitude, melancholy and similar themes.

1786 Scotland *Poems Chiefly in the Scottish Dialect* by Robert Burns (1759–1796). He wrote English verse in the already outworn Augustan tradition, but his best work was Scots, and included satire, narrative and love lyrics, written with warmth and vigour.

1786 Sweden Foundation of the Swedish Academy by King Gustav III, who encouraged literature, of which poetry was the only form which really fl. at that time.

1787 U.S.A. *The Vision of Columbus* by Joel Barlow (1754–1812), statesman and poet. The poem is an early patriotic epic.

1787 Mauritius *Paul et Virginie* by Jacques-Henri Bernardin de Saint-Pierre (1737–1814), a French government engineer and a disciple of Jean-Jacques Rousseau. He wrote novels which combined an admiration for nature and the simple life with the conviction that sentiment is superior to reason. The book foreshadowed Romantic fiction.

DANCE & DRAMA

1785 Czechoslovakia Františck Bulla, manager of the Prague theatre, was the first Czech to present plays in that language. He used the theatre to encourage the revival of a national culture which had been stifled for over 150 years by the Hapsburg rule.

1786 France The choreographer Jean Dauberval (1742–1806) created *La Fille Mal Gardée* at the Bordeaux Theatre. He had been driven from the Paris Opéra ballet, by opposition to his ideas, in 1783.

1786 Germany *Yaldut Ubahrut* by Menahem Mendel Bresselau (1760–1827), a Hebrew imitation of the work of Luzzatto. There was a revival of interest in Hebrew plays in the late eighteenth century as a result of the *Haskala* movement, which introduced Jews to the culture and learning of other nations while at the same time attempting to revive Jewish culture.

1787 France Debut of the actor François-Joseph Talma (1763–1826) at the Comédie Française. He was an ardent supporter of the French Revolution. In the theatre he introduced new ideas in costume, such as wearing a toga instead of modern dress in Roman parts, and used a natural speech delivery instead of the familiar declamatory style.

1787 Germany *Don Carlos* by Schiller.

1787 U.S.A. *The Contrast* by Royall Taylor (1757–1826), the first native American comedy for professionals, was produced in New York by the American Company led by Lewis Hallam Jnr (1740–1808) and John Henry (1738–1794).

MUSIC

1785 England The Caecilian Society was formed in London, where it continued until 1861. During this time it gave the only public performances of oratorios by George Frederick Handel and Franz Joseph Haydn.

1785 Italy Birth of Giovanni Ricordi (d. 1853) who founded a music-publishing house at Milan.

1785 Italy Niccolo Antonio Zingarelli (1752–1837), Italian composer, established at Milan.

1786 Austria First performance, in Vienna, of Mozart's *Le Nozze di Figaro*. It was highly acclaimed there, and in Prague where it was performed very shortly afterwards.

1786 Austria The opera *Una Cosa Rara* by Martin y Soler (1754–1806) the Spanish composer produced in Vienna. His first Italian opera was performed in Florence (1781).

1786 England Goulding & Company, the London music-publishing house, founded by George Goulding.

1786 England First complete edition of George Frederick Handel's works commenced by Samuel Arnold (1740–1802), organist, composer, conductor and musical editor.

1786 England Sir William Parsons (1746–1817) appointed Master of the King's Music.

1786 Germany Birth of Karl Almenräder (d. 1843), bassoonist, responsible for considerable improvements to the instrument.

1786 Germany Birth of Carl Maria Friedrich Ernst von Weber (d. 1826), German composer.

1786 Germany Birth of Iwan Müller, Russo-German clarinettist, (d. 1854); he made many improvements to the clarinet and wrote a method for it which is still used today.

1787 Czechoslovakia First performance, in Prague, of Mozart's opera, *Don Giovanni*.

1787 Germany Death of Christoph Willibald von Gluck, composer (b. 1714).

ARCHITECTURE

1785–1796 USA Virginia State Capitol by Thomas Jefferson and Benjamin Latrobe (1764–1820) was the first major public building in the USA built to resemble the Maison Carée at Nîmes, France, which Jefferson had seen.

1786 Norway Sr Fron Church, Gudbrandsal, by Svend Aspaas is an example of baroque architecture as interpreted in timber in Norway.

THREE DIMENSIONAL ART

1785 France Guillaume Benerman (d. after 1811) became master cabinet-maker: he was principal cabinet-maker to Louis XVI.

1786 U.S.A. Myer Myers (1723–1795) became chairman of the Gold and Silver Smith's Society; he worked mainly in New York and his most famous work was commissioned for the Newport Synagogue; his style reflected the transition from rococo to neo-classical.

1787 Italy Death of Vincenzo Belli (b. 1710), Roman goldsmith whose family continued to make fine gold and silverware for more than a century.

VISUAL ARTS

1786 England Death of Alexander Cozens (b. 1717), a landscape artist who composed from 'blots' of ink which suggested natural forms and ideal landscapes. His monochrome drawings use intense light and shade to convey atmosphere.

1786 England James Gillray (1757–1815) drew his cartoon *A New Way to Pay the National Debt*, a satire on the royal family, which established him as a popular caricaturist. He went further than Hogarth in his use of the grotesque to make personal, rather than general, criticisms.

1787–1784 Italy The English sculptor John Flaxman (1755–1826) studied antique art in Rome and drew illustrations to the *Iliad*, the *Odyssey*, Aeschylus and Dante. These were engraved and met with immediate success.

1787 England Robert Barker patented his 'Panorama', a cylindrical painted scene surrounding the audience and lit to produce a three-dimensional effect.

1787 Scotland Sir Henry Raeburn (1756–1823) became the leading portrait painter in Edinburgh. He painted in a strong, direct style that was mainly self-taught.

INVENTIONS & DISCOVERIES

1785 Matthew Boulton applied steam engine to cotton spinning.

1787 First ascent of Mont Blanc by Horace Saussure.

HISTORICAL EVENTS	LITERATURE	DANCE & DRAMA	MUSIC

HISTORICAL EVENTS

*1788
First British
penal settlement
founded at
Botany Bay,
Australia.*

*1789
George
Washington
inaugurated as
first President of
the U.S.A.
Outbreak of
French
Revolution.*

LITERATURE

1788–1792 Greece *Koray's Letters Written from Paris* by Adamantios Loraes (1748–1833), man of letters. Greek scholars and writers were at this time trying to find a language that could be used by all Greeks for all purposes. The choice was between classical (Church) and spoken (demotic) Greek. Koraës attempted a compromise between Church language and spoken Greek, but the result was too artificial.

1788 Hungary *Etelka* by András Dugonics (1740–1818), playwright, novelist and mathematician. He deplored foreign influences and tried to preserve the native traditions, especially dialects. This was the first popular novel in Hungarian.

1789 England *Songs of Innocence* by William Blake (1757–1827), mystic, painter and poet. He developed a private mythology which he wrote about in his symbolic later poems. He believed that all creation was one, however diverse the elements. Philosophically, he linked the tiger and the lamb; in his creative work, he linked poems and illustration as part of the same conception.

1790–1801 Russia *Letters of a Russian Traveller* by Nikolai Mikhaylovich Karamzin (1766–1826): the book is modelled on Sterne's *Sentimental Journey*. Karamzin based his prose on the colloquial speech of the Russian gentry, excluding all Church-Slavonic influences. Interest in his work created a Russian reading public.

1790 Hungary Translation of *Hamlet* into Hungarian by Ferenc Kazinczy (1759–1831). He began a reform of the language, and used his translations and his original verse to demonstrate the new standards. He wrote copious letters to other writers, discussing his ideas.

1790 India Sir William Jones published his translation of the Sanskrit drama *Shakuntala*. This was the first time the West had encountered Indian literature. The British in India made a study of local languages.

DANCE & DRAMA

1789 Australia *The Recruiting Officer* by Farquhar was performed in Sydney by convicts, the first recorded performance in Australia.

1789 Germany *Egmont* by Göethe.

1789 Germany *Menschanhass und Reue* by August Friedrich Ferdinand von Kotzebue (1761–1819): with a keen awareness of what the public really wanted, he kept them supplied with sensational melodramas. Göethe and Schiller disapproved of him, and of similar writers.

1789 India An English translation by Sir William Jones of the fifth-century drama *Shakuntala* aroused much Western interest in Sanskrit drama: the great period was from the third to eighth centuries A.D.

1790 France Retirement of the ballerina Madeline Guimard (1753–1816), leading dancer of her time, who danced in London in 1784–1786. She is thought to have worn an early version of the *maillot*, skin-coloured tights, which came into general use in the early nineteenth century.

MUSIC

1787 Scotland First volume of *The Scots Musical Museum* published by James Johnson (c.1750–1811), Scottish music engraver who for nearly 40 years had a monopoly of music engraving in Scotland.

1788 Austria Mozart wrote, in six weeks, his last three symphonies, in E flat, G minor and C (*Jupiter*).

1790 Mexico José María Aldana (c.1765–1810), composer, was made leader and director of the Coliseo orchestra.

ARCHITECTURE

1788 Sweden The Botanicum, Uppsala, by Jean-Louis Desprez (1743–1804) is unadorned neo-classicism by a French-trained architect.

England: design for garden of Aspley House by Humphrey Repton

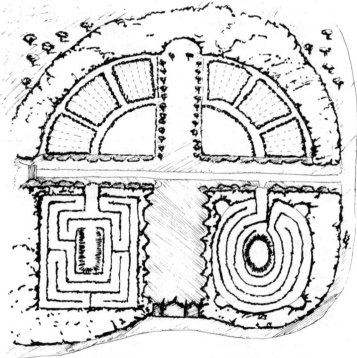

1790 USA Washington was planned by Pierre L'Enfant (1754–1825), a French engineer, on the scheme of a French hunting park.

THREE DIMENSIONAL ART

1788 U.S.A. Death of William Savery (b. 1721), cabinet-maker and carver of the Philadelphia school, noted for his elaborate ornament.

1788 England Humphrey Repton (1752–1818) began to practise as a landscape-gardener. His work was on lines derived from Lancelot Brown but on a smaller scale and with more details added to Brown's broad sweeps. In later life he returned to the formal terraces and beds of French style for the area immediately surrounding the house.

1790 Germany, Poland and Italy Appearance of the neo-classical style in metalwork, with subsequent shift of emphasis from wrought to cast iron. These countries had all had an exceptionally strong rococo tradition and the change came later than in France and England.

VISUAL ARTS

1788 Japan Kitagawa Utamaro (1753–1806) made a new departure in *Ukiyo-E* colour prints with his *Insects*, which exploited the accurate observation of Japanese naturalistic painting; he anticipated the work of Hokusai and Kiroshige in this respect, but was chiefly famous for depicting the world of women.

1789 England *Songs of Innocence* by William Blake (1757–1827) was the first of his major pieces of 'illuminated printing', with handwritten text and illustration engraved together as a decorative whole. Blake's choice of medium was part of his deliberate nonconformity.

1789 England Thomas Lawrence (1769–1830) was commissioned to paint Queen Charlotte. The portrait brought immediate success to this self-taught artist who was earlier considered a child prodigy. He became the most successful portrait painter of his day in England, bringing something of the romantic spirit to the eighteenth-century tradition.

INVENTIONS & DISCOVERIES

1789 Antoine Lavoisier produced first table of chemical elements.

HISTORICAL EVENTS

1791 Canada given representative government by British.

1792 Denmark became the first state to abolish Slave Trade.

LITERATURE

1790 Netherlands Collection of poems by Peter Joost de Borchgrave (1758–1819), Flemish poet and playwright. His best works were elegies and meditative lyrics which showed the beginnings of Romanticism. There was a dearth of Flemish literature in the eighteenth century, partly because French and not Flemish was used by the highly educated.

1790 Russia *Journey from Petersberg to Moscow* by Alexander Nikolayevich Radishchev (1749–1802), poet and prose writer. For writing this book, which was a bitter attack on autocracy and serfdom, he was exiled to Siberia.

1791 France *Justine, ou les Malheurs de la Vertu* by Donatien Alphonse François, Marquis de Sade (1740–1814), writer of erotic books. His work showed the eighteenth-century concern for individualism carried to extremes.

1791 Portugal *Idyllios Maritimos* by Manuel Maria Barbosa de Bocage (1765–1805), whose poetry treated of themes later developed by the Romantics— love, death and personal misfortunes.

1791 Scotland *The Life of Samuel Johnson* by James Boswell (1740–1795), lawyer and man of letters. This is considered one of the world's great biographies, keenly observed and minutely recorded. Boswell also wrote memoirs and kept a diary.

1792–1793 Denmark *Labyrinthen* by the poet Jens Immanuel Baggesen (1764–1826). Some of his poems are in German. He wrote in a variety of modes, humorous, sentimental, elegaic, and for a time embraced Romanticism. *Labyrinthen*, his only prose work, is a travel book, in the manner of Sterne.

1792 Bohemia *Gesichte Der Böhmischen Sprache und Litteratur* by Josef Dobrovský (1753–1829), a literary historian and philologist writing mainly in Latin or German. He wrote about the Czech language and literature of an earlier period, the 'golden age' of Veleslavin. Partly through his efforts, both language and literature began to revive after a long period of decline.

DANCE & DRAMA

1791 Hungary The first dramatic performance in Hungarian was given at Buda, with the support of the leaders of the Hungarian Nationalist movement, who were seeking to establish a native culture.

1792 France *Pamela* by François de Neufchâteau (1750–1828), caused a riot when performed at the Comédie Française because it contained anti-revolutionary sentiments. The company was imprisoned and the playhouse closed.

1792 France Introduction to Paris of the *carmagnole*, a short workman's coat from Carmagnola in Northern Italy, adopted by the revolutionary marchers from Marseilles: a contemporary round dance was named after it and associated with the revolution.

1792 Germany The Duke of Weimar gave entire responsibility for the Weimar court theatre to Göethe, who drew up rules for speech and gesture, insisting that the actor should always be aware of his audience. The stage setting and group playing improved under Göethe, but his rigid application of his own rules led to stilted though well-drilled acting.

MUSIC

1791 Austria Death of Wolfgang Amadeus Mozart (b. 1756), composer. His last opera, *Die Zauberflöte*, had its first performance two months before his death. The *Requiem* was left unfinished.

1791 England Franz Joseph Haydn visited London and remained for 18 months. His second visit was in 1794 when he stayed for 20 months.

1791 France Birth of Ferdinand Hérold (d. 1833), composer.

1791 Germany Birth of Giacomo Jakob Liebmann Beer Meyerbeer (d. 1864), composer.

1792 Austria Johann Georg Albrechtsberger (1736–1809), organist, composer and teacher, became director of music at St Stephen's Cathedral, Vienna. He was a famous contrapuntist, whose pupils included Beethoven, Hummel, Weigl, Scyfried, Eybler and Mosel.

1792 Austria Ludwig van Beethoven living in Vienna where his first music was published.

1792 Italy Birth of Gioacchino Antonio Rossini, Italian composer. (d. 1868).

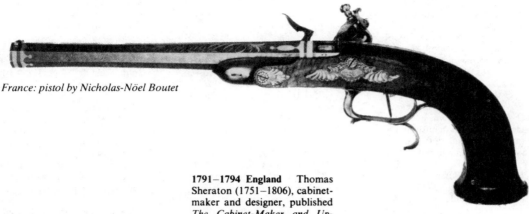

France: pistol by Nicholas-Nöel Boutet

1791–1794 England Thomas Sheraton (1751–1806), cabinet-maker and designer, published *The Cabinet-Maker and Upholsterer's Drawing Book*: this provided a summary of fashionable taste with advice on technical matters and was a source for cabinet-makers in Britain and the U.S.A. Like his later books of 1803 and 1805, it presented styles already popular, not styles which he had originated himself.

1791–1802 England Printer William Bulmer (fl. 1791–1819) printed Boydell's *Shakespeare* in 'modern face', a type similar to that of Bodoni; it became a fashion which lasted for nearly 50 years.

1791 Mexico Spanish sculptor Manuel Tolsa (1757–1816) worked in Mexico: he became a leader of neo-classical reaction against the extravagant Mexican style; typical is his bronze equestrian statue of Charles IV (1803).

1792–1867 USA The Capitol, Washington, by William Thornton (1759–1828) and others was originally Palladian in character; it was enlarged by the addition of the iron dome and the north and south wings in between 1851 and 1867.

1792 England Silversmith Paul Storr (1771–1844) began working in London: he was noted for elaborate presentation pieces such as the Battle of the Nile Cup presented to Lord Nelson; his style was neo-classical.

1792 France Nicholas-Noël Boutet (1761–1833) was made technical director of the state arms factory: he was an artist-gunsmith specializing in decorated swords and fire-arms, and made many pieces for Napoleon I.

1792 Russia The state glass factory and the state porcelain factory amalgamated; they used similar techniques in decorating porcelain and opaline glass.

1792 U.S.A. Gilbert Stuart (1755–1828) painted 124 portraits of George Washington; he established an American school of classical portraiture.

1791
Ordnance Survey established in Britain.

1792
Cable-making machine invented.

LITERATURE

1792 China *Hung Lou Meng*, a novel by the Chinese writer Ts'ao Chan (1715–1763): based on his own family experiences, it was unfinished at his death, and 40 of its 120 chapters were added by Kao 0. The book had considerable influence on modern vernacular literature.

1792 Netherlands Dialogues, after the manner of those in the *Spectator*, by Karel Broeckaert (1767–1826), Flemish writer. He believed that man should be rational, liberal and cosmopolitan, i.e. enlightened.

1793 Italy *Bassvilliana* by Vincenzo Monti (1754–1828), prose-writer and poet. His verse was topical in content but classical in form. This was a poem on the French Revolution in Dante's *terza rima*.

1794 England *The Mysteries of Udolpho* by Mrs Ann Radcliffe (1764–1823), poet and novelist, the most distinguished exponent of the Gothic novel.

1794 France Death of André Chénier (b. 1762), whose poetry was Greek in form and spirit and struck a genuinely personal note. After his death (he was guillotined in the Terror) he was appreciated by the Romantics.

1796 England *The Monk* by Matthew Gregory Lewis (1775–1818), diplomat and Gothic novelist; he was called 'Monk' Lewis, as a result of the popularity of his book.

1796 Germany August Wilhelm von Schlegel (1767–1845) and his brother Freidrich (1772–1829), critics and orientalists, established themselves in Jena, where they became the centre of the early Romantic movement. They believed that poetry was a force that pervaded all life. Neither brother was especially creative, but they provided the ideas and stimulated others to write, August Wilhelm translated Shakespeare, and both brothers helped to arouse interest in oriental literatures. Madame de Staël, greatly impressed by the brothers' theories, passed them on to the rest of Europe.

DANCE & DRAMA

1794 England John Philip Kemble's revival of *Macbeth* had sets by William Capon (1757–1827), who led the trend towards historical accuracy in settings by basing his designs on historical documents.

1794 Poland *The Miracle* by Wojciech Boguslawski (1757–1829): in effect, he was the founder of the Polish theatre. As well as writing plays himself, he encouraged other playwrights, financed and built theatres, and directed actors. A theatre in Warsaw, opened 1902, is named after him.

1794 U.S.A. Thomas Wignell (1753–1802), former leading man with the American Company, began work at the Chestnut Street theatre, Philadelphia. This theatre was modelled on the Theatre Royal at Bath in England; it seated 2000 people and had a well-equipped stage. Its construction marks a great step forward in the history of the American theatre.

1795 India The first theatre for Bengali plays was opened in Calcutta.

1796 England The French dancer and choreographer Charles Didelot (1767–1836) created *Zéphire et Flore*, his most famous ballet. He brought together the teachings of his own masters, Noverre, Dauberval and Auguste Vestris (1760–1842), to produce a *ballet d'action* with comedy, expressed in pure dance without additional mime.

MUSIC

1793 Austria Ludwig van Beethoven studied under Johann Schenk, composer and theorist, and Antonio Salieri, court *Kapellmeister*.

1794 England London debut of John Field (1782–1837), Irish pianist and composer.

1794 France Pierre Gaviniès (1728–1800), French violinist and composer, was appointed first professor of violin playing at the newly opened Paris Conservatoire; he was one of the founders of the great French school of violinists.

1794 Germany Ibach & Sons, pianoforte makers, was founded; the English branch was founded in 1880.

1794 Italy Performance of the first opera by Simone Johann Simon Mayr (1763–1845), Italian composer of German origin. He wrote 61 operas and is said to have been the first to introduce the *crescendo* of orchestra into opera.

1794 U.S.A. First performance in New York of *Tammanny or The Indian Chief*, one of earliest original American operas, by James Hewitt (1770–1827), American (English-born) violinist and composer.

1795 England Publication of *A Concerto for the Harpsichord or Pianoforte* by Thomas Wright (1763–1829). This was probably first music to contain metronome marks, based on his invention of a simple pocket metronome.

1795 France Conservatoire de Musique established in Paris.

1796 France A *Nouvelle Méthode pour la Clarinette* was published by Matthieu Frédéric Blasius (1758–1829), the French composer, who was a professor of wind instruments at the Paris Conservatoire.

1796 U.S.A. *The Archers* by Benjamin Carr (1768–1831), American (English-born) composer and music publisher, performed in New York.

*1795
Directory in
France.*

Australia: 'Government House', Sydney, by Thomas Watling

1795 England Sir Charles Barry born (died 1860), a prolific early Victorian architect in the neo-Renaissance style based on fifteenth-century (Travellers' Club, London) and sixteenth-century (Reform Club, London) models.

1796–1807 England Fonthill Abbey by James Wyatt (1746–1813), the most exotic of all Gothic buildings, collapsed in 1825; Wyatt was equally conversant with the classical style.

c.1794 U.S.A. John Seymour, cabinet-maker in the classical style, began work in Boston: he was considered the outstanding designer and maker of furniture in his day in New England.

1796 Russia Pyotr Korobov set up a factory near Moscow, with imported German craftsmen, to make lacquered boxes: this lacquer-work had formerly been produced in Siberia but was unknown in western Russia.

1793 France Establishment of the Louvre as a public art gallery. The painter Georges Michel (1763–1843) worked there as a restorer, which brought him into contact with Dutch landscape painting of the seventeenth and eighteenth centuries; in them he found a style sympathetic to the portrayal of northern France. Classical landscape painters needed exotic scenery and Italianate buildings for their effects. The northern French and English landscape artists found the Dutch a more congenial model, and applied their influence to local material. The journey to Italy was no longer considered an essential part of an artist's training. Michel was one of the first to paint landscapes in the open air; in this respect he is considered a forerunner of Theodore Rousseau and the Barbizon school.

1794–1796 Japan Utagawa Toyokuni (1769–1825), print designer, made a series of *Stage Representations of Actors*, which is considered his finest work. He led the *Utagawa* school of print-making and was the last of the great artists of *Ukiyo-E* prints.

1794–1797 Spain Francisco Goya (1746–1828) painted portraits, notably that of the actress La Tirana, that were influenced by the style and colouring of Velazquez. He had been made court painter in 1789, but his earlier portraits were in a more formal style influenced by Mengs.

1794 Australia Thomas Watling (1762–*c*.1810) painted the first Australian landscape in oils, *Sydney*.

1795 Japan Death of Maruyama Okyo (b. 1733), a painter who combined Chinese techniques of bird and flower painting with European sketching techniques. His school lasted through the nineteenth century. He was much influenced by the similar work of Shen Nan-p'in, a Chinese artist who worked in Nagasaki 1731–1733.

1796 England Joseph Mallord William Turner (1775–1851) exhibited his first work in oils, *Fishermen at Sea*, a romantic adaptation of the Dutch marine tradition. His previous work consisted of watercolours and topographical drawings.

1794 Eli Whitney invented cotton gin.

1795 Mungo Park explored West Africa and the River Niger. Theory of the Earth by James Hutton outlined new science of geology.

1796 Edward Jenner introduced smallpox vaccination.

1797 Austria Birth of Franz Peter Schubert (d. 1828), composer.

1797 Hungary Birth of Gábor Mátray, Hungarian critic, musicologist and composer (d. 1875); one of the most important figures of his time, he was called 'father of Hungarian musicology'.

1797 Italy Birth of Domenico Gaetano Maria Donizetti (d. 1848), Italian composer of opera.

1798 England *Lyrical Ballads*, a collection of poems by William Wordsworth (1770–1850) and Samuel Taylor Coleridge (1772–1834). Coleridge's contribution was the supernatural treated realistically; Wordsworth wrote on commonplace themes, making them moving and poetic. The poems they produced were in complete contrast to the previous tradition, and the book is usually taken to mark the beginning of the Romantic movement in England.

1798 Russia *Iaropolk and Oleg* by Vladislav Alexandrovich Ozerov (1770–1816). The Russian theatre at this time was completely under Imperial control. Ozerov's plays show a strong French neo-classical influence.

1798 U.S.A. *As You Like It* by Shakespeare, performed at the newly-built Park Theatre, New York, by a company led by William Dunlap (1766–1839). Also in their repertoire was *Andre* by Dunlap himself; it was considered the first American tragedy.

1798 France *Méthode ou Principe Général du Doigté* by Johann Ludwig Adam (1758–1848), Alsatian pianist, teacher and composer, was published in Paris; this was the first of several books by Adam which were important in the development of pianoforte technique.

1798 Germany Ludwig Spohr (1784–1859) made his first tour as a violinist; he was one of finest performers of all time.

1799 Napoleon Bonaparte supreme in France.

1799 China Death of the emperor Ch'ien Lung (b. 1711). He was a writer and patron of the arts. In addition, he exercised censorship of political material.

1799 Spain Collection of poems of Juan Valdes Meléndez (1754–1817). He wrote a wide variety of love and country poems, philosophical works and early Romantic verse. He was remarkable for his delicacy, musicality and wealth of imagery.

1799 Austria First public performance of *The Creation* by Haydn at Vienna.

ARCHITECTURE

1797 Germany Friedrich Gilly's (1772–1800) monument to Frederick the Great was influenced perhaps by the novel classicism of Soane, Ledoux and Boullée; Gilly died young but his major projects were influential.

1798 USA Bank of Pennsylvania, Philadelphia, by Benjamin Latrobe is the first marble Greek Revival building in the USA; it has since been destroyed.

1799 USA Sedgley, Philadelphia, by Benjamin Latrobe is the earliest Gothic revival house in America.

THREE DIMENSIONAL ART

VISUAL ARTS

1797–1804 England Thomas Bewick (1755–1828) published *A History of British Birds*, one of four books with engraved illustrations which he produced between 1784 and 1804 and which are considered his best work. Bewick revived creative wood-engraving in England; his work has strongly influenced modern engravers. He is most famous for his vignettes, miniatures of rural life.

1797 England Death of John Cozens (b. 1752), who was considered the most successful landscape painter in the 'picturesque' style; he exploited the subdued colours of English landscape to poetic effect, and his drawings were admired by Girtin, Turner and Constable.

1798 Scotland Death of Gavin Hamilton (b. 1723), painter and antiquarian; his own paintings were disseminated widely through engravings, and he was influential on neo-classical artists, including Canova and David, as well as on the development of historical painting in Britain.

1799 Spain *Los Caprichos*, a series of prints by Francisco Goya (1746–1828), almost the only great artist of his time to use the aquatint; he was not imitated in this until the Impressionists did so in the late nineteenth century.

INVENTIONS & DISCOVERIES

1798 Herschel discovered infra red band of the spectrum.

England: 'The Peacock' by Thomas Bewick from 'A History of British Birds'

19th Century

HISTORICAL EVENTS

1800
Act of Union united Parliaments of England and Ireland.

1801
Tsar Paul I of Russia assassinated.

1804
Bonaparte crowned Emperor Napoleon I.

LITERATURE

1800 Germany *Hymnen and Die Nacht* by the poet Friedrich Leopold von Hardenberg, called Novalis (1772–1801). Probably the most romantic of all the Romantics, he symbolized their yearnings as 'the blue flower'. This poem expressed another German Romantic idea, the death wish.

1800 India John Gilchrist, principal of the newly-founded college at Fort William, compiled the first Urdu grammar and dictionary. This made possible the translation of foreign literature into Urdu.

1801 India William Carey, protestant missionary, printed his *New Testament* translated into Bengali, on his own printing press. He also translated the Sanskrit classics into Bengali, and printed the first Bengali newspaper.

1802 Denmark *Guldhornene* by Adam Gottlob Oehlenschlager (1779–1850), poet and playwright, leader of the Romantic movement: He used old Norse legends and medieval ballads as a source of inspiration.

1802 France *René* by François René de Chateaubriand (1768–1848) was a short autobiographical novel which was regarded as introducing the romantic hero into French novels. It originally formed part of a volume on Catholicism, *Le Génie du Christianisme*; the author attempted to link the revival of literature with Christian instead of classical sources.

1802 Russia Gray's *Elegy in a Country Churchyard* was translated into Russian by the poet Vasily Andreyevich Zhukovsky (1783–1852). His contribution to Russian literature was to introduce, through his translations, the work of great English and German writers. He also wrote musical lyrics of unrequited love, as well as ballads and folk narratives.

1803 Germany *Alemmanische Gedichte* by Johann Peter Hebel (1760–1826), a poet using the Alemannic dialect. He aimed at a simple readership with work that re-created the atmosphere of his youth. He began a trend for dialect writing.

DANCE & DRAMA

1800 France *Coelina, ou L'Enfant de Mystère* by René Charles Guilbert de Pixérécourt (1773–1844). He was the first writer to use the word 'melodrama' in its modern sense, in his manifesto *Le Mélodrama*. He claimed to write for those who could not read, and his plays call for spectacular effects. His work was widely translated.

*c.***1800 Burma** The government laid down rules controlling the theatre, to ensure that live and puppet performances were respectful to the King and the Buddhist religion. In fact the theatre became a political force; a noted play, *Wizaya* by U Pon Nya, was written to incite support for a usurper.

1801–1811 Russia The French dancer and choreographer Charles Didelot went to St Petersburg, where he concentrated on teaching a new generation of dancers.

1802 England The play *A Tale of Mystery* by Thomas Holcroft (1774–1809), an unacknowledged adaptation of Pixérécourt, performed at Covent Garden: this was the first melodrama seen in England. At that time Covent Garden and Drury Lane were still the only two theatres in London with licences for the performance of legitimate drama. They were huge, so that subtlety of acting and naturalism of style and setting were impossible. Spectacle and melodrama, which was mainly action, flourished.

1802 France Death of Marie Allard (b.1742), noted ballerina.

1802 India The British established their influence in what later became the Bombay presidency. Their relations with native rulers at this time inspired a famous historical play, *Bhau Bandki*, written some 50 years afterwards. It is still popular and contains a strong rôle for a 'virago' actress. This has been played with great success by Durga Khote, whose theatre work in Maharashtra pioneered appearances by women without social criticism.

1803 France The Comédie Française was re-formed.

1803 Transylvania Foundation of the National Theatre.

MUSIC

1800 Arabia Birth of Mikhá'il ibn Jurjís al-Lubnání Musháqa, musical theorist and writer (d. 1888), the most important modern Arabic writer on theory of music.

1800 Austria Performance of the first symphony of Ludwig van Beethoven (1770–1827).

1800 Germany First compositions by Carl Maria Ernst von Weber (1786–1826) included works for piano. In the same year, at Freiburg, he wrote his first opera *Das Waldmädchen*.

1800 Germany The Aeolodion, a keyed wind instrument, is said to have been invented by J. T. Eschenbach of Hamburg. It was subsequently modified by various other mechanicians and eventually superseded by the harmonium.

*c.***1800 Wales** Revival of National Eisteddfod.

1801 Austria Birth of Josef Franz Karl Lanner (d. 1843), violinist and dance composer; he was a contemporary of Johann Strauss senior, and helped lay the foundation of the Viennese waltz.

1801 Italy Birth of Giuseppe Concone (d. 1861), singingmaster, pianist and composer; his singing exercises are still used today.

1802 Austria Ludwig van Beethoven wrote his suicidal *Heiligenstadt Testament*.

1802 France *Traité d'Harmonie* published by Charles-Simon Catel (1773–1830), composer.

1802 Germany *Uber J. S. Bachs Leben, Kunst und Kunstwerke*, first biography of Johann Sebastian Bach (1685–1750) by Johann Nicolaus Forkel (1749–1818). The book has served as a model for all subsequent books on Bach.

1803 France The *Prix de Rome* first awarded for music.

1803 France Birth of Hector Berlioz (d. 1869), composer.

1804 Austria Adalbert Gyrowetz (1769–1850), appointed *Kapellmeister* at Vienna; he was one of most prolific nineteenth century composers.

ARCHITECTURE

1801–1811 Russia Cathedral of the Virgin of Kazan, St Petersburg, by Andrea Voronikhin (1760–1814) is a typical high imperial Russian building of the nineteenth century, modelled on St Peter's, Rome.

1802 France Malmaison by Charles Percier (1764–1838) and P. F. L. Fontaine (1762–1853) was built for Napoleon and is characteristic of the decorative Empire style of which the two architects were the leading exponents.

1802 France *Précis et leçons d'architecture* was published in two volumes by J. N. L. Durand (1760–1834): he advocated functional rationalism in architecture and the work was very influential in nineteenth-century France and Germany.

1803 England Sezincote, Gloucestershire, by Samuel P. Cockerell (1754–1827) was an early example of the briefly fashionable Indian style, applied here to a country house.

1804 France Chaux Ideal City was designed by Claude Ledoux, but not executed; notable is the fact that some buildings were reduced to such pure architectural forms as spheres and cylinders.

1804–1824 Germany Karlsruhe was rebuilt by Freidrich Weinbrenner (1766–1826), it is neo-clasical urban planning in which the Marktplatz has a focal accent provided by a central pyramid between similar but not identical façades.

1804–1816 Russia The Exchange, St Petersburg, by Thomas de Thomon (1754–1813), a French architect who worked for the Tsar, is a major monument of neo-Classicism.

1804 USA Baltimore Catholic Church by Benjamin Latrobe is a fine domed Romantic classical building; he had originally produced an alternative Gothic design for the church.

THREE DIMENSIONAL ART

early 1800–1900 Canada French silversmiths arriving after the French Revolution settled in Quebec which became an important centre of silversmithing: unlike the earlier Huguenot immigrants to America, they were Catholic and most of their work was ecclesiastical.

1800–1900 Russia Figurines in pottery were made at Radonezh, Viatka and Okhta; those from the last two centres were comedy and caricature figures.

1800–1805 Brazil Life-size statue group, the *Twelve Prophets* by António Francisco Lisboa (c.1738–1814), sculptor and architect: he worked in rococo style and, despite paralysis, was considered the most important sculptor in colonial Brazil.

1800 England Beginning of Josiah Spode II's period at Spode's Stoke-on-Trent porcelain factory; he finally formulated the bone-china recipe (hard-paste porcelain modified by the addition of bone-ash).

*c.*1800 **England** Development of gold, silver and copper lustre ware pottery.

1802–1803 Italy The Danish sculptor Bertel Thorwaldson (1768–1884) made his first successful statue, *Jason*, in Rome. He was recognised in his lifetime as the second greatest neo-classical sculptor (after Canova) and as an authority on Greek classical art. His style is considered either supremely noble or excessively cold.

1803 France Death of Jean-Baptiste-Claude Sené (b. 1748), considered the most important chair-maker in his day after Georges Jacob (1739–1814), whom he followed in adopting mahogany and lyre-back forms from the English fashion.

1804–1805 U.S.A. The Gardner-White Pingree house at Salem, Massachusetts was decorated by the wood-carver and architect Samuel McIntire (1757–1811): he was considered the best of the craftsmen-carpenters of New England.

VISUAL ARTS

1800–1900 Europe Magic lanterns were equipped with 'limelights': cylinders of lime heated by an oxyhydrogen flame.

1800–1820 England John Crome (1768–1821) painted his more important large pictures. He and Cotman were considered the major artists of the Norwich school of landscape painting. His pictures of *Slate Quarries*, *Moonrise on the Marshes of the Yare*, *Mousehold Heath* and *Poringland Oak* showed a feeling for the 'spirit of place' which foreshadowed the Romantics.

1801–1804 England Thomas Milton (1743–1827) engraver, published three folios of aquatints; *Views* in Egypt, the Ottoman Empire and Palestine, by Luigi Mayer (d. 1803). English artists and architects were inspired by their imagery.

1801 Japan Death of Sharaku, portrait artist of actors and himself an actor of *Nō* plays. His prints were admired outside Japan for their eccentricity, psychological penetration and qualities of caricature.

1802–1807 France Jacques-Louis David (1748–1825) painted a series of pictures celebrating the achievements of Napoleon. The austerity of his earlier work was here replaced by a more theatrical quality.

1802 England Death of Thomas Girtin (b. 1775), a landscape painter whose watercolour technique was considered revolutionary. He used strong colours in broad washes, painting with the colour in a manner that foreshadowed nineteenth-century style. Watercolour in his own time was conventionally used to tint drawings.

1802 France Following Napoleon's Egyptian campaign of 1798, D.-V. Denon published *Voyage dans la Haute et dans la Basse Égypte*, providing a large collection of illustrated Egyptian motifs to be used in fashionable Western design.

1804 England Death of George Morland (b. 1763), a painter who helped to establish the rough side of country life as part of the artist's repertory. He had much in common with Julius Caesar Ibbetson (1769–1817) in this respect.

1800
Joseph Marie Jacquard invented a punch card loom. Alessandro Volta identified steady electric current.

1802
John Dalton outlined his atomic theory. Johann Ritter discovered ultra violet rays.

1803
Thomas Young proposed wave theory of light.

HISTORICAL EVENTS	LITERATURE	DANCE & DRAMA	MUSIC

1804 Austria First performance of Beethoven's 3rd symphony (*Eroica*) a work unprecedented in its length and the size of its orchestra.

1805 Battles of Trafalgar and Austerlitz.

1805 Spain *Ode To Trafalgar* by Manuel José Quintana (1772–1857), statesman, critic and poet. Unaffected by the Romantic movement, he wrote neo-classical verse on progress, liberty, and patriotic themes. His poetry was majestic and vigorous, and regarded as the model of nineteenth-century Spanish neo-classicism, which dealt with large themes, unlike the more personal poetry of the eighteenth century.

1805 U.S.A. John Jacob Astor and John K. Beekman bought William Dunlap's Park Theatre. They introduced 'stars' to play for short seasons, which began the break-up of the stock company.

1805 Austria First published work by Karl Czerny (1791–1857), pianist, teacher and composer, who wrote a vast amount of teaching music, his best being *Complete Theoretical and Practical Pianoforte School*.

1805 France Birth of Adrien Lenoir de la Fage (d. 1862), composer and writer on music; he was a notable historian and published many valuable works.

1805 France Charles Simon Richault (1780–1866), music publisher, established in Paris. He was first to publish Beethoven's symphonies, Mozart's concertos, and works by Bach, Handel, Schubert, Schumann and Mendelssohn.

1806 Bonaparte abolished Holy Roman Empire.

1806–1808 Germany *Des Knaben Wunderhorn*, a collection of German folk-songs by Ludwig Joachim von Arnim (1781–1831) and Clemens Maria Brentane (1778–1842). The book drew the attention of German writers to a rich folk tradition which they had hitherto ignored, and had considerable influence on the development of lyric poetry.

1806 France Death of the dancer and ballet-master Jean Dauberval (b. 1742), pupil of Noverre: he worked with Noverre and Gaetan Vestris at Stuttgart, and was considered one of the best contemporary choreographers.

1806 Spain *El Side Las Niñas* by Leandro Fernando de Moratin (1760–1828), a neo-classical playwright who greatly admired Molière.

1805 Italy Death of Luigi Boccherini (b. 1743), a violoncellist and prolific composer of cello concerti of which the one in B-flat is the best known.

1806 Italy *De' Sepolcri*, an ode by Niccolo (Uge) Foscola (1778–1837), expressing his philosophy of life and death; it was inspired by a decree of Napoleon concerning the burial of the dead in cemeteries at some distance from dwelling areas. Basically optimistic, the poem was his masterpiece. His poetry was neo-classical.

1807 France Jean-Georges (1727–1809) published *Lettres sur les Arts imitateurs en général et sur la Danse en particulier*, second of his treatises on ballet. He did much to free the art from the inherited conventions of court entertainment, in subject and technique.

1806 Poland Birth of Michal Jozef Guzikow (d. 1837), xylophone player who was regarded as one of the greatest virtuosi in the world.

1807 Treaty of Tilsit between France and Russia.

1807 France Pleyel & Company, pianoforte makers, established in Paris by Ignaz Pleyel.

1808 The United States prohibited import of slaves from Africa.

1808 Denmark *Maskeradeballet I Danmark* by Nikolai Frederik Severin Grundtvig (1783–1872), historian, educationist, linguistic scholar and poet. His most remarkable works were hymns and visionary poems.

1808 Germany Publication of part I of Göethe's *Faust*.

1808 Germany Death of Anna Heinel (b.1752), noted ballerina.

1808 Austria First performance of Beethoven's 5th symphony. He was already engaged in writing the 6th.

1808 Germany *Der Zerbrochene Krug* by Heinrich von Kleist (1777–1811), a German playwright who combined a Sophoclean conception of fate with Shakespearian drama of character.

1808 Germany *Méthode de Premier et de Second Cor* published by Heinrich Domnich (b. 1767), horn player; even today this tutor is only surpassed by that of Louis François Dauprat (1781–1868).

1809 Russia A collection of fables by Ivan Andreyevich Krylov (1768–1844), journalist, critic and playwright. He began by translating the works of La Fontaine, but later wrote his own fables, satirizing in particular the bureaucracy. He used colloquial language and idioms.

1808 U.S.A. *The Indian Princess* by James Nelson Barber (1784–1858), the first American play about Indian life; it concerns Pocohontas.

1809 Austria Death of Franz Joseph Haydn (b. 1732), composer.

1809 Germany Birth of Fredrik Pacius (d. 1891), Finnish (naturalized) composer, regarded as the father of Finnish music.

1809 Sweden *Uno von Thrazenberg* by Fredrick Cederborgh (1784–1835), novelist and playwright. The work was the first humorous/realistic novel in Sweden.

1809 Germany Birth of Felix (Bartholdy) Mendelssohn (d. 1847), German composer, pianist, organist and conductor.

| ARCHITECTURE | THREE DIMENSIONAL ART | VISUAL ARTS | INVENTIONS & DISCOVERIES |

1804 U.S.A. *The Rising of a Thunderstorm at Sea* by Washington Allston (1779–1843) typified his romantic style in landscape painting.

1805 France Halle aux Blé, Paris, by François Bélanger is probably the earliest example of a large iron-framed building in France but some time elapsed before iron as a building material was accepted in France.

1805 Canada Death of the woodcarver Jean Baillairgé (b. 1726), founder of a family of woodcarvers noted for their vigorous adaptation of European styles.

1805 France Jean Auguste Ingres (1780–1867) painted *Bonaparte as First Consul*. He trained under David and became portraitist and decorative painter in classical style. His early portraits were noted for their line.

1805 First factory to be lit by gas, in Manchester.

France: Halle aux Blè, Paris, by François Bélanger

1806–1811 England Downing College, Cambridge, by William Wilkins (1778–1839) is a pioneer work in the Greek revival style in England.

1806 France Arc de Triomphe, Paris, by Jean F. Chalgrin (1739–1811) is monumental neo-Classicism with later nineteenth-century, sculpture adorning it.

1806–1842 France La Madeleine, Paris, by Pierre Vignon (1762–1828) and others is an octostyle peripteral Roman Corinthian temple intended as a memorial to the Napoleonic army; it is top-lit by three saucer domes.

1806–1815 Russia The Admiralty, St Petersburg, by Adrian Zakharov (1761–1811) is a monumental neo-classical building with a façade about 400 m long by the greatest nineteenth-century architects.

1807 Italy The royal palace, Caserta, was decorated by Antonio de Simone. The Sala di Marte and Sala di Astrea are two fine examples of the Napoleonic Empire style outside France.

1808–1829 Denmark The Vor Frue Kirke, Copenhagen, was rebuilt by Christian Hansen (1756–1845). and is the best work by this neo-classical architect; it is notable for the great coffered barrel vault over the nave.

1806 England John Sell Cotman (1782–1842) settled in Norwich. Together with John Crome he became the most important artist of the Norwich school. He was noted for watercolour landscapes of classical structure and broad, flat colourwashes, and for his architectural etchings which he began c.1810.

1806 England *Fighting Horses* by James Ward (1769–1859) was typical of his romantic animal studies, the wildness and energy of which inspired the French romantic school. Ward also painted landscapes with dramatic effects of light and scale.

1806 France Antoine-Jean Gros (1771–1835) painted *The Battle of Aboukir*, as official war artist to the Napoleonic army. He was leader of the classical school after David, but his emotional response to his subjects made him nearer to the Romantics in spirit.

1806 Sir Francis Beaufort designed scale to indicate wind strength.

1808 Dalton first applied atomic theory to chemistry.

1808 U.S.A. Bakewell and Company (Bakewell and Page) of Pittsburgh, glassmakers, began production: they were considered the finest makers of cut and engraved glass.

1809 U.S.A. Binny and Ronaldson set up as type-founders in Philadelphia: before this date American printers used English materials.

1806 Scotland Sir David Wilkie (1785–1841) gained immediate popularity on exhibiting his first anecdotal pictures of village life.

1808 Germany First oil paintings by Caspar David Friedrich (1774–1840), romantic artist: his landscapes and seascapes attracted great attention because of their spiritual content and strong atmosphere.

1809 England Death of Paul Sandby (b. 1725/6), thought to have been the first English artist to use aquatint. Gainsborough said he was the only one to paint actual views from nature.

HISTORICAL EVENTS	LITERATURE	DANCE & DRAMA	MUSIC

HISTORICAL EVENTS

1810
Buenos Aires, Chile and Mexico overthrew Spanish rule.

1812
French invasion of Russia; retreat from Moscow.

LITERATURE

1810 France *De L'Allemagne* by Germaine Necker, Madame de Staël (1766–1817), literary critic and novelist. Widely travelled, she introduced German idealism to the French literary scene and paved the way for the Romantic movement. Her novels were feminist in tone, anticipating Georges Sand.

1810 Germany *Die Marquise von O.* by Heinrich von Kleist (1777–1811), short-story writer and playwright. He was mentally unstable, often morbid and his stories combine horrific subject matter with a dry objective style.

1810 Sweden Foundation of *Phosphorus*, a periodical which was a vehicle for the new Romantics, who called themselves the Fosforister. Their leader was Daniel Amadeus Atterbom (1790–1855), who demanded a return to 'pure' poetry.

1811 Iceland Bjarni Vigfusson Thorarensen (1786–1841), champion of the Romantic movement, published his poems. His output, which was small, included love poems, satire, nature and patriotic poems.

1811 Slovenia Valentin Vodnik (1758–1819), educationist and poet, wrote a poem dedicated to the Illyrian state established by Napoleon. He worked to develop Slovene as a literary language.

1812–1813 Germany *Fairy Tales* by the brothers Grimm: Jakob (1778–1865) and Wilhelm (1787–1859). Jakob was a philologist of repute and also wrote a German grammar and a study of Teutonic legends. The brothers collaborated on a lexicon. Their *Fairy Tales* are perhaps the best-known piece of German literature outside that country.

1813 England *Pride and Prejudice*, a novel by Jane Austen (1775–1817). The scope of her work was limited, by her own choice, to portraying relationships in small communities. She satirized contemporary fashions in literature, basing her own novels on probable events and good sense. She reflects the attitudes of the eighteenth rather than the nineteenth century.

DANCE & DRAMA

1810–1825 England Thomas Wilson, dancing master from the King's Theatre Opera House, published textbooks on eighteenth-century dances. Dancing was the popular amusement after the Napoleonic wars.

1810 Russia Death of Maria Danilova (b.1793), a young dancer of the St Petersburg school who was considered outstanding and celebrated by the poets of her time.

1811 England A London stationer issued the first English Toy Theatre sheets at 'a penny plain, tuppence coloured'. These were cut-outs, mounted on cardboard, and representing scenes from popular productions of the day. They may have originally been intended as souvenirs but soon became popular as children's toys.

1812 England Shakespeare's *King Lear* was performed with songs and incidental music at the Surrey Theatre, London. The addition of music to straight plays was common as they thus became technically 'burlettas' and could be performed at unlicensed theatres.

1812 France Napoleon drew up a new constitution for the Comédie Française. He encouraged the theatre. The celebrated actress Mlle George was one of his mistresses.

1812 Italy Salvatore Vigano (1769–1821) was appointed ballet-master at La Scala, Milan. Of independent means, he was able to carry out his own ideas regardless of pressure from the season-ticket holders and internal intrigue. He achieved a much greater synthesis between dancing and mime and a choreography in which every movement harmonized.

1813 England John Howard Payne (1791–1852) the first American actor to perform in England, appeared at Drury Lane. (In 1815 he was at the Comédie Française.)

MUSIC

1810 Germany Birth of Robert Alexander Schumann (d. 1856), German composer.

1810 Poland Birth of Fryderyk Franciszek Chopin (d. 1849), Polish pianist and composer of French descent, noted above all for the brilliance of his compositions for the piano.

1811 England Novello & Company, music publishers, founded by Vincent Novello (1781–1861) in London.

1811 England Chappell & Company, music publishers, and later pianoforte makers, established in London.

1811 France Birth of Aristide Cavaillé-Coll (d. 1899), organ builder who built the organs in Notre-Dame, Saint-Sulpice, Madeleine and Sainte-Clotilde.

1811 Hungary Birth of Ferencz (Franz) Liszt (d. 1866), Hungarian pianist and composer.

1811 Ireland Johann Bernhard Logier (1777–1846), German pianist, teacher and composer, established his business in Dublin. He invented the chiroplast, a mechanism for training the hands for pianoforte-playing.

1812 Austria Beethoven wrote his 7th and 8th symphonies.

1812 Germany Birth of Friedrich von Flotow (d. 1883), composer.

1812 Germany Production in Munich of the opera *Jephthas Gelübde* by Giacomo Meyerbeer (1791–1864).

1813 England The Royal Philharmonic Society was founded.

1813 Germany Birth of Wilhelm Richard Wagner (d. 1883).

1813 Italy Birth of Giuseppe Fortunino Francesco Verdi (d. 1901), Italian composer.

1813 Russia Birth of Alexander Sergeyevich Dargomizhsky (d. 1869), Russian composer. His early operas were not successful, but *The Store Guest* produced in St Petersburg in 1872 was much admired. It was completed by César Antonovich Cui (1835–1918) and orchestrated by Nicolay Andreyevich Korsakov (1844–1908).

ARCHITECTURE

1810 USA Boston Court House by Charles Bulfinch was built in the Romantic classical style by an architect responsible for several neo-classical public buildings in his native Boston.

1811 England Sir George Gilbert Scott was born (died 1878), the most prolific of the high Victorian architects; he designed both secular and ecclesiastical buildings besides carrying out many, often unsympathetic, restorations of medieval churches.

1812 England Augustus W. N. Pugin born (died 1852), a pioneer Gothic revival architect and passionate advocate for a return to the authenticity of the medieval past; he produced the decorative scheme for the House of Lords, while the building was designed by Sir Charles Barry.

1812 England No. 3 Lincoln's Inn Fields, London, is by Sir John Soane (1753–1837) and was an entirely original interpretation of the classical style, illustrating his interest in planes rather than volumes.

1812–1830 England Regent's Park and Regent Street, London, were replanned by John Nash, a highly versatile and picturesque scheme in which outward appearance was emphasized rather than details.

1813 England St George's Church, Everton, Liverpool, by Thomas Rickman (1776–1841) had a stone-clad, cast-iron interior in Gothic style. In 1817 Rickman published *An attempt to Discriminate the Styles of English Architecture from the Conquest to the Reformation etc*, which established the terms early English, decorated and perpendicular. He pioneered the Gothic revival, based on sound research into buildings as opposed to sentimental revival of Gothic ornament, as in Strawberry Hill, and also cast-iron construction in Gothic styles with Thomas Cragg, whose Mersey Iron Foundry made the prefabricated parts; such prefabricated cast-iron churches were later exported to the USA and the British colonies.

THREE DIMENSIONAL ART

1810 England John Flaxman (1755–1826) was made first professor of sculpture at the Royal Academy: his work, particularly in relief, represents the full strength of neo-classicism in England.

1811 Austria The German glass-enameller Gottlob Mohn (1789–1825) moved to Vienna from Dresden, where he had worked with his equally distinguished father Samuel (1762–1815). In Vienna he worked with Anton Kothgasser (1769–1851) making enamelled beakers: the favourite shape was a simple one which was then elaborately decorated with coloured enamels.

1811 Japan Death of Tomiharu (b. 1723), *netsuke* carver who founded a family of carvers: they worked not only in wood and ivory but in marine fossils and whale's teeth.

VISUAL ARTS

1810–1814 Spain Francisco Goya (1746–1828) made his series of etchings *Los Desastres de la Guerra*, considered some of the most powerful and horrifying scenes of warfare ever drawn.

1811 Japan Death of the painter Goshun Matsumara (b. 1752), whose semi-naturalistic style was combined with an idealism that appealed to the intelligentsia. His followers were called the *Shijo* school.

1812–1820 England Thomas Rowlandson (1756–1827) made two series of drawings: *The Touts of Dr Syntax*. He was considered the most talented draughtsman among English caricaturists.

1811 A. Avogadro proposed molecular theory of matter.

England: the throne from the House of Lords

HISTORICAL EVENTS	LITERATURE	DANCE & DRAMA	MUSIC

HISTORICAL EVENTS
1814
Bonaparte banished to Elba. Congress of Vienna formally opened.

LITERATURE

1814–1815 Germany *Tales* of Ernst Theodor Wilhelm Hoffmann (1776–1822), writer, composer, music critic and illustrator. His stories were a mixture of fantasy, magic and reason, and showed the influence of Scott, Poe and Balzac. Offenbach's opera *The Tales of Hoffmann* is based on them.

DANCE & DRAMA

1814 Austria Joseph Schreyvogel (1768–1832) became head of the Vienna Hofburgtheater. Under him it became one of Europe's most outstanding theatres.

MUSIC

1814 England Birth of Alexander John Ellis [formerly Sharp] (d. 1890), English philologist and mathematician; he greatly influenced English opinion in favour of a standard (concert) pitch.

1814 England Birth of William Pole (d. 1900), English civil engineer and musical scholar who wrote *The Philosophy of Music*, which may be regarded as an introduction to *Tonempfindungen* by Hermann von Helmholtz (1821–94).

1814 Germany C. F. Peters, music-publishing house, founded at Leipzig by Carl Friedrich Peters.

1814 Hungary Birth of Stephen Istvaán Heller (d. 1888), pianist and composer.

1814 Poland Birth of Oskar Kolberg (d. 1890), ethnologist and composer. Writer of more than 33 volumes covering the culture and civilization of Polish people, he is considered to be a leader in the ethnographical and ethnological field of music.

1815
Battle of Waterloo.

1815 Denmark *Hagbarth og Signe* by Adam Gottlob Oehlenschlaeger (1779–1850), Danish writer of romantic tragedies, particularly known for saga-plays. He was influenced both by Schiller and by his study of Greek drama, but his themes are entirely Scandinavian.

1815 Italy *Francesca da Rimini* by Silvio Pellico (1789–1854): it was enormously successful because it appealed to Italian nationalist feelings.

1815 Russia The dancer and choreographer Charles Didelot (1767–1836) gained complete artistic control of the Imperial Theatre ballet. He composed ballets based on Pushkin's poems and generally created a Russian national ballet with native dancers.

1815 Germany Birth of Robert Franz (d. 1892), German organist, conductor and composer.

1815 Hungary Birth of Mihaly Mosonyi (d. 1870), double-bass player, writer on music and composer. He founded first Hungarian musical periodical *Zeneszeti Lapok* and was an important figure of late nineteenth century revival in Hungarian music.

1815 Switzerland The *Bernische Musikgesellschaft* was formed in Berne.

1816
Argentina declared independence of Spain.

1816 France *Adolphe* by Benjamin Constant de Rebecque (1767–1830), politician and novelist: partly autobiographical, this novel analysed the conflict between reason and emotion. Constant came from a Calvinist family who had fled to Switzerland at the time of the Edict of Nantes. Returning emigré and expatriate writers brought the new ideas and emotions which culminated in the Romantic movement in France.

1816 Italy *Lettera Semiseria di Grisostomo* by Giovanni Berchet (1783–1851), poet and patriot. He wrote in support of Madame de Staël, who advised Italians to copy the German Romantics; style should be simple, and appeal to the emotions rather than to the intellect. His own poetry followed these recommendations.

1816 Denmark Antoine Bournonville (1760–1843), French dancer and choreographer, appointed dance director of the Royal Danish Ballet.

1816 England Introduction of the French quadrille as a fashionable dance: the dancers put the figures together by permutations of about 50 different movements. Ultimately one 'set', the one originally introduced, prevailed. Tunes were usually adapted from popular airs.

1816 Austria Franz Peter Schubert (1797–1828) composed his first commissioned work, *Prometheus*.

1816 England Boosey & Hawkes, music publishing and instrument making firm, established in London.

1816 France Johann Nepomuk Maelzel (1772–1838), German inventor, began manufacturing his metronome in Paris.

1816 Germany The first genuine German song cycle, *An die Ferne Geliebte* by Ludwig van Beethoven first performed.

ARCHITECTURE

1814 England William Butterfield born (died 1900), a leading high Victorian Gothic architect, whose work is characterized by its discordant polychromed forms.

1814 France Eugène-Emmanuel Viollet-le-Duc the architect and medievalist was born (died 1879); the Romanesque rather than Gothic was the main inspiration of French revivalism.

1815 England Brighton Pavilion was completed by John Nash (1752–1835) for the Prince of Wales in a mixture of Indian, Chinese and Gothic styles.

1815–1840 Finland The planning of Helsinki was by Ludwig Engel (1778–1840), a German architect working for Tsar Alexander I. The style of the new work is neo-classical.

1815 USA Andrew Downing, born (died 1852), a landscape architect who advocated private building in a style appropriate to their surroundings.

1816–1830 Germany Glyptochek Munich by Leo von Klenze (1784–1864) is a neo-classical gallery influenced in design by Jean-Nicolas-Louis Durand (1760–1834); Klenze also worked in other styles.

1816–1824 Italy San Francesco di Paola, Naples, by Pietro Bianchi (1787–1849) is one of the numerous copies of the Pantheon erected in Europe at this period; the piazza in front of the church is partly surrounded by a curved colonnade in the baroque style.

1816–1831 Italy Caffè Pedrocchi, Padua, by Guiseppi Japelli (1783–1852) and Antonio Gradenigo (1806–1884), is one of the most successful neo-classical buildings in Italy; it also has a neo-Gothic wing of 1837, a rare occurrence of the style in Italy.

THREE DIMENSIONAL ART

VISUAL ARTS

England: Brighton Pavilion by John Nash

1816 England Lord Elgin sold his collection of sculptures from the Parthenon to the British Museum: this was the first time that true, classical Greek sculpture could be seen by the general public, who had grown used to the weaker Roman and Hellenistic copies.

1816 Brazil French artists established an academy in Rio de Janeiro, where French academic taste continued to dominate Brazilian art until c.1920.

1816 Denmark Christoffer Wilhelm Eckersberg (1783–1853) returned to Copenhagen after working in Rome. He became established as a portrait painter, and his use of line influenced the next generation.

1814 George Stephenson constructed first effective steam locomotive.

1815 Humphrey Davy invented miner's safety helmet.

HISTORICAL EVENTS	LITERATURE	DANCE & DRAMA	MUSIC

MUSIC

1816 Germany Carl Maria Ernst von Weber, having been *Kapellmeister* at Breslau and Prague, appointed conductor of German opera at Dresden, a position he held until his death in 1826.

1816 Italy Gioacchino Antonio Rossini (1792–1868) wrote his first opera *Demetrio e Polibio* in 1806 and continued to write operas for the next 30 years. Although not immediately successful, *Il Barbiere di Siviglia* (1816) became his most important work.

LITERATURE

1817–1818 Bohemia Texts purporting to be old Czech manuscripts from the ninth, tenth and thirteenth centuries were issued by Vaclav Hanka (1791–1861). They contained lyrics and epics and were enthusiastically received as examples of the glorious past, this being the period of romantic love of the past. The documents were, in fact, forged by Hanka and his colleagues.

DANCE & DRAMA

1817 England Drury Lane was the first English theatre to be lit entirely by gas. The brighter light necessitated a better standard of scenery, costume and make-up.

MUSIC

1817 Austria Schubert's genius as a song writer was recognized by opera singer Johann Vogl (1768–1840). He composed over 600 songs, *Die Schöne Müllerin* (1823) and *Die Winterreise* (1827) being considered two of the greatest song cycles ever written.

1817 Denmark Birth of Niels Vilhelm Gade (d. 1890), composer and exponent of the romantic spirit in Danish music.

1817 England William Shield (1748–1829) appointed Master of the King's Music.

1817 France Louis François Dauprat, French horn player and teacher (1781–1868), became professor at the Conservatoire, his horn tutor *Méthode de Co-alto et de Cor-basse* is still in use today.

1817 Germany Carl Almenraeder (1786–1843) improved bassoon acoustics in the workshops of Bernhard Schott und Sohne the musical publishers, founded 1773.

LITERATURE

1818 England *Endymion* by John Keats (1795–1821), Romantic poet. His poems, full of sensuous beauty, were on nature, and on mythological and medieval themes.

1818 England *Lectures on the English Poets* by William Hazlitt (1778–1830), critic and essayist. He aimed at both teaching and entertaining his readers.

MUSIC

1818 England Halifax Choral Society was formed; it is one of the oldest in England.

1818 France Jean François Lesueur (1760–1837), French composer, appointed professor of composition at Paris Conservatoire, a post he held until his death. Among his pupils were Berlioz and Gounod.

1818 France Jean-Henri Pape (1789–1875), French pianoforte maker of German origin, established his own business. For nearly 50 years he produced new ideas and inventions, including key-mortices and felt for hammers.

1817 England *An Attempt to Discriminate the Styles of English Architecture* was published by Thomas Rickman, (1776–1841), a book which brought methodical order to the study of English medieval architecture.

1817 England John L. Pearson was born (died 1897), a Gothic revivalist famous for his churches, which were often distinguished by their fine spires.

1817–1822 Italy Braccio Nuovo, The Vatican, by Raffaelle Stern (1774–1820) is a fine neo-classical gallery used as a sculpture museum and built at a time when the Italians were beginning to lose their long pre-eminence in architectural influence.

1817–1857 Russia St Isaac's Cathedral, St Petersburg, by August Montferrand (1786–1858) is neo-classical and was built of costly materials; the dome is technically interesting in that it is framed in iron.

1817–1826 USA The university of Virginia, Charlesville, by Thomas Jefferson and Benjamin Latrobe consists of a group of porticoèd houses linked by colonnades culminating in the Pantheon-like library at one end.

1818–1831 Italy The city of Turin was replanned with wide streets and great squares flanked by arcaded buildings in the seventeenth-century tradition; Trieste, Naples and later Rome were other Italian cities extensively replanned in the nineteenth century.

1817 France Jean Louis Gericault (1791–1844) painted *The Raft of the Medusa.* His dramatic and emotional realism made him one of the founders of French romanticism, and lifted contemporary subjects on to the level of heroic epics. He had a special enthusiasm for painting the horse at speed.

Japan: 'Picnic in Season of Cherry Blossoms' by Hokusai

1818 U.S.A. Founding of the New England Glass Company in Massachusetts: it produced fine free-blown glass; engraved glass (between 1830–1880); and the art glass designed by Joseph Locke (1846–1936). It became the Libbey Glass Company in 1892.

1818 Japan Beginning of the greatest period for Katsushika Hokusai (1760–1849), painter, print designer and book illustrator; he specialized in a direct, imaginative vision of landscape which was new in *Ukiyo-E* prints. He was influenced by Japanese, Chinese and European paintings; his colours were highly original, his designs strong and simple. His 15 volumes of *Random Sketches* have been called an encyclopaedia of Japanese life.

*1818
First iron
steamship
launched.*

1819–1824 England *Don Juan* by George Gordon Noel, Lord Byron (1788–1824). He wrote in the eighteenth-century tradition of poetry, though with a superficial layer of romanticism. This work was a satire on two themes; Don Juan himself, and topical matters, introduced as digressions.

1819 Scotland *Ivanhoe* by Sir Walter Scott (1771–1826), historian, novelist and poet. He was the first to make an extensive study of the ballads of the Scottish border. He inherited the eighteenth-century tradition in his plots and type figures, but excelled in the depiction of eccentric and comic characters. He virtually created the historical novel.

*1820
Liberal
constitutions
declared in Spain
and Portugal.*

1820 England *Prometheus Unbound* by Percy Bysshe Shelley (1792–1822), a Romantic poet, the most passionate and least conventional of the movement. A visionary, he believed in the function of the poet as legislator of the world.

1820 France *Les Mèditations* by Alphonse-Marie-Louis Prat de Lamartine (1790–1869), a collection of lyric poems inspired by a tragic love affair, marked the beginning of the Romantic movement in France. Lamartine's verse also expressed a pantheistic Christianity, which recalled Chateaubriand, and a love of the scenery of Italy and Savoy.

1820 Netherlands *De Ond Ergang der Eerste Wareld* by Willem Bilderdijk (1756–1831), poet and playwright. His best work was his religious poetry (of which this work was an example) and his didactic and epic poetry. A Calvinist and neo-classicist, he had a powerful effect on the development of religious poetry.

1820 India *The Precepts of Jesus, a Guide to Peace and Happiness* by Ram Mohan Roy (1772–1833), a Bengali Brahmin. He saw the value of Western education and helped to found the Hindu college in Calcutta. Although he learned English from the missionaries, he was never a Christian, and great was their annoyance when he published this book, in which Jesus is regarded as a teacher, not divine.

1819 Ceylon The King of Kandy was deposed, and royal patronage of Kandya dance ended. It was replaced by temple patronage.

1820 England Introduction of the Lancers, a dance devised and published by Joseph Hart in a *Set of Quadrilles*, with five additional figures.

1820 Italy Carlo Blasis (1795–1878) published his *Elementary Treatise* on dance, in which he illustrates the ballet position of the feet turned outwards through 90 degrees. What he describes as '*sur la pointe*' is illustrated as resting on the whole, not the point, of the toe.

1820 Italy *Carmagnola* by Alessandro Manzoni (1785–1873), admirer of Shakespeare and creator of Italian romantic drama: the play is unusually accurate historically. He disregarded the Unities completely, and published his views on them in *Lettre sur L'Unité de Temps et de Lieu dans La Tragédie* (1823).

1818 Germany First public appearance as pianist by Felix Mendelssohn.

1818 Sweden Franz Adolf Berwald (1796–1868), violinist and composer, made his public debut as a composer. The first Swedish symphonist, he is considered to be the greatest Swedish composer of the nineteenth century.

1819 Austria Ludwig van Beethoven was almost totally deaf.

1819 Italy Production of the first opera by Guiseppe Saverio Raffaele Mercadante (1795–1870); he wrote 60 operas of which *Elisa e Claudio* (1821) and *Il Giuramento* (1827) were the most successful and had a considerable influence on later composers, especially Verdi.

1820 Germany Robert Alexander Schumann entered Zwickau Lyceum, where he remained for 8 years.

| ARCHITECTURE | THREE DIMENSIONAL ART | VISUAL ARTS | INVENTIONS & DISCOVERIES |

1819–1822 England St Pancras Church, London, by W. (*c*.1771–1843) and H. W. Inwood (1794–1843) is modelled on the Athens Erectheum, the ultimate in Greek revival ecclesiastical architecture.

1819–1834 Russia St Petersburg was replanned and built by Karl Rossi (1775–1849) to a style and scale of imperial Rome.

1820 England St Luke's Chelsea, London, by James Savage (1779–1852) was the first Gothic revival church to be stone-vaulted throughout.

Russia: a view of the St Petersburg skyline on the River Neva

1820–1830 U.S.A. Development of press-moulded glass, which was pressed by plunger into a patterned mould.

c.**1820 Germany** The school of ivory-carving at Erbach first came to prominence through making ivory jewellery. It was founded by Johann Arzt under the patronage of Count Francis I of Erbach-Erbach (b. 1754).

1819 Australia Death of John William Levin (b. 1770), naturalist and landscape painter, who was the first artist to depict the appearance of local vegetation faithfully.

1819 England Rudolf Ackermann (1764–1834), print-maker and publisher, published an English translation of *A Complete Course of Lithography* by J. A. Senefelder, the inventor of the process. Ackermann did much to establish lithography as a fine art.

1820 England John Constable (1778–1842) exhibited *The Haywain* at the Royal Academy. He developed the Dutch landscape tradition of the seventeenth century as the ground for his own original expression of what the eye actually saw; he was concerned with catching the changing light and weather, and did so by applying pure colour in a technique that foreshadowed the Impressionists.

1820 Japan Death of Kubo Shunman (b. 1757), poet and artist, who made *Suri-Mono* miniature colour prints.

c.**1820 India** The ruler Man Singh of Jodhpur commissioned a series of 121 paintings illustrating the seventeenth-century ballad of Dhola and Marvani. He was a notable patron of the arts and his painters signed and dated their work, which was rare in India.

*1820
André Marie
Ampère
expounded theory
of
electromagnetism.*

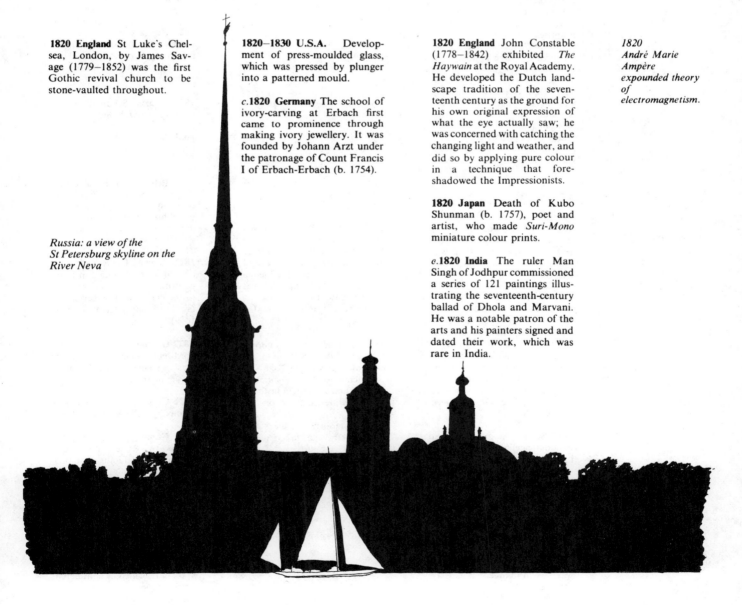

HISTORICAL EVENTS

1821
Greek War of Independence against Turkish rule began.

LITERATURE

1820 U.S.A. *The Sketch Book*, including *Rip Van Winkle* and *The Legend of Sleepy Hollow*, by Washington Irving (1783–1859), historian and writer of short stories. The book brought him international fame; he was the first American writer to be acclaimed in Europe. He was also the first to make extensive use of native American material.

1821 England *A Vision of Judgement* by Robert Southey (1774–1843), prose writer and poet laureate. He wrote long narratives, using blank verse, unrhymed stanzas or complicated rhyme schemes, and original metres.

1822–1827 Bohemia Three volumes of *Slavonic National Songs* were collected by František Ladislav Čelakovský (1799–1852), poet and professor of Slavonic philology at Breslau and Prague.

1822–1837 Hungary *Aurora*, an almanac founded by Karoly Kisfaludy (1788–1830), led the reaction against classicism. Kisfaludy was a playwright, a poet, and author of the first Hungarian short stories.

DANCE & DRAMA

1821 Italy Death of the choreographer and ballet-master Salvatore Vigano (b. 1769) in Milan. Under him La Scala theatre had become the greatest centre of ballet in Western Europe, and its school of dancing attracted dancers from many countries. The school survived him; his repertoire did not, and La Scala lost its pre-eminence as a ballet theatre.

1821 U.S.A. The English actor Junius Brutus Booth arrived to play Richard III in Richmond, Virginia, and settled.

MUSIC

1821 France Pierre Baillot (1771–1842), violinist and composer, was made leader of the orchestra at the Paris Opera, and was the last representative of the great classical Paris school of violin playing; he wrote a method for violin playing with Rodolphe Kreutzer (1766–1831).

1821 France Hector Berlioz (1803–1869), French composer, took up his medical studies in Paris, but soon renounced these in favour of music.

1821 Germany First performance in Berlin of *Der Freischutz* by Carl Maria Ernst von Weber; with this work he laid the foundation of German romantic opera.

1821 Hungary Birth of István Bartalus (d. 1899), Hungarian musicologist, one of the earliest scholars of musical history in Hungary.

1822 Austria Schubert began his '*Unfinished Symphony*'.

1822 Austria First public appearance in Vienna by Franz Liszt.

1822 Belgium Birth of César Auguste Franck (d. 1890), composer and organist, in Liège. He made his career in France and did much for the growth of French instrumental music.

1823
Monroe Doctrine in U.S.A.

1823–1833 England *Essays of Elia* by Charles Lamb, essayist, poet and critic. His style was old-fashioned, rambling and elaborate.

1823 Greece *Hymn to Liberty* by Dionysus Solomos (1798–1857). His early poetry was in Italian, and this was his first poem in Greek. In later life he became preoccupied with form, and this seriously inhibited composition. He planned many works, but finished few. He ranks as the greatest modern Greek poet.

1823 Serbia A collection of national poetry was published by Vuk Stephanovic Karadžić (1787–1864), philologist and lexicographer. He took upon himself the task of shaping a literary language based on the spoken language, and publishing national folk-tales, poetry and proverbs. His work revealed their common heritage to the South Slavs, and showed the way to a unified Yugoslav literature.

1823 Austria *König Ottokars Glück und Ende* by Franz Grillparzer (1791–1872), romantic dramatist and protégé of Schreyvogel, head of the Vienna Hofburgtheater. The play was banned until 1825 because the hero's career was too like that of Napoleon.

1823 England James Robinson Planché (1796–1880) designed costumes for Charles Kemble's production of *King John*: this was the first attempt at historically accurate costume on the English stage. Planché also wrote copiously for the stage, mainly extravaganzas.

1822 England The Royal Academy of Music founded in London (opened 1823), mainly due to the energy and perseverance of Lord Burghersh (1784–1859).

1822 Germany The piano accordion (originally Handäolire) was invented by Friedrich Buschmann in Berlin.

1822 Germany First compositions by Felix Mendelssohn.

1822 Germany First compositions by Robert Alexander Schumann, including a setting of Psalm 150.

1822 Germany Ludwig Spohr (1784–1859) appointed *Hofkapellmeister* to Elector of Hesse-Cassel.

1823 Austria Beethoven completed his *Missa Solemnis*, the Mass in D, which he considered his finest work.

FRANCISCVS SCHREITET VBER DIE WASSER

Austria: 'Lizst Strides Over the Water' from a contemporary drawing

1823–1847 England The British Museum, London, by Sir Robert Smirke (1780–1867) is the most important work by a leading neo-classical architect; the Ionic colonnade is very imposing.

1823–1836 France The Notre-Dame de Lorette, Paris, by L. H. Lebas (1782–1867) is based on the principle of an early Christian basilica with a portico and the inside decorated with murals.

1823–1835 USA Eastern State Penitentiary, Philadelphia, by John Haviland (1792–1852) was the first prison to be planned on the radial cellular system and was castellated – unlike the architect's New York prison (1836–1838) in the Egyptian style.

1822 France Jean-Baptiste Camille Corot (1796–1875) began painting as a professional artist. He composed in the studio from landscape sketches made all over France, working in the classical tradition but with innovatory naturalism. He was influential on most later French landscape painters.

1822 France Eugène Delacroix (1798–1863) exhibited his first painting, *Dante and Virgil in Hell*, which was greatly admired. He had studied the work of Rubens and the Venetian school.

1822 France Louis Jacques Mandé Daguerre (1789–1851) and C. M. Bouton opened in Paris their 'Diorama' theatre of light-projected pictures. Dioramas were adapted in miniature as home amusements.

1823 England George Cruikshank (1792–1878) illustrated *Grimm's German Popular Stories*. His previous success had been as a political cartoonist in the tradition of Gillray; as a book illustrator he was equally successful, and produced an enormous amount of work.

HISTORICAL EVENTS	LITERATURE	DANCE & DRAMA	MUSIC

LITERATURE

1824–1829 England *Imaginary Conversations* by Walter Savage Landor (1775–1864), poet and prose writer. His prose was rich and poetic, though his lyrics were simple. In spirit, his work was classical.

1824 Denmark *En Danske Students Eventyr* by Poul Martin Møller (1794–1888), poet, essayist and short-story writer. A humorous account of student life, it was the first Danish novel to deal with contemporary life.

1824 Slovakia First complete version of *Daughter of Slava* by Jan Kollár (1793–1852): written in Czech, it was a sequence of 151 sonnets and a prologue, and combined the poet's personal love story with a love for the Slav people. Later Kollár added other sonnets on Slavonic history.

1825 Hungary *Zalan Futasa* by Mihaly Vorosmarty (1800–1855), poet, playwright and critic, who wrote national epics in a classical style.

1825 Portugal *Camoes* by João Baptista da Silva Leitão, Visconde de Almeida Garrett (1799–1854), poet, playwright and novelist: a heroic poem, it is regarded as the first work in the Portuguese Romantic movement. Garrett had encountered the poetry of the Romantics during his travels, particularly in England. His work showed some eighteenth-century elements, but the eighteenth-century Portuguese poets had already shown romantic tendencies and the transition from classical to Romantic literature was therefore very smooth. Garrett's prose, informal and flexible, represented a major step forward in Portuguese prose writing.

1825 Russia Anton Antonovich, baron Delvig (1798–1831) became editor of *Severnye Tsvety*, a poetic miscellany. He was one of a circle of poets, contemporaries of Pushkin, known as the Pushkin Pléiade. His own poems were of two kinds: classical forms and folk-poetry.

1825 Russia *Voynarovsky* by Kondraty Fedorovich Ryleyev (1795–1826). He was hanged as a leader of the Decembrist revolt. This poem, a narrative, showed the influence of Byron.

1825 Death of Tsar Alexander I of Russia.

DANCE & DRAMA

1824 Germany Ludwig Tieck (1773–1853) became director of the Dresden court theatre. He improved standards of production by demanding clear diction and simplified staging. He was a leader of the German Romantic movement.

1824 Russia Opening of the Maly (Russian: 'small') theatre in Moscow, with a company originally formed in 1806; it is the oldest Moscow theatre.

1825 Russia *Serkele* by Salomon Ettinger (c.1803–1856), a Russian Jew writing in Yiddish: one of many plays written for the Jewish festival of Purim to replace the traditional, popular festival plays which had become vulgar.

MUSIC

1823 England Performance of *Clari* or *The Maid of Milan* by Henry Rowley Bishop (1786–1855) contained the song *Home Sweet Home*.

1823 England Manuel Garcia (1775–1832), Spanish singer, teacher and composer, founded a school of singing in London.

1823 France Birth of Victor Antoine Édouard Lalo (d. 1892), French composer of Spanish descent.

1823 U.S.A. Chickering & Sons, pianoforte makers, founded.

1824 Austria First performance, in Vienna, of Ludwig van Beethoven's 9th and last symphony, which was commissioned by Royal Philharmonic Society of London in 1818; it was first performed in London in 1825.

1824 Austria Birth of Anton Bruckner (d. 1896), Austrian composer.

1824 Czechoslovakia Birth of Bedřich Smetana (d. 1884), Czech composer.

1824 England J. B. Cramer & Co., music publishing house, founded in London by Johann Baptist Cramer (1771–1858), German pianist and composer.

1824 England *Dictionary of Musicians* compiled and published by John H. Sainsbury. While it contains many errors, it gives valuable information of the period.

1824 Germany Birth of Peter Cornelius (d. 1874), composer and author.

1824 Germany Felix Mendelssohn completed his first symphony.

1825 Austria Birth of Johann Strauss the younger (d. 1899), composer.

1825 France A treatise on the art of accompanying, the first work of its kind, was published in Paris by Ferdinando Carulli (1770–1841), Italian guitarist and composer.

1824 England George Edmund Street was born (died 1881), a Gothic revival architect, specializing in churches; his study of medieval churches on the continent is reflected in his own work.

1824–1844 France St-Vincent-de-Paul, Paris, by J. B. Lepère (1761–1844) and J. I. Hittorf (1792–1867) continues the traditional French interest in early Christian basilican architecture but with the added interest of a two-tower façade and polychrome exterior decoration.

1824–1828 Germany Altes Museum Berlin, by Karl Schinkel (1781–1841) is a superbly proportioned neo-classical masterpiece; behind the Ionic colonnade hides a domed room inspired by the Pantheon.

1824–1880 Germany Cologne Cathedral, the major Gothic revival work in century Germany, was designed by F. A. Ahlert (1788–1833) and others.

1825 France Charles Garnier born (died 1898), who made the most important single contribution to the rebuilding of Paris (1860–1880) by developing the luxury flat, both handsome and convenient.

1825–1829 Scotland Edinburgh High School by Thomas Hamilton (1784–1858) is one of the best Greek revival buildings in Edinburgh New Town, described as the 'Athens of the North'.

1824 U.S.A. John Frazee (1790–1852) carved a portrait bust of John Wells: this was probably the first by a native sculptor.

1825 U.S.A. Founding of the Boston and Sandwich Glass Company by Deming Jarves (1790–1869): it specialized in mould-blown and pressed glass of lacy design, and in cut glass with coloured overlay.

1824–1834 France Jean Auguste Ingres (1780–1867) painted *The Apotheosis of Homer* and *The Martyrdom of Saint Sebastian*. He was then the main champion of academic classicism against the emerging romantic school. He was highly regarded in his own day and very influential. The quality of his line was outstanding and inspired artists into the twentieth century.

1824 France An exhibition of John Constable's pictures was given at the Salon; it was influential on French landscape painters and also on the English painter Richard Parkes Bonington (1802–1828), who trained in France.

Germany: portrait of Mendolssohn by W. von Shadow

HISTORICAL EVENTS	LITERATURE	DANCE & DRAMA	MUSIC

LITERATURE

1825 Sweden *Frithiof's Saga* by Esias Tegner (1782–1846), bishop, scholar and poet. He refused to align himself with any literary school, remaining apart from controversy. This work was a cycle on an Old Icelandic theme. His passionate, lucid poetry made him the greatest Swedish writer of the age.

1826 France *Poèmes Antiques et Moderne* by Alfred Victor, Comte de Vigny (1797–1863), poet, playwright and novelist. His work was pessimistic, stoic, full of biblical themes and symbols. His main concerns were the essential solitude of the great, and the conflict of the poet and society.

1826 Germany *Reise Bilder* by Heinrich Heine (1797–1856), German Jewish lyric poet and satirist. He spent much of his life in France, and was instrumental in effecting an exchange of ideas between France and Germany. Many of his lyrics were set to music by Schumann.

1826 Germany Poems by Johann Christian Friedrich Hölderlin (1770–1843). He wrote in classical forms, or in free verse, expressing his admiration for the Golden Age of classical Greece, which he knew was lost for ever. His poems showed great depth of feeling.

1826 Portugal *Amor e Melancolia*, a collection of poems by António Feliciano de Castilho (1800–1875), Romantic poet. Despite the quality of his own work, his many followers produced colourless work of little value.

1826 U.S.A. *The Last of the Mohicans* by James Fennimore Cooper (1789–1863), a novelist with a strong sense of nationality and feeling for democracy. His work also includes the first truly realistic sea stories, based on his own experiences.

1829 Italy *D'Una Letteratura Europea* by Giuseppe Mazzini (1805–1872), patriot, critic and political theorist. He felt that the Romantic movement was representative of the people and therefore supported it, though he placed morality and patriotism above art.

DANCE & DRAMA

1827 England J. Payne Collier wrote down the text of the English 'Punch and Judy Show', the first written version. Punch may be descended from ancient Greek and Roman mimes *via* the *commedia dell' arte*.

1827 France In the preface to *Cromwell*, not performed, Victor Hugo (1802–1885), poet, novelist and dramatist, set down the principles of the Romantic movement.

1828 U.S.A. T. D. Rice (1808–1860) appeared in black faced make-up, singing a song learned from a Negro, and began the vogue for 'minstrelsy'.

1829 Denmark August Bournonville (1805–1879), son of Antoine Bournonville, choreographed his first ballet for the Royal Danish Ballet: *The Soldier and the Peasant*. He created some 50 ballets of which about 10 are still in the company's repertoire, and was a strong influence on male dancing in Denmark, handing on the classical tradition of his own teacher Auguste Vestris.

1829 France *Henri III et sa Court* by Alexandre Dumas père (1803–1870) was a highly successful production which increased the popularity of the Romantic movement in France.

1829 Germany *Don Juan und Faust* by Christian Dietrich Grabbe (1801–1836), dramatist of the Young Germany movement.

1829 Russia The dancer and choreographer Charles Didelot (1767–1836) was forced to resign as ballet-master of the Imperial Theatre ballet. Its standard declined after he left.

MUSIC

1826 Austria Johann Strauss the elder (1804–1849) best-known for his *Radetzky March*, made his debut as composer in Vienna.

1826 England The English mechanism and the bellows invented by Cumming were introduced into French organs by John Abbey (1785–1859), the English organ builder, when he went to work in Paris.

1826 England Birth of Alfred James Hipkins (d. 1903), writer on musical instruments who was regarded as an authority on matters relating to pianoforte.

1826 Germany Birth of Friedrich Chrysander (d. 1901), music scholar. He edited the complete works of George Frederick Handel, as well as writing various important musical treatises.

1826 Germany Death of Carl Maria Friedrich Ernst von Weber, German composer (b. 1786).

1827 Austria Death of Ludwig van Beethoven at Vienna (b. 1770).

1827 Austria First performance of *Die Winterreise*, a cycle of 24 songs on the subject of unrequited love, by Franz Peter Schubert (1797–1828).

1828 Austria Death of Franz Schubert (b. 1797). His *String Quintet in C*, one of the finest of his chamber works, was completed a few months earlier.

1828 France Jean-Baptiste Vuillaume (1798–1875), violin maker, established at Paris.

1828 Germany Theobald Böhm (1794–1881), flautist, composer for the flute and flute maker, opened a factory in Munich where the Böhm flute was developed.

1828 Germany Robert Alexander Schumann settled in Leipzig to study law, but continued to compose.

1829 Austria The accordion, a portable instrument of the free-reed family, was invented in Vienna by Damian.

1829 England Christian Kramer (c.1788–1834) appointed Master of the King's Music.

1828 Greek independence of Turkey guaranteed.

1829 Catholic emancipation in Britain.

322

1826–1837 England Samuel Palmer (1805–1881) worked at Shoreham and painted some of his finest pictures. He was a mystic and a follower of Blake, expressing his own mystic vision in terms of English rural landscape, often by moonlight.

1826 France Joseph Nicéphore Niépce (1765–1833) made a heliograph of the view from his window at Gras: the earliest surviving example of attempts to fix a photographic image. He used an 8-hour exposure on a pewter plate.

1826
First crossing of the Atlantic under steam.

1827 England William Burges was born (died 1881), a highly individual Gothic revival architect who revelled in exuberant sculptural decoration.

1827 Holland Petrus Cuypers was born (died 1921), one of the most productive architects in nineteenth-century Holland and responsible for a number of Gothic-style works.

1827 USA Richard Morris Hunt, was born (died 1895); he trained in France and produced buildings in a variety of styles, mainly grandiose pastiche, for millionaire clients.

1828–1829 USA Tremont House Hotel, Boston, by Isaiah Rogers (1800–1869) was built of granite, the favourite building material in nineteenth-century Boston; it set new standards in hotel design.

1827 U.S.A. First dated piece of American scrimshaw; sailors on the whaling ships of Europe and America carved scenes and motifs on ivory teeth and whalebone, but American work predominated.

1827–1838 U.S.A. James Audubon (1785–1851) published *The Birds of America*, 435 colour plates from his original drawings, considered to be the most dramatic bird studies yet made.

1827 England John Martin (1789–1854) illustrated Milton's *Paradise Lost*, identifying Satan with the new power of industry, as had William Blake. Martin drew on industrial images of his childhood for scenes of 'sublimity' and disaster.

1828 Scotland Sir David Wilkie (1785–1841) returned after working abroad for three years. Under the influence of Spanish paintings, he began to work on large-scale pictures of historical subjects.

1827
Ohm's law defining current formulated.

USA: a 19th century American trapper, from a contemporary drawing

1829–1831 Germany Potsdam Court gardener's house by Karl Schinkel is a cleverly adapted version of the Anglicized Italian villa, in which basic solids and voids are cunningly juxtaposed; Schinkel designed several buildings in Potsdam for the royal family.

1829–1840 Germany The Ludwigskirche, Munich, is by Frederich von Gärtner (1792–1847) and is Italian Romanesque in style; it was part of the rebuilding of Munich, mainly in the *Rundbogensil*, much favoured in early nineteenth-century Germany.

HISTORICAL EVENTS	LITERATURE	DANCE & DRAMA	MUSIC

1830
Belgium
independent of
Dutch rule.

LITERATURE

1830 Croatia An essay on re-formed Croat orthography by Ljudevit Gaj (1809–1872), philologist. He also founded a newspaper, *Danica*, which printed the work of Slav nationalist writers. His work paved the way for an integrated Yugoslav literature.

1830 France *Le Rouge et le Noir*, a novel by Marie-Henri Beyle, called Stendhal (1783–1842): it portrayed a hero alienated from his environment and resembling the author himself. The 'outsider' was a new type of hero in European fiction. In his greatest books, Stendhal explored different aspects of the political situation.

1831–1848 France Over 50 volumes comprising *La Comédie Humaine* by Honoré de Balzac (1799–1850): the novels are a panorama of French society from Napoleonic times to the end of the reign of Louis-Philippe, full of detail and realistic in treatment. Balzac's theory was that there is a correspondence between the human and the zoological species. He was influenced by Sir Walter Scott, Mrs Radcliffe and Fennimore Cooper.

1831 France *Notre Dame de Paris* by Victor-Marie Hugo (1802–1885), poet, playwright and novelist, regarded as the leading writer of the French Romantic movement. This book helped to establish a new genre, the historical novel, history being an important source of inspiration for the Romantics.

1831 Italy *Canti* by Giacomo, Count Leopardi (1798–1837), a poet and scholar writing in the classical tradition. He believed that for man real happiness was impossible, but that the poet must recreate man's capacity to believe that he is happy. He believed in the happy savage of Rousseau, regarding advanced civilization as decadent. His work showed great depth of feeling expressed in simple, musical language.

DANCE & DRAMA

1830 England *Maria Marten, or Murder in the Red Barn*: one of the best-known English melodramas.

1830 France The first night of Victor Hugo's *Hernani* at the Comédie Française was the scene of riotous clashes between Classicists and Romantics.

1830 Germany Gas lighting introduced into theatres.

1830 Poland Warsaw theatres were nationalized under Russian police officials. The effectiveness and development of Polish theatres varied with the amount of freedom they were given.

*c.***1830 Spain** Dolores Serral introduced a form of Spanish ballet, *baile clasico español*, to French audiences. Spanish ballet combined classical techniques with features from Spanish traditional dances, except flamenco, which was considered vulgar.

1831 France The Paris Opéra, no longer a royal theatre, took a new director, Dr Véron who ran it as a commercial theatre producing popular ballets: these were noted for lavish production, eighteenth-century romantic stories, and a strong emphasis on a star ballerina. Choreography took second place to virtuoso exhibitions.

1831 Russia Publication of *Boris Goudonov* by Alexander Sergeivich Pushkin (1799–1837): the play was not actually performed until 1870. Pushkin set out to create a Russian national drama, working with Russian material and developing the Russian language as a literary vehicle. He was the first great writer to do so.

1831 U.S.A. *The Gladiator* by Robert Montgomery Bird (1806–1854), a romantic melodrama it was the prize-winning entry in a competition organized by actor Edwin Forrest (1806–1872) to stimulate American playwriting.

MUSIC

1829 Germany A bassoon reedcase was advocated by Carl Almenraeder (1786–1843).

1829 Germany Felix Mendelssohn wrote his first volume of *Songs without Words* and the *St Matthew Passion* by Johann Sebastian Bach was rediscovered and revived by Mendelssohn at the Berlin Sirgakademie; it was first performed in 1729.

1829 Germany Robert Alexander Schumann transferred his studies from Leipzig to Heidelberg.

1829 Germany Wagner went to a performance of *Fidelio*, the only opera by Ludwig van Beethoven, which greatly influenced his development.

1829 Russia Birth of Anton Rubinstein (d. 1894), pianist and composer.

1830 France Daniel François Esprit Auber (1782–1871), the French composer of many operas including *La Bergère Châtelaine* and *Fra Diavolo*. His opera *La Muette de Portici* had considerable dramatic intensity, was admired by Wagner and influenced the revolt which established the independence of Belgium.

1830 France J. B. Napoléon Fourneaux (1808–1846), French instrument maker, settled in Paris. He improved the accordion and originated the idea of percussion action in harmoniums.

1830 Germany Robert Alexander Schumann abandoned his study of law and left on a concert tour with Clara Wieck, later to become his wife.

1830 Germany First compositions by Wagner included two overtures.

1830 Scotland A new wind instrument, the Caledonica, was invented by William Meikle of Lanarkshire.

1830 Scotland Felix Mendelssohn's first visit to England and Scotland.

1831 Germany Carl Almenraeder and J. A. Heckel founded a bassoon factory in Biebrich, which is still the chief manufactory of German bassoons.

1830 France Bazar de l'Industrie, Paris, by Paul Lelong (1799–1846) was a very early example of an iron-galleried department store.

1830–1842 Germany Walhalla Regensburg by Leo von Klenze is a magnificently sited Greek revival peripteral Doric temple (i.e. the columns surround the exterior of the building), the style in which Klenze was at his best.

1830–1850 Germany Nikolaikirche, Potsdam, by Karl Schinkel is a centrally planned Classical-styled church, based on the design of the Pantheon but with a dome related to St Paul's, London.

1830 France Théodore Rousseau (1812–1867) began to paint landscapes from nature in the open air. In style he was influenced by the Dutch painter Ruysdael; he became the leader of the Barbizon school of open-air landscape painters who were inspired partly by the Dutch and partly by the English work of Constable and Bonington.

1830
Charles Babbage designed first computing machine.
First use of nitrate as fertilizer.

1831 England Richard Norman Shaw was born (died 1912), an influential and successful architect, particularly of country houses, who worked in many styles but is best known for his late seventeenth-century domestic-style buildings, produced in conjunction with his partner Eden Nesfield (1834–1888).

1831 Australia John Glover (1767–1849) came to Tasmania from a successful career as a landscape painter in England. His work shows the typically Australian conflict between the claims of tradition and realism: sometimes he painted the Tasmanian landscape with clarity and perception, sometimes he tried to treat it in the manner of Claude and Rosa.

England: the chimney of 'Bryanston' by Richard Norman Shaw

HISTORICAL EVENTS	LITERATURE	DANCE & DRAMA	MUSIC

*1832
First British
Parliamentary
Reform Act.*

1832 Germany Completion of part II of *Faust* by Johann Wolfgang von Goethe (1749–1832), poet, novelist, playwright, critic, scientist and philosopher. The work concerned man's attempts to enlarge and deepen his experience. Goethe himself was a kind of latter-day Renaissance 'complete man'. He believed that man's actions are motivated by external rather than internal forces; *Faust* was an expression of that belief. It is regarded as the most important work of German literature, and a world masterpiece.

1832 Italy *Le Mie Prigioni* by Silvio Pellico (1789–1854), a patriot and editor of *Il Conciliatore*, a periodical which was suppressed by the Austrians. This work was an account of his imprisonment for treason, and was pacifist in tone.

1833 Russia *Eugene Onegin* by Alexander Sergeyevich Pushkin (1799–1837). He was influenced by Byron, Shakespeare, and Sir Walter Scott, but although he was fully conversant with all the literary forms of the West, he assimilated them and used them to create an entirely Russian literature. He was never an imitator. He is regarded as Russia's greatest poet.

*1834
Tolpuddle
'martyrs'
transported.
Slavery abolished
in British
Empire.
Indian territory
constituted in
U.S.A.*

1834 England *The Last Days of Pompeii* by Edward Bulwer Lytton, 1st Lord Lytton (1803–1873), statesman, playwright and novelist. He was highly successful, writing on historical subjects, crime, the occult and folklore, all of which had great appeal at the time.

1834 Russia *Literaturnye Mechtaniya* by the critic Vissarion Grigoryevich Belinsky (1811–1848), who was the theorist of the Natural school of Russian literature, insisting that literature should depict ordinary people and 'real life', with a view to exposing evils and pointing the way to a better existence. He based his theories on his reading of Gogol, whose work was realistic, though not in the way that Belinsky understood the term.

1832 France First performance of the ballet *La Sylphide* by Filippo Taglioni: the principal dancer Maria Taglioni (1804–1884) introduced the long white *tutu* of the romantic style and danced long passages 'on points'. Romantic ballet emphasized the ethereal and graceful at the expense of the vigorous; the ballerina took precedence over the male dancer who declined into a supporting rôle.

1832 Poland *Kordian* by Juliuzs Slowacki (1809–1849), first performed 1899. He was a Polish writer who lived in Paris after his exile in 1831. He was a leader of the Polish Romantic movement and his later work shows the influence of Shakespeare.

1832 Russia The Alexandrinsky Theatre was built in St Petersburg on the orders of Tsar Nicholas I. The Tsar used the theatre for political ends and is considered to have virtually invented the patriotic play, a form of drama which permitted playwrights to flatter him.

1833 England The appearance in London of the two ballerinas, Maria Taglioni (1804–1884) of Italy and Fanny Elssler (1810–1884) of Austria, provided a famous contrast in style: Taglioni was celebrated for her ethereal quality, Elssler for robust 'character' dancing.

1833 Italy First partnership of the ballerina Carlotta Grisi (1819–1899) and the French dancer Jules Perrot (1810–1892). Perrot, as a great male dancer, found difficulty working in a period when the ballerina predominated, and eighteenth-century ballets were revived to display his skill.

1833 Russia *Woe From Wit* by Alexander Sergeivich Griboyedev (1795–1829), the first Russian comedy of manners. There was also an abortive attempt to introduce romanticism into Russia with a play on the life of Tasso by Kukolnik.

1834 France *Lorenzaccio* by Alfred de Musset (1810–1847), a French writer whose work was a fusion of the classical and romantic traditions. He was so discouraged by the failure of his first play, *La Nuit Vénétienne*, 1830. that he wrote subsequent plays only to be read.

1831 Italy *La Sonnambula* was first produced in Milan; it is generally regarded as the greatest work of Vincenzo Bellini (1801–1835).

1832 England The Adelphi Glee Club was formed, but merged into the Abbey Glee Club c.1845.

1832 France The revised version of *Symphonie Fantastique*, Op. 14, by Louis Hector Berlioz (1803–1869) was performed in Paris.

1832 France First concert by Fryderyk Franciszek Chopin (1810–1849) in Paris, which established him as a notable figure in the musical life of that city.

1832 U.S.A. Music-publishing firm of Parker and Ditson founded, which became Oliver Ditson & Co. in 1857.

1832 Wales Possibly the first brass band established in Britain, at an ironworks at Blaina.

1833 England First performance of Felix Mendelssohn's *Italian Symphony*, Op 90, in London.

1833 France Birth of Jean François Voirin (d. 1885), bow maker.

1833 Germany Birth of Johannes Brahms (d. 1897), German composer.

1833 Russia Birth of Alexander Porfirevich Borodin (d. 1887), Russian composer.

1834 England Francois (Franz) Cramer (1772–1848) appointed Master of the King's Music.

1834 Germany Publication of *Der Physikalische und Musikalische Tonmesser* by Johann Heinrich Scheibler (1777–1837), a pamphlet which described his work on a very accurate tonometer using 52 tuning forks.

1834 Switzerland/Italy First mature works for pianoforte by Franz Liszt (1811–1866) who was an unrivalled pianist.

ARCHITECTURE

1832–1884 USA Merchant's Exchange, Philadelphia, by William Strickland (1788–1854) is an archeologically correct Greek revival building by an untravelled American architect.

1833 Bulgaria Rila Monastery began rebuilding; it was neo-Byzantine, thus emphasizing independence from traditional Ottoman architecture, as was also apparent in other Balkan countries by the end of the century.

1833–1884 USA The Washington Monument by Robert Mills (1781–1855) is the tallest of the nineteenth-century obelisks that epitomize the Romantic classical ideals.

THREE DIMENSIONAL ART

1832 U.S.A. Horatio Greenough (1805–1852), sculptor, carved the colossal figure of George Washington for the Capitol: he was the first professional American sculptor.

France: 'Chopin Reading a Newspaper' from a contemporary drawing

1833–1836 France François Rudé (1784–1855) sculpted *The Departure of the Volunteers in 1792, (The Marseillaise)* on the Arc de Triomphe in Paris: he was noted for his ability to 'freeze' the dramatic gesture or expression.

VISUAL ARTS

1832 France Honore Daumier (1810–1879), painter and lithographer, was imprisoned for satirizing Louis Philippe. For the next 15 years he turned from political satire to social satire and drew the *Histoire ancienne, Les Baigneuses* and *Les Bons Bourgeois* series.

*c.***1832 Japan** Ando Hiroshige (1797–1858) founded his own school of print design; from then on he concentrated on prints of landscape and of flowers or birds. He was noted for his ability to portray light and his strong feeling for atmosphere which enabled him to evoke the moods of landscape to which the Japanese are traditionally sensitive.

1834 England Development of the 'Zoetrope': images drawn on the inside of a drum were viewed through slits as the drum rotated, giving an illusion of moving pictures.

INVENTIONS & DISCOVERIES

1833 Charles Lyell stated theory of continuing geological change.

1834 Louis Braille perfected system of reading for the blind.

LITERATURE

1834 Spain *El Moro Expósito* by Angel de Saavedra y Ramirez de Baquedano, Ducque de Rivas (1791–1863), poet and playwright. The work is a narrative poem based on a legend, *Siete Infantes de Lara*, which exists today as fragments of a *chanson de geste*. It is a revenge story, and was used by Juan de la Cuevo and Lope de Vega as well as Rivas. Rivas' poem was the first major work of the Spanish Romantic movement.

1835–1837 France *Les Nuits* by Louis-Charles-Alfred de Musset (1810–1857), poet and playwright; a series of romantic poems, inspired by his unhappy relationship with Georges Sand. Musset's early work showed the influence of Victor Hugo; later he was more strongly influenced by Byron. He expressed perfectly the *mal de siècle*, the totally committed search for ideal happiness, and its inevitable disappointment.

1835–1872 Denmark Fairy stories, 168 in number, by Hans Christian Andersen (1805–1875), novelist, playwright and poet. He travelled widely in Europe and attempted almost all forms of literature.

1835 Iceland Foundation of the periodical *Fjölnir*, a vehicle for the patriotic and Romantic reaction against the eighteenth century, by Joans Hallgrimsson (1807–1845), poet and novelist.

1835 India English became the official government language, replacing Persian. Colleges were established to teach English to the Indians; thus Indian writers were exposed to the influences of English literature.

1836–1867 Bohemia *History of Bohemia* in five parts by František Palacký (1798–1876), Czech historian. He played a leading part in organizing Czech cultural life.

1836 Bohemia *May* by Karel Hynek Mácha (1810–1836). His early poems showed the influence of German Romantics and were written in German; later he wrote in Czech. Many of his poems dealt with the history of Bohemia; others were concerned with the relationship between man and nature, and with human love. *May* is regarded as one of the greatest poems in Czech literature.

DANCE & DRAMA

1835 France *Chatterton* by Alfred de Vigny (1797–1863), based on the life of the English poet, Thomas Chatterton. He also translated Shakespeare's *Othello* and *The Merchant of Venice* into French.

1835 Germany *Dantons Tod* by George Büchner (1813–1837), a dramatist of the Young Germany movement.

1835 Spain *Don Alvaro O La Fuerza Del Sino* by Angel Saavedia, el Duque de Rivas (1791–1865), the most important example of Spanish Romantic drama; the movement was short-lived in Spain.

MUSIC

1835 England First public performance of an instrumental quartet presented by Joseph Haydon Bourne Dando (1806–1894), violinist.

1835 England John Hopkinson founded a pianoforte-making firm at Leeds, which removed to London in 1846.

1835 France First production in Paris of *Le Cheval de Bronze* by Daniel François Esprit Auber (1782–1871), French composer; he was the last great representative of *opéra-comique*.

1835 France Birth of Charles Camille Saint-Saëns (d. 1921), French composer, organist and pianist.

1835 Italy Giuseppe Fortunino Francesco Verdi (1813–1901) was appointed *maestro di musica* at Busseto, where he remained for four years.

1835 Italy Gaetano Donizetti (1797–1848) wrote his most famous opera, *Lucia di Lammermoor*.

1835 Norway First Norwegian chorale-book edited by Ole Andreas Lindeman (1769–1857).

1835 Russia Birth of César Antonovich Cui (d. 1918), Russian composer of French descent.

1836 England The Brinsmead firm of pianoforte makers was founded in London by John Brinsmead (1814–1908).

1836 France Birth of Clément Philibert Léo Delibes (d. 1891), French composer.

1836 Russia First performance of *A Life for the Tsar*, the first national opera of Mikhail Ivanovich Glinka (1804–1857), Russian composer who laid the foundation of the modern Russian school of music.

1836 Republic of Texas founded.

1835 Germany Schloss Babelsberg by Karl Schinkel is a picturesque castle, influenced in style by the English medieval castles Schinkel had seen in a tour of England; it was completed by his pupil Persius.

England: illustration by Phiz. 'Mr Dombey Introduces His Daughter Florence'

1835 Australia Conrad Martens (1801–1878) arrived in Sydney. He was considered one of the finest and the most prolific painters of colonial Australia.

1835 England 'Phiz' (Hablot Knight Browne, 1815–1882) began his illustrations of Charles Dickens' books.

1835 Spain The secularization of the monasteries brought to general attention the paintings done for them by Francisco Zurbarán (1598–1664). He was admired particularly by Manet and Courbet.

*1835
Samuel Colt
patented revolver.*

1836 England *Contrasts* was published by Augustus W. N. Pugin; his first book, it illustrated the contrast between the richness of medieval Gothic architecture and the poverty and austerity of contemporary work.

1836 USA Colonnade Row by Alexander Davis (1803–1892) is a New York terrace with the two upper storeys fronted by a row of impressive Corinthian columns; Davis was also responsible for several domed state capitols.

1836–1840 USA Washington governmental buildings by Robert Mills were all sober neoclassical blocks of fireproof construction, dominated by their porticoes.

1836 France Death of Firmin Didot, printer and typefounder: his severe type designs were predominant in French printing for a century.

1836 Germany *Uber den Willen in der Natur* by Arthur Schopenhauer (1788–1860), a German philosopher who held that the human will is wicked but is also the driving force in the universe. His pessimistic philosophy became popular in the 1850s when it accorded with current feeling. He placed great emphasis on the arts, and was highly influential on Wagner, Nietzsche, Mann and Gide.

1836 Iceland Two volumes of poems by Sigurdur Eiriksson Breidfjord (1798–1846), a writer on traditional themes, remarkable for his mastery of form, combined with warmth and humour. His poems were *rimur*, alliterative rhyming verse on mythical or historical subjects. The earliest *rimur* were derived from the French romances.

1836 U.S.A. *Nature* by Ralph Waldo Emerson (1803–1882), philosopher, essayist and poet; he was leader of the Transcendental movement, which called for independent thought and self-reliance in art. It was derived from a variety of sources: oriental philosophy, Plato, the German Idealists and the English Romantics.

France: photograph of Berlioz

*1837
Queen Victoria
succeeded to
British throne.*

1837 Netherlands *De Gids*, a literary review, was founded by Reinier Cornelis Bakhuisen van den Brink (1810–1865), a critic and historian, and Everhardus Johannes Potgieter (1808–1875), a poet, essayist and critic. Their aim was to revive Dutch literature by putting forward the ideals of the seventeenth century to correct the worst trends of the Romantic movement.

1837 Russia *On the Death of Pushkin* by Mikhail Yurovich Lermontov (1814–1841), Romantic poet, playwright and novelist. An idealist, deeply pessimistic in outlook, he resembled Byron in many ways, though he did not imitate the English poet. His analytical novel *A Hero of Our Time* had as its hero a man with no real role to fill, a superfluous man. This figure reappears in many Russian novels of the period. Lermontov ranks as one of Russia's major writers.

1837 England First performance of the ballet *Le Corsaire*, based on Byron's poem. Ferdinand Albert Decombe was the choreographer.

1837 Hungary Opening of the National Theatre.

1837 Italy Carlo Blasis (1795–1878) was appointed Director of the Imperial Academy of Dancing and Pantomime in Milan. Under him it became the most influential ballet school in Europe, with a training system imitated ever since. He first insisted on the feet being turned outwards through 90 degrees, which provided a stable base for acrobatic dancing.

1837 France Hector Berlioz (1803–1869) composed his *Requiem Messe des Morts*, which was performed in Paris the same year.

1837 Hungary Death of Johan Nepomuka Hummel (b. 1778), pianist, conductor and composer.

1837 Russia Birth of Mily Alexeyevich Balakirev (d. 1910) composer.

France: daguerrotype of Daguerre himself

1837–1841 England The Reform Club, London, by Sir Charles Barry is in the Italianate style which came to challenge the Greek revival in England.

1837–1841 Germany The Opera House, Dresden, by Gottfried Semper is neo-cinquecento; Semper's other major works were also in the same city, mainly Italianate in style.

1837 Greece Old Palace, Athens, by Friderich von Gärtner was one of a number of neo-classical buildings built in Athens by northern architects at the beginning of the nineteenth century; many have since been demolished.

1837 France Louis Jacques Mandé Daguerre (1789–1851) made his first 'daguerrotype', a picture of his studio. He used five 45-minute exposures on a plate coated with iodide of silver and developed by mercury vapour. Each 'daguerrotype' was an original; there was no negative from which to print. The process was used mainly to record landscape and architecture; moving figures and traffic did not register on the plate.

1837 France The caricaturist Gavarni (Sulpice Guillaume Chevalier, 1804–1866) began to contribute drawings satirizing social manners to the *Charivari* magazine. He was the most famous and one of the most influential social satirists of his time.

1837 Germany The Norwegian artist Adolph Tidemand (1814–1876) was working mainly in Germany from this date. He concentrated on peasant scenes.

1837
Isaac Pitman
invented system
of shorthand.
First practical
electric telegraph.

HISTORICAL EVENTS	LITERATURE	DANCE & DRAMA	MUSIC

HISTORICAL EVENTS

1838
Anti-Corn Law
League founded
in Britain.

1839
Treaty of London
guaranteed
perpetual
neutrality of
Belgium.

1840
First Opium War
between China
and Britain.

LITERATURE

1837 Spain Death of the journalist Mariano José Larra y Sanchez de Castro (b. 1809): a supporter of Romanticism, he wrote on literature, drama and politics, and satirized contemporary manners. He was an excellent prose writer, and one of the best-paid journalists of the period.

1837 Spain *El Auto da Fé*, a historical novel by Eugenio de Ochoa (1815–1872), statesman, academician and novelist. He also worked on important editions of the Spanish classics.

1837 Sweden *Grannarna* by Fredrike Bremer (1801–1865), a novelist and feminist. Her novels were basically realistic, though inclined to melodrama, and concerned family relationships.

1838 Belgium *De Leeuw van Vlaenderen* by Hendrik Conscience (1812–1883), a Flemish novelist, politician and civil servant. He is considered the most important Flemish Romantic author, and wrote about 100 novels. This work, a historical novel, is said to be the most popular Flemish book. It has been widely translated.

1839 Russia Death of Denis Vasilyevich Davydov (b. 1784), soldier and poet. Tolstoy is said to have used him as the model for Denisov in *War and Peace*.

1839 Sweden *Det Gar An* by Carl Jonas Love Almquist (1793–1866), a novelist, playwright, poet and short-story writer whose work was a mixture of realism and wild romanticism. He used fantasy to cover his attacks on both church and state.

1840–1841 Spain *Canto a Teresa* by José de Espronceda (1808–1842); influenced by Byron, he was a major Romantic poet.

1840–1850 Bohemia Political articles by Karel Havlíček Borovský (1821–1856), a Czech journalist, critic and poet; he was the first writer to use Czech successfully for political ends.

DANCE & DRAMA

1838 Brazil *The Justice of the Peace in the Country* by Martine Pena (1815–1848) ranks as the first Brazilian comedy.

1838 France *Ruy Blas* by Victor Hugo was a triumphant success. Melodrama was accepted as serious theatre.

1838 Serbia Joakim Vujic (1772–1847), called the Father of the Serbian Theatre, created the Novi Sad, an amateur company which later turned professional.

1840 Croatia The Novi Sad gave the first dramatic performance in the Croat language, in Zagreb.

1840 France Death of Pierre Gardel (b.1758), dancer and ballet-master, considered with Dauberval one of the best contemporary choreographers. He and Gaetan Vestris introduced the *rond de jambe* into ballet.

*c.***1840 Siam** Beginning of the *likay* plays in the Moslem quarters of Bangkok: performances still begin with a prayer song, although they are completely secular. There are conventional patterns of movement, but speech is naturalistic and so is action, which has a plot concerning ordinary people. *Likay* is a popular, not an academic, art. It depends largely on improvisation.

MUSIC

1838 France A new model cornet was produced by Gustave Auguste Besson (1820–1875), which still carries his name today.

1838 France Birth of Georges Bizet (d. 1875), French composer.

1838 Germany Birth of Max Bruch (d. 1920), composer and conductor.

1838 Sweden Jenny Lind (1820–1887), Swedish soprano, made her debut in Stockholm in *Der Freischütz* by Weber.

1839 England Charles Barker (1804–1879) took out a patent for his invention of the pneumatic lever for organs.

1839 France Publication of 24 Preludes by Chopin (1810–1849).

1839 Italy Giuseppe Fortunino Francesco Verdi's first known opera, *Oberto*, produced at Milan.

1839 Russia Birth of Modest Petrovich Mussorgsky (d. 1881), Russian composer.

1840 Germany Robert Alexander Schumann and Clara Wiecks were married; during this year he composed *Dichterliebe* and *Frauenliebe und Leben*.

1840 Hungary First performance of *Bátori Mária* by Ferenc Erkel (1810–1893), Hungarian pianist, conductor and composer. It was the first national opera and Hungarian operatic style developed from this.

1840 Norway Ludvig Mathias Lindeman (1812–1887), began his great collection of Norwegian folk melodies.

1840 Russia Birth of Peter Ilyich Tchaikovsky (d. 1893), Russian composer.

1840 Scotland Alexander Glen (b. 1801) established himself in Edinburgh as a bagpipe maker.

1840 Spain A method for the pianoforte was published in Madrid by Pedro Albéniz (1795–1855), who introduced the modern style of pianoforte playing into Spain.

1838–1840 Russia   Kremlin Palace, Moscow, by Konstantin Ton (1794–1881), is a hybrid of Russian and Renaissance, foreshadowing later nineteenth-century eclecticism in Russian architecture.

1838 USA Henry H. Richardson was born (died 1886), the greatest nineteenth-century American architect who was renowned for his massive Romanesque-inspired buildings, and also popularized such native American styles in building as the wood-shingle roof; his larger buildings had a timeless monumental and massive quality, as found in both the Florentine Renaissance and such neo-classical architects as Soane and Schinkel, who stressed the austere, massive geometrical.

1838 USA Alsop House, Middletown, Connecticut, was built by an unknown architect; it is one of the best of the neo-classical villas that abounded on the eastern seaboard of the USA in this period.

1839–1848 Denmark   Thorwaldsen's museum, Copenhagen; by M. G. B. Bindesbøll (1800–1856) is an astylar Greek revival building of extreme severity enlivened by unusually effective polychrome murals.

1839–1852 England   The Houses of Parliament, London, by Sir Charles Barry and Augustus W. N. Pugin are monumental Gothic revival and established the style for civic architecture in preference to the classical in England.

1839–1883 Russia The cathedral of the Redeemer, Moscow by Constantin Ton as the first neo-Byzantine building in Russia.

1839–1861 USA Ohio State Capitol by Thomas Cole (1801–48) and others is possibly the best of the neo-classical nineteenth-century American state capitol buildings.

1840–1842 England Highclere Castle by Sir Charles Barry was rebuilt in the 'Jacobethan' style popular in early nineteenth-century England.

*c.***1840 France** Venetian coloured glass paperweights began to be imported; they became the model for glass made at the factories of Baccarat, St Louis and Clichy.

1838 England John Cotman (1782–1842) published *Lier Studorium*, with 48 soft-ground etchings. This was the last of his books of etchings, and has been thought the most important.

*c.***1838 France** Eugène Delacroix (1798–1863) began to use 'divisionism', a system of colour division inspired by Watteau, juxtaposing pure colours to be blended by the eye. He developed a rough brush-stroke which added to the vigour of his colours, and his mastery of colour for structural and dramatic effect inspired van Gogh.

1839–1846 England   John Cooke Bourne (1814–1896) made two folios of lithographs: *Drawings of the London and Birmingham Railway* and *The History and Description of the Great Western Railway*. He was considered the foremost artist of the railway age.

1839 England Thomas Shotter Boys (1803–1874) published *Picturesque Architecture in Paris, Ghent, Antwerp and Rome, etc.*, a collection of plates which are important early examples of chromolithography, as distinct from hand-tinted lithographs.

1839 England Publication in London of Herschel's method of fixing photographic images on paper with hyposulphate of soda.

1840 Europe Establishment of the 'daguerrotype' as a successful portrait medium, offering intricate detail, after several improvements to the technique. In Austria, the improved Voigtländer lens was developed; in England, Goddard had improved the light-sensitivity of the plate, so reducing exposure time; in France, Fizeau had developed gilding of the photographic plate to deepen the tones of the picture.

1840 England Joseph Mallord William Turner (1775–1851) exhibited *Rain, Steam and Speed*, a painting characteristic of his later style in which he used pure colour to convey impressions, abandoning line and solid form. His work was unlike anything else in Europe at the time, and he is considered the greatest English painter.

1838
Justus Liebig founded science of biochemistry.

LITERATURE

1840 Austria *Der Kondor* by Adalbert Stifter (1805–1868), a painter and writer, especially of short stories. He valued the quiet and humble, both in human character and in landscape. His greatest gift was in expressing the harmony between man and nature.

1840 Belgium Three volumes of poems by Prudens van Duyse (1804–1859), who combined the traditions of the *rederijker* and the Romantics.

1840 Denmark A radical, satirical weekly paper, *Corsaren*, was founded by Meir Aron Goldschmidt (1819–1867), the Jewish novelist. The paper was involved in a feud with the philosopher Soren Aabye Kierkegaard (1813–1855), who claimed to have reached a deeper understanding of Christianity after being ridiculed by Goldschmidt.

1840 Italy Definitive version of *I Promessi Sposi* by Alessandro Manzoni (1785–1873), the poet and novelist. The book is a historical novel of unusual depth with an enigmatic message which still invites study. It was first written in 1827, but Manzoni revised it after coming to regard Florentine as the language of Italy. The book is considered the greatest Italian prose work since Boccaccio. Although he was thought of as the leader of the Romantic movement in Italy, Manzoni was basically a classical writer.

1840 Russia *Liricheskiy Panteon*, poems by Afanasy Afaranyevich Fet (1820–1892), a lyric poet who also translated Horace and Goethe into Russian. At first unappreciated, his poems, which were musical and impressionistic, were finally recognized by the Symbolists, writers who sought to symbolize inner values in their characters and imagery.

1841 Switzerland *Wie Uli der Knecht Glucklich Wird* by Albert Bitzius, called Jeremias Gotthelf (1797–1854), a pastor and writer of short stories. He wrote primarily to instruct, though the literary quality of his work was very high. He virtually created the genre of stories of village life.

HISTORICAL EVENTS

*1841
New Zealand
became separate
British colony.*

DANCE & DRAMA

1841 France First performance, at the Paris Opéra ballet, of *Giselle*, choreographed by Jules Perrot and Jean Coralli. The principal dancers were Carlotta Grisi (1819–1899) and Lucien Petipa (1815–1898). Perrot's choreography was well in advance of the work then usual at the Paris Opéra: *Giselle* is still considered the best embodiment of the romantic ballet then in fashion.

MUSIC

1841 Belgium Birth of Victor Mahillon (d. 1924), Belgian writer on music. He wrote important works on acoustics and musical instruments, and while curator of the museum of Brussels Conservatoire, built up his collection of musical instruments from 78 to more than 1500.

1841 Czechoslovakia Birth of Antonín Dvořák (d. 1904), Czech composer.

1841 England The Abbey Glee Club was founded in London by some of the former choir-boys of Westminster Abbey.

1841 France Birth of Emmanuel Chabrier (d. 1894), French composer.

1841 Germany A turning point in the life of Robert Alexander Schumann when, encouraged by his wife, he expanded his form of composition.

*c.***1840–1866 Canada** Cornelius
Krieghoff (?1815–1872), German painter, toured Canada
painting Indian life and landscape.

*Austria: angel in Saint Leonard am Steinhof church, Vienna, designed by
Otto Wagner*

1841 Austria Otto Wagner
born (died 1918); his architectural style foreshadowed Art
Deco.

1841 England St Giles, Chea-
dle, by Augustus W. N. Pugin,
and one of his best Gothic structures, was built with ample
funds provided by Lord Shrews-
bury.

*1841
David
Livingstone
discovered Lake
Ngami.*

LITERATURE	DANCE & DRAMA	MUSIC

1842–1844 Norway The first collection of Norwegian folktales was made by Peter Christen Asbjønsen (1812–1885) and Jørgen Moe (1813–1882).

1842 Germany *Die Judenbuche* by Annette, Freiin von Droste-Hulschoff (1797–1848), a poet and short-story writer. Her work was both realistic and poetic, similar in some respects to that of Emily Bronte.

1842 Norway A collection of poems by Henrik Arnold Wergeland (1808–1845), poet, playwright and pamphleteer. He was chiefly moved by a love of nature and of freedom. Despite a tendency to over-exuberance, he is considered Norway's most important Romantic writer and probably her greatest poet.

1842 Russia A collection of lyrics by Evgeny Abramovich Baratynsky (1800–1844), whose poetry was terse and elliptical.

1842 Russia *Dead Souls* by Nikolay Vasilyevich Gogol (1809–1852), the playwright and novelist. His work was realistic, exposing the bad aspects of life, but he was also an idealist who had suffered deeply, and he used his writing as a means of revenge. Thus, despite its realism, his work was subjective.

1843 Italy *Il Primato Morale e Civile Degli Italiani* by Vicenze Gioberti (1801–1852), philosopher and patriot. Most of his work was propaganda, aimed at the reform of Italian political and religious life. Italy was united and independent in her literature before being so in other ways.

1843 Portugal *O Bobo*, a novel by Alexandre Herculano de Carvalho e Araujo (1810–1877), historian, poet and distinguished writer of historical novels.

1843 Sweden *Cousinerna* by Sophie, Baroness von Knorring (1797–1848): the first Swedish love story.

1844–1849 Croatia Poems by Branko Radicović (1824–1853), a poet who was particularly skilled as a lyricist, though he also wrote romantic narratives and Byronic epics. His work was a reaction against the patriotic school of writing.

1842 England First performance of the ballet *Alma (La Fille de Feu)*: it was danced by Jules Perrot who choreographed for it a famous *pas de fascination*.

1842 USA Formation of the Christy Minstrels: Minstrel Shows were a native American development and owed nothing to any previous theatrical tradition.

1843 England First performance of the ballet *Ondine, ou La Naïade* by Jules Perrot and Fanny Cerito (b. 1821), to music by Pugni. It contained Ondine's dance with her own shadow, which became a celebrated solo for Cerito. The story inspired the 1958 ballet *Ondine*.

1843 Italy *Arnaldo da Brescia* by Giambattista Niccolini (1782–1861): he wrote to further the cause of a united, independent Italy.

1844 Germany *Maria Magdalena* Friedrich Hebbel (1813–1863), a German playwright whose middle-class and realistic tragedies paved the way for Ibsen.

1842 England Birth of Arthur Seymour Sullivan, English composer (d. 1900).

1842 France Alexandre François Debain (1809–1877), French instrument maker, patented the harmonium or *orgue expressif*.

1842 France Birth of Jules Émile Frédéric Massenet (d. 1912), French composer.

1842 USA Philharmonic Society of New York founded.

1843 Belgium Charles de Bériot (1802–1870) was appointed professor of violin at the Brussels Conservatoire. He is considered to be the founder of the modern Franco-Belgian school of violin playing.

1843 England The Cambridge University Musical Society was founded, as the Peterhouse Musical Society, for regular performance of music at Cambridge.

1843 France Antoine Bord (1814–1888), the French pianoforte maker, invented the *capo tasto* bar.

1843 Germany The opera, *Der Fliegende Hollander*, by Richard Wagner (1813–1883) first performed in Dresden.

1843 Norway Birth of Edvard Hagerup Grieg (d. 1907), Norwegian composer.

1844 Austria Johann Strauss, the younger, made his debut with his own band.

England: contemporary drawing of Arthur Sullivan

1843–1850 France Bibliothèque, Ste Geneviève, Paris, by Henri Labrouste (1801–1875) is one of the first French buildings to use iron on a large scale, although the usage is hidden by a traditional classical façade. The architect used iron again to great effect in 1862 for the Bibliothèque Nationale, Paris.

1843–1849 Germany Petrikirche, Hamburg, by Alexis de Châteauneuf (1799–1853) is one of the most successful of early German Gothic revival churches of great simplicity built of brick.

1843 USA Washington Buildings, Rhode Island, by James Bucklin (1801–90) is neo-classicism successfully applied to commercial use, as often occurred in the USA, whilst public buildings lapsed into dull repetition of classical modes.

1844–1846 USA Trinity Church, New York, by Richard Upjohn (1802–1878) is Gothic revival by an English-born architect specializing in Gothic churches. As a style, however, Gothic revival was never as popular in the USA as Greek revival.

1844 England Caslon type was revived by the Chiswick press; this inspired a new interest in typography as an art.

1843 Scotland The painter David Octavius Hill (1802–1870) used photography as an aid for a group portrait of the Founding Convention of the Free Church of Scotland. He began to work with Robert Adamson (d. 1848), pupil of Talbot's pupil Sir David Brewster. They took outdoor 'calotype' portraits, composed in simple masses of light and shade, not in detail.

1844 England W. H. Fox Talbot published in London his book *The Pencil of Nature*: 24 calotype photographs and an account of their development by a negative to positive process which made copies possible.

1843 James Joule defined conservation of energy (first law of thermodynamics.)

1844 Samuel Morse transmitted first message by U.S. telegraph.

HISTORICAL EVENTS	LITERATURE	DANCE & DRAMA	MUSIC

LITERATURE

1844 France *Les Trois Mousquetaires* by Alexandre Davy de la Pailleterie Dumas, Dumas *père* (1802–1870), playwright and novelist. He wrote lively and ingenious historical adventure tales, issued as serials. He frequently worked with collaborators; between them they produced 300 books.

1844 Hungary *Poems* by Sandor Petöfi (1823–1849), probably the greatest Hungarian lyric poet. His poetry showed the influence of folk literature and embodied his passionate patriotism.

1844 Italy *Arnalda di Roca* by Aleardo Aleardi (1812–1878), a poet regarded by his contemporaries as corresponding to the Romantic ideal of patriot poet. His poetry expresses his hopes for a united Italy.

1845 U.S.A. declared war on Mexico.

1845–1846 Netherlands *De Graaf von Leicester in Nederland* by Anna Louisa Geertruida Bosboom-Toussaint (1812–1886), a novelist and short-story writer. Her early books were historical novels with religious themes. The style was deliberately archaic, the psychology sound.

1845 England *Sybil* by Benjamin Disraeli, Earl of Beaconsfield (1804–1881), the statesman and novelist. His stories had exotic settings and his style was florid; his comments on contemporary life were shrewd and witty.

1845 France *Carmen* by Prosper Mérimée (1803–1870), novelist and short-story writer. His best works were *nouvelles*, long short-stories. He appealed to the contemporary taste for the exotic, describing violent happenings and colourful characters in a detached manner.

1845 Sweden *The History of the Swedes* by Erik Gustav Geijer (1783–1847), historian, composer and poet. He was the champion of moderate realism. He set many of his own poems to music.

1846 Repeal of the Corn Laws in Britain.

1846–1847 Denmark Twelve stories by Steen Steenson Blicher (1782–1848), poet and short-story writer; he was considered the most important writer in the Jutland dialect.

DANCE & DRAMA

1844 Spain *Don Juan Tenorio* by Jose Zorrilla y Moral (1817–1893), Spanish poetic romantic dramatist.

1845 England Introduction of the polka, a Bohemian dance: this and other foreign dances for couples helped to displace the country dance which was already rivalled by the waltz and quadrille.

1845 England The dancers Taglioni, Fanny Cerito, Lucille Grahn (b.1821) and Carlotta Grisi performed Jules Perrot's *Le Pas de Quatre* at the request of Queen Victoria; they were considered the greatest dancers of their time.

MUSIC

1844 France Publication of a method for clarinet by French clarinettist Hyacinthe Éléonore Klosé (1808–1880), which is still a standard work. He also remodelled the clarinet in association with Auguste Buffet.

1844 Russia Birth of Nikolay Andreyevich Rimsky-Korsakov, Russian composer (d. 1908).

1844 Russia Robert Alexander Schumann and his wife went on a concert tour to Russia.

1845 England Publication of *Boosé's Military Band Journal*, by Carl Boosé (1815–1868), a German bandmaster.

1845 France Birth of Gabriel Fauré (d. 1924), French composer.

1845 France Liszt (1811–1866) wrote *Les Préludes* the most well-known of his symphonic or tone poems, a form which he created.

1846 Belgium Antoine Joseph [known as Adolphe] Sax (1814–1894), Belgian instrument maker, patented his new invention, the saxophone.

England: The Queen and Prince Albert polka

1846–1849 England The Coal Exchange, London, by James Bunning (1802–1863) was later demolished; its domed interior was built entirely of glass and iron, with considerable architectural pretensions.

*c.***1846 England**   Development of Parian ware (unglazed biscuit porcelain) by William Copeland at Stoke-on-Trent.

LITERATURE

1846 Belgium *De Drie Zustersteden* by Karel Lodewyk Ledeganck (1805–1847). His early poems were in the *rederijker* tradition. Later he became the first Flemish Romantic poet. This work was a trilogy on three towns: Ghent, Bruges and Antwerp.

1846 Croatia *The Death of Smail-Aga Cengića* by Ivan Mazuranić (1814–1890), politician and poet. His early work was printed in the newspaper *Danica*. This poem was an epic describing the death of a Turkish chieftain, killed by Montenegrins.

1846 Russia Death of the poet Nikolay Mikhaylovich Yazykov (b. 1803), a member of the group called the Pushkin Pléiade. He wrote elegies, nature poems and patriotic verse.

1847–1848 England *Vanity Fair* by the novelist William Makepeace Thackeray (1811–1863). His work was satirical, though his attitude was kindly, and he gave a lively picture of society, written in a graceful, spontaneous style. He was influenced by Fielding.

1847–1853 France *Histoire de la Révolution Française* by Jules Michelet (1798–1874), an essayist and the most important French Romantic historian. His aim was to use his scholarship and imaginative sympathy to re-create the past.

1847 England *Jane Eyre* by the novelist Charlotte Brontë (1816–1855): like all her books, it is a Cinderella story, the heroine being in many respects similar to her creator. It has Gothic elements, and shocked its early readers by its frank analysis of a woman's feelings.

1847 England *Wuthering Heights* by Emily Jane Brontë (1818–1848), the poet and novelist, who was preoccupied with man's helplessness before his own passions and the forces of nature, both of which she portrayed with unusual power.

1847 Hungary *Toldi* by Janos Arany (1817–1882), a poet and critic writing in the classical style. This work was the first of a trilogy of epic poems, in which the hero exemplified all that was best in the national character.

HISTORICAL EVENTS

*1847
Liberia became
an independent
republic.*

DANCE & DRAMA

1847 Denmark Johan Ludwig Heiberg (1791–1860) became Director of the Danish National Theatre. His work ranged from romantic dramas to vaudevilles, a form in which he was especially interested and which he encouraged in Denmark. He was also an influential dramatic critic.

1847 Germany *Uriel Acosta* by Karl Ferdinand Gurzkow (1811–1879), a Young German dramatist: this is a Jewish play which depicts the struggle to achieve intellectual freedom.

MUSIC

1846 England First performance in Birmingham of *Elijah* by Felix Mendelssohn.

1847 England Henry Willis (1821–1901), English organ builder, commenced his career by rebuilding Gloucester Cathedral organ; later he built the organ of the Royal Albert Hall.

1847 Finland First Finnish symphony composed by Axel Gabriel Ingelius (1822–1868), Finnish author, music critic and composer.

1847 Germany Death of Felix (Bartholdy) Mendelssohn (b. 1809), German composer, pianist, organist and conductor.

1847 Scotland Birth of Alexander Campbell Mackenzie (d. 1935), Scottish composer, violinist and teacher.

1846 France The Foreign Ministry, Paris, by Jacques Lacornée (1779–1856) is Renaissance revival, a style then popular in France.

1847 Belgium Galerie de la Reine, Brussels, by J. P. Cluysenaer (1811–1880) was one of a number of early Belgian structures built of iron and glass and also an early example of a shopping gallery vaulted in glass and iron.

1847 England Death of Harvey Lonsdale Elmes, architect of St George's Hall, Liverpool, completed in 1854; his design was an amalgamation of two separate designs for a concert hall and an assize court; it is Roman in form, a variation on the basilica, and Greek in detail. The south pediment originally had sculpture by C. R. Cockerell (1788–1863) and Alfred Stevens (1817–75).

1847–1852 France Gare de l'est, Paris, by F. A. Duquesney (1790–1849) best of the early French railway stations, is distinguished by a large central lunette on the axis of the original iron and glass train shed beyond.

1847 USA Charles McKim was born (died 1909); in partnership with W. R. Mead (1846–1928) and Stanford White (1853–1906), many revival-style buildings were produced, particularly American colonial and Renaissance.

1847 England James Sharples (1825–1892), artist and engineering worker, introduced the 'heroic' treatment of industrial workers with *The Forge* (1844–1847; engraved for publication 1849–1859).

1847
Gold discovered in California led to first 'gold rush'.

USA: casino designed by McKim, Mead and White, 1881-83, Shorthills, New Jersey

1847 Hungary *Gyulai Pál* by Zsigmond, Baron Kemény (1814–1875), journalist, essayist and writer of historical novels. He was influenced by Balzac.

1847 Montenegro *The Mountain Wreath* by Peter Petrovich Njegoš (1813–1851) a poet who was greatly influenced by national poetry. This work, an account of the Montenegrin's struggle against the Turks, contains epic, dramatic, lyrical and philosophical elements, and is regarded as a masterpiece of Yugoslav literature.

1847 Russia The periodical *Sovremmenik* was acquired by the poet Nikolay Alexeyevich Nekrasov (1821–1877). In his hands it became a mouthpiece of the radical intelligentsia. Much of his work was satire. He identified with the people, and many of his non-satiric poems show how completely he had absorbed the spirit of folk songs.

1847 Slovenia Collection of poems by France Prešeren (1800–1849), a poet who combined a European outlook with a deep love of his own country and people, and helped to raise their cultural values. In his hands Slovene became a fully-fledged literary language.

1847 Spain *Escenas Andaluzas* by Serafin Estebánez Calderon (1799–1867), lawyer, scholar, poet, novelist and prose writer. This work is a series of sketches of Andalucia and its customs. One aspect of the Romantic movement was an interest in the picturesque; in Spain this is known as *costumbrismo*.

1848 Year of Revolutions; Louis Napoleon elected President of France. Franz Josef became Austrian Emperor.

1848 Norway *Det Norska Folkesprogs Grammatik* by the philologist Ivar Andreas Aasen (1813–1896). He worked for the development of *landsmal* ('national language'), a form of literary Norwegian promoted as a basis for a national literature. He wrote poems to demonstrate its possibilities.

1848 U.S.A. The *Biglow Papers* by James Russell Lowell (1819–1891), essayist, poet and diplomat, and teacher of modern languages at Harvard. Highly versatile, he was the first editor of the *Atlantic Monthly*.

1848 Russia The French choreographer Jules Perrot (1810–1890) was appointed ballet-master in St Petersburg, where he produced *Esmeralda, Faust, Giselle* and *Catarina* for Fanny Elssler and Carlotta Grisi. His work revived the Russian company which had declined on the removal of Didelot in 1829.

1848 Czechoslovakia Earliest musical periodical in Czech, *Cecilia,* founded by Josef Krejči (1821–1881), Czech organist, composer and teacher.

1848 England George Frederick Anderson (c.1801–1876) appointed Master of the Queen's Music.

1848 England Birth of Charles Hubert Hastings Parry (d. 1918), English composer, scholar and teacher.

1848 Germany Franz Liszt settled at Weimar, where he remained for 13 years.

England: 'Lorenzo and Isabella' by J. E. Millais

1848 USA Union Station, Providence, Rhode Island, is by Thomas Tefft (1826–59), and an example of *Rundbogenstil* in the USA in Lombardic brick.

1848–1853 England The pre-Raphaelite movement fl. with members including Sir John Everett Millais (1829–1896), William Holman Hunt (1827–1910) and Dante Gabriel Rossetti (1828–1882). Their work had a strong literary flavour, combined with a use of poetic symbolism and narrative detail. Rossetti was taught by Hunt, the only one of the three who remained faithful to pre-Raphaelite ideas all his life. Millais continued to paint minutely detailed pictures of great con viction until *c*.1863.

1848 U.S.A. *The Raven and Other Poems* by Edgar Allan Poe (1809–1849), poet, critic and short-story writer. He was preoccupied with abnormality and transience, and fitted ill into the optimistic American scene. He was influenced by Coleridge, and is probably America's most markedly Romantic poet. After his death his influence was particularly strong in France. He also wrote the first detective stories, including *The Murders in the Rue Morgue* (1843).

1848 Poland *Halka*, an opera by Stanislaw Moniuszko (1819–1872), Polish composer, first performed; it was an important work in the development of Polish opera.

1849 Finland Publication of the new *Kalevala*, the Finnish national epic (there had been two previous versions, the first unpublished): it was compiled by the scholar Elias Lönnrot (1802–1884) from his collection of Finnish folk-songs. The work is centred around the exploits of five warrior heroes; alliterative in style and full of repetition, it is written in unrhymed octosyllabic lines.

1849 France *Adrienne Lecouvreur* by Eugène Augustin Scribe (1791–1861) in collaboration with Gabriel Legouvé, a play on the life of the famous actress: the leading rôle was created by Rachel (1821–1858). Scribe invented the 'Well-Made Play,' a model of neat and economic construction.

1849 France Death of Fryderyk Franciszek Chopin (b. 1810), Polish pianist and composer of French descent.

1849 Spain *La Gaviota* by Cecilia Böhl de Faber, called Fernán Caballero (1796–1877): a romantic novel, it is interesting for the intelligently observed pictures of Andalusian life and customs. It helped to revive interest in *costumbrismo*.

1849 U.S.A. First stage appearance of Edwin Booth (1833–1893) one of America's greatest actors, particularly celebrated for his portrayal of Hamlet.

1850
Hung Siu-Tsuen proclaimed himself Emperor of China.

1850 England *David Copperfield* by Charles Dickens (1812–1870), a novelist who set out to expose social evils. His early career as a journalist left its mark on his work, which contains much documentary writing. Dickens excelled in the creation of social setting and in caricature. He made tours, giving readings of his work.

*c.***1850 Spain** The *Sardana*, the Catalonian national dance, was arranged in its modern form by a village musician, Ventura.

1850 Czechoslovakia Birth of Zdeněk Fibich (d. 1900), Czech composer.

1850 Austria The first Slovene Workers' Theatre was opened for the mining community in Idrija.

1850 Germany Bach Gesellschaft established with the object of publishing a complete critical edition of works of Johann Sebastian Bach.

1850 England *In Memoriam* by the poet Alfred, 1st Lord Tennyson (1809–1892). He was most remarkable for his skill in handling metre, and his appreciation of the musical qualities of the English language. Many of his subjects were legendary or historical; he wrote a series of poems around King Arthur in which Arthur appeared as the ideal Victorian man. (The Victorians valued a smooth-running society, and regarded as virtues any qualities which contributed to it.) Tennyson was poet laureate, and his poems were best-sellers.

1850 Germany First performance of Wagner's *Lohengrin* at Weimar. It was produced by Liszt while Wagner was in exile in Switzerland.

1850 Portugal Birth of Alfredo Keil (d. 1907), Portuguese composer of German ancestry and creator of Portuguese opera.

USA: Navajo design

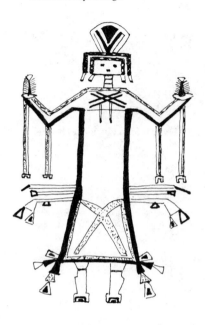

1848 Denmark Death of the painter Christen Købke (b. 1810), noted for his studies of suburban life in Copenhagen.

1848 France Charles-François Daubigny (1817–1879) began to exhibit landscapes at the Salon. He was one of the earliest open-air landscape artists, concentrating on rivers, canals and coastal scenes. Both Boudin and Monet admired his work.

1848 France Revolution inspired Honoré Daumier (1810–1879), painter and lithographer, to return to political satire and create his 'Robert Macaire' and 'Ratapoil' characters. He was considered the greatest caricaturist of his age.

1849 England *Seven Lamps of Architecture* by John Ruskin (1819–1900), an influential book advocating functional planning and honesty in the use of materials and in construction, was published.

1849 USA Laing Stores, New York, by James Bogardus (1800–1874) which was erected in only two months has four storeys and had an early example of a cast-iron façade with Grecian detailing. The use of cast iron in commercial buildings then became widespread in America.

1850–1853 England All Saints, Margaret Street, London, by William Butterfield (1814–1900) was the first Victorian high Gothic church, remarkable for its polychromatic-brick exterior and lavishly decorated interior.

1850–1870 England Lambeth pottery active under H. Doulton: it was his policy to restore the individual artist potter in what had become an industrialized art.

1850–1860 France Restoration of Notre Dame, Paris; this stimulated a revival of wrought-iron work. Attempts were made to revive the art in France, England and Germany during the nineteenth and twentieth centuries, most of them based on recreating period styles.

*c.*1850 **Bohemia** Dominic Biemann active: he was an outstanding engraver of portrait miniatures on Bohemian glass.

*c.*1850 **England** Development of polychrome printing on ceramics by Staffordshire potters, who at first used it mainly on pot lids.

*c.*1850 **U.S.A.** The Navajo Indians learned silver-working from Spanish-Mexican craftsmen: Navajo work is noted for its massiveness and simple design.

1850–1860 Australia Popular lithographs by S. T. Gill (1818–1880) recorded vividly the life of the gold diggings.

1850 France Gustave Courbet (1819–1877) exhibited *The Stone Breaker* and *The Burial at Ornans* which established him as leader of a school of detached realism. Unlike Millet, he saw the lives of working people in terms of their pictorial value and not their emotional impact.

1850 France *The Sower* by Jean Millet (1814–1875) was the first of his paintings of peasant life and the rural working day, seen in all seasons and in all shades of light from dawn until moonlight. His figure drawing gave his subjects a monumental dignity. His emotional involvement with his subjects was not always well received.

1850 Rudolf Clausius outlined second law of thermodynamics.

HISTORICAL EVENTS	LITERATURE	DANCE & DRAMA	MUSIC

LITERATURE

1850 U.S.A. *The Scarlet Letter* by Nathaniel Hawthorne (1804–1864), novelist and short-story writer. One of the classics of American literature, the book is concerned with sin and its consequences in a Puritan society.

1851 France The beginning of a series of weekly articles by the critic Charles Augustin Sainte-Beuve (1804–1869), a champion of the Romantics.

1851 U.S.A. *Moby Dick* by Hermann Melville (1818–1891), poet, novelist and short-story writer. Now regarded as one of the world's great novels, the book, a symbolic tale of sin and expiation, was unrecognized at the time.

DANCE & DRAMA

1851 France *Le Chapeau de Paille d'Italie* by Eugène Labiche (1815–1888) the foremost French humorist of the day.

1851 Germany Franz Dingelstedt (1814–1881) became Director of the Munich Theatre. He used actors from all over Germany and made theatre history with his elaborate productions.

1851 Germany Publication of *Oper und Drama* by Richard Wagner (1813–1883): it expressed his theories that all the music, scenery, stage machinery, movement, costume etc., which he called the *Gesamkunstwerk*, should be under the sole control of one director.

HISTORICAL EVENTS

1852 Second French Empire proclaimed with Napoleon III as Emperor.

LITERATURE

1852 England *Empedocles on Etna* by Matthew Arnold (1822–1888), poet and critic, Son of a celebrated headmaster, and himself an inspector of schools, he was particularly concerned to encourage the growth of culture.

1852 France *Emaux et Camées* by Théophile Gautier, (1811–1872) poet, novelist and art and literary critic. His doctrine was 'art for art's sake', the theory that moral, social or political considerations are irrelevant in the search for ideal beauty.

1852 Germany *Quickborn* by Klaus Groth (1819–1899): a collection of narrative and lyric poetry written in Low German, which Groth handled with masterly skill. He was in part responsible for a revival of Low German literature, and became professor in that subject at Kiel.

1852 Hungary '*Midst the Wild Carpathians* by Mór Jokai (1825–1904), a writer of popular novels with exotic settings, some real, some imaginary. His work combined romance, humour, and easy narrative style. Despite the disapproval of important critics, he was highly successful.

DANCE & DRAMA

1852 France *La Dame aux Camélias* by Alexandre Dumas fils (1824–1895) was an early example of French social drama, Dumas being concerned to bring about social reforms.

MUSIC

1852 Czechoslovakia Birth of Otakar Ševčík (d. 1934), Czech violinist and teacher. His method has influenced generations of violinists, and some studies are still used.

1852 Germany Earliest works composed by Johannes Brahms (1833–1897), including many songs. Song-writing constituted an important part of his early compositions.

1852 Ireland Birth of Charles Villiers Stanford (d. 1924), Irish composer, conductor and teacher. Among his pupils were Vaughan Williams and Arthur Bliss.

1852 Switzerland Birth of Hans Huber (d. 1921), the most important Swiss composer of the second half of the nineteenth century; he was director of the Basel Conservatory 1896–1918.

1850 Germany Adolf Menzel (1815–1905) painted *Frederick at Dinner with his Friends*, one of a series celebrating the life of Frederick the Great and appealing strongly to Prussian nationalism. His sketches from nature, never exhibited, were influenced by Constable and anticipated impressionism, although he said he disliked impressionist painting. His work in this style was later considered more important than his set pieces.

1851–1854 Brazil Palacio Itamarati, Rio de Janerio, by J. M. J. Rebelo (1821–72) is a sophisticated French Empire-styled house: the French tradition in Brazil was then strong, following the arrival of a number of French artists at the beginning of the century.

1851 England Exhibition of cased glass, in which a thin outer layer is cut away to reveal the main body, and of cut glass, by Bohemian glassmakers at the Great Exhibition, London; this has influenced glass manufacture in England ever since.

*1851
Isaac Singer
manufactured
first practical
sewing machine.*

1851–1901 England Sir John Tenniel (1820–1914) drew cartoons for *Punch* magazine which, with his illustrations to *Alice in Wonderland*, are his best known work.

1851 England The Crystal Palace, London by Sir Joseph Paxton (1801–1865), the first prefabricated building in iron, glass and laminated wood, erected in only 9 months, was 548 m long and inspired many similar buildings in Europe; later it was re-erected and extended at Sydenham and finally destroyed in 1936.

1851 England Invention of the collodion or 'wet-plate' process of producing a photographic plate; the fastest process so far, it aided quick, take-away portrait services.

1852–1854 England Paddington Station, London, by Isambard K. Brunel (1806–1859) and Sir Matthew Wyatt (1820–1877) is an early railway station built in iron and glass but with curious additional decorative work.

1852 Russia Death of Pavel Feodotov (b. 1815), who painted scenes from daily life in sentimental or slightly satirical style. He enjoyed great popularity in his time.

*1852
Heinrich Barth
explored Lake
Chad.
Livingstone
started to explore
Zambesi River.*

1852–1857 France New Louvre, Paris, by L. T. J. Visconti (1791–1853) and H. M. Lefuel (1810–80) is a prime example of the Second Empire style, characterized by a boldly plastic façade and end and centre pavilions with high mansard roofs.

1852 Spain Antonio Gaudi y Cornet was born (died 1926), one of the most original architectural talents inspired by Islamic and Gothic sources, whose work is mainly found in Barcelona.

England: 'Alice in Garden of Live Flowers' by Tenniel

1853 U.S.A. *Uncle Tom's Cabin* by Harriet Beecher Stowe (1811–1896): the book's powerful anti-slavery message made it world famous. While Abolition was probably the most important issue, reform of many social injustices preoccupied American writers at this time and later.

1854–1861 Hungary Critical articles by Pál Gyulai (1826–1909), critic, poet and short-story writer: his standards were classical and his views highly influential.

1854 France *Les Chimères*, sonnets by Gérard Labrunie, called Gérard de Nerval (1808–1855), poet, playwright, prose writer and translator. His work contained elements of mystery and showed the influence of the occult, while his travels in Europe and the East provided colour and exotic. He was a forerunner of the Symbolists, who treated characters and images as symbols of abstract qualities.

1854 Portugal *Misterios de Lisboa* by Camilo Castelo Branco (1825–1890), who wrote nearly 200 novels. He tackled a wide variety of types: satirical, historical, romantic (based on his own life, which was stormy), regional (he excelled at these), and serial mysteries, of which this work is an example. Despite weaknesses in plot and construction, his novels remain popular.

1854 Crimean War began.

1854 Switzerland *Der Grüne Heinrich* by Gottfried Keller (1819–1890), a poet, novelist and short-story writer remarkable for his good humour and realistic approach to life. This book was an autobiographical novel.

1854 U.S.A. *Walden; or Life in the Woods* by Henry David Thoreau (1817–1862), essayist and poet, a member of the Transcendental movement; the work is an account of his own experiences, living in a hut in the Massachusetts woods, with reflections on life and society.

1854 Wales *Y Storm*, poems by William Thomas, called Islwyn (1832–1878). His most important work was highly personal, an attempt to make sense of his distress on the death of his fiancée.

1854 Denmark The choreographer August Bournonville created the ballet *Brudefaerden i Hardanger* for the Royal Danish Ballet, using Norwegian folk dances. It was his last production before he left for a 10-year period of work in other countries, feeling that Danish interest in ballet was declining. The company was able to retain his ballets, his teaching and his choreography.

1854 Italy The American dancer Augusta Maywood joined one of the many touring companies which took ballet all over the country, preserving the teachings of Carlo Blasis' Milan school in a repertoire including ballets by Jules Perrot.

1853 England Tonic Sol-fa Association founded by John Curwen (1816–1880), musical educationist.

1853 England Publication of 12 anthems by Samuel Sebastian Wesley (1810–1876), English organist and composer of church music.

1853 France Victor Mustel (1815–1890), French manufacturer of harmoniums, established in Paris. He invented 'double expression' and the métaphone, as well as the celesta.

1853 Germany Julius Blüthner (1824–1910) opened his pianoforte manufactory in Leipzig.

1853 Germany Johannes Brahms (1833–1897) first met Robert Schumann (1810–1856) and became an intimate friend of the family. Clara Schumann was a great influence in his life.

1853 Italy Giuseppe Verdi composed *Il Trovatore* and *La Traviata*.

1853 U.S.A. Steinway & Sons, pianoforte makers, established in New York.

1854 Czechoslovakia Birth of Leoš Janáček (d. 1928), Czech composer.

1854 France First performance of *L'Enfance du Christ* by Hector Berlioz (1803–1869) which, in its use of old musical modes, had an air of serenity, a complete change of mood from his earlier fiery works.

1854 France Earliest known works by Georges Bizet (1838–1875), largely unpublished.

1854 Germany Birth of Engelbert Humperdinck (d. 1921), German composer.

ARCHITECTURE

1853 France Baron Haussman was appointed Prefect of the Seine Department and between 1853 and 1870 supervised sweeping changes to the plan of Paris, notably in the use of broad boulevards and *rond points*.

THREE DIMENSIONAL ART

1853 England John Ruskin (1819–1900), art critic, published *The Stones of Venice* and championed craft, as against industrial, processes for social reasons.

VISUAL ARTS

1853 France The photographer Gaspard Félix Tournachon, called Nadar (1820–1910) opened a Paris studio where he practised until 1880 taking portraits of famous Parisians; he used the camera to reproduce character as well as likenesses.

England: portrait of John Ruskin by H. van Herkomen

1854 France St Eugène Church, Paris, by Louis Boileau (1812–1896) has the arcade and rib vault of iron, without Gothic decoration. Boileau wrote about the uses of iron in architecture.

1854 England John Martin (1789–1854) painted *The Great Day of his Wrath*, an apocalyptic scene said to be inspired by a journey through the 'Black Country' of industrial England, at night.

HISTORICAL
EVENTS
*1855
Death of Tsar
Nicholas I of
Russia.*

LITERATURE

1855 Bohemia *The Grand-mother* by Božena Němcová (1820–1862), a realistic novelist. Particularly concerned with the position of women in society, she based this book on memories of her own grandmother, who was an important formative influence. It is considered a landmark in Czech prose literature.

1855 Denmark *The Flight of the Stag*, a poem by Rasmus Villads Christian Ferdinand Winther (1796–1876). His preferred themes were love of his native Zealand and love of women. He was influenced by Byron and Heine, and led a revival of Danish poetry.

1855 Germany *Kaspar-Ohm un Ik* by John Brinckmann (1814–1870), poet and short-story writer. He was particularly successful with short stories in Low German, and with animal stories. He took as his starting point the humorous anecdote, the *Schnurre*.

1855 Russia *Oblomov*, a novel by Ivan Alexandreivich Goncharov (1812–1891): the hero was an ineffectual man, of no value to society, a type first depicted by Lermontov.

1855 U.S.A. *The Song of Hiawatha* by Henry Wadsworth Longfellow (1807–1882), a poet using both native American and European material. His verse was romantic and moralistic, and in his day he was enormously popular.

1855 U.S.A. *Leaves of Grass* by Walt Whitman (1819–1892), journalist and poet. He modelled his style on Old Testament rhythms, rejecting conventional patterns. He expanded Emerson's ideas, and was the first American poet to celebrate 'the masses'.

1856 France *Madame Bovary*, a novel by Gustave Flaubert (1821–1880). His aim was to give a detached analysis of a situation, offering no moral judgements, and written in flawless prose. The book told the story of a provincial woman discontented with the bourgeois society in which she lived. It caused a legal action to be brought against Flaubert, who was accused of writing an immoral book.

DANCE & DRAMA

1855 Russia *A Month in the Country* by Ivan Sergeivich Turgenev (1818–1883): the first Russian psychological drama.

MUSIC

1855 England *A Method of Harmonium* was published by Thomas Julian Adams (1824–1887), who introduced Debain's harmonium into England.

1855 England *Mr and Mrs German Reed's Entertainment*, a new type of musical drama, was started in England by Thomas German Reed (1817–1888), English musician.

1856 Czechoslovakia A kind of contra-bassoon invented by Václav František Červený (1819–1896), Czech instrument maker of international reputation.

1856 England Birth of John Alexander Fuller-Maitland (d. 1936), a pioneer of the revival of English folk-song and an important contributor to musical literature.

ARCHITECTURE

1855–1859 England Oxford University museum by Sir Thomas Deane (1792–1871) and Benjamin Woodward (1815–61) has iron and glass given the decorative high Victorian Gothic treatment by these Dublin architects.

THREE DIMENSIONAL ART

VISUAL ARTS

1855 England *The Last of England* by Ford Madox Brown (1821–1893) is characteristic of his paintings in the style of the pre-Raphaelites and concerned with social realism.

1855 France Edgar Degas (1834–1917) entered the Ecole des Beaux-Arts and met Ingres, who convinced him of the supremacy of draughtsmanship in painting.

INVENTIONS & DISCOVERIES
1855 Livingstone discovered Victoria Falls.

France: 'Young Spartans Exercising' by Edgar Degas

1856 Scotland Caledonia Road Free Church, Glasgow, is by Alexander Thomson (1817–1875), who was known at 'Greek Thomson', and produced a number of original buildings in the classical style in Scotland, of which this is a singular example.

1856 England Alfred Stevens (1818–1875) began work on his masterpiece, the monument to Wellington in St. Paul's Cathedral, which occupied the rest of his life. He revived the composition style and versatility of the Renaissance.

1856 England A chemist discovered a synthetic mauve dye which provided a completely new colour. This was the first synthetic dye and marked the beginning of a 25-year period of work in the field, important not only in textiles but also in painting because of the use of dyestuff lakes.

1856 Sir Richard Burton and John Speke set out to discover source of river Nile. Louis Pasteur developed germ theory of disease; beginning of bacteriology.

HISTORICAL EVENTS	LITERATURE	DANCE & DRAMA	MUSIC

LITERATURE

1856 Germany *Mozart auf der Reise Nach Prag* by Eduard Mörike (1804–1875), a poet whose work marks the transition from Romanticism to realism. He was considered a superb lyricist.

1856 Hungary *'Neath the Hoof of the Tartar* by Miklos, Baron Josika (1794–1865), the first Hungarian novelist to write historical novels; he was greatly influenced by Scott.

1857 Indian Mutiny. Garibaldi formed the Italian National Association to secure Italian unity.

1857, 1861, 1868 France *Les Fleurs du Mal*, a novel by Charles Pierre Baudelaire (1821–1867), critic and poet; he was remarkable for his subtle use of language and his striking associations. His poetry abounds in oriental images and in references to sea voyages. He was influenced by Poe, whose work he translated. Highly original, he had many followers, and paved the way for symbolism and, later, surrealism. This book caused him to be prosecuted for obscenity.

1857 Denmark *Phantaserne*, the only novel by Hans Egede Schack (1820–1859), lawyer and politician. It is a highly original satire against prevailing literary fashion. Its theme is day-dreaming.

1857 England *Barchester Towers*, a novel by Anthony Trollope (1815–1882). He believed that his job was to create human beings in which the reader could entirely believe. His most popular books (he wrote over 40) are set in a cathedral town, and are mainly concerned with its clergy. In his autobiography (1883) he stated that he wrote for money.

1858 Administration of India transferred to British crown.

1858 Bohemia The literary journal *Maj* was founded by Jan Neruda (1834–1891) and Vitezslav Halek (1835–1874). The journal gave its name to the reformist movement in Czech letters.

1858 India *Sarmistha* by Michael Madhusudana Dutt (1824–1873), a Bengali poet and playwright. His poems include three epics on Indian themes, and show the influence of Milton.

DANCE & DRAMA

1857 Norway Bjørnstjerne Bjørnson (1832–1910) became Director of the Bergen Theatre. He preceded Ibsen in writing realistic plays on social problems.

MUSIC

1856 Germany Friedrich Wilhelm Carl Bechstein (1826–1900) started his pianoforte-making business in Berlin.

1856 Germany Death of Robert Alexander Schumann (b. 1810), German composer.

1856 Italy Birth of Giuseppe Martucci (d. 1909), Italian pianist, conductor and composer a pioneer in the renaissance of instrumental music in Italy.

1857 England Birth of Edward William Elgar (d. 1934), composer.

1857 England Hallé Orchestra formed in Manchester by Charles Hallé (1819–1895).

1858 England Birth of Ethel Mary Smyth (d. 1944), composer of operas and a mass.

1858 France Production in Paris of *Orpheus in the Underworld* by Jacques Offenbach (1819–1880), German/French composer. Offenbach produced 90 operettas including *La Belle Hélène* and *La Vie Parisienne*. His greatest work, *Tales of Hoffman* (1881), was completed after his death by Ernest Guiraud (1837–1892).

1858 Germany Rudolph Koenig (1832–1901), physicist, established own business as maker of acoustical apparatus. He is remembered for his tuning-forks, tuning fork tonometer and clock-fork.

ARCHITECTURE	THREE DIMENSIONAL ART	VISUAL ARTS	INVENTIONS & DISCOVERIES

ARCHITECTURE

1856 USA Louis H. Sullivan was born (died 1924); he was leader of the Chicago school of architecture and a pioneer in skyscraper design.

1857 USA Belle Grove, White Castle, Louisiana, by Henry Howard was, before its destruction, one of the largest of the great neo-classical houses of the Deep South; most have unpedimented porticoes and few were designed by architects.

THREE DIMENSIONAL ART

1856 France Théodore Deck (d. 1891) was established as a potter in Paris: he was the greatest of the French innovators and was instrumental in the revival of handmade decorative pots.

1857 Germany Death of Christian Rauch (b. 1777), sculptor: he was influenced by Thorwaldsen but escaped his master's cold style through his own lively interest in nature. His best known works were portrait busts of great contemporaries.

France: Théodore Deck's pottery—signatures and design from a plate

VISUAL ARTS

1857 England Oscar Gustave Rejlander (1813–1875) made prints from groups of negatives to compose big allegorical pictures, such as *The Two Ways of Life*. Photographers saw in their medium a means of 'instant painting'.

1857 Spain Eduardo Rosales Y Martinez (1836–1873) became head of the Spanish school in Rome. He developed an interest in the work of Dégas and Manet, and their influence appeared in his painting.

1858 England *Fading Away* by Henry Peach Robinson, a narrative photograph of a death-bed scene: Victorians who would have accepted this subject in a painting found it painful and distressing in the realistic medium of photography.

1858 France Eugène Boudin (1824–1898) saw drawings by Claude Monet (1840–1926) and persuaded him to paint from nature. Boudin's own work was mainly inspired by the landscape of Normandy and the Seine estuary.

INVENTIONS & DISCOVERIES

*1857
First steel
steamship built.*

*1858
Auguste Kekule
outlined theory of
molecular
structure, the
basis of organic
chemistry.*

HISTORICAL EVENTS	LITERATURE	DANCE & DRAMA	MUSIC

LITERATURE

1858 Russia *A Thousand Souls* by Alexey Feofilaktovich Pisemsky (1820–1881), a novelist of the Natural school who was remarkable for his good plots and characterization.

1858 U.S.A. *Autocrat of the Breakfast Table* by Oliver Wendell Holmes (1809–1894), novelist, poet and essayist, and professor of anatomy at Harvard. His work was witty and elegant.

1859 Peace of Villa Franca between Austria and Sardinia.

1859 France *Elle et Lui*, a novel by Amandine-Aurore-Lucie Dupin, called Georges Sand (1804–1876), novelist and feminist. Her early books were sentimental romances; later she tackled social problems, pastoral idylls, and personal stories inspired by her many liaisons. Among her many lovers were Musset and Chopin.

1860 Abraham Lincoln elected U.S. President.

1859 Spain The revival of the medieval *Jocs Florals*, an annual literary competition for writers in Catalan, marked a resurgence of literary interest in the language.

1860 England *The Mill on the Floss*, a novel by Mary Ann Evans, called George Eliot (1819–1880). Her books were realistic portrayals of provincial life, and showed concern for the importance of duty and high moral standards. Skilled in portraiture, she was one of the first writers to portray 'intellectual' men.

DANCE & DRAMA

1859 Russia *The Storm* by Alexander Nikoleivich Ostrovski (1823–1886), a writer of realistic plays depicting Russian middle-class life.

1859 U.S.A. *The Octoroon* by Dionysus Lardher Boucicault (1822–1890) is the first play in which the American Negro is treated seriously on the stage.

1860 England *The Colleen Bawn* by Boucicault. He was an Irishman who worked in both England and the U.S.A., knew exactly what the public wanted and how to provide it. Many of his plays are melodramatic, but the background is naturalistic.

1860 Russia Swedish dancer Christian Johansson (1817–1903) became a teacher at the Imperial School of ballet. He had studied with August Bournonville and in turn taught Kchessinska, Preobrajenska and Paul Gerdt. His assistance was valuable to the balletmaster Marius Petipa, who was not a teacher.

1860 Russia Jules Perrot left the Imperial Ballet in St Petersburg. He was succeeded by Arthur Saint-Léon (1815–1870), mediocre as a choreographer but a good diplomat who achieved easier working conditions.

MUSIC

1859 France First performance of the opera *Faust* by Charles François Gounod (1818–1893). Of his operas, *Mireille* (1864) is considered his most successful.

1859 Germany Death of Louis Spohr (b. 1784), German violinist and composer.

1859 Switzerland Nicolas Eugène Simoutre (1839–1908), French violin maker, established at Basel; he made various improvements including the invention of a bass bar.

1860 Austria Birth of Gustav Mahler (d. 1911), Austrian (Bohemian) conductor and composer.

1860 Austria Johann Strauss the younger (1825–1899) began composing his master waltzes.

1860 Austria *Das Pensionat* by Franz von Suppé (1819–1895) was the first Viennese operetta. Others by Suppé were *Light cavalry* and *The Beautiful Galatea*.

1860 Austria Birth of Hugo Philipp Jakob Wolf (d. 1903), Austrian composer.

1860 England First edition of *Hymns Ancient and Modern* published.

1860 Hungary A musical periodical, *Zenészeti Lapok*, was founded in Hungary by Lászlófalui és Mikefoldi Ábrányi (1822–1903), containing the programme of the national movement of Hungarian music; it constitutes one of the most valuable historical documents of the period.

1861 Emancipation of Russian serfs. American Civil War began.

1861 Greenland Foundation of *Atuagagdliutit*, a periodical containing news, articles and translations of Danish, English, French and German novels. Attempts were made during this period to collect the folk tales which had been suppressed when Greenland was colonized.

1861 Spain *El Antiguo Madrid* by the essayist Ramon de Mesonero Romanos (1803–1882), who was probably the best writer of the *costumbrismo* movement. He wrote sober, keenly observed accounts of Madrid life and architecture.

1861 Poland Theatrical début of Helena Modjeska (1844–1909), celebrated Polish actress and one of the leading performers of the day.

1860 U.S.A. The American organ under its present name was introduced by Mason & Hamlin of Boston. The principle of this organ was first discovered in 1835 in the factory of Alexandre of Paris.

1861 Russia Nicolay Andreyevich Rimsky-Korsakov (1844–1908) became acquainted with Mily Alexeyevich Balakirev (1837–1910) who was chief of a group of Russian composers known as the *Kutchka* and this had a profound influence on his future career. Other members of the *Kutchka* were Borodin, Cui and Mussorgsky.

ARCHITECTURE	THREE DIMENSIONAL ART	VISUAL ARTS	INVENTIONS & DISCOVERIES

1859–1888 Austria Ringstrasse, Vienna, by Ludwig Förster (1797–1863) and others necessitated the demolition of the old fortifications of the city to make way for major redevelopment including groups of public buildings erected in various styles, in particular the high Renaissance.

1859–1867 Canada Parliament House, Ottawa by Thomas Fuller (1822–98) and Herbert Jones (1836–1923) is one of the most successful high Victorian Gothic buildings outside England.

1859 England The Red House, Bexleyheath, was built for William Morris by Philip Webb (1831–1915), a leading architect of brick private houses in the revived English vernacular tradition.

1859–1863 Germany The Exchange, Berlin, by Friedrich Hitzig (1811–81) is an imposing building presaging the ponderous neo-baroque popular in Germany at the end of the century, especially in Berlin, the new capital.

1859–1879 USA St Patrick's Cathedral, New York, by James Fenwick (1818–95) is a vast Gothic building by an architect famous for his neo-medieval work.

1860 U.S.A. The figure of 'Armed Liberty' on the dome of the Capitol, Washington, made by Thomas Crawford (1813–1857) and typified his vigorous and simple style.

1859 Spain Death of Jose de Madrazo, a leading academic painter.

1859 U.S.A. Edward Anthony (1818–88) published a series of stereographic photographs of New York city streets. This was the first time an instantaneous exposure had been achieved that would successfully arrest moving subjects.

1860–1900 Netherlands Creative period of the Hague school of painting, a romantic and nostalgic revival of seventeenth-century landscape painting. Antoine Mauve (1838–1888) was considered its most distinguished artist; he painted ordinary scenes in a silvery palette, and impressed van Gogh, who was his nephew.

1859
Origin of Species by Natural Selection by Charles Darwin published.

England: William Morris design for chintz

1861 Belgium Baron Victor Horta was born (died 1947), the leading architect in the Art Nouveau style c.1900.

1861–1874 France The Opéra, Paris, by Charles Garnier (1825–1898) was the most showy neo-baroque building of the Second Empire, prominently sited in Baron Haussman's new high Victorian style.

1861 England William Morris (1834–1896) and associates set up Morris, Marshall, Faulkner and Company to make by hand furniture, metalware, ceramics, glass, textiles and wall-papers.

1861 U.S.A. *Falling Gladiator* by William Rimmer (1816–1879), sculptor: it was characteristic of his vigorous figures with exaggerated forms.

HISTORICAL
EVENTS
*1862
Otto von
Bismarck became
Prussian premier.*

LITERATURE

1862–1869 Russia *War and Peace* by Lev Nikolayevich, Count Tolstoy (1828–1910). A realistic novelist, playwright, short-story writer and philosopher of tremendous creative vitality, Tolstoy developed a philosophy based on the teachings of Jesus and of Rousseau, which he attempted to live out on his own estate. This book, a panoramic view of Russian society during the Napoleonic wars, is the longest nineteenth-century novel, and was unprecedented in its scope.

1862 Belgium *Gedichten, Gezangen, Gebeden*, poems by Guido Gezelle (1830–1899): inspired by love—of God, nature, his native land, and his friends—his poems use a diction and rhythm based on everyday speech. Gezelle was a highly original poet and had a profound influence on other writers.

1862 Bulgaria The American Bible Society commissioned Petko Slaveykov (1827–1895) to translate the Bible into modern Bulgarian. The modern literary language, based on north-east Bulgarian dialects, was established by the publication of this translation.

1862 France *Poèmes Barbares* by Charles-Marie-René Leconte de Lisle (1818–1894), leader of the Parnassians, a group of poets contributing to *Le Parnasse Contemporain*. They were particularly concerned with craftsmanship, and an impersonal approach to their subject. This was in part a reaction against the Romantics' tendency to subjectivity.

1862 Germany *Ut Mine Festungstid* by Fritz Reuter (1810–1874), poet and novelist. Together with Klaus Groth, he was responsible for a revival of Low German literature. He is one of the foremost German humorists.

1862 Germany *Ekkehard*, a novel by Josef Victor von Scheffel (1826–1886), poet and novelist. Much of his work was historical, appealing to the new middle classes who took a rather sentimental interest in their country's past. He also wrote a collection of drinking songs.

DANCE & DRAMA

1862 Japan *Benten the Thief* by Kawatake Mokuami (1816–1893), the last important *kabuki* dramatist.

1862 Russia The ballet-master Marius Petipa (1822–1910) choreographed his first full-length ballet for the Imperial Theatre: *La Fille du Pharaon*, a lavish production for the star ballerina Rosati. Petipa had worked in France and Spain, and in Russia under Perrot. His own ballets were composed to strict formulae with little dramatic flow, but he did conscientiously preserve the Perrot repertoire.

MUSIC

1862 Austria The first of four volumes of *Geschischte der Musik* by August Wilhelm Ambros (1816–1876) was published. The last volume, published in 1881, was compiled from his notes.

1862 Austria Publication of *Chronologisch-thematisches Verzeichniss*, a catalogue of Mozart's works, by Ludwig Ritter von Köchel (1800–1877), Austrian musicographer and naturalist.

1862 Czechoslovakia A provisional theatre of Czech opera was opened, largely through the activities of Bedřich Smetana (1824–1884).

1862 England Birth of Frederick Delius (d. 1934), English composer of mixed continental extraction.

1862 England First public performance of music by Arthur Seymour Sullivan (1842–1900), incidental music to *The Tempest*, which established his reputation.

1862 France Birth of Claude Debussy (d. 1918), French composer.

1862 Germany *Lehre von den Tonempfindungen als Physiologische Grundlage fur die Theorie der Musik* (known in England as 'The Sensations of Tone'), by Hermann Ludwig Ferdinand Helmholtz (1821–1894), German physiologist and physicist.

1862 Norway First published songs and piano pieces by Edvard Hagerup Grieg (1843–1907). He began composing at the age of nine.

ARCHITECTURE

1862 Ireland St Finbar Cathedral, Cork, by William Burges (1827–1881) is a huge French neo-Gothic-style church by an architect acquainted at first hand with continental medieval architecture.

THREE DIMENSIONAL ART

1862 England John Gibson (1790–1866), sculptor, exhibited *The Tinted Venus*: his interest in Greek art led him to experiment with colouring statues. He was internationally influential, after Thorwaldsen and Canova, as a neo-classical sculptor.

VISUAL ARTS

1862 France The painters Boudin and Monet met Johan-Barthold Jongkind (1819–1891), the Dutch landscape painter, and were greatly influenced by the freshness of his style. He did not paint directly from the scene but from preliminary sketches; his pictures nevertheless were considered spontaneous 'impressions'.

INVENTIONS & DISCOVERIES
1862
J. B. L. Foucault measured speed of light.

France: 'Notre Dame, Paris' by Johann Barthold Jongkind (Ashmolean Museum, Oxford)

1862 Russia *Fathers and Sons* by Ivan Sergeyevich Turgenev (1818–1883), novelist, short-story writer and playwright. He was a writer of the Natural school, though there is no element of social propaganda in his work. Many of his stories show the life of the gentry in their country houses; his most interesting characters are failures. His style is impressionistic, with evocative description and subtle character-drawing. Turgenev was the first Russian writer to be well-known in Europe.

1862 Spain *Cantares Gallegos,* poems by Rosalia Castro (1837–1885). Her lyrics, delicate and highly original, were written in the Galician dialect. She was a metrical innovator, using Galician folk songs as a basis for much of her work.

1863 Abolition of slavery proclaimed in U.S.A.

1863 England *The Water Babies* by Charles Kingsley (1819–1875), clergyman, poet and novelist. Much of his work was intended to teach moral values, or promote social reform.

1863 France *Dominique* by Eugène Fromentin (1820–1875), painter, art critic and novelist. The book is an autobiographical novel, following the tradition of La Fayette's *La Princesse de Clèves* (published 1678).

1863 Romania Foundation of Junimea, a literary society whose mouthpiece was the periodical *Literary Talks*. It published the work of well-known writers, many of whom had travelled abroad during their youth and brought back European, particularly French, influences to Romania.

1864 England *Goblin Market and Other Poems* by Christina Georgina Rossetti (1830–1894). This work is the first successful publication by the pre-Raphaelites, a group of writers and painters founded by Christina's brother, Charles Dante Gabriel Rossetti (1828–1882). Their poetry has a mystical feeling and shows a strong sense of colour. They published a periodical, *The Germ*, which was short-lived. They wrote on serious, often religious, subjects.

1864 Hungary The Kisfaludy Society, named after Koroly Kisfaludy (1788–1830) who was the first dramatist to use the peasant characters which were later so popular in Hungary, published the complete plays of Shakespeare in Hungarian.

1863 Belgium *Traité Général d'Instrumentation* published by François Auguste Gevaert (1828–1908), Belgian musicologist, educationist and composer. It is an outstanding work on its subject, second only to that by Berlioz.

1863 England J. Curwen & Sons Ltd., music publishing house, founded.

1864 England Royal College of Organists founded, though not known by this name until 1893.

1864 Germany Death of Giacomo Jakob Liebmann Beer Meyerbeer (b. 1791) German composer.

1864 Germany Birth of Richard Strauss (d. 1949), German composer and conductor.

1864 Germany First performance of Wagner's *Tristan und Isolde* at Munich, with Hans von Bülow conducting.

1864 Mexico Birth of Ricardo Castro (d. 1907), the first Mexican composer to write symphonies.

1864 Spain Spanish pianist and composer, Isaac Albéniz (1860–1909), made his first public performance at the age of four; he is chiefly remembered for his 12 movement suite *Iberia* (1909).

England: 'Whispering Muses Showing the Painter G. F. Watts' by Julia Margaret Cameron

1863 England The Albert Memorial, London, by Sir George G. Scott (1811–78) is an elaborately decorated memorial built with costly materials that epitomises the high Victorian style.

1864 England Oriel Chambers, Liverpool, by Peter Ellis (1804–1884) foreshadows the modern use of cast iron and glass: contemporary use was still inspired by Gothic decoration, while Ellis incorporated curtain walling and functional fenestration.

1864 England Langham Hotel, London, by John Giles (1835–1900) is in a vaguely French Renaissance style sometimes used in Victorian England; the amazing carving on the façade demonstrates the vigour of even non-Gothic architecture of the period.

1864 U.S.A. William Leighton developed a soda glass as clear as lead glass but far cheaper: the difference could only be detected in cut-glass, to which the traditional manufacturers now turned.

1863 France Edouard Manet (1832–1883) painted *Le Déjeuner sur l'Herbe*, a modern version of Giorgione's *Concert Champêtre* with contemporary characters, painted in his characteristic clear, flat colour and precise outline. The picture was attacked as indecent, and Manet became the hero of younger artists as a result.

1863 France Alfred Sisley (1839–1899), an English-born painter, began to exhibit impressionist landscape pictures, mainly concerned with mood and atmosphere.

1864 England First photographic portraits by Julia Margaret Cameron (1815–1879); she used deliberate soft focus and poor definition to bring out character and lose distracting details.

1864 James Clerk Maxwell formulated electromagnetic theory of light.

359

*1865
Abraham Lincoln
assassinated.
American Civil
War ended.*

LITERATURE

1865–1877 Netherlands *Ideën* by Eduard Douwes Dekker, called Multatuli (1820–1887), essayist and satirist. Concerned with truth, justice, and spontaneity of expression, he had a tremendous impact on contemporary writers and helped to destroy the prevailing conventional literary attitudes.

1865 France *Germinie Lacerteux*, a novel by the Huot de Goncourt brothers, Edmond Louis Antoine (1822–1896) and Jules Alfred (1830–1870). As well as art criticism and historical works, the brothers wrote novels depicting contemporary people, often neurotics closely observed and documented, following the line established by Flaubert. Their *Journal* is an important document in any study of the art and literature of the period. The Prix Goncourt, awarded to a promising novelist, was established under the terms of Edmond's will.

1865 France *Philosophie de l'Art* by Hippolyte Adolphe Taine (1828–1893), essayist and philosopher. He was in tune with eighteenth-century thinkers such as Locke, and had a strong influence on Zola.

1865 India *Durges Nandini* by Bankim Chandra Chatterji (1838–1894), a Bengali novelist. His works, particularly his historical romances, show the influence of Sir Walter Scott. His own influence on subsequent Indian writers was considerable.

1865 Portugal The poet Antero Tarquinio de Quental (1842–1891), published *Bom Senso E Bom Gosto*, a pamphlet criticizing the insipid Romanticism of the followers of Castilho. His own poetry showed his preoccupation with philosophical and moral issues. He is considered one of the finest Portuguese poets.

1865 Wales A collection of poems by John Ceiriog Hughes, called Ceiriog (1832–1887); he wrote some of the finest lyrics in the Welsh language. Welsh literature during the nineteenth century was in general hampered by lack of education; although there were many would-be writers, they lacked the proper tools, metre and diction, to be effective.

DANCE & DRAMA

MUSIC

1865 Austria Anton Bruckner (1824–1896), composer, met Richard Wagner (1813–1883) at the first performance of *Tristan* in Munich and this meeting considerably influenced Bruckner's future development.

1865 Austria *The Unfinished Symphony* by Franz Peter Schubert (1797–1828) was performed for the first time, 40 years after Schubert's death.

1865 Czechoslovakia Antonin Dvořák (1841–1904) composed his first two symphonies while a viola player in the orchestra of the Prague National Theatre (1862–1872).

1865 Denmark Birth of Carl August Nielsen (d. 1931), Danish composer.

1865 Finland Birth of Jean Johan Sibelius (d. 1957), Finnish composer.

1865 France Birth of Paul Dukas (d. 1935), French composer.

ARCHITECTURE

1865–1877 Italy Galleria Vittorio Emanuele, Milan, by Giuseppe Mengoni (1829–1877) is a cruciform-planned shopping arcade, the largest and finest of its type in Europe.

1865 Wales Cardiff Castle was restored by William Burges with Castell Coch for the Marquess of Bute and represents the ultimate in theatrical medieval restoration.

THREE DIMENSIONAL ART

VISUAL ARTS

1865 Austria Death of Ferdinand Waldmüller (b. 1793), a painter of landscapes and genre scenes of near-photographic quality. Contemporary academic artists disapproved of his work.

1865 Belgium Death of Antoine Wiertz (b. 1806), a painter of fantastic and erotic subjects whose work later inspired the Surrealists.

Boneshaker bicycles

1866
Peru declared
war on Spain.

1867
Dominion of
Canada
established.

LITERATURE

1866 England *Poems and Ballads* by Algernon Charles Swinburne (1837–1909). He deliberately set out to shock, attacking the conventional morality of the time. His work lacked depth, although technically skilful and melodic, but he did succeed in his aim.

1866 Norway *Storegut*, an epic poem by Aasmund Olafsen Vinje (1818–1870), essayist and poet, one of the first to use New Norwegian, or *landsmal*.

1866 U.S.A. *Snowbound*, poems by John Greenleaf Whittier (1807–1899), journalist and poet. His country poems were in part influenced by Burns. He also wrote strongly, in both prose and poetry, against slavery.

1867 Belgium *Thyl Ulenspiegel* by Charles Theodore Henri de Coster (1827–1879): a colourful modern picaresque novel.

1867 Belgium *Tybaerts en Cie* by Jan Lambrecht Domien Sleeck (1818–1901), a Flemish short-story writer, playwright, essayist and novelist. He was the leading realistic writer in Belgium.

1867 Colombia *Maria* by Jorge Isaacs (1837–1895), novelist and poet: it was the first Spanish-American novel to have more than a purely local interest. Isaacs was influenced by the French Romantics.

1867 Italy Posthumous publication of *I Miei Ricordi* by Massimo d'Azeglio (1798–1866), statesman, painter and novelist. This book was the first of a number of important literary autobiographies by Italian authors. The object of most of his paintings and historical novels was to give Italians a feeling of pride in their past and determination in shaping their future. This object was shared by many contemporary Italian writers.

1867 Italy Posthumous publication of *Confessioni d'un Ottuagenario* by Ippolito Nievo (1831–1861), patriot, novelist, and poet. This book is his masterpiece, a partly autobiographical historical novel telling the story of the movement for Italian unification from Napoleon to Garibaldi.

DANCE & DRAMA

1866 France *La Vie parisienne* by Henri Meilhac (1831–1897) and Ludovic Halévy (1834–1908), to music by Offenbach. The French theatre-going public of the time enjoyed plays which were light, witty and polished.

1867 Norway *Peer Gynt* by Henrik Johann Ibsen (1828–1906), a poetic drama.

MUSIC

1866 Czechoslovakia Bedřich Smetana's first operas, *The Brandenburgers in Bohemia* and *The Bartered Bride*, were performed.

1866 Denmark A concert given by Edvard Hagerup Grieg (1843–1907) in Copenhagen resulted in his being appointed conductor of the Harmonic Society and acknowledged as one of the foremost young musicians of the country.

1866 France Birth of Erik Alfred Leslie Satie (d. 1925), French composer. His music had a great influence on twentieth century French composers.

1866 Italy Birth of Ferruccio Busoni (d. 1924), Italian pianist and composer.

1866 Russia Peter Ilyich Tchaikovsky (1840–1893) was appointed professor of harmony at Moscow Conservatory and began writing his first symphony.

1867 Belgium The Flemish School of Music was formed at Antwerp by Peter Benoit (1834–1901), the chief promotor of the Flemish musical movement.

1867 France The opera *Romeo and Juliet* by Charles François Gounod (1818–1893) first performed.

1867 France The opera *The Fair Maid of Perth* by George Bizet (1838–1875) first performed.

1867 France Birth of Charles Koechlin (d. 1951), French composer and teacher.

1867 Germany Josef Gabriel Rheinberger (1839–1901) Liechtenstein-born organist and teacher, appointed professor of organ and composition at Munich Conservatory. He also conducted the Munich Court Opera (1865–67).

1867 Spain Birth of Enrique Granados (d. 1916), Spanish pianist and composer.

ARCHITECTURE

1866–1883 Belgium Palais de Justice Brussels, by Joseph Poelaert is the most overpowering of all nineteenth-century public buildings; basically classical in style, its Piranesian proportions dominate the entire city.

1866–1870 Denmark National Bank, Copenhagen, by J. D. Herholdt is a masterpiece in the Tuscan *Rundbogenstil*; Copenhagen remains one of the best examples of European cities developed during the Romantic classical period of the nineteenth century.

1867–1874 Germany Munich Town Hall by G. J. von Hauberrisser (1841–1922) is a good example of Gothic revival work in Germany.

1867 USA Frank Lloyd Wright born (died 1959); he was the greatest of American twentieth-century architects with an immensely varied *oeuvre*.

England: after a Gothic design by Bruce Talbert

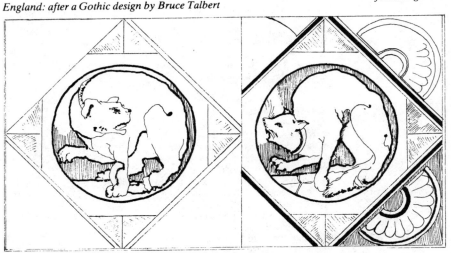

1867 England Bruce Talbert (1838–1881) published *Gothic Forms applied to Furniture*, recommending a simple early style: he became known internationally for his Gothic and, later, Jacobean designs.

1867 France The art critic Charles Blanc published *Grammaire des arts du Dessin* in which he analysed the theories of colour held by Delacroix, and practised to some extent by Turner, and by Michel-Eugène Chevreuil. This became the main source of divisionism, established by Seurat and his neo-impressionist followers (the technique of juxtaposing small areas of pure colour on the canvas so that the eye would mix them, rather than mixing colours on the palette).

1867
Joseph Lister applied germ theory to surgery with the first use of antiseptics.

1867 Switzerland *Zwanzig Balladen von Einem Schweizer* by Conrad Ferdinand Meyer (1825–1892), poet and writer of short stories. Bilingual in French and German, he chose to write in German after the Franco-German war. He avoided writing from direct experience, preferring historical reconstruction.

1868–1869 England *The Ring and the Book*, poems by Robert Browning (1812–1889). He was particularly interested in states of mind, especially the abnormal, and devised the dramatic monologue as a means of exploring them. He tackled difficult subjects, and handled rhyme and syntax in unusual ways, so that his poems demand an intellectual effort. His wife, Elizabeth Barrett Browning, also wrote poetry.

1868–1871 Slovenia Poems and short stories of Fran Levstik (1831–1887), critic and poet. His poetry includes love poems, satire, and children's poems. He worked to promote higher literary standards and linguistic reforms.

1869 Suez Canal opened. End of feudalism in Japan.

1869–1872 Russia Poems by Fedor Nikoleyevich Glinka (1786–1880), a mystical and religious poet. He also wrote some secular poems, one of which, *Troika*, is known throughout Russia as a song.

1869 Bohemia *Kanturčice*, a novel by Johanna Mužaková, called Karolina Světlá (1830–1899). Her early work was influenced by the Young Germany movement. Later she wrote about the northern Bohemian countryside. She was a major novelist of the reform movement headed by the magazine *Maj*.

1869 France *Lettres de mon Moulin* by the novelist Louis Marie Alphonse Daudet (1840–1897). Influenced by Flaubert, Zola and the Goncourts, he wrote closely documented naturalistic fiction; but, being of a sentimental disposition, he never achieved their degree of detachment.

1869 Sweden *Dikter*, poems by Carl Johan Gustav, Count Snoilsky (1841–1903), diplomat and poet: they were elegant lyrics about Mediterranean lands.

1869 U.S.A. Daly's Fifth Avenue Theatre opened in New York. Augustin Daly (1839–1899) was an outstanding theatre manager who engaged the most talented actors of his day. He was also a director, taking immense care with his productions.

1868 England Birth of Ernest Newman (d. 1959), English music critic and author who specialized on Wagner's works.

1868 Germany The result of 11 years work, Johannes Brahms' *Ein Deutsches Requiem* was published, using texts from Luther's translation of the bible.

1868 Germany *Die Meistersinger* by Richard Wagner (1813–1883) performed at Munich.

1868 Italy First production of *Mefistofele*, an opera by Arrigo Boito (1842–1918), Italian composer, still one of the most popular works of the Italian repertory.

1868 Italy Death of Gioacchino Antonio Rossini (b. 1792), Italian composer.

1869 Denmark First performance in Copenhagen of Edvard Hagerup Grieg's *Piano Concerto in A Minor*.

1869 France Death of Hector Berlioz (b. 1803), French composer.

1869 France Durand & Cie, one of principal French music-publishing houses, formed.

1868–1875 Austria Fünfhaus parish church, Vienna, by Friedrich von Schmidt (1825–91) was one of 8 Gothic churches he built in Vienna, usually of the traditional brick-vaulted German hall-church type.

1868–1874 England St Pancras Station Hotel, London, by Sir George G. Scott (1839–1897) has a façade with a fantastic combination of inspired features that hides the functional iron and glass train shed by W. H. Barlow (1812–92). This has a huge vault span of 79·6 m.

1868 England Keble College, Oxford, by William Butterfield (1814–1900) is the epitome of the 'streaky bacon' polychrome style that Butterfield employed, especially in the vast richly decorated chapel.

1868 England Leyswood, Sussex, by Norman Shaw is an influential house, tile-hung and timber-framed, representative of the irregularly planned manorial style that contrasted with the more aggressive Gothic revival.

1868 Germany Peter Behrens born (died 1940); he was noted especially for his early factory designs in the modern style.

1868 Scotland Charles Rennie Mackintosh born (died 1929); he is estimated by some as the last British architect of genius, who worked in a very personal form of Art Nouveau. A few of his buildings survive in and around Glasgow.

1868 England Wallace Martin (1843–1923) began making experimental stoneware, working at Fulham pottery and at Lambeth School of Art. He was influenced by the French artist-potter Jean-Charles Cazin (1841–1901), who came to England to teach at the Lambeth School. Wallace and his brothers, Walter (1859–1912) and Edwin (1860–1915), are considered the first English artist-potters.

1868
Helium identified in the sun's spectrum.

1869
Periodic system of classification first applied to elements.

England: contemporary drawing of inside St Pancras Station

1869 India Sir Syed Ahmad Khan, the Mohammedan social reformer, visited England, where he met a number of distinguished literary figures, including Thomas Carlyle. He was determined to bring Western education to the Indian Moslem community. The final result was the founding of the Mohammedan Anglo-Oriental college in 1877.

1870 Slovenia *Zorin*, a novel by Josip Stritar (1836–1923), critic and poet. His prose work was frequently modelled on foreign writers—this work is modelled on Goethe's *Werther*. He founded a literary review, and was important for his work in introducing foreign masterpieces and encouraging a love of literature.

1870 U.S.A. *Luck of Roaring Camp*, a novel by Francis Brett Harte (1836–1902), who also wrote short stories and humorous verse. He was one of the first American writers to make extensive use of local colour, in this case the Pacific Gold Coast.

1871–1893 France *Les Rougon-Macquart* by Émile Edouard Charles Antoine Zola (1840–1902): a group of 20 novels describing the history of a family during the Second Empire. Influenced by the Goncourts, Zola is regarded as the founder of the naturalistic school of literature.

*1871
French defeat in
Franco-Prussian
war; William I of
Prussia
proclaimed
German Emperor
at Versailles.*

1871–1887 Portugal *As Farpas*, a series of pamphlets on popular culture by José Duarte Ramalho Ortigão (1837–1915), critic, novelist, short-story writer and journalist. He is typical of late nineteenth-century Portuguese writers, who were very conscious of their role as social commentators.

1871 England *Sesame and Lilies* by John Ruskin (1819–1900), art critic and historian. His writings express his belief in the morality of good art. He maintained that happiness could only be achieved through honesty.

1871 Turkey Death of Ibrahim Sinasi (b. 1826), the writer who first brought Western literature to Turkey. He translated from French poets, was a pioneer of Western journalism, and wrote the first play in Turkish.

1870 Austria *Der Pfarrer von Kirchfeld* by Ludwig Anzengruber (1839–1889) began a vogue for the peasant play in Austria.

1870 France Death of François Delsarte (b.1811), innovative teacher of drama: he had sought to re-invigorate tragic acting by an analytical study of the movements and facial expressions which showed the emotions of various types of people. His system became as rigid as the conventions he attacked, but he strongly influenced pioneers of modern dance.

1870 France First performance of the ballet *Coppélia* by Arthur Saint-Léon (d.1870) to music by Délibes for the Paris Opéra ballet. It is characteristic of the large-scale, spectacular ballet which evolved from the romantic school, with a numerous *corps de ballet* and elaborate décor.

1870 U.S.A. *Saratoga* by Bronson Howard (1842–1908), produced by Daly: it ran for 100 performances. Howard was the first American to make a living solely by writing plays.

1871 England Beginning of the ballet seasons at the Alhambra Theatre, London which was one of only two theatres presenting ballet in England. The seasons continued until 1914.

1871 France The dancer Léontine Beaugrand (b.1842) danced Swanhilda in *Coppélia*, which was written for her. She was considered the sole representative of French classical dancing then working at the Opéra; but her influence was limited by continual opposition (she was prevented from dancing the first performance of *Coppélia* by a political feud) and she retired early.

1870 Czechoslovakia Birth of Vitězslav Novák (d. 1949), composer, the most influential teacher of composition in Czechoslovakia since 1900.

1870 England Sir William George Cusins (1833–1893) appointed Master of the Queen's Music.

1870 France The ballet *Coppélia* by Frederick Delibes (1862–1934) first performed in Paris.

1870 Russia *The Volga*, the first string quartet by a Russian composer, was composed by Nikolay Yakovlevich Afanasiev (1821–1898).

1871 Egypt First production of *Aida* by Giuseppe Verdi (1813–1901) at the new Opera House, Cairo; the work was commissioned to celebrate the opening of the Suez Canal.

1871 England A short 'key' to Braille music notation was printed by the British and Foreign Blind Association.

1871 England Royal Albert Hall opened in London.

1871 England Establishment of Royal Choral Society, though not known by this name until 1888.

1870 Czechoslovakia Adolf Loos born (died 1933); primarily a designer of houses, he disdained all forms of ornament.

1870–1880 England St Augustine's Church, Kilburn, London, by John L. Pearson (1817–1897) is a typically spacious church of the period with a fine spire; the brick vault is supported by interior buttresses linked by a gallery as in Albi Cathedral, France.

1870–1886 Germany Schloss Linderhof by Georg von Dollman (1830–95) is one of several palaces built for Ludwig II of Bavaria in extravagant Bavarian neo-rococo style.

1871–1875 USA The State War and Navy Department Building, Washington, by Alfred Mullet (1834–90) is a rare survivor of the many Second Empire-style buildings erected in the USA following the civil war.

1871 Austria Death of Michael Thonet (b. 1796), furniture designer: he originated the idea of bending birchwood into curving lines, the forerunner of bentwood furniture.

1870–1880 England The American-born artist James McNeill Whistler (1834–1903) produced paintings which reflected his interest in Japanese art and in the realism of the French artist Courbet. The *Nocturne* paintings of the Thames show more oriental influence; the painting of *The Artist's Mother* (1872), more realism. Whistler's pictures were noted for subdued tones in harmony.

1870–1880 France Edgar Degas (1834–1917) turned from painting outdoor crowd scenes and race-course scenes and began to paint ballet and the theatre. He said that his Impressionist colleagues needed the natural landscape, but he responded to the artificial.

1870 Argentina Death of the painter Prilidiano Pueyrredón (b. 1823), noted for his pictures of *gaucho* life and other genre scenes recording Argentina before its development.

1870 France *Le Pont Neuf* by Claude Monet (1840–1926) typified his early paintings in which he used techniques learned from his own generation. Monet was not trained by the study of Old Masters; he studied the work of his fellow painters, especially Pisarro, Renoir, Manet and Sisley.

1870 Spain *The Spanish Wedding* by the artist Manano José Bernardo Fortuny Y Carbo (1838–1874), who worked mainly in Rome and also in Morocco: this painting made a great impression because of its brilliant colour.

1871 England Development of the gelatine-coated dry plate, the basis of all future photographic processes. It was perfected in 1878.

1870 Swedish Baron Adolf Nordenskjöld explored interior of Greenland.

Steiner House, Vienna, designed by Adolf Loos

LITERATURE

1871 Spain Posthumous publication of lyrics by Gustavo Adolpho Bécquer (1836–1870). The lyrics are deceptively simple, using everyday words and metaphors but establish him as one of the greatest Spanish lyric writers. He also wrote versions of Spanish legends, full of eeriness and mystery.

1872 Argentina *El Gaucho Martin Fierro* by José Hernandez (1834–1894), the leading poet of 'Gaucho literature': this was a nineteenth-century Argentinian phenomenon, celebrating the life and customs of the cowboys of that region and lamenting their passing.

1872 Peru *Traditions* (first series) by Ricardo Palma (1833–1919), a writer of great originality who devised the 'tradition', a mixture of historical reconstruction, folklore and local history. The development of such work depends on the lack of a strong existing tradition.

DANCE & DRAMA

1872 Denmark Georg Morris Cohen Brandes (1842–1927) became Professor of Aesthetics at the University of Copenhagen: as a drama critic his influence was felt far outside Denmark. One of the first to recognize the greatness of Ibsen, he held that literature should be interpreted in the light of its relation to contemporary problems.

MUSIC

1872 England Birth of Ralph Vaughan Williams (d. 1958), English composer.

1872 England Foundation of Trinity College of Music, London (incorporated in 1875).

1872 France First performance of *L'Arlésienne*, a play by Alphonse Daudet (1840–1897) with music by Georges Bizet (1838–1875).

1872 France First opera by Charles Camille Saint-Saëns (1835–1921), *La Princesse Jaune*, produced in Paris.

1872 Germany The foundation stone laid of the Bayreuth Theatre.

1872 Russia Birth of Alexander Nikolayevitch Skriabin (d. 1915), Russian composer and pianist. His belief in mysticism is reflected in his original use of harmony and rhythm.

1872 U.S.A. Detroit Symphony Orchestra formed.

1872 U.S.A. Carl Fischer (1849–1923) arrived in New York where he founded one of the most important music-publishing houses in the U.S.A.

1873 France *Une Saison en Nefer*, poems by Jean Arthur Rimbaud (1854–1891). A close companion of Verlaine, Rimbaud developed a new theory of poetry: the poet was to disorder all his senses and would then perceive the universe in an entirely new aspect; he would thus become a seer, transmitting these new experiences to his readers. This theory anticipated the Surrealists.

1873 Russia Death of Fedor Ivanovich Tyutchev (b. 1803), poet and diplomat. Most of his working life was spent outside Russia, but his poetry shows a strong patriotic and slavophile spirit. He was described by Dostoevsky as Russia's first philosopher poet. Pantheistic in attitude, he was a forerunner of the Symbolists.

1873 France *Thérèse Raquin* by Emile Zola (1840–1902) was a dramatization of his own novel, and the first 'slice of life' drama in France.

1873 Turkey *The Fatherland* or *Silistria* by Kemal Namik (1840–1888), poet and writer of patriotic plays: he wished to educate and improve the lot of the Turkish people. This play, his first, was an incitement to revolution.

1873 England The ('Royal' in 1897) Carl Rosa Opera Company founded, for the production of opera in English.

1873 England George Grove (1820–1900), English writer and first director of the Royal College of Music, began his editorship of the *Dictionary of Music and Musicians*.

1873 Germany Julius Ferdinand Blüthner (1824–1910) took out a patent for his Aliquot system.

1873 Italy Giuseppe Verdi (1813–1901) composed his *Requiem Mass* after the death of Alessandro Manzoni. It incorporated the *Libera Me*, written for the Rossini Mass in 1869.

1873 Russia Birth of Sergey Vassilievich Rakhmaninov (d. 1943), Russian pianist and composer.

1873 Switzerland Birth of Karl Nef (d. 1935), Swiss musicologist, founder of Swiss musical scholarship.

| ARCHITECTURE | THREE DIMENSIONAL ART | VISUAL ARTS | INVENTIONS & DISCOVERIES |

ARCHITECTURE

1872 Italy St Paul's American Church, Rome, by George Edward Street (1824–1881) is a fine Italian Gothic-style basilica with a striking polychrome-banded campanile; it is one of the best of several Gothic-style churches built by English architects abroad.

1872 USA Sturtevant House, Middletown, Rhode Island, by Dudley Newton (1845–1907) is asymmetric in plan, the verandahs and wooden framework being typical features of the 'stick style' common in American houses during the second half of the nineteenth century.

1873–1877 USA Trinity Church, Boston, by Henry Richardson was inspired by French and Spanish Romanesque and established Richardson's reputation in America.

1873–1875 USA Western Union Building, New York, by George B. Post (1837–1913) was an early skyscraper of 10 storeys in the old-fashioned Second Empire style; it was later demolished.

THREE DIMENSIONAL ART

Germany: Richard Wagner conducting at the Bayreuth Theatre

VISUAL ARTS

1872 France Camille Pisarro (1830–1903) settled at Pontoise after two years in England and worked there together with Cézanne. He was the only Impressionist to be represented in all 8 Paris exhibitions (1874–1886), and a very prolific painter. He was important as a teacher.

1873 England Invention of the platinum photo plate, more permanent than silver and producing a more delicate effect.

1873 Russia *The Volga Boatmen* by Uya Repin (1844–1930) made him internationally famous and considered Russia's greatest painter by contemporaries. He was a leading member of the 'Wanderers', a group of painters not of the Academy who sought by social realism to bring art to a mass audience.

INVENTIONS & DISCOVERIES

1872 George Westinghouse invented automatic air brake.

1873 Franz Josef Land, Arctic, discovered.

LITERATURE

1874–1875 Poland *The Story of a Jew* by Eliza Orzeszkowa (1841–1910), a realistic novelist and short-story writer who was particularly interested in the education of women and in justice for Jews.

1874 Australia *For the Term of His Natural Life*, a novel by Marcus Hislop Clarke (1846–1881): originally published as a serial, the book describes the days of the convicts.

1874 Belgium *Ernest Staes, Advocaat* by Anton Bergmann (1835–1874), a Flemish short-story writer and novelist. He was an important writer of the realistic school.

1874 France *Les Diaboliques* by Jules Amédée Barbey d'Aurevilly (1808–1889), critic and novelist. His work is highly original, in part romantic, in part mystical.

1874 France *Romance sans Paroles* by Paul Verlaine (1844–1896). His early poems were influenced by the Symbolists but later he developed an individual style, expressing great subtleties of mood and feeling in musical, impressionistic language. He was an important influence on the development of symbolism.

1874 Netherlands *Gedroomd Paardrijden* by Everhardus Johannes Ptgeiter (1808–1875), a major poet of the Dutch Romantic movement. His work was idealistic and naturalistic.

1874 Spain *The Three Cornered Hat*, a novel by Pedro Antonio de Alarcón (1833–1891). He excelled in writing short novels, with wit, lively action and vivid character-drawing.

DANCE & DRAMA

1874 Russia Marius Petipa (1822–1910) ballet-master of the Imperial Theatre, St Petersburg, was criticized by Bournonville (of the Royal Danish Ballet) for allowing Russian ballet to decline into mere virtuoso display and divertissement. Petipa replied that the conditions under which he worked prevented any other approach. His ballets, produced until 1903, formed the biggest single contribution to the Russian repertoire for many years.

1875 England *Trial by Jury* by William Schwenk Gilbert (1836–1911) and Sir Arthur Seymour Sullivan (1842–1900): the first of the Savoy comic operas.

1875 Russia The ballet *Swan Lake* first performed in Moscow, choreographed by Reisinger, to music by Tchaikovsky: his score was so far removed from conventional 'hack' ballet music that the company were unequal to it and the ballet failed.

MUSIC

1874 Austria Birth of Arnold Schoenberg (d. 1951), Austrian composer.

1874 Austria First performance in Vienna of *Die Fledermaus* by Johann Strauss the younger (1825–1899).

1874 Czechoslovakia First performance of *My Fatherland*, a cycle of 6 symphonic poems by Bedřich Smetana (1824–1884).

1874 England Birth of Gustav Theodore Holst (d. 1934), English composer.

1874 England The Royal Musical Association founded.

1874 Russia *Pictures at an Exhibition* was composed by Modest Petrovich Mussorgsky (1839–1881), the first great work for solo piano in Russia. The same year, his opera *Boris Godunov* (1870) was given its first performance.

1874 U.S.A. Birth of Charles Edward Ives (d. 1954), American composer.

1875 England Birth of Samuel Coleridge-Taylor, British composer (d. 1912).

1875 England Arthur Seymour Sullivan (1842–1900) collaborated with William Swenck Gilbert (1836–1911) for the production of *Trial by Jury*, the first of a succession of operettas.

1875 France/Austria First production of *Carmen* by Georges Bizet (1838–1875) at Opéra-Comique, Paris. This was his supreme achievement in opera. It ran for 37 performances and Bizet died on the 31st. In the same year there was the first Vienna performance of *Carmen* with recitatives written by Ernest Guiraud (1837–1892), Franco-American teacher and composer.

1875 France Birth of Joseph Maurice Ravel (d. 1937), French composer.

1875 Greece Birth of George Lambelet (d. 1945), Greek composer and musicologist. An authority on folk music, he contributed towards a national school of music.

1875 Russia Birth of Reinhold Moritzovich Glière (d. 1956), Russian composer, conductor and teacher of Belgian descent.

ARCHITECTURE

1874–1888 Austria Burgtheater Vienna, by Gottfried Semper (1803–1873) and Karl von Hasenauer (1833–1894) has been restored and is the best of the Vienna Ringstrasse buildings in neo-baroque style.

1874–1882 England The Law Courts, London, by George Edward Street were built, after a competition, to a design which is a mixture of French high Gothic on a large scale and, on the east and north fronts, polychrome-brick Gothic.

1874–1919 France Sacre-Coeur Church, Paris, by Paul Abadie (1812–84) and others is superbly sited and the best known of French neo-Romanesque churches that are loosely based on the design of St Front, Périgueux.

1874 France Auguste Perret born (died 1954), a pioneer architect in ferro-concrete construction.

1874–1883 Russia History Museum, Moscow, by V. O. Sherwood, one of many foreign architects who worked in nineteenth-century Russia; the building is the culmination of the revival in traditional Russian architecture.

THREE DIMENSIONAL ART

1875 Japan Death of Ohara Mitsuhiro (b. 1810), *netsuke* carver, who originated a style of streamlined bird and plant forms.

VISUAL ARTS

1874 France The critic Louis Leroy coined the word 'Impressionism' after seeing Monet's *Impression: Sunrise* on exhibition in Paris. The artists themselves had previously referred to their work as Impressionistic (attempting to catch the living scene as it presents itself to the eye, in varying focus) but the term had not been formally applied to the school by the public.

La Loge by Auguste Renoir (1841–1919) was also shown in the first Impressionist exhibition. Renoir used the 'rainbow palette' of pure tones, and complete subordination of outlines. He preferred human beings to landscapes as subjects.

1875 U.S.A. *The Gross Clinic* by Thomas Eakins (1844–1916) typified his innovations in scientific realism. He was an important teacher because of his emphasis on drawing from life.

INVENTIONS & DISCOVERIES

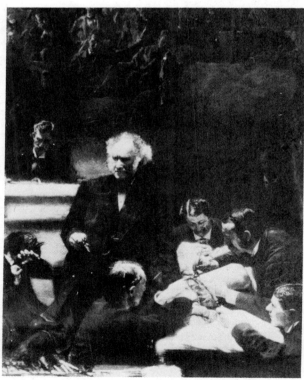

USA: 'The Gross Clinic' by Thomas Eakins

LITERATURE

DANCE & DRAMA

MUSIC

1876 Denmark *Fru Marie Grubbe* by Jens Peter Jacobson (1847–1885), poet, novelist and short-story writer. Denmark's leading naturalistic novelist, he was greatly influenced by the critic Brandes.

1876 France *Marthe, Histoire d'une Fille* by Joris-Karl Huysmans (1848–1907), a French novelist of Dutch descent. He admired the work of Zola, and with him founded the naturalistic school of writing. Later he became more interested in the spiritual aspects of life, and was eventually converted to Catholicism.

1876 Portugal *O Crime do Padre Amaro* by José Maria de Eça de Queirós (1845–1900), regarded as the greatest Portuguese novelist. He excelled at the ironic, realistic novel. Some time spent abroad enabled him to see Portuguese society more clearly.

1876 Russia *Gospoda Golovlëvy* by Mikhail Evgrafovich Saltykov-Shchedrin (1826–1892), the satirist. Much of his work was highly topical, but this book is a novel with universal qualities which make it of lasting value. The name of the hypocritical leading character, Iudushka, has passed into the Russian language as a household word.

1876 France First performance of the ballet *Sylvia* by Louis Mérante, to music by Délibes.

1876 Germany Foundation of the first permanent Yiddish theatre by Abraham Goldfaden (1840–1908). He not only wrote plays and songs, but was an actor, producer and manager. He trained actors and was the first to employ actresses in the Jewish theatre. His plays were simple, but they were what his public wanted.

1876 England Publication of *Instrumentation* by Ebenezer Prout, (1835–1909), English theorist, teacher and composer; the first of many text-books by him, it is still in use today.

1876 England Arthur Seymour Sullivan became first musical director of National Training School, later known as the Royal College of Music.

1876 Germany Johannes Brahms (1833–1897), completed his first symphony, which he had abandoned in 1856, and a year later wrote his second.

1876 Germany The Bayreuth Theatre opened with the first performance of *Der Ring des Nibelungen* by Richard Wagner (1813–1883).

1876 Germany Birth of Bruno Walter (d. 1962), German conductor.

1876 Italy Birth of Ermanno Wolf-Ferrari (d. 1948), Italian composer.

1876 Norway First performance of incidental music to *Peer Gynt* by Edvard Hagerup Grieg (1843–1907).

1876 Spain Birth of Pau [Pablo] Casals (d. 1973), Spanish violoncellist, conductor, pianist and composer.

1876 Spain Birth of Manuel de Falla (d. 1946), Spanish composer.

1876 U.S.A. The beginnings of experimentation leading to the invention of the gramophone. Thomas Edison (1847–1931), American inventor, was largely responsible.

1877
Queen Victoria proclaimed Empress of India.

1877 Iceland *A Glenside Lay* by Steingrimur Thorsteinsson (1831–1913), poet and translator. A Romantic, he wrote on love, nature and patriotism. His translations of great Europeans, including Shakespeare and Goethe, were an important cultural influence.

1877 Serbia Collection of short stories by Milovan Glišić (1847–1903), translator, playwright and prose writer. He translated French and Russian classics; he also wrote realistic stories of peasant life.

1877 Spain *Atlantis* by Jacint Verdaguer Santalo (1845–1902), a Catalan priest and poet. He had a great impact on poetic language, discarding archaic terms and introducing peasant vocabulary and expressions. *Atlantis*, an epic poem, marks the beginning of the renaissance of Catalan literature.

c. **1877 Hawaii** The ukelele was introduced into the Sandwich Islands by the Portuguese.

1877 Germany Birth of Sigfried Karg-Elert (d. 1933), German composer.

1877 Hungary Birth of Ernö Dohnányi (d. 1960), Hungarian pianist, conductor, teacher and composer.

1877 Russia First performance of *Swan Lake* by Peter Ilyich Tchaikovsky (1840–1893) at Moscow.

ARCHITECTURE

1876 England Bedford Park Estate, Turnham Green, London, was planned by Norman Shaw (1831–1912). Earliest of the English garden suburbs, it was composed mainly of detached houses in the brick-built Queen Anne style.

THREE DIMENSIONAL ART

1876 U.S.A. Philadelphia Centennial Exhibition: it showed glass more deeply cut and elaborately patterned than ever and marked the beginning of the American 'brilliant' period in glass manufacture.

VISUAL ARTS

1876 France Invention of the 'Praxinoscope': images were drawn on the inside of a drum and reflected in a central cylindrical mirror which rotated.

INVENTIONS &
DISCOVERIES
1876
Alexander
Graham Bell
patented the
telephone.

USA: Edison's phonograph

1877 Holland Rijksmuseum, Amsterdam, by Petrus Cuypers (1827–1921) is built in the Dutch sixteenth-century Renaissance style but incorporates two courts that make full use of iron and glass materials.

1877 England William Morris began to campaign in public lectures for the renewal of craftsmanship and the dignity of labour: he was the greatest single influence on the Arts and Crafts movement, an artistic philosophy which had been developing ever since Ruskin published *The Stones of Venice*, in 1853. The movement sought to revive the vernacular tradition in crafts, so that functional things would be made beautiful in what the movement saw as a medieval spirit of satisfaction for both maker and user.

1877 England John Thomson and Adolph Smith published *Street Life in London*, a collection of documentary photographs, mainly of the London poor.

1877 France Paul Cézanne (1839–1906) exhibited with the Impressionists for the last time. Thereafter he broke away from the movement, rejecting its emphasis on recording the impression received by the human eye; he wished instead to bring structural order into the expression of visual experience. Structure was to be a matter of the relation of colours to each other.

1877
Thomas Edison
patented the
gramophone.

1877–1889 Italy *Odi Barbare* by Giosue Carducci (1835–1907), critic and poet. He rejected both romantic and Christian influences in Italian literature, regarding them as weakening and corrupting. He advocated a return to the pagan spirit of classical antiquity. His intention was to revolutionize both the form and content of Italian poetry, despite opposition. He received the Nobel Prize in 1906.

*1878
Congress of
Berlin settled
Eastern
Question.*

1877 U.S.A. *Poems* by Sidney Lanier (1842–1881), a musician, critic and poet who wrote on the relationship of poetry to music.

1878 Bohemia *Europe* by Svatopluk Čech (1846–1908), poet and novelist. He excelled in epic poetry, whether romantic, allegorical or idyllic. A liberal and a nationalist, he was representative of his generation, who regarded him as the greatest living poet.

1878 Croatia *Diogenes*, a novel by August Šenca (1838–1881). He represented the liberal middle-class viewpoint, supporting Croat nationalism and the kinship of all Slavs. He is best-remembered for his vivid historical novels.

1878 Russia Poems by Petre Andreyevich, Prince Vyazemsky (1792–1878), poet and critic. His poetry was classical in form, romantic in content.

1878 Turkey Poems of Abdulhak Hamid (1852–1937), romantic poet and playwright; he used Western ideas and forms.

1879–1880 Russia *The Brothers Karamazov*, a novel by Fedor Mikhailovich Dostoyevsky (1821–1881). A naturalistic writer, acclaimed by Belinsky, he was particularly interested in the psychology of the abnormal, because he believed that through a study of abnormality he would come to understand the true nature of man. Passionately interested in religion, he shows in his work a preoccupation with good and evil, and the search for God. His attitude to his characters is one of great compassion.

1879 U.S.A. Opening of the Madison Square Theatre, New York, with stage equipment by Steele Mackaye (1842–1894): this included an adjustable proscenium arch and a movable double stage. Mackaye also invented the folding theatre seat.

1877 Russia Borodin (1833–1887) wrote his B minor symphony.

1878 England A system of compensating pistons for brass instruments was patented by David James Blaikley (1846–1936), English acoustician, who worked for Messrs. Boosey for most of his life.

1878 England Birth of Adam Carse, English composer (d. 1958), teacher and writer. Apart from specializing in writing easy pieces for teaching, he was an authority on old musical instruments; his two most important books are *The Orchestra in the XVIII Century* (1940) and *The Orchestra from Beethoven to Berlioz* (1948).

1878 Hungary Birth of Kalman Isoz (d. 1956), Hungarian musicologist, one of most distinguished of his time.

1878 Scotland Birth of Henry Jackson Watt (d. 1925), Scottish psychologist in music, a pioneer in his contributions to the psycho-physics of sound.

1879 England Birth of Frank Bridge (d. 1941), English composer, conductor and violist, and teacher of composition to Benjamin Britten (1913–1976).

1879 England Birth of John Nicholson Ireland (d. 1962), English composer. He destroyed all his first compositions, prior to 1908.

1879 England Birth of Ernest Read, (d. 1965) English conductor, lecturer and educationist who formed the London Junior and London Senior Orchestras.

1879 England Birth of Cyril Meir Scott (d. 1970), English composer and poet.

1879 Germany Birth of Joseph Haas (d. 1960), German composer and one of the outstanding teachers of composition in Germany.

1878 Spain Casa Vicens, Barcelona, by Gaudi was his first work, a suburban house fantastically decorated with polychrome tiles and sinuous ironwork.

1878 France Auguste Rodin (1840–1917) exhibited his first major sculpture *The Age of Bronze*, which showed his preoccupation with modelling: the character of his pieces was achieved by his work on the modelled figure, casting in metal being necessary for permanency but not his main interest.

1878 U.S.A. John Quincy Adams Ward (1830–1910), sculptor, made his equestrian statue of General Thomas: he was considered the most important of post-civil war sculptors; his work showed a nationalistic spirit and solid, natural forms.

1878–1880 Denmark The Norwegian-born artist Paul Severin Krøyer (1851–1909) painted a series of Spanish and Italian subjects influenced by Velazquez: his work was considered unusual at the time because of its realism and compassion.

1878–1887 Norway The painter Erik Werenskiold (1855–1938) produced his illustrations for *Norwegian Folk Tales*, which are considered one of his outstanding achievements. He was a leading figure in Norwegian art from *c.*1880 until 1900; his style was realistic and severe, his treatment of landscape unsentimental.

1878
First modern
microscope
manufactured by
Zeiss.

1879 USA Provident Life and Trust Company Building, Philadelphia, by Frank Furness (1839–1912) the most vigorously original of the architect's work in the high Victorian Gothic style which flourished in the USA in the third quarter of the nineteenth century; it has since been demolished.

France: 'The Age of Bronze' by
Auguste Rodin

HISTORICAL EVENTS	LITERATURE	DANCE & DRAMA	MUSIC

LITERATURE

1879 England *The Egoist* by George Meredith (1828–1909), poet and novelist. His work was concerned with conflict, social or moral, which he explored through a study of human relationships. He was particularly understanding of women and of sexual problems, but the reticence of the time prevented him from treating these subjects in the naturalistic way he would have wished.

1880 Australia The *Bulletin*, a weekly magazine, was founded in Sidney. It was the mouthpiece of the Nationalist movement, which opposed colonial attitudes.

1880 Belgium A collection of poems by Pol de Mont (1857–1931), a Flemish poet, critic, art historian, folklorist and short-story writer. He brought the concept of 'art for art's sake' to Belgium.

1880 Brazil *Epitaph for a Small Winner* by Joaquim Maria Machado de Assis (1839–1908), novelist and poet. He is regarded as one of the greatest novelists in the Portuguese language.

1880 France *Boule de Suif* by Henry René Albert Guy de Maupassant (1850–1893), novelist and short-story writer. A pupil of Flaubert, he set many of his stories in his native Normandy. They are ironic and realistic, frequently grim, and written with great craftsmanship. He virtually invented the commercial short story.

1880 Iceland Publication of poems by Grimur Thorgrimsson Thomsen (1820–1896), considered one of Iceland's greatest writers on the theme of heroism.

1880 Norway *Garman and Worse* by Alexander Kielland (1846–1906), novelist, playwright and short-story writer. The driving force of his work was indignation at social injustice.

1881 Alexander II of Russia assassinated. Canadian Pacific Railway Company founded. Revolt of Sudan under the Mahdi.

DANCE & DRAMA

1881 England The Savoy was the first London theatre to use electricity.

1881 Germany Appearance at Drury Lane, London, of the Meiningen Players, a private company directed by George, Duke of Saxe-Meiningen and his actress wife, Ellen Franz. Their split-level staging, imaginative handling of crowds, and conception of a production as a whole, to which setting, costume and properties all contributed, were revolutionary in their day and had considerable influence in the theatre throughout Europe.

1881 Japan Women were permitted to act on the stage.

1881 Norway *Ghosts* by Henrik Ibsen, a naturalistic play on the evils of society. Ibsen's social dramas shocked not only Norwegian society but that of other European countries. He was influenced by Shakespeare, Holberg and Scribe.

MUSIC

1879 Italy Birth of Ottorino Respighi (d. 1936), Italian composer.

1879 Russia First production in Moscow of *Eugene Onegin* by Peter Ilyich Tchaikovsky (1840–1893).

1880 Austria Gustav Mahler (1860–1911) completed his first mature composition, *Das Klagende Lied*.

1880 Czechoslovakia Birth of Rudolf Karel (d. 1945), Czech composer and teacher.

1880 England The Guildhall School of Music was founded.

1880 France First piano works by Claude Debussy (1862–1918), whose writing for this medium demanded far more in way of technique than hitherto, and was a lasting influence on both pianists and composers.

1880 Hungary Ödön Farkas (1851–1912), Hungarian composer, conductor, teacher and writer on music, was appointed principal of Kolozsvár Conservatory; he championed the creation of a national school of music, imbued with Hungarian spirit.

1880 Poland Birth of Adolf Chybiński (d. 1952), Polish musicologist. He was a pioneer of musical research, the greatest authority on music in Poland, and educated a generation of Polish musicians and musicologists.

1880 Russia Peter Ilyich Tchaikovsky (1840–1893), whose reputation was already established in Russia, began to receive acknowledgement abroad.

1880 U.S.A. Birth of Ernest Bloch (d. 1959), American composer of Swiss birth.

1881 Czechoslovakia Bedřich Smetana's fourth opera *Libuše* was performed at the new National Theatre.

1881 England Birth of Herbert Lambert (d. 1936), clavichord and harpsichord maker. One of his most important contributions was a portable clavichord.

1881 Hungary Birth of Béla Bartók (d. 1945), Hungarian pianist and composer.

ARCHITECTURE	THREE DIMENSIONAL ART	VISUAL ARTS	INVENTIONS & DISCOVERIES

VISUAL ARTS

1879 France Odilon Redon (1840–1916) made his series of lithographs *Dans la Rêve*, one of many which typified his strange compositions of amoeba-like forms. The Surrealists considered him as a forerunner of their movement.

1880 USA Crane Library, Quincy, Massachusetts, by Henry H. Richardson is a typically chunky stone building and one of several libraries he designed.

1880 France Edgar-Germain-Hilaire Dégas (1834–1917) began to model in wax: he exhibited the bronze *Petite Danseuse de Quatorze Ans* in 1881. In his later years he did more modelling than painting as his fears of blindness increased.

1880–1900 U.S.A. Creative period of Albert Pinkham Ryder (1847–1917), a distinguished painter of imaginative landscapes and marine paintings.

*1880
First electric street lighting, in New York.*

1880 France *The Gates of Hell*, by Auguste Rodin, a work still unfinished in 1900. Many of its 200 figures were used as starting points for individual figures including *The Kiss, The Thinker, La Belle Heaulmiere, Fugit Amor.*

1881 Hungary The massive neo-baroque façade of the East Railway Station, Budapest, by Julius Rochlitz is fairly typical of late nineteenth-century Austro-Hungarian architecture.

1881 USA Louis Comfort Tiffany (1848–1933) formed Louis C. Tiffany and Associated Artists, painters, architects, glass-makers and general decorative artists.

1881–1882 France Etienne Marey (1830–1904) developed a camera which could take 12 instantaneous pictures in one second. They were fixed on to separate areas of one plate.

1881 Netherlands Hendrik Willem Mesdag (1831–1915), a distinguished marine painter of the Hague school, painted his panorama of Scheveningen fishing village.

LITERATURE

1881 Belgium The review *La Jeune Belgique* was founded by Maurice Warlomont, called Max Waller (1860–1889), poet and novelist. It began a literary renaissance in Belgium. Prominent contributors included the novelist and critic Camille Lemonnier (1844–1898), the poet and novelist Georges-Raymond Constantin Rodenbach (1855–1898), the poet Verhaeren, and the dramatist Maeterlinck.

1882–1884 Netherlands *The Land of Rubens* by Conrad Busken Huet (1826–1886), historian, journalist and critic. His literary criticism was directed mainly at the prevailing low standards. This work is the first cultural history in Dutch.

1882 Sweden Poems by Abraham Viktor Rydberg (1828–1895), philosopher, scholar, novelist and poet. A liberal thinker, he challenged the orthodox attitude of the Lutherans. His poems are idealistic, but with a note of despair.

1883/4–1892 Germany *Also Sprach Zarathustra* by Friedrich Wilhelm Nietzsche (1844–1900), poet and philosopher. He rejected existing cultural and moral values, especially religion, and declared that a new civilization was needed, based on a new super-race that would arise out of the rejection of old values. His doctrine of a Will to Power as the mainspring of human effort had a profound influence on subsequent thought and literature. In his early writings, he was particularly scornful of the cultural values of the *parvenu* society which flourished after the unification of Germany.

1883 Australia A collection of poems by Charles Harpur (1813–1868), the first serious Australian poet. Harpur and other early Australian poets wrote about the local countryside but they were strongly influenced in style by English poetry.

1883 France *Contes Cruels* by Philippe-Auguste-Mathias Villiers de L 'Isle Adam (1838–1889), playwright and short-story writer. He was influenced by Hoffmann, Hegel, Baudelaire and Poe. His work, which expresses a romantic idealism, shows his interest in the occult.

DANCE & DRAMA

1881 Spain *El Gran Galeoto* by Jose Echegaray (1832–1916), a playwright whose style owes much to the Romantics, but who wrote about social problems. He made very effective use of theatrical devices.

1881 Russia Appointment of I. A. Vsevolozhky as Director of the Imperial Theatre in St Petersburg. He was the first to take an interest in ballet, and he instructed the ballet-master Petipa to import highly skilled Italian dancers and to stage important ballets already in production elsewhere.

1882 Denmark *A Visit* by Edvard Brandes (1847–1931), writer of analytical social criticism.

1882 France *Les Corbeaux* by Henri François Becque (1837–1899), writer of strong naturalistic dramas. At the time there was no theatre company working in quite this style.

1882 Russia Performance at St Petersburg of the ballet *Useless Precautions* by Marius Petipa and Lev Ivanov: this was a new version of *La Fille Mal Gardée*, first produced in 1786 in France, and most later versions were based on Petipa's.

1883 Bohemia Construction of the Czech National Theatre: before this, drama was found in inn-yards and small halls, often performed by amateurs. It was the peasants and lower middle classes who kept the drama alive.

MUSIC

1881 Russia First symphony composed by Alexander Konstantinovich Glazunov (1865–1936), Russian composer.

1881 Russia Birth of Nikolay Yakovlevich Miaskovsky (d. 1950), Russian composer and the foremost teacher of composition in Russia.

1881 Russia Death of Modest Petrovich Mussorgsky (b. 1839).

1881 U.S.A. The Boston Symphony Orchestra was formed.

1882 Australia Birth of Percy Aldridge Grainger (d. 1961), Australian composer and pianist.

1882 England The Incorporated Society of Musicians founded in England.

1882 Germany The Berlin Philharmonic Orchestra founded.

1882 Hungary Birth of Zoltán Kodály (d. 1967), Hungarian composer, music folklorist and musicologist.

1882 Poland Birth of Karol Maciej Szymanowski (d. 1937), Polish composer.

1882 Russia Birth of Igor Feodorovich Stravinsky (d. 1971), American composer of Russian origin.

1882 Russia The opera *Snow Maiden* composed by Rimsky-Korsakov (1844–1908).

1882 U.S.A. Frederick Delius (1862–1934) settled in Florida and began to study music by himself; later he entered the Conservatory at Leipzig.

1882 U.S.A. Birth of Robert Nathaniel Dett (d. 1943), American pianist and composer, who played a prominent part in musical education of Negroes in the U.S.A.

1883 Austria Birth of Anton von Webern (d. 1945), Austrian composer, possibly the purest exponent of the 12-note technique.

1883 Germany Richard Strauss (1864–1949) met Hans Guido von Bülow (1830–1894) in Berlin, which had a lasting influence on his career.

*1883
Paul Kruger
became President
of South African
Republic.*

ARCHITECTURE

1881 USA Isaac Bell House, Newport, Rhode Island, is by McKim, Mead and White, and is a functionally planned house with wide ornamental detail; the exterior shingle cladding, known as the 'shingle style', was employed all over America in the 1880s and 1890s.

THREE DIMENSIONAL ART

VISUAL ARTS

1881 Belgium Vincent van Gogh (1853–1890) became an artist after working as a preacher. In his remaining years he produced about 1650 paintings and drawings. His early work was an original form of social realism in sombre tones.

England: Mackmurdo's endpiece design for the magazine 'Century Guild Hobby Horse'

1882 England Arthur Mackmurdo (1851–1942) set up the Century Guild to provide craftwork for domestic interiors; its members included the potter William de Morgan (1832–1911), and much of its work foreshadowed Art Nouveau. It influenced the founders of the Deutscher Werkbund in Germany.

1882 England William Morris, in a lecture at the Midlands Institute, Birmingham, laid down principles of pottery-making which were closer to Japanese than European practice, and strongly influenced a rising generation of artist potters.

*1882
Robert Koch
discovered
tuberculosis
bacillus.*

1883 Germany Walter Gropius born (died 1969), a pioneer of the international modern style of architecture and founder of the Bauhaus; he left Germany in 1928.

1883–1902 Hungary Parliament House, Budapest, by Imre Steindl (1839–1902) illustrates how neo-Gothic had spread to eastern Europe by the end of the nineteenth century. The design was influenced by the Palace of Westminster in London.

1883–1884 France *Une Baignade, Asnières*, considered the first important painting by Georges Seurat (1859–1891). It differed from the Impressionists' work in being a planned composition with a scientific approach to colour and monumental figures.

Paul Gauguin (1848–1903) became a professional artist (at that time strongly influenced by impressionism) and Claude Monet (1840–1926) settled at Giverny and began to paint the first of his studies of water lilies. These and his landscapes and seascapes of the same period reflect his growing preoccupation with light atmosphere portrayed in colour.

| HISTORICAL EVENTS | **LITERATURE** | **DANCE & DRAMA** | **MUSIC** |

1883 Italy Death of the critic Francesco de Sanctis (b. 1817), author of the *Storia Della Letteratura Italiana*, an analysis of the course of Italian literature over 6 centuries, viewed as a heroic epic. This was a major work of the Risorgimento, the movement for unification of Italy.

1883 Italy *Novelle Rusticane* by Giovanni Verga (1840–1922), novelist and short-story writer. His best, and later, work was written in his native Sicily, and concerns the lives of the local peasants and fishermen, whom he saw as tragic figures, struggling unavailingly against social forces. He was considered the foremost Italian Realist.

1883 Norway *One of Life's Slaves* by Jonas Lauritz Idemil Lie (1883–1908), novelist, poet and playwright. He wrote on middle-class family life, and although there is implied social criticism in his work, it is not explicit.

1883 Scotland *Treasure Island* by Robert Louis Balfour Stevenson (1850–1894), novelist, poet and essayist. One of the most graceful of prose stylists, he gave a new depth and artistry to the adventure story.

1883 South Africa *The Story of a South African Farm* by Olive Schreiner (1855–1920), a novelist and short-story writer working in English. The first noteworthy South African novel, it shows the influence of *Wuthering Heights*.

1884–1885 Spain *La Regenta* by Leopoldo Alas y Ureña (1852–1901), who held that the novel should reflect real life and bring about reforms. This book, a picture of provincial town society drawn with humour and accuracy, is regarded as a European masterpiece.

1884 Poland *With Fire and Sword* by Henryk Sienkiewicz (1846–1916), novelist and short-story writer. The book is the first of a trilogy of novels dealing with seventeenth-century Poland. It was immediately popular with readers because of its vivid narrative and its appeal to patriotism, but Sienkiewicz was criticized by the Positivists, who felt that literature should deal with current social problems.

1883 Russia All Yiddish plays were forbidden as a part of the anti-semitic measures taken after the Tsar was assassinated. Many dramatists left Russia to settle in America, making New York the new centre of Yiddish drama.

1884 Italy *Cavalleria Rusticana* by Giovanni Verga (1840–1922), leader of the Italian *veristi* (naturalistic) movement: the *veristi* portrayed life in the regions and their plays were often written in dialect.

1883 England Royal College of Music, London, opened.

1883 France The rhapsody *Espàna* by Alexis Emmanuel Chabrier (1841–1894), his best-known work, was first performed.

1883 France Birth of Edgar Varèse (d. 1965), French composer who lived in the United States after 1915.

1883 Germany First volume of *Tonpsychologie* by Carl Stumpf (1848–1936) was published.

1883 Germany Death of Richard Wagner (b. 1813).

1883 Greece Birth of Manolis Kalomiris (d. 1961), Greek composer who exercised considerable influence in Greece by creating 'national' music inspired by folk music, legends and traditions.

1883 U.S.A. Metropolitan Opera House, New York, opened.

1884 Czechoslovakia Death of Bedřich Smetana (b. 1824).

1884 Italy Performance of the first opera, *Le Villi*, by Giacomo Puccini (1858–1924), Italian composer.

ARCHITECTURE

1883 USA In the Home Life Insurance Building, Chicago, by William Le B. Jenney (1832–1907) 'skyscraper construction' was probably used for the first time, with masonry cladding supported on a metal framework attached to the internal metal skeleton. The building gave Chicago the lead in skyscraper design.

THREE DIMENSIONAL ART

England: 'Almina, daughter of Asher Wertheimer' by John Singer Sargent

VISUAL ARTS

*c.***1883 Belgium** The artist James Ensor (1860–1949) abandoned subdued interior scenes and began to paint the grotesque and fantastic. Many of his images were taken from Brueghel and Bosch. He became an increasingly satirical artist, using the monstrous and bizarre to make social comment in painting and graphics. He was a formative influence on the Expressionists.

INVENTIONS & DISCOVERIES

1884 Spain The commission for Sagrada Familia Church, Barcelona, was given to Gaudi and the completed transept façade of the unfinished church, with its four extraordinary ceramic-covered spires, is Gaudi's most fantastic work.

1884 USA Pittsburgh Jail by Henry H. Richardson is in the architect's massive chunky style, admirably suited to the building's function.

1884–1886 France *The Burghers of* Calais by Auguste Rodin.

1884 England Arthur Mackmurdo produced *The Hobby Horse*, a magazine of the Arts and Crafts movement which influenced William Morris in setting up the Kelmscott Press in 1888.

1884 England Sir Edward Coley Borne-Jones (1833–1898) painted *King Cophetua and the Beggar Maid*. He was strongly influenced by Rossetti but also, and more strongly, by Botticelli. Most of his paintings were concerned with a medieval or mythical world which he depicted with flowing lines and subdued colours.

The American-born portrait painter John Singer Sargeant (1856–1925) settled in London, where he became a successful painter of society portraits.

1884 France Paul Signac (1863–1935) founded the Society of Independent Artists. He became the leader of the neo-impressionist, pointillist school on the death of Seurat in 1891.

1884 Sir Charles Parsons invented first practical steam-turbine engine.

381

LITERATURE

1884 Brazil *The Boardinghouse* by Aluizio Azevedo (1857–1913), a writer of realistic novels, often about the lower classes. His material is Brazilian, but the presentation shows the strong influence of Zola.

1884 Spain *Sotilesa* by José Maria de Pereda y Sanchez de Porrua (1833–1906). His early novels were sentimental and full of preaching; later he turned to regional novels, such as this, in which the countryside and the lives of the people were the most important feature. In this he was a master.

1885–1886 Japan *The Essence of the Novel* by Tsubouchi Shoyo (1859–1935), critic, essayist and translator. This highly influential book applies the criteria of the Western novel to Japanese fiction. Shoyo's work included translations of Sir Walter Scott.

1885 Netherlands Foundation of *De Niewe Gids* periodical, the vehicle of the new generation of Dutch poets, who were seeking originality in diction and imagery, and a new expressiveness in rhythm. They were influenced to a great extent by Wordsworth. Important in the movement were Frederick van Eeden (1860–1932), critic, social reformer, poet, novelist and playwright, and Albert Verwey (1865–1937), scholar, critic, playwright and poet.

1885 U.S.A. *The Adventures of Huckleberry Finn* by Samuel Langhorne Clemens, called Mark Twain (1835–1910), humorist, novelist, and writer of short stories and sketches. His most important works were picaresque novels full of local colour. There was at that time a great demand for reading matter, American education having produced an enormous readership, probably larger than that in any other single country, and Mark Twain's books sold very well.

1885 Wales *Rhys Lewis, Minister of Bethel* a novel by Daniel Owen (1836–1895). Fiction was not an approved form of writing in Wales when he began, but he soon won for himself a large public. His early work showed technical defects, but his humorous and sympathetic view of Welsh life outweighed any weaknesses.

HISTORICAL EVENTS

1885
China and Japan gave Korea self-government.

DANCE & DRAMA

1885 U.S.A. Steele Mackaye established the first American Academy of Dramatic Art. His ambitious plans for a playhouse for the Chicago World Fair, never in fact built, had a great influence on subsequent theatre architects.

USA: Mark Twain, whose career encompassed such varied occupations as river boat pilot, journalist and travel writer

MUSIC

1885 Austria Birth of Alban Berg (d. 1935), composer and musical essayist.

1885 England Birth of Benjamin James Dale (d. 1943), English composer best remembered for a cantata *Before the Paling of the Stars* (1912).

1885 France The Piano Concerto, *Variations Symphoniques* composed by Cesar Franck (1822–1890), one of his most important works.

1885 Germany Johannes Brahms composed his 4th and last symphony.

1885 Italy Monument to Victor Emmanuel II, Rome, by Count Sacconi (1853–1905) is perhaps the most elaborate of all nineteenth-century monuments and one of the few notable buildings in Italy of the period, although more for its overpowering pretentiousness and white-marble exterior than any other quality.

1885 Spain Palacio Güell, Barcelona, is by Gaudi; its rectangular grid façade is dominated by a pair of large parabolic-curved entrance arches and topped by chimneys encrusted with coloured mosaic, two features regularly employed by this architect.

1885 USA Marshall Field's Wholesale Store, Chicago, by Henry H. Richardson is a huge block of a building with carefully proportioned windows rising up the rusticated granite walls, the courses graded in size.

1885–1887 France Auguste Renoir (1841–1919) painted *Les Grandes Baigneuses*: it is characteristic of his later, solid manner inspired by Cézanne and the work of Raphael which he saw in Italy.

1885 Australia The Heidelberg school of painting was founded by a group of artists gathered at a painting camp at Eaglemount, Heidelberg, Victoria, and led by Tom Roberts (1856–1931): it was the first art movement with a truly Australian inspiration and idiom and is considered the real beginning of indigenous Australian art. The style was based on impressionism.

1885 France Henri Rousseau (1844–1910) began painting in retirement as an untaught artist. Contemporary artists considered him a powerful 'primitive' painter.

1885 Pasteur made first successful innoculation against rabies.

France: 'Tropical Storm with a Tiger' by Henri Rousseau

LITERATURE

DANCE & DRAMA

MUSIC

1886–1887 Spain *Fortunata Y Jacinta* by Benito Perez Galdós (1843–1920), a novelist remarkable for his insight into human nature, especially in the case of women and children, as well as for his powers of observation and his ability to create atmosphere. His stories are told with humour and compassion, though his characters are often abnormal. He attempted to write the history of Spain in a series of novels. He wrote 80, and has been likened to Dickens, Tolstoy and Balzac.

1886 Belgium *La Wallonie*, a Belgian Symbolist review, was founded by the poet and critic Albert Mockel (1886–1945). Symbolism appealed particularly to Belgian writers; it stressed that characters and events should be shown not for their own interest but as symbols of abstract qualities.

1886 Bohemia A cycle of lyric poems by Emil Frída, called Jaroslav Vrehlický (1853–1912), novelist, playwright, critic, translator and neo-Romantic poet. He introduced English, French and Italian influences into Czech literature, which had hitherto encountered only German influences. His output was enormous, and for a time he was regarded as the greatest Czech writer.

1886 England *The Mayor of Casterbridge* by Thomas Hardy (1840–1928), poet and novelist. Most of his books are set in 'Wessex', the rural areas of south-west England, and depict country people in the grip of an indifferent and inescapable fate. His strong feeling for the countryside is present in both novels and poetry.

1886 France *L'Imitation de Notre Dame la Lune* by the poet Jules Laforgue (1860–1887), a Symbolist; he used free verse (an important technical innovation), with everyday speech rhythms, free association and puns. His work marked the beginning of modern French poetry.

1886 Serbia Publication of short stories by Laza Lazarević (1851–1890), a doctor and short-story writer. His work shows the influence of Turgenev and Gogol, and of his own professional experiences.

1886 Bohemia *Jan Vyrava* by F. A. Subrt was a realistic play by the manager of the Czech National Theatre.

1886 England First compositions of Frederick Delius (1862–1934) though he did not publish until 1892. Delius became well-known through the enthusiasm of Thomas Beecham (1879–1961).

1886 Germany Birth of Heinrich Kaminski (d. 1946), German composer.

1886 Hungary Death of Ferencz (Franz) Liszt (b. 1811).

1886 Spain Birth of Jésus Guridi (d. 1961), Spanish composer who exerted great influence on musical life in northern Spain, through his introduction of European choral works and his interest in Basque folk music.

1886 Switzerland Birth of Othmar Schoeck (d. 1957), Swiss conductor and composer.

ARCHITECTURE

1886 Germany Ludwig Mies van der Rohe born (died 1969), one of several talented German architects of the twentieth century; he moved to the USA in 1938. Every tall glazed office block in the world bears his influence.

1886 USA Tacoma Building, Chicago, by William Holabird (1854–1923) and Martin Roche (1855–1927) is a 12-storey skyscraper that established the Chicago school of architecture as leaders in American skyscraper architecture.

England: Thomas Hardy's house 'Max Gate'

THREE DIMENSIONAL ART

VISUAL ARTS

1886 Australia *The Lost Child* by Frederick McCubbin (1855–1917) was the first 'bush' genre painting from the Heidelberg school. McCubbin showed melancholy and strong national sentiment in early work; after 1904 the influence of Turner stimulated a lighter technique.

1886 England The photographer Philip Henry Emerson (1856–1936) published *Life and Landscape on the Norfolk Broads*, a folio of 40 prints on platinum, the first of his series of ethnic studies. He was considered the first photographer to capture the atmosphere of places and relate it to the nature of their inhabitants. In painting, artists outside the Royal Academy founded the New English Art Club as a stimulus to naturalism. Members dispersed to form schools of painting in Newlyn, Cornwall and Glasgow, Scotland.

1886 France The poet Jean Moréas published his 'Symbolist Manifesto' in the journal *Figaro*. He summed up symbolism for painters as '[clothing] the idea in sensuous form'. Symbolist painters attempted to express visually the spiritual and occult. The symbolist movement inspired a group of journals which all began to appear in 1886: *Pléiade, Decadent, Vogue,* and *Symboliste*.

Paul Gauguin (1848–1903) settled in Brittany and began to work with the Pont Aven group: Émile Bernard, Vincent van Gogh, Paul Sér-usier and Maurice Denis. Under the influence of Japanese art they broke from impressionist realism.

Vincent van Gogh (1853–1890) arrived in Paris, and was also influenced by Japanese art and by the French use of colour.

1886 France Georges Seurat (1859–1891) exhibited *Un Dimanche d'été à la Grande-Jatte*, the first painting in which he had developed his technique of divisionism, juxtaposing pure colours in small dots so that they are blended by the eye. This form of divisionism was later called pointillism.

385

HISTORICAL EVENTS	LITERATURE	DANCE & DRAMA	MUSIC
	1886 U.S.A. *Indian Summer* by William Dean Howells (1837–1920), critic, novelist, writer of travel books, dramatist, and one-time editor of the *Atlantic Monthly*. Howells was the leading writer of realistic novels in America; he encouraged Mark Twain and Henry James, among others.		
1887 Queen Victoria's Golden Jubilee.	**1887–1889 Poland** *Lalka,* a novel by Aleksander Glowacki, called Boleslaw Prus (1847–1912), novelist and short-story writer. He was a Positivist, reacting against romanticism, and the book shows the life of nineteenth-century Polish society.	**1887 England** First of a series of ballet seasons at the Empire Theatre, London: apart from the Alhambra, it was the only theatre then presenting ballet in England. Its ballet school under Katti Lanner achieved a high standard.	**1887 Brazil** Birth of Heitor Villa-Lobos (d. 1959), Brazilian composer, conductor and educationist.
	1887 England *A Study in Scarlet* by Sir Arthur Conan Doyle (1859–1930), Scots novelist, creator of the fictional detective, Sherlock Holmes. This is the first Sherlock Holmes story. He also wrote historical and romantic novels.	**1887 France** André Antoine (1858–1943) founded the Théâtre Libre, Paris, to produce the work of the new naturalistic writers: Becque, Strindberg, Hauptmann, Ibsen. He insisted on complete realism in setting and properties, but also used these to emphasize the mood of the play, a new conception in production.	**1887 England** First performance of *The Crucifixion* by John Stainer (1840–1901). **1887 Finland** Birth of Leevi Antti Madetoja (d. 1947) Finnish conductor, critic, teacher and composer. **1887 Russia** Death of Alexander Porfirevich Borodin (b. 1833).
	1887 France *Poésies* by the poet Stéphane Mallarmé (1842–1898): at first influenced by Baudelaire, he was the originator of the French Symbolist movement, in which an object is not named directly, but indicated by an analogy. A teacher of English, he viewed the French language from a different angle to that of previous writers. He also made experiments in typography and the arrangement of words on the page.	**1887 Sweden** *The Father* by August Strindberg (1849–1912): the first really original Swedish writer, he was responsible for a great increase in the prestige of the Swedish theatre. He was obsessed with the corruptions and abnormalities of the human race.	
	1887 Japan *Drifting Clouds,* a novel by Futabatei Shimei (1864–1909). Following the precepts of Tsubouchi Shoyo, and influenced by his own reading of Russian novels, he produced the first modern novel in Japan.		
	1887 U.S.A. *Zury, the Meanest Man in Spring County,* by Joseph Kirkland (1830–1894), one of several novelists of the period who presented unromantic, realistic pictures of American provincial life.		
1888 William II became Emperor of Germany.	**1888 Sweden** A collection of poems by Carl Gustav Verner von Heidenstam (1859–1940), poet and prose writer. Highly individual and full of feeling expressed in modern rhythms, his poetry led the reaction against naturalism. He was awarded the Nobel Prize in 1916.	**1888 Sweden** *Miss Julie* by August Strindberg.	**1888 Austria/Hungary** Gustav Mahler's first symphony completed.

1887 England New Scotland Yard, London, by Norman Shaw is an unusual combination of polychrome baroque detail applied to a building resembling a Scottish castle; it also illustrates Shaw's developing interest in the baroque style.

1887 France The Eiffel Tower, Paris, by Gustave Eiffel (1832–1923) was built of steel for the 1887 Paris Exhibition and for more than 40 years was the tallest structure in the world.

1887 Holland Maria Magdalenakirk, Amsterdam, is by Petrus Cuypers, who designed several large brick Gothic churches such as this; they often bear great resemblance to each other.

1887 Switzerland Le Corbusier, pseudonym of Charles-Edouard Jeanneret, born (died 1965), the most influential and inventive of twentieth-century architects.

1887 USA Auditorium Building, Chicago, by Louis Sullivan (1856–1924) was the architect's first major work and shows Richardson's influence; it is notable too for an early and very personal use of Art Nouveau interior decoration.

1887 France Théodore Deck (d. 1891), artist potter, was made art director at Sèvres porcelain factory.

1887 USA *Lincoln Memorial* by Augustus Saint-Gaudens (1848–1907) sculptor set up in Chicago; this was one of the earliest of his important commissions, which also included the *Adams Memorial* in Washington, the *Puritan,* Springfield, Massachussetts, the *Shaw Memorial,* Boston, and the statue of Sherman, New York. He was considered the foremost American sculptor of the nineteenth century.

1887 USA The Californian photographer Edward Muybridge (1830–1904) published *Animal Locomotion,* a collection of photographs recording every movement of animal motion. The camera isolated positions held for a fraction of a second and so not discernible to the eye; painters therefore rejected the usefulness of what Muybridge had intended as an artists' visual dictionary. The exact portrayal of a running horse did not give an impression of speed; it only presented to the eye an unfamiliar image.

1887
H. Hertz
demonstrated
existence of radio
waves.

England: bookmark by William Morris for the Kelmscott books

1888 Holland Gerrit Rietveld born (died 1964), architect and member of the de Stijl group of artists which included Mondrian; their buildings were intricate, delicately balanced compositions of line and plane.

1888 England William Morris set up the Kelmscott Press to reinstate printing and binding as a craft: it became the main stimulus of the private press movement.

1888 France Vincent van Gogh (1853–1890) moved to Arles and painted pictures in which colour and lines were no longer representational but expressions of his own violent feelings.

1888 U.S.A. Development of the Kodak camera, with a roll of coated-paper film. This began the age of mass photography for the amateur backed by factory processes.

*c.***1888 France** The Swedish painter Anders Zorn (1860–1920) settled in Paris and began to paint in oils, in impressionist style. His previous paintings, executed on many travels, had been watercolour. He was also noted as an etcher.

1888
John Boyd
Dunlop invented
pneumatic tyre.
Norwegian
Fridtjof Nansen
crossed
Greenland.

387

1888 Belgium *Begga*, a poem by Jan van Beers (1821–1888). His early work was romantic; later he turned to realism. His presentation of folk-customs made him very popular.

1888 Bohemia *Jan Maria Plojhar* by Julius Zeyer (1841–1901), poet, playwright and novelist. Widely travelled in Europe, he brought foreign influences to Czech literature. This book is an autobiographical novel on the difficulties of the artistic temperament.

1889 End of Portuguese empire in Brazil.

1888 Germany *Der Schimmelreiter*, the last and best story by Theodor Woldsen Storm (1817–1888), poet and writer of long short-stories. He believed that the appeal of literature should be emotional rather than intellectual. Much of his work concerns family relationships.

1889 France Paul Fort (1872–1960) founded the Théâtre d'Art, later the Théâtre d'Oeuvre, as a reaction against naturalism. His settings were simple, often stylized, and the dramas he produced poetic.

1889 France *Paléographie Musicale* founded by Dom Andre Mocquereau (1849–1930) French musical scholar. He was an authority on plainsong and influenced methods of studying old manuscripts.

1888 Greece *My Journey* by Giannes Psychares (1854–1929), Greek man of letters. Although he never lived in Greece, but in Paris, he worked hard for the development of Greek language and literature, supporting the spoken, demotic, language against the Church language, and producing philological arguments. He wrote plays and novels which illustrate his theories, though they had little artistic merit.

1889 Germany The Freie Buhne, a private theatre company, formed by Otto Brahm (1856–1912): it was inspired by the French Théâtre Libre. Their first production was Ibsen's *Ghosts*.

1889 Yugoslavia A School of Music in Belgrade founded by Stevan Mokranjac (1855–1914), Yugoslav composer, who may be considered the most important composer in history of Serbian music.

1889 Germany *Papa Hamlet* by Arno Holz (1863–1929), critic, poet and playwright. He was the chief theorist of naturalism, and wrote this book of model stories, and a model play, to illustrate his theories. They were written in collaboration with Johannes Schlaf (1862–1941).

1890 Parliamentary constitution established in Japan.

1890 Bohemia *Jeji Pastorkyna* by G. Preissova, Czech dramatist on rural themes.

1890 Czechoslovakia Birth of Bohuslav Martinů (d. 1959), Czech composer.

1890 Norway *Hedda Gabler* by Henrik Ibsen.

1890 England First production of the *Froissart* overture by Edward Elgar (1857–1934) marked the beginning of his public career. Having spent two years in London, Elgar retired to Malvern in 1891 where he composed the majority of his works.

1890 Belgium *Een Dure Eed* by Virginie Loveling (1836–1923), a poet, short-story writer and novelist considered to be one of the most important of the Belgian Realists. Her novels are sharply observed and well-constructed.

1890 France Birth of Jacques François Antoine Ibert (d. 1962), French composer.

1890 Italy *Profumo*, a novel by Luigi Capuana (1839–1915), critic and novelist. The leader of the Italian Realists, he believed that art should be objective, expressing no emotion. He was particularly interested in the pathological and the abnormal. He had considerable influence on Verga and on Pirandello.

1890 Italy First production of *Cavalleria Rusticana* by Pietro Mascagni (1863–1945), Italian opera-composer.

1890 Spain Birth of Adolfo Salazar (d. 1958), Spanish musicologist and composer who had a great influence upon the musical revival in Spain after 1918.

1888 USA Tower Building, New York, by Bradford L. Gilbert (1853–1911) was 10 storeys high and New York's first skyscraper; it has since been demolished.

1888–1892 USA Boston Public Library by McKim, Mead and White is an Italianate building of smooth granite ashlar, in contrast with Richardson's Trinity Church opposite; it has painted murals within.

1889–1893 Russia Gum Store, Moscow, by A. N. Pomerantsev (1848–98) is an extraordinary eclectic classical building, despite the interior use of iron and glass.

Belgium: after designs by Henri van de Velde

1890–1894 Belgium Henri van de Velde (1863–1957) redesigned the journal *Van Nu en Straks*, which contributed to a revival of book-design. He was influenced by the English Arts and Crafts movement and by Art Nouveau theory.

1890 England Ernest Gimson (1864–1919), furniture designer, formed Kenton and Company, furniture makers, with Sidney and Ernest Barnsley and William Lethaby. Gimson's knowledge of materials and craft processes gave him a strong influence on early twentieth century furniture design.

*c.*1890 **France** Emile Gallé, designer and glass-maker, became first president of the Nancy school of decorative artists: he specialized in decoration based entirely on natural, particularly plant, forms and worked with opaque, or semi-translucent glass.

1889 Australia An exhibition in Melbourne of the work of the Impressionists afforded the first view of paintings by the Heidelberg school of artists from Eaglemount, Victoria. Public reaction was not favourable. The school flourished until 1901, with many of its members leaving for European training and patronage. It inspired Julian Ashton (1851–1942) to found his art school, in which many major Australian artists were trained.

1889 England Philip Henry Emerson published *Naturalistic Photography*. He later renounced many of his theories of vision and art but he strongly influenced art photographers away from composing pseudo-paintings, and towards serious consideration of natural subjects.

1889 France Pierre Bonnard (1867–1947) sold a poster, advertising champagne, and decided to become a professional artist. Until *c.*1910 his work was divided between late-impressionist painting and the graphic arts; in the latter he was influenced by oriental forms and by *art nouveau*.

1889 Sweden The artist Ernst Josephson (1851–1906) became insane. His paintings had shown an outstanding sense of colour; his style was sometimes broad and strong, sometimes meticulous.

The painter Carl Larsson (1853–1919) returned to settle in Sweden after working in Paris. He concentrated on paintings of idealized everyday life in a decorative style with clear, transparent colours. His interiors were popular and influenced fashion in interior decoration.

1890–1900 France Henri de Toulouse-Lautrec (1864–1901) began to produce drawings, paintings and lithograph posters of cabaret, circus and music-hall performers. His poster lithographs were influential on graphic art; he used flat colour and strong outline in designs influenced by the Japanese print.

LITERATURE	DANCE & DRAMA	MUSIC

LITERATURE

1890 Portugal *Oaristos*, poems by Eugénio de Castro (1869–1944), poet and scholar. He introduced Symbolist ideas and French Parnassian anti-Romantic ideas to Portugal.

1890 Sweden *Pepitas Bröllop*, a neo-Romantic manifesto by Heidenstam and his friend Oscar Ivar Levertin (1862–1906). Levertin wrote novels, stories, essays and poetry; he was also an influential critic.

*c.***1890 Australia** *Waltzing Matilda* was among the compositions of Andrew Barton ('Banjo') Paterson (1864–1941), balladeer and collector of old bush songs. His poems are authentic Australian verse and not pale imitations of the work of English poets.

1891
Triple Alliance of Germany, Italy, Austria.

1891–1895 Denmark *The Promised Land*, the first of three novel cycles by Henrik Pontoppidan (1857–1943), novelist and short-story writer. He set out to analyse the Danish character and reveal it to his readers as he saw it, without any attempt to flatter or reassure. In 1917 he was awarded the Nobel Prize.

1891 England *News from Nowhere* by William Morris (1834–1896), craftsman and writer, the leader of the Arts and Crafts movement. The book is a political romance, expressing his distress at the effects of industrialization.

1891 Italy *Da Quarto al Volturno* by Giuseppe Cesare Abba (1838–1910), patriot, poet, novelist and short-story writer. The work, a diary of his service in the Sicilian campaign of 1860 under Garibaldi, exists in several versions, including one for young readers.

1891 Turkey *Servet-I Fünen*, a periodical, gave its name to a literary movement. The writers were cosmopolitan in their approach, but have been considered too literary; they did not appreciate the importance of the colloquial in the development of language and literature.

DANCE & DRAMA

1890 Russia First performance in St Petersburg of the ballet *The Sleeping Beauty*, devised by Marius Petipa, to music by Tchaikovsky. Production was supervised by the theatre director Vsevolozhky so that its various elements were in harmony. This was a new departure and one which influenced the designer Alexandre Benois in developing his ideas on ballet as composed of a number of integrated arts.

*c.***1890 Switzerland** Émile Jaques-Dalcroze (b.1865), a member of the Conservatory of Geneva, developed a system of musical training through physical movement, which he called eurhythmics.

1891 England Jack Thomas Grein (1862–1935) founded the Independent Theatre Club, London, following the example of Antonine's Théâtre Libre.
The Quint-essence of Ibsenism, an article by (George) Bernard Shaw (1856–1950) considered the contemporary theatre juvenile and frivolous and welcomed the work of Ibsen, translated into English by William Archer. He was scornful of the 'Well-Made' play and of melodramatic acting.

1891 Germany *Gestern* by Hugo von Hofmannsthal (1874–1929) who led the revolt against naturalism. He was the librettist of Richard Strauss' *Der Rosenkavalier*.

MUSIC

1890 Switzerland Birth of Frank Martin (d. 1974), Swiss composer.

1891 England Publication of the first of many articles on brass instruments by Walter Blandford (1864–1952), the English amateur horn player.

1891 England Birth of Arthur Bliss (d. 1975), English composer.

1891 Russia Birth of Sergey Sergeyevich Prokofiev (d. 1953), Russian composer.

1891 U.S.A. Carnegie Hall opened in New York.

1891 U.S.A. Birth of Frederick Jacobi (d. 1952), American conductor and composer.

1890–1900 Norway Edvard Munch (1863–1944) painted a series, *The Frieze of Life*, in dark colours and composed of intensely emotional symbolic images. The series included *The Kiss* and *The Shriek*. He also made many woodcuts, lithographs and etchings. His work was remarkable for its use of line for dramatic intensity.

1890 Finland Albert Edelfelt (1854–1905) painted *Christ and Mary Magdalene*, a typical example of his treatment of biblical scenes in modern settings. He had trained in Paris and some of his work, particularly scenes of peasant life, showed the influence of the French painter Jules Bastien-Lepage.

1890 France Pierre Puvis de Chavannes (1824–1898) founded, with Rodin, the Societé Nationale des Beaux-Artes. He was the major mural painter of his time, originating a monumental style of decorative painting in flat colour and elegant line. He was widely esteemed in his own time.

1890 U.S.A. Jacob August Riis (1849–1914) published *How the Other Half Lives*, a photographic study of New York slum life. His photographs, later found to be excellent technically, could not be satisfactorily reproduced in print at the time.

1890 U.S.A. After 9 years working in Europe, Alfred Stieglitz (1864–1946) arrived in America. He carried on Emerson's tradition of art photography and developed American awareness of photography as an aesthetic medium.

1890 Mexico Juan Posada (1852–1913) produced broadsheets and cartoons, many in woodcut, which used the traditional Mexican motif of the skull to express satire. He was influential on the satirical work of Orozco and Rivera.

1891 Australia *Fire's On*, a landscape painting in heroic style by Arthur Streeton (1867–1943), considered the most important landscape painter of the Heidelberg school, established 1885. His square brush technique and predominately blue and gold palette were strongly influential.

Russia: after a design by Rabinovitch for the Prokofiev opera 'Love of 3 Oranges'

1892 Norway *Peace*, a novel by Arne Garborg (1851–1924), a novelist, poet, essayist and playwright writing in New Norwegian (*landsmal*).

1892 Portugal *Só* by António Nobre (1867–1900), a poet influenced by the French Symbolists.

1892 U.S.A. *Don Orsino* by Francis Marion Crawford (1854–1909), a novelist, critic and short-story writer who wrote escapist fiction, particularly historical novels which were very popular.

1893 Bohemia *Tristium Vindobona* by the poet Josef Svatopluk Machar (1864–1942). His poetry is analytical and satirical. This work criticizes romantic patriotism.

1893 France *Les Trophées* by José Maria de Hérédia (1842–1905), a French poet of Spanish extraction. He was a leading Parnassian, particularly remarkable for his sonnets.

1893 Iceland Collection of poems by Hannes Hafstein (1861–1922), a champion of realism. His poems are vigorous and skilful, showing strong patriotic feeling.

1892 France *Pélleas et Mélisande* a play by Maurice Maeterlinck (1862–1949), Belgian dramatist: it was produced at the Théâtre d'Oeuvre by Paul Fort's successor, Aurélien-François Lugne-Poë (1869–1940) who continued the policy of producing symbolist plays (in which the characters have no life of their own but are symbols of certain inner qualities).

1892 Germany *Die Weber* by Gerhart Hauptmann (1862–1946): it was one of the first plays to have as its hero a crowd and not an individual. (This play is naturalistic. Later his work tended towards symbolism.)

1892 Russia Italian dancer and teacher Enrico Cecchetti (1850–1928) became instructor at the Imperial School of ballet. He taught Pavlova, Nijinsky, Fokine, Karsavina and in later life Massine, de Valois, Dolin and Markova. He revised ballet teaching and devised exercises to develop versatility in graceful and in acrobatic dancing.
First performance in St Petersburg of the ballet *The Nutcracker*, by Lev Ivanov, to music by Tchaikovsky.

1892 U.S.A. *Jewish King Lear* by Jacob Gordin (1853–1909) who adapted the work of great European dramatists for a Jewish public. He discouraged improvisation, which was part of the Jewish theatrical tradition, and insisted on the actors following the dramatist's text.

1892 Yugoslavia First ballet performance in Yugoslavia; the art developed in Zagreb during the following five years.

1893 England *The Second Mrs Tanqueray* by Sir Arthur Wing Pinero (1855–1934), a play with a serious subject which was nevertheless successful with audiences used to more frivolous entertainment. In the English theatre at that time serious treatment of double moral standards (for men and women) was an innovation. Pinero also wrote farces and comedies, one of the best-known being *Trelawney of the 'Wells'* (1898).

1892 England Birth of Herbert Howells, English composer and educationist.

1892 France Claude Debussy's mature period commenced when he began work on *L'Apres-midi d'un Faune*, which was first performed in 1894.

1892 France Birth of Arthur Honegger (d. 1955), French-born composer of Swiss parentage.

1892 France Birth of Darius Milhaud (d. 1974), French composer.

1892 Germany Birth of Robert Lachmann (d. 1939), German musician, an authority on Oriental music, especially Arabian music of North Africa.

1892 Hungary Birth of László Lajtha (d. 1963), Hungarian conductor, composer and writer; he is an authority on folk music.

1892 Italy The opera *Pagliacci* by Ruggiero Leoncavallo (1858–1919), Italian composer, produced in Milan.

1892 U.S.A. Antonin Dvořák (1841–1904) accepted the directorship of National Conservatory of Music in New York and his three years there had a great influence on his music.

1893 England Sir Walter Parratt (1841–1893) appointed Master of the Queen's Music.

1893 Finland Jean Sibelius completed the 'Karelia' Overture and Suite.

1893 France Death of Charles Francois Gounod (b. 1818).

1893 France First composition, *Sérénade Grotesque*, by Joseph Maurice Ravel (1875–1937) but the first public performance of his works was not until 1898.

1893 Germany First performance of *Hansel and Gretel*, the most famous opera of Engelbert Humperdinck (1854–1921).

1893 Russia Death of Peter Ilyich Tchaikovsky (b. 1840).

1893 U.S.A. Antonin Dvořák composed his symphony *From the New World*.

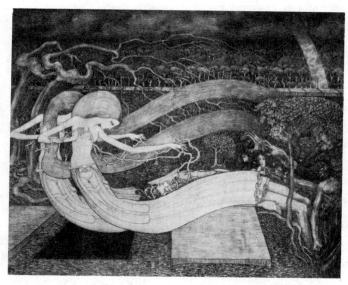

Netherlands: 'O Grave Where is thy Victory?' by Jan Theodoor Toorop

1891 Denmark The Independent Exhibition was established, mainly stimulated by the mystical paintings of Wilhelm Hammershøi (1864–1916), whose work had been systematically rejected by the Copenhagen Academy.

1891 France Paul Gauguin (1848–1903) left for Tahiti, where he painted some of his best known work. He used colour for decorative effect in flat washes with heavy outlines, departing completely from its representational use.

1891 U.S.A. Invention of the kinetoscope, a peep-show in which kinetograph pictures (in sequences shot at 40 frames per second) could be seen by one person at a time. The economic limits to this method were a strong stimulus to developing projection for a large audience.

1892 USA Fine Arts Building, Chicago, by Charles Atwood (1849–95) is one of several academically correct classical buildings built for the World's Fair that contrast sharply with the city's contemporary commercial buildings.

1892 Belgium Tassel House, Brussels, was the first major work of Baron Victor Horta (1861–1947). The interior is particularly remarkable, especially the staircase in which the free-flowing linear patterns of iron-work and painting constitute a fine specimen of Art Nouveau design.

1893 Italy The sculptor Medardo Rosso (1858–1928) made *Conversation in the Garden*, which was characteristic of his desire to capture the play of light on forms. Both he and Rodin claimed to be the first to make Impressionist sculpture, but Rosso was more concerned than Rodin with breaking up the solidity of form.

1893 U.S.A. Daniel Berkeley Updike (1860–1941) founded the Merrymount Press: he was an outstanding printer, typographer and book-designer.

1893 U.S.A. The Columbian Exposition marked a tendency in sculpture to confuse size with quality; *The Republic* (64 feet) was the largest figure constructed in America.

1893 U.S.A. Louis C. Tiffany began to make favrile glass (sprayed with iron salt solution when hot to give it a metallic sheen): he had earlier worked with stained glass and mosaic, and had withdrawn from his Associated Artists company to concentrate on glass-making.

1892 England Philip Wilson Steer (1860–1942), a founder member of the New English Art Club, exhibited landscape paintings influenced by the French Impressionists. His work developed as a combination of the Impressionists' ability to convey light and atmosphere with English naturalist traditions.

1892 France Georges Rouault (1871–1958) began to paint religious subjects. He had trained as a restorer of stained glass, and his religious paintings retained strong colour and strong black outline. His colours were symbolic in the medieval sense.

1892 Netherlands *O Grave Where is Thy Victory?* by Jan Theodoor Toorop (1858–1928): a chalk-drawing characteristic of his flowing style, which influenced many *art nouveau* artists. Roman Catholicism was the main inspiration of Toorop's later work.

1892 Germany A large exhibition of paintings by the Norwegian artist Edvard Munch (1863–1944) caused a sensation. Munch was later regarded in Germany as one of the founders of expressionism.

1893 England James Pryde and his brother-in-law Sir William Nicholson (1872–1949) established 'The Beggarstaff Brothers' as a partnership in poster design.

1893 Nansen led expedition to North Pole. Zip fastener invented.

HISTORICAL EVENTS	LITERATURE	DANCE & DRAMA	MUSIC

HISTORICAL EVENTS

1894
Dreyfus case in France.
Nicholas II became last Tsar of Russia.

1895
Armenian massacres in Constantinople. Japanese defeat of China marked emergence of new power.

LITERATURE

1894 Bulgaria *Under the Yoke* by Ivan Vasov (1850–1921), a novelist, poet, short-story writer, essayist and dramatist whose outlook was traditional and nationalistic. This book is regarded as the best Bulgarian novel and brought Bulgarian literature to the notice of the rest of the world; the period 1890–1920 is known as the Vasov period. He and his followers used simple, everyday language.

1894 England *Esther Waters*, a novel by George Moore (1852–1933), Irish critic, playwright, novelist, and short-story writer. His work was realistic, and he was particularly skilled in portraying women.

1895–1896 Serbia A collection of poems by Jovan Jovanović (1833–1904), a Romantic whose poetry shows the influence of folk literature. He translated from English, German, Hungarian and Russian, and also wrote a wide variety of original poems.

1895 Belgium *Les Villages Illusoires* by Émile Adolphe Gustave Verhaeren (1855–1916), poet, playwright and critic. He experimented with a wide variety of metres and styles. This volume contains free verse and symbolism. Verhaeren believed in the brotherhood of man, and, although impressed by industrial progress, was angered by its destructive effects. He has been considered the greatest Belgian poet writing in French.

1895 Bohemia *The Czech Question* by Tomáš Garrigue Masaryk (1850–1937), philosopher and statesman. He wrote on sociology, religion and ethics, expressing the sceptical attitude of the 1890s.

1895 Russia Poems by Konstantin Dmitrievich Belmont (1867–1943), who used accumulations of words for musical effect. His work shows European and American influences.

1895 U.S.A. *The Red Badge of Courage* by Stephen Crane (1871–1900), a realistic novelist and short-story writer who dealt mainly with war, poverty and death. He was not widely read, although this book is now generally recognized as a masterpiece.

DANCE & DRAMA

1893 France *Madame Sans-Gêne* by Victorien Sardou (1831–1908), who continued the tradition of the 'Well-Made' play, for which Bernard Shaw coined the word 'sardoodledom'. He wrote many of his plays for Sarah Bernhardt (1844–1923).

1894 Norway *The Balcony* by Gunnar Edvard Rode Heiberg (1857–1929), a writer of social problem plays who showed the influence of Ibsen.

1895 England *The Importance of Being Earnest* by Oscar Fingal O'Flaherty Wills Wilde (1854–1900): he wrote the wittiest dialogue in the English theatre for over 100 years, but was completely outside the mainstream of realistic drama.

1895 Germany *Der Erdgeist* by Frank Wedekind (1864–1918), who worked in Munich with his own company: his work tended towards expressionism.

1895 Russia The 'class of perfection' for working dancers was set up by Johannsen and later taken over by Nicolas Legat (1869–1937). Russian dancers at this time learned to combine the technical virtuosity of the Italians with the taste and spirit of their own French-inspired art. Under Legat they achieved a truly Russian art which brought together the French-Danish school of dramatic ballet and the French-Italian school of technical skill.

1895 Russia Mathilda Kchessinska (1872–1917) became *prima ballerina assoluta* at the St Petersburg Theatre. Her powerful admirers gave her a strong influence on policy.

MUSIC

1894 Austria Giudo Adler (1855–1941) founded *Denkmäler der Tonkunst in Österreich*, "Monuments of Music in Austria."

1894 England Publication of *Studies in Modern Music* by William Henry Hadow (1859–1937), English educationist, writer and lecturer on musical subjects. This was the first of many important works which have greatly influenced twentieth century musical thinking.

1894 England Birth of Ernest John Moerán (d. 1950), English composer.

1894 England Birth of Peter Warlock (d. 1930), English composer.

1894 Germany Production of Richard Strauss' first opera *Guntram* at Weimar.

1894 Russia *Russkaya Muzikalnaya Gazeta*, for many years the only musical periodical in Russia, founded by Nikolay Fedorovich Findeisen (1868–1928), Russian musical historian and journalist.

1894 U.S.A. Birth of Walter Piston, (d. 1976) American composer and teacher who has had considerable influence in American musical development.

1895 England Birth of Gordon Percival Septimus Jacob, English composer, conductor and teacher.

1895 England Henry Joseph Wood (1869–1944), appointed conductor of a series of Promenade Concerts at Queen's Hall, opened in 1893.

1895 Germany Birth of Paul Hindemith (d. 1963), German violist and composer, one of the most versatile musicians of his day.

1895 Germany Birth of Carl Orff, German composer, educationist and musicologist; he was one of the founders of the Dorothee Günter School (1925).

1895 Russia The first complete performance of the ballet *Swan Lake* by Peter Ilyich Tchaikovsky (1840–1893) in St Petersburg.

ARCHITECTURE

1894 USA Guaranty Building, Buffalo, by Dankmar Adler (1844–1900) and Louis Sullivan was built on skyscraper principles but decorated with an elaborately coved cornice and rich ornament on the terra-cotta cladding.

1895–1900 Belgium Solvay House, Brussels, is an Art Nouveau design by Baron Victor Horta, here spread to the façade with its curved surfaces and iron work.

1895 England Westminster Cathedral, London, by John Francis Bentley (1839–1902) is polychrome in red brick and stone and based on domed Byzantine models but with an Italian form of campanile; the rich marble and mosaic interior is unfinished.

1895 USA Richard Buckminster Fuller born, who developed the geodesic dome, protecting an interior space, suitable for any arrangement, by a 'space-frame'.

THREE DIMENSIONAL ART

1894 England Foundation of the Ashendene Press by C. H. St John Hornby: the first of a number of private presses founded to carry out the perfectionist principles of William Morris. New types, Subiaco and Ptolemy, were designed for it by Emery Walker (1851–1933).

Belgium: inlaid flower design in Solvay House by Victor Horta

VISUAL ARTS

1893 Germany First annual International Exhibition of Amateur Photography held in Hamburg; this was the first appearance of the art photography movement in Germany.

1894 England Aubrey Vincent Beardsley (1872–1898) drew his illustrations to *Salome*. His original, Japanese-inspired use of black and white for grotesque or decorative effect became an immediate success.

1894 U.S.A. Death of George Innes (b. 1825), who has been considered the greatest American landscape painter of his time. His early work was influenced by the French Barbizon school.

1894 France The Photo-Club de Paris held its first exhibition of photographic art.

1895–1904 U.S.A. Adam Clarke Vroman (1856–1916) made a photo-documentation of the south-western Indians.

1895 Australia *Bailed Up*, the last major painting by Tom Roberts (1856–1931), typifying his work on the pioneering life. His treatment of the bush and of Australian outdoor life was the main influence on developing Australian art.

1895 France Paul Cézanne (1839–1906) was given a one-man exhibition; from this time younger artists became interested in his theories of structure by colour masses, analysing nature in terms of 'the cylinder, the sphere and the cone'.

In cinema, the Lumière brothers, Auguste (1863–1934) and Louis Jean (1864–1948), patented the *Cinématographe* camera and projector and put on the first paying public performance. Films portrayed street scenes, military manoeuvres and sporting events, using trick photography to amuse the audience, e.g. reversing the film to make horses go over jumps in reverse.

1895 USA The 'Ten' group of painters exhibited for the first time; their work was influenced by Impressionism. T. W. Dewing (1851–1938) was thought to be the most original of the group.

1895 Wilhelm Konrad Röntgen discovered X-rays.
First transmission by radio by Guglielmo Marconi.

LITERATURE

1895 Italy *Piccolo Mondo Antico* by Antonio Fogazzaro (1842–1911), poet, playwright and novelist. A Romantic, he aimed at beauty, goodness and truth, believing that his books should have a moral value. He was a Catholic, and his religious writings achieved wide recognition, particularly *Il Santo* (1905). He was regarded by Verga as one of the greatest of European novelists.

1896 Australia *While the Billy Boils*, short stories of Henry Lawson (1867–1922), poet and writer of realistic stories. He stressed the harshness of Australian life, though not without humour.

1896 England *A Shropshire Lad*, poems by Alfred Edward Housman (1859–1936), classical scholar and poet. He wrote bitter lyric poetry, often about rural incidents and frequently tragic.

1896 Nicaragua *Prosas Profanas* by the poet Felix Rubén Garcia Sarmiento, called Rubén Dario (1867–1916), a leader of the Spanish-American 'Modernismo' movement. This had much in common with the early European Romantic movement, and the poets turned to French writers for sources and examples. However, their intention was not to copy, but to revolutionize the literature of Latin America.

1896 Sweden *Stänk och Flikar*, poems by Gustav Fröding (1860–1911), poet and journalist. He believed that God has assigned a function to everything in the world, no matter how evil or ugly. He is regarded as Sweden's greatest lyric poet.

1897 Bohemia *Polar Winds* by Václáv Ignac Jebavý, called Otokar Březina (1868–1929), Czech poet. His early work shows the pessimistic outlook of Schopenhauer; later he became much more vital and optimistic. The development shows in his poems. Stylistically, he was a Symbolist.

1898 Greece *O Tafos*, a cycle of poems by Kostes Palamos (1859–1943). Patriotic and scholarly, he was a supporter of Psychares in his campaign for the use of the spoken, demotic language.

DANCE & DRAMA

1896 England *Michael and His Lost Angel* by Henry Arthur Jones (1851–1929): social drama with a strong element of melodrama.

1896 Germany *Heinrich und Heinrichs Geschlecht* by Ernst von Wildenbruch (1845–1909): his historical plays reflect some of the attitudes to history of the bourgeoisie at that period.

1896 Germany Karl Lautenschläger introduced the first revolving stage.

1896 Russia Vassily Tikhomirov (1876–1956), pupil of Paul Gerdt, became first teacher at the Bolshoi school of ballet. He taught many leading dancers and was considered one of the best teachers of his time.

1897 England *Caste* by Thomas William Robertson (1829–1871): an English realistic domestic drama, far more convincing than anything preceding it.

1897 France *Cyrano de Bergerac* by Edmond Rostand (1868–1918); a French romantic verse play.

1897 Japan *Maki No Kata* by Tsubouchi, a Shakespearian scholar: the play is largely in dialogue, not narrative. He greatly extended the influence of the West in Japan.

1898 England *Plays Pleasant* and *Plays Unpleasant* by Bernard Shaw: he intended his plays to be read as well as acted, and edited and published them to this end. He saw the theatre as a platform for his social and political views, and his plays were intended to appeal not to the emotions but to the intellect.

1898 Italy *La Citta Morta* and *La Gioconda* by Gabriele d'Annunzio (1863–1938): Italian poetical dramas, whose success was in part due to the fact that the heroines were played by the actress Eleanora Duse (1859–1924).

1898 Philippines The islands were ceded to the U.S.A. from Spain: this period produced a brief activity in the *zarazuela*, or Spanish song-play, which is an ideal vehicle for political comment.

MUSIC

1896 Austria Death of Anton Bruckner (b. 1824), Austrian composer.

1896 U.S.A. Edward MacDowell (1861–1908) published his *Indian Suite* which used melodies of the North American Indians.

1897 Austria Gustav Mahler (1860–1911) was appointed *Kapellmeister* at Court Opera in Vienna, largely on the recommendation of Brahms, and remained there for 10 years.

1897 Belgium Performance of the opera *Fervaal* by Vincent d'Indy (1851–1931), French composer, theorist, teacher and author in Brussels.

1897 Finland Fazerin Musiikkikikauppa, Finnish music-publishing house, established.

1897 France *The Sorcerer's Apprentice* by Paul Dukas (1865–1935) was given its first performance, in Paris. It is based on a ballad by Johann Wolfgang von Goethe (1749–1832).

1897 Germany Death of Johannes Brahms (b. 1833).

1897 Hungary Birth of György Kósa, Hungarian pianist and composer. A disciple of Bartók, he has introduced many contemporary compositions to Hungarian public.

1897 Ireland *Feis Ceoil*, Irish Music Festival, founded.

1898 England First performance of a choral setting of Longfellow's *Hiawatha's Wedding Feast* by Samuel Coleridge-Taylor.

1898 England Henry Walford Davies (1869–1941), English organist, composer and educationist, became director and organist at Temple Church; in his 20 years there he considerably developed church music.

1898 England The Folk Song Society founded.

1898 France Pau [Pablo] Casals, the Spanish violoncellist (1876–1974), made his debut in Paris.

1897 Australia Brisbane Cathedral was designed by John L. Pearson (1817–1897); his last work, it displayed his interest in the archaeologically correct on a spacious but spartan scale and is the last and the best of a number of Gothic-styled cathedrals in Australia designed by English architects.

1897–1904 France St-Jean-de-Montmartre, Paris, by J. E. A. de Baudot (1834–1915) was the first church to be built of reinforced concrete and is decorated with faience mosaic.

1897 Holland Amsterdam Exchange by Hendrik Berlage (1856–1934) was built of brick with a stone trim and was a fresh interpretation of Romanesque and sixteenth-century styles; Berlarge had considerable influence on Dutch architects and the Amsterdam school.

1897 Scotland Cranston Tea Rooms, Buchanan Street, Edinburgh, by Charles Rennie Mackintosh (1868–1928) was the first major Art Nouveau work by this architect, who designed a series of such restaurants in Glasgow.

1897–1909 Scotland Glasgow School of Art by Charles Rennie Mackintosh is a highly original building in which the sinuous lines of Art Nouveau were checked by the rectangular abstract shapes of the interior fittings and the later library wing.

1898 Austria Majolika Haus, Vienna, by Otto Wagner (1841–1918) is an original building of Art Nouveau inspiration, in which a faience floral design covers the flat façade.

1898 England Whitechapel Art Gallery, London, by C. Harrison Townsend (1850–1928) is a rare Art Nouveau building in London, possibly inspired by Henry H. Richardson of Boston, USA.

1898 England Broadleys, Lake Windermere, by Charles Voysey (1857–1941) illustrates the architect's independence of period imitation; the house is typically long and low with bands of windows set in white-painted, rough-cast walls.

1896 Belgium Constantin Meunier (1831–1904), sculptor, was commissioned to carve a Monument to Labour, unfinished at his death. His social realism and belief in the dignity of labour were against the popular fashion of his time.

1896 England William Lethaby (1857–1931) was appointed first principal of the Central School of Arts and Crafts: he was an important influence on art education, his theories were those of the Arts and Crafts movement extended to embrace architecture and industrial design.

1897–1912 Scotland Decoration and furnishing of the Cranston Tea Rooms, Glasgow, by Charles Rennie Mackintosh (1868–1928), pioneer designer in art nouveau style. His furniture became known and influential in Europe from 1895; his style combined austerity with grace.

1897 Nigeria A British military expedition made the first Western contact with Benin art: ivories include horns and tusks, armlets, marks and carved figures; bronzes include heads as altar furniture, cast by the *cireperdue* method, statues of animals and men and bronze plaques with figures in high relief. The best were dated as fourteenth to fifteenth century. These and later West African discoveries had a strong impact on twentieth century sculptors.

c.1897 Austria Adolf Loos (1870–1933), furniture designer, attacked the extremes of art nouveau design and championed functional furniture. His ideas were influential on furniture design during the next 20 years.

1898 England Sir Ambrose Heal (1872–1959) brought out his *Plain Oak Furniture* catalogue. This was in the spirit of the Arts and Crafts movement and strongly influenced furniture-making from 1900–1925. Heal's work in machine production made him a pioneer of the Modern Movement in English furniture.

1896 England The first public cinematograph performance in English was given in London. From then on films became popular as music-hall and fairground shows.

1896–1901 Finland Gallen-Kallela (1865–1931) painted a series of pictures in a severe, linear style to illustrate the *Kalevala* epic. This was the beginning of a nationalistic movement in Finnish art.

1896 France George Méliès (1861–1938), a producer of magic and spectacle shows, made his first film in Paris: it was full of trick photography and surreal effects.

1896 India E. B. Havell became head of Calcutta Art School; his interest in old Indian art helped to bring about a Bengali revival. He was succeeded by his pupil Abanindranath Tagore.

1896 Italy The Lumière brothers' film on the city of Venice included a 'sequence shot' by a camera on a moving gondola; this gave the same effect as the theatrical roller-panorama.

1897 France The Lumière brothers opened the world's first permanent film theatre, in Paris.

1898–1903 Austria Gustav Klimt (1862–1918) was a prominent member of the Vienna Secession movement in *art nouveau*. He produced portraits and large paintings in which faces and bodies were modelled, but objects and draperies appeared as two-dimensional ornamental pattern.

1898 Germany Käthe Kollwitz (1867–1945) published a series of prints inspired by Hauptmann's play *The Weavers*. She lived in a poor district of Berlin and for most of her life made sympathetic studies of the poor in engravings, lithographs and woodcuts. She was also a sculptor.

1898 Spain Death of Carlos Haes (b. 1829) a Brussels-born painter who founded a flourishing school of landscape painting.

1897 Discovery of electron, first atomic particle.

397

HISTORICAL EVENTS	LITERATURE	DANCE & DRAMA	MUSIC
	1898 Germany *Der Stechlin* by Theodor Fontane (1819–1898), novelist. He published his first historical novel when he was nearly 60, and his first modern novel at 70. A Realist, he is particularly important for his skilful use of dialogue, which replaced narrative as a means of furthering the plot and revealing character.	**1898 Russia** Constantin Serveivich Stanislavsky (1863–1938) with Vladimir Ivanovich Nemirovich-Danchenko (1859–1943) founded the Moscow Art Theatre. It had an enormous influence on the theatre, and it was itself in part influenced by the work of the German Meiningen Players. Stanislavsky's new method of training actors involved psychological study of the character to be played.	**1898 France** Marcel Dupré (1886–1971), French organist and composer, was appointed to Saint-Vivien, Rouen, from where he went to Saint-Sulpice, Paris and later Notre-Dame. As performer and teacher he has exercised a greater influence than any other contemporary organist.

1898 Russia *The Seagull* by Anton Pavlovich Chekov (1860–1904) was successfully produced at the Moscow Art Theatre, after its initial production at the Alexandrinsky had been a failure. Chekov's subtle, naturalistic style called for a special acting technique, which the Moscow Art Theatre provided.

1898 U.S.A. W. C. Sabine, Professor of Physics at Harvard University, who did much research into acoustics, especially in concert halls, was consulted regarding the building of the Concert Hall in Boston, Massachusetts.

1898 Russia Visit to St Petersburg of the Moscow ballet company of Savva Mamontov: their use of stage design was advanced and depended on the sets painted by Korovin and Golovin with a new use of colour.

1898 U.S.A. Birth of Paul Robeson (d. 1976), noted for his singing of Negro songs and spirituals.

1899 Anglo-Boer War in South Africa began.

1899 Silesia *The Horrid Apparition* and *Palácky's Day*, two poems by Vladimir Vašek, called Petr Bezruč (1867– ?). A Silesian, he is regarded as one of the greatest Czech poets.

1899 Russia Prince Volkonsky appointed Director of the Imperial Theatres: a friend of the designer Alexandre Benois (1870–1960) and the choreographer and producer Sergei Pavlovich Diaghilev (1872–1929), he tried to put their ideas into practice but was defeated by quarrels with them and with the theatre directorate. Diaghilev and Benois aimed at combining the best of music, dancing and painting to make one harmonious work of art on the stage; all three elements were of equal importance to them.

1899 Switzerland *Die Musik und Die Inscenierung*, a treatise by the artist Adolphe Appia (1862–1928): he advocated very simple, three-dimensional sets but emphasized the importance of dramatic and mobile lighting to create atmosphere. Much of modern lighting theory is derived from Appia.

1899 Austria Death of Johann Strauss the younger (b. 1825).

1899 France Birth of Francis Poulenc (d. 1963), French composer.

1899 Germany The designs for Wagner's *The Ring* by Adolphe Appra (1862–1928), a Swiss operatic designer, helped to establish the more abstract presentation of opera involving the reduction of stage clutter and more emphasis on lighting.

1899 Finland Jean Sibelius (1865–1957), completed his first symphony.

1899 Germany International Musical Society founded.

1899 U.S.A. Jazz began to develop in New Orleans.

ARCHITECTURE

1898 England *Tomorrow* by Sir Ebenezer Howard (1850–1928) was published; in it he advocated the advantages of the garden city, several of which were built early in the twentieth century.

1898 Finland Alvar Aalto built Viipuri Public Library with undulating timber roof.

Germany: after a sketch by Joseph Olbrich for exhibition hall of the 'Wiener Sezession', 1899

1899–1904 France Métro stations of Paris were constructed by Hector Guimard (1867–1942), an architect who designed several buildings in which Art Nouveau design is used to great effect.

1899 Germany The Ernst Ludwig Haus, Darmstadt, by Joseph Olbrich (1867–1908) retained the delicacy of Art Nouveau within a more formal framework, reminiscent of Mackintosh in Scotland.

1899 USA J. W. Husser House, Chicago, by Frank Lloyd Wright is an early example of Wright's 'prairie house' style, carefully adjusted to the landscape with low elevation, projecting roofs and rooms merging into each other; it was later destroyed.

1899–1904 USA The Carson, Pirie and Scott department store, Chicago, was by Louis Sullivan; the architect's last great work was built with horizontal emphasis and demonstrated his interest in organically inspired façade ornament; it has characteristic 'Chicago windows'.

THREE DIMENSIONAL ART

1898 France Exhibition of *Balzac*, by Auguste Rodin, a figure violently abused at the time as 'inhuman' but now considered one of the last great works of the dying Romantic movement, and one which confirms Rodin's debt to Michelangelo.

VISUAL ARTS

1898 U.S.A. In Philadelphia the Photographic Society held the first annual exhibition of pictures showing 'individual artistic feeling and expression'. The influence of Japanese art through the European Aesthetic Movement showed strongly.

1899 France George Méliès (1861–1938) began to make story films such as *L'Affaire Dreyfus* and *Jeanne d'Arc*; tableaux were composed for the camera, filmed in one shot each, and linked by titles.

In art, Edouard Vuillard (1868–1940) painted *La Veuve en Visite*, an interior in his mother's home characteristic of his domestic pictures. He considered them to be influenced most strongly by Chardin and Rembrandt.

1899 Japan Film was used to record theatre productions and famous performances of *kabuki* plays.

1899 Acetylsalicylic acid (aspirin) invented.

20th Century

LITERATURE

DANCE & DRAMA

MUSIC

1900 France Foundation of the socialist journal *Cahiers de la Quinzaine* by Charles Péguy (1873–1914) and Romain Rolland (1866–1944). Péguy, a student of the philosopher Bergson, was also a poet. Rolland, who was awarded the Noble Prize in 1916, attempted to bring about understanding between France and Germany. His best-known work is *Jean-Christophe*, a novel about a German composer who placed art before material gains and was acclaimed in France.

1900 U.S.A. *Sister Carrie* by Theodore Herman Albert Dreiser (1871–1945), a writer of realistic novels who had a strong influence on American fiction. This book was regarded as immoral and was withheld for a time.

1900 France Isadora Duncan (1877–1927), American dancer, made her first successful appearance. Her style of 'free' dancing involved miming to music, not specifically dance music, with movements inspired by the music that were not academic dance steps or positions.

1900 Netherlands *The Good Hope* by Herman Heijermans (1864–1924), the first Dutch dramatist to achieve fame outside the Netherlands: his plays deal with contemporary social inequalities.

1900 Spain Pepe Amaya took a flamenco dance company to the Paris Exposition Universale. This began a popular interest in flamenco with dancers appearing in theatres and music-halls. Pastora Imperio was considered the greatest in Spain; Vicente Escudero was the first to achieve wide fame outside Spain.

*c.***1900 India** Beginning of the creative period of Girish Chandra, Bengali playwright and actor-manager. He did much to advance serious appreciation of drama.

*c.***1900 U.S.A.** Evolution of the turkey trot, or one-step, the first of the ragtime dances to spread to Europe. From then on most of the innovations in European social dance came from America, ultimately inspired by Negro rhythms. The one-step, Boston waltz and Latin American tango were the basis of modern ballroom dances.

*c.***1900 Vietnam** Development of a re-invigorated form of *hat boi* theatre, called *cai luong*: this was more popular than the older form, being a kind of operetta based on French and American songs.

1900 Austria Birth of Ernst Krenek, a composer whose work reflects different phases of European music from 1918–1940.

1900 Czechoslovakia Death of Zdenek Fibich (b. 1850). Composer and pioneer of Czech music, he showed great originality of rhythm, harmony and dynamics in his music.

1900 England Granville Bantock (1868–1946), English composer, appointed principal of the Birmingham and Midland Institute School of Music. This marked beginning of his mature musicianship.

1900 England Birth of Alan Bush, pianist and composer.

1900 England First production of *The Dream of Gerontius* by Edward Elgar (1857–1934) who considered this to be his finest work.

1900 England Death of Arthur Seymour Sullivan (b. 1842), English composer.

1900 Germany Birth of Hermann Reutter, German pianist and composer.

1900 Germany Birth of Kurt Weill (d. 1950), German-American composer.

1900 Italy The opera *Tosca* by Giacomo Antonio Domenico Michele Secondo Mario Puccini (1858–1924) first performed in Rome. *La Bohème* had been performed four years before, with Toscanini conducting.

1900 U.S.A. Birth of Aaron Copland, American composer.

1900 U.S.A. Philadelphia Orchestra founded.

*c.***1900 U.S.A.** A type of jazz originating from New Orleans developed known as 'Dixieland'.

1901
Death of Queen
Victoria.
Inauguration of
Australian
Commonwealth.

1901 England *Kim*, a novel by Rudyard Kipling (1865–1936), novelist, short-story writer, poet and journalist. He is best known for his stories of service life in India. His poetry was ballad-like, and most successful read aloud. He was awarded the Nobel Prize in 1907.

1901 U.S.A. *The Jungle* by Upton Beall Sinclair (1878–1969), a novelist and social idealist whose work drew attention to the evils in American life. As a result of this book, the food-packing industry was reformed.

1901 England John Haywood Compton, English organ builder (1874–1857) established his business at Nottingham, moving to London in 1918.

1901 England Birth of Gerald Finzi, English composer.

ARCHITECTURE

THREE DIMENSIONAL ART

1900–1916 England The Doves Press in London published 51 titles; it was founded by T. J. Cobden-Sanderson, bookbinder, and Emery Walker.

*c.*1900 **France** Aristide Maillol (1861–1944) began work as a sculptor. He visited Greece, and his work tempered current romanticism; his interest was in the free-standing sculpted figure, especially the female nude, free of all architectural or other associations. He excelled in controlling the tensions inherent in a plastic form.

Isadora Duncan dancing in the ruins of the theatre of Dionysius in Athens, 1904 (see Dance & Drama)

VISUAL ARTS

1900 England Exhibition held in London of work by American photographers, including Edward Steichen (b. 1879), Clarence H. White (1871–1925) and Alvin Langdon Coburn (1882–1966). Many of the pictures were produced by manipulation of the print or negative to imitate other art forms.

1900 Paris, France The 'Exposition' included systems for synchronizing film with pre-recorded sound; Léon Gaumont demonstrated the chronophone, which continued in use until 1913.

1900 France The Belgian painter Alfred Stevens (1823–1906) was given the first one-man Paris exhibition for a living artist. His work influenced Whistler and the Impressionists.

INVENTIONS & DISCOVERIES

1900 Browning revolver patented. Max Planck proposed quantum theory of energy.

1901 Belgium *L'Innovation* department store by Baron Victor Horta included the great glass and metal Art Nouveau façade, which was considered Horta's most notable achievement in commercial building; it was destroyed by fire in 1967.

1901 U.S.A. Frank Lloyd Wright (1869–1959), architect, lectured in Chicago on 'The Art and Craft of the Machine' as 'the normal tool of civilization': he expressed the conviction that machines could be used to realize the artist's vision of design.

1901–1904 Spain Pablo Picasso (1881–1973) painted the pictures of his 'Blue Period': they were part of a Spanish tradition beginning with Murillo—paintings of the poor and outcast, treated with emotional realism.

1901 Denmark Vilhelm Hammershi (1864–1916) painted a group portrait of five artists, which exemplified his mysticism; he used tones of grey to express an other-worldly quality. His paintings were not appreciated by the public in his earlier years.

1901 Edwin Brandenberger invented cellophane.

HISTORICAL EVENTS	LITERATURE	DANCE & DRAMA	MUSIC

MUSIC

1901 England Birth of Charles Edmund Rubbra, English composer.

1901 France The first mature work by Joseph Maurice Ravel (1875–1937), *Jeux d'Eau*, for piano and string quartet.

1901 Hungary Birth of Ervin Major, Hungarian musicologist and composer who has contributed greatly to our knowledge of Hungarian musical history.

1901 Italy Death of Giuseppe Fortunino Francesco Verdi (b. 1813), Italian composer.

1901 Russia First performance of the *Piano Concerto No. 2* by Sergey Vassilievich Rachmaninov (1873–1943).

1901 U.S.A. Founding of Wa-Wan Press by Arthur Farwell (1872–1952), American composer, for publication of music showing American-Indian influences.

HISTORICAL EVENTS

1902 Peace of Vereeniging ended Boer War.

LITERATURE

1902–1909 Poland *The Peasants* by the novelist Wladyslaw Reymont (1867–1925): a portrait of a peasant community, set in the framework of the four seasons, the novel is noted for its psychological penetration and its combination of myth and and realism. Reymont was awarded the Nobel Prize in 1924.

1902 Brazil *Rebellion in the Backwoods* by Euclydes da Cunha (1866–1909): a piece of creative journalism of considerable artistic merit, the book brought social problems into the open for the first time in Brazil.

1902 England *Typhoon*, a novel by Joseph Conrad (Teodor Jozef Konrad Nalecz Korzeniowski, 1857–1924), the Polishborn and later naturalized English novelist. His novels are all in English, which he learned as a young man. He wrote best about the sea, endurance, and loneliness.

DANCE & DRAMA

1902 Russia *The Lower Depth* by Alexei Maximovich Pyeshkov-Maxim Gorki (1868–1936) was a realistic drama produced by the Moscow Art Theatre.

1902 Russia Début of the ballerina Tamara Karsavina (b.1885), considered the foremost ballerina of her time. She later was one of the founders of Diaghilev's Ballets Russes.

1902 Russia Vsevolod Emilievich Meyerhold (1874–1943) founded the Society of New Drama in Russia. His method of production, known as 'biomechanics', involved reducing the actor to the status of a puppet under the control of the producer. He used a bare stage and stylized gesture. In 1920 he became Head of Theatre in the People's Commisariat for Education.

1902 England Birth of William Turner Walton, English composer.

1902 France First performance of Debussy's only opera *Pelléas et Mélisande*, begun in 1892.

1902 Spain Birth of Joaquín Rodrigo, Spanish composer, noted for his *Conciérto de Aranjuez* for guitar and orchestra.

1902 U.S.A. Birth of Theodore Ward Chanler (d. 1961), American critic and composer, one of the outstanding American song writers.

HISTORICAL EVENTS

1903 Russian Labour Party split into Mensheviks and Bolsheviks.

LITERATURE

1903 Australia *Such is Life* by the novelist Joseph Furphy, called Tom Collins (1843–1912): the book is regarded as the first truly Australian novel; the author himself described it as 'offensively Australian'.

1903 Canada Publication of poems by Emile Nelligan (1879–1941), a French-Canadian poet who was strongly influenced by Verlaine and Rimbaud.

1903 U.S.A. *The Call of the Wild* by John Griffith, called Jack London (1876–1916), novelist and short-story writer. His popular and masterly tales of adventure showed man at odds with the forces of nature, or with society.

DANCE & DRAMA

1903 Austria Performance of Richard Strauss's ballet *Vision of Salome*, by the Canadian ballerina Maude Allan (1883–1956). She was an innovatory dancer influenced by Greek art.

1903 Poland *Akropolis* by Stanislaw Wyspianski (1869–1907) playwright, director and scenic designer, who wrote poetic dramas on national themes. His ideas included a concept of 'total theatre', which necessitated a completely new theatre design.

1903 Russia *The Cherry Orchard* by Anton Chekov (1860–1904).

1903 U.S.A. *Broken Hearts* by Solomon Libin (b.1872): a Jewish social drama about the lives of immigrant workers in New York.

MUSIC

1903 Austria Death of Hugo Philipp Jakob Wolf (b. 1860).

1903 England *The Act of Touch* the first of a series of books which became known as the 'Matthay System', written by Tobias Matthay (1858–1945), English pianist, teacher and composer.

1903 Germany The Heckelphone, a modern orchestral wood-wind instrument, invented by Wilhelm Heckel (1856–1909), German woodwind-instrument maker

1903 Hungary Birth of Pál Kadosa, Hungarian pianist, teacher and composer.

1902 Finland Tampere Cathedral by Lars Sonck was a granite church in a loosely interpreted Gothic style; the quality of the work was very high, as became normal in twentieth-century Finland.

Cargo ships of the type which Joseph Conrad (see Literature) sailed on. His experiences of being at sea provided background for his novels

1903 France 25b Rue Franklin by Auguste Perret (1874–1955) was an early example of a reinforced-concrete-frame construction, designed by an architect who pioneered concrete building.

1903 U.S.A. Louis C. Tiffany began to concentrate on his Long Island house, making it an expression of all his aesthetic theories; he remained manager of his glass company until 1919; the company continued until 1928.

1903 U.S.A. Frederick Carder (b. 1863 in Staffordshire) helped to found the Steuben Glass works; he had been a designer for the English art glass company of Stevens and Williams. He specialized at first in coloured glass in the style of Tiffany, and pioneered the decorative use of glass in architecture; some of his most outstanding work is in the Rockefeller Center, New York.

1901 Europe Camera tripods were fitted with swivel heads for panoramic shots, and put on tracks to reproduce the lantern-slide ('phantasmagoria') effect.

1902 England James Williamson (1855–1933) made his film *Fire*, which still used composed tableaux, but arranged them more flexibly to produce something like a natural sequence of action.

1902 France Maurice Utrillo (1883–1955) began to paint Montmartre and the Paris suburbs. His palette was at first sombre, lightened with whites after 1910 and highly coloured after 1915. He was considered a late Impressionist and, in his treatment of figures and composition, a 'naive' painter.

1902 Japan *Momijigari*, the first narrative film: it was based on a *kabuki* play.

1902 U.S.A. An exhibition of American photographs was mounted in New York by the Photo-Secession Group: their aim was to develop photography as a fine-art medium; their magazine was *Camera Work*.

Death of the artist J. H. Twachtman, a landscape painter who studied light and atmosphere and portrayed them with an unusually cool palette.

1902–1903 U.S.A. Edwin S. Porter made *The Life of an American Fireman*: the first story-film with continuous action in an edited series of shots, it included some actual pictures of fires. He followed this film with *The Great Train Robbery*.

1903 England The film *Runaway Match* made a feature of the chase, a favourite device in early British films.

1903 France Charles Pathé (1863–1957) became the dominant figure of the film industry in Paris, and its first monopolist, controlling production, distribution and exhibition.

1903 U.S.A. Edward Steichen photographed John Pierpoint Morgan: it is the most characteristic of his early portraits.

1902
William Bayliss and Ernest Starling discovered hormones. Pierre and Marie Curie announced discovery of radium.

1903
Orville and Wilbur Wright made first successful flight in aeroplane.

HISTORICAL EVENTS	LITERATURE	DANCE & DRAMA	MUSIC

1904 Outbreak of Russo-Japanese War.

1904 Italy *Alcyone* by Gabriele D'Annunzio (1863–1938), poet, playwright, novelist and short-story writer. Much of his work was based on the philosophy of Nietzsche, which he had misunderstood.

1904 Italy *Ashes* by the novelist Grazia Deledda (1871–1936). Most of her work is set in her native Sardinia. She was awarded the Nobel Prize in 1926.

1904 U.S.A. *Cabbages and Kings* by William Sidney Porter, called O. Henry (1862–1910), a writer of lively and amusing short stories famous for their trick endings.

1904 Ireland Opening of the Abbey Theatre, Dublin, built by Annie Elizabeth Frederika Horniman (1860–1937) as a home for the new Irish dramatic movement. The opening productions were *On Baile's Strand* by William Butler Yeats (1865–1939) and *Spreading The News* by Augusta, Lady Gregory (1852–1932).

1903 Russia Birth of Aram Ilyich Khachaturian, Armenian composer (d. 1978).

1903 Uruguay Birth of Francisco Curt Lange, Uruguayan musicologist and founder of many musical organizations, magazines, conferences, etc.

1904 Austria Alban Berg (1885–1935) first met Schoenberg (1874–1951) and was a pupil of his until 1912.

1904 Czechoslovakia Death of Antonín Dvořák (b. 1841), Czech composer.

1904 England London Symphony Orchestra formed.

1904 France The opera *Hélène* by Charles Camille Saint-Saëns first performed. The title rôle was written for Nellie Melba (1859–1931).

1905 Abortive revolution in Russia.

1905 Japan *The Sound of the Tide*, an anthology by the poet Veda Bin (1874–1916): it contained translations from Victor Hugo and the French Symbolist poets. It was written in colloquial Japanese, which was not usual in poetry.

1905 Russia *B'ir Hacharega* by Hayyim Nahman Bialik (1873–1934), a Russian-born Hebrew poet, essayist and story-writer: this poem, written in reaction to the Kisheneff pogrom, is a moving account of suffering and an admonition to the Jews for their passivity under oppression. In 1924 Bialik settled in Palestine where he was the leader of a cultural revival. He is regarded as the greatest modern Hebrew poet.

1905 China Début of the actor Mei Lan Fang (b.1894), important as the first educated actor in Chinese theatre. He produced historical operas that were properly researched and considerably extended the scope of the theatre, as well as achieving respectability for it and for its actors. Chinese opera relies for effect on actors miming with a few symbolic props; interest lies in the skilful presentation of stock characters by an established repertoire of gestures and songs. It is a classical form concerned with types, not individuals.

1905 England *The Voysey Inheritance* by Harley Granville-Barker (1877–1946) was produced at the Court Theatre, where he was manager in partnership with John Eugene Vedrenne (1867–1930). Non-commercial theatres, intimate theatres, drama festivals and theatre societies proliferated in England at that time, producing the new intellectual drama.

1905 Russia Choreographer Michel Fokine (1880–1942) created *The Dying Swan* as a solo for Anna Pavlova. The ballet was innovatory in its direct expression of feeling.

1905 U.S.A. Arrival of Sholom Aleichem (1859–1916), a Jewish writer who became the protegé of Maurice Schwartz (1888–1960), reviver of Yiddish drama in New York. His plays are mainly about Jewish life in his native Ukraine. One of his comedies, *Tevye The Milkman* was later adapted as the musical *Fiddler on the Roof.*

1904 Italy Birth of Luigi Dallapiccola (d. 1975), Italian pianist and composer.

1904 Italy First performance of *Madame Butterfly* by Giacomo Puccini (1858–1924).

1904 Russia Birth of Dmitry Borisovich Kabalevsky, Russian composer.

1904 South Africa Birth of Gideon Fagan, the first musician born in South Africa to achieve prominence as a conductor.

1905 Austria First performance, in Vienna, of *The Merry Widow* by Franz Lehár (1870–1948).

1905 Brazil Birth of Luiz Heitor Correa de Azevedo, Brazilian musicologist and folklorist.

1905 England Birth of Alan Rawsthorne (d. 1971), English composer.

1905 England Birth of Michael Kemp Tippett, English composer and teacher.

1905 England Ralph Vaughan Williams began musical editorship of *The English Hymnal*.

1905 France Birth of André Jolivet (d. 1974), French composer.

ARCHITECTURE

1904 Austria The Postal Savings Bank, Vienna, by Otto Wagner (1841–1918) was a very modern-looking building, especially the glass-vaulted central hall with tapering metal supports; the use of aluminium in the construction was novel.

1904–1914 Finland Helsinki Railway Station by Eliel Saarinen (1873–1950) was the first major work by this architect; it was built in rugged granite and inspired by the designs of the Vienna Secession.

1905–1911 Belgium Stoclet House, Brussels, was by Josef Hoffman (1870–1956), an architect who had developed from Art Nouveau to simple architectonic compositions; he enhanced this house with marble and bronze on the exterior and marble and mosaic, by Gustave Klimt, (1862–1918) within.

1905 England The Piccadilly Hotel, London, by Richard Norman Shaw illustrates the grandiloquent aspirations of Edwardian neo-baroque architecture.

1905 France The *Samaritaine* department store, Paris, by F. Jourdain (1847–1953) has a façade covered with decorative ironwork and polychrome faience, which is considered the best in the Parisian Art Nouveau buildings.

1905 France *Garage Ponthieu*, Paris, by Auguste Perret was unusual in having its concrete construction exposed on the façade.

1905 Spain Casa Batlló and Casa Milo, Barcelona, by Antonio Gaudi (1852–1926) are blocks of flats with undulating façades and, in the case of the former, glittered with polychrome tiling; the rooms themselves were also unusually shaped.

THREE DIMENSIONAL ART

1904 France Constantin Brancusi (1876–1957), Romanian sculptor, settled in Paris. Early work in wood-carving gave him an interest in the expressive potential of materials; he used bronze for its own qualities and not merely to make clay figures permanent. His ability to reduce forms to essential plane and volume led him to be regarded as the greatest sculptor of his time.

1904 France The potter Auguste Delaherche (1857–1940) first began to throw his own pots; earlier he had designed pots to be thrown by a craftsman potter, as was the practice for artist-potters of the period. Delaherche was more concerned with form than with decoration; his feeling for his material was shared by his fellow potter Ernest Chaplet (1835–1909) and made both of them outstanding among nineteenth century French potters. Art pottery at the time, in France and elsewhere, was mainly concerned with the decoration of pots made by somebody other than the artist, and artist-potters were slow to develop any real affinity with their basic material.

1904 Germany Richard Riemerschmid (1868–1957) was one of the first designers to make furniture which advertised its factory assembly as part of its design.

1905 England American-born sculptor Jacob Epstein (1880–1959) settled in England. Most of his public commissions aroused controversy because of their monumental nature; he was considered the greatest sculptor of his day in the Romantic spirit inherited from Rodin.

1905 France Henri Matisse (1869–1954) exhibited his first sculpture, which was characterized by a simplification of planes influenced by Negro art.

1905 France First one-man exhibition by the sculptor Emile-Antoine Bourdelle (1861–1929), who worked as assistant to Rodin but rejected his romanticism in favour of a classical style. His main interest lay in the relationship between sculpture and architecture in contemporary buildings.

VISUAL ARTS

*c.*1904–1914 **Australia** Most active period of the artist Norman Lindsay (1887–1969) who became a dominant influence in establishing the artist's role in Australian society. His work in painting, ink-drawing and writing was imaginative, frequently erotic and always controversial.

1904 Germany Ernst Ludwig Kirchner (1880–1938) finished his studies in painting at Munich, and came under the influence of neo-impressionism through an exhibition of the same year. He also studied primitive art in the Munich museums, and began to paint in expressionist style with severely simplified primitive images. He also made outstanding woodcuts, influenced in technique by late Gothic artists.

1905–1910 U.S.A. John Marin (1870–1953) worked in Europe as an etcher and water colourist. On his return he came in contact with Stieglitz's 291 Gallery of progressive art (opened 1905).

1905 England Foundation of the Camden Town Group, artists who joined with Walter Richard Sickert (1860–1942) on his return from France. They were inspired by Gauguin and the Pont Aven group to combine realism with strong, decorative colour. Sickert was an important link between French and English painting.

1905 France An exhibition of work by Henri Matisse, Maurice Vlaminck and other artists gave rise to the name 'Fauves', wild beasts, because the paintings expressed feeling directly in pure colour.

1905 France The films of Ferdinand Zecca (1864–1947) began to turn the chase to comic effect, with clowns and trick photography. Many featured André Deed, a clown in the circus tradition.

1905 U.S.A. First documentary picture-stories by Lewis Wickes Hine (1874–1940), a pioneer in photo-journalism, especially on social issues.

1905 U.S.A. Alfred Stieglitz (1864–1946) opened his '291 Gallery' in New York, bringing together the latest work in American and European art. He was a formative influence on American taste.

INVENTIONS & DISCOVERIES

1904
First ultra-violet lamp made.

1905
Albert Einstein published his first (special) theory of relativity.

HISTORICAL EVENTS	LITERATURE	DANCE & DRAMA	MUSIC

MUSIC

1905 Hungary Birth of Mátyás György Seiber (d. 1960), Hungarian-born composer, conductor, violoncellist and writer on music of Hungarian origin.

DANCE & DRAMA

1906 U.S.A. Stuyvesant Theatre, New York, built by David Belasco (1859–1931) who began his career as an actor, but achieved his greatest success as a stage director. His sets and scenic effects were very realistic, and the plays he put on were strong vehicles for the 'stars' of the time.

1906 U.S.A. Ruth St Denis (1877–1968) choreographed her first ballet *Radha*, based on a Hindu theme. She had no contact with authentic Indian work; her own brand of orientalism had many imitators.

HISTORICAL EVENTS

*1906
Transvaal and
Orange Colonies
granted self-
government.
Persian
revolution.*

LITERATURE

1906–1907 Sweden *The Wonderful Adventures of Nils* by Selma Lagerlöf (1859–1940), a novelist and short-story writer whose writing combined sociology and folk-tale. This book was written for children. She was awarded the Nobel Prize in 1909.

1906–1922 England *The Forsyte Saga*, a sequence of novels by John Galsworthy (1867–1933), novelist and playwright. His themes were the acquisitiveness of the middle classes, and social change. He received the Nobel Prize in 1932.

1906 France *Creative Evolution* by Henri Bergson (1859–1941), a philosopher concerned with the nature of experience and the nature of time. He had an enormous effect on the novel because his thinking led to the development of the 'stream-of-consciousness'.

*1907
Triple Entente
between Britain,
France, Russia.*

1906 Hungary *King Midas*, a novel by Zoltán Ambrus (1861–1932), novelist and short-story writer; he was influenced by Flaubert and Maupassant.

1906 Japan *Broken Commandment* by Shimazaki Toson (1872–1943), poet and novelist: the first novel in Japan to deal with social problems, it was about a persecuted minority, and, unlike most Japanese novels of the period did not contain autobiographical material.

1907 Italy *The Little Child*, an essay by Giovanni Pascoli (1855–1912), scholar and poet. His poetry was quiet and pastoral, but anticipated later trends such as the Crepuscular school and futurism. The total effect was almost childlike, hence *The Little Child*, which explained his poetic theory.

1907 Wales *Autobiography of a Super-Tramp* by W. H. Davies (1871–1940), tramp, novelist and poet.

1906 England Birth of Elisabeth Lutyens, composer, a pioneer of 12-note music in England.

1906 Hungary Béla Bartók (1881–1945) and Zoltán Kodály (1882–1967) began a long association, collecting and editing national folk music.

1906 Russia Birth of Dimitry Shostakovich (d. 1975), Russian composer.

1907 England Opening of Miss Horniman's repertory theatre in Manchester. She had seen from her travels in Europe that a subsidized repertory theatre played an important part in the cultural life of the countries she had visited, especially Germany.

1907 Germany *Gott der Rache* by Sholom Asche (1880–1957) produced by Max Rheinhardt: the play introduced the general theatre-going public to Yiddish drama.

1907 Russia The ballet *Le Pavilion d' Armide* by Michel Fokine (1880–1942) produced at the Maryinsky theatre, St Petersburg: it was the first to combine the artistic ideas of Diaghilev and Benois with the original choreography of Fokine. Fokine laid down five principles of dance: (i) new forms fitting the subject matter; (ii) dancing and mime as dramatic expression, not mere exhibition; (iii) the whole body as a means of expression in place of conventional gestures; (iv) the soloist and *corps de ballet* performing as a harmonious whole to carry the action forward, and (v) the combination of dance and other art forms to make an artistic whole. These were all based on the classical technique, on which his choreography was built.

1907 Spain *Los Intereses Creados* by Jacinti Benavente y Martinez (1866–1954), a playwright remarkable for his versatility and for his wide knowledge of contemporary European theatre.

1907 England Gustav Theodore Holst (1874–1934) became musical director at Morley College, London, a post he retained until his death.

1907 England First production of *Toward the Unknown Region* by Ralph Vaughan Williams. This was his first important work for chorus and orchestra and began to establish his reputation.

1907 France Maurice Ravel's first opera *L'Heure Espagnole* produced in Paris.

1907 Hungary Birth of Sándor Veress, Hungarian pianist, musical folklorist, writer on music and composer.

1907 Norway Death of Edvard Hagerup Grieg (b. 1843).

ARCHITECTURE

1906 USA Unity Church, Oak Park, Illinois, by Frank Lloyd Wright was a concrete church with a complex interior space on several levels, a novelty at the time.

1907 Austria The Kartner Bar, Vienna, by Adolf Loos (1870–1933) is considered his best surviving work; much of his pre-war work was confined to remodelling interiors in fine materials, as here in mahogany, marble and glass.

THREE DIMENSIONAL ART

1905 Norway Adolf Gustav Vigeland (1869–1943) began the monumental groups of granite sculpture in Frogner Park, Oslo, which portray the struggle of life. The central obelisk is composed of 100 interlaced figures and all the groups are on a scale only equalled by Rodin's *Gate of Hell*. The work was uncompleted on Vigeland's death.

1906 England First appearance, at the Olympia Exhibition, London, of the Rolls-Royce Silver Ghost motor car.

Edward Johnston published *Writing* and *Illumination and Lettering*, which stimulated interest in calligraphy and lettering especially in Germany.

1907–1908 U.S.A. Alton Manufacturing Company temporarily revived the Boston and Sandwich Glass Company, closed in 1888: it made glass in the style of Tiffany.

1907 Germany Peter Behrens (1868–1940), architect and designer, joined the Allgemeine Elektrizitäts-Gesellschaft (A.E.G.) as designer of electrical equipment, packaging and advertising: he was a pioneer of industrial design in functional style.

1907 Germany Foundation of the Deutscher Werkbund by Hermann Muthesius (1861–1927), to improve the aesthetic standards of engineering and all machine-work.

*c.***1907 Germany** Ernst Barlach (1870–1938) began work as a sculptor; he worked in an expressionist style and showed the influence of German Gothic sculpture in his use of a single unified form to convey an emotion.

VISUAL ARTS

1905 Germany Foundation of the Brücke group of artists, who saw themselves as rebelling against accepted forms, and as a bridge leading to art of the future. They developed no coherent policy. Their work was noted for a primitive expressionism, and they were important in reviving graphic arts, especially woodcut. The main members were Kirchner, Schmidt-Rottluff and Heckel.

*c.***1905 Germany and France** Expressionism emerged as a coherent theory. Earlier artists who had used colour and line as a direct expression of strong feeling, which was intended to arouse the same feeling in the spectator, were Vincent van Gogh, Edvard Munch (particularly in graphics, which he saw to be a most effective medium for dramatic expression of emotion) and the Swiss painter in monumental style, Ferdinand Hodler (1853–1918).

*c.***1906 Denmark** Harald Giersing (1881–1927) began to paint still-life and monumental figure studies in a style inspired by Fauvism. He is considered the pioneer of modern painting in Denmark.

1906 Denmark Ole Olsen founded the Nordisk Film Company: it chose sensational subject matter, and made extensive use of natural locations.

1906 Germany The Swiss artist Paul Klee (1879–1940) settled in Munich and exhibited etchings with the Munich Sezession movement. His early work was mainly in graphics, in which he was influenced by Blake and Goya, and later by Beardsley and James Ensor.

1907 France Georges Braque (1882–1963) began experimenting on forms which developed as cubism. He worked together with Picasso, but he was the leader in developing collages.

1907 France The Spanish artist Pablo Picasso (1881–1973) painted *Les Demoiselles d'Avignon*, which was considered revolutionary in its analysis and separation of form into component shapes. The painting was a fore-runner of his cubist paintings, and reflected his study of Negro sculpture and of the construction of paintings by Cézanne.

INVENTIONS & DISCOVERIES

1906 Norwegian Roald Amundsen completed crossing of North West Passage.

1907 Leo Bäkeland invented bakelite.

HISTORICAL EVENTS	LITERATURE	DANCE & DRAMA	MUSIC

1907 USA Louis Chalif (1876–1948) opened the Chalif Russian Normal School of Dancing: it offered basic dance education to teachers throughout the American continent.

1908
Bulgaria
proclaimed
independent by
Ferdinand I.

1908–1941 Hungary Publication of *Nyugat* ('the West'), a literary periodical, which encouraged European trends in Hungarian poetry. Western literary influences, in particular symbolism, were introduced by Endre Ady (1877–1919).

1908 Cambodia The palace dancers and orchestra went to perform at major Colonial Exposition in Paris: they made a strong impact on French dancers and artists.

1908 France *L'Oiseau Bleu* by Maurice Maeterlinck (1862–1949).

1908 Russia First performance of the ballet *Les Sylphides* by Michel Fokine, choreographed to music by Chopin. He shared with Isadora Duncan the belief that music by the great romantic composers could inspire choreography Fokine derived his images from the music, instead of finding music to fit the images.

1908 Russia Peretz Hirschbein (1881–1949) founded the first Yiddish Art Theatre in Odessa, the ban on Yiddish plays having been lifted.

1908 Russia The dancer Vaslav Nijinsky (1890–1950) made his début at the Maryinsky Theatre, which he left to join Diaghilev's Ballets Russes in Paris when the company was founded in 1911. He was considered outstanding in his combination of dance technique and acting ability; he danced for only 7 seasons in all.

1908 Austria Publication of *3 Pieces for Pianoforte, Opus 11*, by Arnold Schoenberg (1874–1951). This marked his final break with tonality and was of the greatest importance, not only to his own career, but to the world of music in general.

1908 France Birth of Olivier Eugène Prosper Charles Messiaen, French composer and organist.

1908 Russia Death of Nikolay Andreyevich Rimsky-Korsakov (b. 1844).

1908 U.S.A. Birth of Elliott Carter, composer.

1909 Italy *A Futurist Manifesto* by Filippo Tommaso Marinetti (1876–1944), poet, playwright and novelist. The Futurists wanted art to reflect the new machine age. They rejected grammatical rules and used words for their sound rather than their meaning. They glorified war, and welcomed Fascism.

1909 France Serge Diaghilev (1872–1929) brought Russian ballet to Paris, originally for a summer season which was very successful. The Russian school made a strong impression on Western audiences who were by now unaccustomed to taking ballet seriously.

1909 Hungary *Liliou* by Ferenc Molnar (1878–1952), a dramatist writing for international, rather than Hungarian, audiences. This play was later used as the basis of the musical *Carousel*.

1909 Austria Gustav Mahler completed his 9th symphony, considered to be his greatest.

1908 France The comedian Max Linder (1882–1925) introduced into the cinema the suave and elegant comic actor in place of the clown.

1908 USA Gamble House, Pasadena, by Greene and Greene was one of several timber houses built by these brothers under the influence of Japanese architecture: such houses were popular in California.

1908 France Foundation of the Societé Film d'Art, in Paris: it aimed to commission scripts from distinguished writers and to film great literature, establishing a cinema equal to the classical theatre. Actors were recruited from the Comédie Française. The movement spread to other countries; in Britain it had a bad effect on truly cinematic art, in Hungary it marked the real establishment of cinema.

*1908
Sir Ernest
Shackleton
within 100 miles
of South Pole.*

1908 Japan The Yoshizawa film studio opened. Japanese films at this time often mixed live performances with moving pictures; a narrator on stage presented and often dominated the film.

1908 Norway The painter Edvard Munch (1863–1944) settled permanently in Norway following a mental breakdown. His paintings became more extrovert, brighter in colour and subject matter.

1908 Russia Mikhail Larinov (1881–1964) organized the Golden Fleece Exhibition, which combined native traditions in art with new trends in the West. Larinov attempted a synthesis of the two.

1908 U.S.A. The 'Eight' group of artists held an exhibition which had lasting influence. Their leader was Robert Henri (1865–1929), pioneer in a school of social realism that became known as the 'Ashcan' school. Other members were Arthur Bowen Davies (1862–1928), George Luks (1867–1933), William Glackens (1870–1938), John Sloan (1871–1951) and, most prominent of all, the painter and lithographer George Bellows (1882–1925).

*1909
Louis Blériot
crossed English
Channel by
monoplane.
American Robert
E. Peary reached
North Pole.*

Drawing after a futurist sculpture by Giacomo Balla

*c.*1908 **Germany** Franz Marc (1880–1916) began to paint expressionist animal studies, saying that he wished to paint the animals' own perception of their existence.

1909 Germany AEG turbine factory in Berlin by Peter Behrens (1868–1938) was the first of many AEG buildings by Behrens, the firm's architect; it was a strictly functional factory, constructed of concrete, steel and glass without decoration.

*c.*1909 **England** The sculptor Reginald Wells turned to pottery. He was the first English artist-potter to be inspired by traditional English wares; most of his contemporaries attempted high-temperature stoneware after Chinese models, although they had no contact with the original Chinese tradition.

1909–1910 England Cecil Hepworth (1874–1956) made vivaphone films with synchronized sound.

HISTORICAL EVENTS	LITERATURE	DANCE & DRAMA	MUSIC

LITERATURE

1909 U.S.A. *Personae* and *Exultations* by Ezra Loomis Pound (1885–1972), critic and poet. A metrical innovator, he was also concerned with the nature and effect of images in poetry, and founded the Imagist school of poets. His influence was considerable, and he encouraged a number of other poets, among them T. S. Eliot.

DANCE & DRAMA

1909 Italy *Il Piccolo Santo* by Roberto Bracco (1862–1943) a playwright influenced in part by Ibsen: this play is an early forerunner of the Theatre of Silence, in which the audience has to use its imagination to understand what words cannot express.

1909 Italy *Il Re Baldoria* by Filippo Tommaso Marinetti (1876–1944) a playwright writing mainly in French. He was the leader of the Futurists, who were opposed to both classicism and romanticism, and whose plays consisted of unrelated scenes. They made extensive use of sound and lighting effects.

MUSIC

1909 Switzerland Fritz Brun (b. 1878), Swiss conductor, pianist and composer, became conductor of the symphony concerts of the Bernische Musikgesellschaft. Switzerland's only real symphonic composer, he contributed greatly to his country's musical life.

1910 Union of South Africa became a dominion. Japan annexed Korea.

1910 England *Clayhanger*, a novel by Arnold Bennett (1867–1931), novelist and playwright. He is best known for his regional novels, set in the industrial area called the Potteries. He also wrote influential book reviews.

1910 England *Justice* by John Galsworthy (1867–1933), one of several dramatists at the time who were concerned about the problems of the individual in conflict with society and in particular with questions of social injustice.

1910 France First performance of the ballet *The Firebird* by Michel Fokine (1880–1942) to music by Stravinsky. Performed by Diaghilev's company, it was one of the first productions to establish Diaghilev ballet as different from that of the parent Maryinsky theatre in St Petersburg.

1910 England First performance at Leeds of *A Sea Symphony* by Ralph Vaughan Williams (1872–1958).

1910 France First performance in Paris of ballet *The Fire-Bird* by Igor Feodorovich Stravinsky (1882–1971) which established him as a composer of genius.

ARCHITECTURE

1909–1923 Sweden The City Hall, Stockholm, by Ragnar Östberg (1866–1945) was an example of the traditional Romantic nationalist architecture common in Scandinavia at this period; it was superbly sited and well built.

1910–1930 England Castle Drogo, Devonshire, by Sir Edwin Lutyens (1869–1944) was the last English country house to be built on the grand scale by the last of the great English traditionalist architects.

THREE DIMENSIONAL ART

France: 'Portrait of Mme Matisse' by Henri Matisse

1910–1913 Italy Amedeo Modigliani (1884–1920) concentrated on limestone sculpture. Influenced by Brancusi, he believed that the Rodin tradition of clay modelling was decadent, and he returned to direct carving in stone.

VISUAL ARTS

1909–1910 France Henri Matisse (1869–1954) painted *La Danse* and *La Musique*. He believed that art should reflect an 'almost religious' attitude to life and permanent values. He rejected the Impressionists' policy of capturing the fleeting moment.

1909–1910 Italy Giorgio de Chirico (b. 1888) painted his first 'enigmatic' pictures, conveying an air of mystery through strange perspectives.

1909–1914 U.S.A. The Motion Picture Patents Company attempted a complete monopoly and forced independent producers to new locations, e.g. Hollywood, which had reliable sunlight, and cheap land and labour.

1909 Germany Willi Warstat published *Allgemeine Ästhetik der Photographie*, an influential study of the physiology of vision, its psychological impact, and the effects of these on the art of photography.

1909 Italy The painter Gino Severini (1883–1966) came in contact with the Cubists. His own work was concerned with conveying movement by breaking up his picture space into units of different rhythm. He used near-geometrical patches of pure colour.

1909 Sweden Charles Magnusson (1878–1948) became production manager for the film company Svenska Bio, having trained as a cameraman. His films exploit natural backgrounds.

1909 U.S.A. David Wark Griffith (1875–1948) directed *The Lonely Villa*, in which he made the first use of cross-cutting to build suspense. Griffith was the main pioneer of editing and lighting techniques used for dramatic effect. Working with the cameraman G. W. ('Billy') Bitzer, he interpreted nineteenth-century melodrama in cinematic terms.

1910–1912 England Roger Eliot Fry (1866–1934), painter and critic, introduced the French post-Impressionists to the British public in two important exhibitions which greatly stimulated young artists.

INVENTIONS & DISCOVERIES

1910 Arthur Evans excavated Knossos, Crete.

413

LITERATURE

1910 France *Impressions D'Afrique* by Raymond Roussel (1877—1933), novelist, poet and playwright. He had an influence on the development of the *nouveau roman* and on surrealism.

DANCE & DRAMA

1910 U.S.A. Appearance in New York of the Russian dancers Anna Pavlova and Mikhail Mordkin (1881—1944). The visit led to several tours of the U.S.A. by a company led by Mordkin.

c.**1910 Argentina** The tango became socially acceptable and popular. It evolved in the ports of the River Plate from a Central American negro dance, the *tángano*, brought in by migrants.

MUSIC

Couple dancing the tango. From the film 'The Painted Devil', man possibly Rudolf Valentino

ARCHITECTURE

1910 USA Christian Science church, Berkeley, by Bernard Maybeck (1862–1937) was built in a mixture of styles by an architect of great originality.

VISUAL ARTS

1910–1914 Italy Umberto Boccioni (1882–1916) was a leader of the Futurists, who advocated a break with the past and proposed a school of painting where matter would be represented in terms of perpetual movement; they held that artists should not, like the Impressionists, seek to freeze one point in time, but should try to show the subject in a complete time cycle.

1910 Denmark Urban Gad (1879–1947) directed *Afgrunden*, the first film of the actress Asta Neilson, whose popularity created an international demand for Danish films.

1910 England Augustus John (1878–1961) painted his best known portrait, of his wife, *The Smiling Woman*. Considered a brilliant artist in his day, he did his best work in Wales and France between 1911 and 1914. His studies of gipsies created a fashionable image of beauty.

1910 Germany Emil Nolde (1867–1956) painted *Pentecost*, which was rejected for exhibition by the Berlin Sezession and exhibited with the independent Brücke group. He was considered the most forceful German Expressionist, using glaring colours and distorted forms and a highly emotional brushwork. His aim was a revival of forceful religious imagery.

Herwarth Walden founded *Der Sturm* magazine and the art gallery of the same name, which were instrumental in publicizing futurism and the work of the Blaue Reiter group, founded 1911.

1910 Italy The painter Giacomo Balla (1871–1958) was converted to futurist painting after being an Italian pioneer of divisionism.His most famous futurist painting was *Dog on a Leash*, which shows the successive positions of the dog's paws in motion.

1910 Japan *Kabuki* actors refused to appear in films, thus forcing film companies to be independent of the theatre. This reduced their output, and Western films were imported to fill the cinemas. All the companies merged into one, the Nikkatsu company, with a Tokyo studio for contemporary films and a Kyoto studio for historical films, shot on ancient sites.

France: from a design by Leon Bakst

1911
Agadir crisis.

1911 Germany *Weltende* by Hans Davidsohn, called Jakob van Hoddis (1887–1942): it is regarded as the first expressionist poem.

1911 Turkey 'Genc Kalemlev', a literary movement in reaction against the cosmopolitan and over-literary Servet-I Fünen, stressed the importance of a simple, natural style and the use of native culture.

1911 Russia Sergei Pavlovich Diaghilev (1872–1929) founded Les Ballets Russes which gave its first performances in Italy.

1911 England *On the Art of the Theatre* by Edward Gordon Craig (1872–1966) English designer and producer: he wished to see the entire direction of a play — actors, scenery, lighting, music etc. — under the control of one virtuoso director.

1911 Austria The theatre director, Max Rheinhardt took his wordless pantomime drama *The Miracle* to Olympia, London. His productions were on a vast scale, with remarkable handling of crowds, and demanded close collaboration between lighting, music and scenic experts and choreographers. He used stylized architecture in place of scenery.

1911 France First performance of the ballet *Le Spectre de la Rose* by Fokine to music by Weber, designed by Léon Bakst. The dancers were Nijinsky and Karsavina.

1911 France First performance of the ballet *Petrouchka* by Michel Fokine, to music by Stravinsky, for Diaghilev's Ballets Russes. Fokine devised new forms to match the rhythms of the music, which would not accomodate traditional choreography. The décor was by Benois: the principal dancers were Nijinsky, Karsavina and Enrico Cecchetti.

1911 Austria Death of Gustav Mahler (b. 1860), Austrian (Bohemian) conductor and composer.

1911 Austria Arnold Schoenberg (1874–1951) completed his *Harmonielehre* which is one of the most important modern publications on harmony.

1911 England The Russian Ballet was introduced to London by the conductor Thomas Beecham (1879–1961).

1911 France Publication of *Histoire de la Langue Musicale* by Marie François Maurice Emmanuel (1862–1938), French musicologist.

1911 Germany *Der Rosenkavalier* by Richard Strauss (1864–1949) performed at Dresden.

1911 U.S.A. First performance of *Ariadne and Bluebeard*, the only opera by Paul Dukas (1865–1935) conducted by Toscanini.

1911 U.S.A. Irving Berlin (1888–   ) composed *Alexander's Ragtime Band.*

1910 Russia Death of Mikhail Vrubel (b. 1856), an original artist and fine draughtsman whose work prepared the way for cubism in Russia.

1910 Spain José Victoriano González, called Juan Gris (1887–1927) began to paint in cubist style. He originated 'synthetic' cubism: the original analytical Cubists rendered real objects as reduced to their essential cylinder, cone, sphere or cube forms; Gris and the synthesizing Cubists brought together these basic forms to make new, imaginary objects.

1910 U.S.A. Arthur Dove (1880–1946) developed his 'extraction' paintings which pioneered abstract work in America. His pictures were based on natural forms and rhythms.
Death of Homer Winslow (b. 1836) considered the outstanding American landscape, genre and marine artist of his day. He painted in an original naturalistic style uninfluenced by contemporary trends.

1910 U.S.A. An exhibition in Buffalo by the Photo-Secession Group marked the division between photographers who emulated painters' subjects and treatment, and those who were concerned with photographic themes and effects.

*c.*1910 **Austria** Oskar Kokoschka (b. 1886) began to paint 'psychological portraits' which caused a stir. He also made highly original lithographs and posters, and worked for the *avant-garde* Berlin journal *Der Sturm*.

1911–1912 Russia Mikhail Larinov (1881–1964) and Natalie Gocharova developed 'rayonism', stimulated by the Moscow lectures of the Italian Futurist, Marinetti. The 'rays' were parallel lines of contrasting colour set in space, representing force and attraction.

1911 France The film director Louis Feuillade (1873–1925) at Gaumont began a real-life series filmed on location: '*La Vie telle qu'elle est*'.
The Russian-born artist Chaim Soutine (1894–1943) moved to Paris. For him the use of colour was a direct expression of nervous tension.

1911 Germany Fagus factory, Alfeld, by Walter Gropius and Adolf Meyer (1881–1929) was one of the earliest buildings to demonstrate the elements of the international style. It was given a glass-curtain walling and it had no corner piers, both novel features. The term 'international', however, was not generally applied to functionalist architecture until it was inspired by an exhibition of 1932.

1911 India New Delhi by Sir Edwin Lutyens was a project of truly imperial proportions in which the viceroy's house, eclectic in style, provided a suitably impressive centrepiece.

1911 Russia The German Embassy, St Petersburg, by Peter Behrens was built in the classical idiom but so devoid of decoration that Behrens's work in this style is known as 'scraped Classicism'.

1911 England Charles Ashbee (1863–1942) published *Should We Stop Teaching Art* in which he took the view of Frank Lloyd Wright, whom he met in 1900, that modern civilization rests on machinery and the artist must learn to use it. Ashbee had been a leading figure of the Arts and Crafts movement; work from his Guild of Handicrafts (1888–1902) had a European reputation.

1911 France Henri Laurenson (1885–1954), sculptor, associated with Braque and his circle: his work in montage and collage remained influenced by cubist painting.

1911 Hawaii William Brigham of the Museum of Polynesian Ethnology and Natural History published his standard work on bark cloth, indicating its antiquity and geographical extent throughout the Pacific, Africa, South-east Asia, South and Central America: he listed over 300 types of fibre-beaters in use in Hawaii alone.

1911 Amundsen reached South Pole. Ernest Rutherford announced nuclear theory of the atom.

417

DANCE & DRAMA

1911 Germany Rudolf von Laban (1879–1958) set up his Central European School of dance in Munich, teaching by a new method which explored the dynamics of the body: Mary Wigman and Kurt Jooss were among his pupils. He developed a system of movement notation, *kinetographie*, which was widely influential in the scientific approach to dance.

1911 Japan Construction of the Japanese Imperial Theatre, the Teikokuza.

1912 France First performance in Paris of the ballet *L'Aprés-Midi d'un Faune*, choreographed by Nijinsky to music by Debussy and designed by Léon Bakst. Nijinsky was a pioneer of expressionist choreography.

1912 France First performance of the ballet *Daphnis and Chloe* by Michel Fokine to music by Ravel, designed by Léon Bakst; performed by Les Ballet Russes.

1912 India Discovery of the manuscripts of a medieval Sanskrit dramatist, Bhasa. Sanskrit was already a scholastic language by the time the plays were written. The discovery led to a revival of interest in Sanskrit plays. Other important Sanskrit playwrights were King Sudraka, *The Little Toy Cart*, and Kalidasa, *Shakuntala*. The plays were poetry enacted with music and dance. An important figure was the narrator; the plays are thought to have originated in recitations.

MUSIC

1912 USA Birth of John Cage, the composer, in Los Angeles. He applies laws of composition to unprecedented material and is considered extremely experimental particularly noted for aleatory, electronic and silent music.

HISTORICAL EVENTS

1912
China proclaimed a republic.

LITERATURE

1912–1917 France *A La Recherche du Temps Perdu* by Marcel Proust (1871–1922), novelist and critic: a long semi-autobiographical novel, it traced the hero's life and development to the time when he began to write it. His main theme was the subconscious search for eternal values. Highly complex, it is considered a masterpiece.

1912–1922 Austria *The Duino Elegies*, poems by Rainer Maria Rilke (1875–1926), poet and novelist. His subjects were universal—nature, love, death—but his style was individual; his grammar made extensive use of gerunds, present participles and enjambement. These poems dealt with the predicament of the poet, who must be both human and inspired.

1912 England An anthology of contemporary English verse, *Georgian Poetry 1911–1912*, was collected by Sir Edward Marsh. The poems, usually about the English countryside and showing the influence of Wordsworth, were conventional in form and expression. The most representative poet in Marsh's selection was Rupert Brooke (1887–1915).

1912 France *Les Dieux Ont Soif* by Anatole-François Thibault, called Anatole France (1844–1924), novelist, poet and critic. He wrote satirical novels on political and social life. This book is about the French Revolution. He was awarded the Nobel Prize in 1921.

1912 Hungary *Colours and Years* by Margit Kaffka (1880–1918), a poet, novelist and short-story writer who was particularly concerned about social and sexual equality.

1912 Spain *Castilian Fields*, poems by Antonio Machado (1875–1939). His austere verse was influenced by Spanish folklore, and by modernism, Bergson and the French Symbolists.

1912 U.S.A. The magazine *Poetry* was established by Harriet Monroe, who was quick to recognize and encourage native talent.

| ARCHITECTURE | THREE DIMENSIONAL ART | VISUAL ARTS | INVENTIONS &
DISCOVERIES |

THREE DIMENSIONAL ART

1911 Japan Ogata Kenzan, sixth in a line of potters beginning with Kenzan 1 (1663–1743), began to train the English potter Bernard Leach (b. 1887) in the making of *raku* and stoneware pots. Leach, trained originally as an etcher, made a study of the sources and traditions of oriental arts; he came to excel in decoration, and in understanding the relationship of the glaze to the body of the pot.

1912 Austria Gustav Sheu House, Vienna, by Adolf Loos is one of his rare surviving works; the exterior is typically box-like with rectangular windows of various sizes.

1912 Belgium Rik Wouters (1882–1916), painter and sculptor noted for outstanding vitality, completed his bronze *The Mad Virgin*, inspired by the dancer Isadora Duncan.

c.1912 Nigeria German ethnologist Leo Frobenius made the first western discovery of Ife sculpted heads. The one he found was in fact a sand-cast copy; later discoveries were cast in terracotta and bronze by the *cire-perdue* method: they differ from other African art in their naturalistic style. This and earlier West African sculptures had a strong impact on twentieth-century sculptors.

VISUAL ARTS

1911 Germany The Danish film actress Asta Neilson began to work in Germany. Her work helped reconcile the theatre to the cinema as an art, and raised the standard of cinema acting.

In painting, the Blaue Reiter group (Kandinsky, Marc, Macke and Klee were the main members) was formed, concerned with symbolic representation of spiritual values and reacting against the Impressionists. They formed the first coherent policy on replacing structural principle with direct expression of feeling.

1911 Italy Giorgio de Chirico (b. 1888) began to paint 'metaphysical' pictures, in which he investigated the nature of objects by divorcing them from their usual associations.

1911 Spain Death of the painter Isidro Nonell y Monturiol, who had revived the Spanish taste for paintings of poor people, idiots and gypsies.

1911 U.S.A. *Enoch Arden* by Griffith was the first American film of more than one reel: its length was not thought acceptable.

1912–c.1930 India Film studios in Bombay and Calcutta produced over 1500 popular, storytelling films mainly for uneducated audiences.

1912 England Herbert Ponting made the first British documentary film: *With Captain Scott R. N. to the South Pole.*

1912 France Robert Delauney (1885–1941) painted *Le Disque*, a picture without any motif at all: it is a geometrical pattern of colours.

1912 Germany The Russian artist Wassily Kandinsky (1866–1944) published his *Über das Geistige in der Kunst*, in which he declared that 'the inner element, the emotion . . . determines the form'. Form and colour were adequate expression in themselves without a motif. He had painted his first non-objective picture in 1910.

In cinema, Paul Wegener (1874–1948), directed the film *Der Student von Prag*, a visually imaginative treatment of the *doppelgänger* ('ghostly double') theme which had wide appeal.

*1912
Victor Hess
discovered cosmic
radiation.*

Italy: 'The Soothsayer's Recompense' by Giorgio de Chirico

1913–1916 Russia *St Petersburg* by Boris Bugayev, called Andrei Bely (1880–1934), poet, symbolist novelist and critic. He was a disciple of the Austrian educationist Rudolf Steiner.

1913 Australia *The Wanderer*, poetry by Christopher John Brennan (1870–1932), a professor at the University of Sidney. He widened the influences on Australian poetry through his knowledge of French and German literature.

1913 England *Sons and Lovers*, a novel by David Herbert Lawrence (1885–1930), novelist, poet, playwright and critic. His work combined realism, social criticism and symbolism. This book was semi-autobiographical.

1913 France *Alcools*, poems by Guillelmus Apollinarisde Kostrowitzky, called Guillaume Apollinaire (1880–1918), poet, playwright, critic and novelist. Although of Polish/Italian parentage, he wrote in French. He was associated with a number of *avant-garde* movements—cubism, surrealism, dadaism. A friend of Picasso and Braque, he interpreted their art forms in literature.

1913 France *Le Grand Meaulnes* by Henri-Alban Fournier, called Alain-Fournier (1886–1914): a poetic novel about adolescent fantasy and calf-love, it is considered the 'classic' novel on this theme.

1913 India-Europe *Gitanjali*, a mystical verse work by Rabindranath Tagore (1861–1941), Indian poet, novelist and playwright, reached Europe, in translation: it was enthusiastically received. The same year Tagore was awarded the Nobel Prize.

1913 Russia *Stone*, poems by Osip Mandelstam (1892–?1941), a Jewish poet, critic and translator, writing in Russian.

1913 U.S.A. *General William Booth Enters into Heaven, and Other Poems* by Vachel Lindsay (1879–1931), America's first folk poet. He used as his sources revivalist hymns, Negro jazz and the deeds of American heroes, particularly Lincoln.

1913 France Jacques Copeau (1879–1949) founded the Théâtre du Vieux Colombier: his repertoire was based on the works of Shakespeare and Molière. He regarded the proper training of actors as particularly important and did not like naturalistic drama, but wanted to restore beauty and poetry to the French theatre.

1913 France First performance of the ballet *The Rite of Spring* by Nijinsky, to music by Stravinsky for Diaghilev's Ballets Russes. The original choreography was influenced by Dalcroze's theories of eurhythmics and was worked out with the help of Dalcroze's pupil Marie Rambert. It was the first great expressionist ballet.

1913 India Sir Rabindranath Tagore was awarded the Nobel Prize for literature. His works include three important symbolic dramas. He drew inspiration both from his native Indian tradition and from Western influences.

1913 Russia Anna Pavlova (1891–1931) danced her last season at the Maryinsky Theatre and left Russia for England. Her extensive tours from then on introduced classical ballet to many who were unfamiliar with it. She was a traditionalist, rejecting the innovations of Diaghilev.

1913 Switzerland The German dancer Mary Wigman (b.1886) composed her first important work: *Hexentanz*, an expressionist dance performed in silence. She had worked with Dalcroze, developer of eurhythmics. 'Free' dancers emphasized the strain and effort which ballet dancers were trained to hide.

1913 Austria *Pierrot Lunaire*, by Arnold Schoenberg used a 'speaking voice' technique for atonal effect.

1913 England Birth of Benjamin Britten (d. 1976), English composer.

1913 England First volume of *English Madrigal School* (36 volumes 1913–1924) published by Edmund Horace Fellowes (1870–1951), musical scholar and publisher.

1913 Poland Birth of Witold Lutoslawski, composer.

1913 Russia Stravinsky completed his ballet *The Rite of Spring*.

1913 Scotland The Carnegie United Kingdom Trust was established at Dunfermline, for the promotion of, and assistance to, music.

England: 'The Haggs', Miriam's house in D. H. Lawrence's novel 'Sons and Lovers'

ARCHITECTURE

1913–1926 Denmark Grundvig Church, Copenhagen, by P. V. Jensen Klint (1853–1930) is one of the most imaginative 'traditional' style of Scandinavian churches with an expressionist Gothic flavour; it was built entirely of brick.

1913 USA Woolworth Building, New York, by Cass Gilbert (1859–1934) was 259·8m high and for 17 years the highest building in America; it was nevertheless decorated with Gothic details, as were many other contemporary skyscrapers.

THREE DIMENSIONAL ART

1913 England Jacob Epstein (1880–1959) sculpted *Rock Drill* in the style of the Vorticists, a short-lived group inspired by Italian futurism. His work between this and *Christ in Majesty* (1955) was powerful and expressionist in style and made him a strong influence against academic sculpture.

1913 Germany Establishment of the Cranach Press at Weimar by Count Kessler.

1913 German Wilhelm Lembruck (1881–1919) sculptor, carved *Youth Ascending* in bronze. He was a follower of Rodin and was considered a leader of early twentieth century German sculpture.

c.**1913 France** The sculptor Jacques Lipchitz (b. 1891) began to show cubist tendencies in his use of simplified forms: his work remained fully cubist in style until *c*.1925.

VISUAL ARTS

1912 U.S.A. Mack Sennett (1880–1960) founded Keystone Studio to make hectic, anarchistic comedies. Adolph Zukor had commercial success distributing Louis Mercanton's film *Queen Elizabeth*. This and Enrico Guazzoni's *Quo Vadis* (1913) persuaded American companies to accept multi-reel films.

1912 U.S.A. Adolph Zukor had commercial success distributing Louis Mercanton's film *Queen Elizabeth*. This and Enrico Guazzoni's *Quo Vadis* (1913) persuaded American companies to accept multi-reel films.

1913 England The London Group of artists was founded as an exhibiting society with a strong interest in post-impressionism. The artist Wyndham Lewis (1884–1957) was briefly associated with the Group, but formed his own Rebel Art Centre in the same year. He was a pioneer of 'vorticism', a movement arising from Boccioni's statement that all art must be created from an emotional vortex. His own style was semi-abstract and suggestive, even in portraits, of mechanical forms.

1913 France Marcel Duchamp (1887–1968), cubist and futurist painter, exhibited *Nude Descending a Staircase*. His futurism was an attempt to show the mechanics of motion, not the appearance of the moving object. He saw his work as a form of mathematics; painting as a skill did not interest him.

1913 Russia An experimental group including the poet Vladimir Mayakowsky (1893–1930), directed a futurist film, *Drama in Futurist Cabaret 13*: this provided a strong ideological influence for Russian cinema.

1913 U.S.A. Charlie Chaplin (1889–1977) joined the Keystone Studio. His comedy training was in the English music-hall. He introduced 'The Tramp' character into Keystone comedies (1914).

c.**1913–1933 Canada** The Group of Seven founded a school of nationalist Canadian art with their paintings of Northern Canadian landscape in strong forms and colours. James Edward Hervey Macdonald (1873–1932) was one of the members.

1913
F. G. Hopkins isolated Vitamin A.
Niels Bohr applied quantum theory to Rutherford's nuclear atom.

LITERATURE

DANCE & DRAMA

MUSIC

1914 China Publication of poems of Cheng Hsiao-hsu (1859–1938), one of the last outstanding poets using the old literary language, *Ku-wen*.

1914 Germany *Starting Point* by the poet Ernst Stadler (1883–1914), one of the early Expressionists—artists who stressed the importance of internal realities, of which external appearances are an expression. This was in contrast to the work of the Naturalists, who recorded the external only. The Expressionists concentrated on the irrational, and used characters as symbols.

1914 Italy *Canti Orfici*, poems by Dino Campana (1885–1932), who followed Rimbaud's doctrine of disorder of the senses.

1914 Spain *Mist*, a novel by Miguel de Unamuno (1864–1936), Basque philosopher, poet, playwright, novelist and critic. He was pre-occupied with the problems of immortality and free-will, holding that belief in God was vital, though irrational, and one should found one's faith on doubt, and struggle to believe. In *Mist* the novelist points out to the protagonist that he has no will of his own but is manipulated by the novelist, only to have it suggested to him that he may be in a similar situation himself.

1914 U.S.A. *North of Boston*, poetry by Robert Lee Frost (1874–1963). He used a dramatic presentation, incorporating natural speech rhythms, with humour and understatement. At his death he was the United States' most eminent poet.

1914 U.S.A. *The Golden Bowl*, a novel by Henry James (1843–1916), critic, playwright, short-story writer and novelist. More widely read in Europe than in America, he became a British subject in 1915. Much of his work concerned the contrast between the older European standards and the newer American ones.

1915 England *The Good Soldier* by Ford Madox Ford (1873–1939), editor, critic, novelist and poet: with skilful plotting and characterization the book tells a story of evil and human weakness, without any kind of message.

1914 Russia *He Who Gets Slapped* by Leonid Nikolaevich Andreyev (1871–1919), a symbolist drama.

1914 U.S.A. *On Trial* by Elmer Leopold Rice (1892–1967): it was the first American play to use flashback; the technique was familiar in cinema.

1915 France Léonide Massine (Leonid Miassine, b.1896) choreographed his first ballet for Diaghilev's Ballets Russes: *Soleil de Nuit*. His best known works for the company were *La Boutique Fantasque, The Three-Cornered Hat* and *Les Femmes de Bonne Humeur*.

1915 France The Polish dancer Léon Woizikowsky (b.1897) began dancing with Diaghilev's Ballets Russes. He was considered the foremost character-dancer of his time.

1914 England Publication of *Orchestration* by Cecil Forsyth (1870–1941), composer and author. It is the most thorough work on its subject in the English language.

1914 England First performance of *A London Symphony* by Ralph Vaughan Williams (1872–1958); it was his first purely orchestral symphony.

1914 England The two-act opera *The Immortal Hour* by Rutland Boughton, English composer (1878–1960) was first performed at the Glastonbury festival.

1914 France Birth of Paul Tortelier, violoncellist and composer. He invented an angled end-pin for the 'cello, bringing the instrument to a more horizontal playing position, thus, he contended, facilitating bowing.

1914 Latvia Abraham Zebi Idelsohn (1882–1938), musical scholar, started work on *Thesaurus of Hebrew Oriental Melodies* which was completed in 10 volumes. He was a great authority on Jewish music.

1914 Spain Juan Antonio Ruiz Casaux, violoncellist (b. 1889) settled in Lisbon, which gave great impetus to 'cello playing in Portugal. His influence as a teacher extends all over Spain.

1914 U.S.A. Birth of Larry Adler whose fame rests on his ability as a mouth organist. He inspired many writers to compose works for him, including Vaughan Williams.

1915 England *The Interpretation of the Music of the XVII and XVIII Centuries* published by Arnold Dolmetsch (1858–1940) an English musician of French-Swiss origin; he was a pioneer in the recovery of early music, also building and playing early instruments.

ARCHITECTURE

1914 Italy Citta Nuova was planned by Antonio Sant'Elia (1888–1916), the architect of Italian Futurism, who designed cities for the future, complete with skyscrapers, pedestrian precincts and overhead roads.

Russia: 'The Football Match' by Kasimir Malevich

1915 USA Dodge House, Los Angeles, by Irving Gill (1870–1936) and since demolished, was a white-painted composition of blocks reminiscent of contemporary European houses; Gill designed several like it.

THREE DIMENSIONAL ART

1914–1915 England French-born sculptor Henri Gaudier-Brzeska (1891–1915) was a member of the London Vorticist group: his work was influenced by Negro sculpture and by abstractionist theory.

1915 U.S.A. Centaur typeface first used in a book: it was an adaptation of early Roman type and was devised by Bruce Rogers (1870–1957), considered America's greatest book-designer.

VISUAL ARTS

1914–1918 England Official films of the First World War made by J. B. MacDowall and G. Malins constituted the first important documentary film series.

1914 Germany The Swiss artist Paul Klee (1879–1940) visited Tunis and began afterwards to work in colour for the first time.

1914 Hungary Alexander (Sándor) Korda (1893–1956) began directing films.

1914 Italy *Cabiria*, a historical film by the director Giovanni Pastrone (1883–1959): it combined spectacle, dramatic construction and cinematic skills to an unprecedented degree.

1914 Sweden War-time neutrality aided the Swedish cinema which improved beyond other European film industries. Swedish literature provided scripts very suitable for filming, with emphasis on natural landscape and the supernatural.

*c.***1914 U.S.A.** Charles Sheeler (1883–1965) began to photograph American vernacular building.

1915–1920 Italy The major pictures of Amedeo Modigliani (1884–1920) were painted during this period. He developed an original kind of Mannerist elegance and was also influenced by Toulouse-Lautrec; the elegance was subordinated to his interest in the originals of his portraits.

1915 Russia The painter Kasimir Malevich (1878–1935) founded supremism, an abstract art movement in which only geometrical elements were used in construction.

1915 Russia Vsevelod Meyerhold (1874–1940), theatrical producer, made two films now lost: *The Strong Man* and *Dorian Grey*, which are known to have influenced contemporary film-makers. From 1920 Meyerhold had a working studio with pupil directors, including Sergei Eisenstein.

1915–1916 U.S.A. David Wark Griffith (1875–1948) directed *The Birth of a Nation* and *Intolerance*; they are considered his greatest films and were widely influential in their editing techniques.

INVENTIONS & DISCOVERIES

*1915
Hugo Junkers made first all-metal aeroplane. Aurel Stein discovered remains of Marco Polo's 'city of Etzina'.*

LITERATURE

1915 England *Of Human Bondage* by William Somerset Maugham (1874–1965), novelist, playwright and short-story writer. He was an anti-romantic writer, influenced by Maupassant, and remarkable for his vivid evocations of the tropics.

1915 India *Secrets of the Self* by Mohammed Iqbal (1877–1938), a Moslem philosopher-poet writing first in Urdu, later in Persian. He is now called 'the father of Pakistani literature'.

1915 Japan *Rashomon* by Akutagawa Ryunosuke (1892–1927), short-story writer. He based his tales on traditional stories from the tenth and thirteenth centuries.

1915 U.S.A. *The Spoon River Anthology*, poems by Edgar Lee Masters (1868–1950). His early work was influenced by the Romantics, but this poem was in free verse, understated and close to prose.

1915 Wales *My People*, a volume of short stories by David Evans, called Caradoc Evans (1878–1945), Anglo-Welsh playwright, novelist and short-story writer. He satirized hypocrisy in a biblical style.

1916 Italy Death of the poet Guido Gozzano (b. 1883), a leading writer of the Crepuscular school. Their melancholy poetry was considered decadent; they were filled with nostalgia for the past, while their emphasis on the banal was an important step towards more personal expression.

1916 Mexico *The Underdogs* by the novelist Mariano Azuela (1873–1952), the first Spanish American social realist. The book is a portrayal of the Revolution

1916 U.S.A. *The Man Against the Sky*, poetry by Edwin Arlington Robinson (1869–1935). His vision of life was tragic, and had its roots in the previous century. His work contained many psychological studies of failure.

DANCE & DRAMA

1915 Spain First performance of the ballet *El Amor Brujo*, by Manuel de Falla (1876–1946), with choreography by Pastora Imperio, who was principal dancer. De Falla felt that flamenco, excluded from Spanish ballet as vulgar, should be the basis of a national style.

1916 Bohemia Jaroslav Kvapil, manager of the Czech National Theatre, produced 15 plays by Shakespeare in one year. He introduced Western and Russian influences into the Czech theatre.

1916 Germany *Der Sohn* by Walter Hasencleves (1890–1940), the first expressionist play seen in the theatre. Expressionist drama was mainly confined in Germany.

1916 Italy *La Maschera E Il Volto* by Luigi Chiarello (1884–1947) leader of the *Teatro Grottesco* movement, which explored life on two planes, the real and the apparent.

1916 Russia David Hermann (1876–1930) founded the Vilna Troupe for the production of Jewish folk drama. Later the troupe split up, some members remaining with Hermann, the rest going to New York, where they were taken over by Maurice Schwartz. A number of Yiddish art theatres opened in New York, but they ceased to flourish as increasingly large numbers of immigrants used English, rather than Yiddish, as their language.

MUSIC

1915 England Birth of Humphrey Searle, English composer and writer on music.

1916 England Publication of *The Growth of Music* by Henry Cope Colles (1879–1943), music critic and author.

*1916
Battle of Jutland;
Lord Kitchener
drowned.
Easter Rebellion
in Ireland.*

1915 USA *The Chinese Restaurant* by Max Weber (1881–1961) combined cubist and futurist theories in decorative form. His painting later became more realistic, drawing inspiration from his Russian childhood.

*c.***1915 France** Maurice de Vlaminck (1876–1958) began to paint forceful expressionist works combining the pure colour technique of Fauvism with Cézanne's theories of construction. In his earlier work, from *c.*1901, he had concentrated on colour, often using pigment straight from the tube.

England: portrait of W. Somerset Maugham by P. Sheegnian

1916 France Jean Lurçat (1892–1966) began his experimental work in tapestry: he helped to release tapestry from the convention that it should imitate painting.

1916 Switzerland Hans Arp (1877–1966), sculptor and painter, was a co-founder of the Dada 'anarchistic' art movement, and began to make polychrome abstract relief carvings in wood. Later he developed a style of sculpture called 'creative abstraction', which suggested, without reproducing, organic forms.

1916 Belgium The painter and sculptor Rik Wouters (b. 1882) was killed; his paintings have been considered to show an affinity with Renoir's work.

1916 Mexico Jose Clemente Orozco (1883–1949) exhibited a series of wash drawings of *Mexico in Revolution*, which were compared to the work of Goya. Orozco was, unlike Goya, a didactic artist concerned with reaching the masses. To this end he abandoned the academic style for a popular, cartoon-like style.

1916 Switzerland Foundation in Zürich of the Dada movement of 'anti-art': its members wished to stimulate visual imagination through shock. One of its most active members was Francis Picabia (1879–1953).

1916 U.S.A. Thomas Ince (1882–1924) produced the film *Civilisation*; he was a creative producer who is credited with introducing the pre-written total scenario for films.

*1916
First military
tanks used.
Einstein
published general
theory of
relativity.*

HISTORICAL EVENTS	LITERATURE	DANCE & DRAMA	MUSIC

HISTORICAL EVENTS

*1917
February and
October
Revolutions in
Russia.
U.S.A. declared
war on Germany.*

LITERATURE

1916 Russia *The Confession* by Alexei Mikhailovich Peshkov, called Maxim Gorky (1868–1936), literary theorist, novelist, playwright and critic. Although he did not always follow his precepts in his own work, he was an advocate of socialist realism, a doctrine which demanded that the writer portray idealized man, man as he ought to be, and not man as he is. Thus literature is intended to improve men. Gorky is considered a great proletarian writer, because of his sympathy with the working man. He was a naturalistic writer: this was an extension of realism, giving a photographic portrayal of life and showing concern with the effects of heredity and environment.

1917 Brazil *Hallucinated City*, a collection of poems by Mario de Andrade (1893–1945), poet, novelist and critic, the leader of the Brazilian Modernist movement. The Brazilian Modernists wanted to see the Black, Indian and European races fused into one Brazilian nation. They also wanted a vernacular literature freed from Portuguese domination. Brazilian Modernist literature was strongly influenced by expressionism.

1917 China Hu Shih (1891–1962), scholar and critic, became professor at the university of Pekin. His aim was to use the vernacular instead of the old literary language, *Ku-wen*. European writers such as Ibsen and Chekov were translated into the Chinese vernacular.

1917 China A literary revolution was led by Ch'en Ta-hsiu (1879–1942) and Hu Shih. Their most formidable opponents were Chang Ping Lin, historian and philologist and Chang Shih-Chao, a distinguished author using *Ku-wen*.

1917 Egypt *Zaynab* by the novelist Muhammed Huseyn Haykal (1888–1956). Arabic prose had always been didactic and expository; story-telling was considered vulgar and literary Arabic was not suitable for narrative. This novel was the first in which colloquial Arabic was used.

1917 Switzerland *Der Spaziergang* by Robert Walser (1878–1956), poet and novelist. His touch was light, but his work fundamentally serious.

DANCE & DRAMA

1916 USA Short plays by Eugene O'Neill (1888–1953) were produced by the Provincetown Players, one of several groups formed in the hope of breaking the stranglehold of commercialism on the American theatre.

1917 England The Russian dancer Tamara Karsavina (b.1885) moved to London and remained in England; she was influential in the Royal Academy of Dancing, Ballet Rambert and Sadler's Wells.

1917 Germany *Der Bettler* by Reinhard Johannes Sorge (1892–1916): a German social protest drama in expressionist style.

1917 India Rabindranath Tagore (1861–1941) invited a teacher of Manipuri dancing to work at his school. Indian classical dancing was then in bad repute and popularly associated with prostitution. Tagore wrote dance-dramas for his pupils based on Manipuri, Kathakali and Bengali dances; these did much to end prejudice against dance.

1917 Phillippines *Solo Entre les Sombras* by Claro Recto (b.1897), a Filipino playwright writing in Spanish and trained in drama by a Jesuit college. The Philippines have little professional activity in the theatre but amateur groups are traditionally vigorous and expressive of public opinion.

1917 Russia Formation of Habimah ('stage' in Hebrew), a company founded for the production of plays in Hebrew. It originated in Moscow, but in 1931 settled in Palestine, as it had always been intended it should. The Zionists hoped to use a Hebrew theatre company to encourage the use of spoken Hebrew.

1917 U.S.A. First performance of the ballet *Tyl Eulenspiegel* by Nijinsky: an expressionist comedy based on images from the Middle Ages, it was an original work with no model in either the Maryinsky or Diaghilev companies. It was probably influenced by the work of contemporary comedians.

MUSIC

1917 France French composers Auric, Durey, Honegger, Milhaud, Poulenc and Tailleferre formed a group which came to be known as *Les Six*.

1916 U.S.A. Paul Strand (1890—1976) first published photographs in *Camera Work*: his photography was straightforward, with no adjustment of the print, and made frequent use of abstract patterns inherent in objects or natural forms. He printed on platinum paper until 1937.

1917 France *Cité Industrielle Designs* were published by Tony Garnier (1869—1948); the book constituted a revolutionary plan for coping with the problems of modern urban living.

1917 Holland Eigen Haard Housing Estate, Amsterdam, by Michael de Klerk (1884—1923) was one of several housing estates by de Klerk and his colleague Piet Kramer (1881—); it was built of brick, skilfully curved at the corners and elsewhere in a highly personal method.

1917 U.S.S.R. The brothers Antoine Pevsner (1886—1962) and Naum Gabo (1890—1977) returned to the U.S.S.R. from Munich and became founders of the constructivist school of art. Gabo was the most noted sculptor of this school, specializing in constructions of coloured transparent materials which illustrated new theories of sculptural space.

*c.*1917 **Netherlands** An armchair designed by Gerrit Rietveld (1888—1964) applied constructivist theory to furniture; his cubic forms were not joined but merely set together, with extended, cantilevered, surfaces. He influenced the early development of French designer Marcel Breuer.

1917—1920 Finland Tyko Sallinen (1879—1951) painted *Peasants Dancing*, a work characteristic of his violent expressionist style and his feelings for the life of the poor. His later paintings were considered among the most successful Finnish landscape studies.

1917 Canada Death of Tom Thomson (b. 1877), artist of the northern Ontario Landscape.

1917 France Georges Braque (1882—1963) began concentrating on still-life paintings.

1917 Germany The Russian painter Alexis von Jawlensky (1864—1941) painted his series of *Mystical Heads*. This was the beginning of his concentration on abstract studies of the head as religious expression. His style was characterized by simplifying shapes and outlining flat colour areas with strong line.

1917 Germany Ludendorff recommended merging German film studios into one central industry strong enough to project Germany favourably in other countries. This produced the Universum Film A.G. (Ufa).

1917 Sweden Victor Sjöstrom (1879—1960) directed *Terje Vigen*, a film version of a poem by Ibsen. He also made the first of his several adaptations of the novels of Selma Lagerlof, *The Girl from Marsh Croft*, in which he best expressed his own mystical attitude to nature.

1917 Sweden Mauritz Stiller (1883—1928) made his most successful film comedy, *Thomas Graal's First Film*; it showed the influence of Griffith strongly in its technique.

1917 U.S.S.R. Establishment of the first film schools by the state. Lenin considered the cinema 'the most important of all arts for us', but the revolution had dispersed most of the old cinema talent.

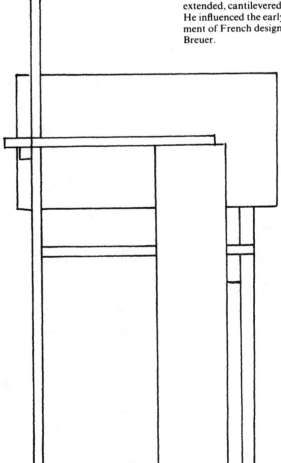

Netherlands: design for an armchair by Gerrit Rietveld

LITERATURE

1917 France *La Jeune Parque*, a long poem by Paul Ambroise Valéry (1871–1945), poet, essayist and critic. He believed that poetry was music, and his work was subtle and symbolist. He was influenced by Mallarmé.

1917 Ireland *The Wild Swans at Coole* by William Butler Yeats (1865–1939), playwright and poet. His work showed his feeling for Irish history and the countryside, and he was influenced by the revival of Gaelic literature which took place early in the century. He was awarded the Nobel Prize in 1923.

1917 Norway *The Growth of the Soil*, a novel by Knut Hamsun (1859–1952), playwright, poet and novelist. His books showed the corruption of the individual by society. He was awarded the Nobel Prize in 1920.

1917 Spain *Silver and I* by the poet Juan Ramón Jiménez (1881–1958). He developed and refined the modernism of Dario, and was later greatly influenced by the Indian poet Tagore. He wrote 'pure' poetry, without rhyme, ornament or conventional form, concentrating on the essential moment, and discarding anything which might distract from it. He was awarded the Nobel Prize in 1956.

1917 Turkey Short stories of Omer Seyfeddin (1884–1920), a writer of the 'Genc Kalemlev' movement, which stressed simple, natural style and vernacular culture.

HISTORICAL EVENTS

*1918
End of the First
World War;
Austria and
Germany
declared
republics.*

LITERATURE

1918 England Posthumous publication of poems by Gerard Manley Hopkins (1844–1889). A Jesuit, he felt it contrary to his duty to publish his poems. His executor, Robert Bridges, delayed publication because he found the poems too 'advanced'. Hopkins used new forms to express his vision of reality: highly condensed language, and 'sprung rhythm'—the accentual verse of Old English. He felt that the meaning should determine the technique and he indicated by stress marks how the poems should sound.

1918 Peru *The Dark Messengers*, poetry by Cesar Vallejo (1892–1938), who identified with the oppressed. Technically, his poetry showed how inadequate were the old forms for expressing deep feeling.

DANCE & DRAMA

1918 Germany *Gas I* (1920 *Gas II*) by Georg Kaiser (1878–1945), leader of the German expressionist school: Kaiser's plays on the ruin of civilization by self-destructive materialism were very influential in Europe and America.

1918 U.S.S.R. Olga Spessivtzeva (b.1895) became ballerina of the Maryinsky theatre She was considered the leading ballerina of her time in the romantic style.

MUSIC

1918 France Death of Claude Debussy (b. 1862).

1918 South Africa Birth of Anton Hartman, musicologist and conductor who is an authority on Afrikaans music.

1918 Switzerland Ernest Ansermet (1883–1969) founded the Orchestre de la Swiss Romande in Geneva. From 1915 he was conductor of Diaghilev's Russian ballet and conducted many of the first performances of the works of Igor Feodorovich Stravinsky (1882–1971).

1918 U.S.A. Cleveland Symphony Orchestra formed under its first conductor, Nikolay Sokolov (1859–1922).

1917 U.S.S.R. Lev Kuleshov (1899–1970) published a series of articles on film theory in *Vestnik Kinematografia.*

USSR: 'Cossacks' by Wassily Kandinsky

1918–1921 U.S.S.R. Wassily Kandinsky (1866–1944), pure abstract artist, was made professor at Moscow Academy of Fine Arts, and later a director of the Museums of Pictorial Culture. He founded the Russian Academy of Arts and Sciences in 1921, but left Russia shortly afterwards.

1918 Denmark Vilhelm Lundstrøm (1893–1950) made collages influenced by those of Picasso and Archipenko; he introduced this kind of work to Denmark.

1918 Denmark Jens Willumsen (1863–1958) painted *The Supper,* which typifies his use of violent colour and distorted form in symbolist painting.

HISTORICAL EVENTS	LITERATURE	DANCE & DRAMA	MUSIC

HISTORICAL EVENTS

1919
Benito Mussolini founded Italian Fascist Party; Adolf Hitler founded National Socialist German Workers' Party.

LITERATURE

1918 Chile *Equatorial* by Vicente Huidobro (1893–1948), a Chilean poet who also worked in Madrid and Paris. He invented the short-lived Creationist movement, in which the poet is a little God, and a poem is autonomous.

1918 China *Diary of a Madman* by Lu Hsin (1881–1936), short-story writer and essayist, regarded as the greatest modern writer in China. He encountered European literature translated into Japanese while he was a student in Japan. His own style was laconic, his sense of humour mordant.

1918 U.S.S.R. *The Twelve* by the poet Alexandr Aleksandrovich Blok (1880–1921), who was the leading Russian Symbolist. This poem concerned 12 Red Guardsmen, representing the Apostles, and was an apologia of the Bolshevik Revolution.

1918 U.S.S.R. *Confession of a Hooligan* by the poet Sergei Esenin (1895–1925). He presented himself as a 'peasant poet' and recited in Moscow salons wearing a peasant smock. He welcomed the Revolution, without really understanding it.

1919 U.S.A. *Winesburg, Ohio* by Sherwood Anderson (1876–1941), novelist and short-story writer: an analysis of the passions underlying small-town life, the book was written in an impressionistic style.

1919 U.S.A. *Jurgen* by James Brunch Cabell (1879–1958), novelist, short-story writer and poet. He wrote about an imaginary medieval kingdom; his books were escapist, but contained serious comment on society.

1920 Poland *Laka*, poems of Boleslaw Lesmian (1878–1937): he wrote in traditional forms, and was influenced by neo-Romanticism and symbolism; his ballads used folk-lore and mythology.

1920 U.S.S.R. *We* by Yevgeny Zamyatin (1884–1937), novelist, short-story writer and critic. He was one of the Serapion Brothers, a group of writers opposed to the intrusion of politics into literature. A highly influential book, *We* prophesied the reign of Stalin.

DANCE & DRAMA

1919 China The vernacular *pai hwa* language of everyday speech was recognized as legitimate for literary and theatrical purposes. Earlier attempts at a modern theatre had been frustrated because the language in written form was unintelligible to all but scholars. Traditional drama was based on music, song and mime, so the problem had not arisen. The first Chinese writer of the new spoken-dialogue plays was Ting Hsi Ling, an amateur.

1919 Germany Leopold Jessner (1873–1945) became Director of the Berlin State Theatre. He used no scenery in his productions, replacing it by different stage levels connected by steps.

1919 U.S.A. The Theatre Guild was formed: its aim was to present distinguished American and foreign plays which deserved performance but were not commercial.

1919 U.S.S.R. Alexander Granovsky (1890–1937) founded the Jewish Theatre Studio in Leningrad: their repertoire was based on the work of Sholom Aleichem. Later they transferred to Moscow as the Moscow State Jewish Theatre. In 1927 Salomon Mikhoels succeeded as director.

1920 France Theatre National Populaire, a theatre for the masses, founded by Firmin Gemier (1865–1933) French actor-manager and disciple of Stanislavsky.

MUSIC

1919 Czechoslovakia Josef Bohuslav Foerster (1859–1951), composer, appointed professor of composition at Prague Conservatory. He was a master of choral music, creating a new style in Czech choral composition.

1919 France Maurice Duruflé (b. 1902), organ virtuoso, began his career as assistant organist at Sainte-Clotilde, Paris.

1919 U.S.A. Juilliard School of Music formed in New York with a bequest from Augustus D. Juilliard.

1920 England Death of Edward Elgar's wife, after which Elgar wrote no further works of importance.

ARCHITECTURE

1919 USSR Memorial to the Third International was designed by Vladimir Tatlin (1885–1953) but never built; it was a 'constructivist' architectural fantasy: a spiral leaning tower. Constructivism was a short-lived ideal in Russia.

Germany: The Bauhaus School

1920 Germany Einstein Tower, Potsdam, by Eric Mendelsohn (1887–1953) was a highly plastic building and its distorted design the outcome of expressionist demands; he also built the Luckenwalde hat factory (1920–1923). using new forms for a new function.

THREE DIMENSIONAL ART

1919 Germany Establishment of the Bauhaus school of design, founded by Gropius to bring all the arts together in creating a building and all its furnishings as one united whole: until 1923 students were trained to explore the potential of their own gifts, tools and materials, with no reference to existing tradition.

1920 England Founding of the Golden Cockerel Press by Harold Taylor.

1920 U.S.S.R. Naum Gabo made a sculpture with a single moving part: it was known as kinetic sculpture and was a forerunner of the true mobile.

VISUAL ARTS

1919 Austria Oskar Kokoschka (b. 1886) painted *The Woman in Blue*: the whole life of the picture is in the colours; the figure is a rag doll. He became celebrated for his expressionist use of colour, especially in landscape and pictures of cities.

1919 France The painter Maurice Denis (1870–1943) was co-founder of the *Atelier d'Art Sacré*. He was a leading Symbolist, and concerned with reviving religious painting.

1919 Germany The caricaturist George Grosz (1893–1959) became a leader of the German Dada group which was anarchistic, destructive and 'anti-art'. His caricatures of Berlin bourgeois society were ferociously satirical. He later developed the calmer realism of the 'new objectivity' school.

1919 Germany Robert Wiene (1881–1938) directed *Das Cabinet des Doktor Caligari*, a film designed by three expressionist painters, H. Warm, W. Röhrig and W. Reimann. It was considered the most characteristic expressionist film drama. Expressionism needed formal studio effects; after 1920, German films were nearly all studio made.

1919 Japan The Art Film Association was founded by Norimasa Kaeriyama (b. 1893), who absorbed many American influences and abolished the mixed stage/screen performances. Directors and cameramen were now trained in America.

*c.*1919 **France** The painter Fernand Leger (1881–1955) began to be pre-occupied with the machine, and to introduce machine parts into abstract paintings.

1920–1931 Germany The Swiss artist Paul Klee (1879–1940) taught at the Bauhaus, Munich. His teachings were published after his death except for one book, *The Pedagogical Sketchbook*, published in 1925. He taught that the artist must wait on an unconscious formative process, but that the painting process itself was not automatic and required technical mastery to re-interpret natural forms as symbols.

*1919
First successful helicopter flight. First non-stop transatlantic flight.*

LITERATURE

DANCE & DRAMA

MUSIC

1920–1923 Czechoslovakia *The Good Soldier Schweik* by Jaroslav Hašek (1883–1923), journalist, editor, short-story writer and novelist. Unfinished at his death, the book was completed by Karel Vanek. Schweik made fools of his superiors by pretending to be stupid, and has been variously interpreted as anti-social, as a little man struggling against bureaucracy, and as a Czech patriot. He has also been criticized for showing the Czechs in a bad light.

1920–1930 Germany *Peasants, Bosses and Bombs*, a novel by Rudolf Ditzen, called Hans Fallada (1893–1947). He was a Realist, writing colloquial prose on the failure of man to do what he knows is good; many of his later books portray what he considered the weaknesses in the German people which enabled the Nazis to obtain power. This book is an account of a farmer's revolt.

1920 England Posthumous publication of poems by Wilfred Owen (1893–1918), whose poetry expresses the horror and futility of war, and disillusionment with patriotic ideals.

1920 France *Chéri* by Sidonie Gabrielle Colette (1873–1954), music-hall entertainer and novelist. She wrote best about her childhood world, the countryside, and animals. Her characters were usually victims of their instincts.

1920 U.S.A. *Main Street*, a novel by Sinclair Lewis (1885–1951), the first American to win the Nobel Prize for literature. He attacked what he regarded as contemporary middle-class characteristics.

1920 U.S.A. *The Age of Innocence* by Edith Wharton (1862–1937), novelist and short-story writer. She had much in common with Henry James, of whom she was a friend.

1920 Germany Mary Wigman (b.1886) established her school of dance and choreography in Dresden. She was a pupil of Dalcroze and Rudolf von Laban and was herself a pioneer of modern dance. Her dancing made more use of spontaneous emotion than did Laban's; she excelled at strong drama, the fierce and the horrifying.

1920 Sweden The Ballet Suédois was formed by the dancer and choreographer Jean Börlin (1893–1930) to present expressionist ballet. The major productions were *El Greco*, *L'Homme et Son Désir* and *La Création du Monde*. Börlin's style had much in common with 'free dance' and broke away from classical dancing.

*c.***1920 U.S.S.R.** Foundation of the Moscow Chamber Ballet, which produced violently expressionist work. It was influenced by European 'free dance' developments and by movements in Soviet theatre.

1920 Germany Death of Max Bruch (b. 1838).

'After the Battle of Ypres.' Scenes such as these inspired many poets during World War I, especially Wilfred Owen

ARCHITECTURE

1920–1928 Sweden City library, Stockholm, by Gunnar Asplund (1885–1940) had architectonic shapes reduced to basic rectangles and cylinders.

THREE DIMENSIONAL ART

*c.*1920 **England** Bernard Leach (b. 1887) founded the St Ives pottery and worked there with the Japanese potter Shoji Hamada (b. 1892). Leach was trained in Japan and became the founder of an English school of art pottery inspired by Japanese and medieval English traditions; he was the main force in a new style of working in which the potter did everything himself — designing, throwing, decorating and firing — and so acquired an intimate understanding of his materials. Among Leach's associates and pupils were Michael Carden and Katharine Pleydell-Bouverie.

VISUAL ARTS

1920–1930 U.S.A. Georgia O'Keefe (b. 1887) was considered a leader in expressive abstract painting, much of it inspired by architectural form.

1920 Germany Kurt Schwitters (1887–1948) invented *Merz*, a development of the Dada anarchistic movement. He worked in collage made up of scraps of newspaper, old tickets and other bits of printed ephemera. His sculptures, *merzbau*, were made from scraps of wood and metal.

1920 Holland Piet Mondriaan (1874–1944) published *Le Neoplasticisme*, summarizing his theories of painting. He was a co-founder of the Dutch *De Stijl* movement and its periodical of the same name; he attempted to portray the structure and equilibrium of creation in geometric forms and lines, and in their relation to each other.

*c.*1920–1930 **Italy** Giorgio Chirico (b. 1888) began to paint his most hallucinatory pictures, inspired by architectural forms. He was much admired by the Surrealists.

*c.*1920 **Uruguay** Pedro Figari (1861–1938) began to concentrate on painting after an early career as a lawyer and amateur artist. He was one of the first Latin American painters to develop an original style, using impressionist techniques to record Uruguayan life.

*c.*1920 **Scotland** The painter John Duncan Fergusson (1874–1961) became a leader of the group called the 'Scottish colourists'; other members were S. J. Peploe (1871–1935), and Leslie Hunter (1879–1931). They were influenced by the French Fauvist movement.

*c.*1920 **U.S.A.** Edward Weston (1886–1958) began to make abstract photographs. He required clear-cut and almost surrealist detail through the picture from the foreground to the distance. Weston exploited the difference between the camera and the eye which earlier photographers had regretted and tried to avoid.

1920–1930 U.S.A. John Marin (1870–1953) became a formative influence in the development of abstract painting.

INVENTIONS & DISCOVERIES

1920
J. T. Thompson invented submachine gun.
Discovery of the skeletons of Peking Man.

1921 Portugal *English Poems* by Fernando Pessoa (1888–1935), poet and critic. Highly eccentric, he was interested in the occult, and in astrology. He separated himself into four different personalities, each of whom was a poet, differing considerably in style from the others. He is considered a major European writer.

1921 Uruguay *Anaconda* by Horacio Quiroga (1878–1938), an expressionist short-story writer influenced by Kipling.

1921 Italy *Six Characters in Search of an Author* by Luigi Pirandello (1867–1936): his work unites a strong sense of theatre with a thought-provoking and pessimistic attempt to explore the nature of reality. His plays express the impossibility of finding absolute truth, and he had a considerable influence on European drama.

1921 Sweden Restoration of the Drottningholm Theatre and Museum near Stockholm, built in 1766. The museum contains a large number of French stage designs from the seventeenth and eighteenth centuries. The theatre has the original 'carriage and frame' machinery for quick scene changes, and over 30 sets dating from the eighteenth century.

1921 U.S.S.R. *The Chief Thing* by Nikolai Nikolaivich Evreinov (1879–1953), a Symbolist, who was concerned to show the drama of the inner self.

1921 U.S.S.R. *Mystery Bouffe* by Vladimir Vladimirovich Mayakovsky (1894–1930) is the first Soviet play, produced by Meyerhold. A Futurist, Mayakovsky aimed at shocking his audience.

1921 France Death of Charles Camille Saint-Saëns (b. 1835).

1921 Switzerland *Le Roi David* by Arther Honegger (1892–1955) completed.

1920–1930 France Raoul Dufy (1877–1953) began to paint by drawing outlines on brilliant washes of background colour. His recurring subjects were racing and boating scenes on the Riviera or at Deauville. He had studied impressionism and Fauvism in his early years.

1920–1930 Germany the *Neue Sachlicheit* 'new objectivity' movement fl. in art and literature. It reacted against symbolic and abstract expression and practised a plain representation of everyday life. Its leading members were George Grosz and Otto Dix (b. 1891).

1921 Holland Dr Bawnik School, Hilversum, was by William Dudok (born 1884); this and other Hilversum buildings by Dudok, the city's architect, were designed as compositions of asymmetrical rectangular blocks prefiguring the international style.

1921 France Louis Delluc (1890–1924) directed *Fièvre*. His films were noted for atmosphere and psychological observation.

1921 Rutherford and James Chadwick disintegrated most elements as preliminary to splitting the atom.

1921 France The German artist Max Ernst (1891–1976) became a founder member of the Surrealists in Paris. He worked in collage and photo-montage, and was one of the originators of *frottage*, making rubbings from rough surfaces, as a starting point for a painting. His images were drawn from the dark side of German romanticism and medieval fantasy.

1921 France The Spanish artist Pablo Picasso painted *Three Musicians*, a cubist picture in which images inspired by the motif were formally arranged in geometrical pattern.

1921 Germany Carl Mayer (1894–1944) wrote the film *Hintertreppe*, first of the *Kammerspiel* films: these films observed the three dramatic unities, of time, place and action, and were set in contemporary life and played with restrained and naturalistic acting. Their theme was social conditioning, their style formal and romantic.

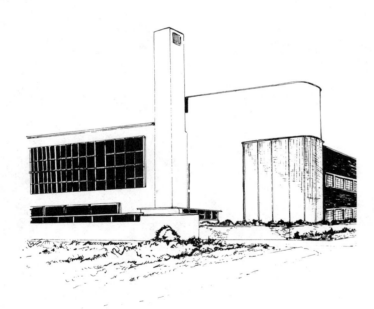

Holland: Snellius School in Hilversum, designed by William Dudok

1921 U.S.A. Henry King (b. 1892) directed the film *Tol'able David*: strongly influenced by the work of Griffith, it was itself influential, especially in Russia.

1921 USA In the film world the 'star' system had become all-important; Rudolf Valentino, Douglas Fairbanks, Mary Pickford and others all established types which were endlessly re-born in new actors who modelled themselves exactly on existing favourites.

HISTORICAL EVENTS	LITERATURE	DANCE & DRAMA	MUSIC

1922
Union of Soviet Socialist Republics established.

LITERATURE

1922–1940 France *Les Thibaults* by Roger Martin du Gard (1881–1958), novelist and playwright: the book was a family chronicle, in 11 volumes, dealing with the attitudes which led to the First World War. He was awarded the Nobel Prize in 1937.

1922–1925 USA Publication of *The Fugitive*, a magazine whose contributors were traditionalist conservative poets, led by John Crowe Ransom (b. 1888), poet and teacher of English at Vanderbilt University.

1922–1927 Wales *My Life and Loves* by James Thomas Harris, called Frank Harris (1856–1931), journalist, editor and novelist. He wrote biographies of people of note, most of whom he knew personally, which combined fact with a great deal of fiction.

1922 China The Creation Society was formed by Kuo Mo-jo (b. 1893), poet and critic. The group was influenced by the European Romantic movement. Kuo Mo-jo himself showed the influence of the Indian poet Tagore and the American poet Walt Whitman.

1922 England *The Waste Land* by Thomas Stearns Eliot (1888–1965), the American-born poet and critic (later a British subject). Influenced initially by Pound, he was himself enormously influential. He developed a new poetic language to express the spiritual barrenness and disorder of the times.

1922 England *The Garden Party* by Katherine Mansfield (1888–1923), a short-story writer whose best work recalls her childhood in New Zealand. She was educated in England and later lived in continental Europe.

1922 Ireland *Ulysses* by James Joyce (1882–1941), novelist, short-story writer, poet and playwright. Realizing the possibilities of the interior monologue, or stream-of-consciousness, he developed it considerably. The book was a tragicomedy, containing parody, fantasy, jokes and realistic passages, all telling a single story in a variety of ways, and reflecting the complexity of human experience.

DANCE & DRAMA

MUSIC

1922 Austria International Society for Contemporary Music formed at Salzburg.

1922 England Robert Mayer (b. 1879) started his series of orchestral concerts for children. From 1923 until 1939 Malcolm Sargent (1895–1967) was particularly associated with these.

1922 Greece Birth of Iannis Xenakis, composer.

ARCHITECTURE

1922 Denmark Øregaard School, Copenhagen, by Edward Thomsen and G. B. Hagen (1873–1941), was traditional architecture in the Romantic classical mould.

1922 France Citrohan House 2nd Project by Le Corbusier (1887–1965) had a design which included raising it on pilotis off the ground.

1922 France Notre-Dame, Le Raincy, by Auguste Perret and his brother is a hall-church design built with reinforced-concrete vaults and glazed walls; it stands at the beginning of modern European ecclesiastical architecture.

Germany: still from film 'Nosferatu' directed by Friedrich W. Murnau

THREE DIMENSIONAL ART

1922 England Stanley Morison (1889–1967) was appointed typographical adviser to the Monotype Corporation. He greatly extended the range of types available to printers, reviving historical types and introducing designs from living artists; the latter included Perpetua, Gill Sanserif, Goudy Modern, Lutetia.

1922 France Head of Madame Derain by Charles Despain (1874–1946), sculptor: this shows the intimate delineation of character for which his work was noted.

VISUAL ARTS

1921 U.S.A. *I Saw Figure Five in Gold* by Charles Demuth (1883–1939) typified the 'poster portrait' of symbolic portraiture which he developed. This picture symbolized the poet William Carlos Williams.

1921 U.S.A. Alfred Stieglitz (1864–1946) gave a one-man exhibition in New York of photographs which stressed the artistic qualities inherent in the subject. Stieglitz believed that the art of the photographer lay in his ability to see a composition and to capture it with perfect technique. No 'art' must come between the subject and the audience.

1922 Germany Fritz Lang (1890–1976) directed the film *Dr Mabuse der Spieler*, which reflected the growing cult of the superman.

1922 Germany Friedrich W. Murnau (1888–1931) directed the film *Nosferatu*, a Dracula story combining expressionism with the use of natural location.

1922 Mexico Murals by David Alfaro Siqueiros (b. 1896) included figures reflecting the spirit of Aztec sculpture. In 1921 he had published a treatise recommending that easel painting be abandoned for murals, and stressing the importance of the doctrine expressed in pictures.

1922 Sweden Death of Karl Isakson (b. 1878) painter of landscapes, still life and nude studies. He was one of the first Scandinavian artists to be concerned with the aspects of structure explored by Cézanne and the Cubists.

1922 Hollywood, U.S.A. Robert Flaherty (1884–1951) directed *Nanook of the North*, a documentary film of Eskimo life which reflected contemporary interest in romantic aspects of primitive societies. Some of his later documentaries were considered over-romantic and escapist.

1922 U.S.S.R. The director Lev Kuleshov (1899–1970) made his first experiments with montage, 'the Kuleshov effect', to show that cutting can completely alter the audience's perception.

*1922
Lord Carnarvon
and Howard
Carter discovered
the tomb of
Tutankhamún at
Luxor.*

LITERATURE

1922 Hungary *Beggar of Beauty*, poems of Attila Jozsef (1905–1937), a poet influenced in his thinking by both Marx and Freud, and in his expression by Ady, Rimbaud, and his country's folk literature. He was both fascinated and repelled by industry, and attempted in his poetry to find a meaning to both life and his own nature. He was a manic-depressive and finally committed suicide.

1922 Spain *Tirano Banderas*, a novel by Ramón del Valle y Peña, called Ramón del Valle-Inclan (1866–1936), an expressionist poet, playwright, novelist and critic.

1922 Sweden *Clouds*, poems by Karin Boye (1900–1941), poet, novelist, critic and editor. She worked on a radical, modernist periodical, and was also a trained psychologist. Her work reflected her own uncertainties.

1922 Turkey *Father Light* by Yakub Kadri Karaosmanoglu (b. 1899), novelist and short-story writer. Influenced by both French and Russian literature, he is regarded as one of the greatest prose writers in modern Turkish literature.

1923 Australia Publication of *Vision*, a magazine of the arts inspired by illustrator and minor novelist Norman Lindsay (1879–1969). The *Vision* group of writers most valued vitality in the arts and were opposed to the values of the new bourgeoisie.

1923 Austria *Ich und Du* by Martin Buber (1878–1965), Jewish philosopher: it expounded his theories on the relationship between man and things and between man and God, and linked atheist and Christian existentialism.

1923 England *Come Hither* by Walter de la Mare (1873–1956), poet and prose writer; he wrote mainly for children.

1923 Italy *Confessions of Zeno* by the novelist Ettore Schmitz, called Italo Svevo (1861–1928). He was a businessman of mixed Italian-Austrian Jewish parentage, and spoke both Italian and German imperfectly. He wrote about undistinguished people in plain Italian, producing fiction which Italian readers were not yet ready to appreciate. Later he was 'discovered' by James Joyce.

DANCE & DRAMA

1922 India Anna Pavlova, who had long been interested in Indian dancing, visited India for the first time. She did not, in fact, see the best of classical dancing; but her visit is important because her own performances interested Indians in Western classical dance and did much to remove feeling against women dancing in public.

1922 U.S.S.R. *The Dubbuck* by Solomon Ansky (1863–1920) was produced by the Habimah company. Ansky was an ethnologist and the play was inspired by his researches into Central European folklore.

1922 U.S.S.R. Asaf Messerer (b.1903) danced his first major role: Siegfried in *Swan Lake*. He became an important teacher of dance and greatly extended the dramatic range of the male dancer.

1923 France First performance of the ballet *La Création du Monde*, by Jean Börlin, performed by Ballets Suédois. It was typical of expressionist ballet in its emphasis on décor and costume.

1923 France First performance of the ballet *Les Noces* by Bronislava Nijinska (1891–1972) to music by Stravinsky for Diaghilev's Ballets Russes. Her choreography was based on her brother Nijinsky's work in *Sacré du Printemps* and *Les Jeux*, but with a greater tendency to abstract pattern.

1923 U.S.A. The Russian dancer Mikhail Mordkin (1881–1944) settled in New York and founded his own company.

1923 U.S.A. *The Adding Machine* by Elmer Rice (1892–1967): an expressionist fantasy on the domination of man by the machine.

MUSIC

1923 Czechoslovakia *Czech Nonet*, a chamber-music ensemble of international reputation, founded at Prague.

1923 England New studios for the B.B.C. opened at Savoy Hill and the first, opera was broadcast.

1923 Hungary First performance of *Psalmus Hungarious* by Zoltán Kodály (1882–1967).

HISTORICAL EVENTS

1923 Turkish republic established under Atatürk, end of Ottoman empire. Chinese Nationalist government established.

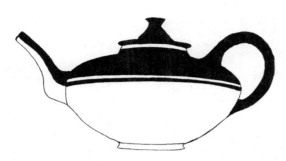

Germany: Bauhaus tea-pot, designed by Otto Lindig

1923 France *Vers une architecture* by the Swiss architect Le Corbusier was published: it was one of many works by him on the philosophy of modern architecture and town planning.

1923 Germany Chilehaus, Hamburg, by Fritz Höger (1877–1949) was a dramatic expressionist skyscraper, built when Expressionism influenced German architects; the irregular site allowed for both curved and sharp-angled façades.

1923 USA Mrs G. M. Millard House, Pasadena, by Frank Lloyd Wright is a compact vertically planned house – unusual for Wright – built of decorative concrete blocks during the baroque period in his career.

1923 Germany The exhibition of work done at the Bauhaus since 1919 coincided with a new direction in its policy; the Hungarian artist László Moholy-Nagy (1895–1946) became director, and introduced an emphasis on industry and the machine in place of the former feeling for craftwork and self-expression. The Bauhaus became a centre of functionalism, in which the form of an object is dictated by the use to which it is put and ornament or decoration is shunned. The style dominated design until *c.*1975.

1923 Japan The painter Shoji Hamada (1892–1978) returned to Japan from England. He came to be considered the greatest twentieth century potter; he settled in the village of Mashiko (where pots were already made) and concentrated on stoneware.

1923 U.S.A. William A. Dwiggins (1880–1956) became influential in book production through his work for Alfred Knopf.

1923–1926 U.S.A. The principal formulae of the 'Western' film were established by three Hollywood directors in a succession of films: *The Covered Waggon* and *Pony Express* by James Cruze (1884–1942); *Three Bad Men* and *The Iron Horse* by John Ford (b. 1895), and *Tumbleweeds* by King Baggott.

1923 France The Russian painter Marc Chagall (b. 1889) returned to Paris to work, his art being unacceptable in Russia. He combined dream-like fantasy with figurative portrayal of images from Russian peasant art.

1923 Japan An earthquake destroyed all film studios except the Nikkatsu studio at Kyoto, which had to increase production to meet the demand alone; standards suffered.

1923 U.S.A. Buster Keaton made his first film in Hollywood: *Our Hospitality.*
  The German-Born film director Ernst Lubitsch (1892–1947) made *The Marriage Circle* in Hollywood, using a German scriptwriter. From then on Hollywood deliberately attracted European directors, writers and actors. The loss to Europe, particularly to Germany, was felt to be more significant than the gain to Hollywood.
  The film director Cecil B. de Mille (1881–1959) revived the biblical spectacle with *The Ten Commandments.*

*c.***1923 Spain** Joan Miro (b. 1893) became one of the leaders of surrealism, painting forms of organic shape in abstract composition. His style went on developing on essentially the same lines after the Spanish Surrealists had broken up.

1924 England The film producer Michael Balcon (1896–1977) established Gainsborough Pictures.

1924 France Louis Delluc (1890–1924) founded *Cinéclub* to stress film as an art and create an independent film criticism.

1924 France René Clair (b. 1898) made *Entre'acte*, as a film interlude for a Dadaist ballet, *Relâche*. Erik Satie wrote the film music.

*1923
John B. Tytus
invented
continuous hot-
strip rolling of
steel.*

LITERATURE

1924 Chile *Twenty Poems of Love and One Desperate Song* by Neftali Ricardo Reyes, called Pablo Neruda (b. 1904), a poet influenced by Walt Whitman and by surrealism, and remarkable for his subtle rhythms. In the 1930s he became a communist. He was awarded the Nobel Prize in 1971.

1924 England *A Passage to India* by E. M. (Edward Morgan) Forster (1879–1970), novelist, essayist, short-story writer and critic. This complex and poetic book, considered his masterpiece, showed how ill-will and fear frustrate human attempts at communication.

1924 France *Manifeste du Surréalisme* by André Breton (1896–1966), poet and novelist, one of the founders of the Surrealist movement in literature. His novel *Nadja* (1928) is regarded as a masterpiece of surrealist writing. He dispensed with reason and logic, and by juxtaposing incongruous ideas, and using 'automatic' writing, attempted to express his subconscious thinking.

1924 Germany *The Magic Mountain*, a novel by Thomas Mann (1875–1955). His books, which portrayed early twentieth-century German society, were concerned with the conflict between Life and Art. He was awarded the Nobel Prize in 1929.

DANCE & DRAMA

1924 China Women were re-admitted to the stage as a profession. They had been banned in the eighteenth century when the theatre was considered indecent.

1924 France *Orphée* by Jean Maurice Cocteau (1889–1963) dramatist, film director, artist, novelist, poet and critic.

1924 Ireland *Juno and the Paycock* by Sean O'Casey (1880–1964), dramatist of the Dublin slums.

1924 Japan Opening of the Tsukiji Little Theatre in Tokyo, as a deliberate attempt to bring modern Western theatre to Japan. Naturalism and realism were foreign to the existing dramatic forms. *Nō* drama, popular *kabuki* and the nineteenth-century *shimpa* plays (strong, commercial melodramas). The Little Theatre had Soviet inspiration and was closed down by 1934 as a Communist organization.

1924 Monaco First performance, in Monte Carlo, of Bronislava Nijinska's ballet *Les Biches*, to music by Poulenc: it was designed by Marie Laurencin and performed by Les Ballet Russes.

1924 U.S.S.R. Death of Léon Bakst (b. 1866), painter and stage designer. He designed many of Diaghilev's ballets, including *The Sleeping Beauty*, *Carnaval*, *Schéhérazade* and *L'Apres-Midi d'un Faune*.

1924–1926 Germany Kurt Jooss (b.1901) choreographed the repertoire for the *Neue Tanzbühne* ballet group; it was his first important work. Jooss used lighting for visual effect rather than scenery or costume, and developed movements outside the range of classical ballet.

MUSIC

1924 Czechoslovakia Book on musical forms written by Karel Boleslav Jirák (b. 1891), composer, conductor and writer, which has had lasting influence on young Czech composers.

1924 England Edward Elgar (1857–1934) appointed Master of the King's Music.

1924 England First public performance of *Hugh the Drover*, a ballad opera by Vaughan Williams.

1924 France Death of Gabriel Urbain, Fauré (b. 1845), French composer and one of the most original minds of his time.

1924 Finland Jean Sibelius (1865–1957) composed his 7th and last symphony.

1924 U. S. A. Curtis Institute, Philadelphia, founded, one of the most outstanding conservatories in U.S.A.

ARCHITECTURE

1924 Holland Schröder House, Utrecht, by Gerrit Rietveld (1888–1964) was a small but unusual house, reminiscent in its intersecting planes and angles of a Mondrian painting; it was an indicator of the direction European modern architecture was to follow.

THREE DIMENSIONAL ART

1924 Denmark Kaare Klint (d. 1954) was appointed professor of furniture design at the Copenhagen Academy of Fine Arts: he was concerned with re-stating classical values in terms of every-day contemporary needs.

1924 England The Golden Cockerel Press was taken over by Robert Gibbings (1889–1958), who made illustration as important as typography in the Press's productions: the most famous of these was the *Four Gospels* of 1931, with wood engravings by Eric Gill (1882–1940).

England: artist's impression of one of Eric Gill's designs for 'Canterbury Tales', 1928, published by the Golden Cockerell Press

VISUAL ARTS

1924 Germany Friedrich Wilhelm Murnau (1888–1931) directed, and Carl Mayer (1894–1944) wrote, *The Last Laugh*, in which realistic images were manipulated to expressionistic effect. The camera saw for the characters; the content of the shot took precedence over the editing.

1924 Germany Development of the Ernostar very fast lens made possible instant or brief-time exposures without flashlight. 'Candid' un-posed photography became fashionable; the first important exponent was E. Salomon (1886–1944) who took 'candid' shots at state occasions with this technique.

1924 Sweden Mauritz Stiller (1883–1928) directed *Gosta Berling's Saga*, the film which introduced Greta Garbo.

1924 U.S.A. Walt Disney (1907–1966) began making cartoon films in Hollywood, with *Alice in Cartoonland*.
  Erich von Stroheim (1885–1957) directed *Greed* for MGM in Hollywood, who cut it to about a third of its length. None of his films were distributed as he made them; he sought to capture on screen the illusion of a whole world which is offered by the realistic novel, and this produced films of up to 40 reels. His main pre-occupation—conflict between instinct and outside forces—was that of the Expressionists.

1924 U.S.S.R. *The Adventures of Octyabrina*, the first film made by the Factory of the Eccentric Actor (FEKS), had forms created from a mixture of puppet theatre, circus and music-hall. The directors were students of Vsevelod Meyerhold's theatre school.

1924 U.S.S.R. *Kino Eye*, directed by Dziga Vertov (1896–1954): a fore-runner of *cinéma-vérité* which Vertov called 'the organization of the seen world'. His theory of cinema came to be known as 'Kino Eye' also.

1924 U.S.S.R. Yakov Protazanov (1881–1945) directed *Aelita*, the only film designed in 'constructivist' style. Constructivism originated in sculpture; it was an abstract style exploring movement in space and using the materials of the machine age.

LITERATURE

1925 Czechoslovakia Posthumous publication of *The Trial* by Franz Kafka (1883–1924), novelist and short-story writer. His major works were all published after his death by his friend, Max Brod, although Kafka had instructed him to destroy them. He was preoccupied with the predicament of man in a hostile and incomprehensible world.

1925 England *Pastors and Masters*, a novel by Ivy Compton Burnett (1892–1969). She wrote about family relationships in a dry, polished and civilized style. Her plots were akin to Greek tragedies and constructed on the same principles; they dealt with all manner of crimes.

1925 South Africa *Gedigte*, poems by Eugene Nielen Marais (1871–1936), poet and story writer, the first serious writer in Afrikaans.

1925 Sweden *Guest of Reality* by Pär Fabian Lagerkvist (1891–1974), poet, playwright and novelist, who described himself as a religious atheist. His work was expressionist, and combined both naturalistic and symbolic elements. His mood was generally pessimistic. He was awarded the Nobel Prize in 1951.

1925 U.S.A. *The Great Gatsby* by Francis Scott Key Fitzgerald (1896–1940), novelist and short-story writer: the book was a portrait of the American rich in the 1920s, at once realistic and symbolic.

1925 U.S.A. *Manhattan Transfer* by John Roderigo Dos Passos (1896–1971), novelist, playwright, and writer of travel and political studies. He used an original technique, combining stream-of-consciousness writing with poetic prose, objective reporting, a collage of newspaper headlines and currently popular expressions to portray his left-wing view of society.

1926 Scotland *Penny Wheep*, poetry by Christopher Grieve, called Hugh MacDiarmid (b. 1892), who rejected Anglo-Saxon values and led a revival of Scottish poetry. He helped to found the Scottish National Party which aimed at independence.

DANCE & DRAMA

1925 Indonesia Beginning of a popular modern theatre movement, paving the way for a nationalist theatre.

1925 Palestine Foundation of Ohel (Hebrew: 'tent'), the Jewish Labour Federation Theatre Company in Tel Aviv. Ohel is a touring company, playing throughout Israel in a portable theatre.

1925 Siam Death of King Rama VI (b.1880), royal patron of dance-drama: he developed a form of traditional Khon dances which his own household danced. Khon dance-dramas are based on themes translated from the Indian *Ramayana* epic, and have always been an aristocratic art.

1925 U.S.A. Martha Graham (b.1893) was appointed as a teacher at the Eastman School of Music, New York; there she began to experiment in dance forms, seeking movements expressive of feeling and not necessarily based on classical steps and gestures. She came to be considered the greatest American expressionist dancer.

1925 U.S.A. *The Golem* by Halper Levick (1888–1962), major Yiddish writer in the United States.

1926 England Ninette de Valois (b.1898) founded the Academy of Choreographic Art in London. She had danced at Covent Garden (1919) and with Diaghilev's Ballets Russes (1923).
 Lilian Bayliss (d. 1937) opened Sadlers Wells Theatre to house productions of opera and ballet formerly staged at the Royal Victoria Hall ('The Old Vic'). The Old Vic from this date concentrated entirely on drama, and particularly on Shakespeare and the English writers of 1600–1800.

1926 South Africa Formation of the first Afrikaans theatre company led by Paul de Groot (1882–1942). They performed native folk drama and translations of English plays.

MUSIC

1925 England Gustav Holst (1874–1934) achieved his greatest public success with production of his opera *At the Bour's Head* and his *First Choral Symphony*.

1925 England and U. S. A. First electrical records issued by H.M.V. (England) and Victor (U.S.A.).

1925 France Birth of Pierre Boulez, French composer.

1925 Germany Première of *Wozzeck* by Alban Berg at the Berlin Opera.

1925 Italy Birth of Luciano Berio, composer.

1926 Germany Birth of Hans Werner Menze, composer.

1926
General Strike in Britain.

ARCHITECTURE

1925 England 'New Ways', Northampton, by Peter Behrens (1868–1938) was the first international-style house in Britain at a time when British architects shied away from such austere cubic geometry.

1925 Germany The Bauhaus, Dessau, by Walter Gropius was the first important example of the new international-style architecture to be built.

1926 England Silver End, Essex, by Sir John Burnet (1857–1938), Thomas Tait (1882–1954), and Lorne was an early English-designed house in the international style, built when public commissions in this style were rare.

1926 France No. 14 Avenue Junod, Paris, by Adolf Loos has a more complex plan than his earlier houses, with split-level rooms and a curved bifurcated façade.

1926 Holland Hook of Holland Housing Estate by Jacobus Oud (1890–1963) is his first important work in which the rigid discipline of the de Stijl artists was less apparent, particularly in the simple curve-ended façades.

THREE DIMENSIONAL ART

1925 England The potter William Staite Murray (1881–1962) became head of the Pottery School at the Royal College of Art. He worked for the acceptance in England of pottery as a form of art, exhibiting his own pieces as individual, named works. He was trained mainly through his own experiments, but acknowledged the Japanese potter Shoji Hamada as a strong influence. His own style was highly inventive, and he had no interest in useful ware.

1925 France Paris Exposition Internationale des Arts Décoratifs et Industriels Modernes laid stress on fine work by the individual workman and launched the art deco style.

1926 Germany Publication by the Cranach Press, Weimar, of Virgil's *Eclogues*, illustrated with woodcuts by the French sculptor Maillol.

*c.***1926 Italy** Marino Marini (1901–1966) turned to sculpture, having trained as a painter and engraver: he worked largely in bronze, his main interest being to exploit the sensuous qualities and surface texture of the metal.

VISUAL ARTS

1925–1927 France Abel Gance (b. 1889) directed *Napolèon*: cameras were used with unprecedented freedom, batteries of them moving in all directions at once, with thousands of shots cut to one-twelfth of a second, superimposed and multiplied on the screen. He introduced 'polyvision', three images side by side on a panoramic screen, sometimes forming a continuous scene and sometimes showing different scenes.

1925 France The Spanish artist Pablo Picasso (1881–1973) painted *Three Dancers*, a surrealist picture in which images taken from the motif were dislocated, not for formal pattern but for emotional impact.

1925 Germany Ewald Andres Dupont (1891–1956) directed *Variété*, which a real-life subject like the *Kammerspiel* but was shot without artificiality and shows a highly subjective use of the camera. Georg Wilhelm Pabst (1885–1967) directed *Joyless Street*, a drama of social realism in a style which came to be known as *Neue Sachlicheit*, a hard documentary style.

1925 Norway Death of the artist Christian Krohg (b. 1852), who had painted the poor, prostitutes and social outcasts. He acknowledged inspiration by the novels of Zola.

1925 U.S.S.R. Sergei Eisenstein (1898–1948) directed *Battleship Potemkin*, intended as one episode in a full coverage of the 1905 revolution. He edited to produce an emotional reaction in his audience by a startling juxtaposition of real and symbolic images. Such carefully manipulated successions of shots were important in Soviet didactic films.

1926–1934 England Stanley Spencer (1891–1959) painted the murals for the War Memorial Chapel at Burghclere, using the Resurrection theme which he frequently repeated, setting it in contemporary terms, in this case in terms of his own experience in the First World War. His style displayed distortion and exaggeration.

1926 U.S.A. Warner Brothers presented the film *Don Juan* with synchronized sound effects and music.

INVENTIONS & DISCOVERIES

1925
Clarence Birdseye extended deep-freezing process to pre-cooked foods.
W. Heisenberg presented matrix formulation of quantum mechanics.

1926
J. L. Baird first demonstrated television in London.
E. Schrödinger reconciled wave and matrix theories of quantum mechanics.

1926 Argentina *Don Segundo Sombra* by Ricardo Guiraldes (1886–1927), a novelist and poet of the *modernismo* movement: the book is considered a masterpiece of Gaucho literature.

1926 France *Les Faux-Monnayeurs* by André Gide (1896–1951), novelist and critic. His work showed the conflict between the puritan and pagan aspects of his personality; he was influenced by Nietzsche and by Christianity alike. One of his main preoccupations was *l'acte gratuit*, the motiveless act. He was awarded the Nobel Prize in 1947.

1926 Norway *Alberta and Jacob*, the first of a trilogy of novels by Sara Fabricius, called Cora Sandel (1880–1974). They were autobiographical, and dealt with the situation of a sensitive, intellectual woman in a male-dominated society.

1926 South Africa *Whiplash*, a satirical magazine, was founded in South Africa by the poets Roy Cambell (1901–1957) and William Plomer (b. 1903), who was also a novelist. They discarded the British tradition, and found inspiration in Africa itself and the modern Europeans.

1927–1934 Hungary *Life of a Man* by Lajos Kassák (1887–1967), editor, novelist and poet. Influenced by the Italian Futurist, Marinetti, he was opposed to the liberal humanism of Babits and the group of writers associated with the periodical *Nyugat*.

1927 England *To the Lighthouse*, a novel by Virginia Woolf (1882–1941). She found the traditional English novel inadequate for her purpose, and used Bergson's 'stream of consciousness', endeavouring to record all the day's impressions as they registered in an ordinary mind. She and her friends were known as the Bloomsbury Group, but they did not constitute a movement; they were like-minded people who discussed current artistic ideas.

1927 U.S.A. *The Bridge of San Luis Rey*, a novel by Thornton Niven Wilder (b. 1897), novelist and playwright, his work is technically skilful and original.

1927 England *Danger* by Richard Hughes (1900–1976), a play written specially for radio and owing nothing to stage traditions. Radio drama producers began to exploit sound to create a type of play with a unique appeal to the imagination.

1927 France Theatre Alfred Jarry was founded by Antonin Artaud (1896–1952) and Roger Vitrac (1899–1952). Vitrac was a writer of surrealist plays. Artaud wanted to use the theatre to liberate man's unconscious, so that he recognized his true self. To this end he developed the Theatre of Cruelty, where movement, sound, and symbolic gesture replace coherent language.

1927 England School of English Church Music founded by Sydney Hugo Nicholson (1875–1947), organist and educationist.

England: platen press on which Virginia and Leonard Woolf printed works by the 'Bloomsbury Group'

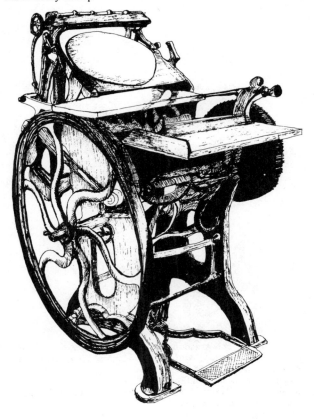

1927 Holland Van Nelle factory, Rotterdam, by J. A. Brinckmann (1902–1949) and L. C. van der Vlugt (1894–   ) was a rare monumental work in the 1920s in the international style, demonstrating its admirable adaptation to factory design.

1927 Spain The sculptor Julio Gonzalez (1876–1942) began to work in iron; his work varied from realistic to abstract.

1926 France Arrival in Paris from Hungary of the photographer André Kertész (b. 1893), who specialized in unposed pictures of people in natural surroundings. New fast technique and unobtrusive cameras enabled photographers to capture an image that might last only an instant.

1926 Germany The Russian artist Wassily Kandinsky (1866–1944) published *Point and Line to Plane*, a theory of drawing based on the symbolic value of signs: they stood not for inner emotion but for constant impersonal spiritual values, making a language of symbols comparable to mathematics.

1926 Germany Fritz Lang (1890–1976) and his wife, the scriptwriter Thea von Harbou (1888–1954), made *Metropolis*, a film of a futuristic city state, considered a major work of German expressionist cinema.

1926 U.S.S.R. Vsevelod Pudovkin (1893–1953), pupil of Kuleshov, directed *Mother*, with scenarist Nathan Zarkhi and cameraman Anatoli Golovnya. This was the first of a trilogy (*The End of St. Petersburg* and *Storm over Asia* followed). Pudovkin edited for continuity and not, like Eisenstein, for shock effect. He was thus able to develop his characters and their emotional growth smoothly.

1927–1930 U.S.S.R. Alexander Dovzhenko (1894–1956) made *Zvenigora*, *Arsenal* and *Earth*, the last being considered his best film. He used a variety of techniques all subordinated to a poetic lyricism.

1927 France Death of Jean-Eugène-Auguste Atget (b. 1856), documentary photographer of Paris: he used nineteenth-century technique and his photography was considered free of influence by any other medium.

1927 France René Clair directed the film *Un Chapeau de Paille d'talie*, a successful visual equivalent of a verbal farce.

1927 Japan *Sword of Penitence*, the first important film of Yasujiro Ozu (1903–1963), a director later known for films on contemporary society.

1927 Charles A. Lindbergh made first solo transatlantic flight.

1927 Germany *Der Steppenwolf*, a novel by Hermann Hesse (1877–1962), novelist, essayist, poet and painter. He was concerned with the tension between man's spiritual and material. The book contained realistic and fantastic elements, and owed much to Hoffman's *Tales*. He was awarded the Nobel Prize in 1946.

1927 Romania *Suitable Words* by Ion N. Theodorescu, called Tudor Areghezi (1880–1967), novelist, journalist and poet. His work drew on his experience as a monk and, later, as a political prisoner. He combined sensibility with a peasant tradition.

1927 U.S.S.R. *Jewish Tales* by Isaak Babel (1894–1941), Jewish novelist, playwright and short-story writer. He wrote mainly about violence and brutality, from the standpoint of an intellectual both fascinated and repelled by his material, yet striving to be objective.

*1928
Salazar took
over Portuguese
government.*

1928–1929 India *Pather Panchali* by Bibhutibushan Banerji (1894–1950), a novelist writing in Bengali: the book is in part autobiographical, and is considered a masterpiece of changing moods and styles.

1928 Belgium *The First Book of Schmoll* by Paul van Ostaijen (1896–1928), Flemish poet and short-story writer. His work showed a variety of contemporary influences: expressionism, dadaism, and the work of Verhaeren, and Kafka Apollinaire.

1928 England *The Childermass* by Percy Wyndham Lewis (1884–1957), poet, painter, novelist and critic. In his early years he was associated with vorticism, a cultural movement which called for clear-cut images and striking geometric patterns; it was an extension of imagism. This book is the first of a trilogy, *The Human Age*, in which humanity is shown outside heaven, awaiting judgement.

1928 England *Memoirs of a Foxhunting Man* by Siegfried Sassoon (1886–1967), poet and critic. His poetry expressed his fury at the pointlessness of trench warfare and the stupidity of officers. This book was part of his autobiography.

1928 America The Argentinian dancer La Argentina (Antonia Mercé y Luque, 1888–1936), made her first successful tour of north America. Her tours aroused a wide interest in Spanish dancing and led to a revival. She attempted a 'balletized' form of flamenco.

1928 Belgium *Barabbas* by Michel de Ghelderode (1898–1962), a playwright writing both in Flemish and French: the atmosphere of his plays is medieval and grotesque.

1928 England First performance of the ballet *Les Petits Riens* by Ninette de Valois: it was her first major success.

1928 U.S.A. Foundation of a school of dance by Doris Humphrey (1895–1958) and Charles Weidman: Doris Humphrey aimed at a basic language of movement which would be universally understood.

1928 U.S.A. Agnes de Mille (b.1908) began to give recitals of solo dances: they were mainly naturalistic mime, possibly influenced by the acting styles of silent cinema.

1928 Austria *Symphony for Small Orchestra* composed by Anton von Webern (1883–1945) in which he used the 12-note technique with great economy.

1928 Czechoslovakia Death of Leoš Janáček (b. 1854), Czech composer.

1928 England Eric Fenby (b. 1906), composer, became *amanuensis* to Delius, a position he held until Delius' death in 1934.

1928 France Maurice Martenot (b. 1898), musician and inventor, brought out his radioelectric instrument called Ondes Musicales ('now' Ondes Martenot). Many modern composers have written works for this instrument.

1928 France First performance of *Bolero* by Maurice Ravel (1875–1937).

1928 Germany Birth of Karlheinz Stockhausen, composer, noted for his explorations into electronic music.

1928 Mexico Carlos Chávez (b. 1899), composer, appointed director of National Conservatory and conductor of Orquesta Sinfónica de México. He has had great influence on development of modern music in Mexico.

India: scene from 1954 film by S. Ray of Banerji's 'Pather Panchail'

1927 U.S.A. Introducing sound into films brought radical changes. William Fox presented short films in Fox Movietone, with sound recorded on the film, including the first dialogue film, *They're Coming to Get Me*. The full-length film *The Jazz Singer* had synchronized music and some dialogue. Early 'talkies' stultified cinema art: the camera-work became secondary to the manipulation of heavy recording equipment; action became static. Theatre actors were brought in, who alone could produce the new natural acting style in place of old miming techniques. Realism was increased by dispensing with titles.

1927 U.S.A. William Wellman (1896–1975) won the first Academy Award, for his film *Wings*, which showed aerial warfare with documentary realism.

1927 U.S.S.R. Development of the Tager sound system. Early Russian sound films pioneered film reporting with direct recording of actual events; the first was Abram Room's *Plan of Great Works* (1930).

1927–1928 U.S.A. Josef von Sternberg (1894–1968), Austrian-born director, made three gangster films: *Underworld*, *The Dragnet* and *Docks of New York*; their strong atmosphere set the pattern for the gangster films of the 1930s. His best-known film, equally atmospheric, was *Der Blaue Engel*, made in Germany in 1930. It starred Marlene Dietrich, whom he directed in several films.

1928 France Luis Buñuel (b. 1900) directed *Un Chien Andalou* with Salvador Dali, who wrote it: a surrealist fantasy film, using images from the subconscious.

1928 France Carl Theodor Dreyer (1889–1968) directed *La Passion de Jeanne d'Arc* on new panchromatic film which would register facial expressions without make-up; this was a great stimulus to realism, and to the dramatic use of faces in close-up.

1928 Germany The photographer Albert Renger-Patzsch (1897–1966) published *Die Welt ist Schon*, showing his use of the camera to explore and interpret nature.

1928–1932 England American book-designer Bruce Rogers (1870–1957) worked in England and designed the Oxford lectern *Bible*, Stanley Morison's *Pacioli* and T. E. Lawrence's translation of the *Odyssey*.

1928 Finland Alvar Aalto (b. 1898) established Artek furniture in collaboration with his wife Aino Marsio: he applied Breuer's cantilever principle to wood and became, with the Swede Karl Bruno Mathsson, a formative influence on Scandinavian furniture.

1928 France Marcel Breuer (b. 1902) designed for the Thonet Company a cantilevered tubular steel chair: he was an innovatory designer of all metal furniture and of bent and moulded plywood and became head of furniture design at the Bauhaus in 1924.

*c.*1928 England The potter Michael Cardew (b. 1901) began to produce successful earthenware from his kiln at Winchcombe, Gloucestershire. He had trained at the Braunton pottery in North Devon, and with Leach. His main interest was in the revival of English slipware and he concentrated on useful ware, all made in quantity.

1928 Alexander Fleming discovered penicillin. H. Geiger and W. Müller constructed the Geiger counter.

LITERATURE	DANCE & DRAMA	MUSIC

1928 Germany *All Quiet on the Western Front* by Erich Maria Remarque (1898–1970), considered by many the greatest novel on war ever written.

1928 U.S.S.R. *Envy*, a novel by Yuri Olesha (1899–1960), novelist, short-story writer and playwright: it was a satire on a technological society.

1928 U.S.S.R. *And Quiet Flows the Don* by the novelist Mikhail Sholokhov (b. 1905): an epic novel of Cossack life from 1912–1922.

1928 U.S.A. First performance of the musical, *Showboat*: at this time, the serious theatre in the United States was beginning to decline, and the great musical was becoming America's prime contribution to contemporary theatre. (There were showboats on the Mississippi and the Ohio from 1817 to the 1920s, taking the theatre to pioneer settlements. They are not found in any country other than the United States.)

1928 Poland First of a series *Cantica Selecta Musices Sacrae in Polonia* published by Waclaw Gieburowski (1877–1943), ecclesiastic, musicologist and conductor. In this series he revived Polish music of fifteenth, sixteenth and seventeenth centuries.

1928 Switzerland Publication of *Historisch-biographisches Musikerlexicon der Schweiz*, a basic work of reference for Swiss musical history by Edgar Refardt (1877–   ), musical historian.

1929 Wall Street Crash; beginning of world economic crisis.

1929 England *Goodbye to All That*, an autobiography by Robert Graves (b. 1895), poet, essayist, translator and critic. He was one of the Georgian poets, writing in the period following accession of George V in 1910, mostly about the First World War. He also wrote novels which reflect his interest in history and mythology.

1929 England *The Good Companions* by John Boynton Priestley (b. 1894), novelist, essayist, playwright, journalist and critic. He dealt with modern problems, but not in modern techniques, his work being traditionalist in form.

1929 Germany *Berlin Alexanderplatz* by Alfred Döblin (1878–1957), psychiatrist, essayist and novelist. His main concern was why individuals would consent to lose their identity in mass movements. He used stream-of-consciousness, collage and flashback in the modernist technique created by the American writer Dos Passos.

1929 Japan *The Cannery Boat* by the novelist Kobayashi Takiji (1903–1933). A communist, he was considered Japan's leading writer of proletarian literature.

1929 U.S.A. *The Sound and the Fury* by the novelist William Faulkner (1897–1962), who was a Nobel prize-winner in 1949. He used the 'interior monologue' to present his vision of the American South.

1929 U.S.A. *Look Homeward Angel* by the novelist Thomas Clayton Wolfe (1900–1958). His books, on the theme of man's search for a father-figure, were autobiographical.

1929 Arabic theatre *The Death of Cleopatra* by Ahmad Shawqui (1888–1932), Arabic poet and playwright: educated in Europe, he was influenced by French classical theatre, especially Corneille.

1929 Norway *Konkylien* by Helge Krog (1889–1962), a dramatist whose sympathetic portrayal of women and their problems furthered the cause of the emancipation of women.

1929 U.S.S.R. The ballerina Galina Ulanova (b.1910) danced Odette in *Swan Lake*, her first important rôle. Her dancing represented a survival of the best pre-revolutionary Russian school. She was taught by Agrippina Vaganova, who was in turn taught by Nicolas Legat; her parents were dancers at the Imperial Theatre in St Petersburg, the Maryinsky.

1929 France George Balanchine (b.1904), choreographer, arranged the last Diaghilev ballet, *The Prodigal Son*. He went on to choreograph for the Ballets Russes de Monte Carlo.

1929 Belgium Birth of Henri Pousseur, composer.

1929 England *A History of Arabian Music to the 13th Century* published by Henry George Farmer (b. 1882), conductor, musicologist and Orientalist.

1929 England First performance of *The Rio Grande*, most famous work by Constant Lambert (1905–1951), composer, conductor and writer on music.

1929 Portugal Fernando Lopes Graça (b. 1906), musical scholar and composer, made his debut. He was the first in Portugal to systematically apply atonal and polytonal principles.

1929 U.S.A. Birth of George Crumb, American composer.

1928 U.S.A. The Hungarian director Paul Fejös (1898–1963) directed *Lonesome*: he worked with a handheld camera, and used improvisation and location-shooting.

1928 U.S.A. King Vidor (b. 1894) directed *The Crowd*, a film on the life of a city clerk, using unknown actors and free camera-work.

1928 U.S.S.R. Congress on Film Matters produced a tightening censorship.

1929 England John Grierson (1898–1972) directed the film *Drifters*. He defined documentary as 'the creative treatment of reality'.

Alfred Hitchcock (b. 1899) directed *Blackmail*, using natural sound to convey atmosphere and make psychological point. His gift was the exploitation of ordinary things and settings to sinister effect.

1929 Finland Paimio Sanatorium by Alvar Aalto (1899–1978) was one of the first hospitals built in the international style by one of the few European architects of calibre working outside France, Holland and Germany.

1929 Germany Chair designed by Ludwig Mies van der Rohe (1886–1969) for the German pavilion at the International Exhibition in Barcelona became famous as the 'Barcelona' chair: it was considered one of the most beautiful modern chairs, with a framework of curving steel bars.

1929 France Villa Savoye, Poissy, by Le Corbusier is typical of the private houses then built by him: it was freely planned in basic geometric shapes and using modern construction techniques; he called such houses 'machines for living'.

1929 U.S.A. The Metropolitan Museum exhibition in New York 'The Architect and the Industrial Arts' consolidated the art deco movement.

1929 France The Spanish artist Pablo Picasso painted *Woman in an Armchair*: it is characteristic of the monumental style he began to use at this time.

1929 Spain German Pavilion, Barcelona Exhibition, by Ludwig Mies van der Rohe is the first important work by the architect; it was built on one level with carefully articulated space and all in high-quality materials; it has since been demolished.

Finland: Paimio Sanatorium designed by Alvar Aalto

1929 Germany The *Film und Foto* exhibition in Stuttgart showed much experimental work with light-projected images. L. Moholy-Nagy (1895–1946) and Man Ray (d. 1976) had begun to experiment in this field (*c*.1921) to produce abstract art by light projection.

1929 U.S.A. The painter Stuart Davis (1894–1964) returned after working in France; he introduced elements of French synthetic cubism into American art, using natural forms.

1929 USA The Chrysler Building, New York, by William van Alen, was designed in 'moderne' style which combined massive form, inspired by ancient architecture, with Art Deco motifs and streamlined shapes; van Alen used engineering materials, steel and aluminium, to celebrate the machine age.

1929 U.S.A. Rouben Mamoulian (b.1898) directed *Applause*. He restored mobility to the camera in sound films and introduced the superimposed sound track.

1929 U.S.A. MGM produced *Broadway Melody*, the first film musical.

c.**1929–1931 U.S.A.** Development of the noiseless and smokeless flash bulb, for photography synchronized-flash techniques and electronic lamps. Light could now take an active part in photographic composition.

HISTORICAL EVENTS	LITERATURE	DANCE & DRAMA	MUSIC

1930
Mahatma Gandhi opened civil disobedience campaign in India.

1930–1940 England Short stories of H. E. (Herbert Ernest) Bates (1905–1974), short-story writer, novelist, playwright, poet and critic. He was influenced by Maupassant.

1930–1943 Austria *The Man Without Qualities* by Robert Musil (1880–1942), novelist, short-story writer, playwright and critic: the book is a tragicomic picture of an empire in decline, but it can be interpreted on many levels. Two of its themes are sexuality after Freud, and music as an evil force; it also has mythological overtones. There is no plot, but rather a series of inter-related facts. The novel is unfinished; some passages exist in several drafts.

1930 Australia *The Fortunes of Richard Mahoney* by Ethel Florence Lindesay Richardson, called Henry Handel Richardson (1870–1946), a novelist living in England but writing on an Australian theme. The book was entirely naturalistic.

1930 Portugal *The Jungle* by José Maria Ferreira de Castro (1898–1974), novelist and journalist. His style was objective, and much of his writing concerned working people in Portugal or Brazil.

1930 England Foundation of the Camargo Society, with the aim of making a national ballet. Frederick Ashton, Ninette de Valois and Antony Tudor all created ballets for the society, which was dissolved in 1933.

First performances by the Ballet Rambert: it was founded by Marie Rambert (b.1888) who had studied with Cecchetti and Jacques Dalcroze, and danced with Diaghilev's Ballets Russes.

1930 France Serge Lifar (b.1905) appointed ballet-master at the Paris Opéra ballet. He continued there, with a gap 1944–1946, until 1959 as a choreographer, ballet-master and dancer, designing ballets to suit his own athletic, staccato style.

1930 France Michel Jacques Saint-Denis (1897–1971) nephew of Jacques Copeau, founded the Compagnie de Quinze, producing the work of, among others, André Obey (b.1892).

1930 Brazil Heitor Villa-Lobos (1887–1959) began composing his *Bachianas Brasileiras*.

1930 England Sir Adrian Boult (b. 1889), conductor, appointed Musical Director to the B.B.C. and conductor-in-chief of the newly formed B.B.C. Symphony Orchestra.

1931
U.S. President Herbert Hoover's plan for one-year moratorium for reparations and war debts.

1930 Cuba *Motives of Sound* by Nicolas Guillen (b. 1902), a mulatto poet. He used Cuban Negro folk-lore and is considered the leading writer of South American Negro poetry.

1930 Denmark *Havoc*, a novel by Tom Kristensen (b. 1893), poet, critic, novelist and short-story writer. He was a leading Expressionist.

1930 France *Corps et Biens*, poems by Robert Desnos (1900–1945), one of the early Surrealists.

1930 U.S.A. *The Bridge* by the poet Hart Crane (1899–1932): an American epic, it was successful even though the poet had little education and little knowledge of American history.

1931 France *Vol de Nuit*, a novel by Antoine de Saint-Exupéry (1900–1944). He was a pioneer airman, and his experiences flying dangerous mail routes are used in this book.

1931 England First performance of the ballet *Façade*, choreographed for the Camargo Society by Frederick Ashton (b. 1906) to music by Walton. Ashton was at this time influenced by George Balanchine and by the attitudes of the Diaghilev company after 1924, when Diaghilev abandoned his principle of the harmonious whole, and began to stage deliberate mixtures of style he called 'cocktail' ballets.

First performance of the ballet *Cross-Gartered*, by Antony Tudor (b. 1908) for Ballet Club; it was his first ballet. He returned to the ideal of bringing together movement, music, lighting and costume into a total effect.

A new ballet school, to replace the Academy of Choreographic Art, was founded at Sadler's Wells by Ninette de Valois. It became known as the Vic-Wells Ballet and later as Sadler's Wells Ballet. It was considered a major influence on British ballet.

1931 England The reconstruction and opening in London of the Sadler's Wells Theatre, largely due to the efforts of Lilian Baylis (1874–1937).

1931 England First performance of *The Canterbury Pilgrims* by George Dyson (1883–1964), English composer and educationist.

1931 England First performance at Leeds of *Belshazzar's Feast* by William Walton (b. 1902).

1931 France Death of Vincent d'Indy (b. 1851), French composer, theorist, teacher and author.

1931 Germany Wolfgang Fortner (b. 1907), German composer, appointed professor of composition at the Institute for Protestant Church Music of Heidelberg.

ARCHITECTURE

1930 Czechoslovakia Tugendhat House, Brno, by Ludwig Mies van der Rohe was remarkable chiefly for the interior planning in which living space was divided only by screen walls.

1930 Germany Siemensstadt Housing Estate, Berlin, by Walter Gropius was the prototype housing estate, with flats contained in tower blocks and terraces.

1931 Germany St Engelbert, Cologne-Riehl, by Dominikus Böhm (1880–1955) was an expressionist church by an architect who designed several like it.

1931 Italy The railway station, Milan, by Eugenic Montuori (b.1907) is a massive building in streamlined Roman Classicism, typical of the official architecture of Mussolini's totalitarian regime.

THREE DIMENSIONAL ART

1930 Germany Architecture became predominant at the Bauhaus, which was no longer producing furniture or industrial designs in other forms.

1930 Sweden The Orrefors glass company developed the Ariel glass technique, i.e. obtaining a design by trapping air and pigments in an outer layer of glass and then fusing this to an inner layer. There are two other techniques exclusive to Orrefors: Graal glass (three layers, clear and patterned alternating); and Ravenna (successive layers trapping coloured decoration).

1930 Switzerland Alberto Giacometti (1901–1966), sculptor, began to work in a surrealist style, in which he developed his characteristic open-cage constructions and elongated forms these were considered to typify surrealism, being 'profoundly disturbing' mechanisms constructed in space.

*c.***1930–1945 England** Henry Moore (b. 1898), sculptor, was considered the most important figure in English art and began to develop an international reputation: he studied the ancient sculptures of Sumeria and the Americas and developed a style independent of the classical tradition.

Australia: 'Mrs South Kensington' by William Dobbell

VISUAL ARTS

*c.***1929–1938 Spain** Salvador Dali (b.1904) was recognized as a leader of the surrealist movement. He evolved a systematic presentation of hallucinatory experience. The Surrealists rejected him as his style developed.

1930–1931 Germany Georg Wilhelm Pabst (1885–1967) directed *Westfront 1918* and *Kameradschaft*, two films in which he perfected his unobtrusive editing (he cut on movement, not on static images) to produce naturalism. He and other directors found that imposing a soundtrack inhibited rapid cutting; they reverted to longer shots, moving the camera (instead of cutting to a new angle) for emphasis.

1930–1932 The Russian film directors Eisenstein, Alexandrov and Tisse travelled in Europe and America lecturing and filming.

1930–1939 U.S.A. Most films (95%) were now produced by 9 organisations controlled by the Morgan and Rockefeller financial groups. Sound produced a boom in audiences, followed by a slump; the finance houses demanded technical perfection and predictable ingredients to win audiences back; no risks could be taken, individuality was discouraged. Films came to have a studio style rather than a director's style; the studio team was all-important. The period produced light entertainment of high quality.

1930–1940 U.S.A. Ivan Albright (b.1897) became one of the most successful nationalist painters.

1930 France Jean Cocteau (1889–1963) directed *Le sang d'un poète*, a film assembly of poetic images.

1930 U.S.A. The Russian-born director Lewis Milestone (b. 1895) directed *All Quiet on the Western Front*, considered his finest film.

*c.***1930–1945 Australia** Period of the most important paintings by William Dobell (b.1899), a portrait artist in expressionist style. He used colour, texture and exaggerated forms to make social as well as personal comments on his subjects.

*1930
Acrylic plastics were invented.*

LITERATURE

1931 Greece *Strophe* by George Seferiades, called George Seferis (1900–1971), poet, critic and translator. With this volume, he made a break with the poetry of the past, which had become stilted and ponderous. Influenced by Eliot and the French Symbolists, he aimed at simplicity. He was awarded the Nobel Prize in 1963.

1931 Persia *Ziba* by Muhammad Hijazi (b. 1898), a novelist particularly concerned with the lot of women.

1931 Romania *L'Homme Approximatif* by the poet Sami Rosenstock, called Tristan Tzara (1896–1963), one of the founders of the dada movement. Co-founders were Hans Arp (1887–1966), a German artist and poet, and Hugo Ball (1866–1927), also a German poet. The Dadaists scorned culture; they combined literature with the plastic arts, and developed a form of simultaneous poetry which involved collage, various original typographical devices, and montage.

1932–1947 France *Les Hommes de Bonne Volonté* (27 volumes) by Louis Farigoule, called Jules Romains (1885–1972), novelist, poet and playwright. The work was a study of the nature and evolution of French society in this century. Romains' book of poems *La Vie Unanime* gave the name to the 'Unanimist' movement, a group of poets who believed in the collective life of human groups. Most of his work concerned group consciousness and communal life.

1932 Austria *Radetzskymarsch* by Joseph Roth (1894–1939), novelist, short-story writer and critic: the novel told the story of three generations of a family at the end of the Austro-Hungarian empire. Roth was concerned not with politics but with people.

1932 England *Brave New World* by Aldous Huxley (1894–1963), essayist, novelist, poet, playwright and critic. His early books were sardonic and intelligent accounts of English intellectual life in the 1920s. This work was prophetic, and had much in common with Zamyatin's *We*.

DANCE & DRAMA

1931 France Foundation of the Ballet Russe de Monte Carlo by René Blum and Colonel de Basil.

1932 Denmark Harald Lander (1905–1971) became balletmaster of the Royal Danish Ballet. He revived the repertoire of August Bournonville (1805–1879) with its stress on the vigorous male dancer.

1932 France First performance of the ballet *The Green Table* by Kurt Jooss: a notable example of ballet as political satire, its subject was the First World War.

1932 India Rajamanickam established his theatre group at the Walltax Theatre, Madras, as the first modern theatre in the State of Tamil Nadu. His company was all male, his plays predominantly religious.

1932 Spain Foundation of the Madrid Ballet by La Argentinita (Encarnacion Lopez, 1898–1945) and the poet Federico Garcia Lorca. La Argentinita trained in Spanish folk dance, flamenco and Spanish ballet. Garcia Lorca had a deep interest in flamenco and the company presented much flamenco in an authentic spirit.

MUSIC

1931 Spain A complete edition of *Huelgas Codex*, a Spanish collection of medieval music, published by Higini Anglès, the only collection of polyphonic manuscripts preserved in place of origin.

1931 U.S.A. *Star-Spangled Banner* became the official United States national anthem.

1932 England London Philharmonic Orchestra formed by Thomas Beecham (1879–1961).

1932 Switzerland Publication of *Die Schweiz in der Deutschen Musikgeschichte* by Antoine-Élisée Cherbuliez (b. 1888), Swiss musicologist; it was the first comprehensive account of Swiss musical history.

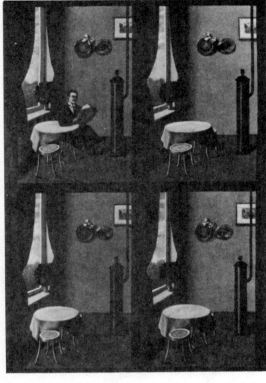

Belgium: 'Man Reading a Newspaper' by René Magritte

1930 Belgium René Magritte (1898–1967) painted *On the Threshold of Liberty*, one of the best-known surrealist paintings. Magritte broke from the surrealist doctrine of 'automatic painting' to release images from the unconscious. He sought instead to point out new significance in objects by setting them in startling juxtaposition.

*c.***1930 England** Graham Sutherland (b.1903) turned from etching to painting. He worked between 1933 and 1939 on a series of pictures based on the Pembrokeshire landscape.

*c.***1930 Japan** Hiroshi Hamaya (b.1915) began working in Tokyo and the 'snow country' of northern Japan as a photographer. He was considered the foremost of his time in Japan.

1931–1933 U.S.S.R. Pudovkin directed *The Deserter*, an elaborate experimental exercise of all his theories on sound films. It was criticized by the authorities as 'intellectual'; he became cautious thereafter.

1932–1938 England Boots factory, Nottingham, by Sir Owen Williams was a rare example in England at the time of a large industrial building in the international modern style.

1932 France Pavillon Suisse, Paris, by Le Corbusier was, as so often in his early work, built on pilotis; innovations were the use of a curved wall as well as cubist blocks and a random rubble wall to contrast with the usual white concrete.

1932 Italy Casa del Fascio, Como, by Guiseppe Terragni (1904–43) is an early example in Italy of the international style.

1932 USA Savings Fund Building, Philadelphia, by George Howe (1886–1955) and William Lescaze (1896–1969) was one of the first skyscrapers designed in the international style in the Sullivan slab tradition.

1932 England First appearance of Times Roman typeface, designed by Stanley Morison.

1932 U.S.A. First exhibition of mobile sculpture by Alexander Calder (1896–1976), who invented them: he became the leading sculptor in welded metal.

32 England Grierson established the G.P.O. Film Unit, later the Crown Film Unit (from 1940): it was a leading influence in creative documentary film until 1945. He persuaded Government and industry to sponsor films. The resulting regular units provided stable training bases.

1932 France Luis Buñuel (b.1900) directed his documentary *Las Hurdes*: this film, and the French film *A propos de Nice* (1930) directed by Jean Vigo (1905–1934), were considered the two major *avant-garde* documentaries.

1932 France René Clair directed *A nous la liberté*, considered one of the first French films to make creative use of sound.

1932 U.S.A. Lewis Wickes Hine (1874–1940) published *Men at Work*, a collection of photographs taken 'on the job' during the building of the Empire State Building in New York.

*c.***1932 U.S.S.R.** The work of the painter Ilya Repin (1844–1930) became the model for artists of the new, officially decreed, socialist realism.

*1932
Neutron
discovered.*

453

HISTORICAL EVENTS

1933
Hitler appointed
German
Chancellor.

LITERATURE

1932 France *Voyage au Bout de la Nuit* by Henri-Louis Destouches, called Louis-Ferdinand Céline (1894–1961), physician and novelist. His work was based on his own experiences, which he distorted through the cubist technique of breaking up and juxtaposing images.

1932 France *The Knot of Vipers* by François Mauriac (1885–1970), novelist, poet, playwright, critic and journalist. His most important books were set in respectable society and showed the psychological drama hidden beneath the decorous surface. His chief theme was redemption. He was awarded the Nobel Prize in 1952.

1932 USA *An Objectivist's Anthology*, edited by Louis Zukofsky (b. 1904), poet and critic. Objectivism, in which the poem is seen as an object defined by its form, developed from imagism: its chief exponents were Zukofsky, William Carlos Williams and Ezra Pound.

1933–1941 France *Le Chronique des Pasquier* by Georges Duhamel (1884–1966). For a time he was associated with the Unanimists. This book was semi-autobiographical, both comic and pathetic.

1933 Belgium *Cheese*, a novel by Alfons de Ridder, called Willem Elsschot (1882–1960), Flemish poet and novelist. His work, comic and laconic in style, was particularly appreciated in Holland.

1933 China *Water* by Ting Ling (b. 1907), a novelist and short-story writer, probably the best known of woman communist writers. She dealt with personal difficulties in a time of political upheaval.

1933 France *La Condition Humaine*, a novel by André Malraux (1901–1976), politician, critic, novelist and art historian. A communist in the Chinese Revolution of 1926 and in the Spanish Civil War, and a resistance fighter in the Second World War, his life was active and often dangerous. This is reflected in his books, though Malraux was detached and able to present a balanced view of conflict.

DANCE & DRAMA

1933 England First appearence in London of Rikuhei Umemoto's Japanese classical dance company.

1933 Germany *Mutter Courage* by Bertolt Friedrich Brecht (1898–1956) German poet and dramatist: he intended his plays to appeal not to the emotions but to the intellect, and employed various alienation devices – film, notice boards, cartoons, songs – to ensure that the audience did not identify with the characters. The social and political settings of his plays are more important than the fate of individuals; the plots are a string of incidents. This is in line with the work of Buchner and Piscator, and is known as Epic Theatre.

1933 Spain *Blood Wedding* by Federico Garcia Lorca (1898–1936) Spanish poet and playwright and founder/director of La Barraca, a travelling amateur company: his plays are folk tragedies.

1933 U.S.A. Ted Shawn (1891–1972), who had worked together with Ruth St Denis (1877–1965) as the Denishawn Ballet, founded his own company of male dancers. Their work restored the prestige of the male dancer in America.

MUSIC

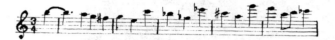

Germany: an example of 12–note music from Hindemith's opera 'Cardillac'

1933 England Thomas Goff (b. 1898) established himself as a clavichord and harpsichord maker in London.

1933 Poland Birth of Krzystof Penderecki, composer.

1933 USA First production, in New York, of *Emperor Jones* by Louis Gruenberg (1884–1964), American pianist and composer of Russian origin, whose compositions were greatly influenced by Negro music.

*c.***1933 Germany** Paul Hindemith (1895–1963) developed his music using the 12-note scale.

Mural by Diego Rivera on the Insurgentes Theatre, San Angel, in Mexico City (see USA Visual Arts)

1933 Germany The Bauhaus was closed and its style condemned: dictatorships in Germany, Italy and Russia preferred monumental buildings on a gigantic scale, often neo-classical.

1933 Brazil Roberto Burle Marx (b. 1909) began to study garden design: his work in landscape and garden design is considered an important setting for Brazilian architecture.

1933 England Alexander Korda (1893–1956) directed *The Private Life of Henry VIII*. Its success marked the beginning of a revival in British films.

1933 France 'Brassai' (G. Halasz, b.1899) published *Paris de Nuit*, a collection of spontaneous photographs of Paris street life, using even torn posters as pictorial form.

1933 Mexico Rufino Tamayo (b.1899) painted a mural for the National Conservatory of Music. He was a champion of the aesthetic qualities of painting as opposed to its message.

1933 U.S.A. First exhibition by the photographer Henri Cartier-Bresson (b.1908), in New York. He, like Alfred Stieglitz, emphasized the ability to see a composition and isolate it in the view-finder; the camera was not used to add to what his eye saw, only to preserve it.

1933 U.S.A. Ben Shahn (1898–1969) worked with Diego Rivera (1886–1957) of Mexico on murals for the Rockefeller Centre, and also worked as a photographer. His early graphic training developed into poster art.

1933 Polythene discovered.

LITERATURE

DANCE & DRAMA

MUSIC

1933 Greece Death of the poet Konstantinos Kavafis (b. 1863) sometimes known as Cavafy. His work was mainly circulated privately during his lifetime. He wrote about himself and his own interests — a learned homosexual, living in Alexandria, interested in Byzantine history — and his work showed no trace of the influence of contemporary Greek poetry. He is considered one of the greatest of lyric poets.

1933 Jamaica *Banana Bottom* by Claude McKay (1890–1948), poet and novelist, the first professional novelist in the West Indies. West Indian literature had been slow to develop because of the high illiteracy rate. Many writers preferred to work in London, where there was at least a readership.

1933 USA *The Autobiography of Alice B. Toklas* by Gertrude Stein (1874–1946). She is less important for her own writings than for her encouragement of younger writers whom she called 'the lost generation', such as Fitzgerald, Hemingway and Wilder, and for the effect that her abstract work, based on the theories of abstract art, had on others.

1933 U.S.S.R. *Youth Restored* by Mikhail Zoshchenko (1895–1958), playwright, novelist and short-story writer. A humorist, in this book he satirized the idea that socio-economic progress will change mankind.

1934–1950 Netherlands *Anton Wachter* by Simon Vestdijk (1898–1971), Dutch poet, essayist, translator and novelist. He was influenced by Dostoyevsky, Proust, and the theories of Freud. This book was a semi-autobiographical novel on the relationship between mother and son.

1934 Canada *Such is my Beloved* by Morley Callaghan (b. 1903), a realistic novelist encouraged by Hemingway. He was Canada's first important novelist writing in English.

1934 Denmark *Seven Gothic Tales* by Karen Blixen (1885–1962), novelist and short-story writer. She was a modernist, witty and sophisticated, but using the Gothic convention.

1935 New Zealand The Caxton Press was founded by Denis Glover (b. 1912).

1934–1937 China The trilogy of plays by Ts'ao Yü (b.1905): *Thunderstorm, Sunrise* and *Wilderness* brought great popularity to modern theatre in China.

1934 Arabic theatre *Scheherezade* by Tewfiq-al-Hazim (b.1902), Arabic novelist and writer of both symbolic and conventionally modern plays.

1934 England The ballet *Swan Lake* was choreographed for Sadler's Wells by Nicholas Sergeyev (1876–1951): he based his choreography on the first successful version at St Petersburg in 1895. Sergeyev was important in preserving original versions of classical ballets, especially those of the Maryinsky Theatre where he became *premier danseur* in 1904.

1934 France Birgit Åkesson, Swedish dancer, gave her first 'free dance' recital. She trained with Mary Wigman, but broke away from the violent form of expressionism in which there was no definite vocabulary of movements. She aimed at a classical harmony and restraint based on a sophisticated technique that could be handed on.

1934 U.S.A. *Rain from Heaven* by Samuel Nathaniel Behrman (b.1893), the leading American writer of comedy of manners.

1934 U.S.A. Establishment in Hartford, Connecticut, of The American Ballet, by Lincoln Kirstein and Edward Warburg. They worked with the choreographer George Balanchine. The company became the opera ballet at Metropolitan Opera, 1935–1938, and was influential in forming the policies of the later New York City Ballet.

1934 U.S.S.R. Agrippina Vaganova (1879–1951) ballerina and teacher, published *Fundamentals of the Classic Dance.* She was an influential teacher who stressed that technique is grounded in developing bodily strength, balance and coordination.

1934 U.S.S.R. First performance of the ballet *The Fountain of Bakhchisarai,* by Rostislav Zakharov (b.1907) who made many ballets from Pushkin's works. The principal dancer was Galina Ulanova (b.1910).

1934 England Festivals of opera established at Glyndebourne, Sussex, by John Christie.

1934 England Walford Davies (1869–1941) was appointed Master of the King's Music.

1934 England Birth of Peter Maxwell Davies, composer.

1934 England Death of Frederick Delius (b. 1862), English composer.

1934 England Death of Edward Elgar (b. 1857), composer.

1934 England Death of Gustav Theodore Holst (b. 1874), English composer.

1934 U.S.A. The American Musicological Society was founded in New York with Otto Kinkeldey as its first president.

1934 U.S.A. Invention of the Hammond organ.

1934 U.S.A. *Rhapsody on a Theme by Paganini* by Sergey Vassilievich Rakhmaninov (1873–1943), Russian composer and pianist.

1934 U.S.S.R. Sergey Sergeyevich Prokofiev (1891–1953) returned to the Soviet Union, having left at the time of the revolution in 1918.

*c.***1935–1940 U.S.A.** Boogie-Woogie, a style of jazz in the blues manner, developed. Also a particular sentimental style of singing known as crooning became popular.

1935 Austria Death of Alban Berg (b. 1885) a few months after completing his famous *Violin Concerto,* 'To the Memory of an Angel'.

| ARCHITECTURE | THREE DIMENSIONAL ART | VISUAL ARTS | *INVENTIONS & DISCOVERIES* |

ARCHITECTURE

1934 England Penguin Pool, London Zoo, by Berhtold Lubetkin (born 1901) and Tecton Group is the best known of several zoo buildings designed by this successful team of architects in the modern style.

Design for a chair by Marcel Breuer

THREE DIMENSIONAL ART

1935 England French designer Marcel Breuer made the first successful table cut from one piece of plywood: furniture made of a single piece by one industrial process has been the aim of many modern designers.

VISUAL ARTS

1934 France Cinémathèque Française began to give daily showings of traditional French films. The founders, Henri Langlois and Georges Franju, inspired a new generation of directors.

1934 Mexico The election of Lazaro Cardenas, leader in liberal reforms, created an atmosphere conducive to socialistic art.

1934 Mexico José Clemente Orozco (1883–1949) returned from the U.S.A. and began producing the great murals which best characterize his work. His main concern was to express in visual symbols the sufferings and oppressions of the human race. His type of expressionism went far beyond the socialist art of his contemporaries.

1934 U.S.A. Frank Capra (b.1897) directed *It Happened One Night*, which influenced the whole direction of American film comedy.

1934 U.S.S.R. Grigori Alexandrov (b. 1903) directed the film *Jazz Comedy*, which typified the new official attitude that all films should be comprehensible even to the dullest. 'Intellectualism' was banned.

1935 Belgium Paul Delvaux (b.1897), painter of neo-impressionist and expressionist pictures, was converted to surrealism, in which he was influenced by Chirico and Magritte; he followed them in gaining his effects by juxtaposition and in the use of architectural settings. His most persistent motif was the female nude.

1935 England Arthur Elton (b. 1906) and Edgar Anstey (b. 1907) directed the documentary film *Housing · Problems*; their techniques did not appear again until the post-war television reporters used them.

1934 J. F. and I. Joliot-Curie discovered induced radioactivity.

1935 Robert Watson-Watt built first practical radar equipment for detecting aircraft. First regular television service in Britain.

457

HISTORICAL EVENTS	LITERATURE	DANCE & DRAMA	MUSIC

LITERATURE

1935 France *Que Ma Joie Demeure* by the novelist Jean Giono (1895–1970), whose writings were inspired by the life of his native Provence. His work showed the influence of Homer and the Old Testament.

1935 Switzerland *When the Mountain Fell*, a novel by Charles-Ferdinand Ramuz (1878–1947). His books were regional, and he used a deliberately simple style and the Vaudois dialect. His themes, however, were universal.

1936 Brazil *Anguish* by Graciliano Ramos (1892–1953), a novelist who used the interior monologue; his work was recognized as convincing both psychologically and socially.

1936 Canada *New Provinces* was an anthology of English-Canadian poetry. The leading poet of the period was E. J. Pratt (1883–1964) who wrote on urban themes as well as the more traditional nature poetry.

1936 France *Le Journal d'un Cure de Campagne*, a novel by Georges Bernanos (1888–1948). A Catholic, he was concerned with the struggle between good and evil.

1936 France *La Chanson de Jean-sans-Terre*, a cycle of poems by Isaac Lang, called Iwan Goll (1891–1950), poet, playwright, novelist and critic. His early work was in German; later he wrote in French. He was greatly influenced by Joyce.

1936 U.S.A. *Look, Stranger!* by Wystan Hugh Auden (1907–1973), English-born poet and critic. He became an American citizen in 1939. In the 1930s he was influenced by Marxism; later his poetry became more meditative, and his later poems still were about morality and religion.

1937 Hungary *A Journey Round my Skull* by Frigyes Karinthy (1888–1938), humorist and journalist. He translated Heine, Swift and Mark Twain. Good-humoured, intelligent and objective, he was considered one of Hungary's leading writers. This book was about his experiences after the diagnosis of a brain tumour, which killed him.

DANCE & DRAMA

1935 England Appointment of Frederick Ashton (b. 1906) as chief choreographer of the Vic-Wells Ballet, until 1939. He trained as a dancer under Massine and Marie Rambert, and studied choreography under Massine and Nijinska. His first work was *A Tragedy of Fashion* (1926), for Ballet Rambert.

1935 England *Murder in the Cathedral* by Thomas Stearns Eliot (1888–1965) American-born English poet and playwright, who began a revival of poetic drama in England. His later plays were based on ancient Greek drama but with modern settings.

1935 Finland Performance of the ballet *Scaramouche*, choreographed by Irja Koskinen, who was the first Finnish choreographer, to music by Sibelius.

1935 U.S.A. *Porgy and Bess* by Dubose Heyward (1885-1940) with music by George Gershwin: a musical based on Heyward's dramatization of his own novel *Porgy*, considered the first true portrayal of the southern negro.

1935 U.S.A. *Awake and Sing* and *Waiting for Lefty* by Clifford Odets (b.1906): he was a member of the Group Theatre which set out to create a theatre devoted to social realities and group playing.

1935 U.S.S.R. The State Academic Theatre of Opera and Ballet became the Kirov Theatre of Opera and Ballet: it was formerly the Maryinsky Theatre, an important centre of ballet in imperial St Petersburg.

1936 England First performance of the ballet *Jardin aux Lilas* by Antony Tudor (b.1908): his first completely original work, noted for its economy of style and the characterization of the female rôles.

1936 India The dancer Menaka presented Kathak dancing at the Berlin Olympiad; it was a successful and influential appearance. Menaka had trained in European dancing and in the oriental style of Ruth St Denis; she had then returned to India to learn the authentic Kathak style.

MUSIC

1935 Hungary Hungarian String Quartet formed.

1935 U.S.A. First performance, in Boston, of *Porgy and Bess* by George Gershwin (1898–1937).

*c.***1935 USA** 'Swing' became popular and with it the 'big' bands using contrasts of saxophone and clarinet.

1936 England The first regular television service in the world started operating from Alexandra Palace, London.

1936 France Foundation of 'La Jeune France' by a group of composers aiming at 'sincerity, generosity and artistic good faith'.

1936 Palestine Palestine (later Israel) Philharmonic Orchestra founded by Bronislaw Huberman (1882–1947).

1936 U.S.A. Copland wrote an orchestral fantasy *El Salon México* in what he described as his 'more accessible style', based on popular Mexican themes.

1936 U.S.S.R. Dimitri Shostakovich (1906–1975) fell into disfavour with the authorities with his tragic opera *Lady Macbeth of Mzensk* (1934).

1937 England Publication of *Text-book of European Musical Instruments* by Francis William Galpin (1858–1945), English clergyman and archaeologist; it is the most concise and comprehensive book on the subject in the English language.

1937 France Death of Joseph Maurice Ravel (b. 1875), French composer.

1937 Germany First production, in Frankfurt, of *Carmina Burana* by Carl Orff (b. 1895).

1937 U.S.A Death of George Gershwin (b. 1898).

1936 Outbreak of Spanish Civil War.

1937 Rome/Berlin Axis formed.

1935 England Lawrence Whistler (b. 1912) began to work as a glass-engraver, at first on window glass. He became celebrated for a style of work on windows and goblets which was inspired by the idyllic tradition in English art.

1935 U.S.A. Ansel Adams published *Making a Photograph*, an influential manual illustrated with his own work. He specialized in portraying natural textures.

Black Iron, a painting by Charles Burchfield (1893–1967) typified his portrayals of the power and drama of industry. Burchfield took a romantic approach to realism.

The artist Mark Tobey (b. 1890) returned after working in China and Japan, where he had studied Chinese calligraphy. He began to paint in calligraphic strokes in white.

1936 England Impington Village College, Cambridgeshire, by Walter Gropius and Maxwell Fry (born 1899) was a more relaxed example of modern architecture built of brick and incorporating coloured tiles and ironwork; all-glass walls kept its pupils in touch with natural surroundings. European architecture was commissioned frequently by government as part of a planned improvement in surroundings or living standards, while American artists worked mainly for private patrons and built-up areas were unplanned.

1936 Canada Death of Homer Watson (b.1855), landscape painter.

1936 England The photographer Bill Brandt (b.1906) published *The English at Home*, a collection of photographs exploiting surreal aspects of mundane images.

1936 Italy Aircraft hangars, Orbetello, by Pier Luigi Nervi (born 1891) were a reinforced concrete structure of intersecting beams; Nervi was an engineer and an important figure in the development of reinforced concrete buildings. The hangars have since been demolished.

1936 France The playwright Marcel Pagnol (b. 1895) wrote a trilogy of plays set in Marseilles and filmed the third, *César*, himself. It was considered an important example of poetic realism. (The other two plays, *Marios* and *Fanny*, were filmed by other directors from Pagnol's adaptations and were considered too theatrical.)

1936 Germany Leni Riefenstahl (b. 1902) directed the film *Der Triumph des Willens*; national socialist propaganda films copied Max Reinhardt's use of moving masses in his stage productions.

1936 USA Falling Water, Pennsylvania, by Frank Lloyd Wright is cantilevered out over Bear Run in horizontal sections: it was not unlike the European international style.

1936 U.S.A. Beginning of *Life* magazine. Some of its photographic assignments produced picture-stories good enough to be published separately in permanent form, e.g. *Spanish Village* by W. E. Smith (1951).

1937 Frank Whittle invented jet engine.

1937–1942 Brazil Ministry of Health and Education, Rio de Janeiro, by Lucio Costa (1902–1963), Oscar Niemeyer (born 1907) and others is a modern-style tower block modified by the introduction of sunbreaks, devised by Le Corbusier, the consultant architect: they were to become normal features in buildings in hot climates. Niemeyer was a pupil of Le Corbusier but more interested in buildings as sculpture.

1937–1938 Romania Ensemble of sculpture by Constantin Brancusi at Turgu Jiu; the *Table of Silence*, *Gate of the Kiss* and *Endless Column*: these are architectural sculptures of enormous mass and simple visual impact.

*c.*1936 England John Piper (b. 1903) began to paint romantic studies of great houses, made into fantasies through his use of colour and texture.

1937 Canada David Milne (1882–1953) changed from his Fauvist style to work in watercolour under oriental influence, expressing his deep feeling for nature.

1936 Norway *Nederlaget (The Defeat)* by Nordahl Brun Grieg (1902–1943) Norwegian poet, novelist and playwright: he experimented in dramatic techniques, but was killed in action in World War II before he had fully shown his powers.

1937 Canada *Regards et Jeux dans L'Espace* by Hector de Saint-Denys-Garneau (1912–1943), a French-Canadian poet, the first of the modern movement in Canada.

1937 U.S.A. Publication of poems by Emily Dickinson (1830–1886), a poet and a recluse for the last 30 years of her life. She published only five poems during her lifetime, and was not recognized until 40 years after her death. Considered a great lyric poet, she has been compared to Blake.

1936 U.S.S.R. The ballet *La Symphonie Fantastique* was choreographed by Léonide Massine: it contained some of his most successful work, in which he combined expressionist effects with classical economy.

1937–1941 U.S.S.R. Leonid Lavrovsky (1905–1967) was artistic director of the Kirov Ballet, where he had worked as dancer and choreographer. He created *Romeo and Juliet* to music by Prokofiev in 1940, with Galina Ulanova (b.1910) and Konstantin Sergeyev (b.1910) as principal dancers.

1937 U.S.A. *The Daring Young Man on the Flying Trapeze* by William Saroyan (b. 1908), short-story writer and playwright. His short stories, which appeared formless, were intended to reflect the chaotic and contradictory nature of life.

1937 U.S.A. *The Man with the Blue Guitar* by Wallace Stevens (1879–1955), a poet concerned with expression rather than emotion; his work is polished, literary and abstract.

1937 England First performance of the ballet *Dark Elegies* by Antony Tudor, an abstract ballet composed to Mahler's *Kindertotenlieder*; Agnes de Mille (b.1908) appeared as guest artist. Tudor used expressionist devices where appropriate but retained a strong sense of working in a classical tradition.

1938 Australia Foundation of the *Jindyworobak Review*, a magazine stressing Aboriginal culture; it appeared until 1948.

1938 England First performance of *Symphonic Studies* by Alan Rawsthorne (1905–1971).

1938
Inönu elected
President of
Turkey on
Atatürk's death.
German
annexation of
Austria.

1938 Australia *Chosen People*, a novel by Kenneth Mackenzie, called Seaforth Mackenzie (1913–1955), poet and novelist: he introduced a new element of symbolism into Australian fiction.

1937 U.S.S.R. Foundation of the State Folk Dance Ensemble under the direction of Igor Moiseyev (b.1906), a dancer and choreographer who had specialized in comic and character rôles in ballet. His work combines the traditions of ballet and folk dance.

1938 France Death of Fedor Ivanovich Chaliapin (b. 1873), Russian bass singer, particularly noted for his interpretation of *Boris Godounov*.

1938 England *The Death of the Heart* by Elizabeth Bowen (1899–1973), an Irish short-story writer and novelist influenced by Henry James and Virginia Woolf.

1938 Canada Foundation of the Winnipeg Ballet Company by Gweneth Lloyd and Betty Farrally.

1938 England *Brighton Rock* by the novelist Graham Greene (b. 1904). A Catholic, his novels were concerned with remorse, failure and guilt, set against seedy or violent backgrounds.

1938 India Uday Shankar (b.1902) opened a dance centre at Almora to train dancers in Western and Indian styles. His own work in Indian classical dancing owed as much to Ruth St Denis's 'orientalism' as it did to authentic Indian dance, but he was important in stimulating Indian interest in its own dance tradition and in contemporary Western ballet. He was also a pioneer of good theatrical presentation of dance.

1938 U.S.A. *Understanding Poetry* by Cleanth Brooks (b. 1906), critic, and Robert Penn Warren (b. 1905), poet, novelist and critic. The book brought an entirely new approach to the teaching of poetry at American universities, stressing textual analysis in place of the history of ideas.

1937 Denmark The Town Hall, Aarhus, by Arne Jacobsen (1902–1971) and Erik Møller is a refined, well-proportioned, international-style building, typical of Jacobsen's work.

1937 USA Johnson Wax factory, Racine, Winsconsin, by Frank Lloyd Wright used curves to play an important part in the building's planning, particularly in the later extension (1949), when Wright pursued the circular theme.

Germany: '1914-18 War Memorial, Magdeburg Cathedral', 1927-28, by Ernst Barlach

1938 Germany Death of Ernst Barlach (b. 1870), expressionist sculptor in ceramics, bronze and wood: he developed the expressive potential of Gothic styles, particularly for tragic subjects.

1937 France *Nude in the Bath* by Pierre Bonnard (1867–1947) was one of his many studies of the static figure made two-dimensional as viewed through water. Bonnard was the last of the Impressionists: he made the mundane setting poetic by seeing it in terms of colour variations.

1937 France Julien Duvivier (b.1896) directed *Pépé le Moko*, the prototype for French films of pessimism and the character doomed by fate.

1937 France Jean Renoir (b. 1894) directed *La Grande Illusion*. He said he was more and more in favour of setting up a scene in depth and altering the image by moving the camera around within it, as opposed to changing the image by the now established montage technique of cutting from one shot to another. This and *La Règle du Jeu* (1939) are considered his greatest films.

1937 Spain Pablo Picasso painted *Guernica*.

1937 U.S.A. The photographer Margaret Bourke-White (b. 1904) published *You Have Seen Their Faces*, a study of the southern States. At this time there was a strong interest in documentary photographs in America; the picture was held to be a document in itself and to need no text. Other outstanding documentary photographers were Walker Evans (b. 1903) and Dorothea Lange (1895–1965).

1937 U.S.A. The German-American artist Lyonel Feininger (1871–1956) returned to work in America after painting in Germany and France. He was associated with 'golden section' cubism and also worked at the Bauhaus 1919–1933.

1937 U.S.A. Death of Irving Thalberg, the creative producer responsible for the opulent style of MGM studio pictures.

1938 U.S.S.R. Mark Donskoi (b. 1897) began the trilogy of films on Maxim Gorky: *Childhood of Gorky, Among People, My Universities.*

*1938
J. Ladisla and George Biro made first practical ball-point pen. Nylon discovered.*

HISTORICAL EVENTS	LITERATURE	DANCE & DRAMA	MUSIC

1938 France *La Nausée* by Jean-Paul Sartre (b. 1905), philosopher, novelist, playwright, essayist and editor: the book was a semi-autobiographical novel, propounding his theories that man's existence has no essence, no pre-determined purpose, so he must create a meaning for it, assuming responsibility for his own destiny. Sartre was considered the leading existentialist writer.

1938 Poland *Ferdydurke* by Witold Gombrowicz (1904–1969), modernist novelist and playwright.

1938 England Agnes de Mille (b.1908), American choreographer, first produced her ballet *Rodeo* as a short comedy of great vigour. She later produced an extended version for Ballets Russes de Monte Carlo (1942). It became the first important American ballet.

*1939
German invasion
of Poland began
Second World
War.
Franco pre-
eminent in Spain.*

1939 Czechoslovakia *John the Fiddler* by Josef Hora (1891–1945), poet, novelist and journalist. He began as a Communist, writing political poetry; but later he turned to socialism and his poetry became more specifically Czech. This work was a narrative poem about a returning exile.

1939 England *Goodbye to Berlin* by Christopher Isherwood (b. 1904) novelist and playwright: the book was a series of stories, all observed by a passive character, who recorded events as does a camera.

1939 Hungary *The Book of Jonah* by Mihály Babits (1883–1941), poet, novelist, translator, critic and editor of the literary magazine *Nyugat*. He endeavoured, though without success, to create a non-political literature.

1939 Martinique *Return to my Native Land* by Aimé Cesaire (b. 1913). The poem showed strong surrealist influence, and is probably the best known expression of 'Blackness' and African values.

1939 Spain *Laura, O La Soledad Sin Remedio* by Pio Baroja y Nessi (1872–1956), realistic novelist. His work was deliberately poor technically, because he maintained that life is not stylistically perfect, and the novel should represent life.

1939 U.S.A. *The Grapes of Wrath* by John Steinbeck (1902–1968), novelist and short-story writer. He wrote on the theme of injustice, often setting his stories in his native California. He was awarded the Nobel Prize in 1962.

1939 India The dancer Menaka founded a school at Khandala to teach Kathakali, Manipuri, Kathak and Bharata Natyan dancing. Her own ballets were based on Indian mythology and classical drama; her choreography was influenced by Western ballet and free dance. She attempted a mixture of Indian dance styles within one ballet.

1939 Mexico First performance in Mexico City by the dancer Anna Sokolow (b.1915) of the Martha Graham company. She founded a modern dance school in Mexico shortly afterwards.

1939 Monaco First performance of *Capriccio Espagñol*, ballet by Léonide Massine and La Argentinita to music by Rimsky-Korsakov, designed by Mariano Andrèu.

1939 Yugoslavia Return of the dancers Ana Roje and Oscar Harmoš who had both studied under Nicolas Legat in London. Ana Roje became Legat's assistant and the perpetuator of his system of teaching; Oscar Harmoš had also studied free-dance choreography with Ballet Jooss. They became prima ballerina and choreographer of the Zagreb Ballet, which had been under strong Russian influence.

1939 England Daily lunch-time concerts were inaugurated at National Gallery, London, by Myra Hess (1890–1965), English pianist, and they continued until 1946.

1939 England/Germany Popular songs at the beginning of World War II in Britain: *Hang Out the Washing on the Siegfried Line* and *The Last Time I saw Paris*; in Germany: *Wir Fahren Gegen England* and *Lili Marlene*, the latter gaining great popularity in Britain.

1939 U.S.A Establishment of the All American Youth Orchestra under Leopold Anton Stanislaw Stokowski (1882–1977).

| ARCHITECTURE | THREE DIMENSIONAL ART | VISUAL ARTS | INVENTIONS & DISCOVERIES |

VISUAL ARTS

1938 Canada Death of Horatio Walker (b. 1858) painter of landscape and peasant scenes.

1938 England Anthony Asquith (1902–1968) directed *Pygmalion*, an adaptation of Shaw's play which was considered his best pre-war film. He returned, successfully, to filming plays later in his career.

Carol Reed (1907–1976) directed *The Stars Look Down*, which showed documentary influence in its choice of subject matter: a mining village.

In photography beginning of *Picture Post* magazine encouraged the use of the miniature camera by any available light, instead of flash; pictures had dramatic impact at the expense of perfect definition.

1938 Germany The painter Max Beckmann (1884–1950) left Germany as a refugee and went to the Netherlands. His large-scale allegorical paintings expressed a concern for social and philosophical values; his work was strongly influenced by experience of the First World War.

*c.***1938 U.S.A.** Jackson Pollock (1912–1956) turned away from American nationalist painting under the influence of the Mexican mural artists and the Surrealists. He began to develop his own version of surrealist 'automatic' painting by dripping paint on to canvas.

1939–1945 England The Crown Film Unit wartime documentaries included work by Richard Massingham (1898–1953) and Humphrey Jennings (1907–1950), who has been called a 'poet of documentary film', and had an unusual eye for symbols of English life and thought.

1939 Australia The *Melbourne Herald* Exhibition brought contemporary arts to the general public for the first time. The modern movement had flourished since *c.*1913, but not in the public eye.

1939 Belgium Death of Frits van den Berghe (b. 1883), pioneer of Belgian expressionism. His fantastic, nightmare images were also fore-runners of surrealism.

ARCHITECTURE

1939–1954 USA Institute of Technology, Illinois, by Ludwig Mies van der Rohe was a new campus planned with cubic simplicity and logic: the buildings were of steel-skeleton construction with brick wall panels.

THREE DIMENSIONAL ART

1939 U.S.A. The Allen Press was founded in San Francisco as a private printing house.

INVENTIONS & DISCOVERIES

1939 Paul Müller synthesized D.D.T. Uranium atom split.

USA: Seagram building in New York city designed by Mies van der Rohe

1939 U.S.A. *The Day of the Locust*, a novel by Nathanael West (1903–1940), was a grim, spare yet compassionate picture of Hollywood.

*1940
Battle of Britain
at its peak.
Japan invaded
French Indo-
China.*

1940–1970 England *Strangers and Brothers* by C. P. (Charles Percy) Snow (b. 1905), novelist, scientist and civil servant: a sequence of 11 novels, narrated by 'Lewis Eliot' (Snow himself), and concerned with ethics, science, and public affairs.

1940–1962 U.S.S.R. *Poem Without a Hero* by Anna Gorenko, called Anna Akhmatova (1889–1966), a leading member of the Acmeists, a group of poets who reacted against symbolism and demanded a return to a harder, more precise mood and expression.

1940 Canada *Hath Not a Jew . . .* by A. M. Klein (b. 1909), a poet and novelist writing from the standpoint of a committed Jew. His work was truly original, and he discarded all nineteenth-century influences.

1940 England *Darkness at Noon*, a book on Soviet communism by Arthur Koestler (b. 1905), Hungarian-born British novelist, playwright, philosopher and journalist. He is concerned with the capacity of the human mind for both creativity and destruction.

1940 Norway *The Seed* by Tarjei Vesaas (1897–1970), a poet, playwright, critic and novelist writing in the 'New Norwegian' or *landsmal*. He wrote regional novels about peasant life.

1940 U.S.A. *For Whom the Bell Tolls* by Ernest Miller Hemingway (1898–1961), novelist and short-story writer. Pre-occupied with death and the necessity of living a futile life with courage, he wrote a spare narrative style with laconic dialogue.

1940 U.S.A. *The Man Who Loved Children* by Christina Stead (b. 1902), an Australian-born novelist living in America; she was influenced by the French tradition.

1940–1941 Australia First ballets presented in Melbourne by Edouard Borovansky (1902–1959) who came to Australia with Ballet Russe de Monte Carlo in 1936–1937. A company was also started in Sydney by Hélène Kirsova, of the same Ballet Russe, who presented her first season in 1941.

1940 England First performance of *Peter and the Wolf*, successful comic ballet by Frank Staff (b.1918). Post-expressionist choreographers using their own understanding of the classical tradition were considered more successful in comedy than in serious dramatic or abstract ballet.

1940 U.S.A. Foundation of Ballet Theatre, a touring company in the tradition of the Russian repertory company. It developed from an earlier company led by Mikhail Mordkin.

1940 U.S.A. Publication of *Kaleidophone*, a manual on musical theory which has become known as the 'Schillinger system', by Joseph Schillinger (1895–1943), American conductor, theorist and composer of Ukrainian birth.

1940 U.S.A. Béla Bartók (b. 1881), Hungarian pianist and composer, went to America, where he remained until his death in 1945.

1940 Switzerland Alberto Giacometti, sculptor, began to make human forms of a skeletal, emaciated appearance: these were influential on contemporary sculpture.

1940 U.S.A. Charles Eames (b. 1909) and Eero Saarinen (1910–1961), furniture designers, were prizewinners at the Museum of Modern Art competition for 'Organic Design in Home Furnishings': they entered shell-form moulded chairs uniting back, seat and arm-rests in one.

Switzerland: 'Man Pointing' by Alberto Giacometti

1939 England Lectures given by Roger Fry (1866–1934) at Cambridge were published posthumously, and are considered among the greatest works of art criticism in the twentieth century. Fry had been a strong formative influence on taste since *c*.1910.

1939 France Marcel Carné (b. 1909) directed *Le Jour se Lève*, considered the best of contemporary French studies in romantic pessimism.

1939 Mexico David Alfaro Siqueiros (b. 1896) returned after working as a propaganda artist, and fighting, in the Spanish Civil War. He began the series of vast murals which occupied him until 1947 and embodied his realist theories. He was considered the leader of left-wing art in Mexico; his work was overwhelmingly concerned with the theme of struggle.

1939 USA Ernst Lubitsch (1892–1947), the German-born film director, directed *Ninotchka*, his comedies remained European in spirit and often in setting.

1940–1942 England Henry Moore (b.1898), sculptor and draughtsman, drew studies of the London Tube air-raid shelters while he was an official war artist. The drawings, in pen, wash and gouache, convey a three-dimensional solidity in the forms of the sheltering civilians.

1940–1948 U.S.A. The German-born painter Joseph Albers (b. 1888) made a series called Graphic Tectonics (black-and-white prints), exploiting the vertical and horizontal line. He had always been interested in rectangular shapes and later concentrated on coloured squares.

c.**1940 Australia** Beginning of the active period of G. Russell Drysdate (b. 1912), painter of landscapes in the 'outback' with a strong abstract and surrealist influence. He is considered next after Tom Roberts as an innovator in Australian landscape.

1940 England The artist Ben Nicholson (b. 1894) settled in Cornwall and became the centre of a school of artists in St Ives. His best-known work was abstract, in a style similar to that of Mondrian.

HISTORICAL EVENTS

1941
U.S.A. declared war on Axis powers after Japanese bombed Pearl Harbor. German invasion of Russia.

1943
Mussolini fell from power in Italy.

LITERATURE

1941 Italy *The Fancy Dress Party* by Alberto Pincherle, called Alberto Moravia (b. 1907), novelist, short-story writer, playwright, journalist and critic. His themes were the moral decadence of the middle classes and the loneliness of men. He was also a critic of Fascism; this book poked fun at Mussolini.

1941 Italy *Conversation in Sicily* by Elio Vittorini (1908–1966), short-story writer, critic and novelist. He believed that literature should be concerned with social ethics. Through his translations he helped to increase Italian awareness of the American novel.

1941 Turkey Publication of *Bizarre*, a volume of poetry by three poets: Orhan Veli (1914–1951), who was a satirist; Melih Cavdet Anday (b. 1915), a socialist realist; and Otkay Rifat (b. 1914), whose work was experimental, often surrealist. The book revolutionized Turkish poetry.

1942 England *Put Out More Flags* by Evelyn Waugh (1903–1966), essayist, biographer and novelist. His early books were black satires on fashionable society; his later works were more tolerant, reflecting religious feelings (he was converted to Catholicism).

1942 New Zealand *Landfall in Unknown Seas* by Allen Curnow (b. 1911), a poet steeped in New Zealand history, and influenced by English Elizabethan and Jacobean poetry.

1942 Spain *The Family of Pascal Duarte* by José Camilo Cela (b. 1916), editor, travel writer, novelist and short-story writer. His style, which he originated, was called *tremendista*, because his accounts of horror and brutality provoked a tremendous reaction.

1942 Sweden *The Man Without a Way*, poetry by Erik Lindegren (1910–1968), poet, librettist, critic and translator. He helped to establish modernism in Sweden.

1943 Japan *The Makioka Sisters*, a novel by Tanizaki Junichiro (1836–1965): it is a *roman fleuve*, without any plot or any account of emotion, but giving a photographic description of life.

DANCE & DRAMA

1941 The Netherlands The Amsterdam Muncipal Opera Ballet Company was formed from the Georgi Ballet, founded by Yvonne Georgi in 1936.

1941 U.S.A. Ted Shawn (1891–1972) began to organize an annual dance festival at Jacob's Pillow. He was strongly influenced by primitive and other ethnic dances as well as by sophisticated oriental dance. He used classical ballet choreography, but not its traditional music. His festival was important in extending the range of American dance; and he was a strong influence on Martha Graham.

1941 U.S.S.R. Vladmir Bourmeister (1904–1971) appointed chief choreographer and balletmaster of the Stanislavsky and Nemirovich-Danchenko Lyric-Theatre Ballet.

1942 Indonesia The Japanese occupying army encouraged the national theatre group Maya, which was the first to take modern, realistic drama on tour. The group, which was led by Usmar Ismail, dissolved in 1950.

1942 U.S.A. First performance of the ballet *Pillar of Fire* by Antony Tudor (b.1908), his first successful ballet in America.

1943 Brazil *The Wedding Dress* by Nélson Rodrigues (b.1912) novelist and playwright. His early plays were modelled on Greek drama and included a chorus.

1943 England Vera Volkova (b.1904) began teaching ballet in London, following the methods of her own teacher Vaganova. She later taught at Teatro alla Scala, Milan, and the Royal Danish Ballet.

1943 France *Le Soulier de Satin* by Paul Claudel (1868–1955), diplomat and dramatist, working in close collaboration with actor/director Jean-Louis Barrault (b.1910). Claudel was a Catholic who expressed his religious philosophy in his plays. He began writing for the stage in 1899, but was far ahead of his time in requiring a form of 'total theatre' which was not then developed. He did not become known to the public until his plays were produced by Barrault.

MUSIC

1941 England Arnold Bax (1883–1953), prolific, English (self-confessed) romantic composer, appointed Master of the King's Music.

1941 England First performance of *A Child of Our Time* by Michael Kemp Tippett (b. 1905).

1943 England Committee for the Promotion of New Music formed in London.

1943 England Publications of *Annals of Opera: 1597–1940* by Alfred Loewenberg (1902–1949), British musical bibliographer, lexicographer and historian of German birth.

1943 Israel *Concerto for Oboe and Orchestra* by Alexander Uriah Boscovich (b. 1908), Israeli composer, was the first effort made by any composer to introduce genuine Oriental elements into a musical score.

ARCHITECTURE

USA: The Guggenheim Museum designed by Frank Lloyd Wright

1943–1960 USA Guggenheim Museum, New York, by Frank Lloyd Wright was one of his best known works, with the exterior an outward expression of the interior arrangement.

THREE DIMENSIONAL ART

1941 U.S.A. Death of Gutsom Borglum, sculptor: he was responsible for the mountain-sculpture memorials to Washington, Jefferson, Lincoln and Roosevelt at Mount Rushmore. They were executed with pneumatic drills and dynamite, and were unfinished at his death.

VISUAL ARTS

1941–1946 Australia Publication of the *Angry Penguins*, an *avant-garde* journal of the arts. It supported the early work of Australian expressionists.

1941 India Death of the painter Amrita Sher Gil (b. 1913), who was influenced by Gauguin and painted the humbler people of India in large-scale, brightly coloured pictures. Her influence on contemporary artists was considerable.

1941 U.S.A. John Huston (b. 1906) directed *The Maltese Falcon*, the prototype for a series of distinguished gangster films.

1941 U.S.A. Orson Welles (b. 1915), directed *Citizen Kane*. He used more camera movement than montage, filming whole scenes in one shot. He combined experience of radio and theatre with an extravagant use of cameras.

1942–1945 France The cinema under occupation was escapist, decorative and fantastic, e.g. Marcel Carné's *Les Enfants du Paradis*.

1942 Italy A new movement for social realism in cinema was begun by Luchino Visconti (1907–1976) with *Ossessione*, and christened 'neo-realism' by Giuseppe di Santis and Umberto Barbaro.

1942 U.S.A. Robert Motherwell (b. 1915) exhibited paintings for the first time (at the International Surrealist Exhibition, New York). He worked in a variety of techniques, including collage, and showed a strong interest in the European tradition of modern art.

1942 U.S.A. Death of the painter Grant Wood (b. 1892): he had studied as a stained-glass artist in Germany, and his later work was influenced by the Flemish and early German painting he saw there.

1943 Belgium Death of Gustave de Smet (b. 1877), pioneer of Belgian expressionist painting. His later paintings, landscapes, were noted for their lyrical quality.

INVENTIONS & DISCOVERIES

1942 Magnetic tape invented. First nuclear reactor constructed.

HISTORICAL EVENTS

*1944
'D-Day' landings in Normandy.*

*1945
Germany surrendered following Hitler's death.
U.S.A. dropped atomic bomb on Hiroshima and Nagasaki; Japan surrendered.*

LITERATURE

1943 England *The Near and the Far* by L. H. (Leo Hamilton) Myers (1881–1944): a collection in one volume of four novels, set in India in the sixteenth century. The world it portrayed was imaginary and not historical reconstruction. Myers' chief concern was why people choose to stay alive.

1943 Greece *Amorgos* by Nikos Gatsos (b. 1915), poet and translator: a surrealist poem, written 'automatically' in a single night.

1944 Australia *100 Poems* by Kenneth Slessor (1901–1971), a member of the Vision Group. His most important poem was *Five Visions of Captain Cook*.

1944 Belgium *The Space Within* by Henri Michaux (b. 1898), poet, prose writer and artist. He is best known for his short-story sketches about Mr Plume, a Chaplinesque 'little man'.

1944 England *Left Hand, Right Hand* by Osbert Sitwell (1892–1969), poet, novelist and short-story writer. He was the brother of Sacheverell (b. 1897), essayist and poet, and Edith (1887–1964), poet, biographer and critic. This book is one of a series of autobiographies.

1944 Ireland *There Were No Windows* by Norah Hoult (b. 1898), a novelist influenced by Henry Handel Richardson and Christina Stead. The book was about an old woman in the London Blitz.

1945 Austria *Der Tod Des Vergil* by the novelist Hermann Broch (1886–1951). He was concerned mainly with the value of art to humanity.

1945 Canada *Two Solitudes*, a novel by Hugh Maclennan (b. 1907), an English-Canadian writer concerned with the problems of Canada's divided French/English culture. He first published because he felt the lack of contemporary Canadian fiction.

1945 Italy *Il Canzoniere* by the poet Umberto Poli, called Umberto Saba (1883–1957). He lived in Trieste, which he felt was cut off culturally from the rest of Italy. He dealt with homely subjects, his own childhood, marriage and family, in simple language.

DANCE & DRAMA

1943 Switzerland *Das Heilige Experiment* by Fritz Hochwalder (b.1911), Viennese born playwright. He writes on moral conflicts or conflicts of ideas, and observes the Unities.

1944 France *Huis Clos* by Jean-Paul Charles Aymond Sartre (b.1905) playwright and leader of the Existentialist movement, whose philosophy is contained in his plays.

1944 U.S.A. First performance of the ballet *Fancy Free* by Jerome Robbins (b.1918), to music by Leonard Bernstein: it combined classical choreography with dance-hall movements and acrobatic dancing. His first important comedy ballet, it was influential on American dance. He expanded it into a stage musical *On the Town* and later worked on the film version.

1944 U.S.A. First performance of the ballet *Appalachian Spring* by Martha Graham, to music by Aaron Copland.

1944 U.S.A. First performance of *Danses Concertantes*, a ballet by George Balanchine to music by Stravinsky: it was performed by Ballet Russe de Monte Carlo.

1945 England Foundation in Kendal of Theatre Workshop, under the artistic director Joan Littlewood (b.1914): the members were dissatisfied with the commercial theatre artistically, socially and politically. At first a touring company, they settled at the Theatre Royal, Stratford, London in 1953.

1945 India The All India Dance Festival in Bombay attracted important dancers from all over India. Bombay was a centre of ballet between 1940 and 1950: the Indian People's Theatre Association presented propaganda expressionist work; the Indian National Theatre and New Stage presented historical and mythological dramatic ballets using traditional song and dance forms, or popular adaptations of them.
First of the occasional presentations by Prithvi Theatre, which was composed of Prithviraj and his son Raj Kapoor, both cinema stars. Their plays were in Hindi and normally dealt with an issue of national concern; the most famous, *Pathan*, was about the effects of Partition on personal life.

MUSIC

1944 England The B.B.C. took over the trusteeship of the 'Proms' from Henry Wood.

1944 U.S.S.R. First performance of the opera *War and Peace* by Sergey Sergeyevich Prokofiev (1891–1953) in Moscow.

1944 U.S.A. Yehudi Menuhin (b. 1916), American violinist, commissioned Belá Bartók's (1881–1945) violin concerto.

1945 England Benjamin Britten (1913–1976) composed *Young Person's Guide to the Orchestra*, variations and fugue on a theme from Purcell's *Abdelazer*. The score was commissioned by the Ministry of Education as music for a film *The Instruments of the Orchestra* but it soon established itself as a concert piece in its own right. Each of the 13 variations spotlights a different instrument or group of instruments. Also the opera *Peter Grimes* was first performed.

France: artist's impression of a comb designed by René Lalique

1945–1950 U.S.A. David Smith (1906–1965), painter who turned to sculpture, began to make welded steel, slightly surrealist, constructions: his sculpture related to abstract expressionist painting.

1945 France Death of René Lalique (b. 1860), jeweller and glass-maker whose work embodied the Art Deco style.

1945 Gold Coast The English potter Michael Cardew (b. 1901), after working as a college instructor, moved to the village of Vume-Dugame on the Volta River and began making stoneware from local resources. The pots were mainly bronze-green or blue, ash-glazed and decorated with colour from iron oxide. Cardew left the Gold Coast in 1948 but later returned to West Africa to work in Nigeria.

1943 Canada Death of Maurice Cullen (b. 1866), impressionist painter of landscape and city scenes. He had worked in France between 1889 and 1895.

1943 U.S.A. Rufino Tamayo (b. 1899), the Mexican artist, painted an abstract mural at Smith College, New York. From this point he turned to an original and violent expressionism.

1943 U.S.A. William Wellman (1896–1976) directed *The Ox-Bow Incident*, a Western much praised and made as a deliberate attempt to work outside the studio system and the conventions that system imposed.

1943 U.S.S.R. Alexander Dovzhenko (1894–1956) and his wife Yulia Solntseva (b. 1901) directed *Battle for the Ukraine*, an important war documentary made by giving personal instruction to 24 different cameramen distributed along the battle front.

1944 France The Hungarian graphic artist Victor de Vasarely (b. 1908) began painting. He had been taught by Moholy-Nagy; his style was severe and simple. Later he developed an interest in kinetic painting (pictures with the illusion of movement).

1944 England *Three Studies of Figures for the base of a Crucifixion* by Francis Bacon (b. 1910) aroused an instant controversy. Bacon's paintings made use of timeless images of the repulsive and disturbing.

1944 England Graham Sutherland (b. 1903), painter of landscapes and abstract studies, began to be interested in the thorn, thistle, tree and other organic motifs that dominated his work from then on.

1944 U.S.A. Billy Wilder (b. 1906), who had worked as a writer for Ernst Lubitsch, made *Double Indemnity*. It typified the American 'film noir'—films treating issues of human and social corruption in a glamorous visual style.

1945 Canada Death of the landscape painter Emily Carr (b.1871), who was inspired by Indian art and the nationalist Canadian art of the Group of Seven (1913–1933).

1945
First atomic
fission bomb
exploded.

HISTORICAL EVENTS	LITERATURE	DANCE & DRAMA	MUSIC

LITERATURE

1945 Canada *Bonheur d'Occasion* by Gabrielle Roy (b. 1909), the first French-Canadian realistic novelist of any standing.

1945 Chile Lucila Godoy Alcayaga, called Gabriela Mistral (1889–1957) became the first woman, and the first Latin American, to be awarded the Nobel Prize for literature (1945).

1945 China *Rickshaw Boy* by Shu Ch'ing Ch'un, called Lao-She (b. 1897), a novelist, short-story writer and playwright highly regarded as a satirist.

1945 England *Animal Farm* by Eric Blair, called George Orwell (1903–1950), novelist, journalist and critic: an allegory on Stalinism in the form of a fable, it is considered a classic and unique in English literature.

1945 France *Le Plupart du Temps*, early poems by Pierre Reverdy (1889–1972), poet and critic. His poetry reflected cubist techniques.

1945 Persia *Haji Aqa* by Sadiq Hidayat (1902–1951), novelist and short-story writer. Strongly influenced by French culture, he was also keenly interested in Persian history and folk-lore, which he used in his work.

1945 Switzerland *L'Homme Foudroyé* by Frédéric Sauser Hall, called Blaise Cendrars (1887–1961), poet and novelist. His early poetry was translated by Dos Passos, on whom he had a strong influence. This book is a quasi-autobiographical novel self-exploratory in mood.

1945 U.S.A. *Black Boy* by Richard Wright (1908–1960), a Negro novelist writing critically of the Negro predicament.

1945 Yugoslavia *The Bridge on the Drina* by Ivo Andrić (b. 1892), novelist and poet. Set mainly in the period of Turkish rule in his native Bosnia, his work was epic in scope and naturalistic in style, softened by lyricism. He was awarded the Nobel Prize in 1961.

1946 Guatemala *Mr President*, a novel by Miguel Angel Asturias (b. 1899): the book is about tyranny. Asturias was awarded the Nobel Prize in 1967.

DANCE & DRAMA

1945 Italy Eduardo de Filippo (b.1900) actor, director and playwright, founded his own theatre company. His production methods follow those of the *commedia dell' arte.*

1945 U.S.S.R. The ballet *Gayané* was created by Nina Anisimova (b.1909), one of the first women to work as choreographer in the Soviet Union.

1946 England Sadler's Wells Ballet moved to Covent Garden, with Frederick Ashton as chief choreographer. His *Symphonic Variations* was successful as an abstract ballet to music by Franck.

1946 France Boris Kokhno and Christian Bérard encouraged Roland Petit (b.1924) to form the Compagnie des Champs-Élysées: a ballet company which produced work in the late Diaghilev style of 'cocktail' ballets, composed of deliberately mixed incongruous features.

1946 India The dance-drama *Discovery of India* was produced by Indian National Theatre on tour. They were originally amateurs who used drama to put across nationally-important issues to the widest possible audience, using a style that was less academic than the classical but still a traditional pantomime style.
Krishna Kutty (b.1924) choreographed his first major ballet, *Chitra*, for the dancer Hima Kesarcodi. He had been a noted Kathakali dancer and teacher, working with Menaka at her school where he took the unusual step of learning the other classical styles as well as teaching his own.

1946 Siam The end of the Second World War produced a brief period of American-influenced modern theatre. Its most successful playwright was the American-educated Kamut Chandruang.

MUSIC

1945 England Philharmonia Orchestra formed in London.

1945 Federal Republic of Germany Musica Viva, an organization for promoting contemporary music, founded by the German composer Karl Amadeus Hartmann (1905–1963).

1945 U.S.A. Death of Béla Bartók (b. 1881), Hungarian pianist and composer.

*c.***1945 U.S.A.** Bop, a style of jazz, also known as bebop, evolved in New York.

1946 England The Third Programme, entirely devoted to music and broadcasts of a cultural nature, was opened by the B.B.C.

1946 Nuremberg Trials. First meeting of U.N. General Assembly.

| ARCHITECTURE | THREE DIMENSIONAL ART | VISUAL ARTS | INVENTIONS & DISCOVERIES |

1945 U.S.A. *Kouros* by Isamu Noguchi (b. 1904), Japanese-American sculptor: his work was mainly in sheet metal, abstract but inspired by natural form.

1945 Italy Roberto Rossellini (1906–1977) directed *Roma, città aperta*, a reconstruction of the anti-fascist resistance. It was the first 'neo-realist' film to make an international impact.

1945 England The watercolourist Edward Burra (1905–1976) turned away from surrealism to a more naturalistic style. His work was unusual in English watercolour because of its comment on the darker side of contemporary life.

1945 Mexico Alfredo Zalce (b. 1908) painted the mural *Estampas de Yucatan*. He was one of the more successful members of a propagandist art group, Workshop of Popular Graphic Art, formed in 1937.

1946–1952 France Unité d'Habitation, Marseilles, by Le Corbusier is more aggressive than his earlier work, and in a style later architects developed into 'brutalism': emphasis on mass and on the untreated surface of the material, which was often concrete; the proportions of the building were worked out on his modular system and it contained all community needs.

1946–1947 England Henry Moore, sculptor, had his first one-man exhibitions in America: he broke new ground in English sculpture through his interest in direct carving and in the nature of his materials.

1946 England Lynn Chadwick (b. 1914), sculptor, began to experiment with mobiles, followed by metal structures with a rough finish and some mobile element.

1946 U.S.A. Charles Eames produced his first 'body-moulded' curved plywood chair for the Hermann Miller Furniture Company. He also began to develop storage units and tables, all light, colourful, and derived from stock industrial parts. Eero Saarinen developed a shell-chair in fibreglass, the 'womb' chair.

1946 Australia Sidney Nolan (b. 1917) began his series of paintings of the outlaw Ned Kelly, a subject characteristic of his pre-occupation with legends of Australian history. His main concern was the juxtaposition of symbols of European civilization and Australian landscape, the latter shown mainly by the use of colour wash.

1946 England David Lean (b.1908) directed *Great Expectations*; the film marked a change in his style from the economical to the expansive.

Death of the artist Paul Nash (1889–1946), landscape painter and official war artist of two world wars. He saw himself as a successor to Blake in expressing mystic visions with an absolute clarity and realism.

1946 Finland Death of Helene Schjerfbeck (b.1862), painter of interior scenes. Her work between 1890 and 1900 was noted for her use of colour. Her later work became progressively simpler.

USA: chair designed by Charles Eames

HISTORICAL EVENTS	LITERATURE	DANCE & DRAMA	MUSIC

HISTORICAL EVENTS

1947
India and Pakistan gained independence.

1948
Communist rule established in Czechoslovakia.

LITERATURE

1946 Greece *Zorba the Greek*, a novel by Nikos Kazantzakis (1885–1957), poet, playwright, critic, essayist, translator and novelist. He studied under Bergson, and was also greatly influenced by Nietzsche.

1946 South Africa *Mine Boy* by Peter Abrahams (b. 1919), a novelist of mixed South African/Abyssinian blood who was concerned about the exploitation of South Africans.

1946 U.S.A. *Paterson* by William Carlos Williams (1883–1963), novelist and poet. He recorded the local and particular, often the commonplace, in idiomatic language, believing that American life can only be expressed in the American, not the English, language.

1946 Wales *Deaths and Entrances* by the poet Dylan Thomas (1914–1953). His exuberant poetry was in marked contrast to the poetry of the late 1930s, being full of imagery and glorying in language. He also wrote autobiographical accounts of Welsh life. He gave readings of his own work and became a 'popular' poet.

1947 England *Under the Volcano* by Malcolm Lowry (1909–1957), novelist and poet. The book, about an alcoholic former consul, was set in Mexico. It was symbolic, but treated realistically.

1947 France *La Peste* by Albert Camus (1913–1960), novelist, essayist, journalist, playwright and short-story writer. He was born in Algeria. His early work showed existentialist sympathies; later he developed a more humanitarian attitude. He was awarded the Nobel Prize in 1957.

1947 Italy *Life of a Man*, poems by Giuseppe Ungaretti (1888–1970), poet, essayist and translator. He was influenced by Leopardi and Mallarmé. He was the founder of the Hermetic school of poetry, in which purity of language and the texture of sounds and words were of paramount importance.

1947 South Africa *Mafeking Road* by H. C. Bosman (1905–1951), an Afrikaner novelist and short-story writer, writing in English, giving objective pictures of Afrikaner life.

DANCE & DRAMA

1946 Sweden Birgit Cullberg (b.1908), trained at the Jooss-Leeder school, became director of Swedish Dance Theatre.

1947 France *Les Bonnes* by Jean Genet (b.1909), a playwright who developed Artaud's concept of the Theatre of Cruelty. Ritual and the acting-out of fantasies are an important part of Genet's theatre.

1947 India Establishment in Bombay of Theatre Unit, a group originally aiming to present plays in English. They formed a link between Indian and Western theatre, from which they imported plays, staging methods and acting techniques.

1947 Mexico *The Gesticulator* by Rudolpho Usigli (b.1905), a playwright critical of the Mexican character: his approach to drama is not unlike that of Bernard Shaw.

1947 Monaco American impresario George, Marquis de Cuevas (1886–1961) took control of the Grand Ballet de Monte Carlo, which was particularly successful in the classical repertoire. It became the Grand Ballet du Marquis de Cuevas in 1950.

1947 Scotland Foundation of the Edinburgh International Festival of Music and Drama.

1947 U.S.A. *A Streetcar Named Desire* by Thomas Lancer (Tennessee) Williams (b.1914), writer of controversial and outspoken drama.

1948 Canada *'tit Coq* by Gratien Gélinas, whose stage name was Fridolin (b.1910), French/Canadian actor and playwright: this play's entirely convincing atmosphere and characters make it a landmark in Canadian theatre.

1948 Canada First Canadian Ballet Festival; it was sponsored by the Winnipeg ballet company, which remained non-professional until 1949.

1948 Denmark First performance of the ballet *Études* by Harald Lander (1905–1971) to music by Czerny.

1948 England *The Lady's Not for Burning* by Christopher Fry (b.1907), English poetic dramatist.

MUSIC

1946 Spain Death of Manuel de Falla (b. 1876), Spanish composer.

1946 Wales The Welsh National Opera Company founded.

1947 England First performance, at Glyndebourne, of (Edward) Benjamin Britten's (1913–1976) *Albert Henry*; the libretto by Eric Crozier was taken from Guy de Maupassant's story *Madame Husson's May King*.

1947 England Formation of the English Opera Group, the National Youth Orchestra of Great Britain and the New Era Concert Society.

1947 England The Royal Philharmonic Orchestra was formed by Thomas Beecham.

1947 England The African Music Society was founded by Hugh Tracey and Dr Winifred Hoernlé.

1947 France Publication of *Schoenberg et son Ecole* by René Leibowitz (1913–1972), Franco-Polish composer and conductor of Russian parentage. It was first full length account of the Schoenberg school in any language.

1947 Scotland First International Festival of Music and Drama in Edinburgh.

1948 England First long-playing records introduced by Columbia Company of America.

1948 England The Aldeburgh Festival was founded by Benjamin Britten, Eric Crozier and Peter Pears. It is held for about a week in June each year, featuring modern music, predominantly by Britten, and also lectures, poetry readings and exhibitions of painting.

1947 Italy The railway station, Rome, by Eugenio Montuori and Associates is considered one of the best post-war Italian buildings, built to a design of clarity and economy.

1947 England Sir Gordon Russell (b. 1892) became director of the Council of Industrial Design. His work was an application of Arts and Crafts Movement principles to machine production.

1947 Italy The sculptor and painter Lucio Fontana (1899–1968) founded the spatialist movement. He argued that the artist should use all available modern materials and discoveries and should abandon the accepted boundaries between art forms: art would then reflect the new surroundings of post-war society.

*c.***1947 Denmark** Beginning of an outstanding period in furniture-making: Danish hand-made furniture is made not by a single artist but by collaboration between a designer and a cabinet-maker, of whom Hans Wegner and Finn Juhl, designers, Johannes Hansen and Niels Vodder, cabinet-makers, were noteworthy.

*c.***1947 Finland** The Arabia ceramics company was the first Scandinavian company to make a strong impact on European taste in table pottery; its elegant, austere style pioneered a popular fashion which is still flourishing.

England: chest of drawers designed by Sir Gordon Russell

1947–1952 England The film magazine *Sequence* campaigned for a cinema that reflected the whole of British life, rather than south-east English urban life. It was edited then by Lindsay Anderson (b.1923), Gavin Lambert, Karel Reisz and Penelope Houston.

1947 England Alex Mackendrick (b.1912) directed *Whisky Galore* for Ealing Studios. The 'Ealing Comedies' were considered the most imaginative English films of 1947–1955. Directors included Charles Crichton (b. 1910) who made *The Lavender Hill Mob*, Robert Hamer (1911–1963) who made *Kind Hearts and Coronets*, and Henry Cornelius (1913–1958) who made *Passport to Pimlico*.

1947 France André Masson (b.1896) began to paint landscape in Provence. He had previously experimented with cubism and surrealism.

1947 France Jean Rouch (b.1917) began a series of documentaries: they were influenced by the Russian documentarist Dziga Vertov but improved by the smaller less obtrusive equipment now available.

1947 France Jacques Tati (b.1908) directed *Jour de Fête*, his first full-length comedy film in which an innocent central character unwittingly creates havoc in an organized world. Tati writes, directs and acts in his films.

*c.***1947 England** Victor Pasmore (b.1908), who was known for lyrical landscapes, moved from figurative to abstract painting.

1948 France The Dutch painter Karel Appel (b.1921) became a founder of the Cobra group of action painters in Paris. He worked on a huge scale, with some figurative content in his pictures. He considered the action of painting as an expression of emotion.

1948 Italy Vittorio di Sica (b.1907) and Cesare Zavattini (b.1902) made *Ladri di biciclette*, a film acted by non-professionals in real and often poor locations. They followed it with *Miracolo a Milano* (1951) and *Umberto D* (1952).

*1947
First supersonic
air flight.
Discovery of
main series of
Dead Sea
Scrolls.*

*1948
Peter Goldmark
invented the long-
playing record.
Transistor
invented.*

HISTORICAL EVENTS	LITERATURE	DANCE & DRAMA	MUSIC

LITERATURE

1948 Belgium *Pedigree* by the novelist Georges Sim, called Georges Simenon (b. 1903), master of the psychological crime novel.

1948 Iceland *The Atom Station* by Halldór Laxness (b. 1902), novelist, poet, playwright and essayist. His country's history was the main influence on his work, which included historical novels, modern stories of farmers and fishermen, and political satires. He was awarded the Nobel Prize in 1955.

1948 Senegal *Anthology of New Negro and Malagasi Poetry* by Leopold Sedar Senghor (b. 1906), poet and politician, Catholic and pan-Africanist. His poetry recalled that of Claudel. Although a poet of 'Blackness' he was concerned with integration, not black power.

1948 South Africa *Cry The Beloved Country*, an anti-apartheid novel by Alan Paton (b. 1903), a South African novelist writing in English.

1948 Sweden *Burnt Child* by Stig Dagerman (1923–1954), journalist, poet, playwright and novelist. A powerful and versatile writer, he had affinities with Strindberg.

1948 Turkey Poems of Yahya Kemal Beyatli (1884–1958), a professor at the university of Istanbul writing in the traditional manner with great vigour.

1948 USA *The Naked and the Dead* by Norman Mailer (b. 1923): it has been regarded as the best American novel of the Second World War.

1949 Argentina *The Aleph* by Jorge Luis Borges (b. 1900), poet and short-story writer. An anti-realist, and sometimes described as a mystic, he was influenced by Schopenhauer and R. L. Stevenson.

1949 England *The Edge of Being* by Stephen Spender (b. 1909), poet, critic, translator, editor and novelist. His earliest poems were Georgian but he soon came under the influence of his friend, Auden, and wrote about his chief concern, the state of society in the 1930s.

DANCE & DRAMA

1948 France *L'Etat de Siège* by Albert Camus (1913–1960): it was adapted from his own novel, *La Peste*. Camus wrote of the human conditions, which he regarded as absurd.

1948 France Foundation by Roland Petit (b 1924) of his own ballet company, with which he stayed until 1952. (The company was re-organized in 1953.) Its first production was *Les Demoiselles de la Nuit* in which the leading rôle was danced by Margot Fonteyn (b.1919), British ballerina trained by Ninette de Valoïs' Vic-Wells ballet, London.

1948 Japan Death of the actor Baigyoku, of the *kabuki* theatre in Osaka. His death was the end of a long tradition and the occasion of new experiments to modernize *kabuki*. New acting techniques were introduced and 'New Kabuki' scripts have been written by Hojo Hideji and Funahashi Seiichi.

1948 U.S.A. Formation of the New York City Ballet: founded, directed and strongly influenced by George Balanchine (b.1904), ballet-master of Diaghilev's Ballets Russes 1924–1929.

1948 U.S.A. First performance of the ballet *Fables of Our Time*, based on the work of James Thurber, by Charles Weidman (b.1901). He had trained with Ted Shawn and danced with Martha Graham's company before forming a company with Doris Humphrey (1927–1945). He was an influential teacher of modern dancers.

1949 Brazil *General Strike* by Guilherme Figueiredo (b.1915), a playwright who uses classical stories and legends as a basis for his work.

1949 France First performance in Paris of the ballet *Carmen* by Roland Petit, with Renée Jeanmaire dancing the leading rôle. Petit's ballets were important for the opportunities they gave to ballerinas.

1949 U.S.A. *Death of a Salesman* by Arthur Miller (b.1915) writer of tragedies about ordinary people. Classical tragedy always concerned great and noble characters.

MUSIC

1949 England Death of Richard Tauber (b. 1892), Austrian-born tenor.

1949 England First English long-playing records introduced by Decca.

1949 France International Music Council (UNESCO) founded in Paris.

1949 Federal Republic of Germany Death of Richard Strauss (b. 1864), German composer and conductor.

1950 U.S.A. Aaron Copland wrote *Piano Quartet*, one of his more complex works, in the serial manner.

1949 Communists controlled China; Chinese People's Republic proclaimed in Peking. North Atlantic Treaty signed.

1948 U.S.A. Jules Dassin (b.1911), directed *Naked City*. He exploited economic difficulties which necessitated small-scale films, and location shooting instead of studio sets. Social and psychological studies became the most suitable subjects for films that had to be cheaply made. The intrinsic quality of the script was therefore important.

1948 U.S.A. Willem de Kooning (b.1904), a Dutch-born artist, had his first one-man exhibition which established him as a leading abstract artist. He used abstract forms in black and white.

1949 USA Eames House, Santa Monica, California, by Charles Eames (born 1907) was an influential building because of its construction from prefabricated standard components in a totally modern style.

1949 USA New Canaan House, Connecticut, by Philip Johnson (born 1906) saw the style of Mies van der Rohe reach its ultimate development: it was a glazed box in which only the bathroom was enclosed.

1949–1950 USA Graduate Centre, Harvard University, Cambridge, Massachusetts, by Walter Gropius was one of several buildings he designed in America whilst Professor of Architecture at Harvard.

1949 USA Christ Lutheran Church, Minneapolis, by the Saarinens is an elegant and spacious brick-built church and one of their best known works.

1949 USSR Lomonosov State University, Moscow, by Rudiev and others is a typical Russian skyscraper of the twentieth century, combining American modernism with neo-Baroque.

1950 France Notre-Dame-du-Haut, Ronchamp, by Le Corbusier is moulded in concrete to create a huge sculptural form penetrated by windows placed at random; the church illustrated the architect's post-war aggressive or brutalist style.

1949 England First exhibition by the Austrian-born potter Lucie Rie (b. 1902). She and the German-born Hans Coper (b. 1920), with whom she worked, produced a highly sophisticated pottery inspired entirely by the designs and architecture of modern urban society. This distinguished them from their English contemporaries, whose work was mainly rooted in rustic folk traditions.

1949 England Graham Sutherland (b. 1903) painted his first portrait of Somerset Maugham.

1949 England Carol Reed (b.1906) directed *The Third Man*, which established the style already used in *Odd Man Out* (1947): he used realistic images, particularly of the decorative, and heightened them into symbolism.

1950–1955 India Satyajit Ray (b.1921) directed the film *Pather Panchali*, the story of a Bengali life, which won the 1956 Cannes Grand Prix.

1949 Philip Hench discovered Cortisone (compound E) as treatment for rheumatism.

1950–1960 England Reg Butler (b. 1913), sculptor, began to produce figurative works in place of his earlier abstract and constructivist pieces.

1950 Bolivia Death of Cecilio Guzmán de Rojas (b.1900), painter of landscape and Indian life, who was considered a pioneer of Bolivian national art.

1950 France The painter Roger Bissière (1888–1964) achieved international recognition for large-scale compositions presenting natural scenes in terms of colour patterns. he had painted natural landscape since before moving to Paris in 1910, when he experimented with cubism. His influence as a teacher was great, his work virtually unknown until 1950.

HISTORICAL EVENTS	LITERATURE	DANCE & DRAMA	MUSIC

1950
*Korean War
began.*

LITERATURE

1950 France *Un Barrage Contre le Pacifique* by Marguerite Donnadieu, called Duras (b. 1914), novelist and playwright. She was born in Indo-China. Concerned with the nature of time, she rejected the chronological narrative.

1950 Italy *The Moon and the Bonfire* by Cesare Pavese (1908–1950), novelist, poet, critic and translator. He translated Melville, Defoe, Faulkner and Joyce, and their influence was apparent in his own work. His books combined realism with symbolism.

1950 Uruguay *Short Life* by Juan Carlos Onetti (b. 1909), a novelist influenced by Faulkner, Dos Passos and Céline.

DANCE & DRAMA

1950 Burma Death of the actor U Po Sein, considered one of the greatest Burmese actors and important in establishing the good character of the theatre; actors were previously regarded as less than respectable. The most important type of dance-drama in Burma is the Indian-derived *zat pwé* which tells stories from Burmese history, centred on a virtuoso display by the leading dancers and accompanied throughout by an orchestra.

1950 Canada *At My Heart's Core* by Robertson Davies (b.1913), the most popular native Canadian dramatist.

1950 Canada Foundation of the National Ballet of Canada under Celia Franca (b.1921), who danced with Ballet Rambert, Sadler's Wells and the Metropolitan Ballet, of which she was ballet-mistress and principal dancer.

1950 England Formation of Festival Ballet by Anton Dolin (b.1904) and Alicia Markova (b.1910). (This developed from a company formed the previous year.)

1951
*Kingdom of
Libya
established.*

1951–1973 England 12 volumes comprising *A Dance to the Music of Time* by Anthony Powell (b. 1905): they are intricate and subtle comedies on English middle-class life.

1950 France *La Cantatrice Chauve* by Eugene Ionesco (b.1912), Romanian-born French playwright who describes himself as an objective observer of life, writing pure theatre with no social or political message. He virtually created the Theatre of the Absurd.

1950 Italy Teatro Popolare Italiano founded by Vittorio Gassmann (b.1912), actor/manager.

1950 U.S.A. Lee Strasberg (b.1901) became director of the Actors' Studio, which follows the principles of Stanislavsky (the Method).

1951 France *La Ville Dont le Prince est un Enfant* by Henri de Montherlant (b.1896), writer of psychological drama, usually within the context of the Catholic religion.

1951 India Foundation of the Nritya Darpana ballet company with Krishna Kutty and the dancer Shirin Vajifdar as co-directors. They took the company to Europe in 1952, providing the first sight of modern Indian ballet outside India.

MUSIC

1951 England First performance of the opera *Billy Budd* by Benjamin Britten (1913–1976).

1951 England Royal Festival Hall opened in London.

1951 England First Performance of the ballet *Donald of the Burthens* by Ian Whyte (1901–1960), at Covent Garden.

1951 France Pierre Boulez (b. 1925) composed *Polyphonie X* for 18 solo instruments.

1951 U.S.A. First performance of *Projections* and *Projections 2* for 'cello, flute, trumpet and violin by Morton Feldman (b. 1926), U.S. composer who introduced elements of chance into his music.

1951 U.S.A. *Amahl and the Night Visitors* by Gian Menotti (b. 1911) was the first opera to be written specially for a television production.

1951 U.S.A. Death of Arnold Schoenberg (b. 1874).

1951 U.S.A. Premiere of the *Second Symphony* of Charles Edward Ives (1874–1954) conducted by Leonard Bernstein.

ARCHITECTURE

1950 USA Lever House, New York, by Louis Skidmore (1897–1962) Nathaniel Owings (b.1903) and John Merrill (b.1896) is the first important post-war skyscraper, distinguished by its isolated site and green-glazed curtain walls on three sides.
India: design for part of the Kasmir tapestry made to cover wall in one of the Courts of Justice at Chandigarh, buildings designed by Le Corbusier

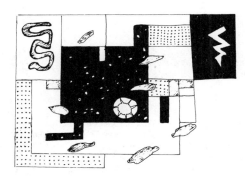

1951 England Royal Festival Hall, London, by Leslie Martin (1908–1977) and Sir Robert Matthew (born 1906) survives from the Festival of Britain, which finally converted English public taste to the modern style.

1951 India Chandigarh, East Punjab, was planned by Le Corbusier as a new state capital but only three principal buildings by the architect were completed, in a chunky sculptural concrete.

1951 USA General Motors Technical Institute, Warren, Michigan, by Eero Saarinen is a group of buildings of Miesian severity but softened by the incorporation of a central lake and the use of coloured glazed brick.

THREE DIMENSIONAL ART

1950 Italy Giacomo Manzu (b. 1908), sculptor, was commissioned to make a door for St Peter's Rome: his sculptural style was formed under the influence of Rodin and Maillol.

1950 Mexico The government organized a Salon de Plastica Mexicana where independent artists could exhibit free of charge and sell without commission.

1951 Japan Designs in reinforced concrete for two bridges in Peace Park, Hiroshima, by Isamu Noguchi, sculptor.

1951 U.S.A. *Hudson River Landscape*, David Smith (1906–1965), painter and sculptor; this was a 'drawing' of rods and wires in space. During the next decade he concentrated on the human figure.

VISUAL ARTS

1950 France Robert Bresson (b.1907) directed *Le journal d'un curé de campaigne*, the prototype for his films using classical tragic themes and austerity of presentation.

1950 Federal German Republic Photographic exhibition at Cologne showed work by Otto Steinert (b.1915), in which form and pattern predominated.

1950 Mexico Luis Buñuel (b.1900) directed *Los Olvidados*, his first notable film since 1932.

1950 Norway Henrik Sörensen (1882–1962) began his mural for Oslo Town Hall, one of the largest in Europe. His later work was allegorical and emotional; his early landscapes continued the nineteenth-century nationalist tradition and were influential on younger painters.

*c.***1950 Scotland** Alan Davie (b.1920), painter and goldsmith, began his active period in decorated, vividly coloured paintings which reflected his interest in Zen Buddhism and in magic.

*c.***1950 England** Beginning of the mature period of Terry Frost (b.1915) a painter who concentrated on abstracts exploring the nature of colours. Many of his paintings were inspired by St Ives in Cornwall.

*c.***1950 U.S.A.** The Russian-born expressionist painter Mark Rothko (1903–1970) began to develop his mature style, using juxtaposed rectangular panels of colour, although he avoided a hard, defining edge and aimed instead to create sensations in the spectator by the interaction of his colours where they came together. His style was in direct contrast to the frenzy of the 'action painters'.

1951–1952 USA *Adam*, a painting by Barnett Newman (1905–1970) characteristic of his style—a huge canvas of one colour divided into rectangles by vertical lines of a second colour. He was considered the most important American abstract expressionist painter, concerned with colour and flat-field composition.

1951 U.S.A. *Clarinets and Tin Horn* by Ben Shahn (1898–1969) typified his later concern with still life.

*1951
Electric power produced from atomic energy at Arcon, Idaho, U.S.A.*

HISTORICAL EVENTS	LITERATURE	DANCE & DRAMA	MUSIC
		1951–1956 Denmark First appointment of Niels Bjørn Larsen (b.1913) as artistic director of the Royal Danish Ballet. He held the post again 1960–1966.	
		1951 England John Cranko (1927–1973), South African dancer, choreographed *Pineapple Poll* to music by Sullivan for Sadler's Wells Theatre Ballet. It was his most successful comic ballet.	
		1951 England *Saints Day* by John Whiting (1915–1963) actor, playwright and dramatic critic.	
		1951 England *The Love of Four Colonels* by Peter Alexander Ustinov (b.1921) English actor, producer and playwright, who was trained in France under Michel Saint-Denis.	
1952 Queen Elizabeth II succeeded to British throne. European Coal and Steel Community founded.	**1952 Australia** *Between Two Tides* by Robert David Fitzgerald (b. 1902), an Australian poet, associated, though not closely, with *Vision*, and aware of European influences in poetry.	**1951 Italy** *La Regina Gli Insorti* by Ugo Betti (1892–1953), a playwright influenced by Pirandello.	**1952 U.S.A** First performance of the opera *Trouble in Tahiti* by Leonard Bernstein (b. 1918), U.S. conductor, composer and pianist, followed in 1953 by a musical, *Wonderful Town*.
	1952 Nigeria *The Palm Wine Drinkard* by Amos Tutuola (b. 1920), a Nigerian novelist writing his own idiosyncratic English. The book combined poetry, folk-lore, childish exaggeration and naive comment on modern life.	**1952 England** *The Deep Blue Sea* by Sir Terence Mervyn Rattigan (1911–1977) who was not interested in experimental theatre, but said he wrote for 'Aunt Edna', the ordinary member of the public who wants to be entertained.	
	1952 South Africa *Museum Pieces* by William Plomer (b. 1903), the first South African writing in English who was able to give an accurate, clear-sighted picture of the black man.	**1952 France** *Waiting for Godot* by Samuel Beckett (b.1906), Irish-born dramatist writing mainly in French. His plays express the view that life is meaningless and that human beings are unable to communicate. There is neither logical plot nor coherent dialogue.	
	1952 Turkey *The Moscow Symphony* by Nazim Hikmet (1902–1963), poet and novelist. A Marxist, he was particularly influenced by Mayakovsky. He wrote free verse, in modern language.	**1952 India** Formation of the Nat Mandal theatre group in Ahmedabad: it was influential in fostering interest in the theatre in Gujarat, which had little traditional drama. Important figures in Gujarati drama of this century were the playwright K. M. Munshi, who wanted to use theatre for political and social reform and to revive pre-colonial culture, and the actor-director Sundari, whose work combined folk elements and modern theatre.	
	1952 U.S.A. *Invisible Man* by Ralph Ellison (b. 1914), a black novelist writing about the negro's awareness of his predicament: the novel was surrealist, resembling both James Joyce and Kafka.		
1953 Death of Stalin in Russia.	**1953 Mali** *The Dark Child* by Camara Laye (b. 1928), an African novelist writing in French: the book was a largely autobiographical recollection of Malinke traditions.	**1953 England** Kenneth Macmillan (b.1930) choreographed his first ballet for Sadler's Wells: *Somnambulism*. He did no full-length ballets until *Romeo and Juliet* in 1965.	**1953 England** Arthur Bliss (1891–1975) was appointed Master of the Queen's Music.

| ARCHITECTURE | THREE DIMENSIONAL ART | VISUAL ARTS | *INVENTIONS & DISCOVERIES* |

1951–1953 Mexico Juan O'Gorman (b. 1905) designed mosaic decorations in University City. He was an architect, painter and designer.

1951 Japan Akira Kurosawa (b.1910) won the Venice Grand Prix with *Rashomon*; this opened the Western market to Japanese films.

1951 U.S.A. Elia Kazan (b.1909) directed *A Streetcar Named Desire*. His Actors' Studio taught the Stanislavsky method, brought to public attention by Marlon Brando and James Dean.

USA: 'Untitled (yellow is lands)' by Jackson Pollock

1951 U.S.A. The painter Jackson Pollock (1912–1956) began to paint in black and white only. He was the best known 'action painter', considering that the action of applying the paint was itself a work of art and the finished painting was less important.

1952 Finland Tapiola New Town was designed by Aarne Ervi (born 1910) as one of several planned urban developments in post-war Finland.

1952 England First exhibition by the sculptor Elizabeth Frink (b. 1930). She treated bronze in a near-expressionist way, giving a sometimes almost sinister character to her human and animal figures.

1952 Belgium Death of Constant Permeke (b.1886), pioneer of Belgian expressionism, which he combined with traditional Flemish realism. His paintings were sombre and based on forceful drawing.

*1952
The U.S.A.
exploded the first
hydrogen bomb
at Eniwetok
Atoll, Pacific.*

1952 France Henri-Georges Clouzot (1907–1976) directed *La Saleur de la Peur*, one of his most successful films. He was considered a master of the atmospheric thriller.

1952 Japan Akira Kurosawa directed *Living*. Most Japanese directors made only one category of film; Kurosawa was the exception.

1952 U.S.A. The artist Helen Frankenthaler (b.1928) began to use colour dyes poured on to unprimed canvas, so that her colours are in and not on the surface of the picture. At first she made designs of accidental shapes; later on she produced larger areas of controlled shape.

1952 Mexico *The Nightmare of War and the Dream of Peace*, the last great mural painting by Diego Rivera (1886–1957): it was painted in polystyrene on canvas and covered more than 500 square feet. Rivera absorbed contemporary techniques in Europe between 1907 and 1921, and then appeared to abandon them so as to produce a didactic art.

1953 France UNESCO Headquarters, Paris, by Marcel Breuer (born 1902), Bernard Zehrfuss and Pier Luigi Nervi (born 1891) had a particularly fine trapezoidal conference hall in concrete.

1953 England *The Unknown Political Prisoner*, characteristic sculpture by Barbara Hepworth (1903–1975): she worked in abstract forms in stone and bronze, expressing natural forms and forces through a geometric perfection.

DANCE & DRAMA

1953 Puerto Rico *The Ox Cart* by René Marques (b.1919) a playwright using patriotic themes.

1953 Spain The dancer Antonio (Antonio Ruiz Soler, b.1922) formed his own company: he was the first non-gipsy to be a truly successful flamenco dancer.

1953 U.S.A. Merce Cunningham (b.1919), solo dancer with the Martha Graham company 1939–1945, formed his own company of modern dance.

1953 Yugoslavia Foundation in Split of a ballet school run by Ana Roje and Oscar Harmoš, as a continuation of the Nicolas Legat school.

1954 Australia Foundation of the Elizabethan Theatre Trust to train actors, encourage plays and provide touring companies to cover the entire continent.

1954 England First appointment of Robert Helpmann (b.1909) as director and choreographer of the Royal Opera House, Covent Garden. He held the post again in 1956 and 1958–1959.

1954 France Formation of Les Ballets de L'Etoile by Maurice Béjart (b.1928) and Jean Laurent. Béjart's most famous ballet for the company was *Symphonie pour un Homme Seul* in 1955; it was performed to *musique concrète*.

1954 Japan Death of Nakamura Kichiemon, great *kabuki* actor and the first to gain Imperial recognition of his talent.

1954 Japan The exceptional success of the People's Art Theatre production of *Death of a Salesman* marked the sudden popularity of Western-style 'modern' theatre at the time. Actors were employed in stable troupes offering salaried work all the time; playwrights had more chance of production since plays were changed monthly. (Work in the classical theatres was handed from father to son, and playwrights could only alter existing stories.)

1954 Wales *Under Milk Wood*, the poetic drama by Dylan Thomas (1914–1953), was broadcast by B.B.C. radio.

MUSIC

1953 U.S.A. Production of *Kismet*, a musical based on Alexander Porfirevich Borodin's (1833–1887) music for *Prince Igor*.

1954 Italy First performance, in Venice, of the opera *The Turn of the Screw* by Benjamin Britten (1913–1976).

1954 U.S.A. Death of Charles Edward Ives (b. 1874). His large output of work only began to become widely known through publication and recordings after his death.

HISTORICAL EVENTS

1954 Nasser assumed power in Egypt.

LITERATURE

1954–1955 England *The Lord of the Rings* by J. R. R. Tolkien (1892–1974), a philologist and specialist in Old Norse language and literature whose fictional books have become the subject of a cult.

1954 China *The Rice Sprout Song* by Eileen Chang, a Chinese novelist not living in China: the book is nevertheless considered the best Chinese novel of the period.

1954 England *Lucky Jim* by Kingsley Amis (b. 1922), a novelist and poet remarkable for his sharp observation and comic gifts. The book was in tune with the attack on English life of the 1950s which was the dominant note of literature of the period.

1954 England *Lord of the Flies*, a novel by William Golding (b. 1911): a realistic account of the degeneration into savagery of boys stranded on a desert island, the book was a parody of a Victorian classic, Ballantyne's *Coral Island*.

1954 England *The Go-Between*, a novel by L. P. Hartley (1895–1972). He had affinities with Henry James. Many of his books were about children.

1954 England *Under the Net* by Iris Murdoch (b. 1919), Irish novelist and philosopher. Her novels incorporate fashionable psychological and sociological concepts.

1954 France *Les Mandarins* by Simone de Beauvoir (b. 1908), philosopher, sociologist, essayist, novelist, travel writer and playwright. Her chief concern was the importance of freedom, as it is understood by the Existentialists.

ARCHITECTURE

1953–1959 Venezuela Edificio Polar, Caracas, by Martin Pacheco is an example of skyscraper building in South America, in this case supported on ferroconcrete piers, a material that was then beginning to replace steel.

1954 Mexico Church of the Miraculous Virgin, Narvarte, by Felix Candela (born 1910) was an expressionist building by an architect-engineer who made brilliant use of concrete.

THREE DIMENSIONAL ART

1954 Holland *The Destroyed City* by the French sculptor Ossip Zadkine (1890–1967) was considered one of the most dramatic European war memorials: Zadkine's aim was to combine gigantic scale with dramatic animation by reducing mass and portraying movement.

England: scene from 1957 production of Dylan Thomas' 'Under Milkwood', adapted from the stage play by Eric Crozier for BBC television

VISUAL ARTS

1952 U.S.A. Fred Zinneman (b.1907) directed his best-known film, *High Noon*. Born in Austria, he had worked with the 'new realism' school in Germany until 1930.

1953 Italy Neo-realism in the cinema had been undermined by its own commercial success, which attracted American investment and star players. The back-street locations became picturesque backgrounds for comedy and sentiment. Its influence however remained strong in new directors; Federico Fellini (b.1920) made *I Vitelloni*, a study of disaffected middle-class youth.

1953 Japan Yasujiro Ozu (1903–1963) directed *Tokyo Story*, considered his best film. His style was static and austere; a still camera observed the naturalistic playing with no apparent artistry.

1953 Poland Alexsander Ford (b.1928) made the first film reflecting post-Stalin relaxation: *Five Boys from Barska Street*.

1953 U.S.A. Willem de Kooning (b.1904) first exhibited his paintings of female figures in expressionist style.

1954 Greece Michael Cacoyannis (b. 1922) directed *Stella*; his other important films were *Windfall in Athens* and *The Girl in Black*.

1954 Hungary Zoltán Fábri (b. 1917) directed the film *Fourteen Lives Saved*, which marked the beginning of a new creative period after the Rakosi censorship.

1954 Italy Federico Fellini (b. 1920) directed *La Strada*, which he described as 'the first complete catalogue of my mythical world'. It was an entirely literal film; after this he began to use the surreal.

1954 Japan Teinosuke Kinugasa (b. 1896) won the Cannes Grand Prix with *Gate of Hell*, praised for its 'painter's use of colour'.

1954 Poland Andrzej Wajda (b. 1926) directed *A Generation*, the first film of a trilogy examining the effect of the Second World War on men who survived it. *Kanal* (1956) and *Ashes and Diamonds* (1958) completed it.

INVENTIONS & DISCOVERIES

1953 Edmund Hillary and Norkey Tenzing climbed Mount Everest. J. D. Watson and F. Crick explained helical structure of DNA molecule.

1954 U.S.S.R. built first nuclear power station.

1954 U.S.A. Formation of the Robert Joffrey Ballet Concert by Robert Joffrey (b.1930) who began his dancing career with Les Ballets de Paris de Roland Petit in 1949.

1955
East European Defence Treaty signed in Warsaw.

1955 Australia *The Wandering Islands* by the poet A. D. (Alec Derwent) Hope (b. 1907), who confined native vigour in formal Augustan modes.

1955 Canada *Snake Wine* by Patrick Anderson (b. 1915), an English poet who was for a time a Canadian citizen, and introduced to Canadian poets the influence of English writers of the 1930s, such as Auden and McNiece. He founded a Canadian literary magazine, *Preview*, in which the work of Canadian poets, among them P. K. Page and Louis Dudek, appeared.

1955 Canada *Son of a Smaller Hero* by Mordecai Richler (b. 1931), an English/Canadian novelist concerned with Jewish life and problems. Like a number of other Canadian writers, he does not live in Canada.

1955 England *The Less Deceived*, poems by Philip Larkin (b. 1922), poet, novelist and jazz critic. His work is concerned with decay and defeat.

1955 Mexico *Pedro Parama* by Juan Rolfo (b. 1918), a novelist and short-story writer influenced by Faulkner and modern Europeans. A naturalist and a regionalist, he also explored the myths of his native land.

1955 Turkey *Memed My Hawk* by Yasar Kemal (b. 1922), writer of realistic novels.

1955 U.S.A. *Howl* by Allen Ginsberg (b. 1926), poet of the Beat Generation.

1955 USA *Lolita* by Vladimir Vladimirovich Nabokov (1899–1977), a Russian émigre novelist and poet (an American citizen) writing in both Russian and English. He was detached and analytical; his style included verbal tricks, puns and anagrams.

1955–1961 U.S.A. Paul Taylor (b.1930) was leading dancer with Martha Graham's modern dance company. He went on to found his own company, stressing the comic and entertaining powers of modern dance.

1955 Australia *Summer of the Seventeenth Doll* by Ray Lawler (b.1922) an actor and writer of realistic drama.

1955 Canada Formation in Montreal of Les Ballets Chiriaeff under Ludmilla Chiriaeff (b.1924) who had formed Les Ballets des Arts in Geneva. The company became Les Grands Ballets Canadiens in 1956.

1955 Cuba Formation of the National Ballet of Cuba from the former Ballet Alicia Alonso, started in 1948. Alicia (b.1909), her brother Alberto Alonso (b.1917) and her husband Fernando (b.1914) established the ballet in Cuba; their teaching, choreography and dancing is based on American and Russian ideas.

1955 England Performance at Sadler's Wells of a short plotless ballet to the score of *Danses Concertantes*, choreographed by Kenneth Macmillan (b.1930). It was his first notable ballet.

1955 Finland *Systrarna (The Sisters)* by Walentin Chorell, a Finnish author writing in Swedish: the play won first prize in a playwriting competition with entries from Denmark, Norway, Sweden, Finland and Iceland.

1955 India The dancer Balasaraswathi opened a school of Bharata Natya dancing in Madras. She aimed to preserve the authentic classical style in a period when the search for novelty seemed to threaten the purity of the four schools of classical dance.

1955 Austria First performance, in Salzburg, of the opera *Irische Legende* by the German composer Werner Egk (b. 1901); the opera was inspired by W. B. Yeats.

1955 German Democratic Republic The State Opera House was opened after re-building.

1955 Italy First stage performance, in Venice, of Serge Prokofiev's (1891–1953) opera *The Angel of Fire*. Composed in 1925, it was considered by Prokofiev, and others, his finest work.

1955 Italy Luciano Berio (b. 1925) and Bruno Maderna (b. 1920) founded an electronic Studio di Fonologia at the Italian Radio in Milan.

1955 U.S.A. Marian Anderson (b. 1902) who sang the part of Ulrica in Verdi's *Masked Ball* was the first Negro singer to perform at the New York Metropolitan. Toscanini said of her that it was 'the voice that comes once every hundred years'.

1954 U.S.A. *Flag,* a picture by Jasper Johns (b. 1930), attempted to break down the difference between representation and reality. He widened the subject matter of contemporary American art by his interest in commonplace objects. The painter Elsworth Kelly (b. 1928) returned from working in France and settled in New York, where he became a strong influence on 'post-painterly abstraction'—a detached style using few and simple forms, hard-edged and in pure colour, as a reaction against the emotional 'action painters'. Some of his paintings were monochrome; none used more than three colours.

1955 England Langlebury School, Hertfordshire, by James Cubitt (born 1914) and Partners typified many schools in the country using a successful system of prefabrication.

*c.***1955 Scandinavia** Work in stainless steel tableware began to have a strong influence on European design in steel and silver.

1955 Christopher Cockerell invented hovercraft.

1955 Italy Pirelli Building, Milan, by Gio Ponti (born 1891) and Pier Luigi Nervi is considered one of the most spectacular post-war skyscrapers; it is built around a concrete core and tapered at each end.

1955 Denmark The film director Carl Dreyer (1889–1968) made *Odet,* considered his greatest film on spiritual intuition versus organized religion.

1955 Spain Juan Antonio Bardem (b. 1922) directed *Death of a Cyclist*; his conscious aim, with Luis G. Berlanga (b. 1921) was to revive the moribund Spanish cinema.

1955 U.S.A. Robert Rauschenberg (b. 1925) began using large three-dimensional objects in collage. Together with Jasper Johns he is considered the most influential artist of the movement leading towards Pop Art. He abandoned collage for silk-screen work and *frottage* in *c.*1962.

1955 France Max Ophuls (1902–1957), the German film director, made *Lola Montez,* his last film and the climax of his visual style. He was considered a master of camera and subject movement within the long, complex shot. His style has been described as ornate.

1955 U.S.A. The photographic exhibition *Family of Man* at the Museum of Modern Art, New York, brought the work of world-wide documentary photographers to public attention.

The Robe was the first film on the cinemascope screen, shot with an anamorphic lens: widescreen films were unsuitable for classical montage technique (altering the images by cutting from one to another); such frequent cuts are only acceptable to the eye in a small area.

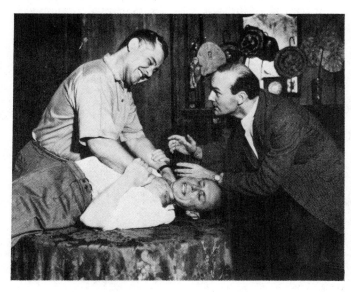

Australia: scene from the 1956 production of 'Summer of the Seventeenth Doll' by Ray Lawler performed in the Elizabethan Theatre, Sydney

483

LITERATURE

DANCE & DRAMA

MUSIC

1956 Brazil *The Devil to Pay in the Backlands*, a novel by Joao Guimaraes Rosa (1908–1969): an interior monologue, the book linked the wild and strange interior of the country with the inner recesses of a man's mind.

1956 England *Anglo-Saxon Attitudes* by Angus Wilson (b. 1913), novelist, playwright and critic. In his lengthy novels, which contain a large number of characters, he studied intelligent society.

1956 Italy *The Storm and Other Things* by Eugenio Montale (b. 1896), poet and critic. His poetry showed his interest in music, and in a development from the Crepuscular school.

1956 Italy *The False and the True Green* by Salvatore Quasimodo (1901–1968), poet, critic and translator, a leading member of the Hermetic school.

1956 South Africa *Six Feet in the Country* by Nadine Gordimer (b. 1923), short-story writer and novelist. Her work is concerned mainly with the human problems, not the political aspects, of Apartheid.

1956 South Africa *Germanicas*, a verse drama by N. P. Van Wyck Louw (b. 1906), a poet and critic writing in Afrikaans. His work showed the influence of German expressionism.

1956 Sweden *The Songs of Aniara* by Harry Martinson (b. 1904), poet, playwright and novelist. Though interested in science and technology, he was alienated from modern industrial society; he lived for a time as a tramp. This work was a narrative poem about a spaceship which went off course into the void. He was awarded the Nobel Prize in 1974.

1957–1960 England *The Alexandria Quartet* by Lawrence Durrell (b. 1912), Irish novelist, travel writer and poet: the four books, which deal with the nature of love and art, tell the same basic story from different angles. He was influenced by Joyce.

1957 Italy *That Awful Mess on the Via Merulana* by Carlo Emilio Gadda (1893–1974), novelist and short-story writer. His work was satirical and disillusioned.

1956 Canada Ruthanna Boris (b.1918), American dancer and teacher, became director of the Royal Winnipeg Ballet Company, which she revived.

1956 England John Field (b.1921) appointed director of the Royal Ballet: he had been principal dancer with Sadler's Wells Ballet.

1956 England *Look Back in Anger* by John James Osborne (b.1929) was a complete contrast to the 'polite' plays then current on the English stage. With direct and vigorous language it marks a turning point in taste in the English theatre.

1957 England John Cranko choreographed *The Prince of the Pagodas* for the Royal Ballet. This was a three-act work, continuing Frederick Ashton's emphasis on the full-length, big-scale ballet.

1957 France *La Cimetière des Voitures* by Fernando Arrabal (b.1933) Spanish-born, French playwright of the Theatre of the Absurd.

1957 Scotland Formation of Western Theatre Ballet by Peter Darrell (b.1932) and Elizabeth West (d.1962).

1957 Sweden Birgit Åkesson (b.1908) staged her first ballets for the Royal Swedish Ballet: *The Minotaur, Icaros, Rites* and *Play for Eight*. She was trained by the German dancer Mary Wigman.

1957 U.S.A. Ballet Theater (founded 1940) became known as American Ballet Theater.

1957 U.S.A. First production of the ballet *Agon* by New York City Ballet: the music was by Stravinsky; the choreographer George Balanchine used sarabandes, galliards and double branles.

1956 U.S.A. The musical *My Fair Lady*, based on George Bernard Shaw's *Pygmalion*, opened in New York.

1957 Austria Herbert von Karajan (b. 1908) became musical director of the Vienna State Opera and later established the Salzburg Easter Festival.

1957 Finland Death of Jean Johan Julius Christian Sibelius (b. 1865), Finnish composer.

1957 Italy Death of Beniamino Gigli (b. 1880), an outstanding singer in the style of Enrico Caruso (1873–1921).

1957 Italy Death of Arturo Toscanini (b. 1867), one of the greatest musical conductors of all time.

1957 U.S.A. First performance, in New York, of the ballet *Agon* by Igor Stravinsky (1882–1971); this marked a turning point in Stravinsky's career, towards serialism and away from the neo-classical works.

| ARCHITECTURE | THREE DIMENSIONAL ART | VISUAL ARTS | INVENTIONS & DISCOVERIES |

ARCHITECTURE

1956 Finland Vuosenniska Church, Imatra, by Alvar Aalto was a complex and highly individual design by the greatest of modern Finnish architects.

1956 German Federal Republic Thyssenhaus Hochhaus, Düsseldorf, by Helmut Hentrich (born 1905) and Petschnigg (born 1913) displayed the influence of Mies van de Rohe on a grand scale.

1956 Scotland Cumbernauld New Town by Geoffrey Copcutt (born 1928) and Hugh Wilson (born 1913) was one of a number of post-war British new towns; here, living and working areas were integrated very successfully.

1956 USA Seagram Building, New York, by Ludwig Mies van der Rohe and Philip Johnson was considered the culmination of the former's streamlined style; it was a rectangular slab of bronze, marble and grey-tinted glass.

1957–1973 Australia The Opera House, Sydney by Jørn Utzon (born 1918) a controversial building with a sail-like roofscape. It was architecture as sculpture, but strongly influenced by function.

1957 France Monastery of la Tourette, Évreux, by Le Corbusier is a late work by the architect in raw brutalist concrete.

1957 USA Richards Laboratories, Philadelphia, by Louis Kahn (1901–1974) has a bold silhouetting of towers, a reaction to Miessian simplicity, which led to Kahn's being defined as an early brutalist architecture.

VISUAL ARTS

1956 England Young film directors continued their efforts to widen the scope of British films, by their work in 'Free Cinema', a series which included the documentaries *O Dreamland* by Lindsay Anderson (b. 1923) and *Momma Don't Allow* by Tony Richardson (b. 1928).

1956 Japan Kon Ichikawa (b. 1915) directed *The Burmese Harp*; his later films included *Alone in the Pacific* (1962) and *Olympiad* (1964).

1956 Sweden Ingmar Bergman (b. 1918) directed *The Seventh Seal*, first of a group of his films with period settings which revived the Swedish tradition in their examination of the spiritual and their feeling for nature. His later films explored contemporary psychological problems.

1956 U.S.S.R. Grigori Chukrai (b. 1921) directed *The Forty-First*, a re-make of a 1927 film by Protazanov. The 20th Party Congress had relaxed censorship; films emerged which had human, non-political themes.

1957 France The photographer Marc Riboud (b. 1923) made his first working visit to China. In 1965 he produced a one-man exhibition and a book of his work there.

1957 Mexico The Argentinian director Leopoldo Torre-Nilsson (b. 1924) directed *La Casa del Angel*: it is characteristic of his mannered, atmospheric films portraying bourgeois life in decay.

1957 U.S.A. Stanley Kubrick (b. 1928) began his major work with the film *Paths of Glory*, in which he manipulated realism to express compassion. His later films were concerned with futuristic fantasy.

France: the monastery of La Tourette, Évreux, designed by Le Corbusier

LITERATURE

DANCE & DRAMA

MUSIC

*1958
General de Gaule
became President
of France.
European
Economic
Community
established.*

1957 France *La Jalousie*, a novel by Alain Robbe-Grillet (b. 1922). A leading exponent of the *nouveau roman*, which dispenses with the plot, time-scale and characterization of what is normally regarded as a novel, he believed that the novelist should be like a camera, simply recording objects.

1957 Italy *The Leopard* by Giuseppe Tomasi de Lampedusa (1896–1957), a Sicilian prince who wrote this novel and some stories. The book was set in Sicily at the time of Garibaldi's invasion.

1957 U.S.S.R. *Dr Zhivago* by Boris Pasternak (1890–1960), poet, playwright, novelist and translator. The novel, which is about the intelligentsia at the time of the Revolution, was offensive to officialdom because it was not socialist realism and because it was on the side of the individual. Pasternak was offered a Nobel Prize in 1958, but was not allowed to accept it.

1958 England *Collected Poems* by John Betjeman (b. 1906), who became poet laureate in 1962. The book was a bestseller. His work was mainly concerned with suburban living. Much is parody of nineteenth-century verse.

1958 England *Saturday Night and Sunday Morning* by Alan Sillitoe (b. 1928), novelist and short-story writer: the book was about working-class life in his native Nottingham.

1958 Nigeria *Things Fall Apart* by Chinua Achebe (b. 1930), novelist and short-story writer, an active supporter of the Biafran cause. Although a self-confessed protest writer, his style was restrained and his manner detached.

1959 England *Cider with Rosie*, an autobiography of a country up-bringing by the poet Laurie Lee (b. 1914), who writes lyrical and pastoral poems.

1959 France *Le Planetarium* by Nathalie Sarraute (b. 1902), novelist, playwright and critic. She wrote *nouveaux romans*, though she was more interested in psychology than is usual in this type of book.

1958 England First performance of the ballet *Ondine* by Frederick Ashton, to music by Hans Werner Henze, for the Royal Ballet. Margot Fonteyn danced Ondine. The story was inspired by a ballet of 1843, Perrot's *Ondine, ou La Naïade*.

1958 France American dancer and choreographer George Skibine (b.1920) became balletmaster of the Paris Opéra ballet. He resigned in 1962.

1958 Switzerland *Biedermann und Die Brandstifter* by Max Rudolf Frisch (b.1911) who is an acquaintance and follower of Brecht. Although Switzerland has produced few great names in the history of theatre, the country has a long and vigorous tradition of amateur drama.

1958 U.S.A. Foundation of the Institute for Advanced Studies in the Theater Arts, New York, which gives foreign directors opportunities to show their techniques to American directors.

1959 England *Serjeant Musgrave's Dance* by John Arden (b. 1930), one-time Fellow in Playwriting at the University of Bristol. Bristol was the first English University to open a Department of Drama (1946/47). Arden was in reaction against the realistic school of English theatre, using period settings and a poetic interpretation of events.

1959 England *One Way Pendulum* by Norman Frederick Simpson (b.1919), an example of the English Theatre of the Absurd.

1959 Netherland Benjamin Harkarvy (b.1930 in America) left Het Nederlands Ballet, of which he was ballet-master, and founded Het Nederlands Dans Theater which performed much new work.

1959 U.S.A. *The Connection* by Jack Allen Gelber (b.1932) was presented by the New York Living Theater: this *avant-garde*, off-broadway company has been very influential in the American theatre.

1959 U.S.S.R. Galina Ulanova (b.1910) was appointed balletmistress of the Bolshoi Ballet, Moscow.

1958 England Death of Ralph Vaughan Williams (b.1872), English composer.

1958 England First performance of the opera *Noye's Fludde* by Benjamin Britten (1913–1976).

*1959
Unsuccessful
rising in Tibet
against Chinese;
Dalai Lama fled
to India.*

1959 Brazil Death of Heitor Villa-Lobos (b.1887), Brazilian composer, conductor and educationist.

1958 France CNIT Exhibition Hall, Paris, is by J. Prouvé (born 1901) and Pier Luigi Nervi (born 1891), two engineers who built here the largest concrete vaults in the world; the walls are glazed.

1958 USA Geodesic dome, Baton Rouge, by Buckminster Fuller had a diameter of 125·9 m and was the largest such dome designed by the man who invented this cheap and functional form of shelter.

1958 USA Dulles Airport, Chantilly, Virginia, by Eero Saarinen is considered one of the best new airport buildings; it has a curving roof of concrete laid on cables, reminiscent of flight.

1959 England The University Engineering Block, Leicester, is by James Stirling (born 1926) and James Gowan (born 1923), who were architects of many post-war English university buildings and leaders in the vogue for brutalism.

1959 Japan Hammi Apartment Block, Tokyo, by Kunio Maekawa (born 1905) was an early brutalist block by the doyen of modern Japanese architects.

1959 England The sculptor Antony Caro (b. 1924) began to make non-figurative work, using metal sheets and girders to define space. He was influenced by David Smith and was in turn a strong influence on younger British sculptors.

1959 Germany The first one-piece plastic table was designed by Walter Papst: plastic furniture requires entirely different skills from wooden, relying on casting, moulding and shaping for its effect and not on the old aesthetic of construction. Outstanding furniture-makers in the new material were Luigi Colani, Verner Panton and J. Steen Østergaard.

1958–1959 England Jack Clayton (b. 1921) directed *Room at the Top*, a Yorkshire tragedy. British directors followed the documentary lead in subject matter towards authentic, non-romantic portrayal of contemporary life; many films adapted contemporary novels.

The British documentary film was revived and humanized with *We Are the Lambeth Boys* by Karel Reisz (b. 1926) and *Every Day Except Christmas* by Lindsay Anderson (b. 1923).

1958 France The film critic and theorist André Bazin (1918–1958), in his *Qu'est-ce que le Cinéma?*, praised von Stroheim and Murnau for their lengthy, probing shots; there was now a trend away from montage. Bazin had founded and was the editor of *Cahiers du Cinéma* magazine, which employed as critics Claude Chabrol (b. 1930), François Truffaut (b. 1932), Jean-Luc Godard (b. 1930) and Eric Rohmer (b. 1920). They became film directors themselves, practising the magazine's teaching that a film should be a personal statement of the director's feelings for his subject. Together with other directors, notably Alain Resnais (b. 1922), they became known as the *nouvelle vague*. Their films manipulated accepted formulae to the point of disruption.

1958 Stereophonic gramophone recordings in production. Introduction of electronic computers.

1959 Russian spacecraft Lunik III photographed moon. Discovery of Arctic submarine plateau.

England: the engineering block of Leicester University, designed by James Stirling

1959 Federal German Republic
Billiards at Half-past Nine, a novel by Heinrich Böll (b. 1917), poet, playwright, novelist and short-story writer. He is a Catholic, concerned mainly with what he sees as the emptiness of modern West German society. His early work was realist; his later books were modernist, using flashback and stream-of-consciousness techniques. He was awarded the Nobel Prize in 1972.

1959 Federal German Republic
The Tin Drum by Günther Grass (b. 1927), Polish-born novelist, playwright and poet. The book was a survey of German history from the Third Reich to the period of the 'economic miracle', seen through the eyes of an insane dwarf.

1959 Paraguay *Son of Man* by Auguste Roa Bastos (b. 1917), novelist and short-story writer: a tragic portrait of greed in Paraguay, the book was also an allegory of human selfishness the world over.

1960
John Kennedy elected U.S. President.

1959 U.S.A. *The Naked Lunch* by William Burroughs (b. 1914), a Beat novelist writing on the theme of drug addiction. His technique was basically surrealist.
Life Studies, a collection of poems by Robert Lowell (1917–1977), American poet; it marked the change from academic poetry to more direct, personal and colloquial verse, not only in Lowell's work but in American poetry generally.

1960 France Collected poems of Aléxis Léger, called Saint-John Perse, (1887–1975) poet and diplomat. His poetry is learned and rhetorical, written in rhythmic prose. He was awarded the Nobel Prize in 1960.

1960 Italy *The Gold-Rimmed Spectacles* by Giorgio Bussani (b. 1916), a realistic novelist whose main concern was with the sufferings of Italian Jews under the Fascist regime.

1960 Poland *The Magician of Lublin* by Isaac Bashevis Singer (b. 1904), Jewish journalist, short-story writer and novelist. He wrote in Yiddish, mainly about Polish ghetto life between the seventeenth and twentieth centuries.

1960 England *The Caretaker* by Harold Pinter (b. 1930), playwright in the Theatre of the Absurd tradition.
First performance of an English version of the ballet *La Fille Mal Gardée*, choreographed with English folk dances by Frederick Ashton (b. 1906).

1960 U.S.A. *O Dad Poor Dad Momma's Hung You in the Closet and I'm Feeling So Sad* by Arthur L. Kopit (b.1938) dramatist, then a student at Harvard.

*c.*1960 **France** *Musique concrète* made possible by the use of tape recordings.

*c.*1960 **Greece** The bouzouki, a Greek strung instrument, became internationally known as a result of compositions for this instrument.

USSR: Kalinin Prospect, Moscow

1960 Brazil Brasilia was begun by Lucio Costa (1902–1963) and Oscar Niemeyer (born 1907) and planned in the shape of a bird with the parliamentary buildings at its head; the influence of Le Corbusier is seen in the buildings themeselves.

1960 USSR Kalinin Prospect, Moscow, was begun by M. Posokhin and others; a very wide street bordered by skyscraper blocks, it was typical of modern housing in Russia and eastern Europe.

1960 Italy Michelangelo Antonioni (b. 1912) directed *L'Avventura*. He used geographical settings to establish a tension between character and landscape; the character sees his surroundings as a projection of his own state of mind, but in realistic, not expressionist, images.

1960 U.S.A. John Cassavetes (b. 1929) directed the film *Shadows*, with mainly improvised acting.

The photographer Roman Vishniac (b. 1897 in Russia) began working with new techniques of photomicroscopy, in which he had been interested since 1906. His aim was to release to the eye the beauty of the normally invisible microscopic world.

1960 U.S.S.R. Josip Heifets (b. 1905) directed *The Lady with a Little Dog*, a film independent of any official tradition.

*c.***1960 Europe** Beginning of a revival in animated film as an art form. The main centres were France, Britain (mainly stimulated by the advertising industry) and eastern Europe. Animation as an art had declined since the achievements of the Canadian Norman McLaren in the 1930s.

1960
Laser developed.

LITERATURE

DANCE & DRAMA

MUSIC

1961
*Berlin Wall
constructed.
Union of South
Africa became
republic.*

1961 Australia *Riders in the Chariot* by Patrick White (b. 1912), novelist, poet and playwright, and a Nobel Prize-winner. His writing was symbolic, the themes showing the influence of Nietzschean thought.

1961 Scotland *The Prime of Miss Jean Brodie* by Muriel Spark (b. 1918), novelist.

1961 U.S.A. *Herzog* by Saul Bellow (b. 1915), a Canadian-born novelist, playwright, writer of short stories, and essayist, of Russian Jewish extraction. His work was existentialist, pre-occupied with man as a victim of life.

1962–1968 France *Poésies* by Pierre Jean Jouve (b. 1887), poet, novelist and literary and music critic. His work is strongly influenced by Freudian concepts.

1962 Spain *Desolation of the Chimera* by Luis Cernuda (1904–1963), poet, translator, critic and prose writer. He wrote on the conflict between reality, with which he could not come to terms, and desire, which was unobtainable.

1962 U.S.A. *Ship of Fools* by Katherine Anne Porter (b. 1894), a novelist and short-story writer of great versatility in technique and subject matter.

1962 U.S.S.R. *One Day in the Life of Ivan Denisovich* by Alexander Isayevich Solzhenitsyn (b. 1918), novelist and poet: the novel described life in a labour camp in the Stalin era. Others of his writings were 'protest' works, revealing Soviet treatment of dissident writers and thinkers. He was awarded the Nobel Prize in 1970, but the Soviet authorities refused to allow him to accept it. He was expelled from Russia in 1974.

1961 England Sir Laurence Kerr Olivier (b.1907) actor and producer, became the first director of the National Theatre.

1961 Federal German Republic Appointment of John Cranko (1927–1973), South African dancer and choreographer, as director of ballet at Württemberg State Opera, Stuttgart. He worked in German companies until his death.

1961 Netherlands Combination of Amsterdams Ballet and Het Nederlands Ballet to form Het National Ballet, with Sonia Gaskell as artistic director. In the same year Hans van Manen became artistic director of Het Nederlands Dans Theater; his work, until 1970, included much plotless ballet featuring dance as emotional expression.

1962 Australia Establishment of the Australian Ballet under the directorship of Peggy van Praagh, British ballet-mistress who had been artistic director of Borovansky's company (founded 1940), since his death in 1959.

1962 England John Gilpin (b.1930) appointed artistic director of London's Festival Ballet.

First partnership of the dancers Margot Fonteyn and Rudolf Nureyev (b.1938), in *Giselle* at Covent Garden.

Next Time I'll Sing to You by James Saunders (b.1925) was presented by the Questors Theatre, London, an amateur group founded in 1929. They train amateur actors, and have presented a large number of new plays.

Arnold Wesker (b.1932) writer of naturalistic drama, attempted to set up a working-class theatre at the Roundhouse, London. The venture failed.

1962 Netherlands American dancer and choreographer Glen Tetley (b.1926) joined Nederlands Dans Theater.

1962 Switzerland *Die Physiker* by Friedrich Durrenmatt (b.1921) a dramatist influenced by both Brecht and the Expressionists.

1962 U.S.A. *Who's Afraid of Virginia Woolf?* by Edward Franklin Albee (b.1928).

1961 Federal Republic of Germany Henri Pousseur (b. 1929) began his variable "operatic fantasy" (completed in 1967), *Votre Faust.*

1962 England First performance of the opera *King Priam* by Michael Kemp Tippett (b. 1905), at Covent Garden.

1962 England First performance of the choral work *War Requiem* by Benjamin Britten (1913–1976).

ARCHITECTURE

1961 England St James's Place Flats, London, by Denys Lasdun (born 1914) is a luxurious block designed uncompromisingly in the modern style by one of the most successful contemporary British architects.

1961 Finland Hyvinkä Church by Aarno Ruusuvnori (born 1925) is a good example of modern Finnish church building in an original triangular form, built of white-painted concrete and glass.

1961 Japan Metropolitan Festival Hall, Tokyo, by Kurio Maekawa illustrates the influence of Le Corbusier in Japan.

1962–1967 England Liverpool, Roman Catholic Cathedral by Sir Frederick Gibberd (born 1908) is built over the crypt of the original Lutyens design; the cathedral is centrally planned and tent-like in appearance, crowned with a metal and glass lantern.

England: St James' Palace flats, designed by Denys Lasdun

THREE DIMENSIONAL ART

1962 U.S.A. The Japanese-American sculptor Isamu Noguchi (b. 1904) made *The Cry*, one of his best known sculptures. He began work as an assistant to Brancusi and had also studied Japanese art, but no single influence ever dominated his work; he was also successful as a stage designer and landscape gardener.

VISUAL ARTS

1961–1970 U.S.A. *Life* magazine published a series of photographic features by Gordon Parks (b. 1912), which were outstanding in their treatment of black America.

1961 Spain Luis Bunuel made his film *Viridiana*: he used surrealist horror and comedy to state the theme, that living the Christian faith in today's society is impossible.

1961 Australia The *Edmund Campion* series of paintings by Leonard French (b. 1928): they are considered outstanding in Australian religious painting. His style is semi-abstract.

1962 Brazil Glauber Rocha (b. 1939) made his first feature film *Barravento*. He wrote a history of Brazilian cinema in which he laid down rules for a new movement, *Cinema Nôvo*.

1962 Hungary Miklós Jancsó (b. 1921) directed *Cantata*, first of a number of films debating values in society in a philosophical sense.

1962 India James Ivory (b. 1928), American-born director, made the film *The Householder*. He and Satyajit Ray (b. 1921) were the two directors of Indian films to make an international impact.

1962 U.S.A. The Austrian Ernst Haas (b. 1921), considered one of the greatest photographers of his time, was given a one-man exhibition at the Museum of Modern Art, New York. Haas made many photographic essays for magazines 1952–1960.

The painter Robert Rauschenberg (b. 1925) began using silk-screen printing to provide repeating images. A single image was used in *Marilyn*, a silk-screen print by Andy Warhol (b. 1930), the best-known of the 'Pop' artists, who were concerned with reprocessing popular images. Other 'Pop' artists were Roy Lichtenstein (b. 1923) and Claes Oldenburg (b. 1929).

INVENTIONS & DISCOVERIES

1961
Major Yuri Gagarin of U.S.S.R. became first space-man.

1962
US communications satellite Telstar launched.

HISTORICAL EVENTS	LITERATURE	DANCE & DRAMA	MUSIC

HISTORICAL EVENTS

1963
Nuclear test ban treaty between U.S.A., U.S.S.R. and Britain. President Kennedy assassinated.

1964
Outbreak of war in South Vietnam.

1965
U.S. troops in Vietnam authorized to take offensive action. Unilateral declaration of independence from Britain by Rhodesia.

LITERATURE

1963 Netherlands Collected poems of Gerrit Achterberg (1905–1962). He used traditional verse forms, but his approach to words has been described as surrealist. Much of his poetry is based on his own interpretation of the myth of Orpheus and Euridyce.

1963 Japan *The Sailor who Fell from Grace with The Sea* by Mishima Yukio (1925–1970), novelist and playwright. His work was sensational and showed the influence of American psychoanalysis.

1963 Scotland A collection of Gaelic poems by Iain Crichton Smith (b. 1928), poet, novelist and short-story writer; he also writes in English.

1963 U.S.A. *The Group*, a novel by Mary McCarthy (b. 1912), a writer concerned with the lack of true wisdom in the intellectual.

1963 U.S.S.R. *A · Precocious Autobiography* by Yevgeny Yevtushenko (b. 1933), a poet stylistically influenced by Mayakovsky. Following Kruschev's denunciation of Stalin, literary censorship in the Soviet Union was somewhat relaxed. Yevtushenko's poetry is a product of that period.

1964 England *The Snow Ball* by Brigid Brophy (b. 1929), Irish journalist, critic and novelist.

1964 Trinidad *A House for Mr Biswas* by V. S. (Vidiadhur Surajprasad Naipaul (b. 1932), a Hindu novelist and short-story writer born in Trinidad: the book portrayed the decay of Indian family life in the West Indies.

1965 Czechoslovakia *A Night with Hamlet* by Vladimir Holan (b. 1905), translator and poet. His early work was surrealist; then he turned to social realism. His latest poetry, in free verse, expressed his feelings of alienation from others and from himself. He is influenced by Eliot.

1965 Czechoslovakia *A Close Watch on the Trains* by Bohumil Hrabal (b. 1914), novelist and short-story writer. Like Hašek, he wrote about little people swallowed up in incomprehensible events. His techniques are modernist.

DANCE & DRAMA

1962 U.S.A. Alvin Ailey, modern dancer, choreographed *Feast of Ashes* for the Robert Joffrey Ballet Concert. His work began as a celebration of negro dance and influenced a new development in energetic theatrical dance about black America.

1963 Nigeria Publication of *The Lion and the Jewel* by Wole Soyinka (b.1934) playwright, lecturer in English literature at the University of Ife: his plays are ritualistic in pattern but his themes are modern.

1964 Federal German Republic *The Persecution and Assassination of Marat, as Performed by the Inmates of the Asylum of Charenton under the Direction of the Marquis de Sade* by Peter Weiss (b.1916) playwright and director of experimental films: the play is one of the major works in the tradition of the Theatre of Cruelty.

1964 Turkey *The Feet and Legs Factory* by Sermet Cagan (b.1929) writer of plays of politics and ideas in the style of Brecht.

MUSIC

1964 Korea Isang Yun (b. 1917) composed *Om Mani Padme Hum*, a setting of texts by Buddha.

1964 First public performance of Gustav Mahler's (1860–1911) tenth symphony, unfinished at his death but completed by Deryck Cooke (b. 1919) from Mahler's notes.

1964 U.S.A. Death of Cole Porter (b. 1893), composer of popular songs and works for the stage including *Anything Goes* and *Kiss me Kate*.

1964–66 U.S.A. Stravinsky wrote the *Requiem Canticles*.

1965 England First performance of the children's opera *Julius Caesar Jones* by Malcolm Williamson (b. 1931).

| ARCHITECTURE | THREE DIMENSIONAL ART | VISUAL ARTS | INVENTIONS & DISCOVERIES |

USA: sculpture by Carl Andre

1963 Czechoslovakia Milós Forman (b. 1932) directed *Peter and Paula*; he led a group of new directors who aimed to revitalize national films. He collaborated with Ivan Passer (b. 1933).

1963 England The American-born film director Joseph Losey (b. 1909) made *The Servant*. English cinema in 1960–70 exploited the image of 'swinging Britain' projected in the early films of Richard Lester (b. 1932), and the social malaise that was thought to accompany it. Losey was considered one of the most imaginative directors; other outstanding film-makers of the period were John Schlesinger (b. 1926), Ken Loach (b. 1936) and Tony Richardson (1928). Richardson also encouraged younger directors and provided stable working conditions for them at Woodfall Films.

1963 Italy Luchino Visconti (1907–1976) directed *The Leopard*, abandoning neo-realism for a decorative style.

*c.***1963 Sweden** The newly-formed Swedish film Institute began to encourage work by new directors, of whom the best-known were Bo Widerberg (b. 1930) and Vilgot Sjöman.

1963 Development of first supersonic military airplane.

1964 Japan Olympic Buildings, Tokyo, by Kenzo tange (born 1913) had a tensile catenary roof spanning the National Gymnasium; Tange began with radical changes in construction methods and created buildings round them.

1964 U.S.A. First exhibition by the sculptor Carl André (b. 1935), who defined sculpture as 'Form = Structure = Place': he sought to define an area by arranging objects rather than creating them.

1964 Italy The sculptor Giacomo Manzu (b. 1908) completed the *Portal of Death* for St Peter's, Rome: it combined traditional Christian subjects with contemporary events, sketched in low relief. He had made a similar piece for Salzburg Cathedral, but most of his earlier work was figure sculpture.

1965 U.S.A. The term 'minimal art' was invented to describe work (mainly sculpture) composed of simple objects arranged to give an awareness of space, mass, texture, light and colour. Minimal sculpture is influenced by constructivism; its best known exponent is Robert Morris (b. 1931).

1964 Hungary András Kovács (b. 1925) directed *Difficult People*; he was considered an innovator in filming current social problems.

1964 Italy Death of Giorgio Morandi (b. 1890), a painter who specialized in still life and achieved a pure aesthetic style independent of contemporary trends.

Pier Paolo Pasolini (1922–1975), directed *Il Vangelo secondo Matteo*. He used a harsh, austere style of camera-work to record tangible realities.

1964 U.S.A. Robert Rossen (1908–66) made his last film, *Lilith*. He used a visual style in direct contrast to the nature of the subject matter (insanity), using the camera to make clear, formal patterns.

1965 Norway Death of Peter Krohg (b.1889), a painter trained in Paris whose most important work was in cubist style.

1964 Discovery of quasars as sources of radio waves.

1965 Federal Republic of Germany Church of the Atonement, Dachau, by Helmet Striffler (born 1927) is built on the site of the concentration camp, and is a brutalist building with a low horizontal profile.

1965 Soviet cosmonaut Alexei Leonov became first man to walk in space. Natural gas discovered in North Sea.

HISTORICAL EVENTS	LITERATURE	DANCE & DRAMA	MUSIC

LITERATURE

1965 England *Ariel* by Sylvia Plath (1932–1963), an American-born poet and novelist later living in London: the poems, published posthumously, and inspired by her own mental condition, were about a sick society.

1965 New Zealand *Memoirs of a Peon* by Frank Sargeson (b. 1903), a novelist using the vernacular with great sensitivity and skill. The book was the first antipodean picaresque novel.

1965 West Indies *The Castaway* by Derek Walcott (b. 1930), poet and playwright. He presented a truthful, not romanticized, picture of West Indian life.

1966
Mrs Gandhi became Prime Minister of India. Start of Cultural Revolution in China.

1966–1967 U.S.S.R. *The Master and Margarita*, a novel by Mikhail Bulgakov (1891–1940), playwright and novelist, was published posthumously. Bulgakov was concerned with the nature of the opposition to Bolshevism and the position of the artist in a bureaucracy. His books were fantasy in a realistic setting, expressed in a series of short scenes—a cinematic technique.

1967 Czechoslovakia Poems of Miroslav Horub (b. 1923), research chemist and poet; he was a supporter of Dubcek, though he later recanted.

1966 Canada The Royal Winnipeg Ballet Company presented *Rose Latulippe*, the first full-length Canadian ballet.

1966 England Re-organization of Ballet Rambert as a company mainly concerned with new work.

1966 Federal German Republic *Die Plebejer Proben den Aufstand* by Gunter Grass (b.1927) novelist and playwright in the Theatre of the Absurd tradition.

1967
Military coup in Greece; Constantine II fled to Rome. Six-day War between Israel and Arab states.

1967 Mexico *One Hundred Years of Solitude* by Gabriel Garcia Marques (b. 1928), a Colombian novelist living in Mexico. He abandoned realism in an attempt to express the fantastic nature of the country.

1967 Sweden *Guide to the Underworld* by Gunnar Ekelöf (1907–1968), poet, essayist and translator. He used *avant-garde* techniques to express his sense of insecurity.

1967 England *Rosencrantz and Guildenstern Are Dead* by Tom Stoppard (b.1937): a Theatre of the Absurd play which was a great success with the general public.

Zigger Zagger by Peter Terson (b.1932) was written for the English National Youth Theatre. The final version of this and other of Terson's plays evolved from the original script through the collaboration of author, actors and producer.

1967 Federal German Republic *Soldaten: Nekrolog auf Genf* by Rolf Hockhuth (b.1931) writer of plays on contemporary history.

1967 U.S.A. First performance by the New York Philharmonic Orchestra of *November Steps* by Toru Takemitsu (b. 1930), Japanese composer who included both European and Japanese styles in his work.

1968
Russian invasion of Czechoslovakia.

1968 Poland Poems of Zbigniew Herbert (b. 1924), poet and playwright. His poetry showed a strong sense of classical and Polish history.

1968 South Africa *Selected Poems* by Ingrid Jonker (1933–1965), an Afrikaans woman poet concerned chiefly with the connection between violence and birth. Her poetry showed the influence of Dylan Thomas.

1968 Poland Publication in English of *Towards a Poor Theatre*, a collection of writings by and about Jerzy Grotowski (b. 1933) theatre director. He developed the theories of Stanislavsky in what he called a psychophysical direction. A 'poor' theatre relies entirely on the actor.

1968 U.S.A. Publication of *Early Jazz: Its Roots and Musical Development* by Gunther Schuller (b. 1925). His earlier publication *Horn Technique* (1962) is also a standard text.

1968 U.S.A. Pulitzer Prize awarded to George Crumb (b.1929), for his *Echoes of Time and the River*.

494

| ARCHITECTURE | THREE DIMENSIONAL ART | VISUAL ARTS | INVENTIONS & DISCOVERIES |

1965 U.S.A. The exhibition 'The Responsive Eye' provided the first international survey of 'Op art', *i.e.* art based on optical illusion through the juxtaposition of colours and shapes. Its leading exponents were Kenneth Noland (b. 1924) and the British artist Bridget Riley (b. 1931).

1965 Bulgaria Dusan Makavejev (b.1932) directed *A Man is not a Bird*, which admitted that human affairs are often directed by nature and by accident, not by the Party.

1965 Hungary Miklós Jancsó directed *The Round-Up*; he abandoned montage and used instead a series of long unbroken shots each lasting several minutes and resembling ballet sequences.

1966 USA Lincoln Centre, New York, was completed; The most opulent of post-war entertainment centres, it involved four architects: Philip Johnson, Wallace Harrison (born 1895), Max Abramovits (born 1908), and Eero Saarinen (1910–1961).

1966
First landing on moon, by U. S. Surveyor I.

1966 Italy Death of the painter Carlo Carrà (b. 1881), whose working life had covered classicism (until 1910), futurism, cubism and the 'metaphysical' style of Chirico (*c.*1915–1920). A series of seascapes (1921–1925) was considered his major work, in which all former experimental extremes were abandoned.

1967 Canada Habitat Housing, Montreal, by Moshe Safdie (born 1936) consisted of prefabricated-concrete housing units fitted together in an experimental design.

1967 Federal Republic of Germany Bensberg Town Hall by Gottfred Bohn (born 1920) blended with the old castle and successfully departed from the Miesian tradition by having a multi-angular façade and central tower.

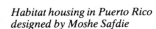
Habitat housing in Puerto Rico designed by Moshe Safdie

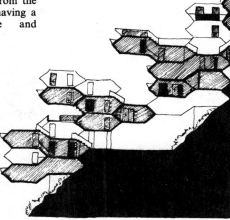

1967 U.S.A. Arthur Penn (b.1922) directed *Bonnie and Clyde*, using a theme (sympathetic study of a bank robber and his girl-friend) first exploited by Fritz Lang in the 1930s.

1967
First heart transplant.

1967 U.S.S.R. Censorship tightened again; the historical film *Andrei Roublev* by Andrei Tarkovsky (b. 1932) was not released because of its 'negative' view of history.

1968 Australia Death of Sir Hans Heysen, landscape painter. His early work was in heroic style and developed from the paintings of the Heidelberg school; later work was mainly inspired by desert landscapes of the interior.

1968
Pulsar discovered.

1968 England Lindsay Anderson's film *If*: a move away from literal realism to a semi-fantastic epic film.

HISTORICAL EVENTS	LITERATURE	DANCE & DRAMA	MUSIC
	1968 U.S.A. *Tell Me How Long the Train's Been Gone* by James Baldwin (b. 1924), a black novelist writing about two groups he saw as persecuted-negroes and homosexuals.		
	1968 Wales *Not That he Brought Flowers* by R. S. Thomas (b. 1913), clergyman and poet. His writing is in English, although he learned Welsh, and his work shows Welsh Nationalist feeling.		
1969 Death of Ho Chi Minh in Hanoi.	**1969 Japan** *Face at the Bottom of the World* by Hagiwara Sakutaro (1886–1942), the first poet of any stature to make successful use of spoken colloquial Japanese. Influenced by Baudelaire, he fused European and Japanese elements in his work.	**1969 England** Buckminster Fuller designed the Samuel Beckett Theatre for experimental works in drama, art and music, to be built under the quadrangle of St Peter's College, Oxford.	**1969 Switzerland** Death of Ernest Ansermet (b. 1883), Swiss conductor and founder of the Orchestre de la Suisse Romande.
	1969 Japan *House of the Sleeping Beauties*, a novel by Kawabata Yasunari (1899–1972), Nobel Prize-winner; he was particularly concerned with sexual feelings.		
1970 Death of de Gaulle in France.	**1970 England** *Crow*, poems by Ted Hughes (b. 1930). His work is influenced by folk-tales and anthropology.	**1970 England** *Black Mass*, an anti-apartheid play by Edward Bond (b.1935).	**1970 England** The opera *Knot Garden* by Michael Kemp Tippett (b. 1905) performed in London.
	1970 Hungary/England *The Boy Changed into a Stag*, an English translation of poems of Ferenc Juhasz (b. 1928), Hungarian poet of international stature. His work is a mixture of the cruel and the tender.	**1970 South Africa** *People are Living Here* by Athol Fugard (b.1932) a playwright who also directs his own theatre company.	**1970 Federal Republic of Germany** Bernd Alois Zimmerman died (b. 1918); he composed the opera *Die Soldaten*.
	1970 South Africa *The Wanderers* by Ezekiel Mphahlele (b. 1919), a black South African writing in English. The book is semi-autobiographical. He felt that so much of South African energies went into racial conflict that there was nothing left for creative work.		**1973 England** First performance of the opera *Death in Venice* by Benjamin Britten (1913–1976) at the Aldeburgh Festival.
			1973 Switzerland Otto Klemperer, conductor and composer died, (b. 1885).
			1973 Germany Wolfgang Schmieder died, (b. 1870). He indexed Bach's works beginning each piece with the letters BWV, *Bach Werke-Verzeichis*.
			1973 Puerto Rico Pablo Casals, Spanish cellist died, (b. 1876).
			1974 U.S.S.R. Death of David Oistrakh (b. 1908), Russian violinist.
			1975 England Malcolm Williamson (b. 1931) appointed Master of the Queen's Music.
			1975 U.S.S.R. Death of Dimitry Shoshtakovich (b. 1906).

1969 Switzerland An exhibition called 'When Attitudes Become Form' provided the first international survey of 'conceptual art', in which art is seen as an attitude to experience, even if that experience is not recorded in a conventional art form. Going for a walk thus becomes an act of creative art but the artist no longer feels obliged to record the walk in forms or images.

*1969
Man first landed
on moon.
First flight of
supersonic
civilian airliner
Concorde.
Human egg
fertilized in test
tube.*

Man walks on the Moon, July 1969

1970 U.S.A. Bruce Davidson (b. 1933) published photographs of *East 100th Street*, New York. He used a 4 × 5 tripod camera, completely abandoning the usual 'unseen eye' approach of the documentary photographer.

1970 Italy Bernardo Bertolucci (b. 1941) directed *Il Conformista*, using lightly surreal compositions to link sexual disturbance with fascist behaviour.

1970 Japan Akira Kurosawa (b. 1910) made his first colour film, *Dodeska Den*, using colour to show the moods of inner fantasies. The creative use of colour has always been well understood in Japanese cinema.

*1970
Nuclear-powered
heart pacemaker
introduced.*